A PRACTICAL GUIDE
TO QABALISTIC
SYMBOLISM

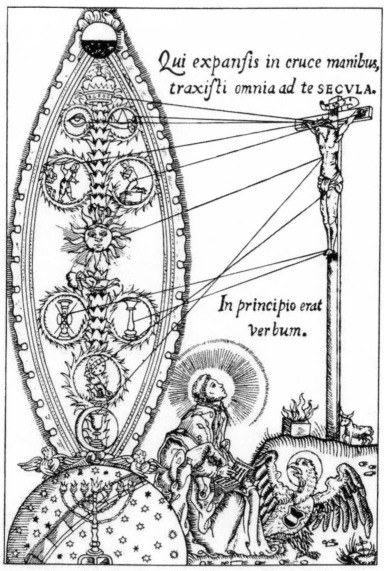

Qui expanſis in cruce manibus,
traxiſti omnia ad te SECVLA.

In principio erat
verbum.

Tree of Life from Syriac New Testament, Vienna, 1555

'Magic has power to experience and fathom things which are
inaccessible to human reason. For magic is a great secret
wisdom, just as reason is a great public folly.'

—PARACELSUS

A PRACTICAL GUIDE TO QABALISTIC SYMBOLISM

ONE-VOLUME EDITION

Volume I
ON THE SPHERES OF THE TREE OF LIFE

Volume II
ON THE PATHS AND THE TAROT

by
Gareth Knight

WEISERBOOKS
Boston, MA/York Beach, ME

First published in 2001 by
Red Wheel/Weiser, LLC
368 Congress Street
Boston, MA 02210

Collected hardcover edition first published in 1978.
First edition, in two volumes, published in 1965 by Helios Book
Service (Publications) Ltd.

10 09 08 07 06 05 04 03 02 01
10 9 8 7 6 5 4 3 2 1

Library of Congress Catalog Card Number: 66-71818

ISBN 1-57863-247-1

Printed in the United States of America
MV

The paper used in this publication meets the minimum requirements of
the American National Standard for Information Sciences—permanence
of Paper for Printed Library Materials Z39.48–1992(R1997).

To ROMA

*without whose love
and faith in me
this book would not
have been*

CONTENTS

Part One

Part Two

Part Three

DIAGRAMS

TABLES

AUTHOR'S PREFACE
TO THE PAPERBACK EDITION

It has been forty years since I put pen to paper to write *A Practical Guide to Qabalistic Symbolism*. My book and I seem to be appreciated by a younger generation, which is a great joy, even if in some respects we begin to show our age.

While it is most rewarding to have written a book that retains its appeal down the years, it has, at times, felt rather like an albatross around my neck when I have been challenged to justify some idea that crossed my mind more than a generation ago. The economics of publishing a large book of somewhat specialist interest have not permitted any alteration to the text, so both I and my readers have had to live with a number of opinions (sometimes stated as fact) that are now considerably dated, or were even, in the first place, just plain wrong. May this short preface go some way to atone for any shortcomings in this respect.

Please bear in mind that this book was written by an enthusiastic young man who had just made his way through the grades of an initiatory fraternity, and who had yet to learn that there might be considerably more to understanding "life, the universe and everything" than he had gleaned from absorbing fraternity knowledge papers. That is the reason the work might appear to you to be rather too credulous of authoritative sources.

However, it is these knowledge papers rather than my own contributions of the time that provide much of the strength of the book. In this respect, also bear in mind that esoteric fraternities have their own life cycles too, and at that time, the Society of the Inner Light was going through something of a mid-life crisis. Much of the traditional approach of a magical fraternity within the Western esoteric tradition was being called into question—some of it not without good reason—and, combined with the current fashion in alternative forms of psychotherapy, a more mystical ambiance was being engendered.

A Practical Guide to Qabalistic Symbolism mirrors this state of affairs, which had its upside as well as its downside. The Western

Mystery Tradition has always been a changing, organic synthesis of inner and outer experience, without which it would be ossified and devoid of life. So let the modern reader be aware of this, carefully weigh up what is being said, reject the doubtful, and hold fast to that which is good. With this in mind, let us highlight some specific points of the "not so good."

The draconian remarks on homosexuality seemed fairly commonplace at a time when this form of sexual expression was still a criminal offense. Society has since moved on quite radically in this respect, and it is a cause of great regret to me if, as a result of my words, anyone has been given a bad time on account of their sexual orientation. Not that I necessarily endorse all that I see or hear about the wilder frontiers of human sexual activity, particularly when allied to quasi-magical practice (which was one of Dion Fortune's concerns), but I have no desire to set myself up as an arbiter of public morals.

Scientology is glibly assumed to be a panacea for all "evils" in parts of the book. This I now regard as far too sanguine an assessment but the techniques happened to be very popular with the leadership of the Society at the time of writing, as Jungian psychology had previously been in Dion Fortune's day.

The system of correspondences presented in this book is based upon that of the Hermetic Order of the Golden Dawn. It is certainly not the only valid system, although in my experience it has worked very well for me, and there is room for considerable flexibility in its use. There was no good cause for dismissing any other system that I did not understand, as I did with that of C. C. Zain. However, I am indebted to Mr. Prier Wintle for providing me with a courteous explanation of its rationale.

Finally, I would like to answer the criticism that the text sometimes wanders into speculative side-alleys. This was because, at the time of writing, I was seeking the slightest excuse to include as much material as possible from the knowledge papers of the Society of the Inner Light, a policy encouraged by the Society, and which, at the time, we felt to be perhaps the most important element within the book.

—Gareth Knight
Vernal Equinox 2001

AUTHOR'S PREFACE

This two volume book deals with the Sephiroth and Paths of the Tree of Life as a basis for a study of many branches of esoteric symbolism. It is not an academic or historical treatise but is intended to be a practical guide to those who wish to use Qabalistic symbolism as a means to explore fields of consciousness beyond the physical.

I would like to thank the Society of the Inner Light for permission to incorporate extracts from various unpublished papers in the Society's archives, particularly in Volume I. However, the work represents my own views only, as they were at the time of writing, and does not necessarily represent those of the Society, past or present.

My own views have changed in some respects over subsequent years, but the book remains what it always was, an example of meditative work upon the ground plan of the Qabalistic Tree of Life, and insofar as this reveals the all important structure of the Tree it should serve its purpose, individual quirks of interpretation notwithstanding.

My later direction of thought has since been recorded in EXPERIENCE OF THE INNER WORLDS, which serious students are recommended to read in conjunction with the present work; and THE CHRIST, PSYCHOTHERAPY AND MAGIC by Anthony Duncan has also much relevance. The main difference in emphasis, or outlook, is in a return to a closer concern with the original Jewish Qabalah and the European tradition that springs from it, through the Christian Qabalists of the fourteenth to nineteenth centuries with some admixture of Sufi influences as a result of the Crusades. In philosophical terms we have moved from a monist to a theist standpoint.

With regard to the present text, some experienced occultists have written to say that they use other correspondences than the ones I use, and I have no doubt that other systems can be used successfully and that there is, in fact, no 'one and only true'. I am indebted to Mr. Prier Wintle who has taken much trouble to explain that C. C. Zain's attributions, that I dismiss somewhat shortly, are in fact based on well thought out principles, however far removed his resulting correspondences are from the traditional systems that I favour.

Some have also taken me to task with regard to my fulsome remarks about scientology. It may be that they are made on insufficient evidence but I can only in all honesty record that my own personal experiences of this technique have been very helpful. It may be that I have been singularly fortunate.

G.K. 23.11.1975

Part I

Chapter I

THE USES OF THE QABALAH

1. "If we would know the inner nature of man by his outer nature; if we would understand his inner heaven by his outward aspect; if we would know the inner nature of trees, herbs, roots, stones by their outward aspect, we must pursue our exploration of nature on the foundation of the Qabalah. For the Qabalah opens up access to the occult, to the mysteries; it enables us to read sealed epistles and books and likewise the inner nature of men."* Thus wrote Philippus Aureolus Theophrastus Bombastus von Hohenheim, called Paracelsus, the medieval physician, philosopher and mystic.

2. The purpose of this book is to prove that what Paracelsus claimed on behalf of the Qabalah is as true in our day as it was in his. The method of proof will not be by any attempt at a history of its usage, or an analysis of whence it stems; for the proof of any pudding is in the eating of it and not in any catalogue of previous illustrious partakers of it, nor a treatise on the source of the various ingredients.

3. As a theosophical system, the Qabalah and its basic diagram, the Tree of Life, works. The sole purpose of these pages is to put the reader in a position to try it for himself and then to make his own judgment from his own experience. This book is therefore a practical guide as well as a theoretical treatise. It is intended for those who seek a psychic quest and spiritual adventure, rather than for those who seek merely an acquisition of knowledge.

4. But in order to prevent any initial misunderstandings

1

* *Paracelsus*, Selected Writings (edited Jacobi) published by Routledge and Kegan Paul. London. Also American publishers. Pantheon. 1951. New York.

it may be as well to examine Paracelsus' claim in more detail.

5. His first claim is that by means of the Qabalah we can know the inner nature of man by his outer nature and understand his inner heaven by his outward aspect. He then goes on to include the external world of trees, herbs, roots, stones and nature in general.

6. From this we can gather a basic concept that there is an inner reality or essence to things apart from their outward appearance, and that further, the nature of the inner can be deduced from the outer. This is by no means an exceptional concept; it is fully in line with all idealist philosophy. It includes however, the refinements of the Hermetic schools that as God made man in His own image, so can the examination of man lead to the knowledge of God. And as God created Nature, so it, at the same time, hides and reveals God.

7. Thus all manifestation in the material world is an effect of causes operating from a higher plane, and these causes can be deduced from the effects produced, right back to the Primal Cause, God Himself. This is in accordance with the Hermetic axiom 'As above—so below'.

8. It is obvious that within man, the level of causation is higher than the material world unless one is to regard man as an automaton. For instance, a man's actions are ruled by his mental decisions or emotional directions. It may be said that his decisions and directions are in turn an effect of the environment, and this is of course true, for all who live in the material world are affected by it —though some more than others. The great majority of humanity are ruled by their external circumstances, but the superior man is he who works out his own direction and then changes his environment, or his reaction to it, accordingly. He is a master of his destiny.

9. In the same way, the multitudinous forms of Nature can be conceived as various experiments in what has been called the Great Laboratory of life. The materialist hypoth-

esis of 'natural selection' is all very logical on its own level, but it pushes logic a very long way, almost as far as the proverbially long arm of coincidence. One is asked to look upon a rose, or the iridescent beauty of a peacock's tail for instance, and then believe that the one was the form ultimately most attractive to certain insects, and the other the one particular pattern that most excited the erotic desires of the peahen, and that all other variations died out. Similarly, coincidence is invoked to explain how the physical nature of this planet just happened to be that in which life could be supported. Surely, a Plan behind it all is really the most logical and satisfying explanation? (Some will say that logic and satisfaction are not necessarily criteria of truth and of course this is certainly true in regard to philosophical speculation. If one drives the mind far enough, one is eventually faced with the choice of nihilism or faith. One then comes back to logic and satisfaction to justify one or the other—according to irrational choice.)

10. However, the belief in a Divine Plan—except perhaps to a Christian Scientist—does not entail an attempt to deny the limitations that the physical world imposes. The Laws of the physical world cannot be gainsaid, and anything that goes against them suffers accordingly. The Laws of physics, chemistry and biology antedate the coming of life, and life has to adapt to them. But these Laws do not prevent the manifestation of great beauty, or any other purposes of life, any more than they cause it. They are, at most, conditioners.

11. In view of this, it is possible to conceive that there are forms of life on other stars and planets which are adapted to flourish in those conditions. One could conceive of beings with bodies of fire in the Sun for example. This is certainly more probable than the idea that ours is the only inhabited planet within thousands of lightyears. If life desires to manifest, it will manifest, whatever the conditions; and then having adapted itself to those conditions, it will

pursue its own way of expression in accordance with, not as a result of, those conditions.

12. This brings us back to Paracelsus' statement that the inner nature, which caused the outward form, can be deduced from that outward form. The method he recommends is that of the Qabalah, which, although being a system built up on symbolical correspondences, is nothing to do with the pseudo-sciences that grew up in the Middle Ages, except that the latter are ignorant applications of its general doctrine. Even Paracelsus, being a man of his time, was guilty of this kind of error. He believed for example that as the leaves of the thistle are prickly, it was an excellent herb for the cure of internal prickling, and that as another herb has roots wrapped in an envelope like armour it would give protection against weapons. It would need very great faith nowadays to put one's trust in such cures and preventions but there are many who pay good money for books purporting to tell character or fortune from the letters of their name, the residue in their tea cups, their coffee cups and so forth, all of which superstitions stem from the same source.

13. The pity of it is that such manifestations cause many intelligent people of today to condemn anything smacking of the occult as foolishness, just as our less tolerant forefathers condemned it as witchcraft. The moral in both cases is not to throw out the baby with the bath water—though our ancestors burned it at the stake for good measure.

14. Paracelsus then goes on to state that "the Qabalah opens up access to the occult, to the mysteries; it enables us to read sealed epistles and books and likewise the inner nature of men."

15. It is interesting to note that after his catalogue of 'occult', 'mysteries', 'epistles and books', he comes back to man again. Man is the whole key to all these things, for, the famous motto written in gold in the entrance to the Delphic Oracle—GNOTHI SEAUTON, (Know Thyself,

or Get to Know Thyself)—is the beginning, and also the end, of all spiritual development.

16. The word 'occult' means hidden and is often used synonymously with the word 'esoteric'—for the few. And they are both used in conjunction with what is often called 'the Mystery Teaching'. It may be as well to expand these concepts a little.

17. In common usage the word 'mystery' can mean something either secret or inexplicable. In its ecclesiastical sense it is a religious truth above human reason but revealed by God; and in its archaic sense it was a handicraft or trade. In talking of the Mysteries as a school of initiation one is using the word as a combination of all these meanings.

18. The teachings of the Mysteries, in that many of them are religious truths, are beyond the rational mind. To the logical mental processes, with which so many people insist on operating entirely, they may well appear nonsensical. The Mystery of the Holy Trinity for example is a religious truth which is beyond the reach of the mind. Most have to take it on faith, but for the few, the mystics of the Church, it can be a great reality, a profound experience which cannot subsequently be adequately described in words. But words are the data upon which the rational mind works and the only means of communication of such things in words is by analogy, allegory and symbol. And even this conveys little to the normal mind processes, as anyone who attempts to interpret the Book of Revelations, for example, can well prove for himself.

19. It is for similar reasons that the words 'occult' and 'esoteric' are used. Much portentous nonsense has been written about 'occult secrecy', the 'Keys of Power' and the like in past years, mainly to cloak ignorance in the writer, or else for cheap self-aggrandisement. The reason why the Mysteries, which are really the Yoga of the West, are called hidden, and for the few, is because they *cannot* be explained to outsiders. The barrier is purely one of

communication. To try to describe a mystical experience is like trying to describe the scent of a flower; one cannot do it. The best one can do is tell the enquirer how best he can obtain the particular flower so that he can smell it for himself. If he cannot be bothered to follow your directions or flatly refuses to believe that the flower exists there is nothing one can do about it. The Qabalah could therefore be described as a ground-plan of the flower garden of mystical experience. One can present it to an enquirer if he is interested, but it ultimately rests with him if he will use it. That is, it is no good his having a purely intellectual grasp of its ramifications; he has to make practical use of it. The merely intellectual approach is like expecting to smell flowers direct from a seedsman's catalogue.

20. Where secrecy does come in is in the practical use of the Qabalah on a group basis. It is possible to make a fair degree of progress on one's own account, but in a Mystery School the process is quicker. Here, a Group Mind is set up which affects the unconscious mind of each of its members. The ideas of each member of the group are pooled, as it were, so that they can be picked up telepathically by all the other members. This is a purely automatic process and occurs in any group of people to a greater or lesser extent, but more so when what is known is kept a secret, strictly withheld from any outside the group, and particularly so when the things held secret are matters which profoundly affect the subconscious i.e., symbolism, religious beliefs, mythological images, etc. In this case then, secrecy is necessary or the work becomes valueless. But it is only secrecy of practical usage relevant to that particular group.

21. Thus in practical esoteric work, as in religious worship—and there is a close connection between the two—a group is a distinct advantage. As Our Lord said: "For where two or three are gathered together in my name, there am I in the midst of them." And in more advanced work, particularly where the symbols used are not merely subjectively contemplated, but ritually enacted, some high

degree of skill is required. There is more to a Roman
Catholic Mass for example than dressing up in vestments
and reciting the words. It is in this development of skill
that 'the Mysteries' can be regarded in the archaic meaning of the word, as a craft or trade. The training is one of
apprenticeship. Thus to form a ritual group requires at
least one person who is already expert who can train the
others. If a crowd of amateurs get together and try to do
ceremonial working the result will be either nothing or
more than they bargained for. And the latter is no joke, for
the subconscious potencies behind mystical symbolism are
psychological dynamite.

22. The Qabalah, then, is a system of relationships among
mystical symbols which can be used, as Paracelsus says,
to open up access to the hidden reaches of the mind—
beyond the frontiers of reason. It enables us to read 'sealed
epistles and books', by which is meant writings of a mystical nature couched necessarily in symbolic language,
because the Qabalah gives us the means to penetrate to
the meaning behind the symbolism.

23. It could be regarded as the mystical process in
reverse. A natural mystic will have his visions by what he
would no doubt call 'the grace of God' and would then
attempt to write them down in symbolism or analogy—
the nearest approximate metaphors in the language of the
mind. The Qabalah, by a study of symbolism, helps the
Qabalist to break through to the reality that the mystic
has attempted to describe.

24. This applies not only to Christian mysticism but to
all other religious faiths including the pagan. Thus one
can obtain the experience of what the Greeks meant by
Pallas Athene, Zeus, Demeter and all the other Olympians;
what the Egyptians meant by Isis, Ra, Osiris, Horus;
what the Celts meant by Keridwen; the American Indians
by the Manitou, Hiawatha, and so on throughout the
whole history of man's search for the Divine. Of 'the
sealed epistles and books' there is not only the Bible but

other mystical treatises such as 'The Egyptian Book of the Dead', 'The High History of the Holy Grail', 'The I Ching, or Book of Changes', to name but a few.

25. In short, although primarily a Judaic system, by its systematic layout it acts as a key to the study of comparative religion—and not merely as an academic pursuit but as a practical theosophy. The reason why this can be done is because the inner structure of human psychology being the same whatever the race or creed, and God being One, all approaches to God must be similar. The diversity of men could be considered to be spread all round the circumference of a wheel, with God at the centre. Then, although the approaches to God would be from different angles, as the spokes of a wheel, and some apparently diametrically opposed to each other, one spoke would be much like another though perhaps painted in different colours or carved in a different shape.

26. It may be thought that it is impossible to reconcile Christianity, for example, with pagan religions, one being a monotheistic system and the pagan religions worshipping a diversity of gods. The point is that God works in many ways and even the most orthodox Christian prays to God in many aspects, as Father, Son, Holy Spirit, Judge of the Wicked, Redeemer of Sins, Maker of Rain, Protector of the Harvests, to say nothing of the Virgin Mary and the intercession of Saints. None of these is incompatible with the belief in the One God. And the pagan had many gods each of which was a particular aspect of the One God, Who existed then as now, except that among the pagans more did not realise it. Pagan and modern worship are in a way diametrically opposite. The modern Christian thinks only of one God and yet prays to many in the various aspects of the One. The pagan thought only of many aspects of God and yet prayed to the One God through them. It is all really a question of terminology, the reality is the same.

27. Where the Judaic system is so valuable is that it was one of the earliest, if not the earliest, of monotheistic

systems and therefore has a foot in both worlds. God, although being One, is considered to manifest through ten emanations which are carefully described, and under the presidency of each emanation is an Archangel and Choir of Angels. Nothing if not thorough, they also provided details of a whole system of demons to correspond to each emanation of God to represent the associated averse aspects, but these need not detain us at the moment, in fact the less they detain us the better.

28. In connection with each emanation or aspect of Divinity, apart from the writings on it, there was also allocated a number of symbols, verbal or pictorial, around which others have grown in the course of Qabalistic study through the ages. Of the later symbolism, some is more reliable than other, and some still subject to research and experiment. The Qabalah is a living system, its proofs are in practical working, not in historical research.

29. Symbolism in general can be classified under two headings, Arbitrary and Universal.

30. Arbitrary symbols are used extensively in many fields, in science and mathematics, in musical notation, in words themselves. They occur in art. In medieval times Judas used to be painted with a yellow robe to signify envy, while the Virgin Mary had a cloak of blue.

31. The latter symbolism of the Virgin Mary being associated with blue is almost a Universal symbol—but not quite. In some cases there is no sharp dividing line between one and the other.

32. Universal symbolism is more or less immutable in basic significance. Numerical symbolism is a good example in that the number three, for instance, or the triangle, signifies triplicity in all things, the Three-in-One of the Divinity; the thesis, antithesis and synthesis of Hegelian philosophy; the possible modes of manifestation of force, active, passive or equilibrated. The Sun is another example, the centre of a system, a source of light, sustainer of life, all of which can also apply to Deity of which it is a symbol.

It should not be thought that our pagan ancestors necessarily worshipped the Sun itself, they were capable of a high degree of civilisation and philosophical subtlety, as their writings show. One could equally unjustly accuse Christians of worshipping a cross, merely because it appears on their altars. In fact, it is a symbol, and a Universal one at that, though varying in its forms. A Calvary Cross calls up different associations from an Equal-armed Cross or a Swastika.

33. The examples given here are all simple symbols, but it is possible to have highly composite ones. The story of Adam and Eve, for example, is a vast symbol of the beginnings of human life, and the Revelation of St. John the Divine an even vaster one of the ending. There is a wealth of symbolism in pagan mythology, as, for example, Prometheus stealing Divine Fire to bring to man. This could be taken at one level to mean the discovery of physical fire but there is really a great deal more to it than that. It throws a revealing light on the meaning of Free Will and on premature revelation.

34. There are two movements afoot at the present time with regard to mythology. One is to explain it away by means of depth psychology, which is an exploration in the right direction but which, in the last analysis, does not go deep enough. The other is to explain it away by attributing it to the history of the movements of tribes with the subsequent rise and fall of various deities and forms of worship. This no doubt has some truth in it but is a very shallow approach.

35. The majority of myths hold a wide diversity of meaning, natural and artistic, moral and ethical, philosophical and metaphysical, religious and theological, mystical and occult. They may apply to man or the Universe or both. What appears to be a simple story can lead to an apprehension of infinite truth with applications in all realms of consciousness.

36. The same applies to the composite symbol of the

Tree of Life, which is the basis of the Qabalah. And not only is it a comprehensive symbol in itself, it allows other symbol systems to be interpreted in the light of it. Therefore in its ability to relate varying mythologies and religious beliefs, and occult symbol systems such as astrology, numerology, alchemy and the Tarot, it is the foundation stone of the Western Mystery Tradition.

Chapter II

A YOGA FOR THE WEST

1. The Western Mystery Tradition is the counterpart of what is known as Yoga in the East, and it is unfortunate that most people have never heard of the first and know very little about the second.

2. In the Occident, neither of these systems received much attention outside their devotees until the latter end of the nineteenth century, since when there has been a gradually increasing interest in ways of inner development, together with a gradually increasing promulgation of foolishness, as any examination of the bulk of the wares in any occult bookshop will show. The public always demands what is sensational, whether it be true or not, and there are plenty of people willing to supply the demand.

3. According to the Qabalah, the first quality needed before any spiritual progress can be made is discrimination. And discrimination is needed to sort out the true mystic from the false.

4. In the East, what is usually considered by the Westerner to be a yogi is, in fact, a fakir. A fakir subjugates his physical body by dominating it with his will, through suffering. Many of them proudly exhibit withered arms that have been caused by holding the arm in the air for fantastic lengths of time, or blinded eyes from staring at the Sun. They are either ignorant fanatics torturing themselves in order to attain heavenly grace, or conjurors performing 'miracles' based on skill, patience and physical contortion. Many of them claim to be yogis but the true yogi is neither fanatic nor sectarian, nor does he perform

tricks for money. It is true he may have developed abnormal physical powers, particularly if he is a follower of Hatha Yoga, but these powers are a means not an end.

5. The goal of Yoga is what the word Yoga means, Union, which corresponds with the ultimate experience of the Qabalah—Divine Union. And the way to this goal is by the control of the will and the functions of thought, emotion, and internal or external bodily movement, all of which ordinarily operate without any great degree of control. The whole system is really a combination of philosophy, science, religion and art. It has its system of doctrine which constitutes its philosophy, yet it requires something more than an academic appreciation, namely, an active religious faith, and, like the practice of medicine, it is at the same time a science and an art.

6. What has been said of the Yoga of the East also applies to that of the West. The goal of the true practitioner is the same, and in both cases, the true is masked by the clamour and exhibitionism of the false. In the West the situation has been further complicated in that the Church effectively stamped out any written exposition of the Mysteries. Thus, what literature there is, the various alchemical treatises for example, is extremely cryptic where it is not deluded— for there were as many, probably far more, false alchemists than true; and of the various Magical Grimoires, most are medieval rubbish, or copyings of copies of copies, with successively increasing mistakes, right up to the present day.

7. All in all, there is little original work in the literature of Western illuminism and what there is is unreliable, through caution or folly, so that we cannot compare with the East and its vast amount of esoteric lore. Perhaps this is all to the good for it throws us onto our own resources. We must derive our theory from practice, instead of having our practice unconsciously limited by theory.

8. The Qabalah, as practised, is derived almost entirely

14

from one simple diagram, the Tree of Life, and that is all
that is basically needed.

9. The uses to which the diagram can be put can best be
described by reference to the Eastern system of Yoga. This
falls into five main categories:

i) *Raja Yoga*—the education of consciousness through
meditation and contemplation.

ii) *Bhakti Yoga*—the religious way of devotional mysticism.

iii) *Gnana Yoga*—the pursuit of enlightenment through
philosophical speculation.

iv) *Karma Yoga*—the application of Yoga through right
living.

v) *Hatha Yoga*—the control of the body and development
of the inner physical resources.

10. The Western system has parallels to all these techniques but generally is applied in a different way, for the
conditions of East and West and the physical and psychological make-up of Eastern and Western man are to some
extent different.

Raja Yoga: It is expected of most people in the civilised
world today that they have sufficient control over their
emotions not to break out into physical violence. Even this
is difficult for some, and impossible, it seems, on a group or
national level. Raja Yoga is a system of training whereby
the emotions and the mind are placed under conscious
control so that not merely physical harmony is achieved,
but there is no riot on the subjective emotional or mental
levels.

11. Any average person who cares to take an honest look
at the condition of his own psychological processes will be
aware of the teeming confusion that lies there. The process
has been described quite fully in the 'stream of consciousness' literature between the wars. Also, to ascertain the
general condition of human consciousness, one has only to
count the number of advertisements in magazines by firms

which seem to do a good trade in helping people to overcome 'grass-hopper minds', 'nerves' and so on. It is
generally recognised also that an ulcerated stomach, to
name but one disease, can have its roots in emotional stress.
There is clearly much to be gained in the control of the
mind even from a point of view of material profit, to say
nothing of the spiritual aspects involved.

12. The techniques of Raja Yoga in the early stages are
purely callisthenics of the mind, and they are basic to any
kind of occult training. In fact the initial exercises are
precisely those which are used by most of the firms that
advertise cures for mind-wandering, weak will, etc. There
is no easy road either. If one is physically flabby the only
cure is hard exercise and the same applies to the muscles
of the mind.

13. There are three stages to the training of the mind by
Raja Yoga—i) concentration, ii) meditation, iii) contemplation.

14. Without concentration any occult work is impossible,
for it requires the faculty to hold an image in the mind,
often for long periods.

15. The only way to learn how to hold an image in the mind
is to do it. One can set oneself a graded system of exercises
starting by imagining an object, say a football, and holding
it before the mind's eye for ten minutes. Then one can go
onto more complicated images until one can hold in the
mind's eye a detailed painting or a roomfull of furniture.
Eventually one can graduate to taking a short story, and
having read it thoroughly, going through it as a spectator,
seeing all the scenes and hearing the words spoken. This
should be possible after short practice daily over three or
four months. The secret of success is short regular practice
rather than long bouts at irregular intervals.

16. Once the power of concentration has been achieved
meditation is possible. Meditation is the concentrated
examination of something, whether it be an image or an
idea, and while the mind is fixed upon it, allowing ideas to

rise around it. In this manner a well is sunk into the unconscious, as it were, and the related ideas allowed to rise to the surface.

17. This process allows the significance of any symbol to be elucidated, and notes can be taken of the ideas that arise. Furthermore, the ideas that come from meditation are 'realisations' rather than concepts. To have a mental concept is merely to have a piece of information held within the mind which may be useful or may be not and is easily forgotten. To have a realisation of something means that it becomes a part of oneself. One has taken an idea and made it real—'real-ised' it.

18. Meditation is therefore an important mental process in using the Qabalistic Tree of Life, for it allows the significance of the ramifications of symbolism attached to it to be understood and to become a part of one. And as the Tree of Life is a diagram of the Divine Plan, a lifetime's meditation on it, building its concepts into the soul, will take any student a long way along the Path of Attainment.

19. Here we have gone beyond purely mental callisthenics and the mind is being used for esoteric purposes. It is important therefore to open and close any meditation with some holy sign such as the sign of the Cross, for the mind is being used in a receptive manner in connection with very deep symbolism, some of which is not untainted by previous dubious usage.

20. Contemplation follows on from meditation and can well be used in conjunction with it. It is difficult to describe because it is such a simple process—it is really only a question of 'being aware'. In addition to the concentration and receptivity of meditation it has in it the qualities of faith, love and tranquillity. Meditation is analytical, it dwells upon statements, principles or ideas *about* something. Contemplation is of a synthesising nature, it is simply a calm gaze *upon* something that has been previously realised. It is really a spiritual perception—"Be still, and know . . ."

21. Meditation is more artificial. Contemplation is an easy

natural process that cannot be strained after. Perhaps many people have contemplated all their lives without consciously realising it. After some awareness of the nature of the 'invisible realities' has been hewn into consciousness by active meditation then the presence and power of these realities can be allowed to flow into the mind by contemplation. It is acting as a channel for the Divine. It will be remembered from the first chapter of Genesis: "And God saw every thing that He had made, and, behold, it was very good." It is a similar state of mind, a state of acceptance, a practice of the Presence of God, and nothing to do with self-satisfaction or blind optimism.

22. While meditation is best done in a dimly lit room free from noise and interruption, contemplation can perhaps best be done sitting over a bottle of beer and a cigarette in one's own back yard—and if this statement shocks anyone it is as well for them to bear in mind that, for the adept of the Western Mysteries, occultism is a twentyfour hours a day, seven days a week business, as it is for the Eastern guru. Only in the West the adept lives in the world, not in a monastic retreat. It is this consideration which is really at the base of the differences between the Eastern and Western systems, though both systems are followed with the same dedication and aspirations, and both lead to the same goal.

Bhakti Yoga: This is the Yoga of devotional mysticism. It teaches how to believe and how to pray and can be applied to any religion, for differences of religion do not exist for it, there is only 'the religious Way.'

23. It has been made known through the works of disciples of Ramakrishna, an avanced exponent of it. Ramakrishna spent twelve years following the way of each great religion in turn and always came to the same result, a state of divine ecstasy. He thus claimed to prove from personal experience that all the great religions are one, that they all lead to the One God.

24. In that the Tree of Life can be used as a compendium

of comparative religion it will be seen that the use of it by a devotional mystic is a Western way of Bhakti Yoga. It is, in a way, similar to Raja Yoga except that the accent is placed on the emotions. For those with strong emotions it breaks the emotions in and harnesses them in a religious direction, while at the same time it can develop the religious emotions in those in whom they are weak.

25. As there is an extensive literature in the West on the practice of religion, the concepts of Bhakti Yoga are quite familiar to most people, but it may be as well to summarise them.

26. To the devotional mystic prayer is not merely a kneeling down at certain times with a recital of prescribed words often grown meaningless through constant repetition, nor is it a detailed solicitation or petition. Prayer is a yearning of the soul for union with its Divine source, an articulate expression of aspiration. It is at one and the same time, aspiration, compunction, reverence, adoration, praise, gratitude, communion, invocation, loving desire, oblation and worship.

27. Methods of prayer have been laid down by various mystical writers but generally speaking they follow a similar basic pattern:

i) Preparation by means of preliminary sacred reading or meditation.

ii) Vocal prayer, which can be spontaneous or prescribed, uttered audibly or formulated in the thoughts.

iii) Fervent meditation or voiceless aspiration of the heart.

iv) Mystical experience in which the soul is drawn into interior communion and colloquy with the Divine in silence of words, thoughts and desires.

28. These are the principles of prayer to God in whatever form the Divine is conceived, either as the Christ, or in the aspect of God known as Zeus, Isis, Woden, Ahura-Mazda or what have you. It is not idolatry for the One God is behind all the aspects that have been formulated by man,

but for those in the West under the Christian dispensation and drawn particularly to devotional mysticism, the Christian way is without doubt the best, for the Lord Jesus is something far more, to say the least, than an idea of man's of an aspect of the Godhead as were the pagan god-forms. Also, Our Lord said, "I am the way, the truth and the life: no man cometh unto the Father, but by me." and "Lo, I am with you always, even unto the end of the world."

29. This is not written as a sop to orthodoxy but as a result of mystical experience on an individual and group level.

30. Whilst on the subject of Bhakti Yoga it is as well to examine another form of religious practice which does not occur in the East but which has been laid down by St. Ignatius of Loyola, the founder of the Society of Jesus, in his 'Spiritual Exercises'.

31. This system of training recommends the strong visualisation of being present during scenes in the life of Our Lord. It has, however, other applications and is used extensively in occult schools. It is a further development to the advanced exercises in concentration in that instead of running over a short story, a work of literary fancy, one is using as a basis powerful emotive symbolism.

32. It can be further developed in that spontaneous events, symbols and personages can be allowed to arise in consciousness whilst dwelling on a certain scene—a temple constructed in the imagination for example. It calls for a high degree of technical skill, the fruit of much practice in more elementary exercises, and is not a thing to be fooled around with. To some people it comes more easily than others and it is sometimes called 'scrying' or 'astral clairvoyance'. Some people find building-up and holding images in the imagination easier, whilst others find reception to spontaneous images simpler. The highly skilled operator can use both methods at once with equal facility.

33. With regard to the Qabalah it is of use mainly in

treading the Paths of the Tree of Life and will be gone into in more detail in the second volume of this book. It is a useful technique but can lead easily to abuse or self-delusion.

Gnana Yoga: This Yoga is the way of knowledge and uses the methods of Raja Yoga, concentration, meditation and contemplation, to arrive at a conception of the reality of things and their inter-relationship.

34. It teaches the mind to travel in unaccustomed directions and on new planes—in other words, not on the outward aspect of things but on their inner principles. It teaches a man that only what he has experienced as true can be true for him, that what seems true to the logical mind need not be true at all when viewed from a higher level, and that words can be a greater hindrance than help to truth.

35. The Qabalistic Tree of Life is a system *par excellence* for realising all this. As a composite symbol of underlying relationships it enables one to collate what one knows and then to deduce what one does not know, partly from intuition and partly from first principles. It is a kind of metaphysical algebra.

36. It must always be remembered however that metaphysical symbols, like algebraic ones, represent something and are not ends in themselves. The great limitation of the intellectual type is that he cannot break free from his reason. Once he has a concept or label for something he thinks he knows it. Thus he may be aware of the symbol of the Black Isis leading to the White Isis; but when faced with the reality behind the symbol, the hideous red-in-tooth-and-clawed aspect of Nature, he is apt to forget all he learned from symbol and the glorious revelation beyond of the White Isis.

37. Occult meditation, leading to a hyper-developed intuition, is one cure for this, as opposed to ratiocination or mental juggling, which is all too easy with symbols. Symbols can be a great help to the mind in leading it in the right direction, but they can also be a terrible barrier. The whole aim of symbolism is its own destruction so that one can get

to the reality which it represents.

38. This is a point which is all too easily forgotten by the intellectual type of person who is attracted to this branch of study and it mars many books on the subject of the Qabalah, for without practical experience all philosophical discourses on the subject are just words, words, words, which, as said above, are a greater hindrance than help, particularly to the higher realms of truth.

Karma Yoga: This is the Yoga that teaches right living, and in view of the fact that the Western occult student lives out in the world, is all-important in the West. It is the direct opposite of the concept of 'Sunday religion'.

39. To a student of the Qabalah, all that he learns from it should be expressed in his daily life. He lives his life in the light of spiritual principle.

40. The aim of the ordinary man is to live his life avoiding all difficulties, discomforts and unpleasantness within the bounds of his conscience. The esoteric student should be a man with a very demanding conscience and so his life is more difficult. This does not mean that he goes about seeking for or making difficulties for himself, but he meets all obstacles as a challenge, and the greater the obstacle the greater the opportunity it is for him to overcome the weaker aspects of his nature.

41. The patterns for living are shown forth in many of the hero legends of a race, for example in the adventures of King Arthur and his Knights of the Round Table. An esoteric student is expected to develop ordinary virtues to the heroic level. And in modern life the difficulties are more subtle. In the legendary stories the evil is easily identifiable. There is less definition in ordinary life and also there is no aspect of medieval glamour. The dragon he has to meet may be his employer or his wife, which is a far more subtle challenge than any knight had to face in the ancient stories.

42. Also, the main direction of spiritual development leads

by the Way of the Cross, which was the pattern laid down by Our Lord and also in the legends of sacrificed gods before him. It is a way of self-sacrifice, a Path on the Tree of Life trod over and over again, and though the Crucifixion may not mean a physical death it is in some respects far harder to live out one's life for a cause than to die for one.

43. In case this should seem too depressing for anyone it should not be forgotten that after the Crucifixion comes the Resurrection and subsequent Ascension.

Hatha Yoga: This Yoga is the development of power over the body and is unsuited for the West. The various postures and breathing exercises of Hatha Yoga have a direct effect upon the etheric centres and endocrine glands and produce abnormal sensitivity. To develop such a high degree of sensitivity whilst living a normal life in the hustle and bustle of Western civilisation is to court a nervous breakdown.

44. There is no strict physical regime needed for the pursuit of occultism under Western methods. It is merely a question of common sense; and questions of vegetarianism, teetotalism and abstinence from tobacco are best left for the individual to make up his own mind—after all, he should know what suits him. The principle is one of moderation and balance, and the results in daily living should be ease of function, so that there is no bodily distraction from getting on with the job in hand.

45. The sensitivity that is brought about in the East by Hatha Yoga is induced, for temporary periods, in the West by ceremonial ritual. This is a highly skilled business as mentioned before and should not be attempted outside a Mystery school. To anyone who is not a student of one but is curious to see the technique in action, it can be seen and experienced by attending a Roman Catholic Mass, particularly one conducted by priests of a Contemplative Order. Attendance at a Greek or Russian Orthodox service can also be an interesting experience. But even here, little may be gained if one takes the attitude of a mere spectator.

With all aspects of occultism and mysticism as with religion, it is basically a way of life; one must commit oneself to active participation. After the first steps are taken in faith, the following steps become plain, and the proofs of the validity of the teaching become evident.

46. Unless the first steps are taken, nothing can follow. That is why science, up to now, has made so little of the inner reality behind appearances.

Chapter III

AN OUTLINE OF THE TREE OF LIFE

1. We have, so far, posited the existence of a whole range of existence behind the appearances of physical reality. We have also made a brief survey of the method by which this reality can be made accessible to consciousness. We can now proceed to an examination of the Tree of Life, by means of which a plan of direction can be formulated so that these methods can be used to best advantage.

2. The Tree of Life (Fig. 1) consists of ten spheres, plus an 'invisible' eleventh, with twentytwo paths interconnecting them. Constant reference is recommended to the basic diagram of the Tree and further help will be gained by making further diagrams and placing subsequent information upon them. The aim is to get the basic diagram well bedded into the unconscious mind, and persistent conscious working and brooding over the symbol is the only way to do this. Once this foundation has been well laid any further symbolism can be thrown into the subconscious mind to gestate, where it will, after a time, take its place on the appropriate part of the Tree and thus reveal its meaning and relationship to other symbolism previously assimilated.

3. The Tree of Life purports to be a symbol of the soul of man and of the Universe. As the Bible says, God made man in His own image and likeness, so whatever is relevant to the structure of the soul and body of man is relevant to the soul and body of God, the Universe. Thus the Tree can act as a tool of philosophical speculation as well of psychological discovery.

24

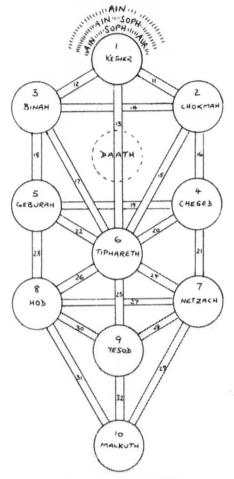

Fig. 1. THE TREE OF LIFE
The Ten Sephiroth and the TwentyTwo Paths

4. The spheres, or Sephiroth (singular:- Sephirah) are stages in the emanations of the Spirit of God or man in its progress from noumenal existence to its building of a physical vehicle in the phenomenal world. Each Sephirah represents a stage on the way, which remains as a centre of force after it has established itself and then overflowed to form the next centre. The Sephiroth were established in

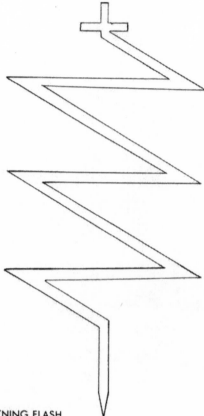

Fig. 2. THE LIGHTNING FLASH

numerical order and this is shown in the glyph of The Lightning Flash or Descent of Power. (Fig. 2) A glyph, in the sense used in Western occultism, is a picture representing an idea or ideas; Mystery teaching is put in pictorial form for this is the only language the unconscious mind understands. As Malkuth, the tenth Sephirah, represents the whole of physical existence, including the body of man, some idea of the vast range of the whole symbol can be gleaned.

5. In addition to the glyph of The Lightning Flash there is a further basic symbol which can be superimposed on the Tree. That is the glyph of The Pillars of Manifestation.

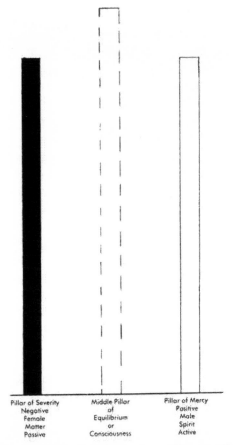

Fig. 3.
THE PILLARS

Pillar of Severity	Middle Pillar	Pillar of Mercy
Negative	of	Positive
Female	Equilibrium	Male
Matter	or	Spirit
Passive	Consciousness	Active

(Fig. 3) The Qabalah teaches that all manifestation is based on duality; and the right hand Pillar represents the positive, masculine or active pole and the left hand Pillar the negative, feminine or passive pole. This duality is in everything; as well as there being a duality on the Tree there is also a duality in every Sephirah. It is the principle of polarity.

6. This principle can be seen in a myriad forms in the physical environment: the polarity of the sexes; the nucleus and encircling electrons of the atom; any physical action has it, the mover and the moved; before a physical action is even performed there is polarity, the desire to

move or not to move; the thesis and antithesis of Hegelian philosophy; relationships between people, performer and audience, leader and follower, father and son—countless examples come to mind with a few moments' thought.

7. The point to remember from all this variety is that the concepts of the Tree of Life are not static easily defined things, but concepts of movement, change and relationship. The Pillars are presented as covering each of one side of the Tree but it must be remembered that they also operate in each Sephirah and between one Sephirah and any other. The only Unity is in the Unmanifest—that is the pure state of non-existence from which existence arises—symbolised on the Tree by the three veils behind Kether, the first Sephirah, The Veils of Negative Existence.

8. A veil is something you can see through but dimly, if at all, so one must not expect to come to an easy understanding of the concept of Negative Existence. It is veiled from understanding because our understanding is part and parcel of positive existence. But it is by no means entirely futile to try to come to some understanding. Some dim glimmering can be attained. If one likes to try the experiment one might obtain some realisation by watching crystals materialising out of a saturated solution as it cools. Alternatively, one could visualise a spider's web, symbolising the unmanifest mind of God, upon which dew begins to form from the atmosphere in shimmering crystal globes until it is a radiant network of light. In such a manner might the worlds have formed.

9. There remains however the Middle Pillar, which, when placed upon the Tree, covers the central Sephiroth. This is the Pillar of Equilibrium, poised between the Pillars of Function.

10. It might be as well at this point to take an example from the basal Sephiroth of the Tree as these should be within conscious reach of anybody. Amongst other things, the Sephirah Netzach at the base of the right hand Pillar represents the creative imagination. Hod, at the base of the

left hand Pillar represents the image making concrete mentation of the human mind. In a properly balanced person these two factors should be equilibrated. If a person has too much 'Netzach' and too little 'Hod' you will have the highly imaginative but impractical so-called 'arty' type; and if there were too much 'Hod' and little 'Netzach', the dry-as-dust academician, very good at passing examinations but with little imagination. The result of the combination of these two side Sephiroth will manifest itself in Tiphareth as the philosophical or religious attitude of the person, in Yesod as his instinctual behaviour and in Malkuth as his physical being and affairs of the world.

11. Thus it will be seen that the Tree can be used as a diagnostic instrument, but what is more, it can also be used for treatment. For should the person be a student of the Tree of Life, having diagnosed his unbalance, he can set it to rights by sustained meditation upon the Sephiroth in whose powers he is lacking. Furthermore, when we come to a study of the Paths between the Sephiroth, considerable subtleties are possible, but this must be left until Volume II.

12. Also, as the higher Sephiroth on the Tree represent the superconscious and spiritual aspects of the psyche, expansion of awareness and spiritual growth is achieved by meditation on these. The Tree is therefore a means whereby anyone can, in time, attain his fullest potential. Its danger is that people who are badly unbalanced will be naturally attracted to those parts where they already have an overplus of force, thus causing more unbalance in themselves. It is a powerful tool for good, but not a thing to be idly played with.

13. As life is a great complex of relationships, so is the Tree of Life. Its advantage is that it enables aspects of life to be sorted out and placed under the psychic microscope. However, this does not make the process of understanding very much the easier. The study of the Tree of Life demands more than a lifetime's work for, being what it is, if you have full understanding of the Tree of Life, then you

have full understanding of life itself. This is no easy short term matter, however good your tools of elucidation.

14. The point is that as no aspect of life can be fully understood devoid of its relationship with a great complex of other aspects, so no Sephirah on the Tree can be described without reference to all the other Sephiroth. And the same thing applies to the Paths between them.

15. In order to form some kind of basis of understanding it will be necessary, therefore, to cover the whole Tree cursorily from different aspects before dealing with each Sephirah in detail.

16. Behind Kether is Negative Existence from which all things came. From this pregnant void emanated Kether by means of a kind of crystallising process symbolised in three stages by The Veils of Negative Existence. These are called in Hebrew, Ain, Ain Soph, and Ain Soph Aur in order of advancing concretion. Translated, these words mean Negativity, The Limitless, and The Limitless Light. Concrete thought can make little of this, though meditation is recommended, for the unconscious knows far more than the conscious mind gives it credit for.

17. Negativity is nothingness. Yet it is already something, for we are able to posit it if not define it. Then comes The Limitless—limitless nothingness. It could be called infinity—a circle with no circumference whose centre is everywhere. Its nearest and purest symbol is perhaps zero—the number before numbers commence. Then this nothingness becomes a blaze of light—The Limitless Light. "God said, Let there be light: and there was light."

18. From this limitless light crystallises Kether—meaning The Crown. A centre has crystallised in nothingness—a point, which according to Euclid's axiom has position but no size. It is self existent, alone, and therefore can be allocated the number one.

19. Then, when the Crown of Creation is established, it becomes conscious of itself, having nothing else to be conscious of, and projects an image of itself, the second

Sephirah, Chokmah—meaning Wisdom. There is now a duality in being and so we have the number two. The 'Spiritual Experience' of Chokmah is called 'The Vision of God face to face'. As it is stressed many times in the Old Testament that no man shall look upon the face of God and live it can be surmised that a real experience of the Sephirah Chokmah would be shattering. Only the highest mystics are likely to get anywhere near it without heavy protective veils of symbolism.

20. Next comes Binah, making the first triangle, the simplest plane figure, and thus the idea of form. Up to now all has been pure force. And even Binah is force, but force with the latent idea of form because an archetypal idea has been created by three forces which, by their very number, make possible the concretion into form. Binah has been described as the idea or possibility of form, or limitation of force—each Sephirah works out one new 'idea'. The number of Binah is, of course, three; and its name means Understanding. An idea of the subtlety of these levels can be inferred by considering the titles of Chokmah and Binah, Wisdom and Understanding. Understanding has a slightly more concrete implication than Wisdom. Wisdom can be a pure state, but Understanding implies that there is something to understand.

21. We now have a triangle formed which can be called the Supernal or Archetypal Triangle, in contradistinction to the Moral or Ethical Triangle of Chesed, Geburah, Tiphareth and the Astral or Psychological Triangle of Netzach, Hod, Yesod. Malkuth, the physical world, is on its own diagramatically, as a pendant to the Astral or Psychological Triangle. These triangles demonstrate which functional Sephiroth polarise into which central Sephiroth. An example has already been given of Netzach and Hod seeking their balance in Tiphareth, Yesod and Malkuth. Similarly the pure force of Chokmah and the archetypal idea of form of Binah have their point of equilibrium in Kether, the original source of upwelling life pressure from the Unmani-

fest, and, coming further down into concretion, in Tiphareth, the central balancing point of the whole Tree. The Paths interlinking the Sephiroth show the manifestation of this triangular principle.

22. There is a further division of the Tree into four levels known as the Four Worlds. These are Atziluth, the Archetypal World; Briah, the Creative World; Yetzirah, the Formative World; and Assiah, the Material World.

23. The Archetypal World consists only of Kether, the point where the original life urge wells up, holding within itself as an archetype the latency of its future potentialities as a seed holds the archetype of the grown plant.

24. The Creative World consists of Chokmah and Binah, the pure force and idea of form from which further creation ensues.

25. The Formative World, the world of forms, contains the remaining Sephiroth except Malkuth, for although physical concretion has not yet taken place, all manifestation below the Supernal Triangle is in terms of forms, whether mental concepts or imaginary images or pure nodes of energy.

26. The Material World, the Sephirah Malkuth, is where physical manifestation takes place.

27. To revert to the descent of the Tree, following the course of The Lightning Flash, the next stage from Binah is the formation of the Sephirah Chesed. Here what was supernal force takes on form and the point of transmutation is over what is called the Abyss. The Abyss is the void between force and form and the place where the transmutation takes place is the 'hidden' Sephirah Daath— meaning Knowledge. The Mysteries of Daath are profound and were little touched on in earlier writings on the Qabalah. The Sephirah has no number allocated to it and by Knowledge is meant not so much what we understand by the word, but the word in its biblical usage of sexual union, only here the meaning is a kind of Divine Union where differing planes of being impact and there is a resultant

change of state brought to birth—a transformation or transmutation of power.

28. In Chesed is the pristine form laid down. Chesed means Mercy or Love but its alternative title, Gedulah, Greatness or Magnificence perhaps gives a better idea. Its number is four, with the implied associations of four-squaredness, or a foundation stone upon which all further development in form is based.

29. From this fundamental sphere of stability is emanated Geburah, the fifth Sephirah, meaning Strength, or Pachad, Fear. It is the onward thrust into dense manifestation and is a sphere of vast force in form, as its diagonally opposite, Chokmah, is vast force without form. It will be seen that the stability of Chesed is likewise a reflection of its diagonal opposite, Binah, the archetypal idea of form.

30. The attribution of the word Pachad, Fear, to Geburah can be misleading. It is not fear as commonly understood but what might be called the 'fear of God', the feeling of awe one feels in the presence of a great kinetic force of Nature such as an erupting volcano, a raging sea, a tornado or an earth tremor.

31. Chesed and Geburah are respectively the latent and kinetic energy of the Universe. We use the term energy as opposed to force because force we have stated to be the state of life beyond form; by energy we mean force indwelling form. And in the spheres of Chesed and Geburah the forms are not concreted into images yet; at these levels pure energy is a form. In psychological terms it is 'will to action' before any plan of action has been formulated. The images assigned to Chesed and Geburah may make understanding easier—Chesed is represented by a king sitting on a throne in state, Geburah, by a king in his chariot.

32. From the prickly five-sided form of Geburah, evolved symbolically from the stable square of Chesed, we have the six-sided figure of Tiphareth. Tiphareth is the central Sephirah on the Tree, the point of equilibrium for all that has gone before it and all that is to come after. All the side

Sephiroth balance into it and it also holds the balance between Daath and Yesod, and Kether and Malkuth. It is thus appropriately named Beauty. It is the force of the Supernals brought down into manifestation in perfect equilibrium.

33. The state of equilibrium finally overbalances in the course of the descent of power and the seventh Sephirah, Netzach, meaning Victory, is formed. It is an active Sephirah, reflecting its diagonal, Geburah, which in turn we have seen reflects the kinetic nature of its higher diagonal opposite, Chokmah. The figure seven, attributed to Netzach, calls to mind the seven bands of the spectrum and it is in Netzach that the equilibrated power of Tiphareth splits into diversified aspects.

34. These diversified aspects of energy develop into forms in Hod, Glory. The figure eight can be considered a development of the first coming into form symbolised by the four of Chesed. There is a link between Hod and Chesed as they are diagonally opposite; they are, like Binah, 'form' as opposed to 'force' Sephiroth.

35. From the conjunction of the powers of Netzach and the forms of Hod comes The Foundation, Yesod. As its name implies, it is the foundation of the .physical form, the framework of stresses which later concrete into the tenth Sephirah, Malkuth, the physical world. With the figure ten is the end of the series of numbers and also the completion of the descent of force into form.

36. To recapitulate, we have seen how force upwells in Kether, flows forth in Chokmah, takes on the idea of form in Binah, descends into form via Daath, manifests as energy, latent, kinetic and equilibrated in Chesed, Geburah and Tiphareth, diversifies in Netzach, takes on concrete forms in Hod, forms a basic pattern in Yesod and physically manifests in Malkuth.

37. This is the bare bones of the philosophy of the Tree of Life. Applying the Sephiroth to the psychology of man we have Kether representing the essential self of the soul

of man, his innermost being, the spark of divine fire we call the Spirit. In Chokmah is reflected the type of the basic power of the Spirit and in Binah, how that type will manifest in the worlds of form.

38. Across the Abyss, in Chesed, the force of the Spirit is first equilibrated in form, a direct reflection in psychic energy of the spiritual pattern of itself. In Geburah this energised image or 'eidolon' takes more concrete form by expression of its nature, and the equilibrium resulting from the perfect image performing perfect expression for its nature results in Tiphareth, the sphere which in psychological parlance has been called the Superconscious.

39. Tiphareth manifests to man in the world as the proddings of conscience, and most religious experiences of a more or less common occurrence are experiences of consciousness touching the sphere of Tiphareth. William James' classic treatise 'Varieties of Religious Experience' collates many examples of this.

40. As a genuine contact of the ordinary conscious mind with Tiphareth can result in sudden conversion and mystical revelation, it will be gathered that experiences of Geburah and Chesed, let alone Daath and the Supernal Triangle, will be even more potent. It could change the whole life and even shatter it, hence the warnings against dabbling with ceremonial magic which are found in books on that subject. If consciousness is powerfully concentrated by artificial methods such as high ritual there may well be a dangerously powerful influx of force unless the whole thing is carefully controlled, as in a Roman Catholic Mass, which is of course a ritual designed to evoke in the soul the powers attributed to the Sephirah Tiphareth.

41. There should be no danger for most students practising individual meditation on the Tree however unless they are ultra-psychic. Indeed, given good sense and good intention the Tree is a fine spiritual therapy but like all things which are potent for good it can be misapplied. If any diffusion of consciousness is experienced as a result of working upon

it then it is as well to let it alone for a time, or even abandon it altogether until such time as one can study under the personal supervision of an experienced teacher. These words are not said for dramatic affect, nor are they meant to frighten anybody—they mean exactly what they say. There is no greater risk than in any other system of mystical development for the average student but it is well to be aware of the possibilities and potencies involved. It is no parlour game for over-imaginative fools.

42. In Netzach is the force of the creative imagination and the emotions in general; in Hod, the concrete images of mental concepts and all that is usually meant by 'mentality'. Yesod holds the subconscious mind and the instincts, and Malkuth, the physical man.

43. Thus we have covered the Tree superficially in its philosophical and psychological aspects, but it must be remembered that the Tree exists in its own right as an archetypal plan and that the ideas of increasing concretion in form implied by the Sephiroth can be applied at any level. We can posit a Tree in each Sephirah for instance. A Sephirah when it is first formed manifests first as a point of upwelling force, its own Kether, and from this archetypal level, or Atziluth, procedes to produce its own Creative, Formative and Material Worlds through the formation of its own Sephiroth. The term Material World here means its densest possible aspect, there is no physical form for Kether for instance, but the Malkuth of Kether is that which precedes the formation of the Kether of Chokmah and so on down the Tree. Though one must not forget the analogues of the Veils of Negative Existence which precede the Kether of each Sephirah.

44. In this manner the use of the Tree can be further extended. In the abstruser ranges of occult metaphysics for example, the whole of the Universe, from Spirit to Matter, can be placed in Malkuth, that is, Malkuth is considered to be the entire Seventh Cosmic Plane. Kether then would be the Central Stillness on the First Cosmic Plane and

the other Sephiroth the stages between. This is an application which will be of use and interest only to advanced esoteric students however.

45. Students with some knowledge of other theosophical systems may care to attempt to correlate these systems with the Tree of Life. Attempts to do this are very good practice in becoming familiar with the concepts of the Tree. As a general guide, the Tree can be split into a sevenfold system by taking it level by level: 1—Kether, 2—Chokmah and Binah, 3—Chesed and Geburah, 4—Tiphareth, 5—Netzach and Hod, 6—Yesod, 7—Malkuth. Alternatively, Daath can be included as a separate level and Yesod and Malkuth lumped together. Another way is to include the Supernals together as the highest level and Yesod and Malkuth together as the lowest, with each individual Sephirah as a level between. The three functional Triads, and the Four Worlds have already been mentioned and suggest correlations with three and fourfold systems. The Middle Pillar can also be used to correlate with the Chakras of the Eastern teaching. It will be found in some cases that no straightforward correspondence can be made that is not open to debate but this is all to the good. It is far better for anyone attempting this kind of exercise to work out the problems for himself than to look up books and read other people's opinions. It is better to have a little genuine understanding about the Tree of Life than much second-hand learning.

Chapter IV

THE SEPHIROTHIC ATTRIBUTIONS

1. The attributions of symbolism assigned to the various Sephiroth are best considered under certain classified headings.

2. At first sight some of the headings and the attributions may appear arbitrary or nonsensical, but this is purely a conscious mind reaction. The Tree of Life speaks to the unconscious mind which has its own lines of reasoning that the conscious mind cannot readily understand. It will be found that after working at the Tree for a time the attributions will fall into place quite naturally without any efforts of conscious memory. And after all, if the Tree is what it is claimed to be, a diagram of the inner structure of man, then this is only what one has a right to expect.

3. It must always be remembered that it is a *Tree of Life* and not a Framework of Mentality. Mere mental juggling with symbolism will lead nowhere, it has to be made a part of one by meditation, contemplation, prayer, or fasting, sack-cloth and ashes if necessary. The implications of the symbolism, as well as being considered by the mind, must be felt in the heart, groped for by the aspirations, embedded in the viscera almost. The Tree of Life is not merely a lifetime's study, it is a way of life.

4. In view of this it will be plain that any so-called 'objective' study of the Tree of Life would be, if not impossible, certainly of little consequence. The remarks on the attributions throughout this book then must be taken, not as an attempt at logical proofs to the rational mind, but as the often unclassified results of practical experience, including

38

great chunks of symbolism which have not been fully explored, and also tentative intuitions of further possibilities. The implications of the Tree of Life are so vast that no definitive treatise is possible.

5. However, a brave attempt will be made at a rational approach so that the student can find his bearings. And if anything is found which appears too fantastic, or just incomprehensible, it is best to leave it alone and come back to it at some future time, when it may have become clearer. Of the attributions, only the Hebrew Divine Names are part of the original Tree and thus with claims to be divinely inspired. The remainder of the attributions have been built up by subsequent research through the intervening centuries, and as incorporated here, include some of the most recent concepts of advanced esotericism. The latter are included as being a possible help to occult students of some experience; they should not be allowed to become a barrier to anyone who comes to esotericism for the first time via this book.

6. On contemplating the problems involved in getting across some of the concepts of the Tree of Life one is strongly tempted merely to list the basic symbolism, give a few simple instructions on meditation, and then tell the reader to get on with it. This might perhaps be too bald an approach, but it is hoped that the reader *will* set down and get on with it after having read this book—otherwise it will have been written in vain. What matters is what one receives from the Tree oneself and one only gets that by working on it.

7. In view of this, nothing which appears within these pages should be taken as authoritative. The only real authority rests within oneself, and it has to be searched for "Ask, and it shall be given you; seek, and ye shall find; knock, and it shall be opened unto you. For everyone that asketh receiveth; and he that seeketh findeth; and to him that knocketh it shall be opened." And it is perhaps not always realised that the giving of what is asked, and the

revealing of what is sought, and the opening of the Way it is desired to tread, is done by the same being that does the asking, the seeking, and the knocking—to wit, oneself.

8. *The Title of the Sephirah:* This gives, in so far as is possible, a root idea of what the Sephirah stands for in one word, e.g. Wisdom, Understanding, Beauty etc. It is given first in anglicised Hebrew and then in English, and a table of the letters which go to make up the Hebrew titles and Divine Names is given at the back of this volume.

9. It is well to become familiarised with the Hebrew letters because they play an important part in practical working upon the Paths between the Sephiroth, which will be dealt with in Volume II. Much was made of the numerical value assigned to each letter by early Qabalists and by an elaborate system of codes and anagrams, hidden significances and secret teaching was said to be revealed.

10. As an example, Genesis xviii 2, "And lo, three men" in the original Hebrew has a numerical value of 701, which is equal to the numerical value of the Hebrew sentence, "These are Michael, Gabriel and Raphael"—three of the Sephirothic Archangels. Further, the first word of the Old Testament, used as an acrostic by the medieval Jewish Qabalist, Solomon Meir Ben Moses, was taken to hold the following secret meanings:

a) "The Son, the Spirit, the Father, Their Trinity, Perfect Unity."

b) "The Son, the Spirit, the Father, ye shall equally worship Their Trinity."

c) "Ye shall worship My first-born, My first, Whose Name is Jesus.

d) "When the Master shall come Whose Name is Jesus ye shall worship."

e) "I will choose a virgin worthy to bring forth Jesus, and ye shall call her blessed."

f) "I will hide myself in cake (baked with) coals, for ye shall eat Jesus, My Body."

11. By means of these he apparently converted another Jew, previously bitterly opposed to Christianity. However, the number of permutations and combinations used in this branch of Qabalism make it possible to prove almost anything and there is probably more superstition, special pleading and logic chopping in it than anything of value. But like most superstitions, it has a basis of truth to it. It seems that certain words, usually Proper Nouns, were specially constructed originally with this kind of thing in mind. As an example, the name for the metaphysical concept, 'the great sterile Mother' is AMA, (Aleph, Mem, Aleph.) The letter Yod, as a symbol, represents the fertilising aspect of nature and so the name for 'the great fertile Mother' is the same, but with a Yod added to show that it has been impregnated with fertility—namely, AIMA, (Aleph, Yod, Mem, Aleph.) This is quite apart from any numerical significance or coding.

12. But to pursue a comprehensive line of research in these matters would require a knowledge of the Hebrew language and access to the Qabalistic literature, the Old Testament in the original, the Zohar, the Sepher Yetzirah, the Sepher Sephiroth, the Asch Metzareph and all their dependencies. This is beyond the scope of most students including the present writer. It is also beyond the scope of this book which is concerned primarily with the Qabalistic diagram, the Tree of Life, which, from experience, is quite enough to keep anyone occupied for a very long time.

13. However, in the case of obvious significances, tentative interpretations will be attempted. It is a field which has been little tilled and there appear to be some strange growths in it. Anyone who has the necessary qualifications is invited to reap what he can find but he will have to go it alone. There is little modern literature on the subject and most references seem to be derived from Magregor Mathers' 'The Kabbalah Unveiled', written in 1887, or Christian Ginsburg's 'The Kabbalah' of 1865.

14. It is interesting to note however, the vast wave of

popular superstition that has arisen from this Judaic tradition. There are any amount of books purporting to tell future and character from the letters of one's name, or adding the digits of one's date of birth and so on. These are of little, if any, worth and are merely suffocating and foul-smelling smoke from, and concealing, a very dim-glowing fire. Even the know-it-all Crowley abandoned the comparison of modern alphabets with early ones as hopeless.

15. *Subsidiary Titles:* These are further titles culled from Qabalistic literature which expand the concept of a Sephirah, often from a different point of view.

16. *The Magical Image:* Magic is the term used for building mental images and is perhaps an unfortunate term as it has a glare of glamour about it. The Magical Image then, is the mental picture which can be built up to represent a Sephirah. The unconscious mind works primarily in pictures and so it is a useful device. Like all symbolism that has been used for long ages, a pool of force and ideas grows up around it so that one has only to tap that central symbol and all the related ideas will flow up from the unconscious. The technique for doing this is, of course, meditation.

17. *The God Name:* This, together with the Archangelic and Angelic Names is an original part of the Tree of Life and thus has claims to divine inspiration.

18. The God Name represents the most spiritual form of the Sephirah and thus is conceived as functioning in the Kether, or Atziluthic World, of that Sephirah. In commencing a meditation or practical operation on one of the Sephiroth the spiritual force of the God Name should be dwelt on first. One should always, as a matter of principle, start from the most spiritual aspect and work downwards. Concentrated work purely on the God Name is not recommended because it represents a direct force, untempered by any intermediary, and thus can well prove too hot to

handle unless the operator is well experienced.

19. It must be borne in mind also that all the God Names are aspects of the One God. Thus one would think in terms of 'the One God, in His Name . . .'.

20. These Names all appear in the Old Testament but for the most part have been translated by the single word 'God', though with occasional attempts at more literal translation such as Lord, The Ancient of Days, Lord of Hosts etc. It is interesting to note that in the original Hebrew, God can be both masculine and feminine, singular and plural. For instance, in Genesis iv 26 the literal translation is "And Elohim said: Let Us make man . . . ." The word Elohim is a feminine singular stem with a masculine plural ending. Thus the principle of polarity is taken well into account, a point which is lost in the translation.

21. The approximate English equivalent is given in the table of God Names but in practical work the Hebrew version should be used. One can visualise the Name in its Hebrew form, not forgetting that Hebrew reads from right to left, and if it is said aloud or mentally, experience has shown that pronunciation is not important, the Hebrew Names anyway consist mainly of consonants.

22. *The Archangel:* This may cause some initial difficulty to those brought up on Protestant theology or on no theology at all.

23. The Archangel organises the forces inherent in a Sephirah and the direction of motivating forces that come under its presidency. It thus works on the Briatic level, the Creative World, of a Sephirah, and certain of the symbols and titles of a Sephirah relate to that level. Reflection on these symbols or titles can bring a contact with the corresponding Archangel. Thus 'Ama' has a special relationship to Tzaphkiel, and the orb and tetrahedron have a special relationship to Tzadkiel. Experiment is recommended with regard to the other Sephiroth.

24. Archangels are real beings though they have not

physical bodies. Their anthropomorphic forms, as represented in religious painting for example, come from the human mind, which has to have a mental form acceptable to the understanding. More appropriate forms would be pillars of vast force, or profound geometric shapes in accordance with the basic nature of the Sephirah—such would be more in accordance with the real 'appearance' an Archangel would assume.

25. An Archangel is a Lord of Flame, the Lords of Flame being a life evolution previous to humanity—in fact the primal evolution—which laid down the prime stresses of the Universe which are the basis of the physical laws discovered by science. It is impossible to enter into these fascinating fields of esoteric cosmology here, but they can be examined in Dion Fortune's 'The Cosmic Doctrine' (Aquarian Press, London.) The Flame referred to in the title, Lord of Flame, is Divine Fire, which is a highly abstract condition of Will—the myth of Prometheus has relevance to it.

26. It is, generally speaking, easier, and as said before, more suitable, until a fair degree of experience has been attained, to invoke the Archangel of the Sphere rather than the God Name—though the God Name should be dwelt on briefly first to base the meditation or operation on a spiritual level. The force of the Archangel is easier to handle should the potency invoked cause too great an influx of power. The force of the Archangel will, strong as it is, dissipate and disappear more quickly. In invoking angelic help, visualisation of the appropriate colour and playing appropriate music is of great assistance. One can also dwell mentally on those whom the Archangel has helped, for example, with Raphael, the young Tobias, or, with Gabriel, Daniel or the Virgin Mary.

27. In case this should appear as sheer superstition to any reader it might be as well to reiterate that experience is the only proof. And if mental contact is attempted in a spirit of scepticism then the result will be failure—though

this failure will be considered success no doubt from the sceptical point of view. In mystical work certain steps have to be taken in faith and this is one of them. The critical faculties should by all means be used *after* a psychic experiment—blind credulity is of use to no-one—but when doing actual work along these lines, belief is necessary, and the controlled use and receptivity of the creative imagination. In Qabalistic words, one does the work in the spirit of Netzach, the Occult Intelligence, but uses one's Hod, whose ethic is Truth, afterwards in analysing the results.

28. Those who are more inclined to credulity on the other hand should beware the superstition that the Archangel is standing there in the room before them. The contact is an inner one. By visualising the appropriate symbols and performing the appropriate invocations one is tuning in one's mental radio to a particular wavelength and this analogy explains how it is possible for several people in different places to get onto a particular contact at the same time. Much misunderstanding has been caused by taking state-ments of mystics too literally—the seeing and hearing is done with the inner eye and ear and not with the physical organs. In other words, with the creative imagination.

29. It should be said though that an objective shell can be built up for a psychic force to indwell, but this is not likely to be achieved by anyone who has not undergone a long course of mental training. And anyway, the form would be visible only to someone having 'etheric vision'— a natural psychic. This form of psychism is fairly un-common and the lack of it causes much heartburning to many esoteric neophytes. However it is no particular advantage to have it—in fact it can be more of a hindrance for it tends to draw the attention entirely to the glamour of astral forms. Esoteric schools train people to perceive on a higher level, to develop a hyper-sensitive intuition, and this, although less sensational to the perceiver, is a far more reliable method of psychic perception.

30. *The Order of Angels:* Much that has been said about the Archangels applies also to the Angels. The Angels are responsible for what might be called the 'mechanics' of a Sephirah and operate in its Yetzirah, or Formative World. God has been called The Great Architect of the Universe, the Angels are His builders. By the same metaphor the Archangels could be regarded as His foremen or overseers.

31. There are, besides the Sephirothic Angels, other Orders, including great and beautiful Nature Beings of the higher types under whom Elementals work. The order of their hierarchy is Archangel, Angel, Elemental Spirit. In the East they are generally known as Devas.

32. Certain Angels work especially with Group Souls of animals, others with Group Souls of nations, that is, under the presidency of the National Angel of the country. A National Angel is best built in the form that holds the ideals of that nation. For example it could take the form in Britain of Britannia or St. George, and in the United States of the Statue of Liberty. Remember that the forms that the potencies indwell are man made.

33. There are other Angels that ensoul the essence of beauty in the various forms of art, whether music, painting, sculpture, poetry or drama. If these arts really touch the higher levels they bring down a great amount of Angelic force which intensifies a hundredfold the appeal to the hearer or onlooker. Ready-built man-made forms for these are, for example, the Nine Muses.

34. It is quite useless expecting contact with these beings if one never thinks of them, therefore if one wants Angelic contacts one must think of the Angels, feel with them, imagine them as they are, great and wonderful forms of light and glory, deep protective presences in contact with God and man, forming a link between. Where Angels speak or send messages to man, they do not exactly send a message in language, but they impress the idea or the meaning of the message very strongly on the mind of the recipient and his subconscious mind supplies appropriate

words. They are also much concerned with immediate after-death conditions of man and the beasts.

35. An Angel is a perfect entity, it does not evolve. In a way, the lesser Angels are divine automata. In this they are superior to man but they do not have man's potentialities. Man has plucked the fruit of the Tree of the Knowledge of Good and Evil which makes him potentially a God, though only after a long period of travail being strung halfway between the condition of the Angels and the beasts. Man's Path is one of the equilibrium between the opposites, forging the pattern of his humanity. The bestial type of person is really no worse than the one who deviates to the side of the Angels and is 'too good to be true'—in fact the latter can be even more, and literally, inhuman. The glyph of the Pillars is very much of personal as well as Universal application.

36. *The Mundane Chakra:* This is not a good name for the idea it tries to convey, but must be used for want of something better. The Mundane Chakras are, for the most part, planetary attributions, but the astrological forces associated with the planets are properly allocated to the Paths between the Sephiroth, which are psychological states, microcosmic, as opposed to the Sephiroth themselves which are primarily Universal or Macrocosmic.

37. What is implied by the Mundane Chakra is that each of the Sephiroth has some resemblance to the Divine Plan behind certain planets or astronomical forces. The writers of science fiction speak truer than they think for there are life forces on or in or 'in-forming' all the other planetary and stellar bodies but perhaps not in a way readily imaginable to man. Whenever a certain concept takes a grip upon the mind of man in the mass it is a good indication that there is a truth behind it, however fantastic the imaginative speculations may appear. And the truth often turns out to be stranger than the fiction; the limits of man's mind are, in a certain sense, his protection.

38. While astrology is by no means a certain science, there being so many variable factors involved, the development and constant change of the 'zeitgeist' or 'spirit of the times', the similarity in branches of art work and the frequent cases of simultaneous scientific discovery can be considered largely the result of extra-terrestrial influences.

39. *The Spiritual Experience:* This title explains itself and each one is called a Vision. This is misleading because it does not mean a picture thrown into consciousness, but a state of mind or expansion of awareness brought about by realisation of the powers of a Sephirah. It is similar to being 'informed' by an Archangel, as Daniel was by Gabriel, which does not necessarily mean the hearing of any words, or a seeing of any pictorial visions, but a process of being 'in-formed' so that one's psyche acts as a vehicle for, or is permeated by, the powers concerned. Thus is spiritual growth steadily but unspectacularly made.

40. *The Virtue and Vice:* These are not strictly part of a Sephirah itself but are the reactions of the human psyche to it. The Virtue is the quality that the Sephirah should confer and which is essential to the proper working of the powers of that Sephirah. The Vice is the type of unbalance that a Sephirah may cause through human weakness; really a Sephirah has no vice, but the 'Mundane Chakra's' astrological bad influence is put there, sometimes with dubious correctness. However the Vice can sometimes serve as an interesting indicator in an occult school, for human nature being what it is, the unbalance usually manifests first, so that when a student well established in the harmony of Tiphareth starts becoming unaccountably contentious then one can mark it down as a possible symptom of spiritual growth, for it may mean that he is approaching Geburah but has not attained full control of its potencies yet.

41. *The Symbols:* These are images subsidiary to the Magical Image and as already mentioned in the section on Archangels, can be used to make contact with certain aspects of a Sephirah. They can also throw further light on a Sephirah from a different angle pictorially, as the subsidiary titles do verbally.

42. *The Yetziratic Text:* These texts are descriptions of the Sephiroth and Paths as given in a supplement to the Sepher Yetzirah, or Book of Formations, an early Qabalistic document. The language, though obscure, yields much to meditation.

43. The book of texts designates as 'Paths' all the facets of the Tree—the ten Sephiroth and the twentytwo Paths—hence the expression 'The Thirtytwo Paths of Concealed Glory'. It also gives each one a title, called an 'Intelligence', which acts as a very useful subsidiary title to the Sephirah or Path.

44. The translations used are those of Dr. Wynn Westcott, taken from the Hebrew version of Joannes Stephanus Rittangelius printed in Amsterdam in 1642, and with reference to numerous other versions. Dr. A. E. Waite has criticised them as being too eclectic and has offered his own translations which he claimed to be more accurate, but experience has shown the Westcott versions to be more valuable. It can hardly be repeated too often that the Qabalah is a living practical system, not a cut and dried body of authority. Even if Waite's contention is true, that his scholarship is superior to Westcott's, it does not alter the fact that, as far as the modern practical Qabalist is concerned, an intuitive reconstruction of an ancient and probably corrupt text is superior to an unimaginative literal translation.

45. *The Flashing Colours:* These are colours attributed to each Sephirah, one for each level within it. In visualisation it can be a help to use the appropriate colour. Thus God

manifesting in a Sephirah could be pictured as an effulgence of the Atziluthic colour, the Archangel as a pillar of the Briatic colour, the Angels as geometric shapes of the Yetziratic colour, and a general background could be used of the Assiatic colour.

46. It is best to build up a vocabulary of colour in the mind from the natural world by contemplating the brilliant colours of sunrise or sunset for example, or the subtle colourings of the flora and fauna of Nature. Radiant light should be the concept to get at rather than the reflected dull light of pigments. The clichés of the mind should be overcome by the freshness of first hand observation.

47. In practical working, when pictures build up spontaneously in the imagination, it may be found that the colours do not correspond with the traditional ones. This need not cause any great concern for, from experience, the colours seem to be largely arbitrary for they often vary from person to person. Sometimes an important symbol will come up in the appropriate colours.

48. For general purposes in meditation upon the Tree it is customary to think of each Sephirah in its Briatic colour. This is no doubt in accordance with the fact that the Archangelic force is the easiest to handle.

49. *Pagan Mythology:* The gods and goddesses of pagan mythology are so numerous and diversified that immense scholarship would be needed to attribute each to its place on the Tree, and, being composite, each could go on more than one Sephirah, for example, Artemis on Geburah, Yesod or Netzach, depending on each one's idea of the God. In all cases it is the idea that counts. No time is wasted in studying mythology however for all myths and legends are expressions of a race's attempt to classify the powers of God as they work through the subjective and objective worlds. All the gods and goddesses are aspects of the One God, but they are not codified so neatly as the

Ten Emanations of the Jewish Qabalah. It is a useful exercise to correlate the different systems though, for one throws light on another, not only from the point of view of intellectual understanding but also from the stimulation of the imagination. A person who could make little of the idea of Chokmah, for instance, might get closer to an awareness of its nature by considering the attribution of Zeus hurling thunderbolts. But then in his other aspects Zeus could equally be considered as a Kether figure, as King of the gods, or in Chesed as the beneficent ruler, or in Geburah etc, etc, etc. Again one sees the impossibility of cut and dried cataloguing. No systematic attributions will be made therefore throughout the text unless to emphasise a particular point. It is strongly recommended that students try to work out correspondences for themselves for this will produce facility in using the Tree. Also attributions may vary, quite validly, from person to person, and so there is little to be gained by hunting up supposed authorities, such as Crowley's '777' or even the text of this book. With the Qabalah it is a question of 'no ticket—no laundry'— and the only valid ticket is personal experience.

50. *The Tarot:* As correspondences to the Tree of Life, the twentytwo Trumps of the Tarot relate to the Paths, the sixteen Court Cards to the Four Worlds, and the forty small cards to the Sephiroth according to number. As the Tarot is a complete system within itself it will be dealt with as a whole, including the Sephirothic attributions, in the second volume of this book.

51. *The Grades:* An esoteric grade is assigned to each Sephirah but as there is so much misunderstanding with regard to the conception of esoteric grades they demand a special chapter to themselves.

52. *The Qliphoth:* These demonic forces are best left until a good general idea of the Tree has been assimilated. They

are thus also treated separately.

53. *Miscellaneous:* This includes precious stones, plants, animals, perfumes, alchemical terms etc., most of which are highly arbitrary and in any case more in the province of the experienced ritualist. Thus a separate chapter is allocated to this subject also.

Part II

Chapter V

THE UNMANIFEST AND THE VEILS
OF NEGATIVE EXISTENCE

1. Before the manifestation of the first Sephirah is the Unmanifest, which, through the condensation of the Cloud-Veils of Negative Existence, finally concretes Kether, the first manifest of the manifest Universe.

2. The Unmanifest is that which is, before anything was, and to which all things will return. It is the alpha and the omega, the Beginning and the Ending. It is not a thing that can be explained because it is beyond the reach of the rational mind. It is a concept which defies the reason because it is above reason. It is perhaps to break people of the domination of reason that Zen Buddhism uses aphorisms like 'imagine the sound of one hand clapping'. An attempt to imagine the Unmanifest throws a similar spanner into the works of the mind.

3. The first chapter of 'The Cosmic Doctrine', the cosmological treatise received from the inner planes through the mediumship of Dion Fortune, attempts to describe it as follows:

4. "The Unmanifest is pure existence. We cannot say of it that is is *Not*. Although it is not manifest, it IS. IT is the source from which all arises. IT is the only 'Reality'. IT alone is substance. IT alone is stable; all else is an appearance and a becoming. Of this Unmanifest we can only say 'IT IS'. IT is the verb 'to be' turned back upon itself. IT is a state of pure 'Being', without qualities and without history. All we can say of IT is that it is not anything that we know, for if we know anything it must be in manifesta-

54

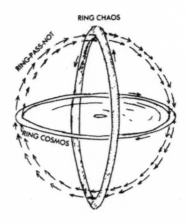

RING CHAOS

RING-PASS-NOT

RING COSMOS

Fig. 4a. The Three Primary Rings of
'The Cosmic Doctrine.' The
Ring Cosmos subsequently
becomes a disc, concreting a
centre—'The Central Stillness.

tion for us to know it, and if it is in manifestation, it is
not unmanifest. The Unmanifest is the Great Negation;
at the same time IT is the infinite potency which has not
occurred. It is best conceived of under the image of inter-
stellar space."†

5. It is well to note that the image of interstellar space
is but a symbol to assist understanding. The same source
goes on to describe the process of first manifestation as
'space' beginning to move in a ring, if one can conceive of
nothingness moving, and the 'movement' of this ring
setting up 'movement' at 'right angles' to it so that another
ring is formed outside the first. The interaction of the
forces of the two rings then causes the inner ring to rotate
on the axis formed where the two rings interconnect, thus
causing a third spherical ring to be formed by the transverse rotation of the primary ring. The symbol thus
described resembles a gyroscope. (Fig. 4a) The central
ring, spinning in two directions at once then concretes a
centre.

The Cosmic Doctrine—Dion Fortune. Published by Aquarian Press, London.

Fig. 4b. The Cloud-Veils of
Negative Existence
Concreting Kether.

6. The first ring, from which is eventually created the whole Cosmos, is called the Ring Cosmos; the second ring, which acts as a thrust-block for the first ring's secondary movement, is called the Ring Chaos; and the third ring, described by the transverse spin of the first, is called the Ring-Pass-Not because it transcribes a sphere of limitation for all future development. The centre then formed by the Ring Cosmos corresponds to Kether.

7. It must be remembered that this is all metaphor.

8. These three Rings can be equated with the Veils of Negative Existence on the Tree of Life. The Ring Cosmos to AIN, the Ring Chaos to AIN SOPH, and the Ring-Pass-Not to AIN SOPH AUR.

9. This concretion of a centre, Kether, by AIN through the development of AIN SOPH and AIN SOPH AUR can be further illustrated by the traditional Qabalistic diagram of the Cloud-Veils of Negative Existence. (Fig. 4b) It will be seen that the correspondences from these two sources are exact.

10. In the original Hebrew, the names of the Three Veils

are of three, six, and nine letters respectively, with each three letters occurring in the next denser Veil. AIN—Aleph, Yod, Nun. AIN SOPH—Aleph, Yod, Nun. Samekh, Vau, Peh. AIN SOPH AUR—Aleph, Yod, Nun. Samekh, Vau, Peh. Aleph, Vau, Resh. This has reference to the Three Pillars, which are the three possibilities of the way in which force can manifest—active, passive or equilibrated. The Four Worlds of the Sephiroth only exist when they have been achieved, and when manifestation ultimately withdraws up the planes they cease to exist. The Pillars, as possibilities, exist whether there is manifestation or not.

11. Thus the glyph of the Pillars should not be thought of as part of the glyph of the Tree of Life. They are separate entities. The Sephiroth are established modes of existence, the Paths between them are established experiences in consciousness, but the Pillars are possibilities of manifestation and have their root in the Unmanifest.

12. In pursuit of further metaphors for the concepts implied by the Veils of Negative Existence it may prove helpful to turn to the early verses of the Old Testament. It has been said that the Bible can be fully explained only in the light of the Qabalah, the latter being a mystical interpretation of it, as the Talmud is a learned commentary upon it. Whether this is true or not would need very advanced understanding to judge, but in our elementary studies, the Bible, which we do know fairly well, may throw some light upon the Qabalah, which we do not.

13. Verses two to five of the first chapter of Genesis read as follows:

"And the Earth was without form, and void: and darkness was upon the face of the deep. And the Spirit of God moved upon the face of the waters. And God said, Let there be light: and there was light. And God saw the light, that it was good: and God divided the light from the darkness. And God called the light Day, and the darkness He called Night."

14. Unless one is a confirmed Fundamentalist, it will be

obvious that 'Earth', 'waters', and 'light' are not meant to be understood in their everyday sense. As a suggestion, the dark void can be equated with AIN, Nothingness; the Spirit of God moving upon the face of the waters with AIN SOPH, the Limitless; and the light with AIN SOPH AUR, the Limitless Light.

15. Here it is interesting to recall the Eastern teaching which conceives of Days and Nights of Manifestation. After a Day of Manifestation the whole Cosmos is withdrawn back to its source, where it rests in a Night of Pralaya. "And God called the light Day, and the darkness He called Night."

16. In almost all religious creation myths, creation first occurs as the manifestation of light. But the Veils of Negative Existence refer to the pre-dawn period before darkness has fully given birth to light, and in this shadowy area there are many symbols which attempt to give some understanding of the primordial darkness before anything was. All of them, however, are variations upon the circle or sphere, from the serpent with its tail in its mouth to the 'rotundum' of the alchemists.

17. It is the circular figure, the endless line, which best gives the idea of something which is self-contained, without beginning or ending; with no before or after, that is, timeless; with no above nor below, without space. Space and time, beginning and ending, come only with the coming of light, or consciousness, and this is not yet present.

18. It is also, as shown in the symbol of the Cosmic Egg, the germ from which all creation arises. It is also a state in which the opposites are united as is shown in the Chinese t'ai chi t'u sign. (Fig. 4c) It is the perfect beginning because the opposites have not yet flown apart and the perfect ending because the opposites have come together again. It is at the same time the primal germ and the final synthesis of all creation.

19. The first stanza of 'The Secret Book of Dzyan' given in Hillard's abridgement of H. P. Blavatsky's 'Secret

58

Fig. 4c. Chinese t'ai chi t'u sign,
'the supreme ultimate.'

Doctrine' gives another description of this condition:

"The Eternal Parent, wrapped in her ever-invisible robes, had slumbered once again for seven Eternities. Time was not, for it lay asleep in the infinite bosom of duration. Universal Mind was not, for there were no Intelligent Beings to contain it . . . The causes of existence were no more; the visible that was, and the invisible that is, rested in eternal Non-Being—the One Being. Alone, the One form of Existence stretched boundless, infinite, cause-less, in dreamless sleep; and Life pulsated unconscious in universal Space, throughout that All-presence which is sensed by the 'Opened Eye' of the Seer. But where was the Seer when the Over-Soul of the Universe was absorbed in the Absolute, and the great Wheel was parentless?"

20. Here we have, implicit in the description of the Un-manifest, the idea that there is a great Cyclic Law by which manifestation occurs and then is withdrawn into the Unmanifest to come forth into manifestation again at some later time—although of course, at these levels, there is no such thing as time as we understand it.

21. Stanza III of this sacred book describes the first coming into manifestation — that is, in Qabalistic terms, the formation of the first emanation, Kether:

"The last vibration of the seventh Eternity thrills through Infinitude. The Mother swells, expanding from within without, like the bud of the lotus. The vibration sweeps along, touching with its swift wing the whole universe, and the Germ that dwelleth in Darkness; the Darkness that breathes over the slumbering Waters of Life. 'Darkness' radiates Light, and Light drops one solitary Ray into the Mother-deep. The Ray shoots through the virgin Egg, the Ray causes the eternal Egg to thrill and drop the non-eternal Germ, which condenses into the World-egg."

22. This passage calls to mind the section of Genesis previously quoted, "and darkness was upon the face of the deep. And the Spirit of God moved upon the face of the waters. And God said, Let there be light: and there was light." And we have already equated this with the Three Veils of Negative Existence and the Three Primary Rings of 'The Cosmic Doctrine'.

23. The Stanza continues: "Then the three fall into the four." The 'three' refers to the Veils of Negative Existence, in which are held the three possibilities of force in action, positive, negative or equilibrated, which is symbolised in the glyph of the Pillars. The 'four' refers to Kether, which, as we shall see in the next chapter, is of a four-fold nature. As Kether is the crown of creation this four-fold nature is relevant to all levels of manifestation and is what the ancients called 'the Four Elements'. Their idea that all substance was composed of varying mixtures of earth, air, fire and water was a philosophical concept—the Elements being modes of being. They of course tried to apply these ideas to primitive chemical science and much error resulted. But it is even more erroneous for moderns to think them more mistaken than they were and that the elements as they considered them were only the four physical ones.

24. The Stanzas of Dzyan are well worth correlating as far as is possible with the aspects of the Tree of Life. They are said to be the original work from which the religious books of all nations are compiled, including 'The Book of

Concealed Mysteries' which is one of the main Qabalistic
texts. This need not be taken too literally as it is unlikely
that the copying was done physically. What is probably
meant is that the inner source of divine writings is the same
and that the Stanzas of Dzyan are the oldest and purest
transcription of ideas from this source. By comparing
sacred texts and symbol systems much enlightenment can
be gained. The language of most of them is so obscure and
symbolic that it is often difficult to tell the difference
between what is profound symbolism beyond one's present
understanding and what is just corruption in the text
through faulty copying or translation. But if apparent
differences are approached in a creative way, seeking to
find resemblances and an over-all synthesis, much will be
attained. A critical approach, seeking to expose discrepancies is not likely to be productive of anything but a catalogue of discrepancies.

25. Many scripts for example set out to symbolise different things, and from different viewpoints and thus there
are bound to be differences of detail. Also it is well to
make one's own interpretation of symbolism through
meditation, and not to accept other people's ideas. Not only
are there differences in people's psychology, causing them
to see things in a different light, but also much symbolism
has reference to many different levels, and as one opens
consciousness to different levels of being then the understanding of particular symbolism may well change or
expand also. Always, the only valid meaning to a symbol
is the meaning that one has wrested from it oneself. A
second-hand meaning is of as little value as no meaning—
and possibly a considerable positive hindrance.

26. As certain races have more aptitude for metaphysical
speculation than others it will be found that some mythologies have comparatively naive creation myths; but on the
other hand, many that sound naive are really highly
abstruse when the key to the symbolism is found. Also the
important point, as mentioned above, is what a particular

god or goddess means to the student, not necessarily what it is supposed to have meant to the original worshippers. The latter will have varied from place to place and time to time, and it is present time that is important to the esoteric student, not the past, or even the future.

27. A close correspondence with the conception of the Unmanifest is to be found in the Greek Hesiod, who wrote his 'Theogony' in the eighth century B.C. It is the oldest known Greek attempt at a mythological classification.

28. "In the beginning," he writes, "there was Chaos vast and dark." This term Chaos comes from a root meaning 'to gape' and thus designates open space. Later confusion has arisen because of a false derivation from a word meaning 'to pour' so that the word came to mean a confused and unorganised mass of elements scattered through space. The original and true meaning is a pure cosmic principle devoid of god-like (or any) forms.

29. From Chaos, continues Hesiod, there first appeared Gaea, the deep-breasted Earth. Gaea thus came to be an Earth goddess, which would place her Qabalistic attribution in Malkuth, but further examination of her characteristics suggests that the Earth meant is the solid basis of prime manifestation, not the solid basis of the growth of life on this planet. There is a symbolic analogue between earth and cosmic space as is shown in the ancient worship of stones, by no means a mere totemistic religion.

30. Apart from Gaea there also appeared Eros—not the later minor god of human love but a grander cosmological conception. There is a parallel between them though if one considers that there is Divine as well as profane love—Divine Union as well as sexual union. And Union with God is the Spiritual Experience of Kether. One could conceive of a mighty Eros rising and loosing a great arrow which, winging through space, creates the planes while descending them like the Lightning Flash upon the Tree.

31. Thus Gaea and Eros could both be considered as Kether figures, bringing attention to the bi-polarity of God.

In support of this attribution there is the fact that Gaea gave birth to Uranus, 'the starry sky', and Pontus, 'the sterile sea', which tie in well as correspondences of Chokmah and Binah.

32. Chaos also brought forth Erebus and Night who, in turn, mated and gave birth to Ether and Hemera, the day. This also corresponds with the first manifestation of light as described in the texts already examined.

33. In the Egyptian pantheòns, the Heliopolitan system describes the god Nu as the primordial Ocean in which the germ of all creation lay. He was called the 'father of the gods' but had no temples built for him and was a purely intellectual concept, though sometimes shown as a figure waist-deep in water holding up the gods he had created. It was taught that inside Nu, before the creation, there lived a formless spirit called Atum, who bore within him the totality of all existence. When he finally manifested from Nu as a separate entity he gave birth to all gods, men and living things and was then known as Ra or Atum-Ra—obviously in this myth a Kether figure.

34. Hathor, in that she was described by some texts as a great celestial cow who created the world and everything in it, including the Sun, can also be aligned with the Unmanifest. There is apt to be a certain overlapping of concepts, particularly with Mother goddesses, because what is considered as the Mother of Forms, and a Binah figure, can also, on a higher level, be considered a Mother of All, and thus a form-giving aspect of the Unmanifest; in Qabalastic terms, the AIN SOPH. One must accustom oneself to these transpositions, for though they may appear confusing at first they give many useful clues to the relationships between aspects of the manifest Universe; moreover, whilst the Sephiroth are simple 'mono-ideas', the god-forms, being made by humans, are inevitably complex and so fit several simplicities.

35. Another example of this transposition formula, which is found most frequently in the Egyptian pantheons, is

the scarab or beetle god, Khephera. He was said to emerge from his own substance and was therefore a symbol both of the Sun and also of life, which is continually reborn of itself. But bearing in mind the cyclic rhythm of Days and Nights of Manifestation it could equally be applied to the Unmanifest. A non-Egyptian analogue of this would be the pheonix, rising from its own ashes. This is primarily a symbol of religious regeneration but all life has its analogues on higher and lower levels in accordance with the Hermetic axiom 'As above—so below'.

36. So in attempting to get behind the symbolism to the reality of a myth the terms used must not be taken at their face value only. We have already seen that 'Earth' can also mean the prime basic substance of manifestation. It is not uncommon for moderns to think it rather quaint that the ancients should have believed in a cosmology in which the Sun and stars were created after the Earth. And it is true that before Copernicus the majority of mankind believed this—some still do. But many myths are parables invented by the priesthood and the initiatory schools to embody teachings of cosmic principles, and are not meant to be taken at their face value any more than the Christian parables. The parable of the Sower has not been invalidated by modern advances in agricultural techniques any more than ancient cosmogony is invalidated by astronomy, or alchemy by modern chemistry. The terms of reference are different.

37. Similarly with some myths where the Sun is referred to, or the Moon, they may have reference to psychological states or to anything radiant, positive and life giving and anything reflective, negative and magnetic respectively. One has to learn to think in analogy as the ancients did. It is true that thinking by analogy is viewed with great suspicion by logic—but in these matters of shifting symbols and variable psychological equations logic is often more hindrance than help.

38. The Sun that appears in some symbols, even if it

should apply to a stellar body, may have reference to other stars than our Sun. This is particularly to be watched for in connection with winged Egyptian figures. Wings appear seldom among the Egyptian gods for it was a concept beyond the exoteric religion of the period, but where they do, it signifies the cosmic principle of a particular force. Thus the solar disk worn on the head-dress of Isis or Hathor, particularly the Winged Isis, refers to Sothis, now more commonly known as Sirius, the Dog Star, which was a star particularly sacred to Isis.

39. Esoteric students of some experience will see the implications of this, for Sothis, along with the Great Bear and Pleiades, is a source of power behind the twelve zodiacal constellations, which in turn radiate influences to our Solar System via the mediation of the Solar Logos— our God.

40. In the esoteric psychology of man, the Veils of Negative Existence correspond to that part of his being where forces from outside the Solar Logoidal jurisdiction can contact him, usually from Universes where previous evolutionary experience has been undergone. Such a contact, if very strong, coming from such a foreign source, might cause strange aberrations within that soul. Sometimes a Black Adept starts his career thus, though not all such contacts are out of line with the Plan of this Solar Logoidal System and may be desirous of serving it.

41. To help to gain a conscious conception of Negative Existence, speculative meditation is recommended on the texts and diagrams given and on any of the early creation myths with which the student may be familiar. It may also help to work on the following seed ideas and images:

a) a vacuum of pressure.

b) a limitless ocean of negative light.

c) nothingness crystallising a centre.

d) an invisible web upon which shining dew forms.

Chapter VI

KETHER—THE CROWN

"The First Path is called the Admirable or Hidden Intelligence because it is the Light giving the power of comprehension of the First Principle, which hath no beginning. And it is the Primal Glory, because no created being can attain to its essence."

MAGICAL IMAGE:	An ancient bearded king in profile.
GOD NAME:	Eheieh.
ARCHANGEL:	Metatron.
ORDER OF ANGELS:	Chaioth he Qadesh, Holy Living Creatures.
MUNDANE CHAKRA:	Primum Mobile. First Swirlings.
VIRTUE:	Attainment. Completion of the Great Work.
TITLES:	Existence of Existences. Concealed of the Concealed. Ancient of Ancients. Ancient of Days. The Smooth Point. The Primordial Point. The Most High. The Vast Countenance. The White Head. The Head Which Is Not. Macroprosopos.
SPIRITUAL EXPERIENCE:	Union with God.
ATZILUTHIC COLOUR:	Brilliance.
BRIATIC COLOUR:	Pure white brilliance.
YETZIRATIC COLOUR:	Pure white brilliance.
ASSIATIC COLOUR:	White, flecked gold.
VICE:	
SYMBOLS:	The point. The point within a circle. The crown. The swastika.

1. Kether is the fount of Creation, the point where life wells up from the deeps of the Great Unmanifest. It is manifestation on the point of becoming manifest, the centre crystallised in the midst of Non-being, containing within it the potentialities of all to come. It is the supreme height of Godhead although it must not be forgotten that all the Sephiroth are equally holy, being emanations of the One God. Thus Malkuth, the physical world, is as divine as the highest spiritual sphere, Kether, the Crown of Creation.

65

2. Those who consider Malkuth holy without reference to the higher Sephiroth fall into the error of pantheism, which is a half-truth. Those who consider Kether to be holier than the subsequent creation fall into the equal error of denying the Unity of God, of setting up a dichotomy between Spirit and Matter. All subsequent creation from the pure force of Kether is a gradual concretion into form of the one divine force. Form is force locked up into patterns of its own making. Force is that which is released when the patterns or forms are broken. Force and form, are one and the same—'As above—so below'.

3. This is the principle of the unity of opposites and of the processes of life and death. Force on one level acts as a duality, functioning either actively or passively. When opposing forces meet they mutually attract and repel one another, form a spinning ring after the manner of the process described in the extract from 'The Cosmic Doctrine' in the preceding chapter, and thus descend a plane, creating a form through the interlocked equilibrium of their potencies. In a like manner, if the stabilised form is broken, the forces inherent in it become free-moving, on a higher plane.

4. To an entity conscious on the lower plane where the form is built, the interlocking of the higher forces, causing a form on the lower level, will appear to be a birth. When the form is broken and the forces return to their original higher level the process will appear as a death.

5. To an entity conscious on the higher plane however, the descent into form of free-moving forces will be considered a death, and the break up of a form to release the forces will be a birth.

6. In this way it will be seen that birth and death are two sides of the same coin. The empty shell of the built-up form remains on the lower plane, to resolve back into the basic matter of that plane, and the forces return to their higher level, now vibrating with the experience of manifestation in the denser form.

7. This is the basic pattern of all manifestation and un-manifestation, which we have already seen to be cyclic. It is also the process of the human soul coming down the planes into densest form and subsequently dying to this form and being reborn to the inner worlds, and then, after a time of assimilation of past experience in densest form, coming to birth into it again by the death of its freedom of the less dense forms of the higher planes. This is the basic doctrine behind the theory of reincarnation. It is also the rationale behind the primitive religious practice of blood sacrifice—by destroying the form, force was released to wing its way to the higher worlds.

8. The fossilised remains of extinct species are the cast off forms of life which were no longer adequate to the expression of life-force. But the life has achieved rebirth in higher types of vehicle. It was only by abandoning simpler forms that life could enter more complex expressions of existence. A consciousness inhabiting a doomed simpler form would look upon the decline of its genus as a tragedy. A consciousness inhabiting a more advanced evolutionary form, growing in power at the expense of the old, would rejoice. In this way do species and races and nations rise and fall. From the standpoint of Kether it is all one, for Kether is the basic life-force at the root of all forms. Thus this level is beyond the good and evil as conceived of by consciousnesses limited in forms. In Kether is the Spirit that knows it is immortal whatever the triumphs and vicissitudes of the expressions of form.

9. In this way it can be considered as the Crown of Creation as the Crown in a modern monarchy is above the rough and tumble of party politics. This indeed could be regarded as an aspect of Kether in the sphere of Malkuth —and the Crown is a symbol of Kether.

10. The other symbols, the point and the point within a circle, indicate the manifestation of Kether to be both the simplest form of manifestation, as a point is the simplest geometrical figure, and also the concretion of a centre in

the Great Round of the Unmanifest. The subsidiary titles also bear out this attribution, particularly The Primordial Point and The Smooth Point. The latter title is one of those conceptions which are nonsensical to the concrete mind, for a point, by definition, has no surface to be rough or smooth. It implies a sphere of no magnitude and takes into account the Unmanifest side of Kether which is also implied by the titles Concealed of the Concealed and The Head Which Is Not. As there is a dark side of the Moon which is ever invisible to man on Earth so is there a side to Kether which, being of the Unmanifest, is incomprehensible to the rest of creation.

11. As the Yetziratic Text says, it is the Primal Glory, because no created being can attain to its essence. Were any created being to attain to its essence, which according to the Spiritual Experience is Union with God, it would by that very fact become uncreate. Yet this is the goal of all evolution as the Virtue of Kether reveals, Attainment, Completion of the Great Work. The Great Work, a term often met with in magical and alchemical writings, is the great work of life itself, the death of free-moving spirit into form and its subsequent regeneration.

12. "The First Path is called the Admirable or Hidden Intelligence because it is the Light giving the power of comprehension of the First Principle, which hath no beginning."

13. This main statement of the Yetziratic Text confirms the Spiritual Experience, for only Union with God can give the power of comprehension of the immortal Spirit, which is the first principle behind manifestation and being immortal, without beginning or ending. Thus is this Sphere called the Admirable Intelligence for created beings can only adore—or admire—in the presence of God. And the Hidden Intelligence again signifies that the Spirit stems from the unknowable Great Unmanifest. The Text also refers to the Sephirah as 'the Light giving the power of comprehension'; again we see that Light is the first thing

manifest, and in Kether the Light gives comprehension of itself to itself. It will be remembered from Genesis that on the creation of Light, the Darkness comprehended it not. It must also be borne in mind that the Light referred to is not the type of etheric disturbance that we call light, but a high metaphysical concept of which the light of the Sun and stars is only a symbol and lower analogue. Light as we perceive it through our physical senses could be conceived of as a dense aspect of the Kether of Malkuth, but the Light of the Kether of Kether is Spirit; just as the Fire that Prometheus stole from Heaven is a type of Spiritual Will.

14. Light being the First Manifest it is also obviously the oldest thing in creation, except that these spiritual levels are outside our conceptions of space and time. The titles Ancient of Ancients and Ancient of Days bring out this point. The days referred to are obviously Cosmic Days of Manifestation. The Magical Image, an ancient bearded king shown in profile, is a pictorial symbol of these titles, but can be misleading. From this Magical Image, which has obviously through long contemplation of God by the exoteric church, filtered through to the popular conception, has grown the naive representation of God as an old man with flowing white beard and gown.

15. This is a concrete example of the power behind these Qabalistic symbols, for the colour white is also a Kether colour—as for instance in the title, The White Head; white contains all the other colours as Kether contains all subsequent manifestation. But it is also an example of how symbols can lead people astray, for many profess to deny religion on the grounds that its anthropomorphic concepts are too naive. The truth is, of course, that the critic is too naive, and, as so often happens, projecting his own failings onto the outside world, the only way most of us can face our own inadequacies, by blaming them on others.

16. However, while God is a real being, and not a mere metaphysical abstraction, He is obviously not an old man

in a white gown either. In the Magical Image He is conceived of as in profile, for the other side of Kether is unmanifest, and he is considered old because Kether is the first manifest. But one should glean a shred of wisdom from the myth of Tithonus, who obtained the gift of immortality from the gods but forgot to ask for eternal youth. Consequently he got more and more senile and decrepit until his life was a burden to him. As an act of mercy he was changed to a cicada—which he presumably still is to this day. This was no doubt a lesson to him, but the lesson for us is not to think of great divine beings as subject to the physical laws of time, biology and chemistry and thus old fashioned and decrepit; they also have 'eternal youth'.

17. The Name of God in Kether is Eheieh which has been likened to the outflowing and indrawing of the breath, thus symbolising Kether as the root from which all flows and to which all returns. The Divine Breath is a widely used symbol amongst Eastern mystics and much of the teaching behind Hatha Yoga is based upon it.

18. The Hebrew letters which make up the Name are Aleph, Heh, Yod, Heh. In the symbolism of the Hebrew alphabet the letter Aleph denotes the beginnings of things and Heh the reception, or stabilisation at a level of form. Yod represents the fertilising principle. Thus the Name itself implies the initial going forth of force which is then stabilised, and then a further fructifying emanation resulting in a final stabilisation. This can be considered either as increasing manifestation in slightly denser stages, or, perhaps better, manifestation and then return to stability in the Unmanifest. Yod and Heh can also represent the positive and negative aspects of force and thus could be equated with Chokmah and Binah. Thus one could consider the Name to represent the coming forth of life (Aleph) resulting in the stabilisation (Heh) of the principles of manifestation, positive (Yod) and negative (Heh). There are no doubt further possible interpretations.

19. Eheieh has been variously translated as I AM, or I AM THAT I AM or I BECOME. All of which corresponds with the title assigned to Kether, Existence of Existences.

20. The colour assigned to the Atziluth of Kether is Brilliance, which transcends all colours, as Kether transcends all creation.

21. The Archangel of the Sephirah is Metatron, who presides over the whole Tree of Life as well as over Kether. Traditionally, it was Metatron who gave the Qabalah to man. This can be taken to mean that from his inscrutably high heavenly world he sent through an idea chart of evolution which was imprinted on the higher levels of man so that it could subsequently be brought through to the conscious mind by the techniques of meditation.

22. It was not what could justly be called 'telepathy' for it was above the realms of the concrete mind. Such a high being as Metatron would not deal directly in mental concepts or pictorial forms but would make direct contact with the spirit of man. On the abstract spiritual levels on which such a being operates, mental ideas would appear as solid and concrete as lumps of rock do to us, and when we wish to communicate to each other we look for easier methods than carving messages on stone.

23. This does not mean that it is impossible to make contact with one such as Metatron; one should never allow one's practice to be limited by theory in these matters. He can be pictured in the Briatic colour of Kether, a vast powerfully radiating pillar of pure white brilliance.

24. The Order of Angels assigned to Kether is The Holy Living Creatures. These are classified into four types in accordance with the Biblical system which describes them as having the forms of a Bull, a Lion, an Eagle and a Man. The Angels are concerned with the Formative World of a Sephirah and this is the clue to much, for what is formed in Kether will be reflected throughout the whole of manifestation. This is the basis behind the much maligned Four Elements of the ancients which the Jungian school of

analytical psychology is now doing much to restore to respectability.

25. Esoterically speaking, God manifests in Four Aspects as opposed to the Three Aspects or Persons of the exoteric church. These Four Aspects are the Father, Son, Holy Spirit and the Destroyer or Disintegrator. The Aspect of the Father is the Power Aspect or the Spiritual Will. The Aspect of the Son is Love, that is, complete understanding of the needs of all, not sweet sentimentality. The Aspect of the Holy Spirit is Wisdom, Active Intelligence or Illumination. The Fourth Aspect is the Withdrawer of Life from the death of form and ultimately of all manifest life to the Unmanifest.

26. All the words used to describe the Four Aspects in the above paragraph are inadequate. The powers of God are beyond the grasp of words so instead of being limited by them one should, by meditation, try to get beyond them to the truth that they so poorly represent.

27. The symbols of the Holy Living Creatures will be recognised by astrological students to correspond with the zodiacal signs of Taurus, Leo, Scorpio and Aquarius. These are the Fixed Signs of the Four Elements of Earth, Fire, Water and Air respectively for in Kether are the roots of the Elemental powers which are represented by the Tarot Aces of Coins, Wands, Cups and Swords, which were the original designation of the Diamonds, Clubs, Hearts and Spades of modern playing cards.

28. The ancients said that all things were basically made up of the Four Elements and this is literally true, for the Elements are modes of action and not just the four physical elements, although these are reflections of the archetypal principles involved.

29. The interlinking correspondences of the Elements are numerous and it would be of little use to examine them in detail before a complete examination of the Tree has been undertaken. Students familiar with Jungian psychology can get some conception of their application by considering the

four Jungian psychological functions of intuition, feeling, intellect and sensation, which correspond to Air, Water, Fire and Earth and which on the lower Sephiroth of the Tree can be equated with Tiphareth, Netzach, Hod and Malkuth.

30. For contacting the angelic powers of Kether it is not really necessary to go into a long analysis of correspondences though. Perhaps the best image to build up is the Swastika, which is an emblem of the Equal-armed Cross of the Elements in circular motion. One can picture a swastika of pure white brilliance, with a picture of one of the Holy Living Creatures in each arm, and then visualise the swastika spinning rapidly on a brilliant axis against a background of white flecked with gold.

31. This spinning motion will call to mind the Mundane Chakra of Kether, the Primum Mobile, or First Swirlings. This attribution means that an idea of Kether can be gained by going out and contemplating a whirling nebula in the night sky, for it will be an astronomical analogue of the cosmological creation. This symbol may also serve to show that the ancients were not all so dumb, astronomically speaking, as we like to make out.

32. The title assigned to Kether of Macroprosopos, or The Vast Countenance, is a purely Qabalistic one, relating to one of the ways of dividing the Tree. These patterns on the Tree will be dealt with in a later chapter but the title of The Vast Countenance can be used as an image without reference to metaphysical theory. Imagine a great head arising from the depths of a calm still sea until it completely covers the space above the horizon. Then see the image of this vast countenance reflected in the waters.

33. Alternatively, one can identify oneself with the vast countenance rising, perceiving one's reflection on the surface of the great deep from whence one has arisen. Or, identify oneself with the reflection. Most symbols can be used in this subjective way, whatever their form, but used in this way their effects may be far more potent than the

usual method of visualising them objectively. The process should be used with discretion.

34. In mythology Kether can be aligned with all prime creators springing up from the abyss of water or space, self-created, and creating all other gods, men and living things. There can be a certain amount of overlapping, for where a prime creator is male he could also have claims to be aligned with Chokmah, and if female, with Binah. The state of Kether is really androgynous and we have already examined this dual nature in the cosmological conception of Hesiod, where both Gaea and Eros can be considered Kether figures. Cronos, also, could be considered a Kether figure, in that he devoured his children as Kether finally indraws all that has been created through it.

35. Cronos is however of the second divine dynasty of the Greeks and although the above attribution is valid for anyone who cares to make it so, Cronos has reference to a much later stage of manifestation. He was one of the Titans, who can be considered human memories of a pre-human race. They took part in the Greek version of The War in Heaven which appears in so many mythologies, including the Bible. Cronos in turn was overthrown by Zeus, who, with the other Olympians, was the main manifestation of God to the Greeks.

36. In the Orphic cosmogony Cronos is an entirely different concept, being called the First Principle—Time, from which came Chaos, the infinite, and Ether, the finite. Chaos was surrounded by Night, and in the darkness an egg was formed of which Night formed the shell. The centre of the egg was Phanes—Light, creator, in conjunction with Night, of heaven and earth and also Zeus.

37. This creation fantasy can be considered as a résumé of the concretion of Kether. The distinctions of Time, Infinite and Finite, Light and Darkness are philosophical abstractions which demonstrate this conception to be a metaphysical structure rather than genuine primitive myth. These writings were attributed to Orpheus, whose original

teachings were probably of Eastern origin, though it was Dionysos who became the supreme god of Orphism.

38. In the Egyptian pantheons Thoth, Ra, Ptah and Osiris amongst others were all credited by their followers with creating the Universe. But the Heliopolitan system seems to correspond with the Qabalistic concept best in Atum-Ra, who lived inside Nu before anything was, and whose name Atum derives from a root meaning both 'not to be' and 'to be complete' which corresponds well with the dual manifest and unmanifest, alpha and omega, beginning and ending aspects of Kether.

Chapter VII

CHOKMAH—WISDOM

"The Second Path is called the Illuminating Intelligence. It is the Crown of Creation, the Splendour of Unity, equalling it. It is exalted above every head, and is named by Qabalists, the Second Glory."

MAGICAL IMAGE:	A bearded male figure.
GOD NAME:	Jehovah, or Jah.
ARCHANGEL:	Ratziel.
ORDER OF ANGELS:	Auphanim. Wheels.
MUNDANE CHAKRA:	The Zodiac.
VIRTUE:	Devotion.
TITLES:	Power of Yetzirah. Ab. Abba. The Supernal Father. Tetragrammaton. Yod of Tetragrammaton.
SPIRITUAL EXPERIENCE:	The Vision of God face to face.
ATZILUTHIC COLOUR:	Pure soft blue.
BRIATIC COLOUR:	Grey.
YETZIRATIC COLOUR:	Pearl grey iridescence.
ASSIATIC COLOUR:	White, flecked red, blue and yellow.
VICE:	
SYMBOLS:	The lingam. The phallus. Yod. The Inner Robe of Glory. The standing stone. The tower. The uplifted Rod of Power. The straight line.

1. Chokmah is the dynamic thrust and drive of spiritual force. It is the upwelling spirit of Kether in positive action, the power house of the Universe. One does not have to be much of a Freudian psychologist to see the idea of masculine sexuality behind most of the subsidiary symbols assigned to the Sphere. At the same time Chokmah is the Sephirah of Wisdom, which may seem rather strange at first sight, for in much of the workings out of the drive of sexuality, Wisdom is usually the one thing which is noticeable by its absence. However, it must be remembered that

76

we are dealing with cosmic principles behind manifestation and not with their reflection in the greatly aberrated actions of man.

2. In its passive aspect Chokmah is a reflection of the primal upwelling of force in Kether, and in its positive aspect it is the divine force in positive function as opposed to its passive mode of action in Binah. When the glyph of the Pillars is placed upon the Tree, Chokmah is at the head of the Positive Pillar and Binah at the head of the Negative one, so we can expect to find all symbols of a positive and masculine nature assigned to the former, and all symbols of a passive and feminine nature assigned to the latter.

3. Before making an examination of the phallic Chokmah symbols though, it will be best to examine its aspects as a reflection of Kether. In all matters of spiritual analysis it is best to work from the highest point downwards in order to get a genuine understanding, for the higher precedes the lower in point of creation and is thus its cause. Thus Chokmah is a dynamic Sephirah because it is a reflection of Kether and all the subsequent symbolism stems from this fact. By examining the male sexual symbolism first and then proceding from that to the cosmic factors one is liable to fall into the error of many followers of Freud who try to describe religious symbolism as mere projections of human sexuality.

4. To use the language of metaphorical symbolism, one could say that the God-head manifests, a Vast Countenance, from the nothingness of the Great Unmanifest. It is therefore alone and self-created with nothing else in manifestation to attract its attention. It therefore reflects upon itself and this reflection causes an image of itself to be formed, and as the Mind of God is so powerful, this image takes on an objective existence—anything that God thinks, is. Thus the whole of manifestation could be conceived of as the thought process of God. "We are such stuff as dreams are made on."

5. It is this first projection of an idea of itself that is

what we call the Sephirah Chokmah. It is the action of the Mind of God in manifestation, and this great image of God, being a perfect image, is also self-conscious, so that a great polarity of mutual recognition is set up between Kether and Chokmah. As God in Kether becomes aware of the image of itself in Chokmah so does Its own mentation change, thus producing a change in Its image, Chokmah, which again produces a change in Kether, and so on ad infinitum.

6. "The Lord our God is a living God". The Mysteries of this great primal polarity are part of the great Eleventh Path of Concealed Glory which leads between Chokmah and Kether and whose Tarot symbol is perhaps the profoundest in the whole pack—The Fool.

7. It may be noticed that we refer to God as It. This is not meant in an attempt to reduce the Universe to a conception of mechanics—though mechanics, like geometry, can give a useful field of symbolism, "God geometrises."— but because God is the Great Androgyne, both masculine and feminine and yet transcending them.

8. It is in view of this pure prime reflection of the Godhead, Kether, that the Yetziratic Text describes Chokmah as "the Crown of Creation, the Splendour of Unity, equalling it. It is exalted above every head, and is named by Qabalists, the Second Glory."

9. It also explains the nature of the Spiritual Experience of Chokmah, the Vision of God face to face. It is unlikely that any living person could attain to such a high mystic vision, for as is said in the Bible in several places, no man can look upon the face of God and live. And when one realises how difficult it is for man to look upon himself as he really is, one can imagine how much more of a shattering experience it would be to look upon his Creator. However, the parallel is not exact, for man finds it difficult to look upon himself because of the tawdry shabbiness of his own sins, whereas the Vision of God face to face would be a realisation of searing omnipotent perfection—or naked

Truth. Yet as man is built in the image of God, he has his own God-head within him, his Spirit which first created him. This he has to look upon also in the end. But what stops him is his own self-made blockages, the barriers he has created within himself through his deviation from the Divine Plan. Thus he has first to face his own Dweller on the Threshold, to disperse his own Shadow and False Darkness before he can go on eventually to face the Light. The Light that is usually referred to in religious writings is that of Tiphareth, and the facing of the Dweller comes on the Paths between Tiphareth and Geburah, and Geburah and Chesed, far below the exalted visions of Chokmah.

10. In further confirmation of this analysis of Chokmah, its Virtue is Devotion, and one can imagine that any Vision of God face to face would impel devotion. At such a high level of mystical realisation as this there could be no evil manifesting and so, as with Kether, there is no Vice assigned to Chokmah. And looking at the world today it is pretty obvious that general conditions are so tainted that no-one could live an active life without dirtying his hands spiritually in some way—the only exception being one such as Our Lord. So if anyone claims to be of the esoteric grade of Magus or Ipsissimus, the grades assigned to Chokmah and Kether, he proclaims himself either as a Christ, a liar, or a fool. And if in justification he should say that the assignation of the Path between Chokmah and Kether is The Fool, then he is further guilty of a sheer ignorant abuse of symbolism. It is the meaning behind symbolism that is important, not the mere outward form of the symbol as we must realise if we are to understand the phallic symbolism of Chokmah and the yonic symbolism of Binah correctly.

11. The positive masculine side of Chokmah is the All-Father as is suggested by the Magical Image of a bearded male figure, and the subsidiary title of The Supernal Father.

12. The Name of God in the Sphere of Chokmah is Jehovah, or, as it appears in transliterated Hebrew script, JHVH.

(Yod, Heh, Vau, Heh.) Much has been written on this Name, it is the pedantic Qabalist's delight. It is this particular Name of which it is said that were it to be pronounced correctly the Universe would be destroyed. It is not recommended that students attempt the experiment as their vocal chords will be worn out with effort long before the attempted cataclysm is achieved. Silence will come upon them, but not the Unmanifest Silence.

13. The more credible idea behind this story is that anyone able to function in the Sephirah Chokmah, which is the Sphere of the Vision of God face to face, would be, through the absolute purity of Devotion of this experience, drawn into Union with God, and would thus, from the point of view of manifestation, no longer exist. He would attain an entirely noumenal rather than a phenomenal reality and thus his own manifest Universe would be destroyed.

14. This is not to deny that there is great power behind certain words, particularly Holy Names. On the contrary there is often great power; that is what the Names are for and they should not be used indiscriminately. There are many Words of Power in occultism which are kept as guarded secrets for this reason. This is not only for fear that someone might do himself harm by using them foolishly, but such foolish use would also tend to disperse their power. It is really for the same reason that one would not use an altar covering for a dish wiping cloth.

15. Orthodox Jews do not pronounce the Name of God when reading from their texts, but either make a pause or substitute another word. Although this might facilely be considered superstition it is really an act of reverence, and reverence should be paid to occult symbols if one is to make best use of them, and words are also symbols.

16. JHVH, (or IHVH or YHVH—the Hebrew letter Yod being transliterated as a J, I or Y by various authorities) like the God Name for Kether, Eheieh, (Aleph, Heh, Yod, Heh.) is a tetragrammatonic or four letter word which signifies the idea 'to be'. It can be variously written in

twelve different ways and, according to Magregor Mathers, all these transpositions retain the meaning 'to be', a fact which is not applicable to any other word. The twelve permutations of the four letters are called 'the twelve banners of the mighty name' and are said by some to correspond to the twelve zodiacal signs. This theory is interesting in the light of the fact that the Mundane Chakra of Chokmah is the Zodiac.

17. The Name can be interpretted symbolically in many ways but the usual method is to equate it with the Four Worlds: Yod to Atziluth, Heh to Briah, Vau to Yetzirah and the second Heh to Assiah. Once a grasp of the meaning of the Hebrew letters is attained there is great scope for metaphysical speculation in this one word, but it is a line of research for specialists and so cannot be entered upon in the present context.

18. As regards the practical pronunciation of the word it is really a matter of personal choice. The usual forms are Jehovah or Yahway, or the spelling out of each letter, Yod, Heh, Vau, Heh. Sometimes the word Tetragrammaton is substituted for it. MacGregor Mathers claimed to know over twenty different ways of saying it but there are no prizes offered for exceeding this score.

19. The Archangel of the Sephirah is Ratziel and the title Ab or Abba is perhaps of help in contacting this potency. These titles, consisting of the first two letters of the Hebrew alphabet, Aleph and Beth, signify the formation of a second principle from the first principle and the term Ab is thus the first coming forth of divine power, and Abba, its reflection. The Archangel could be conceived as a grey pillar against a light blue background, and the best source of the real quality of the colours is in the clouds in the sky on a bright day. This visual context will bring in the association of interstellar space which is very pertinent in relation to the higher levels of the Tree of Life.

20. The Order of Angels is the Auphanium, or Wheels, their colour an iridescent grey. The word grey is perhaps

not a good one as it contains an allusion to nondescriptness or dirtyness, but it is the nearest verbal equivalent to the real colour intended. The description of this Order of Angels as Wheels gives the conception of cyclic action, unending power through motion; and an idea of their mode of being can perhaps best be obtained by contemplating the eternal wheeling of the stars in the night sky, for the Mundane Chakra of Chokmah is the Zodiac. The white, flecked red, yellow and blue which is the colour assigned to Assiah also suggests the stars, which appear white to the naked eye, though many are red, yellow or blue on closer examination. One way of building an image of the Auphanim would be to picture whirling grey iridescent wheels against a background of the night sky.

21. Of the subsidiary symbols, perhaps the simplest is the straight line, which gives the idea of the point, a symbol of Kether, now in dimensional motion.

22. The letter Yod, the first letter of the God Name of Chokmah, is the letter signifying initiatory fecundating power. The Hebrew symbol for the letter Yod is the Hand. Crowley has considered this to be a euphemism for the male sperm, and there is much to be said for this interpretation, but it also signifies the Hand of God which stretches forth and sets creation in motion. The painting of the Creation of Adam by Michelangelo in the Sistine Chapel gives a good visual conception of this. This is further expanded by the title The Power of Yetzirah, or The Power of Formation, for it is the power of Chokmah which animates all subsequent form.

23. The Inner Robe of Glory is one of a series of symbols or titles which conceives of the various Sephiroth as having correspondences in the technical equipment of a ritual magician. The meaning intended here is that God is a Great Magician bringing higher powers down into lower forms, thus the Tarot Card, The Magician, is assigned to the Path between Kether and Binah, the Godhead and the Archetypal Idea of Form. Form, in this particular symbol-

ism, is said to be The Outer Robe of Concealment, but as Chokmah is above even the idea of form, and yet is not Godhead Itself, though a reflection of It, it is naturally called The Inner Robe of Glory.

24. The remaining symbols are phallic, or phallic derivatives, and signify the Male Principle of the Universe or the Universal Male. The subject of sexual symbolism in religion is a vast one, overlaid with many false trails and confusing ramifications. The fact that many of the visions of the saints are expressed in sexual symbolism has led some to infer that religion is nothing more than a sublimated expression of inhibited sexual desire. This of course may be true up to a point, and many of the saints were probably pathological, but this by no means proves the thesis, which is indeed that most treacherous of things, a half-truth.

25. Sexuality is a means of expression of the life-force within a person, just as any other creative activity is, whether it be in religion, art, or an executive capacity in the fields of science or commerce. And if the life-force is blocked off on one level it will seek expression on another. This life-force is often confused with sexual force, for sexual expression is common to all mankind, being rooted in the instincts, but it must be remembered that sex is a function, not a force, even though life-force usually seeks this means of expression as the line of least resistance.

26. It is this life-force, on all its levels, which is the correspondence of the life-force of God, in Chokmah. Life-force up-wells originally from the Unmanifest, not from the physical.

27. This fact is not immediately obvious because there are two 'threads' of life in an organism. One is the life thread and the other is the consciousness thread. Esoteric psychology teaches that when an entity such as man comes into incarnation the relatively immortal part of himself— variously called the Higher Self, Evolutionary Self, the Soul etc.—projects a rod or thread-like process into the

lower levels which forms the basis of personality, and this develops a life of its own and is kept alive by means of this life thread which has been described as a 'silver cord' not only in the Bible but also in recorded experiences of etheric projection, the details of which are available in many books on psychical research. As the personality develops towards maturity the Higher Self begins to take over to a greater or usually lesser extent and this is by means of opening up the thread of consciousness between the two levels of being.

28. The aim of esoteric training is to make this dual consciousness a single reality. The consciousness of the Lower Self is raised by means of meditation, contemplation, and prayer, and the Higher Self is brought down by attention, intention and, in the West, ritual methods. As the Lower Self may not be, for varying reasons, an accurate projection of the Higher Self there will be natural limits to the extent that this ideal can be achieved. The lack of a conscious link between the two levels is one of the results of man's Original Sin, but whatever the causes, it can be seen that it is because of this occluded link that man has such a limited idea of his own psychology and normally no awareness of any existence before his present physical life.

29. On the Tree of Life, used as a symbol of man's psychology, the link is made at Tiphareth, the central Sephirah. So normally man is not conscious of anything above this level—indeed, his whole conception of himself must be less than half truth. But it can be seen then how easily he can make the mistake of assigning the forces which stem from Chokmah and Kether to the drive of the instincts, which correspond to the Sephirah Yesod, because unless he is guided by faith, he will consider he does not exist above the levels of Hod and Netzach, the Sephiroth of the mind and creative imagination respectively.

30. So to avoid this mistake we must remember that in religious and occult symbolism, most sexual emblems relate to the Supernals, the basic pattern of duality and

polarity throughout all manifest existence. In early sects where these principles were represented by actual representations of the genitalia it is obvious that, human nature being what it is, most of them would decline into orgy. In many cases this may have been deliberate by the priesthood, for frenzied orgy gives off great quantities of raw emotion and etheric extrusion which can be directed occultly. This is the rationale behind the Witches' Sabbats, which also used blood sacrifice as a source of raw power.

31. Needless to say such methods are not used in esoteric groups nowadays, apart from in Black and Dirty-Grey Lodges. Although they are no doubt effective methods, apart from the social and legal difficulties of organising such a procedure, the degradation of human individuality involved could not be countenanced. Where etheric force is needed it is to be obtained much more salubriously and simply by having a group of people sitting quietly in a circle so that their etheric force is concentrated. This is the technique of the seance table in spiritualism. The power to move light objects such as paper trumpets and similar paraphernalia comes from the sitters themselves, or from an ectoplasmic medium, that is, a person with an unusually high degree of free etheric magnetism. Even this method is not generally used in esoteric training groups though, for their aim is the development of higher consciousness, not the manifestation of apparent wonders to the lower consciousness. And where messages are concerned, telepathic contact is far superior to the ouija board or planchette, and easier to operate than the technique of deep trance.

32. In view of the dangers of direct phallic symbolism it can be seen that the reasons for the derivatives of it are not just prudery. In the course of time the principle became symbolised in such forms as the standing stone, the tower, the wand, the snake, the bull, the goat, the cock and the spire etc. It may be rather maliciously amusing to speculate how many good church-goers realise

the origin of the cockerel on the top of their church and which justifies its existence nowadays as a wind vane or as the cock which crew thrice for Peter, but one must not make the error of thinking that the original idea is purely sexual; the original idea is the Creative Power of God. And anyone who is disposed to try to reduce religious ideas to mere sexual projections is counselled to take to heart the 38th chapter of Job where the Lord, answering Job out of the whirlwind, thundered: "Who is this that darkeneth counsel by words without knowledge? Gird up now thy loins like a man; for I will demand of thee, and answer thou Me. Where wast thou when I laid the foundations of the earth? Declare if thou hast understanding. Who hath laid the measure thereof, if thou knowest? Or who hath stretched the line upon it? Whereupon are the foundations thereof fastened? Or who laid the corner stone thereof; when the morning stars sang together, and all the sons of God shouted for joy?"

33. This passage, apart from its literal meaning, is full of Chokmah symbolism.

34. In the pagan mythologies obviously all the Great Father figures can be referred to Chokmah, and in their higher aspects, all the Priapic gods such as Pan. But perhaps the best god-form to meditate upon is that of Pallas Athene—the virgin goddess of wisdom, who sprang fully armed from the brow of Zeus much as Chokmah sprang from the reflection of Kether. The meaning of the title Chokmah is Wisdom. Or, if the Egyptian god-forms are preferred, her Egyptian counterpart Isis-Urania can be used, winged, to show her cosmic affinities, and with the disk of Sothis above her head. Both goddesses can be visualised against a background of the night sky, and this idea of cosmic reality can be assisted by putting the Earth into this picture in the form that it really is, a sphere spinning and spiralling through inter-stellar space.

Chapter VIII

BINAH—UNDERSTANDING

"The Third Path is called the Sanctifying Intelligence, the Foundation of Primordial Wisdom; it is also called the Creator of Faith, and its roots are in Amen. It is the parent of faith, whence faith emanates."

MAGICAL IMAGE:	A mature woman.
GOD NAME:	Jehovah Elohim.
ARCHANGEL:	Tzaphkiel.
ORDER OF ANGELS:	Aralim. Thrones.
MUNDANE CHAKRA:	Saturn.
VIRTUE:	Silence.
TITLES:	Ama, the dark sterile mother. Aima, the bright fertile mother. Khorsia, the Throne. Marah, the Great Sea.
SPIRITUAL EXPERIENCE:	Vision of Sorrow.
ATZILUTHIC COLOUR:	Crimson.
BRIATIC COLOUR:	Black.
YETZIRATIC COLOUR:	Dark brown.
ASSIATIC COLOUR:	Grey, flecked pink.
VICE:	Avarice.
SYMBOLS:	The yoni. The kteis. The Vesica Piscis. The cup or chalice. The Outer Robe of Concealment.

1. Binah is the first 'form' Sephirah. That is, although it is far above any kind of form as we know it, there is implicit in it the archetype or idea of form. Form can be defined as the interlocking of free-moving force into patterns which then operate as a unity. In this way a unit of force no longer is unconditioned but has to operate in conjunction with the other forces which go to make up the pattern of which it is a part.

2. From this can be deduced the reason for evolutionary manifestation. Spiritual entities, or Divine Sparks, although perfect, are incapable of growth in the perfectly free

conditions of Unmanifestation, or manifestation above the form levels. In order for there to be any development there must be some limitation of possible action. Pure virgin spirit has no, or very few, distinguishing characteristics from other sparks of first manifest spirit. Capacity for individualised action is gained by the entry into the limiting factors of form, firstly the relative high degree of freedom of the spiritual levels, then the more limited freedom of mentation—(and any writer struggling to find a word to fit a concept knows this)—then the even greater limitations which the emotional levels impose, and finally the extreme limitation, physical existence, (and anyone who has ever missed the last bus home will be well aware of this.)

3. Thus the whole purpose of life is the gaining of experience in form. The spiritual babes—the Divine Sparks— enter manifestation, much as human babies, with certain inherent characteristics, but lacking experience of life. Their involutionary and evolutionary experience is like the moulding of character in the life of man. And their final withdrawal from manifestation corresponds to the death of a man, who, unless he has spent most of his life in an easy rut, carries far more practical wisdom out of this world than ever he brought into it.

4. So it will be seen that spiritual growth is best attained by getting fully to grips with life in the world. It is a common pathology with esoterically inclined students that they want to find the easiest way out of it. This accounts for many of the 'muzzy mystical' societies which give such a bad name to occultism. In a genuine occult school the student should be rammed good and hard into the maelstrom of life; and until he can cope efficiently with the physical plane the higher planes of experience should be barred to him—for his own sake as well as others. A student who cannot handle his mundane responsibilities will only reap confusion worse confounded if he starts opening himself to the forces and responsibilities of the supramundane levels of life. It is not always realised that the

higher worlds, owing to the deviation of man, are by no means all sweetness and light, and it is part of an occultist's job to compensate unbalanced forces on these levels and bring them through in harmonised balance to physical living. If, through ignorance or lack of competence, he brings them through unbalanced the effect on his physical circumstances will be chaotic. And the implications of such an action go far deeper than any discomfort to him and his immediate associates and relations. This is why high standards are expected of occult students. And if the standards of a training group are not high then one can deduce from that very fact that its inner powers are negligible, for if it did have real power being expressed through it, any lowering of standards would burst the organisation wide open by internal dissensions. This is usually the reason why occult groups sometimes founder; they get onto a level of power which they cannot handle. The development of an occult group, as with an individual, must be undertaken with great circumspection, and any undue haste can be fatal. Therefore do not believe anyone who offers to teach you the Wisdom of the Ages in six months—he is only after your money. You may gain wisdom from the transaction, but not the kind you expected.

5. The title of Binah is Understanding which is the form side of the Wisdom of Chokmah. This Wisdom and Understanding are not merely the wisdom and understanding of the human mind as ordinarily meant by these words. The Understanding here indicated is more a higher type of Faith. The Yetziratic Text states that Binah is 'the parent of faith, whence faith emanates.' And the other attributions of the Yetziratic Text: the Sanctifying Intelligence, the Foundation of Primordial Wisdom, the Creator of Faith, amplify this statement, while the phrase 'its roots are in Amen', which means 'So be it.' indicates the first manifestation of form.

6. As the human mind, being composed of forms itself, must give shape to anything in order to understand it, it

is obvious that Binah is the absolute highest level which the mentality could attain. All our considerations of the levels beyond Binah have been in the form of concept and symbol and yet form only enters into the scheme of things at Binah. All our awareness of cosmic force, therefore, must be filtered to us by form representations—"for now we see through a glass, darkly; but then face to face." At its higher levels, this statement of St. Paul's applies to the cosmic initiations beyond Binah; the Spiritual Experience of Chokmah, it will be remembered, being The Vision of God face to face.

7. Binah is the form giver to all manifestation and thus also is the Archetypal Temple behind all temples, the Inner Church behind all churches, the Basic Creed behind all creeds. It is the Womb of Life, and this archetypal feminine quality of the Sephirah manifests in two aspects, as Ama, the dark sterile mother, and Aima, the bright fertile mother.

8. Ama is composed of the Hebrew letter Mem, which signifies Water, the Waters of Form, between two Alephs, signifying the beginnings of things. Aima is the same word with the fertilising Yod impacted in it.

9. Ama, the Dark Mother, is the aspect of Binah which binds the free-moving force of Chokmah into limiting form. Aima tends more to the future condition when the imprisoned force has achieved harmonised function in form and the form is therefore no longer a necessary limitation for its development. Considering Chokmah and Binah as the Supernal Father and Mother, Aima would be the mate or spouse of Chokmah and Ama the corrective disciplinarian for it imprisons and breaks up the free-moving Chokmah force.

10. As Ama is the aspect of Binah which 'trains' the Spirit it is an important side of the function of the Sephirah and should be deeply considered. In its essence it is the force of travail in all types and levels of bringing to birth, the labour that is required to bring about any goal in the worlds of form. This aspect can be visualised in the form of a

gigantic Mother Superior, completely shrouded from head to foot in black, the face partly concealed, and holding in the *left* hand a correcting rod formed of a short, slightly tapering, rounded bar of unpolished black wood. The impression that the figure should give is of splendour and beauty veiled by this voluminous sombre robe—The Outer Robe of Concealment.

11. It must not be forgotten that the spiritual side of the Ama power is part of the action of the Cosmic Christ, the regenerating and reconciling Aspect of God. Regeneration could be defined as the facing up to individual reality honestly combined with the genuine desire to change. It can be a painful process for the personality; few people care to look at their failings honestly, and many fear change of any kind as it appears to be a threat to security. The dross in human nature goes up in flames when exposed to this regenerative fire, and the Dark Mother, the Mother of Sorrows, who mediates this force to the character over a greater or lesser period of time is really a figure of great compassion compared to the direct application of a cosmic force as potent as the Cosmic Christ, the searing heat of which, applied to the soul, would be akin to applying an oxy-acetylene torch to the body.

12. The Cosmic Christ force should not be confused with the Lord Jesus, the Master of Compassion. What is meant here is the blind cosmic force which was mediated in one of its greatest forms in the history of mankind by Our Lord in his capacity as the Bearer of the Christ force. The Lord Jesus mediates this force as does the Ama figure, which is represented in Christian worship by the Virgin Mary. Through the course of ages representations of Our Lady have become sentimentalised to a large extent, the early Byzantine paintings and mosaics of her give a truer indication of her Binah aspect as the 'Mater Dolorosa'. And her description in the Litany as 'Mater Boni Consilii' is very apt for the Understanding of Binah.

13. It is on the character building which this force brings

about that so much depends, for without it, the forces of the Great Father, the higher wisdom of Chokmah, cannot be brought through to the mind and thus bring about the living of the 'higher life'—the continual conscious mediation of Spirit in Earth of the initiated adept.

14. The archetype of the initiated adept is also held in Binah, the esoteric grade of which is the Magister Templi —Master of the Temple. This term applies to one who is absolute master of the arbitration and manipulation of force and form and who has complete understanding of cosmic power and the creation of the requisite forms in which this power may manifest. Also, who has the ability to gauge conditions from day to day and to accept people as they are at any given moment, seeing the stage that they have reached and taking into account the difference between a soul as it is and what it will become as a result of further training; and including in the assessment the effects of karma on the personality or physical vehicle. The archetype of such a one can be conceived as a seated figure with a greyish Egyptian head-dress and uraeus, or snake symbol, perhaps in the form of a serpent twined staff, above the brow. The face like that of a great sphinx, but illuminated from within in a kind of luminous grey. The robes should be black and the figure should bear a stone sceptre with a roughly shaped object suggestive of a heart at the top.

15. The 'Temple' of the title of the grade also implies the vehicles of the Spirit in manifestation, including the physical body as well as the psychic structure. Our Lord was one who demonstrated the powers of the Magister Templi in his words "I will destroy this Temple and rebuild it after three days." and it will be recalled that at the end of the Crucifixion "the Veil of the Temple was rent in the midst." The ability of this grade is to build a temple out of the structures of the personality and to dwell in it until the time comes to destroy it so that a better form can be built. This destruction comes under the Fourth Aspect of the

Deity and also under the Dark Mother, and is by no means evil.

16. The Spiritual Experience of Binah is the Vision of Sorrow and an alternative Magical Image to that of a mature woman is a heart pierced vertically with three swords. There are certain pictures of the Virgin Mary which show her heart pierced with swords and this is really a combination of the two magical images.

17. The Sorrow of the Vision has many levels of meaning. It does not mean merely a temporary emotional disturbance over some minor misfortune, but more an absolute and complete realisation of the road to be travelled, of all that will happen and that has happened along that road, and how and when and if achievement will come. Thus the Vision of Sorrow as the Spirit comes down into the form building principles of Binah is the realisation of the toilsome way of involutionary and evolutionary progress. The Sorrow is made all the greater of course by the subsequent Fall of Man so that what was before the Fall a toilsome struggle is now a contorted agony. But this deviation of man's, having no place in the Divine Plan, has no noumenal reality, and so its results are not, strictly speaking, to be assigned to Binah—or indeed to the Tree at all in that the Tree is a Divine Pattern. The sins of man are more correctly assigned to the Pit of the Qliphoth in which are the distorted reflections of the Holy Sephiroth.

18. However, the manifestation of sorrow in the human personality can be regarded as the work of Ama, the Mother of Sorrows. Grief is a purgative and strongly disruptive force, and when the essential work of breaking down adhesions and dispersing poisons has been done by it, it gives place to a deep lassitude and feeling of emptiness which can act as a purified basis for new growth. People are so made that they will not or cannot realise a thing fully unless they are hit in the most vital part in some deep emotional sense. And so only by sorrow, and by going from sorrow to sorrow can an individual's evolution

proceed. The man who cannot or will not feel sorrow or face it in others cannot proceed at all.

19. There is, however, no value in grief for its own sake. Through some quirk of the human make-up it tends to be regarded as a static image instead of a process which leads on to a higher level of enlightenment and rest and thus transformed from a negative destructive force into a positive constructive one. Exoteric Christianity has tended to make this mistake and become fixated in the Crucifixion without going on to the subsequent Resurrection and Ascension.

20. These may seem hard sayings, but if they evoke a violent emotional reaction of disbelief, then one would do well to examine oneself as to why these particular statements should produce an emotional reaction rather than mere indifference. A strong emotional antagonism towards something usually denotes a psychological blockage and a refusal to face what is implied by it.

21. But whether one accepts these statements of the necessity of sorrow or not, if one should be undergoing a period of grief it can be of great help in more ways than one to picture the Mother of Sorrows. She can be seen as a mighty maternal figure of majesty and sorrow, robed in black, and seated in the centre of a sphere of purple light, graduating from translucent violet and lilac to the deep purple of grapes in the centre—an excellent symbol in itself for it signifies one who has trod the wine-press alone. This figure can be considered as Christian or pagan, for the sorrow of the feminine side of Divinity is the same through the ages, whether it be Demeter sorrowing for her daughter, Ishtar descending the seven hells for her lover, Isis searching for the dismembered parts of her husband, or Mary watching her son die.

22. On the higher levels the Sorrow of Binah is the knowledge and understanding of the great cosmic factors behind the incarnation of man and also of Christ. It is the realisation and revelation of the Great Mother herself. An aware-

ness of this condition can be made by building the picture of the Crucifixion with Our Lady and St. John on either side of the Cross. The skies are seen to grow black and the Crucifixion takes place between earth and sky in some strange condition of space. Mary herself steps forward as if to take on herself the weight of the symbolism, and overshadowing all is Tzaphkiel, the Archangel of Binah, and the deep crimson, black, dark brown and grey flecked pink of the Sephirah's colours.

23. This image should lead to an understanding of the whole of the manifested Universe as a form encompassing pure cosmic force; a gigantic Cross upon which this force is crucified. And the whole of life is lived under the Shadow of this Cross. This is the primary Cross of Life of which the Cross of Golgotha is a lesser manifestation; a shadow cast by the Great Shadow.

24. Contemplation of Binah may bring a very real sense of being surrounded by Great Waters, and in this connection the Temple of Binah is as an Ark upon the Supernal Seas. This is the 'Ark of Isis', a symbol of the Womb of the Great Mother. There may also come an awareness of the inner aspects of the soul, a feeling that the ordinary personality is but the visible part of a gigantic iceberg, huge in the submerged depths below consciousness. A geometrical form may be perceived in relation to this and is well worth working on in meditation for it will be a potent symbol of the inmost structures of one's being upon which all the rest is built. It could be considered as the Rock upon which the foundations of the Temple of one's being are built.

25. The God Name of the Sephirah, Jehovah Elohim, is usually translated as 'The Lord God'. God is referred to under the title of Elohim in the first chapter of Genesis, but in chapter II, after the seventh day has been blessed, becomes Jehovah Elohim. Elohim is a feminine word with a masculine ending, implying bi-polar duality, and as Jehovah can be considered as the action of God in the

Four Worlds the combined title gives the idea of the principle of polarity functioning on all levels and thus the basis of form.

26. The Archangel of Binah has been called the 'Keeper of the Records of Evolution' and as the influence of Binah develops forms from the Akashic Sea of Consciousness, which is the basic matter of life, this presumably has reference to the Cosmic Akashic Records, the Memory of God which records all things that occur during the course of manifestation. The geometric form that one might come across in meditation on Binah which relates to the inner structure of the self could thus come from an individual segment of this spiritually primeval level. Thus the Archangel Tzaphkiel, in that all the karmic records are under his jurisdiction, is a higher analogue of the Dark Angel of the Soul of Man who mediates the Ama force of discipline and regeneration to him, just as the Archangel of Chokmah, Ratziel, represents archetypally the Bright Angel of the Soul of Man who brings illumination and guidance. These two Angels have been handed down in popular belief as the 'Good' and 'Evil' Angels that accompany man through life. But they are basically divine principles and it is the shortsightedness of the lower mind that describes correction and retribution as evil, or bad luck. Actually the Dark Angel holds the repository of a soul's karma and the Bright Angel its destiny. Destiny is the task the Spirit undertook to carry out on entry into manifestation, and karma is the action necessary, often painful, to readjust past errors that have occurred through the Fall of Man in order that he shall be in a position to take up his work of destiny— to return his hands to the plough. On the Tree used as a chart of the psychology of man, these two personal Angels are usually ascribed to the spheres of Chesed and Geburah.

27. The Archangel Tzaphkiel can also be considered to preside over all the planes of the Cosmos, just as Ratziel, the Archangel of Chokmah, presides over the Cosmic Rays,

whose analogues are the zodiacal signs. Tzaphkiel could also be considered as the Altar of Manifestation and Ratziel as the Fires of Creative Force descending upon it. And, as this attribution implies, Tzaphkiel is behind the formulation of all the mystical groups that have emanated from the Great White Lodge. He is the Archangel of the Archetypal Temple.

28. The Choir of Angels of Binah are called Aralim, Thrones, a title which is apt when one considers that a throne is a seat of power. A king without a throne is power-less and thus a subsidiary title of Binah is Khorsia, the Throne. Form is the throne which Divinity must occupy in order to control Its own powers which otherwise would dissipate, having no thrust-block. Steam is a useful analogy for the force of the Spirit, which when confined can drive vast machinery but which when not confined accomplishes nothing.

29. Saturn, the Mundane Chakra assigned to Binah is not an entirely satisfactory attribution for the Sephirah really refers to a condition of Space. In fact a far better Mundane Chakra would be interstellar space—when one realises that such space is a form. The traditional Mundane Chakra is apposite however in that Saturn is a planet with several moons and Binah is the principle behind all moon force, which is almost universally regarded as presiding over the feminine functions. Saturn is also a planet of limitation on the lower planes, astrologically considered, and yet on the higher levels it does draw down power from the Limitless Void toward the spheres of form. This corresponds well with Binah in that this Sephirah gives primal form or expression to the great stellar forces of Chokmah, drawn down through Kether out of the Unmanifest.

30. Forces of stellar magic can therefore be contacted through Binah and the constellations of the Great and Little Bear have particular significance for this Universe as our Solar Logos is said to have undergone previous evolution on those stars we associate with these constellations. Thus

in the stars of these constellations are the prototypes of
evolutionary destiny of the planets of this Solar System.
The Great Bear also has reference to the Round Table and
the Little Bear to the Holy Grail. Investigation of the
Samothracian Mysteries will prove fruitful in this sphere
for they were much concerned with stellar magic.

31. Samothrace was also a stronghold of Ama, as were
certain Egyptian Temples, particularly those concerned
with the 'dark' sides of Isis and Osiris. Isis is also, as the
spouse of the priest-king Osiris, an excellent example of
Aima, the 'bright' side of Binah. And the 'dark' side could
be delegated to her companion Nephthys.

32. It should be remembered that the dark and bright,
Ama and Aima, work in conjunction, being two sides of the
same coin. Thus weaving goddesses are applicable here
such as the Gaelic Orchil, weaving the Thread of Life;
with one hand spinning it up through the mould and with
the other weaving it down again beneath the earth. Thus
Orchil represents the dark and bright aspects within the
same image.

33. As Chokmah, as Masculine Principle of the Universe,
has a wealth of phallic symbols assigned to it, so Binah, as
the Feminine Principle, is assigned feminine sexual symbols.
As with the male symbolism, this can vary considerably
in its subtler ramifications. Thus apart from the vulva, the
womb and the breasts there are also the cup or chalice,
the cauldron, the cave, the moon, the sea, the tomb, certain
fruit such as figs or pomegranates, enclosing forms such
as cities, houses, gates or fences, ponds and wells, water
in general as opposed to the masculine fire, and so on and
so forth.

34. Finally, the Virtue and Vice attributed to the Sephirah
may appear to be quite arbitrary at first sight. There is a
certain anomoly in assigning a vice to a Supernal Sephirah
—or, indeed, to any Sephirah—but perhaps it was felt that
a vice should be assigned to any Sephirah which is in
Form, and so Binah was included as being the Mother of

Form. Or more likely, the vice may have been assigned because of confusion of the Sephirah with the astrological factors of the Mundane Chakra. Avarice is the vice that is concerned with an obsession with form and Binah is the form behind all forms. However, it might be better to consider the vice as the vice behind all vices—'forming and holding the wrong idea of oneself'. That is, making a false eidolon or image of the Spirit with which to work in the worlds of form. This is the root of the Prime Deviation.

35. The Virtue of Binah is Silence and this implies silence on all levels of being, not only the physical. It is necessary to still all the clamouring noises of the lower levels in order to hear the voice of the Spirit, and so the ideal state of form in order to make the vertical contacts is one of quietude. On another more practical level, if one is performing magical work and building up forms in subtle matter, silence and secrecy are essential in order not to break the psychic stresses. The easiest way to ruin esoteric work is to talk about it, and as Binah is the Archetypal Temple where forms are built for force to indwell, it is natural that the Virtue should be Silence. The Virtue is exemplified in the great Binah figure of the Virgin Mary—she who knew the wonderful and terrible experiences beyond the esoteric knowledge and experience of any ordinary woman and could sufficiently possess the inner wisdom to keep all such things to herself. A young Jewish girl who confided in no-one, who led, apparently, an ordinary life, looking after her own household, seeing her own women relations and friends occasionally, watching with terrible knowledge the mission of her son and knowing what the final achievement in the world would be, and doubtless knowing at least some part of the other achievements in the other worlds as well.

36. It is to be wished that many esoteric students had similar power and wisdom. Usually they learn by experience that, though the barriers of unbelief are thrown down within themselves, they will reap nothing but ridicule by

running round trying to spread the Light to their friends and relations. Every soul has its own pace, and the true adept has to know, and accept, that the only thing he can do is to keep silent, watching until the time is ripe for revelation to particular individuals or groups.

Chapter IX

DAATH—KNOWLEDGE

YETZIRATIC TEXT:	—
MAGICAL IMAGE:	A head with two faces, looking both ways.
GOD NAME:	A conjunction of Jehovah and Jehovah Elohim.
ARCHANGEL:	The Archangels of the Cardinal Points.
ORDER OF ANGELS:	Serpents.
MUNDANE CHAKRA:	Sothis or Sirius, the Dog Star.
VIRTUES:	Detachment. Perfection of Justice and the application of the Virtues untainted by Personality considerations. Confidence in the future.
TITLES:	The Invisible Sephirah. The Hidden or Unrevealed Cosmic Mind. The Mystical Sephirah. The Upper Room.
SPIRITUAL EXPERIENCE:	Vision across the Abyss.
ATZILUTHIC COLOUR:	Lavender.
BRIATIC COLOUR:	Silvery grey.
YETZIRATIC COLOUR:	Pure violet.
ASSIATIC COLOUR:	Grey, flecked yellow.
VICES:	Doubt of the future. Apathy. Inertia. Cowardice, (fear of the future.) Pride, (leading to isolation and disintegration).
SYMBOLS:	The Condemned Cell. The Prism. The Empty Room. The Sacred Mountain of any race. A grain of corn. The complete absence of symbol.

1. Daath, regarded as a Sephirah, is a comparatively modern conception. It is mentioned in early Qabalistic writings but is considered as the conjunction of the Masculine and Feminine Principles of God, Chokmah and Binah. Indeed the early texts state most explicitly that there are ten Holy Sephiroth, not nine and not eleven, but ten. However, modern research has led to sufficient evidence to justify its being regarded as a Sephirah in its own right, but in rather an especial way. It is thus termed the Invisible Sephirah and Crowley suggested that it might be best considered as in another dimension to the other Sephiroth.

On the Tree it could be said to be 'astride' the Abyss, the Abyss being the gulf—a higher analogue of the Gulf below Tiphareth—which divides noumenal from phenomenal reality.

2. Daath is the sphere where pure force takes on form. Binah represents the archetypal idea of form and the fourth Sephirah, Chesed, is a Sephirah of forms; Daath represents the state where actual forms are precipitated from the interaction of supernal forces. Daath could thus be conceived of as a lower analogue of Kether, but a state where form and not force first manifests. The forms implied here are of course in still a very abstract condition, being more in the nature of nodes of energy. Actual images and shapes as we generally understand them do not occur until the Sephirah Hod.

3. Daath is thus the highest unity in the world of forms. One could say that in Daath the Logoidal Meditation takes place, for from Daath the supernal forces are brought down across the Abyss to manifest in form as 'abstract knowledge'. Thus the Knowledge referred to in the title, as with the titles of the Supernal Sephiroth, means far more than the ordinary human mentation, abstract knowledge being almost synonymous with faith. But faith emanates ultimately from Binah and could well be called 'unmanifest knowledge'. In Daath is the transition of the Logoidal Plan from a state of unmanifestation to a state of abstraction so far as the human mentation is concerned.

4. Daath is the highest point of awareness of the human soul regarded as a soul (or in other terminologies Higher Self, Evolutionary Self, etc.) for awareness of the supernal levels can only be possible to the Spirit or Divine Spark itself. It is the gateway to what is called Nirvana in the East, and thus represents the point where a soul has reached the full stature of his evolutionary development, has attained perfect free will and can make the choice between going on to further evolution in other spheres or remaining to assist in the planetary Hierarchy. 'The Rays

and the Initiations' received through the mediumship of Alice A. Bailey gives a fascinating account of the choices of Path open to a soul at this point. It will be obvious that the esoteric grades assigned to the Supernal Sephiroth are grades of Masterhood and thus inner plane grades.

5. Before the grade of Daath the experience of a soul is devoted to bringing about a fusion of itself with the Spirit —to 'becoming'. After the powers of Daath are fully operative in a soul there is no further process of 'becoming' for that soul 'is'.

6. Daath is thus rightly called the Mystical Sephirah for it brings about the correct understanding of that much abused word 'mysticism'. Mysticism is *not* a confused state of purposeless or ill directed 'spirituality', it is a clear-cut realisation of the various potencies of life and their unity with God and with the soul. In this Sephirah the balance and realisation and *absorption* of these potencies meet together in the light of the abstract mind.

7. In Christian language Daath is the sphere of the Upper Room at the descent of the Pentecostal Flames. In pre-Christian times it was the sphere of the Creative Fire in the realm of Mind. For example in Druidism it was connected with Beltane though Beltane was the festival of the earthly creative fire as well.

8. The symbol of the cloud-hidden peak of the Sacred Mountain of any race is apposite to Daath for it was Daath consciousness that Moses contacted when he received the Tables of the Law from the top of Sinai, the Moon Mountain. This consciousness could be shown under the symbol of a grain of corn—the sense of being *in* everything, containing, in essence, the sacramental bread.

9. Daath, then, is the sphere of Realisation in its supremest meaning, understanding united with knowledge—and these two words are chosen with care. The human mind at this most abstract level attains to a complete awareness of All and in this complete awareness is absorbed by the Eternal Mind and made one with it, so that Daath, as a

Sephirah, represents supreme Wisdom and supreme Power of Realisation. And Realisation at its greatest height is Illumination, and all the supernal revelations of ancient times that have come to great spiritual leaders have been acquired through contact with the consciousness attributed to Daath.

10. There is another aspect to Daath by reason of the great Wisdom and Realisation that it holds and that is Justice. Again this is a far greater thing than ordinary human justice, or perhaps one should say attempts at justice. The Justice of Daath is the absolute balance inherent in the Cosmos which takes account of all factors within it from the relationships of the simplest atom to the remotest and largest suns. This Justice is exact, for by its very nature, as absolute Adjustor and Balancer, it cannot veer to left or right, but must be perfect.

11. It is well to bear in mind that the human soul, being by no means perfect, would be severely disrupted if brought into premature contact with the active side of this Justice. It is the kind of Justice that shows no mercy to any transgression of Cosmic Law. This may sound hard, but one would not expect mercy from being burned if one put one's hand in the fire; one has to accept the laws of the physical world and similarly one cannot contravene Cosmic Law unscathed. This is the principle behind karma. It has been said that one could abreact all one's karma in an hour, but this is highly unlikely to be achieved for the agony of spirit would be so intense as to shatter the personality.

12. Because of this aspect, the Daath power tends to upset previous conditions in the body or mind. It is really a balancing force, but this is in the long view and its temporary results will be disrupting. Not only will the inner vehicles be severely shaken up but the lower levels may become completely out of hand. This can be deduced from the Virtues and Vices attributed to the Sephirah. The effect of the force of Detachment upon the personality will tend to cut off the person from the standards of social living

which are built up about him in his present life and the consequences of these higher levels being stimulated will be completely regardless of any considerations of the welfare of the personality. The higher levels of his being will drive him into situations without any regard for the future comfort of the lower vehicles.

13. The Daath powers in balanced function, of course, give the type of person with a mission or sense of destiny who will have sufficient detachment to cut his way through any obstructions to his aims, at no matter what cost, and who has absolutely no concern for what danger the future may have in store such is his faith in his powers and acceptance of his destiny. The prime exemplar of this is Our Lord and also the Apostles and of course there are many others, in the fields of science, art, medicine, social welfare, political reform, evangelism and so on. It is not an attitude of fanaticism, though the condition can lead to this. Fanaticism is at root intense pride which will eventually lead to isolation from human contact and ultimate self-destruction. The fanatic is always inhuman. Our Lord, in spite of his many hard sayings and his undeviating course towards his destiny, could never justly be called inhuman. The fanatic is really a blasphemous caricature of the exemplary life for he pushes virtues so far that they become vices, and in the end he destroys himself—as Our Lord destroyed himself. But there is a great difference between the life and death of a Jesus, or a Socrates or a Thomas More and the life and death of a Hitler or any other fanatic, religious, political, scientific or what have you. Of course many fall between the two categories, but the real fanatic is he who is so proud and self-centred in the supposed rightness of his personal convictions that he lacks compassion.

14. Evil always pays good the compliment of masquerading as it but the unfailing diagnostic indicator of it is lack of compassion, or, those other much misunderstood terms, charity, humanity, or the Love of God.

15. From all this it will be obvious that meditations on Daath, unless very carefully decided upon beforehand and directed, are not very safe, particularly if they impinge upon the Cosmic Justice aspect of the Sephirah. The colours of the Sephirah, lavender, silvery grey, pure violet, and grey, flecked yellow are well enough to work with, particularly on Isis mythology, but should one come across strange reds and greens, a speckled brown and white, or electric blue, one should cease work immediately, for these relate to the Justice aspect and have a strange rate of vibration which can do much damage to the inner vehicles. There is also a dark side of Daath relating to what might be called the subconscious mind of God and this could have strange results on the soul. Contacts with the personal subconscious can be disturbing enough, so one can well imagine how much more explosive would be contacts with the Universal Subconscious, containing the whole past history and inner stresses of the Logos.

16. The safest way to work with Daath is through the Isis mythology for this relates generally to the bright positive side of Daath in which is held the Supernal Planning of the whole Universe and the shining goals of the future. Isis is a very ancient goddess, far older than the Egyptian pantheons. This is indicated in the myth where Isis, by the power of her magic, induced Ra, the Father of the Gods, to impart his secret name to her whereby she obtained power over him. She was said to have her home in the star Sept, which is the star we now call Sirius or Sothis, the Dog Star. And students of advanced esotericism will know that Sirius is the sphere of the Greater Masters, and the Sun behind our Sun.

17. Although all the myths concerning Isis can be correlated with many parts of the Tree it is through the Daath Sephirah within these Sephiroth that the Isiac force functions. This is really the key to an understanding of the power and methods of the Isis formula, though there are other aspects to it.

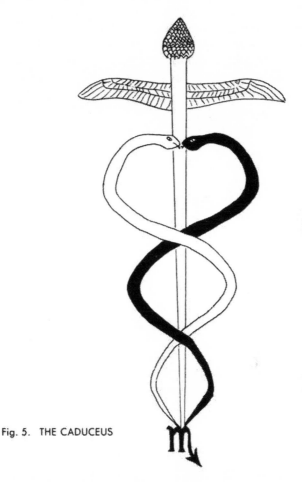

Fig. 5. THE CADUCEUS

18. Isis could be called, in a way, the Ether of the Spirit, and she can be correlated with The Priestess of the Silver Star which is the full title of the Tarot Trump which is assigned to the Path which leads up across the Abyss through Daath from Tiphareth to Kether. There is also a connection with the glyph of the Caduceus, a winged staff entwined with two serpents, having a pine cone at its head and the sign of Scorpio, the scorpion, at its base. (Fig. 5) Aligned with the Tree of Life, the pine cone covers Kether, the wings embrace Chokmah and Binah, and the serpents

heads unite in Daath. The serpent symbolism of this figure denotes the manifestation of force at any level. This serpent symbolism is well explained in the myths of Isis if meditated upon, and it is well to remember the seven scorpions attributed to Isis in the light of the seven planes of manifestation and the symbol at the base of the Caduceus.

19. The complete Isis mythology goes through several cycles—for instance after her journeyings to find the body of Osiris she had to go on another journey to hide her son and then on another journey to find the scattered fragments of Osiris and so on. In psychological terms, these various cycles give contact with the archetypes on different levels. And so if a course of meditation is essayed on them in order to elicit their inner meaning, the path of transmutation and sublimation of the psyche towards the consciousness of Daath can be trodden with the minimum of danger, for this particular line of meditation will build forms into the psyche which will hold the forces contacted whether in the depths of the instincts or the heights of superconsciousness.

20. It was because of the clear run-through of power possible with this formula that Isis often appeared winged in Egyptian sacerdotal art. Although the profound symbolism of those wings might not be appreciated by the populace of the day, their influence and meaning could be. 'felt'— and still can be. They have relation to the wings of the Caduceus.

21. The Isis formula is particularly worth working on because it is relatively complete and it gives the feminine side to the more usual masculine symbols of esoteric development—it can be used as a complement to the Osiris and Christ teachings relating to the Sephirah Tiphareth. There is symbolism in other goddess formulae, particularly the Grecian and Assyrian, and in Mary, the Mother of Jesus, where different aspects are more developed, but the teaching of Isis, apart from its great wisdom, power and inspiration, is one of the most stabilising, and that is a very necessary contribution towards inner development,

particularly where Daath is concerned.

22. There will be no difficulty in unravelling the popular teachings of Isis in the light of ordinary states of consciousness but these states have to be worked over again and again on a higher arc and what may seem to be the most obvious parables about Isis will be found to be repositories of profound esoteric knowledge.

23. The Isis myths contain references to different grades of initiation, to principles of sexual polarity, to contact with the Higher Self, to contact with the Spirit, and even to the Spirit of God Itself. Isis was able to perform miracles, to heal, to bring the dead to life. She was a great traveller and also goddess of the sea. One of her gifts was the imparting of sweet perfume to those she touched. This has deep reference to the Sephirah Daath, which is an analogue of Yesod, (one of whose attributions is perfumes and incense), on a higher level. It refers to the 'perfume' of the Spirit of man, and though this may at first appear to be a strange concept, it indicates the ability to impart to others, even through the senses, the wonder and the beauty, the glory and the joy and the power of the immortal Spirit.

24. The form of Isis can be built up in the Daath colours or alternatively in blue, for the force has much to do with the 'Blue Ray' of the higher mind. For general purposes the best way is to visualise a huge pillar of Egyptian sculpture and within it the clear-cut lines of the goddess seated upon her throne with vast wings that would encircle the Universe; on her head the Solar disk of Sirius. The column should tower up to the uttermost limits of the Universe and equally penetrate to the uttermost depths. One should feel particularly an aura of vast strength.

25. Of the other pagan pantheons Janus gives the best Magical Image for the Sephirah as the god who looks both ways; down into manifestation, seeing all that occurs therein, and also towards the Supernals, thus giving the Spiritual Experience of The Vision across the Abyss.

26. Balder the Beautiful and Horus equally have aspects

relating to Daath, the pure Spirit coming down into manifestation; and Heimdall, who guards the rainbow bridge which leads from the world of man to the world of gods, also has relevance.

27. The potentially dangerous aspects of Daath to the ordinary human personality are well illustrated in the heroes whose adventures are obviously Daath experiences—these are Prometheus, Galahad and Perseus, to name but three.

28. Prometheus stole Divine Fire from Heaven assisted by the goddess of Wisdom, Pallas Athene. This can be regarded as an aspect of Free Will, by which primitive man took a step forward in physical evolution from the near animal level. According to Zeus, or the powers reigning at the time, this was a premature act and Prometheus was chained to a mountain in the Caucasus, tormented by an eagle devouring his liver. The eagle of course was a symbol of Zeus, but it is also another form of Scorpio, the scorpion, which is associated with divine force coming down to manifest in a plane of form in both the Caduceus and Isiac symbolism.

29. The feminine side of Prometheus is Io, who, ravished by Zeus, was turned into a white heifer, and wandered over many lands tormented by a gad-fly sent by Hera, the leading female divinity. Eventually Io was restored to human form in Egypt, where she bore a son and was worshipped there as a fore-runner of Isis.

30. Galahad was the perfect knight of the Arthurian cycle and the Grail winner and he has been over-spiritualised by later Christian commentators in just the same way that the Lord Jesus has been rendered 'meek and mild'. He was however the greatest knight of all, overwhelming all comers, and completely single-pointed in dedication, so much so that when he had completed his Quest, his one wish, which was granted, was to die.

31. Perseus was the hero who captured the Medusa's head which changed all who saw it to stone, and is a good symbol of the dark side of Daath. He was assisted by

Hermes, who also had a hand in rescuing Io from Hera, and also by Pallas Athene, the aider and abettor of Prometheus. Pallas Athene thus also has her place in considerations of Daath although, like Isis Urania, she is also aligned with Chokmah. Her relevance to Daath and those who aspire to its powers is well summarised in the passage about her from Kingsley's 'The Heroes': "I am Pallas Athene; and I know the thoughts of all men's hearts, and discern their manhood or their baseness. And from the souls of clay I turn away, and they are blest, but not by me. They fatten at ease, like sheep in the pasture, and eat what they did not sow, like oxen in the stall. They grow and spread, like the gourd along the ground; but, like the gourd, they give no shade to the traveller, and when they are ripe death gathers them, and they go down unloved into hell, and their name vanishes out of the land."

"But to the souls of fire I give more fire, and to those who are manful I give a might more than man's. These are the heroes, the sons of the Immortals, who are blest, but not like the souls of clay. For I drive them forth by strange paths, Perseus, that they may fight the Titans and the monsters, the enemies of Gods and men. Through doubt and need, danger and battle, I drive them; and some of them are slain in the flower of youth, no man knows when or where; and some of them win noble names, and a fair and green old age; but what will be their latter end I know not, and none, save Zeus, the father of Gods and men.'

32. As Daath was not considered to be a Sephirah by the original Qabalists the sphere has no God Name, Archangel or Order of Angels traditionally assigned to it. However the God Name can be considered to be a synthesis of the God Names of Chokmah and Binah. Also as it is a reflection of Kether it could be said to represent all three Supernal Sephiroth at the fount of the worlds of form.

33. The Archangel can be taken as a combination of the Archangels of the Four Cardinal Points, Raphael, Michael, Gabriel and Uriel, the Archangels of East, South, West

and North respectively. Gabriel and Uriel have particular reference to the Sephirah on their more profound less obvious sides.

34. The Angels of the Sephirah are a kind of Seraphim, only not flaming as the Seraphim of Geburah. To clairvoyant sight they have the appearance of silvery grey serpents with golden darting tongues and a type of force emanating from them which can only be described as 'Incandescent Knowledge'.

35. All attempts at a description of the states of consciousness of Daath can at best be only metaphorical, for really it is the state of awareness devoid of all symbols. This is why the great formula that expresses the nature of Daath is 'The Empty Room'. This is the nearest symbol which implies absence of symbol, and thus contact with Reality. It is an awareness of the 'Complete Denudation of God' into that which is neither force nor form but contains both. It is a 'condition' beyond all other conditions—a Supreme State, and this state is approached when the phase of the abstract mind is entered. The approach to this state, which can be analysed into several stages, is along a 'secret' Path of the Tree of Life, from Chesed towards Daath. It is an initiatory process for the Adeptus Exemptus —one who has learnt all that Earth has to teach—and the way can be a terrible one, being the well known Dark Night of the Soul of the mystic, but on a higher arc than is usually experienced.

Chapter X

CHESED—MERCY

"The Fourth Path is called the Cohesive or Receptive Intelligence because it contains all the Holy Powers, and from it emanate all the spiritual virtues with the most exalted essences. They emanate one from another by virtue of the Primordial Emanation, the Highest Crown, Kether."

MAGICAL IMAGE:	A mighty crowned and throned king.
GOD NAME:	El.
ARCHANGEL:	Tzadkiel.
ORDER OF ANGELS:	Chasmalim, Brilliant Ones.
MUNDANE CHAKRA:	Jupiter.
VIRTUE:	Obedience.
TITLES:	Gedulah, Love. Majesty. Magnificence.
SPIRITUAL EXPERIENCE:	Vision of Love.
ATZILUTHIC COLOUR:	Deep violet.
BRIATIC COLOUR:	Blue.
YETZIRATIC COLOUR:	Deep purple.
ASSIATIC COLOUR:	Deep azure. flecked yellow.
VICE:	Bigotry. Hypocrisy. Gluttony, Tyranny.
SYMBOLS:	The solid figure. Tetrahedron. Orb. Wand. Sceptre. Crook.

1. Chesed, before Daath was considered to be a Sephirah, was the first Sephirah of the Formative World and this explains the Yetziratic Text, which still holds good, for Chesed receives all the Holy Powers from the Supernals rayed through Daath, one of whose symbols is the Prism.

2. The Text affirms that all the Emanations, or Sephiroth, have their ultimate root in the prime upwelling of divine force in Kether. This force, which is activated and given potentiality of form in Chokmah and Binah, is then refracted through Daath into Chesed, which is thus called the Recep-

tive Intelligence. It is also called the Cohesive Intelligence because it is in this Sephirah that the forces first cohere into forms, although on a subtle level. In Binah is the idea of form, and in Daath the process of transmutation into form, but the forces actually cohere into forms in Chesed.

3. From Chesed these forms gradually, through the remaining Sephiroth, attain greater density of manifestation and thus is it also said that from Chesed 'emanate all the spiritual virtues with the most exalted essences.' In other words, Chesed is the supreme height of manifestation in form, although form has been foreshadowed, and has its place to a certain extent, in Daath and Binah. But Chesed is the first Sephirah below the Abyss.

4. Thus it will be seen that from this Sephirah emanates all rulership over the worlds of forms although the prime force emanates from the Supernal Sephiroth transformed through Daath. Because of this, the sphere of the Masters is said to be in Chesed.

5. The history of the concept of the Masters is a stormy one. Before the end of the nineteenth century they were rarely, if ever, mentioned. Anyone who contacted them prior to this either kept the fact secret or else was unaware of what or who it was they contacted. Where the inner planes are concerned the actual form conceived is usually coloured by the mental bias of the perceiver. A parallel to this can be seen in the annals of psychiatry where it will be found that patients under Jungian analysis turn up with fine Jungian symbolism, while patients under Freudian analysis turn up with Freudian symbolism and so on. Similarly in scientological processing where a pre-clear has a flash-back in memory to a time when he was a free Spirit without, or with only very abstract form in interstellar space, he will often clothe the memory with the trappings of modern science fiction and 'remember' himself as in a space-ship and so on, simply because his mind cannot conceive the idea of being without form. In a like manner the Jews always considered any discarnate entity

to be an angel or archangel—or devil or archdevil—in order to conform to their theology and maintain a monotheistic bias.

6. So the Masters, as we picture them, are images in our imagination, as indeed are all inner plane entities, human, angelic or elemental. *But this does not mean that they are the product of our imaginations. They are real beings on their own level.* And the level of the Masters corresponds to the Sephirah Chesed, which is a sphere where forms are of the density of the processes of the abstract mind or intuition.

7. When one pictures an inner plane entity in astral consciousness one is operating in the sphere of Yesod—the Treasure House of Images—but one is contacting a being who is really a potent centre of abstract force in the case of a Master. The picture that one projects in the imagination acts as a focus for this force, which will animate the imagined picture—thus it is possible to hold conversations with this imaginary projection and this is the technique of 'astral psychism'.

8. However it is a method which has its dangers and delusions. There are few who can work at this dense level of mentational form without subconsciously injecting some of their own ideas and conceptions into it. The directest method of communication is the most efficient and that is by raising one's own consciousness to the level of the communicating entity and thus receiving impressions direct from abstract mind to abstract mind which will filter down into concrete consciousness as one's own ideas or thoughts.

9. From this it will be seen that the techniques of communication are such that it is impossible to give proofs of the existence of these high inner plane beings under laboratory conditions, for physical science has no means of gauging what is the emanation of one mind or another. The only proof is direct experience, which requires initial faith, which is not an approved scientific instrument or even attitude. The only form of psychic communication with

which science can get to grips is deep trance which is not a condition that is required either for astral psychism or mental telepathy.

10. The two latter methods of communication are within the reach of anybody, given a certain degree of mind training, and many probably do it unconsciously, though it is found that some people have much more aptitude than others. The Masters themselves favour the higher mental approach for it is less subject to error once properly developed. The astral method has led in the past to some ludicrous errors which has made the word 'occultism' stink in the nostrils of many who might otherwise be favourable towards it.

11. Obviously if one is going to start holding interior conversations with projections of one's own imagination it does not require much dissociation of consciousness to land one into the strange worlds of schizophrenia and hallucination. That is why practical occultism should be carried out under strictly controlled conditions and with a definite purpose in mind, and it is the reason for opening and sealing rituals before and after practical work.

12. Whilst early propagandists on behalf of the existence of the Masters may not have fallen into schizophrenia it appears that many were the victims of hallucination in that they confused their planes, mistaking astral consciousness for physical reality. Thus one reads accounts of meetings with such and such a Master in a railway train or public park, with detailed descriptions of dress, including top-hat, umbrella and all.

13. Anyone having any conception of what the Masters really are must realise that accounts of such alleged physical manifestations are complete balderdash. However the fact is that there is truth behind the folly and self-deception and it is an appalling tragedy that the foolish way in which the facts have been presented in the past has led many to dismiss the whole subject out of hand—and frankly one can hardly blame those who have done so.

14. The Masters, or Inner Plane Adepti, are human beings who have gained all the experience, and all the wisdom resulting from experience, necessary for their spiritual evolution in the worlds of form. They are thus 'just men made perfect'. All souls, when they have become free of the necessity for birth and death, can go on to higher evolution in other spheres, but some elect to stay behind in Earth conditions in order to help on their 'younger brethren' in their progress through cyclic evolution on this planet. These are the Masters, and there are many of them, though only a few are known to humanity by name for it is only the 'teaching Masters' who communicate directly with us.

15. It is this 'College of Masters' that forms the upper reaches of the planetary Hierarchy of human beings, just as the Archangels form the upper reaches of the Angelic and Elemental Hierarchy. The function of the Masters is to mediate divine forces, or the Will of God, to humanity and thus can they be considered to operate in the Sephirah Chesed.

16. The 'Inner Council of Masters' however, commonly referred to as 'The Great White Lodge' is more of a Daath condition, for when the 'Council' is in full session the contacts with the higher Supernal levels are made and with the Un-nameable and Un-knowable beings who have their existence in those remote spheres. It must be remembered that these terms are at best approximate and that the nature of the 'Council' and its higher contacts is more in the fashion of a high telepathic rapport than a council meeting as we commonly understand it.

17. The sphere of Chesed can further be seen to be a Sephirah especially related to the Masters in that the esoteric grade assigned to it is that of Adeptus Exemptus. That is, one who is exempt, or free, from the limitations imposed by physical and lower form existence and the need to reincarnate.

18. The function of the Sephirah is similar to the function of the Masters as can be seen by the Magical Image of a

mighty king, crowned and throned; the Flashing Colours, which are the purples and blues normally associated with kingship; and the subsidiary symbols of the orb, wand, sceptre and crook.

19. However it must not be thought that the rulership implied is that kind of authority which human beings usually inflict on one another in the world—so often manifesting as bossiness and even persecution. The Will of God is also the Love of God and the Spiritual Experience of the Sephirah is the Vision of Love. Crowley was perfectly correct when he said "Love is the Law, Love under Will," even though that phrase has been much misunderstood, not least of all by Crowley himself.

20. It is a similar case with his other axioms, "Every man and every woman is a star" and "Do what thou wilt shall be the whole of the Law." The whole of the Law implied here is the Will of the Spirit, which is synonymous with the Will of God. It does not mean "do what you like" according to the dictates of the lower vehicles.

21. It must not be thought that all Crowley's writings are full of wisdom. There is much of worth in them but he is a treacherous authority to follow unless one has a very good idea of what occultism is all about. Like Eliphas Levi, the nineteenth century French occultist whom he admired so much, he was a practical joker of the *'pince sans rire'* variety. As an adept he was very third rate as his life story shows, and apart from a brilliant intellect, his main contribution to occultism was that he was a good medium. An adept has to be able to control the forces he invokes and Crowley could not. In spite of all his rare talents he succumbed to the forces he rashly invoked with the usual result of a gross inflation of the self-importance of the personality and gradual decline into drug addiction and magical impotence. He is still admired by many, but his example is more in the nature of what not to do, and so he can best be regarded as a lesser Mordred, one who was his own Judas Iscariot—as indeed to a greater or lesser extent we all are.

22. "Do what thou wilt shall be the whole of the Law" and "Love is the Law, Love under Will" apply well to Chesed, for at the level of this Sephirah the will of the individual is completely in harmony with the Will of God. Thus Obedience, which is the Virtue of this Sephirah, does not mean the willingness to take orders. What is implied is that the soul who has achieved the grade of the Chesed initiation is so aligned with the Will of God that his own will is the same as the Will of God and so he can do no evil—it is completely foreign to his nature.

23. Thus the Masters, when they train pupils, do not train them to take orders, but to develop themselves to the degree that they can make up their own minds what to do, and the result of which will be in accordance with the Will of God and the aims of the Hierarchy. Human free-will is sacrosanct.

24. In view of this last factor there is no compulsion in White occultism. If a person is headed for a nasty fall he may be warned about it. If he persists nonetheless in his course of action then that is his affair, though if the damage he is likely to do to himself and others is likely to injure the Group he is in too badly, he may be asked to leave it in the interests of all concerned. He is then free to leave, pursue his course of action and have his smash-up, and if he is in a fit state after it and has developed a little wisdom from the experience he may be re-admitted. It is often the only way that some will learn.

25. As the Will of God in ruling his creation is the Law of Love, Gedulah, Love is perhaps the better title for this Sephirah, and it is quite often so termed. However, Chesed, Mercy, is the more common usage and is probably derived from the fact that when the glyph of the Pillars is super-imposed upon the Tree, this Sephirah is in the centre of the Pillar of Mercy at the 'Ethical' or 'Moral' level. Geburah, Severity, corresponds in a like manner to the Pillar of Severity. The subsidiary titles of Majesty and Magnificence are also well to bear in mind.

26. Looking around at the world in the physical level of

Malkuth it may appear strange to some that the Will of God should be Love, for the world is far from being a loveable place at times. But it must be remembered that according to this Law of Love human free-will cannot be gainsaid and most of the horror of physical existence stems from man himself. "Man's inhumanity to man makes countless thousands mourn". And no doubt countless thousands more will mourn until the majority of the human race learns to contact the Chesedic sphere, whether they call it by the Qabalistic title or not.

27. Apart from the more obvious human inventions such as neuroses, psychoses, gas chambers, concentration camps, slums, torture chambers, hydrogen bombs and so on, on the subtler levels, by his deviation from the Will of God, man is also responsible for introducing certain of the parasitic and saprophitic entities to this planet which manifest as some diseases. However, man has baked his cake and he must eat it, every last crumb, and when he has done so then he can clap the plate on his head and use it for a halo.

28. These may seem very hard sayings and some will no doubt ask "Why does God allow it?" And the only answer one can give is that they had better ask God. It is perhaps in his Mercy that He sent the last deluge, but the fresh start humanity gained from it does not seem to have improved matters. Faced with the situation as we are the only thing we can do is to try to right it, and the only way that can be done is by seeking the Will of God within. No easy task.

29. Perhaps it is better to reserve one's sympathy for the animal and Elemental kingdoms, which had no part in the Fall but have had to suffer much of the consequences in that they share the planet with us. It is also a grisly truth that what may be good from the point of view of the Spirit can be most unpleasant when viewed from the personality orientation. This again is a result of man's deviation, for had he not abused free will, he would still have the links operating between all the levels of his being and

he would be able to see with the eyes of the Spirit.

30. But in our considerations of Cosmic adjustment we are verging on the borders of the Sephirah Geburah. It must be said that compared to the realities of man's cosmic situation, the *'angst'* or anguish of the atheist existentialist is very small beer—but there are compensations. Very great ones indeed—for "every man and every woman is a star", basically, and potentially.

31. The Name of God in this Sephirah is El or Al, composed of the Hebrew letters Aleph and Lamed. Aleph, as we have already discussed, signifies the beginning of things and one of the symbols of Lamed is the wing of a bird, so that the name can be said to convey the idea of power and potentiality, (Aleph), combined with uplifting and outspreading force, (Lamed). Viewed in this light a symbol could be constructed of the Name whereby Aleph is represented by a point within a circle, for this is a representation of beginnings of things, and Lamed by a wing. The resultant composite symbol would resemble the winged disk of the ancient Egyptians. Alternatively, using the traditional Qabalistic symbolism for these letters, Aleph is called the Ox and Lamed, the Ox-goad, so that here we have the idea of primal driving force under control.

32. The Archangel of the Sephirah, Tzadkiel, as well as the Order of Angels, Chasmalim, or Brilliant Ones, can be built up in imagination, the Archangel having an especial link with the symbol of the Orb, and the influence of these beings will be valuable to anyone suffering from instability, whether of mind or emotions. Generally speaking, an inability to be punctual or to control the time factor is a symptom of mental confusion, while general untidiness or inability to control the space factor is a sign of emotional confusion. The soothing, constructive forces of the Chesedic sphere can do much to relieve these conditions.

33. The planet Jupiter, which is the Mundane Chakra of Chesed, has long been considered in astrology as the great beneficent influence among the planets and this is no doubt

122

a result of the fact that this planet is that on which the evolution is in terms of 'concrete Spirit'—not a term that conveys much, but which can be seen to apply well to Chesed which is the first of the form-Sephirah proper and receives the pure abstract spiritual forces from the Supernals. Thus one can perhaps obtain an idea of what 'concrete Spirit' is by considering the Sephirah Chesed, and this is one of the ways of working that make the Tree of Life such a valuable symbol for unknown concepts can be defined and understood by reference to the known.

34. The Vices of the Sephirah are those vices commonly shown by people who set themselves up in authority or who are set up by others as an authority, and they often manifest in very subtle ways. There is the common saying that "Power tends to corrupt." and anyone who is given power, in that he must be to some degree aberrated or he would not be in incarnation at this time, will inevitably be but a poor caricature of the Divine Rule of Chesed. Some of course will be more successful than others but there is no record of a faultless ruler in the known history of humanity. Bigotry, hypocrisy and tyranny are all vices that stem from identifying oneself with the ruling principle whilst refusing to face the reality of those parts of the self that are unworthy of rulership. Gluttony is a sheer abuse of the whole principle, as indeed is Tyranny also, in that rulership over others or over objects is orientated entirely for the 'benefit' of the self rather than for the benefit of the ruled. It must not be thought either, that these vices and temptations apply only to those in high positions of authority—they apply to everyone, for everyone has rulership over something even if it be only the physical body.

35. The symbol of the solid figure indicates an added dimension to the plane figures relating to the Supernal Sephiroth. The added dimension of course being form.

36. In the pagan mythologies the relevant gods will obviously be those that are beneficent rulers over gods and men, or those aspects of any god or goddess which so rule.

From this it can be seen how the pagan deity attributions frequently overlap various aspects of Divinity. Zeus, for example, as the All-Father figure would relate to Chokmah, but as the ruler of gods and men would be a Cheşed figure. Again this is one of the advantages of the Qabalistic system for it gives greater ease of classification and differentiation than the teeming chaotic profusion of most mythologies.

Chapter XI

GEBURAH—SEVERITY

"The Fifth Path is called the Radical Intelligence because it resembles Unity, uniting itself to Binah, Understanding, which emanates from the primordial depths of Chokmah, Wisdom."

MAGICAL IMAGE:	A mighty warrior in his chariot.
GOD NAME:	Elohim Gebor.
ARCHANGEL:	Khamael.
ORDER OF ANGELS:	Seraphim, Fiery Serpents.
MUNDANE CHAKRA:	Mars.
VIRTUE:	Energy, Courage.
TITLES:	Pachad, Fear. Din, Justice.
SPIRITUAL EXPERIENCE:	Vision of Power.
ATZILUTHIC COLOUR:	Orange.
BRIATIC COLOUR:	Scarlet red.
YETZIRATIC COLOUR:	Bright scarlet.
ASSIATIC COLOUR:	Red, flecked black.
VICE:	Cruelty. Destruction.
SYMBOLS:	Pentagon. Five petalled rose. Sword. Spear. Scourge. Chain.

1. The Yetziratic Text of Geburah is similar to that of Chesed in that it lays stress on the source of power in the Supernals. Where the Text of Chesed specifically mentions Kether however, the Text of Geburah specifically mentions Chokmah and Binah. Kether is the Atziluthic or Supernal World of the whole Tree, while Chokmah and Binah both constitute the Briatic or Creative World. From this one can gather that as Chokmah and Binah represent the Divine Force of Kether in action, so does Geburah represent the more active side of the rulership principle of Chesed. This is borne out by the Geburic Magical Image—a mighty

124

warrior in his chariot, the Spiritual Experience—the Vision of Power, and the Virtues of the Sephirah—energy and courage.

2. The attributions of Geburah are almost all martial ones, and though, because of this, it is perhaps easier to gain an elementary conception of Geburah than of the other Sephiroth, it can lead to some misunderstanding for this Sephirah has its subtleties and profundities equal to those of any of the other spheres of the Tree.

3. Geburah is basically a Sephirah of adjustment and assessment; it is a sphere of absolute and unmitigated Truth. One could say that it would have been in the light of Geburah that on the seven days of creation God looked at what He had done and saw that it was good. One tends to gloss over this action of God almost as a needless formality, but in any mystical treatise of the quality of the Book of Genesis, nothing is put in merely for the sake of effect. After the creative effort of putting things into form, there follows the necessity of scrutinising the result intensely and purging the form of any excrescences or defects.

4. The process can best be considered in the sphere of creative art. A painter, say, works at a canvas, building up colours and forms in inter-relationship until he has created what he considers may be a finished picture. He does not send it to a gallery for sale immediately he has laid down his brush—he takes a walk and then returns to look at the picture with fresh eyes. He may turn its face to the wall and re-examine it again and again over a period of days, weeks or even months before he declares it a finished work worthy to bear his signature. The standards he will use in judging various aspects of the picture will be set by the laws of the picture itself. A patch of one colour in a particular shape and position will be valid or invalid according to its context in the rest of the picture, whether it balances up and complements all the other colours and shapes in other positions over the canvas.

5. One can conceive that the Creation of a Universe by

an Intelligent Entity would follow much the same process. The building up of the forms and relationships of a painting, like the formulation of the forms and relationships of a Universe can be posited as under the presidency of the Chesedic sphere. The clear eyed assessment of the work of art or of the Manifested Universe and the erasure or correction of any falsities would thus be an action of Geburah.

6. In a well conceived and executed work of art there would be little need of corrective action, though the principle of Geburah would be applied with equal force in the assessment of it. In a botched work the subsequent corrective action, which is a different aspect of Geburah, would need to be greater. The same applies to the Universe. One can imagine that the creative work of God would require little subsequent adjustment, but some of the 'colours' God has used are human and capable of independent action. If man had acted throughout his evolutionary life in accordance with Divine Law all would be relatively well, but he did not, so the result, in this planet at least, has been like a painting in which the colours arbitrarily change their hues, lighten, darken, or spread over the canvas to areas where they should not be. This of course calls for constant assessment and readjustment on the part of the Creator, and the attempts to keep the Universal work of art from becoming an unredeemable mess are what we call the workings of the Laws of Karma, or more properly, Readjustment, and these Laws are attributed to the Sephirah Geburah.

7. It is in view of this that there is an aspect of Geburah known as 'The Hall of Justice' or 'The Hall of the Lords of Karma'. Justice, as the perfect balance between Mercy and Severity, is properly assigned to Daath, the conjunction of Chokmah and Binah, the two Sephiroth mentioned in the Yetziratic Text of Geburah. Geburah is the sphere where that Justice is applied in the worlds of form.

8. This aspect of Geburah can be imagined as a great

hall, completely empty, but radiated throughout with scarlet light. Here the soul stands stripped naked of every shred of excuse or possibility of evasion while the piercing shadowless light penetrates to every part of its being. In the utter silence of the Scarlet Hall, Justice is revealed. The soul *is* in such and such a state and is revealed to be so. In this revelation everything is taken into account, automatically, inevitably and pitilessly. It is a Hall of Justice, not Judgment, and no sentence is pronounced, no doom decreed. Silence reigns supreme — the silence of Binah, Understanding, to which, as the Yetziratic Text says, Geburah is united. And Geburah is resembled to Unity, for the part is taken into account as being a part of the unified whole.

9. The result to the soul is the presentation of an inescapable fact—what that soul really is. In this assessment factor of Geburah there is no conception of a punishment forced upon a soul. The Hall of Justice is like an immensely complicated and infallible calculating machine, it delivers the answer and that is all, though the whole omnipotence of the Cosmos is behind that answer. There is equally no consideration of whether the soul has the strength to bear the Truth revealed, or whether it will be crushed beneath the burden. The answer comes and the soul can take it or leave it as long as it chooses, as long as choice remains.

10. The subsequent actions necessary to bring the soul into correct alignment with what it should be are no part of this particular force of Geburah. The necessary balancing, compensating or adjustment may well come under the action of the destructive side of Geburah but could equally be under some other sphere of the Tree of Life. Thus a soul which continually refused to face up to the facts of life of the instincts would probably best profit from the influences of the constructive side of Yesod; a harsh application of pure Geburic force might do more harm than good. It is in guiding and helping souls to eradicate their failings and

excrescences that the Hierarchy of Masters is concerned. These 'elder brethren' of humanity, knowing the strengths and weaknesses of a soul, may advise and help it so that the expunging of 'the scarlet letters on the scroll of the machine of Truth' may be as little shattering as possible. Whether the soul asks that aid or seeks that advice is a matter for that soul alone to decide—but however long the Truth is evaded it still has to be faced in the end, whether in the hard way or by easier ways, it matters not to the Forces of Cosmic Balance.

11. In its more positive corrective side Geburah shows the joint action of the Active and Passive Pillars within itself probably more clearly than any other Sephirah. There are souls which can face a terrible death in some religious, political or other cause, a death which by reason of the physical make-up cannot cause very prolonged agony. This is the sharp Geburic action symbolised by the spear and sword. The passive aspect of Geburah can be very slow, and indeed its slowness is one of its most potent methods, implying *constant* vigilance and iron control of its *continuous* working over a very long time. This is to be seen in the *gradual* evolutionary forces of karma, the *gradual* development through trial and tribulation of the human being, the *gradual* development and break-up of racial groups. The relevant symbols here are the Scourge, which lashes to continuous action, and the Chain, which holds captive through great stretches of time and prevents any escape.

"The Mills of God grind slowly, yet they grind exceeding small;
"Though with patience He stands waiting, with exactness He grinds all."

12. The inevitability of this process of Geburah is shown in the title assigned to it in the Yetziratic Text—the Radical Intelligence. This implies that the works of Geburah have to do with root sources and origins, forming part of the

essential nature of things; and are also thorough going and unsparing, so that anything which does not align with the basic pattern is detected and completely eradicated.

13. However one title of Geburah may be very misleading and that is Pachad, Fear. If there is one thing that has absolutely no part in the Divine Plan for evolution, and which is in itself unreservedly evil, in origin and manifestation, that thing is Fear. One could almost say it was from Fear that all other deviations and evil arose, that it provides the foundation for the Powers of Evil.

14. Where there is Faith, or Knowledge of God, there is no Fear. It will be remembered that the Virtues and Vices of Daath, the Sephirah of Knowledge, are much concerned with the absence or presence of Fear. As has been well said: "The Truth shall make you free.", as it seems were the early Christian martyrs, going singing to their deaths, and yet of course many fear Truth, and fear it so much that they cannot even admit to themselves the existence of their fear. Fear of course is very deep rooted and is common to animals and man, so it is not primarily a result of man's Fall. It has been said that it was a prime cause of the legendary War in Heaven, when certain great beings, Angelic and otherwise, revolted against the Will of God, fearing their extinction or exceeding change. This event, primeval as far as humanity is concerned, has been handed down in popular legend as the revolt of Lucifer—though Lucifer has been much maligned by this attribution as he is really an aspect of the Promethean forces, his name signifying 'the Light'—though he is said to have fallen through Pride. Pride however is one side of a coin whose other side is Fear, and Fear is a result of lack of Faith, a betrayal of the Love of God.

15. Geburah is one of the Holy Sephiroth and so Fear should have no part in it—nor should Fury and Anger, for all these things are aberrative and not part of the Divine Plan. They are symptoms and products of departure from the Plan. Assessment and corrective action are part of the

Plan but this does not mean destructive criticism or fury and anger to produce fear, these are typically human distortions.

16. It is interesting to consider the Tone Scale of human ability put forward by Hubbard and used as a basis for scientology and dianetics. Here, the human being functioning at the height of his powers is said to be in a condition of eagerness and exhilaration and it is obvious that the analytical and corrective work of Geburah could best be done by a human being functioning at this level. As aberration increases so the human being becomes less efficient, and instead of the eager exhilaration, one has drops in ability ranging from strong interest, mild interest, indifference, boredom, resentment and so on, through anger and fear, to grief and apathy, which in its most apathetic form is death—the complete indifference to survival. Now obviously one of the Ten Holy Sephiroth, the Emanations of God Imminent, could have little to do with a state of such heavy human psychological occlusion as anger or fear.

17. The ideas of anger and fear being associated with Geburah probably come from the typically human associations derived from a superficial study of its symbolism. The title, Pachad, Fear, refers more to the awe that encompasses one in contemplating a vast manifestation of God's power in nature, what also might be called the Fear of God, which is not at all the same as ordinary fear.

18. Anger and fear may also be human reactions to the forces of Geburah at work. That is, anger at the reality revealed, and fear of the consequences necessary to bring that reality into alignment with Spiritual Truth or Spiritual Reality.

19. Although Energy and Courage are true enough as Virtues of this Sephirah, for they represent the forces of the fully functional unaberrated human being in action as put forward by L. Ron Hubbard, Anger and Fear might well be included in its Vices. Cruelty is obviously a Geburah

vice, for apart from the cruder varieties of physical cruelty, on its subtler levels it is a distortion of the powers of assessment and correction into carping criticism and mental and emotional bullying.

20. The attribution of Destruction as a Vice though can lead to misunderstanding, and it would be better to consider the Vice as Wanton Destruction. Destruction where destruction is needed is a necessary and holy thing and is indeed under the presidency of the Fourth Aspect of the Deity.

21. There are many people who look upon anything destructive as evil, but this is only because they take the short instead of the long view and consider any change as a threat to their security. Thus we have the old bogey, Fear, cropping up again.

22. But a moment's thought will show the fallacy of this fear of Destruction. If one has a cancer the desirability of the destruction of that growth should be obvious to anyone. On more subtle levels, the forces of change are always about us, pressing us on through the centuries, and new forms have to be found to give expression to these new forces. As Our Lord pointed out, one is asking for trouble by pouring new wine into old bottles. Yet despite this it seems that humanity needs wars and disasters before it gets the impulse to break down the old and build the new. It required the devastation of two wars to clear many European slums. It required revolution at least once in the history of almost every Western nation to break up the old thought forms and prepare the way for democracy in one form or another. Yet the principle is so simple—you cannot have an omelette without first breaking eggs.

23. The same resistance to change occurs in the make-up of the human being on his quest for spiritual enlightenment. Perhaps the greatest barrier to every student is the refusal to let go of past emotional and mental habit patterns. In the Revelation of St. John the Divine, He who sat upon the throne said, "Behold, I make all things new." but one

cannot make all things new within oneself without changing the old.

24. It is when an esoteric student invokes the forces which will make things new, and then tries to oppose the resultant changes, that he gets himself into trouble. The spiritual force comes boring in like a drill through wood, and if it meets any blockages then the heat and friction starts which can be not only uncomfortable but even injurious to the soul.

25. Where conscious duplicity is concerned the resultant catharsis will be even greater and the Biblical story of Ananias and Sapphira gives an example. In the early days of Christianity when members of the Church contributed all their wealth and possessions to the community, Ananias and his wife sold a plot of land yet withheld part of the price. When confronted by St. Peter with an accusation of their hypocrisy they persisted in denial of it and were both struck dead. This is an example of the Geburic action of the Holy Spirit and it must be remembered that it did not seek them out in the first instance. Ananias and Sapphira took the initiative in seeking for the higher knowledge and then refused to accept the price for getting it. They tried to hold on to their old security whilst seeking for the new.

26. There is a great lesson here for whoever seeks to invoke the powers of the Spirit. Changes will be necessary in the orientation of the soul, and if that reorientation is denied or resisted then the product of the resultant conflict can be unpleasant in the extreme, resulting in bad cases in nervous or physical breakdown, insanity or even death. And whilst evil intentions reap their own evil reward, where the higher forces are concerned even good intentions are no guarantee of safety. That is why supervision and long training is necessary for anyone who seeks the higher realms of practical occultism.

27. It must be borne in mind that minor karmic adjustments are often as painful as a major balancing up. In any

adjustment that is made it is necessary to pull down and tear apart the aspects concerned and then to replace them in correct alignment. The Force of Geburah is one which, possibly above all others, needs calm and detachment in its application. It is all too easily confused with brute violence but it really represents the Majesty of the Law on the inner planes.

28. The symbol of the great Balance held by the figure of Justice can be elucidated in the light of another image. That image is of a ship in distress in which the sailor must adapt himself to the worst circumstances, doing all he can to keep himself afloat and finally, when he has done all in his power to help himself, putting his trust in God alone.

29. The results of work on the Sephirah Geburah will vary according to the temperament of the one endeavouring to contact its forces. With some it will upset physical plane conditions, with others emotional states, and it is bound to bring conflict on the mental level. But this is all to the good for it shows that the forces are working and readjustments are being made. Eventually of course everyone will have to face these readjustments whether they desire the contacts of Geburah or not.

30. A bearded warrior is one of the Magical Images of Geburah and it is well to link it up with some ideal figure such as St. George, Ares, Mars, or one of the Arthurian or other knightly heroes. Sir Galahad, the perfect knight of the Round Table and Holy Grail, clad in iron armour and standing in a star ruby is a very good form to use.

31. The esoteric grade attained in Geburah is that of the Adeptus Major, who is one fully skilled in working magic. It differs from the higher grade of Chesed in that in Chesed the adept *is* magic. By magic is meant the building of appropriate forms for spiritual forces to indwell.

32. The God Name of the Sephirah is Elohim Gibor, per-haps best translated as Almighty God, implying the Might of Cosmic Law which cannot be evaded. The towering scarlet figure of the Archangel Khamael, and the Fiery Serpents

134

or Seraphim are perhaps the safest ways to contact this omnipotent and omniscient readjusting and balancing force. Khamael is protector of the weak and wronged and also the Avenging Angel who pursues transgressors of human or cosmic law. This does not mean that he is an employee of the police, but that he works on the consciousness of the wrongdoer. Few breakers of law rest easy in their beds and Dostoevsky's 'Crime and Punishment' gives an account of how the workings of the criminal's own mind can lead him on to retribution.

33. We have already considered the Bright and Dark Angels of the soul of man and attributed their sphere of action to Chesed and Geburah. Perhaps the best form in which one could visualise these two entities allotted to every human being would be as members of the Chesedic and Geburic Orders of Angels. The Bright Angel as an ovoid orb-like figure of brilliantly shining purple, and the Dark Angel as a bright scarlet serpent of fire. These may serve better than anthropomorphic representations which popular tradition has served to taint with the epithets 'Good' and 'Evil'.

34. The Mundane Chakra of Geburah is the red planet Mars, one of the so-called 'malefics' of popular astrology. The planet has been described by the Tibetan in Mrs. Bailey's 'Esoteric Astrology' as producing great struggles but leading finally to great revelation. The Martian evolution is one based on the passional and instinctual levels— as the Earth is based on the physical—and so its effects on this planet often occur at a passional and therefore often group level. The statement that a planetary evolution is founded upon a certain plane may sound strange but is based on the teaching on Planetary Beings in 'The Cosmic Doctrine' mentioned previously. The whole subject is a vast one and so can only be mentioned in passing in the present context.

35. The number five plays an important part in the geometrical symbolism of Geburah and the use of the Penta-

gram as a sign for delimiting a circle and banishing unwanted forces clearly is in accordance with the principles of the Sephirah. Another symbolic way of looking at the Sephirah geometrically is by conceiving the solid figure of Chesed now in motion, dynamic.

36. Of the pagan pantheons, the Gods of War, Ares, Mars, Thor and so on are usually applied to Geburah in view of its general martial symbolism but this must not lead to an oversimplification of the idea of the Sephirah. Ares was not well thought of by the Greeks because of his brutality and blind violence and Thor was also very much the rude simple warrior. Perhaps the Roman Mars gives a better allround figure in that he was first a god of Spring, which is the new movement and vitality of Geburah, then father of Romulus and Remus, the founders of the great empire which brought law and order to most of Europe after conquering it under the aegis of Mars as God of War.

37. It is a mistake to think of Geburah entirely in terms of war-like symbolism for it also has its aspects of justice, assessment, analysis, endurance and so on. Thus one could also attribute to the Sephirah many god-forms and heroes, from the Avenging Furies or Erinyes of the Greeks, through the fortytwo Assessing Gods of the Egyptian Book of the Dead, to the jester knight Dinadan of the Arthurian cycle, for laughter also comes under the presidency of Geburah. Humour is the destroyer of painful emotion, its opposite face, as the Greek linked comic and tragic masks imply, and even apart from its satirical cutting aspect it is one of the greatest weapons against tyranny. The pen is mightier than the sword and the type of vainglory that often sets itself up as an authority can survive snubs, curses or even direct persecution, but laughter and ridicule never. It has been found also that people with a well developed sense of the ridiculous are not easily 'brainwashed' and so laughter should perhaps be considered a prime force of Geburah, for it is ameliorative and more cutting than the

iron burin or the martial weapons of traditional Geburic symbolism. There might be much value in meditating upon 'God's laughter.'

Chapter XII

TIPHARETH—BEAUTY

"The Sixth Path is called the Mediating Intelligence, because in it are multiplied the influxes of the Emanations; for it causes that influence to flow into all the reservoirs of the blessings with which they themselves are united."

MAGICAL IMAGE:	A king. A child. A sacrificed god.
GOD NAME:	Jehovah Aloah va Daath.
ARCHANGEL:	Raphael.
ORDER OF ANGELS:	Malachim. Kings.
MUNDANE CHAKRA:	The Sun.
VIRTUE:	Devotion to the Great Work.
TITLES:	Zoar Anpin. The Lesser Countenance. Melekh, the King.
SPIRITUAL EXPERIENCE:	Vision of the Harmony of Things. Mysteries of the Crucifixion.
ATZILUTHIC COLOUR:	Clear rose-pink.
BRIATIC COLOUR:	Yellow.
YETZIRATIC COLOUR:	Rich salmon-pink.
ASSIATIC COLOUR:	Golden amber.
VICE:	Pride.
SYMBOLS:	Lamen. Rose Cross. Calvary Cross. Truncated Pyramid. Cube.

1. Tiphareth is the central Sephirah of the Tree of Life, the keystone of the whole creation, holding the balance between all the other Sephiroth which it connects: between God in the Highest in Kether and the physical Universe of Malkuth; between the upper and lower poles of the psyche in Daath and Yesod; between the opposites of Chokmah and Binah, Chesed and Geburah, Netzach and Hod; between the similar potencies of Chesed and Hod, Geburah and Netzach; in fact it is truly the Mediating Intelligence assigned to it by the Yetziratic Text. There is fruitful scope for medita-

137

tion in all the triangles formed by the Paths leading between Tiphareth and the other Sephiroth and without knowledge of what all these Paths represent and their inter-relationship there can never be full understanding of Tiphareth. The same applies to the other Sephiroth, of course, but the inter-relationships of Tiphareth are so fundamental and various that an understanding of Tiphareth is almost synonymous with an understanding of the whole Tree. It is the Sephirah of Beauty, which means the Divine Plan carried through into manifestation as it should be.

2. The Yetziratic Text states that all the influences of the other Emantions, or Sephiroth, flow into Tiphareth where they are blessed with an imprint of over-all unity. This Sephirah then is the integrating aspect of the whole Tree, leading towards synthesis and unity, which is a state towards which humanity has been struggling for thousands of years and the lack of which is the prime cause of pain and suffering. It is because Tiphareth represents the goal to which all must attain that its Virtue is that of Devotion to the Great Work. And as, within the soul of man, the Great Work is regeneration, or rebirth, the Sephirah is full of the symbolism of death and resurrection. It is the Sephirah of all the Redeemer Gods, including of course the Supreme exemplar of human redemption, Our Lord Jesus Christ.

3. The Spiritual Experiences of the Sephirah are two in number instead of the usual one. This signifies that there are two sides to Tiphareth and indeed it is *par excellence* a linking Sephirah, reconciling the upper part of the Tree to the lower. There is a split in 'normal' human consciousness brought about by the Original Fall and this is symbolised by The Gulf, placed just below Tiphareth. The average man has little conception of the vast sphere of his divine consciousness above the levels of the work-a-day mind and will only be aware of Tiphareth consciousness if he is of a religious persuasion. Even then he may have no great functional awareness of the realisations of this great

sphere which confers a Vision of the Harmony of Things and an understanding of the Mysteries of the Crucifixion. And it is realisation which is the important thing, not a mere intellectual theoretical conception.

4. The colours of the Sephirah are pinks, yellows and ambers which can be best perceived in the supreme beauties of the horizon at sunset and dawn. The Name of God in this Sephirah is Jehovah Aloah va Daath, meaning God Made Manifest in the Sphere of Mind, but unfortunately God is little manifest in the mind of man at the present time.

5. Harmony, or Beauty, implies health and healing and so Raphael, the Archangel 'which standeth in the Sun' is obviously an integral part of Tiphareth. In ritual working he is the Archangel who guards the Eastern quarter which is the quarter of the Element of Air. The East has always been regarded as the source of holiness; it is the point where the light of the sun first appears after the long hours of night, just as the Spiritual Light dawns in the darkness of unillumined consciousness. The Element of Air is also a symbol of the Spirit, free-moving and unconfined, penetrating everywhere.

6. Raphael can be visualised, as an alternative to the Sephirothic colours, in the colours of gold and blue of the shining disc of the sun in a clear sky, raying the healing and sustaining powers of sunlight, which include the forces of radiant heat, infra-red and ultra-violet besides the spiritual enlightenment and quickening of life of the Sun behind the Sun. He can be pictured with wings which fan the air causing a rush of fire and air which revitalises the forces of any aura it contacts—it is a great contact of healing, spiritual and psychological as well as physical.

7. The order of Angels are called Malachim, Kings, and can be considered as healing and life-bringing agents under the presidency of Raphael. There is great healing power in nature of course, the Sphere of the Elements, and the Four Elemental Kings, the Rulers of the peoples of each Element can be assigned to Tiphareth, though the Sphere

of the Elements pertains really to Malkuth.

8. The tradition is quite well known that Elementals, being units of life created by the early Building Powers of the Universe and not emanating from the realms of Spiritual Reality, have only phenomenal and not noumenal existence. Thus when the Day of Manifestation comes to an end they will become extinct unless in the meantime they have picked up the vibration of spiritual being during the course of it. They can obtain this chance of immortality from any evolution inhabiting the planet whose bodily shell they hold in being and so on Earth they rely on contacts with humanity. One has only to take a look round at humanity to be filled with a grave doubt as to their chances. The large proportion of humanity is ignorant of its own spirituality, let alone aware of the need for mediating this quality. And even where man has achieved high spiritual awareness it has been all too often accompanied by a contempt and horror of the physical being. Medieval theology branded all Elemental beings as devils and in modern times their very existence is denied. Thus the adept has always been considered the initiator of the Elemental Kingdoms as the only one qualified by reason of spiritual stature and realisation so to do. The strange old book 'Comte de Gabalis' by the Abbe N. de Montfaucon de Villars contains very great truths on these matters under the guise of making fun of them, often the only way that truths on these matters can be got across through the hard shell of man's cosmic parochialism.

9. When an Elemental has attained spiritual awareness it can be said to have Tiphareth consciousness and the Elemental Kings, those Elementals that have attained this state, are also Way-showers to them. The Elemental Kings go by the names of Paralda, for Air; Niksa, for Water; Ghob, for Earth; and Djin, for Fire; but a full consideration of the Elemental evolution really belongs to Malkuth.

10. The Mundane Chakra of Tiphareth is the Sun, which is the source of light and life to its Universe and so a

physical manifestation of the powers of God Himself and the spiritual worlds. The Conditioner and Sustainer of our Solar System is the Solar Logos—commonly referred to as God—and though He is the One God as far as humanity and the rest of the Solar System is concerned, He is God only over that System, and the Sun can be considered His physical body, though all the rest of physical existence of the Solar System is under His presidency.

11. Where esoteric theology differs from exoteric theology is that the latter regards God as unchangeable and supreme over all existence. Esoteric theology on the other hand considers God, great as He is, to be evolving. Also it considers that every star is a God presiding over Its own creation and that over the God of our Solar System there are other Gods rising in greatness to the God presiding over the whole Galactic System, which, like the Solar Systems, is a gigantic revolving wheel; and that presumably there may be a God presiding over all Galactic Systems throughout the whole of inter-stellar and inter-galactic space.

12. This is not a denial of monotheism for the God or Solar Logos of our System is omnipotent, omniscient and omnipresent within this System and so is the One God for all over which It presides. All the extra-Logoidal influences, whether from Sirius, the Great Bear, the Pleiades, Andromeda or the constellations of the Zodiac, affect the Solar System only through the mediation of the Solar Logos, not direct.

13. All these matters relating to Tiphareth just considered, God Made Manifest in the Sphere of Mind, the great healing harmonising powers of Raphael, the divine consciousness of the Elemental Kings, the life giving light and heat of the Sun, have reference to the Vision of the Harmony of Things. There is however the other Spiritual Experience —the Mysteries of the Crucifixion.

14. It is in Tiphareth that the Spirit makes its contact with the mind of man and this contact will at first be small. The supreme symbol for the birth of spiritual conscious-

ness is provided in the Christmas story of the Christ child born in a manger watched over by the beasts of the field. Man is a being strung halfway between god and beast and the spiritual consciousness is at first weak as a small child in the animal world of the psyche—the still small voice which can be so easily ignored.

15. But the child, given protection, grows, gradually learning the facts of its new physical existence until eventually it becomes as a man, and with the Spirit, not only a man, but as a king amongst men. Following the Christian symbolism, which is the exemplary Way, Truth and Life, it will be remembered that Christ was called the King of the Jews, though, as he said, his Kingdom was not of this world. In his intellectual jugglings over what is Truth, Pilate might have realised that many a true word is spoken—or in his case, written—in jest.

16. Following upon the principle of kingship, which is the rulership of the Spirit over the rest of the psyche, the soul treads out the Way of Love which is the sacrifice of the self for the benefit of others, as Our Lord was crucified—though the Crucifixion is not the end, but the means whereby the subsequent Resurrection and Ascension comes and the establishment of Divine Kingship.

17. This is the sequence of ideas behind the Magical Images of this Sephirah, the Child, the King and the Sacrificed God, and it is a way that every soul has to tread, not once, but many times. The whole pattern is laid down in the life of Our Lord. In the progress of the soul the Crucifixion is but a symbol for a mode of action, though it is nonetheless real for that. The odd thing is that there are many souls seemingly permanently fixated in the Crucifixion; souls who make of their whole lives a weary pattern of self-sacrifice and self-inflicted suffering, completely deaf to the cries of the 'spirits in prison' of the animal side of their own personalities and refusing to go on through the Descent into Hell to give these aspects of themselves realisation of the spiritual principles involved, and to the

release and illumination of the Resurrection and Ascension. It is a kind of spiritual masochism — definitely pathological and probably resulting from a refusal to face certain areas of the soul which were responsible for, or are a result of, the initial deviation from the Divine Plan.

18. Everyone has his own Crucifixion, or 'Cross to bear' as the saying goes, according to his strength, and it is usually only in one or more of the last earthly incarnations that life itself is sacrificed in devotion to a principle for the welfare of others. The death of the physical body is one of the supremer forms of the principle of Crucifixion. One which equals it is the 'death of initiation'. This is the comparatively high initiation where the whole life is dedicated to the service of the Spirit, which is the service of all others, and the initiate instead of dying for a principle, lives out his life in accordance with a principle, and this can be a far harder thing. He becomes 'a living dead man', that is, he lives out fully a life in the world but after his unreserved dedication he is living on borrowed time. The Great Work comes first, whatever the cost, and so the Virtue of Tiphareth is Devotion to the Great Work. And Devotion does not mean intellectual interest, part-time work, vague good intentions. These are well enough for the lay-man or the minor aspirant but hopelessly inadequate for the higher initiate who has made his dedication, served his term of probation, and finally been accepted by the Inner Plane Hierarchy for individual training and work.

19. On the other hand, although an unreserved dedication is called for this does not mean that the esoteric fraternities should be coteries of fanatics. Fanaticism is an aberration. As has already been mentioned fanaticism is a form of Pride which is the Vice assigned to Tiphareth and one very likely to come up in the initiate newly taken on individual probation by a Master. The Great Work requires human beings and when one devotes one's life to a principle there is a right way and a wrong way to go about it.

20. The wrong way is to become completely identified

with the function of the principle so that one becomes more of a functioning object than a human being. The commonest form of this is the poor village schoolteacher, who is not allowed to be anything but the schoolteacher whether on or off duty. The other members of the community will not let her be anything else. Whenever they talk to her it is always to 'the schoolteacher' they talk and not to a flesh and blood human being.

21. The right form of dedication is to retain all the human characteristics and yet to live a life entirely directed by principle. It may not call for any great outward acts of heroic virtue or showy self-sacrifice; however, it is expected that the virtues of the initiate be raised to the heroic level. Not only does it require completely ethical actions on the physical plane in the smallest details—and persistent virtue in so-called small matters is equally as important as, and even more difficult than, a short burst of virtue on the grand scale—but it also requires control of the thoughts and emotions. As Our Lord said: "Ye have heard that it was said by them of old time, Thou shalt not commit adultery: But I say unto you, That whosoever looketh on a woman to lust after her hath committed adultery with her already in his heart." To the occultist every plane of being is of equal importance and a life outwardly virtuous on the physical plane is worthless if there is not equal virtue on the inner planes. Such a condition would be one of great hypocrisy and almost spiritual pathology, for it would imply a conformance to outer law with a split in the being dividing the outer conformity from the real chaotic and anarchic condition of the soul.

22. This is the real function of the magician, to construct the right forms out of his own being for his own spiritual force to indwell. The ritual workings of ceremonial magic are but a special technique for raising a particular potency of life to the nth degree to give a correct orientation to it. The real ritual is a twentyfour hours a day process of living out life according to spiritual principles so that, by

this talismanic action, patterns of right living are formed in the unconscious mind of the race so that this right way of living becomes easier for those who follow after.

23. It may be thought that a few initiates living life according to principle could have little effect on the vast mass of people living their lives in various degrees of chaos, seeking only after pleasure and profit rather than principle. The point is, though, that a life lived with talismanic intention has far greater force than one that has its patterns based, not on spiritual reality, but on day to day physical expediency. Also the initiate has a trained mind and his clear-cut thought-forms and the vibrancy of his aura have a profound effect on the environment. The thought-forms of the average man are generally too weak and vacillating to have much permanent effect, except through weight of numbers. Also the whole force of the Great White Lodge mediating the Will of God is working behind and alongside and through the initiates in the world.

24. It should be remembered that after the death of Our Lord, the way of life that subsequently formed all Christendom was started off by eleven men of an obscure Middle Eastern subject nation. Also one can consider the ideals of the Round Table, so much with us now in the principles of democracy, albeit with many shortcomings. One can imagine how little of his ideals the original Arthur could have consistently achieved physically, yet the ideal lived on through the hey-day and decline of feudalism, through the rise and decline of the merchant guilds, through the rise and decline of the nineteenth century factory owning bourgeoisie until our own more or less democratic times of 'round table conferences' and equality for all in theory if not yet in practice. Of course, humanity being as it is, these things come in with variously distorted applications. Thus instead of being a circle where all represented contribute to the general solution, a round table conference is usually a gang of people all pulling their own separate ways, jealously guarding their own minor interests so that

all that is left is a heap of discords and bitter recriminations and at best a dubiously workable universally hated compromise. Also the general trend of the fighters for equality for man has been to pull down the superior to the level of the mob instead of raising the mob to the quality of the aristocratic in heart, mind and deed. But there is plenty of evolutionary time left to run even if humanity does give itself a set-back of several hundred or thousand years by temporarily solving its difficulties with hydrogen bombs.

25. The only final solution to humanity's problems is by the universal realisation of the Vision of the Harmony of Things in Tiphareth, which implies the supreme ethic of Service, and this is symbolised by the Way of the Cross. Thus one of the most important symbols of Tiphareth is the Cross, whether in its form of the Calvary Cross of black with three black steps leading up to it, or the gold Equal-armed Cross with a rose of red blooming at its centre.

26. The Calvary Cross represents the way of self-sacrifice for the benefit of others and it is the only way by which man can return to his spiritual home. As Our Lord said: "No man cometh to the Father but by Me." Only after the Way of the Cross has been accepted and experienced can come the knowledge of the Rose Cross, when the Rose of the Spirit blooms on the Universal Cross of manifestation in dense matter. In this latter symbol the Vision of the Harmony of Things and the Mysteries of the Crucifixion are one. On the Calvary Cross is the man sacrificed as a separate being; on the Rose Cross is the Spirit of man in harmony with the whole Universe, including densest manifestation.

27. The principle behind the Calvary Cross is that of the Way-shower who descended into the corruption of human existence on Earth and showed the formula of Redemption. The principle behind the Rose Cross is that of the Way-shower who remained out of manifestation holding the perfect pattern of what man should be, untainted by cor-

ruption. Had there been no fall of man the Calvary Cross would have been unnecessary, there would have been no illusion of separateness and lack of brotherhood and mutual service between men. The Spirit would have budded and then burst forth into flower like a fragrant rose on the golden cross of a harmonious physical existence. As we now stand, the Rose Cross is unobtainable without accepting the Calvary Cross first.

28. The Qabalistic Title for Tiphareth is Zoar Anpin, the Lesser Countenance, as opposed to the title Arik Anpin, the Vast Countenance of Kether. Thus Tiphareth in this symbolism is conceived as Kether on a lower arc, the source of the Spirit, not at the fount of creation, but in the midst of it.

29. Alternatively these titles of the Vast Countenance and the Lesser Countenance are put in their Greek form of Macroprosopos and Microprosopos, and then Malkuth, the physical world, is known as the Bride of Microprosopos. Or, when Tiphareth is referred to as the King, Malkuth is the Queen. This shows plainly that the physical world has an important place in the Plan of God, for it is the physical world, Malkuth, which will be joined in 'marriage' and 'rulership' with God-made-manifest-in-the-midst-of-creation.

30. It is this which is implied in the Revelation of St. John the Divine: "And I John saw the holy city, new Jerusalem, coming down from God out of Heaven, prepared as a bride adorned for her husband." and further, "And there came unto me one of the seven angels . . . and talked with me, saying, Come hither, I will shew thee the bride, the Lamb's wife. And he carried me away in the spirit to a great and high mountain, and shewed me that great city, the holy Jerusalem, descending out of heaven from God." The New Jerusalem is the Garden of Eden on a higher arc, and it is the purpose of God and man spiritually to civilise the prime simple form of creation represented by the garden of Eden to the expression of spiritual realities in the densest levels of manifestation as represented by the building of the New

Jerusalem on Earth.

31. The same idea inspires much of William Blake's verse:

"The fields from Islington to Marybone,
    To Primrose Hill and Saint John's Wood,
"Were builded over with pillars of gold;
    And there Jerusalem's pillars stood."

"Her Little Ones ran on the fields,
    The Lamb of God among them seen,
"And fair Jerusalem, His Bride,
    Among the little meadows green."

"Pancras and Kentish Town repose
    Among her golden pillars high,
"Among her golden arches which
    Shine upon the starry sky."

32. Anyone having any knowledge of some of these London districts will have a very fair conception of the gap between vision and reality.

33. It should be unnecessary to state, of course, that the ultimate aim of the initiated adept is not the use of gold as a building material, nor a reconstruction of the world in a kind of pre-Raphaelite mish-mash. However, it is perhaps well to emphasise the fact for it is little more fatuous than the idea that because they often use Judaic symbolism and impose oaths of secrecy that Western Esoteric Schools are secret agents of International Zionism—which was an accusation made against them some years ago when anti-Semitism was more fashionable.

34. Of the remaining symbols commonly assigned to Tiphareth, the cube, though at first sight a Chesed symbol, can correspond to Tiphareth because of its six faces. The truncated pyramid, also a six sided figure, has implicit in its form the suggestion of the apex, which would be Kether, though the higher levels are not actually in the form of the

solid figure, which represents form below Tiphareth, broad-based and diverse at the lowest level and ascending towards the Unity of the apical point—the God-head. The Lamen is the symbol upon the breast of the magician which has written upon it the exact nature of the force with which he is working, thus it corresponds to Tiphareth, which is the Vision of the Harmony of all the forces of nature, particularly as it is worn on the breast which is the Tiphareth centre when the Tree of Life is applied to the human body.

35. In the pagan pantheons all sun gods, healing gods, and sacrificed redeeming gods can be applied to Tiphareth and in their diversity can give useful clues to the many aspects of this Sephirah, whose ramifications are tremendous. One of the attributions not immediately obvious is Percival, one of the Arthurian Knights of the Round Table. In his youth he was kept well away from knighthood by his mother, who had lost all her other menfolk in battle, but Percival eventually met some knights, and fired by their example, went, a rude country youth, to Arthur's Court. There he slew a knight, though without armour himself, and was so ignorant of the facts of knighthood, that unable to undo his victim's armour, he built a fire and tried to roast him out of it. He was eventually taken in and trained by a kindly vavasour and subsequently became one of the greatest knights and a Grail-winner. This is another slant on the first early attempts of the Spirit to manifest in the lower worlds as symbolised by the Child of Tiphareth and subsequently gaining control and performing the works of its Father in Heaven.

Chapter XIII

NETZACH—VICTORY

"The Seventh Path is called the Occult Intelligence because it is the refulgent splendour of the intellectual virtues which are perceived by the eyes of the intellect and the contemplations of faith."

MAGICAL IMAGE:	A beautiful naked woman.
GOD NAME:	Jehovah Tzabaoth.
ARCHANGEL:	Haniel.
ORDER OF ANGELS:	Elohim. Gods.
MUNDANE CHAKRA:	Venus.
VIRTUE:	Unselfishness.
TITLES:	Firmness. Valour.
SPIRITUAL EXPERIENCE:	Vision of Beauty Triumphant.
ATZILUTHIC COLOUR:	Amber.
BRIATIC COLOUR:	Emerald.
YETZIRATIC COLOUR:	Bright yellow green.
ASSIATIC COLOUR:	Olive, flecked gold.
VICE:	Unchastity. Lust.
SYMBOLS:	Lamp and girdle. Rose.

1. The Seventh Path, being the Occult Intelligence, and 'occult' meaning hidden or secret or full of mysteries, the Sephirah Netzach, like occultism, is fraught with glamour and misunderstanding. Whenever the human mind comes up against things mysterious it projects all kinds of misconceptions and superstitions into that void.

2. The term 'intellectual' in the Yetziratic text means not so much the logical processes of the concrete mind but the human mind as a whole, the psyche below Tiphareth. The Sephirothic Triad of Kether, Chokmah, Binah was translated by Mathers similarly as the Intellectual Triad thus leading to great risk of misunderstanding because these three Supernal Sephiroth are quite above the intellectual mind,

150

whose real sphere is Hod. So it is with Westcott's translation of the Yetziratic Text and it would be less misleading to render the latter half as "because it is the refulgent splendour of the psyche, which psychic refulgence is perceived by the lower mind both by mental discernment and religious awareness."

3. This refulgent splendour of the psyche is really the force of the creative imagination, and so Netzach is the sphere whence emanates the inspiration not only of the artist but of all who work creatively. It is a Sephirah of perfect balance of force and form, though anteceding the concretion of mental forms in Hod, and the awareness of the perfect balance produces ecstasy, joy, delight and fulfilment, or, in other words, the Spiritual Experience of the Vision of Beauty Triumphant. The result of approaches to this perfection of balance manifests ultimately not only in great works of art but also in the beauty of well designed tools, machinery, scientific instruments and so on, for perfection of precision in use gives beauty of form. One has only to compare the beautiful lines and efficiency of the modern supersonic airliner with the gawkiness and inefficiency of the early 'heavier-than-air machines' to see this principle in operation. There is an alliance between art and scientific invention—as has been demonstrated by the genius of Leonardo da Vinci—and this is because both emanate from the 'psychic refulgence' of Netzach, the creative imagination.

4. The Victory of the Title of Netzach is the victory of achievement and there is a link between Netzach, the Seventh Sephirah, and the Seventh Day of Creation of Genesis: "Thus the heavens and the earth were finished, and all the host of them. And on the seventh day God ended His work which He had made; and He rested on the seventh day from all His work which He had made. And God blessed the seventh day, and sanctified it: because that in it He had rested from all His work which God created and made."

5. The achievement of perfection in form and force requires both Firmness and Valour, two further titles of Netzach, and which can be looked upon as two sides of the symbol of the Balance—Geburah on a lower arc. One could call Firmness and Valour the two side Pillars as they manifest in Netzach. The Atziluthic and Briatic colours are amber and emerald and the two Pillars of the Tyrian Temple were gold and green. There is also a link with the Hibernian Mysteries, the Pillars of whose Temples represented Science and Art.

6. The Rose—a symbol of Netzach—is in itself a complete symbol system and is usually considered to be the perfect flower, combining scent, colour and shape in great beauty; also, it is a sphere containing semi-spheres within it and is in truth a Cosmic Pattern centred about the golden heart of its system—hence, the Rosa Mystica.

7. Anyone who has ever attempted creative work will know the feeling of vast inertia that has to be overcome. Not only is there inertia in the material in which expression is sought but there is also inertia in the means of expression, the lower nature, which being more animal than god, is not basically concerned with higher forms of creation. However this inertia is overcome and the means of its overcoming is the flaming creative energy of Netzach, for Netzach is an active Sephirah, being assigned to the Element of Fire as is its higher diagonal opposite, Geburah, and Geburah's higher diagonal opposite, Chokmah.

8. With the urge of creation successfully overcoming the inertia of the denser levels comes the joy of creation, a satisfying delight in the awareness of the life-force whether it be used in sex, art, ritual magic or whatever. Netzach has much to do with magic, and until the energy of Netzach is at work, the images of Hod will not be ensouled and thus any ritual will be mere empty gestures and words, and any art, lifeless.

9. Thus the magical weapons assigned to Netzach are the Lamp and Girdle. The Girdle, that which girds up the loins

for action, and the Lamp, the Eternal Lamp of the Mysteries bringing Illumination. The operations of ceremonial magic are creative work in the best sense.

10. Jehovah Tzaboath, the Lord of Hosts, is the Name of God in the Sephirah Netzach and indicates the diversifying aspect of the Sephirah, which, like a prism, splits up the Sun light of Tiphareth, the One force of the Spiritual Light, into the beauteous aspects of the lower worlds. A good symbol for the Sephirah could be gained from contemplating the morning sky with the rising sunlight on the clouds evoking the image of a glorious army with banners—particularly if the Morning Star, the planet Venus, the Mundane Chakra of Netzach, is also in the sky.

11. The Archangel Haniel is not so widely known as the other Archangels of the lower Sephirah such as Michael, Gabriel, and Raphael, the protector, the bringer of visions. and the bringer of healing. This is a great pity for all the contacts of Netzach can be gained from him, not only the awareness of harmony and beauty in the lower worlds but also a great wisdom of the inter-relationships of all things whether of planets, plants, spheres or men. He can be pictured as shining with a green and golden flame with a rose coloured light at the top, or over his head, if an anthropomorphic form is used, and emanating generally an aura of archetypical sympathetic vibration.

12. The Order of Angels is the Elohim, or Gods. Netzach, being the sphere where the One appears in diversity, is the sphere of formation of all the mythological god-forces of whatever pantheon. When astral clairvoyance, or 'scrying' in the pictorial imagination, is used, the god forms play an important part and may take on a life of their own. Such an occurrence is not a direct manifestation of God Imminent. The Vision of God face to face is a Chokmah experience, not to be gained by such a dense form of working as that of the pictorial imagination. However, something is motivating the forms and forces of the gods, which are aspects of the One God, and so one can conceive the

agency to be the Order of Angels of Netzach, the sphere of the creative imagination, the Gods. One could picture these angels as actual pagan god-forms therefore.

13. The Mundane Chakra of Netzach is the planet Venus. This planet has vast implications, esoterically considered, in its relationship to Earth, mainly stemming from the fact that the Planetary Ruler of Earth, known in the East as Sanat Kumara, came to Earth from Venus. It is a planet which will profoundly affect the incoming of what is called the Aquarian Age for it concerns the sympathetic coalescing and inter-relationship of all. It can be seen that the general trend of human affairs is towards a final unification of the races now on Earth. The earlier tribal and feudal ideas of relationship out of which grew the family system is well on into the phases of disappearance. Even the racial barriers of blood are being broken down more and more with the increasing ease of intercommunications and travel and also the increasing occurrence of inter-marriage.

14. The latter factor still provides many bones of contention, for the keeping of the blood of a race pure is a very ancient instinct which arose in the early days when the authority of certain tribes, families and races was building up, and its aim then was to forward evolution. From an esoteric standpoint, the blood was kept pure to increase the strength of its contact with the Oversoul of the race. From this concept came the covenants of dedication between the 'Blood Entity' and its inner plane guardians such as was made, for example, by the ancient Jews, the Mayans and the Chinese, with their tutelary spirits. This covenant particularly extended to the Royal Family of a race and this custom has now become the sentiments felt toward the Blood Royal.

15. In earlier times the gift of etheric clairvoyance—now largely an atavism though to return more naturally in the far future as a development—was maintained by heredity in the lineage of the Priest-Kings, thus purity of blood was

actually the means of the power to communicate at will with the inner planes. Also, as the blood holds the life-force it is linked with the Spirit. But as, with the evolutionary development of man, Spirit becomes more easily consciously linked with matter, so does the need for the activities of the Blood Entity lessen. As has been long realised in the East, the relationships of the various personalities of subsequent reincarnations are more important than hereditary relationships.

16. The overall factor of Netzach is polarity, and by polarity is meant relationship in any of its many and various forms. It might be as well to list some of the more common forms to show the great diversities possible.

i) Polarity on spiritual or mental levels between two of the same sex, i.e. between two aspects of the same force. The 'formula' of this is 'friendship' which was once as important an aspect of chivalry as the knight's relations with women. There is also of course the well known relationship between David and Jonothan. This is a form of relationship bearing very great gifts to both parties concerned. There are many men who have served in the armed forces who will testify that one of the greatest things they miss in civilian life is the comradeship in adversity of the Services. On its more intense levels it can be dangerous with undedicated people for, by a confusion of the planes, a high powered mutual stimulation on the mental and higher emotional levels can degenerate into homosexuality. In spite of the modern spate of apologetics for this form of lower emotional and physical relationship it is a perversion and evil. It is perhaps as well to state this quite categorically as it is a form of vice likely to be on the increase with the lesser differentiation in physical sexual characteristics of the Aquarian type of human being now coming into the world. This increasing lack of differentiation is becoming quite common, there are increasingly fewer men nowadays who could grow a really patriarchal beard, and women, from the buxom mammalians of classical painting are becoming more boyish and angular in figure, to say nothing of the occasional much publicised actual changes from one sex to another. Homosexuality, like the use of drugs, is one of the techniques of black magic. In the homosexual act two streams of force are called forth with all the power of the instincts and as these two streams of force are of the same type there is no circuit of force possible, so that the combined forces are available for magical direction. It is a much more potent way of working than the use of incubi and succubi, lower elementals of sensuality, which are formed by the solitary technique of fantasies of masturbation.

ii) Polarity between two of a different sex. Here again occultism is much on the side of 'old-fashioned' morality. Whilst there is no point in upholding a bad marriage for the sake of Mrs. Grundy unless there are children concerned, (and their right to a home is paramount, outweighing any considerations of convenience for the father or mother), and whilst semi-permanent sexual relationships can be productive of much benefit to both parties concerned, there is little to be said for promiscuity. A temporary union rarely touches anything deeper than the senses and the emotions. The union of the tender affections, intellectual sympathies and spiritual ideals is the fruit only of a long-standing relationship. This could be said to be a counsel of perfection and rare and lucky are they who can achieve it. There may be nothing but good to be gained from breaking up a relationship which has become stale with usage, and has degenerated into mere mutual toleration out of force of habit.

iii) Polarity between 'force' and 'form' proceeding from the same source.—e.g. the relationship between brother and sister, and by the word relationship is meant a real psychological rapport, not a mere biological categorising. Thus the brotherhood and sisterhood between members of an esoteric fraternity can be every bit as real as that between two offspring of the same physical parents. As mentioned before in this chapter, there is relationship in 'spirit' as well as in 'blood'.

iv) Polarity between 'higher' and 'lower' aspects of the same force—e.g. relationship of father and son, or mother and daughter. Here again the same applies in spirit as well as blood. There is the relationship of all men and women to God the Father and God the Mother. It often happens therefore that a child who is on very bad terms with the father may be upon a cycle of karma relating to an original rejection of God the Father in spiritually primeval days.

v) Polarity between 'higher' and 'lower' aspects of 'force' and 'form' drawn from the same source—e.g. relationship of mother and son, or father and daughter. Here again the same principles apply as with the above.

vi) Polarity between aspects of 'force' and 'form' drawn from another level of the source—e.g. relationship of aunt and nephew or uncle and niece. On high esoteric levels the relationship between humanity and earlier evolutions could be catalogued under this heading. The overshadowing of a high initiate by a Lord of Mind for example, or the over-shadowing of the Lord Jesus with the Christ force.

vii) Polarity between the source of a power and one of its levels through an intermediary—e.g. relationship of god-parent and god-child. This relationship contains the whole function of priesthood also.

viii) Polarity between teacher and pupil on different levels as in the esoteric sense or on the same level as in the exoteric sense.

ix) Polarity between a group and an individual as in the relationship of the leader to the other members. This can be applied esoterically to the conception of Manus of ancient races.

17. There is much teaching on polarity in mythological stories and also in great literature. Lancelot and Guinevere, Tristram and Iseult, Paolo and Francesca, Romeo and Juliet are all initiatory types. One of the human abuses of the polarity principles of Netzach is the exaggeration of

158

one particular aspect at the expense of other aspects and this can lead to great tragedy as exemplified in the great romances. Very often trouble may stem from sexual magic in ancient times. The courtesan holds in modern times a very debased position and deservedly so, for the motives are entirely commercial, but in former times the Temple courtesan was a priestess whose work was distinctly religious. Money and gifts were not given to her personally but as a thank-offering to the Divinity in whose name she acted. Function carried out in combination with ritual becomes a sacrament, as for example the eating and drinking of bread and wine allied with ritual are sacramental acts in Christianity today, and in the same way the sexual function was used in ancient days to bring through divine power to a high degree. So if such a thing be done today, unconsciously perhaps through vague memories and promptings of a past incarnation, the power brought down may well be too great to be controlled and thus the partner will be worshipped as a divinity, and will be expected to behave like a divinity, and a general situation produced which has all the elements within it for great tragedy.

18. The contra-sexual image of the Jungian psychology, of course, can be attributed to the Sephirah Netzach though strictly speaking all the magical power of the archetypes belongs here. However, Netzach being the sphere of Venus-Aphrodite the anima has particular relevance. The action of this archetype is quite commonly known—that it is a projection of the man's ideas of the All-Woman onto any particular woman who happens to be around and who bears sufficient resemblance to the archetypal figure for it to use her as a hook for it to be hung on. Thus the woman, who may be quite a shallow creature, is invested in the love-blind eyes of the lover with all the attributes which represent the ideal essence of womanhood to him. If the projection is mutual, a hasty and ill-advised marriage is often the result—a marriage which is extremely unlikely to last, for marriage is one way of really getting down to

reality and neither partner in such a case can live up to the lofty conception held within the other's psyche.

19. It is not generally realised though that the contra-sexual image is often the image of the higher aspects of the soul itself which are seeking union with the lower self. Thus the best way to overcome the domination of a powerful contra-sexual image is through the way of religion. Thus the high reverence for the Virgin Mary in Roman Catholicism, apart from its religious aspects, is also a psychological therapy. If the god-like attributes of the contra-sexual image are being safely projected onto a religious object—which is really the true direction of projection anyway—there is less likelihood of them being projected onto another human being with all the subsequent disillusion and possible tragedy that this will entail. There is considerable danger in the all-masculine bias of Protestant theology and it no doubt is itself a symptom of the Anglo-Saxon puritan heritage which borders very closely on spiritual pathology.

20. The subject of polarity, sexual or otherwise, is a vast one and volumes could be, and have been, written about it. All its subtleties however are under the province of Netzach and in view of this, Netzach is perhaps the most subtle and intricate Sephirah on the whole Tree, and there is scope for much research upon it in the light of the many mythological cycles relating to it.

21. Aphrodite is the main god-form of the Sephirah, and like all the gods and goddesses has a 'dark' and 'bright' side. As a rough classification the 'White Aphrodite' can be assigned to the Atziluth and Briah of Netzach, and the 'Dark Aphrodite' to the Yetzirah and Assiah. A useful glyph for meditation deriving from this is a pillar, or a figure of Venus or Aphrodite, in which the upper half is white and the lower half black. Also, the two great symbols of Aphrodite, the dove and the leopard, can be assigned to the 'higher' and 'lower' aspects respectively. Broadly speaking, in sexual relationships, these represent the happy

160

and fruitful mate of the bountiful bright side, whose obverse aspect is the wanton; and the dominating mate of the dark side, whose obverse aspect is the calculating wanton who uses the destructive aspect of Aphrodite for selfish ends. There is no rigid classification however, and the combinations of aspects are infinite in real life as the same person can manifest different aspects at different times. The great figures of myth, legend and literature provide more consistent types for study, for example, Guinevere, Morgan le Fay, Desdemona, Lady Macbeth, Juliet, Clytemnestra, Electra and so on. The Queens and Ladies of the Arthurian cycle give a very full overall picture of the various types of female functioning in the relationships of Mother, Maiden, Mistress, Aunt and so on, and the occupations of Guide, Guardian, Wise Woman, Magician, Recluse etc.

22. There are also very subtle and advanced teachings held in other mythologies such as the mating of Isis and Osiris *after the latter's death* to give birth to Horus, which might be described as the 'Regenerated Force of Mating emerging from Destruction'. There is similar teaching in the Mysteries of Hecate, relating to the forces released when a woman's reproductive period is ended which so often, owing to wrong attitudes and teaching, results in an upsetting of physical conditions, causing failing health in one way and another. Were the force, freed from reproduction, guided to work consciously and powerfully on the inner planes, the individual should be even better in body and mind than before. It is so often forgotten that there is a 'vertical' as well as a 'horizontal' aspect to all forms of polarity working.

23. In view of this, Venus-Aphrodite is sometimes called 'The Awakener'. This does not only refer to the awakening of the horizontal polarity of sex, but also to the vertical polarity of inner plane consciousness and contacts. Another aspect of this 'awakening' force is evident particularly in the arts, where the creative imagination is always bringing in new forms and conceptions, usually resulting at first

in great antagonism from those who are not readily awakened to new experience, hence the battle against indifference and hostility that almost every great creative artist has to face before his work is first accepted and then drawn into the bulk of established academicism which later artists in turn have to fight against. Similar difficulties occur in other branches of human creative activity, the pioneer is always resented whether he be scientist, doctor or occultist.

24. This can be symbolised by Lucifer the Light-bringer, who is closely associated with Venus, the Star of Promise rising over the stormy waves—and it is not to be expected that the Victory of Netzach should be achieved without Valour, Firmness, and struggle. It is interesting to note that Lucifer has been readily associated with the Devil.

25. Another very esoteric formula is that of 'The Son of his Mother' having reference to the Goddess bringing forth a Son, who, when adult, is re-absorbed into her womb on the highest arcs. This is behind the Isis, Nephthys and Horus formula—'the Bull begotten of the Two Cows.' A similar formula is in the Book of Revelations referring to the book which when eaten is sweet as honey in the mouth but in the belly bitter. This has reference to the inner relationship between Netzach and the 'great bitter Sea' of Binah.

26. In Assyrian mythology Ishtar is an aspect of the 'force' side of the 'Dark Goddess' and might be described as the 'Archetypal Courtesan'. Her mythology is well worth study.

27. A mythological figure having much to do with the forces of Netzach is Orpheus. This great being brought harmony to the Elements, birds, beasts and trees, though in the myth did not bring it to man—this latter might be called the work of the 'Aquarian Orpheus'. Orpheus is the presiding figure over what is called the Green Ray, which might be considered as having three facets—fair proportion or philosophy; power; harmony, including serenity and poise. Orpheus can thus be regarded as the Balancing

Power in the lower planes as Thoth is in the higher planes. These two great beings are the Supreme Balancers, just as Osiris and the Lord Jesus might be termed, each in his own way, Holders of the Balance.

28. Furthermore there is much significance in the great Seven-stringed Lyre of Orpheus, seven being the number of Netzach and also the number of planes in the Universe and Cosmos.

29. All these suggestions may not mean much at first reading but they are meant only to indicate fruitful lines off individual meditation and research.

30. There remain the Vice and the Virtue of the Sephirah to consider. Unselfishness is really the prime necessity for any success in any polarity working and this should be readily obvious even though difficult of application. The Vices of Unchastity and Lust are not meant to be taken only in their sexual connotation. Unchastity is impurity and lack of clear definition in the use of force, resulting in 'blurred edges' and general muddle, the opposite of the Firmness of Netzach. It is this fault which often leads to that wishy-washy conception of niceness, sweetness and light which is a travesty of the clear-cut glorious hard beauty of Netzach. Lust is an over-emphasis and exaggeration of force and thus a contravention of the perfect balance which results in the true Beauty Triumphant of the Sephirah.

31. It is easy to interpret Netzach entirely in terms of sex as it is, equally superficially, to interpret Geburah in terms of war. The beautiful naked woman of the Magical Image can be identified with Venus-Aphrodite as long as one remembers that there is more to the goddess than a kind of patron saint of cabaret and striptease shows. The Dance of the Seven Veils is usually associated in the Western mind with frightful Oriental sensualism, or naughty night-clubs, but if one considers the seven veils to be the Seven Planes of the Universe then the revealed naked Goddess is obviously something far more than an object of eroticism,

just as the Cosmic Eros is something much more than a chubby little love-cherub.

32. The Victory of Netzach is really the victory over all the false ideals evolved since and because of the Fall, such as, for example, the 'great lovers'—the conception that an overwhelming passionate love for another human being is a purifying and enobling thing. Heloise and Abelard, Romeo and Juliet and all the rest were just victims of sheer glamour. And there are the many other false ideals which are generally generously coated with a thick syrup of this same glamour. The brass bands and flying colours that incite men to kill one another for example. Real war, like real love, is not a thing of glamour. The extermination of evil requires more the surgeon's attitude rather than the popular conception of a bloodstained patriotic hero going singing to his victory or death. There is a great difference between being fired with the glamour of battle over a newspaper at home and actually meeting an enemy in a muddy field with fixed bayonet, face to face.

33. The Victory of Netzach, over all these false ideals,— can come fully only after the Sacrifice of Tiphareth; and before it can come, all the false ideals of 'Beauty' and 'Peace' will have also to be destroyed—those perversions of truth and beauty one sees in their grossest form in nineteenth century 'salon' art or the Earth denying type of 'mysticism' which still clings to occultism. More crudely, 'pie in the sky' religion.

34. The false ideas of Beauty have effectively prevented the Many from becoming the One, for Beauty *must* be in accord with Truth. Thus the Spiritual Experience could better be called 'The Vision of the Triumph of Truth and Law'—for that *is* Beauty.

Chapter XIV

HOD—GLORY

"The Eighth Path is called the Absolute or Perfect Intelligence because it is the mean of the Primordial, which has no root by which it can cleave or rest, save in the hidden places of Gedulah, from which emanates its proper essence."

MAGICAL IMAGE:	A hermaphrodite.
GOD NAME:	Elohim Tzabaoth.
ARCHANGEL:	Michael.
ORDER OF ANGELS:	Beni Elohim. Sons of God.
MUNDANE CHAKRA:	Mercury.
VIRTUE:	Truthfulness.
TITLES:	—
SPIRITUAL EXPERIENCE:	Vision of Splendour.
ATZILUTHIC COLOUR:	Violet purple.
BRIATIC COLOUR:	Orange.
YETZIRATIC COLOUR:	Red russet.
ASSIATIC COLOUR:	Yellowish black, flecked white.
VICE:	Falsehood. Dishonesty.
SYMBOLS:	Names and Versicles. Apron.

1. Hod is primarily the Sephirah of the forms of the concrete mind and intellect, and as form was first formed in Chesed or Gedulah, which is its diagonal opposite, the relationship between these two Sephiroth is stressed in the Yetziratic Text. It will be seen that Chesed is also a diagonal opposite of Binah, where the idea of form is first conceived and so these three Sephiroth are linked in this way, being regarded as under the presidency of Water just as Chokmah, Geburah and Netzach are referred to Fire and the line of central Sephiroth to Air.

2. As the human mind works in terms of form it is obvious that Hod is the Perfect or Absolute Intelligence, for

when the forms are true, then they are the means by which man can come to grips with the formless verities of the Primordial or Supernal regions of being. Yet form, when viewed from the Primordial, Supernal or Spiritual standpoint has no reality, it has phenomenal, not noumenal existence, and so the Yetziratic Text states that these lower forms, however valuable they may be, have no basic reality save 'in the hidden places of Gedulah' which would be more or less a Daath condition where the spiritual forces are first taking on conditions of form.

3. Thus it is that man anthropomorphises his gods. The diverse aspects of God have their sphere of action in the lower worlds in the Sephirah Netzach, but Netzach is a force, not a form Sephirah. Therefore the forces of nature and the internal forces of man are given picture images, and these images are formed in the Sephirah Hod. It matters not whether the form be a gross or naive one such as the image of God the Father as an old man with patriarchal beard and robes, or whether it be highly symbolic and subtle such as the representation of the same concept as a point within a circle or 'the smooth point'; an image is used and all mental images are formed under the lower cohering principle of Hod. So all the god-forms belong to Hod just as all the god-forces belong to Netzach.

4. The sceptic may object that all forms are reflected images of the physical world, and so in the unlikely event of a sceptical materialist being a Qabalist, he would no doubt insist that all forms belong to Malkuth. Given the materialist's premises, this would be correct, but the Qabalah is based implicitly on an idealist philosophy and holds that forms are first conceived on the inner levels and subsequently concrete into forms. This is no place to go into an analysis of the main watershed of philosophical speculation—a materialist or idealist conception of the Universe—even if such an analysis would be likely to be of any value. Most philosophies are sound logical structures and their diversity stems basically from whatever premisses

they are built on. And as most premisses, even when they contradict each other, are held to be self-evident and thus axiomatic, there is little to be gained from logical disquisitions on them. In the last analysis 'you pays your money and you takes your choice', and the choice of the Qabalist is the idealist viewpoint.

5. All philosophies, in that they are structures of formalised concepts, come under the presidency of Hod, and their only ethic is whether they are true or false, which is the essence of the Virtue and Vice of this Sephirah. Falsehood can be termed an error, and could be conceived as part of the scheme of things, for it is a fruit of inexperience, and the aim of evolution is to gain experience. Dishonesty however, where it is conscious, and even when it is unconscious for that matter, is a deliberate perversion, therefore Qliphothic and evil, and thus has no real part in the scheme of things but is another foul fruit of man's prime deviation.

6. The God Name of the Sephirah Hod is similar to that of Netzach, being Elohim Tzabaoth, God of Hosts, as compared to Jehovah Tzabaoth, Lord of Hosts. In Netzach the Hosts are the myriad forces of the lower worlds whereas in Hod they are the myriad forms which serve to clothe these forces. There is an interesting field of speculation in why Netzach should have Jehovah as the first part of the Name of God and Hod have Elohim. As we have already discussed, Jehovah refers to the manifestation of forces on different planes and so the Name is applicable to Netzach as it gives insights to relationships of forces at all levels. Elohim, on the other hand, is a Name having polarity and plurality implicit in it, the many in the form of one, and Hod is a Sephirah where logical structures are made, which process is one of finding a coherent unity to diverse aspects. It will be noted that the Magical Image of Hod is the Hermaphrodite, a form which, like Elohim, has duality and polarity implicit in one form. Also the Names Jehovah and Elohim first appear in Chokmah and Binah respective-

ly, of which, according to the principle of similarity of diagonally opposite Sephiroth, Netzach and Hod are lower forms. When the glyph of the Pillars is superimposed on the Tree of Life, Chokmah and Netzach are at the head and base of the Ach've Pillar of Force and Binah and Hod at the head and base of the Passive Pillar of Form.

7. The Archangel of Hod is Michael, the great Guardian who holds at bay the forces of the Underworld. In magical working he is assigned to the South, the Fire Quarter, and can be visualised as a great columnar figure blazing with all the reds of fire. Alternatively the familiar anthropomorphic form can be used of a mighty winged being, with sword upraised, crushing a dragon or serpent beneath his feet. This Archangel is the one to be called upon when assaulted by danger or unbalanced force of any nature, including the uprush of averse and demonic aspects within oneself.

8. The Element of Fire is that Element which transmutes forms to a higher level and so is associated with Michael by reason of the fact that he deals similarly with unregenerate forms and forces. Fire is the purging Element as Michael is the purging Archangel. As Hod is a 'Water' Sephirah it may seem strange that the Archangel of Fire should be assigned to it, but the processes of mentation of Hod, logic and science, the categorising the unknown into knowable structures, is a shedding of light into dark places and one of humanity's greatest fears is the fear of the unknown. It is this past passion for logical categorising that has led to the existentialist jibe that all pre-existential philosophies have been attempts to escape from facing a Universe which is illogical or absurd. Be that as it may, and there is more than a grain of truth in it even if the Universe is not a structure of meaningless absurdity, there remains the fact that ignorance is the breeding ground of much evil and that ignorance is dispersed by the light of the mind in Hod. Thus the attribution of Michael, the Disperser of the Forces of Darkness is a correct one.

9. It is an interesting fact that the Christian Church has

long used Michael as a protector and guardian, though prefixing his name with the title of Saint. There must be hundreds of places dedicated to St. Michael and they are usually sites of pagan worship and thus places frequented, according to medieval Christian belief, by devils. These sites are often on high places or hillocks and the most famous are St. Michael's Mount, near Penzance, Cornwall, and Mont St. Michel off the coast of Brittany. Also the tower on Glastonbury Tor—part of 'the holyest erthe in Englande'—is part of a church originally dedicated to St. Michael. The rest of the church, it is said, was demolished by earthquake leaving only the standing tower—a pagan symbol, so perhaps the old forces have won here. One does not need to take this too seriously though for the differences between pagan and Christian worship of God are really quite superficial. Basically it is one worship and one God.

10. The Order of Angels, the Beni Elohim or Sons of God or Sons of the Gods, can be conceived as working in conjunction with the Order of Angels of Netzach, the Elohim, or Gods. These two Orders of Angels could be considered as the force and form aspects of all the various gods and goddesses conceived by the mind of man. The term 'Son' means an esoteric relationship as can be seen by Christ's naming two of his disciples Boanerges, Sons of Thunder; and Christ himself is known as the Son of God and Son of Man, the former not being entirely derived from the belief in the Immaculate Conception by the Holy Spirit.

11. The Mundane Chakra of Hod is the planet Mercury, the physical planet which stands closest to the Sun and receives more light than any other. It is closely involved esoterically with Venus and the Earth and is associated with the psychic level of the abstract mind. It has much to do with the Mysteries of Hermes.

12. Hermes has given his name to a complete occult tradition—the Hermetic Ray, which is the way of enlightenment through the mind. Hod then is very much the sphere of esoteric philosophy and magic. The three main Paths of

Western occultism can be aligned with the lower Sephiroth. The Green Ray of nature mysticism and art refers to Netzach, the Purple Ray of devotional mysticism to Yesod, and the Orange Ray of magic and occult philosophy to Hod. All three Paths unite however at the level of Tiphareth. The key figures on each Path are Orpheus, Our Lord, and Hermes, respectively.

13. Hermes Trismegistus goes under several variations of name, Mercurius Termaximus and Thrice-greatest Hermes being Roman and English equivalents of the Greek form which probably derived from the Egyptian Thoth-Tehuti. The highest aspect was as the 'Divine Pymander'. 'Pymander' means 'Shepherd of men' and signifies the archetypal leader, teacher and illuminator of mankind. He is a being however who works principally through teaching of the mind rather than through the emotions or religious faith, as is hinted in an extract from some of the Hermetic writings: "Have Me in thy mind and whatever thou wouldst learn, I will teach thee." and Emerson was moved to write: "I cannot recite, even thus rudely, laws of the Intellect, without remembering that lofty and sequestered class who have been its prophets and oracles, the high priesthood of the pure Reason, the Trismegisti, the expounders of thought from age to age. When, at long intervals, we turn over their abstruse pages, wonderful seems the calm and grand air of these great spiritual lords, who have walked in the world—these of the old religion . . . This band of grandees, Hermes, Heraclitus, Empedocles, Plato, Plotinus, Proclus, Synesius, Olympiodorus, and the rest, have somewhat so vast in their logic, so primary in their thinking, that it seems antecedent to all the ordinary distinctions of rhetoric and literature, and to be at once poetry, and music and dancing, and astronomy, and mathematics."

14. The secret of the logic of these Hermetic philosophers is that it is based upon Truth and so speaks to the intuition as well as to the lower mind. Unenlightened philosophies

can be farragoes of nonsense although their structure may be completely logical, simply because they are not based on Truth. One can build up a great imposing logical edifice but the ultimate worth of it will depend upon its foundations, whether it is built upon the rock of Truth or the shifting sands of personal opinion. Again this refers us back to the Vice and Virtue of the Sephirah Hod, Truth and Falsity.

15. According to Clement of Alexandria the whole of Egyptian religious philosophy was contained in the Books of Thoth. Thoth, the Lord of Books and of Learning, was regarded as the inspirer of all sacred writings and the teacher of all religion and philosophy. Furthermore, as Iamblichus tells us, Thoth was the president of all priestly discipline and every Egyptian priest was held to be a priest of Thoth over and above his other priestly functions because Thoth was the archetypal priest or hierophant—the Oversoul of all priests.

16. As has already been mentioned under Netzach, Thoth can be regarded as the Balancing Power on the higher planes as Orpheus is on the lower. This does not imply that one is greater than the other for all the Sephiroth, and thus all the planes, are equally holy. Hod, as it is a lower reflection of Chesed, is a link between humanity and all teachers on the higher planes whether they be Masters, (that is, highly evolved humans,) or Lords of Mind. The Lords of Mind are perfected beings of a previous evolution, and Hermes, Merlin, Buddha and the individual Spirit of Jesus of Nazareth (i.e. Jesus as apart from the Christ force) have been said to be of that evolution. The technique of teaching of the Lords of Mind is always the linking up of some of the Divine Reason with the higher mind of man; in other words, they give *knowledge* of God as distinguished from *awareness* of God which last is the method of the Venus teachers such as Orpheus. The inner priesthoods known as the Order of Prometheus and the Order of Melchizedek derive from Mercury and Venus respectively,

though there are the forces of certain constellations working behind these planets.

17. It may seem strange that Jesus should be considered in relation to the Hermetic Ray as he is primarily a teacher on the Love Aspect of God. However it must be remembered that no Aspect can be considered without the others and that they all interlink. Many people are anxious to give themselves up to Wisdom in spite of the fact that they lack the necessary basis for it. This basis is Love, for compassion, in its true sense, fertilises Wisdom so that right use is made of it. Many leaders of esoteric groups who, by their Wisdom bias, are led to the field of teaching, have personalities in which the Love Aspect is not adequately developed. True Wisdom cannot be present without the other Logoidal Aspects, for, as the Athanasian Creed says of the Wisdom Principle of the Logos: "(It) is neither made, created, nor born, but proceeding."

18. The images of Hod are not the same as those of Yesod —the Treasure House of Images. They are forms made and controlled by mind and will and reflected in the great Water Temple of Hod. They are images of eternity often conceived and placed there by higher beings to be picked up by man and meditated upon to give subsequent revelation and the Vision of Splendour that is the Spiritual Experience of Hod. The Water of Hod is not the Elemental Water but the crystal-clear Well of Truth.

19. In this category of symbolic forms can be placed all the main pictorial systems of esoteric teaching such as Hebrew letters, the astrological signs and the Tarot, which latter is often called the Book of Thoth. The origin of the Tarot cards is shrouded in obscurity, being placed by some authorities as far back as the Egyptian Mysteries and by others as late as the sixteenth century. However, this type of scholastic research matters nothing for their true origin comes from the inner planes and their authority derives not from the date of their physical inception but from their use as a practical system here and now.

20. The mythological attributes of the Egyptian Thoth give a general picture of the attributions of the Sephirah Hod. He was depicted with the head of an ibis whose long beak can be likened to the analytical mind picking out the morsels of Truth from the swampy waters of falsity. He was also a moon-god, having the crescent moon upon his head, the heavenly body which brings reflected light to the dark hours of Earth as the reflections in symbols of the higher powers of Chesed bring light to the mind of man in Hod. Apart from being the Demiurge in Hermopolis, the 'City of Eight', he was also a Divine Judge or Balancer, and his action at the heavenly tribunal before which the implacable enemies Horus and Set appeared, earned him the title of 'He who judges the two companions'. He also helped Isis to defend the child Horus from danger and drove out the poison from the child's body when it was stung by a scorpion. This is analogous to the duties and powers of the Archangel Michael. Thoth was also inventor of all arts and sciences and of hieroglyphs, and the first of all magicians—also distinctly Hod attributes, besides being herald of the gods, as was Hermes, the Greek counterpart of Thoth, and also the Roman Mercury. In that the images of Hod are symbols of divine import the attribution of messenger as well as magician is fairly obvious.

21. In analysing the attributes of a god in this way relationships of divine aspects can be deduced. There is much significance in the relationship of Thoth with Isis, Horus, Osiris and Set, for example, and of Hermes with Pallas Athene, Perseus, Apollo and Zeus. Generally speaking, the Egyptian myths are purer because the Egyptian civilisation was a very rigid one, always strictly under the control of the priesthood. The Greek was not so, and while the Greek divinities may be more human and appealing one has to guard against Greek popular distortion and levity. Hermes, for example, was the patron of merchants, travellers, glib talkers and thieves, which attributions probably derive at second hand from the fact that he was Divine

Messenger. There was no aspect of cunning and trickery in the Egyptian Thoth.

22. The Egyptian god-forms were carefully prescribed by the priesthood who had a great knowledge of the psychological effects of angles and line. Thus much can be gained from contemplation of Egyptian imagery and its simplicity of form makes it easy to remember, visualise and hold in the imagination. The Greek gods on the other hand are very much more human, being in fact idealisations of human types. Thus, of the main Western pantheons, the Egyptian tends to give the inner esoteric side to the divine forces, and the Greek the outer more human side. Roman mythology is largely derivative from Greek, the Romans being too pragmatic to bother much about inner forces save as a means of furthering their material ambitions. The Assyrian gods and goddesses are worth study for the East does not tend to repress its subconscious as the West does, while the Norse is valuable in that it may have more appeal to the Nordic mentality and it looks the harder facts of life straight in the eye, for life in the North was, for purely climatic reasons, much harder than life around the Mediterranean.

23. By a careful consideration of the whole variety of god-forms a considerable store of occult knowledge and wisdom can be built up and this is essentially a process under the province of Hod.

24. The other method of Hod-working is that of magic, for magic is essentially a process of building forms for forces to indwell and Hod is the Sephirah of magical forms. The Names and Versicles, symbols of Hod, are the writings the magician has which symbolise and describe the potencies with which he is working, they are, in fact, talismanic forms of those potencies.

25. The Apron, which has Masonic associations, is the characteristic garment of the craftsman, the maker of forms, which of course the magician is. That the forms may be mental or astral rather than physical is only a

174

difference of level, not of function. The Apron also covers
the Moon centre, or loins, as the Lamen covers the Sun
centre, or breast, and it will be remembered that Thoth
is a god of the Moon, from which he derives his name of
Tehuti.

26. As a last consideration there is an interesting tradition which says that the Beni Elohim, the Sons of God,
were Sons and Daughters of other Spheres who came down
to Earth in very early times and mated with humans, producing a race of Wisdom the like of which has never been
seen since. The mating and the offspring, though holy at
first, degenerated into evil beings of great power who had
in the end to be destroyed. This fact is said to lie behind
many strange legends of all races and the fact that these
beings were androgynous and could use either sex at will
is no doubt the foundation of such legends as that of Sodom.
The Magical Image of Hod is, of course, the Hermaphrodite,
and the tracing through of such correlations, often very
strange, of the magical alphabet of symbols is a pursuit of
great interest and fascination. Though as with all fascinating pursuits, particularly esoteric ones, it is well not to let
one's enthusiasm go too unleashed for there is a very
treacherous and shifting boundary between the Virtue and
the Vice of Hod—Truth and Falsity.

Chapter XV

YESOD—THE FOUNDATION

"The Ninth Path is called the Pure Intelligence because it purifies the Emanations. It proves and corrects the designing of their representations, and disposes the unity with which they are designed without diminution or division."

MAGICAL IMAGE:	A beautiful naked man, very strong.
GOD NAME:	Shaddai el Chai.
ARCHANGEL:	Gabriel.
ORDER OF ANGELS:	Kerubim. The Strong.
MUNDANE CHAKRA:	The Moon.
VIRTUE:	Independence.
TITLES:	Treasurehouse of Images.
SPIRITUAL EXPERIENCE:	Vision of the Machinery of the Universe.
ATZILUTHIC COLOUR:	Indigo.
BRIATIC COLOUR:	Violet.
YETZIRATIC COLOUR:	Very dark purple.
ASSIATIC COLOUR:	Citrine, flecked azure.
VICE:	Idleness.
SYMBOLS:	Perfumes and Sandals.

1. Yesod is the Sephirah of the etheric plane and so not only is it the powerhouse or machinery of the physical world it also holds the framework in which the particles of dense matter are enmeshed.

2. The study of the etheric is a vast one, for it is co-extensive with the whole range of the physical sciences but its effect in the physical world can be regarded approximately as Vitality. It is an energy of integration which co-ordinates the physical molecules, cells and so on into a definite organism, and so without it our physical bodies would be nothing but collections of independent cells. It is

not a product of physical life, for Yesod is nearer the source of things than Malkuth, but living creatures, plants and even minerals are its products. And even as a lack of it in the nervous system would lead to exhaustion and death, so an overplus of it would cause disease and subsequently death.

3. It is the controlling agent in the chemico-physiological changes of protoplasm and shows its presence by the power of organisms to respond to stimuli, and is thus the basis behind those fibrous cells which constitute the nerves and give the power to feel pleasure and pain. It is held by esoteric science that it is the etheric vehicle and not the physical body which has the power to feel, and this is the principle behind certain anaesthetics; they drive the etheric double out of the physical body as occurs in sleep, deep trance and finally at death. The physical body is the receiver of physical sense impressions only and has no acute sensory awareness except as vague, dull, diffused feelings such as general fatigue. The formation of a nervous system is caused by an admixture of astral with etheric force and so there is only rudimentary nervous structure in plants and none at all in minerals. All however, have their structure built and held by the etheric web or network, thus it is the foundation of physical existence, and 'The Foundation' is the Title of Yesod.

4. In this way Yesod can be said to hold the image of everything that exists in the physical world, and thus it is the Storehouse of Images. And yet it not only contains these images, it has the power of altering them, and it is by means of this fact that the Yogi, for example, can produce changes within the physical organism by means of the meditation and postural techniques of Hatha Yoga. This particular aspect of Yesod is that which is stressed in the Yetziratic Text: "The Ninth Path is called the Pure Intelligence because it purifies the Emanations. It proves (i.e. tests) and corrects the designing of their representations . . ." which results of course in functional forms in

the physical world, Malkuth. The integrating function over cellular and molecular life is covered in the remainder of the Text, which reads: "(it) disposes the unity with which they (the emanations) are designed without diminution or division." Ultimately, the supreme integrated image of Yesod is that of 'the Luminous Image of the Creator' which is shown forth and concealed in the physical world. Thus the God Name of the Sephirah Yesod is Shaddai el Chai, the Almighty Living God.

5. Naturally as Yesod is a Sephirah much concerned with the etheric, the images of pre-physical manifestation of all the higher emanations, and also the vast body of teaching developed about the Moon—the great reflector of the Sun's light—the Archangel of the Sephirah is the Archangel of the Annunciation, Gabriel, who gives the powers of Vision.

6. He can be imagined as a beautiful blue-green figure with silver flashes of light and a tremendous swirl of colours of various shades of peacock tints shot with silver which are his wings, or a part of his extensive aura, and about his head and beneath his feet, streams of liquid silver. It may be noted that these are not strictly speaking the Sephirothic colours, but one should not let the imagination be bound too closely by tradition, particularly with symbols like the Flashing Colours which are to a large extent arbitrary. The colours given above in connection with the Archangel Gabriel should evoke much of the Sea and Moon power which is an integral part of the Sephirah Yesod.

7. This anthropomorphic form can then be seen to change into a tremendous pillar of silver light, perhaps with a mauve-grey tinge, reaching up as far as the sky and standing on the Earth, and around the pillar again clouds of peacock blue and green. This tremendous pillar should be conceived to be like a battery of the Universe—an electric battery—and all actions of the Universe are switched, as it were, onto you through this great battery, for this is the basis of Vision, whether clairvoyance or clairaudience.

8. The mighty silver pillar can then be changed to a nine-fold figure, a solid figure with nine sides of crystal, but reflecting silver and blue-green light. Imagine in that ninefold figure a large amount of force from the former great silver and blue-green pillar and watch it; watch this solid as you would look into a crystal globe and see what appears. As a conclusion to this experiment it is best to change the form back once more to the protecting beautiful Angelic form radiating the powers of the Moon and of Water which are qualities in tune with the visionary faculties that can give real and right understanding of the inner life. It is Gabriel who rules 'the Living Water streams that well from out the Highest Throne'. (cf. Revelations XXII i: "And he showed me a pure river of water of life, clear as crystal, proceeding out of the throne of God and of the Lamb." and also Genesis II x "And a river went out of Eden to water the garden: and from thence it was parted, and become into four heads.")

9. The Order of Angels of Yesod are the Kerubim, the Strong, which title is apposite when one considers that Yesod holds the etheric levels and stresses on which physical form depends. It is this conception which is also behind the Magical Image—the beautiful naked man, very strong, who could be equated with Atlas, who held the whole world on his shoulders, having the strength of those other classical 'Foundations' of the Universe, the Elephant and the Tortoise and the Eagle. In a way, these three creatures plus the man Atlas could be conceived of as reflections of the Four Holy Living Creatures of Kether. Also, the strong beautiful man can be considered as Our Lord as a counter-balance to the Sunday-school 'gentle Jesus meek and mild' conception which has unfortunately grown up around him. Jesus, the strong man who had the passive strength not to resist his persecutors when all the time he had the power to do all those things that the devil tempted him with in the Wilderness; who had sufficient 'presence' of power to impress and impel faith into a hardbitten Roman centurion

whose servant was sick; who had the power and knowledge over the etheric levels to heal the sick, perform 'miracles', raise the dead, and reconstruct his body again, glorified, after three days.

10. The Kerubim work on the building of knowledge and the harnessing of force in etheric or Yesodic methods, of which one is the use of symbols relating to Yesodic understanding within the depths of the subconscious mind. With the progress of time these symbols become less 'ritualistic' and more mental—that is, they become tools in the hands of the various schools of psychoanalysis. Nevertheless, these images of psychological healing are still present day versions of the contents of 'The Treasure House of Images' and the forces behind this therapy are the Order of Angels of Yesod however fantastic that may sound to the scientific mind. The great powers in the etheric sphere are the Angels themselves, the Kerubim, and as the etheric powers are the great formative forces of the world and of man, these great forces must be taken into account by medical research if it is to have any value. Apart from the subconscious aspects, which result in much psycho-somatic disease, the complete understanding of the mechanism which works the body so that it may be cured in sickness, kept in good condition when it is well, and rejuvenated when it is old, are all contained in Yesod and must be sought in Yesod, the etheric foundation behind the physical kingdom of Malkuth.

11. It is in this direction that the new 'unorthodox' methods of healing are progressing such as anthroposophy, radionics and the Alexander techniques. Often, certain of these techniques work better with people who have some conscious awareness of their astral and etheric levels and whose lower levels are thus less dense. People who have made a fetish of drugs on the other hand are less likely to be helped by vegetable and homeopathic treatments. However, on the inner levels, the increase of radio-active fallout is having the effect of rendering the etheric levels less

dense so that there is some good coming from this evil it seems, though of course it can lead to terrible disease if not adequately controlled, as is well known.

12. The Mundane Chakra of Yesod is the Moon and the Moon is intimately connected with the growth of plants, and there is much forgotten lore regarding herbs and plants and their influence on sickness and other matters which Paracelsus tried to revive and which are still revived today though lack of scientific method does not help the cause much, and it is a happy hunting ground for cranks and faddists.

13. The Moon is intimately connected with the Earth as the etheric plane is intimately connected with the physical. The power of the etheric vitality is as the power of the Moon which produces the great movements of the tides of the sea on the face of the Earth; and the cyclic activity of the etheric 'Machinery of the Universe' is as the cyclic activity of the Moon and the physiological cycle of woman —the Moon sex.

14. In addition to this there is also the vast amount of esoteric teaching which centres about the Moon, for the Moon and the Sun are two great principles which have their analogues in the Pillars behind the whole of manifestation. It can be said that Pan and Isis are aspects of the Yesodic sphere because Pan gives the idea of archetypal strength which is characteristic of the etheric and of the action of the Moon on Earth; and Isis gives the idea of the archetypal virginity of the Feminine side of God, the whole receptive side of things which is shown forth by the reflection of the Sun's light by the Moon, and by the Sephirah Yesod being the receptacle of all the higher emanations for them to be formed into the images which are the basis of forms in the physical world. Also the main function of Yesod, the mechanism by which the human race lives and dies, is born and is mated, is also the function of the Great Mother, or Isis, for Isis contains all other goddesses.

15. There is also the magical side of the Moon, and Yesod is more important magically than any other Sephirah except possibly Hod. It being a Moon Sephirah, the god Thoth is also intimately connected with Yesod. This fact is behind some of the legends which tell of Thoth being a helper of Isis. As Yesod is so intimately connected with the purification and unification of forms its relevance to practical magic will be obvious, for all higher forces have to pass through Yesod before they can manifest physically in Malkuth.

16. The attribution of the Sandals to Yesod also shows the close magical link with the Sephirah Hod, for one aspect of them is the Winged Sandals of the Great Messenger, which refers to Hermes, Mercury and Thoth. In another sense, the Sandals are magical implements which enable one to walk with ease on the Foundations of the various psychic levels.

17. The Perfumes, also assigned to Yesod, contain another whole branch of the understanding of the etheric vibrations behind minerals and plants. This again is part of the Moon aspect of Yesod and a sphere which has been little investigated in spite of the profound changes of consciousness that can be effected by means of various perfumes— as indeed with music. As Dion Fortune remarked, "How quickly do our thoughts turn away from earthly things when the drifting smoke of incense comes to us from the high altar; how quickly do they return to them again when we get a whiff of patchouli from the next pew!"† Furthermore there is the higher esoteric side to perfume, which we have already touched upon with reference to Isis and Daath. There is a strong connection between Daath and Yesod and they are said to be 'opposite poles of the magical circuit'. That is, Daath is the highest and Yesod the lowest part of the psyche when the physical body in Malkuth and the spiritual levels of the Supernal Triad are discounted; they are the extreme poles of the link between Spirit and Matter.

18. In the chapter on Daath mention was made of Moses and the Moon mountain of Sinai, and the Old Testament as

†The Mystical Qabalah by Dion Fortune—published by Williams and Norgate, London.

a whole contains a vast compendium of Yesodic symbolism. Much has been obliterated through the course of the ages and by translation but the great symbols of Moon worship are there for those who care to look for them.

19. To begin with, as Genesis tells us, the nomadic tribe which became known as the Jews came forth originally from Ur of the Chaldees. Ur was the great Moon-city of Chaldea and carried great teaching of the Water and the Moon in the worship of that strange being, Ea, the Divine Man-Fish, who, according to Berosus, the Babylonian priest and historian, "wrote a book on the origin of things and the beginnings of civilisation, and gave it to men." This book probably gave those accounts of the Deluge and the Tower of Babel which appear in fragments from the Royal Library at Ninevah as well as in the Bible. Ea, or Oannes as the Greeks later called him, says, Berosus, "used to spend the whole day amidst men, without taking any food, and he gave them an insight into letters, and sciences, and every kind of art; he taught them how to found cities, to construct temples, to introduce laws and to measure land; he showed them how to sow seeds and gather in crops; in short, he instructed them in everything that softens manners and makes up civilisation, so that from that time no-one has invented anything new. Then when the sun went down, this monstrous Oannes used to plunge back into the sea and spend the night in the midst of the boundless waves, for he was amphibious."

20. Shrouded as it is in the depths of legend and mythology we cannot be sure whether the sea is meant as such, or whether the etheric sea is meant. In legend many things can be implied by the apparently physical descriptions— for example Daath consciousness is usually symbolised by the seer ascending a mountain or going to an upper room. From the description of his functions however, Ea was obviously what esoteric tradition calls a Manu or leader and civiliser of an early race. These beings are said to have had no permanent physical bodies but to have materialised

etherically, somewhat after the fashion that ectoplasmic materialisations occur in the séance room. In those days too it is said that all men had etheric vision so that the Manu was visible to all. Be that as it may it was from this background of tradition that the early Jews descended.

21. The Moon powers and the Sea powers were worshipped as gods before men worshipped the full force of the Sun power, and though Jehovah eventually became strongly identified with the Sun, from early days he was a Moon force. Thus the great power of the Moon regarding fertility became with the ancient Jews a sacred thing as for example in the ritual of circumcision instituted by Abraham.

22. In the early days the Moon was worshipped as a god as well as a goddess, and certain races inclined more to one side or the other. The Jews of course tended towards the male side and some confusion generally resulted when the race encountered rival tribes who worshipped a female representation of the same force such as Ishtar or Astarte. The strange book The Song of Solomon probably stems from one of these encounters, for its real meaning undoubtedly refers to the dark aspects of the Moon goddess: "I am black, but comely, O ye daughters of Jerusalem, as the tents of Kedar, as the curtains of Solomon. Look not upon me, because I am black, because the sun hath looked upon me . . ."

23. Solomon and Huram are two examples of magical figures where, although historically certain men corresponding with them can be said to have existed, they are really great archetypal figures ensouled by great forces to a degree far beyond that which any mortal could have borne. These figures occur in all races as for example King Arthur, Robin Hood and so on, and the process even works with fairly contemporary figures such as the heroes of the Wild West.

24. The Second Book of Chronicles tells of the construction of the Great Temple of Solomon which was built with the assistance of Huram the King of Tyre who had also

assisted David. The Temple was constructed with very intricate and precise measurements—a great Moon ritual of measurement and the pure and exact forms of Yesod—and the symbolism is well worth study for it embodies such things as representations of the Kerubim—the Yesodic Order of Angels, and pillars surmounted with pomegranates —definite feminine symbols, and in the midst was placed the Ark of the Covenant.

25. The Ark is a great Moon and Sea symbol and thus early origins of this cult can be traced in the story of Noah's ark, which was also constructed according to precise measurement, and to the strange story of Jonah and the whale. Although the Moon symbols refer much to fertility it is not only a matter of physical fertility but also of fertility of the mind and imagination and soul as well. The higher teaching of the Ark is that it is a vessel of Mystery, a primitive and Eastern type of the Holy Grail, and the Holy Grail is the point of fusion between planes, where a receptacle is made in lower consciousness that can act as a container or giver of form to forces of higher consciousness.

26. There is also the whole tradition of stellar teaching connected with the Sea Mysteries, for the Sea, like Stone, is a symbol of cosmic space. Knowledge of the stellar bodies reached a great height among the priests of Cháldea. Number plays a significant part in the Old Testament and in connection with the story of David there is the tale of a mortal skirmish between twelve men against twelve and in a subsequent battle the death of threehundred and sixty men. (2. Samuel. Ch. II.) Obscured by translation and re-translation and commentary this probably relates to early zodiacal symbolism and to the calendar for the number of days in the year was held to be threehundred and sixty in early times. David also was anxious to fetch the Ark of the Covenant so that it should be set in a worthy place and received into the nation with proper state, and to do that he danced before it. We can take it that this was not mere primitive exuberance but a definite ritual act and probably

the ancient 'Dance of the Stars', an imitation of the movement of the stars in the sky.

27. Finally there is the great racial leader Moses who like so many Jewish leaders had been in Egypt, the centre of Mystery training. Being the man he was it is extremely likely that he had studied in the Egyptian priesthood and may well have been a priest of the great Moon-god Osiris, the Great Ruler, as Moses himself was to become.

28. A strong Yesod contact can be made by visualising this great teacher of Moon Mysteries upon the Moon Mountain of Sinai. He can be imagined after the manner of the wellknown statue by Michelangelo; a somewhat spade-like face, very thick hair which has almost a vital strength as if a living creature in itself, and from the pineal gland, stretching out from either side of the forehead can be imagined two great sword-like streams of light. Mount Sinai can be pictured as a great mountain of volcanic origin, grey and dark in colour and stretching up far into the clouds.

29. This image strongly built may well bring a kind of Daath contact for it must have been a state of Daath consciousness that Moses was in, to receive direct Divine contact and formulate the potent supernal forces impacted on his higher consciousness into language and precepts to be handed down as the basic laws of the race.

30. The resulting Ten Commandments are said to correlate with the ethics of the Ten Holy Sephiroth of the Qabalah. The following is a personal analysis on the Commandments as given in the Authorised Version of the Bible. The interpretation makes no claims to authority but according to it it will be seen that the listed order of the Commandments also has Qabalistic significance.

1 *Thou shalt have no other gods before me refers to the unity of Kether.*

2 *Thou shalt not make unto thee any graven image refers to the formless Devotion of Chokmah*

where the only image is the Vision of God face to face.

3   *Thou shalt not take the name of the Lord thy God in vain has reference to the Virtue of Silence in Binah, the root of Faith.*

4   *Remember the Sabbath day, to keep it holy. Six days shalt thou labour etc. Six is the number of Tiphareth and the observance of the Sabbath or seventh day has reference to the Devotion to the Great Work and the Vision of the Harmony of things in Tiphareth.*

5   *Honour thy father and thy mother refers to Chesed whose Virtue is Obedience.*

6   *Thou shalt not kill obviously relates to Geburah.*

7   *Thou shalt not commit adultery although superficially it may seem to refer to the Vice of Netzach really applies better to Yesod, the Sephirah of purification—the Pure Intelligence.*

8   *Thou shalt not steal is an exhortation to the Virtue of Netzach, Unselfishness, and the Firmness and Valour of this Sephirah. Theft is an underhand weakness and a sheer abuse of all principles of polarity, for theft can apply to other levels besides the physical.*

9   *Thou shalt not bear false witness relates to Hod. The Qliphothic aspect of Hod is referred to as 'the False Accuser' and in the Greek pantheon the averse side of Hermes was considered to be the patron of thieves.*

10   *Thou shalt not covet thy neighbours house . . . nor anything that is thy neighbours refers to the Vice of Malkuth—Avarice.*

31. In this order of the Ten Commandments we have the formulation of first Kether, Chokmah, Binah, an upward pointing triangle; then successively Tiphareth, Chesed, Geburah and Yesod, Netzach, Hod, both downward pointing triangles, and lastly, Malkuth. Reference to the glyph of the Tree of Life will show that these triangles are the same as the three Triads of the Sephiroth.

32. With regard to systems of legend and mythology other than the Biblical the ramifications are vast for they include all deities of Sea, Moon, Stars, and measurement.

33. Bearing in mind the Magical Image of Yesod, the very strong man, Hercules is an important figure, a figure indeed standing for all humanity. The Twelve Labours of Hercules can be said to represent the evolutionary tasks of man and can be aligned with the Twelve Signs of the Zodiac.

34. The Egyptian goddess Maat is likewise worthy of mention. She was often depicted as a woman sitting on her heels—a suggestion of the Sandals of Yesod and the Foundation. It was she who, usually in the form of a feather, was placed in the pan of the Balance of the Judgment Hall of Osiris opposite the heart of the one newly dead to test its truthfulness. Here again we have the accent on measure and the purity of Yesod. She was also intimately connected with Thoth, who was sometimes called 'the Master of Maat'—the Master of Truth and Justice.

35. There is also the triple aspect of the Moon and the triple aspect of woman, virgin, mate and ancient crone. These are represented in the Greek pantheon by Artemis, Selene and Hecate, although other goddesses do have overlapping aspects; Pallas Athene for example could qualify as Virgin of the Moon in her lower aspects. Thus references in certain old grimoires of magic to having a young virgin or a hag to assist the magician may well originally have been guarded references to certain moon symbolism and the potencies behind it. From this it will be seen that one needs an experienced magical method of mentation before dabbling with certain occult matters for the true inter-

pretation of much magical lore depends on analogy, allegory and symbol rather than straightforward logic.

36. In practice this unfortunately works out in the fact that the scientifically minded person considers the occultist to be completely devoid of any powers of logic of sensible reasoning. However occultism is in reality a very exact science—it must be, or the practical operator is soon in trouble, and the training of an adept is every bit as rigorous and lengthy as an advanced graduate of one of the sciences. It is to be hoped that in the future the two methods of mind-working and research will coalesce as indeed they seem to be doing through the field of modern psychiatry and the increasing interest in symbolism and myth.

Chapter XVI

MALKUTH—THE KINGDOM

"The Tenth Path is called the Resplendent Intelligence because it is exalted above every head and sits upon the throne of Binah. It illuminates the splendours of all the Lights, and causes an influence to emanate from the Prince of Countenances, the Angel of Kether."

MAGICAL IMAGE:	A young woman, crowned and throned.
GOD NAME:	Adonai Malekh, or Adonai ha Aretz.
ARCHANGEL:	Sandalphon.
ORDER OF ANGELS:	Ashim, Souls of Fire.
MUNDANE CHAKRA:	Sphere of the Elements.
VIRTUE:	Discrimination.
TITLES:	The Gate. Gate of Death. Gate of the Shadow of Death. Gate of Tears. Gate of Justice. Gate of Prayer. Gate of the Daughter of the Mighty Ones. Gate of the Garden of Eden. The Inferior Mother. Malkah, the Queen. Kallah, the Bride. The Virgin.
SPIRITUAL EXPERIENCE:	Knowledge and Conversation of the Holy Guardian Angel.
ATZILUTHIC COLOUR:	Yellow.
BRIATIC COLOUR:	Citrine, olive, russet and black.
YETZIRATIC COLOUR:	Citrine, olive, russet and black, flecked gold.
ASSIATIC COLOUR:	Black, rayed yellow.
VICE:	Avarice. Inertia.
SYMBOLS:	Altar of the double cube. Equal-armed cross. Magic circle. Triangle of evocation.

1. The Sephirah Malkuth represents the entire physical world and though it might seem that the fact of the physical world is obvious to everyone there are probably few people who are really capable of living in it at will; that is, whose consciousness is focussed in present time and place and not wandering to happy or traumatic condi-

189

tions of the past or wish-fulfilment dreams or vague worries of the future. So many people have all their faculties centred on their mental life or their emotional life rather than the sensory life of the physical world. There is even a kind of religious aversion to sensuousness—the word itself has unsavoury overtones to it in many quarters, so that it tends frequently to be confused with sensuality, the undue indulgence in the grosser pleasures of sense. It is interesting to note that originally the word 'sensual' was quite an innocent one, but that its meaning became corrupted so that Milton had to coin the new word 'sensuous' which has now also deteriorated in popular usage, if not in academic definition. Milton's own phrase to describe great poetry, "simple, sensuous and passionate" for example might well be seen nowadays as a selling slogan on the cover of any paperback novel or blazened forth in the trailer of any semi-erotic film. Again this is one of the symptoms of the puritan pathology—an unconscious compulsion to rub dirt into the gates of the senses. The soul of a race can be judged from its use of language just as the psychology of an individual can be assessed by the newspaper and magazines he reads.

2. The ambivalent attitude to the world of physical sensation is a strange one. It is, at the same time, a running away from it into past, future or sanctimony, and also a strange unhealthy fascination and feeling of guilt which characterises the Anglo-Saxon mentality in particular. Yet, looking at things from an evolutionary and re-incarnationary standpoint, the physical world is the world which should be thoroughly grasped by the soul—there is ample time for emotional and mental meanderings after death. The physical world, in that one has to return to it time and time again, must hold the key to spiritual development. And this development is surely not to be gained in regarding all physical nature as a trap and temptation which must be strenuously denied and put away from one.

3. According to esoteric teaching, man descends on the

involutionary arc from the planes of Spirit, forming functional vehicles on all the descending planes. On the evolutionary arc it is his destiny to gain control objectively of all the planes in ascending order. The first plane on the evolutionary path then is the physical but how many aspirants to spiritual growth have effective control of it? All too often the mystically inclined person is an ineffectual on the physical plane and so the apparent affinity with things sacred is in reality a running away from and attempted evasion of the next step on the Path—the expression of the Spirit functioning effectively in the mundane world, which could be called 'the Initiation of the Nadir'.

4. The Yetziratic Text of the Sephirah Malkuth shows the importance of the physical world in the Divine scheme of things. "The Tenth Path is called the Resplendent Intelligence because it is exalted above every head and sits upon the throne of Binah."

5. The reference to Binah shows that Malkuth is the supreme manifestation of the form which was first conceived as a possibility in the Supernal World of Binah. It is thus "exalted above every head" for Malkuth is the end result of the Divine impulse into manifestation—the spiritual pattern made physically manifest.

6. Its title, the Resplendent Intelligence, is explained in the latter half of the text: "It illuminates the splendours of all the Lights, and causes an influence to emanate from the Prince of Countenances, the Angel of Kether." The Lights can be considered either as the Divine Sparks of men or else the other nine Sephiroth, which cover the whole gamut of created being. There is much teaching implied in this short text for it indicates that physical objective existence is needed before the true potentialities within the Spirit of each human being can be drawn forth. It 'illuminates the splendours' of all of us, or should do. Many, it seems, are in the habit of carting round hefty bushels of unreality to hide their lights under. The Text really gives a picture of

what physical existence should be—and indeed must be before further evolutionary progress can be made.

7. There is also great import in the sentence; "(it) causes an influence to emanate from the Prince of Countenances, the Angel of Kether." The material world can be considered as being a focussing or earthing point for the creative powers of the Spirit—for the Angel of Kether is Metatron, the great being superintending the Creative World of Kether. Thus Spirit and Matter are as great poles in a vast cosmic battery, each has to be functional before current can flow in the magical circuit between Daath and Yesod. This further implies that all knowledge of spiritual realities can be gained from contemplation of the physical world—the reflection of the Vast Countenance in Kether. Again we come back to the prime Hermetic axiom: 'As above—so below.'

8. This revelation has been mentioned by Blake in his 'Auguries of Innocence':

"To see a World in a grain of sand,
"And a Heaven in a wild flower,
"Hold Infinity in the palm of your hand,
"And Eternity in an hour."

9. The various titles of Malkuth which refer to it as a Gate show that the physical world is a definite stage in spiritual development or a thing which one must *go through*.

10. The Gate of Death and the Gate of the Shadow of Death refer to the great boundaries of Malkuth as far as man's physical existence is concerned—birth and death. By birth we come into the world and by death we go out of it. Birth and death however are two sides of the same coin, for when one dies physically one is born into the higher worlds, and when one is born physically, from the point of view of the higher worlds one is dead.

11. The aspect of Malkuth as the Gate of Death can be considered in two ways, for there is the Gate of the Death

of the Physical Body and the Gate of the Death of Illumination. These two aspects have been admirably explained in 'The Cosmic Doctrine' and so one can do no better than to quote the references in full.

12. *Physical Death:* "Each individualised consciousness lives to die and dies to live. It is only by death that we can reap the fruits of life. We graze in the fields of Earth, and we lie down in the fields of Heaven to chew the cud. It has been said 'for one hour's study do three hours meditation.' In death is the soul's meditation and in life its study."

13. "Did you only 'live', all experiences would pass through consciousness and leave but little impression after the first few pictures had filled all available space. All would be concrete, unrelated, unsynthesised; in the meditation which is 'death', the abstract essence of life is extracted, and instead of a million concrete images there is the abstract concept. Learn to trust death. Learn to love death. Learn to count upon death in your scheme of things, and regularly perform the exercise of visualising yourselves as dead and conceiving how you shall then be, for thus you will learn to build the bridge between life and death, so that it shall be trodden with increasing ease. See yourselves as dead and working out your destiny. See yourselves as dead and continuing your work from the plane of the dead. Thus shall the bridge be built that leads beyond the Veil. Let the chasm between the so-called living and the so-called dead be bridged by this method, that men may cease to fear death."

14. The spiritual exercise of imagining oneself at death is of course a well known one in the Roman Catholic Church. Also, the practice of going back over the day's happenings just before going to sleep is widely recommended in various esoteric groups for in this way much of the 'abstracting' work of death is done in life. It should also be noted that the bridging of "the chasm between the so-called living and the so-called dead" should be achieved by meditation work within oneself and not by indiscriminate calling back

194

of the dead in the seance room. To interfere continually with a dead soul in this way is to risk doing it very great injury for it may well become 'earthbound', which accounts for certain types of hauntings.

15. *The Death of Illumination:* In this death "consciousness is withdrawn from the Personality and made one with the Individuality and then a man ever beholds the face of his Father Which is in Heaven, even when he himself sojourns upon Earth. Thus it is that the illuminated Initiate is not as other men. Complete Initiation is a living death."

16. "Those who desire the things of the senses and the pride of life use the words 'living death' to denote the most terrible fate that can befall man; but those who have knowledge know that the 'living death' means the freedom of the spirit brought through to the plane of matter. It means awareness of Heaven while dwelling upon Earth. Therefore the Initiate goes to the living death which is freedom whilst still in the body, for death annuls the Law of Limitation, frees the potentialities of the spirit, gives sight to the blind and power to the impotent. That for which we longed vainly in life we realise in death, for death is life and life is death."

17. "To the wider consciousness the womb is a grave and the grave is a womb. The evolving soul, entering upon life, bids farewell to his friends who mourn him, and taking his courage in both hands and facing the great ordeal and submitting to suffering, enters upon life. His first action in life is to draw breath. His second action with that breath is to set up a cry of distress, because he has entered upon the task of life with grief; and his aim in life is to make life bearable. But when he enters the grave he passes through a gateway into the wider life of consciousness; and when the Initiate would pass to the wider life of consciousness, he passes to it through a gateway which symbolises death; and by his death to the things of desire he obtains freedom, and as one dead he walks among men. In the death in life, which is the freedom of the spirit in

the bonds of flesh, he transcends the Law of Limitation; being dead, he is free; being dead he moves with power among those buried in the flesh; and they, seeing the Light shining brightly through him, know that he is dead, for the Light cannot shine through the veil of flesh. While consciousness is incarnate in the body the Light cannot shine through that consciousness; but when consciousness is discarnate the Light shines through it. If the discarnate consciousness is still manipulating its body, then that Light shines through into the world of matter and illuminates men. But remember this, and meditate upon it—the illuminated Initiate is a dead man who manipulates his body that he may thereby serve those who cannot otherwise be approached."

18. This passage refers of course to the fully initiated adept—and these are few. Even so, this does not mean that the adept goes about lit up like a Christmas tree, with pineal gland ablaze like the headlights on a car. The Light is the Inner Light of Illumination, and though it profoundly affects all who come into his environment, it will affect them unconsciously and they will frequently react with hostility. It will be remembered that even Jesus of Nazareth, the most illuminated of men, was laughed at in Nazareth, where his own kin and neighbours could not overcome their preconceptions about his humble familiar origin, due to long habit; and in the city of Jerusalem, he was first hysterically feted and subsequently just as hysterically scourged and done to death.

19. That, in kind if not in degree, is very much the reception the modern adept receives. Though he is unlikely to be physically persecuted nowadays he usually meets with indifference, mockery or hostility on the one hand, and exaggerated reverence on the other.

20. The reference to Malkuth as the Gate of Tears emphasises its connection with the Sephirah Binah, whose Spiritual Experience is the Vision of Sorrow. The understanding of Sorrow is one of the lessons of Malkuth and it

must be realised that it has nothing to do with self pity or sentimentality which are the roots of most human sorrow. The full realisation is implied by the division made by the Abyss; it is the Divine Sorrow which comes with the delays and separations implicit in evolution and in the development of form. It is perhaps best expressed in the German word 'Weltschmerz'.

21. The Gate of Justice is a reminder that it is in Earth conditions that karma is usually worked out, the average soul being largely in a subjective or even unconscious state whilst dead to the physical world.

22. Prayer is an active result of the fact of Faith, as Malkuth is of Binah, the Parent of Faith, so this is probably the basis of the title assigned to Malkuth—the Gate of Prayer. The title Gate of the Garden of Eden refers of course to the original state of perfect creation to which the Earth must attain once more under the symbolism of the New Jerusalem.

23. The remaining titles, the Inferior Mother, the Queen, the Bride, the Virgin have the common denominator of femininity. This attribution is obvious when one considers that Malkuth is receptive to all the higher emanations of the Tree. The Queen and the Bride are references to the relation of Malkuth to Tiphareth, the King and the Lesser Countenance, the Harmony of which Sephirah must become manifest in Malkuth, which is also the Cross of dense matter upon which the Spirit is crucified; thus we have a further link with Tiphareth in the Mysteries of the Crucifixion.

24. The Inferior Mother indicates again the link with Binah, the Supernal Mother, and the title of Virgin could be applied either to the pristine condition of the Garden of Eden or to the condition of Earth before becoming the Bride of Tiphareth.

25. Most of these feminine titles are assumed in the Magical Image of Malkuth which is that of a young woman, crowned and throned. The Throne is really that of Binah

and the maiden can be identified with a goddess of the Earth such as Persphone, the daughter of Demeter, the Earth Mother.

26. The God Name of the Sephirah Malkuth is Adonai Melekh, the Lord who is King, or Adonai ha Aretz, the Lord of Earth. And it must be remembered that Adonai is a holy emanation of God just as is Eheieh or any other of the Names. Thus Malkuth is in no wise less holy than Kether —for it is an expression in manifestation of the same force. If this fact had always been remembered there would have been less unhealthy and pathological forms of asceticism in the history of religion and mysticism. This fact can be seen in the dogma of the Roman Church of the Physical Assumption into Heaven of the Virgin Mary. There is great spiritual truth behind this dogma, which becomes evident when one remembers the Magical Image and feminine titles of Malkuth and also its destiny.

27. The Archangel of the sphere is Sandalphon and his colours are citrine, olive, russet and black. A good idea of these colours can be gained from looking at the skin of an apple. This Archangel is the Guide or Intelligence of the planet Earth and herein lies teaching of very great importance.

28. The formation of the planetary spheres is a subject which belongs more to a treatise on esoteric cosmogony than to an outline of the Qabalah. However it can be said briefly that the planetary spheres were formed one after the other by the earliest evolutions, the Lords of Flame, Form and Mind, who built the initial stresses and structures of form. Each planet was built first on a certain level, for example Jupiter on the plane of the denser spiritual levels; Mercury on the plane of abstract mind; Saturn, concrete mind; Venus, the higher emotions; Mars, the instinctual and passional levels; and the Earth and its Moon on the etheric/physical. Subsequently each planet develops the lower sheaths or vehicles so that they all manifest physically and can be seen in the night sky. Each one though

has to rely on the entities inhabiting it for the higher levels of it to be built.

29. The practical implication of this is that the etheric/physical structure of the Earth, which is built out of the projections of consciousness of Elemental entities, relies on humanity to put it in touch with spiritual realities. As the Elementals are 'creations of the created', that is, they are units of consciousness created by the Evolutions of Flame, Form and Mind and not by their own development from the spiritual reality of the Great Unmanifest, they are doomed to extinction at the end of a Day of Manifestation unless they have picked up spiritual vibration by that time, and the only way they can do this is through the mediation of humanity. As the majority of humanity seems blissfully ignorant of its own spirituality, let alone the existence of the Elemental kingdoms, it will be obvious that the plight of these Elemental entities is a grave one.

30. The sum total of all these Elemental entities which hold together the etheric stresses of the planet is called the Planetary Being. (In some cosmogonies it is referred to as the Planetary Spirit, but in the light of the facts just stated the title is a misleading one, for it has no inherent contact with spirit.) The Archangel Sandalphon is its guide, for he holds the concept of what it should become, and this concept, which has objective existence on its own level, can be called the Planetary Entity. However, the bridge between Planetary Being and Planetary Entity has to be built by humanity itself, and this constitutes one of the tasks of the initiated adepts, though it is really the responsibility of all humanity.

31. The Planetary Being is helped much by the right attitude to earthly things—that is, the application of spiritual principles in ordinary life. The ethic of Malkuth, Order and Efficiency has to be consciously pursued all day long, and it is little use inducing it for short periods only as in ritual working, or regarding the task grudgingly, as a duty or convention. Also, the Planetary Being cannot

be helped much by the intellect, for it has no mind, but it is contacted and helped by what might be called the constant dedication of the instincts. This does not apply only to the sexual instinct but also to the taking of food and the tilling of the Earth to make it bring forth fruits, for all these are sacramental in their correct understanding—and the life of the adept is the sacramental life, dedicated to the greater glory of God, and Man, and Planetary Being.

32. In all these considerations the distinction must be borne in mind between Earth as a planet, Earth as one of the Four Elements, and Earth as Malkuth—the physical plane of the whole Universe. Thus the traditional Archangel of Malkuth is Metatron, the same being who is Archangel of Kether, which again shows the strong link between Spirit as Spirit and Spirit as Matter. Sandalphon is really the Archangel of the planet Earth; and the Archangel of the Element Earth is Uriel.

33. Uriel is one of the great Archangels of the Four Quarters. In the East is Raphael; in the South, Michael; in the West, Gabriel; and in the North, Uriel. The first three Archangels have already been described. Uriel is a great figure built up with the dark greens and browns of Earth and who, in his inner aspects, represents the primeval Light of God Himself, and who is much concerned with the great teachers who have periodically come to Earth. Thus in the East is the great source of healing, in the South the great source of balance and protection, in the West the great source of vision, and in the North the great source of teaching. Uriel is also connected with Michael as a great balancing force and is behind the great cataclysms of Earth such as are described in the legends of Atlantis, Sodom and Gomorrah.

34. In building up the forms of the Archangels of the Four Quarters they are best conceived as great fortresses or towers coloured in the *active* colours of the Element concerned, viz. Yellow, Red, Blue, Green respectively as opposed to the passive colours, Blue, Dark Red, Silver,

Black. Interpenetrating all can be conceived the Archangel Sandalphon in citrine, olive, russet and black, pulsing with the slow vibrations of Earth.

35. One can also build up the Kings of the Elemental Forces, surrounded by the lesser denizens of the Element in whatever form most appeals to the imagination. The King represents what might be called the spiritually illuminated Elemental.

36. In the East is the Air-King, Paralda, presiding over the Sylphs. He can be pictured as standing in eddies of air which are almost like the waves of the sea standing upright on end; air and wind streaming from him in radiant light.

37. In the South is the Fire-King, Djin, presiding over the Salamanders. He can be pictured with waves of heat surging up around him and points of fire and flame searing the atmosphere and reaching towards the ceiling.

38. In the West is the Water-King, Niksa, presiding over the Undines. He can be pictured permeated with moisture and currents of foam swinging round his feet and pouring from his aura.

· 39. In the North is the Earth-King, Ghob, presiding over the Gnomes. He can be pictured with waves of 'Earth-power'—not so much an idea of soil as an intermediate state of matter, slow-moving but vastly strong.

40. The Elements can be conceived of as forming a great Equal-armed Cross, which is a symbol of the Elements and of the Sephirah Malkuth, and in the centre of the Cross one can picture the Rose of the World which slowly blooms with the development of the Elementals and whose dew falling helps these beings to manifest.

41. A whole treatise could be written on the subject of the Elementals alone, for like humanity, they form a whole evolution, as diverse as humanity is diverse. Although they share the planet Earth with man they are little known or acknowledged by man save in folk-lore or literature. e.g. "We who are old, old and gay, O so old! Thousands of

years, thousands of years if all were told." (W. B. Yeats.) In order to avoid superstition one must remember that the forms assigned to them are man-made, for man anthropomorphises everything, including God. What is required however is recognition of their existence and this is best done by an *intelligent* use of primitive anthropomorphism and animism.

42. The Four Cardinal Points, or Quadrants, also can be considered under the astrological headings of Fixed, Cardinal and Mutable. The Fixed aspect is the 'temperament' of the Quadrant and is based on the nature of one of the Four Holy Living Creatures of Kether. The Cardinal aspect is the Great Intelligence behind the Quadrant which is the ruling power of the Archangel. The Mutable aspect is ruled by the Elemental Kings who work through 'change'.

43. The Order of Angels of Malkuth, the Ashim, or Souls of Fire, can be considered as the 'atomic consciousnesses' which hold physical matter together, and the Mundane Chakra, the Sphere of the Elements, has been adequately covered above.

44. The Spiritual Experience of Malkuth is the Knowledge and Conversation of the Holy Guardian Angel. The Holy Guardian Angel is often confused with the Higher Self or Individuality, (Daath, Chesed, Geburah, Tiphareth.) behind the Lower Self or Personality. (Netzach, Hod, Yesod, Malkuth.) In reality however, it is very different.

45. In the very early days of manifestation before humanity had started upon the journey of evolution, the Divine Plan was projected by the Mind of God into the consciousness of the swarm of Divine Sparks which constituted the basis of humanity. With the coming of evolutionary life the swarm broke up to act as individual units and at the same time the conception of the Divine Plan also 'broke up', a small piece going with each Divine Spark.

46. This, of course, is very much in metaphorical terms, but the implications are of very real import. The true Spiritual Experience of the Knowledge and Conversation

of the Holy Guardian Angel is no astral vision but an awareness of the true destiny that each human being has to fulfill as his evolutionary task. Usually this will manifest as an inner urge within a man, and such a one goes through physical life with a mission, he is a 'man of destiny'. Occasionally this impulsion to a definite form of activity may be conceived as a separate entity as in the case of Socrates and his 'daimon', which was probably an aspect of his Holy Guardian Angel.

47. The subsidiary symbols of Malkuth include the Magic Circle and the Triangle of Evocation which imply the actual manifestation of magical work. The Magic Circle is the area of delimitation that the magician chooses to work in and the Triangle is the area in which he conjures an entity to appear. This is more of symbolic than practical importance for the etheric evocation of discarnate entities is a very low form of magic little used nowadays.

48. The Altar of the Double Cube is a six-sided figure though having the implication in its name of ten, the number of Malkuth. Malkuth is of course in itself an Altar, for it is the place where-on or where-in higher forces descend and in another sense an altar is also a Gate, particularly where the whole being is offered in dedication on the Altar of Sacrifice—which does not imply blood-letting though it is equally drastic.

49. The Vices of Malkuth are Avarice and Inertia. The Avarice is obvious, one has only to look at the condition of the human race today; and the Inertia will be met with by anyone who tries to change things, or to do any kind of creative work. The Virtue is Discrimination, which is really the key, and first essential, to esoteric development, for it is not all who cry "Lord, Lord." who are to be listened to —and this includes aspects of oneself besides the charlatans of the outer world.

50. Of the mythological teaching, obviously all the Earth gods and goddesses have great importance with regard to the Sephirah Malkuth. Demeter and Persephone perhaps

most of all, for these were the deities of the Eleusinian Mysteries which was one of the greatest centres of the inner aspect of the Earth Cult. There is also much to be gained from investigation of the Kabiric Mysteries and the gods of the Underworld.

51. This concludes our analysis of the Ten Holy Sephiroth, and Malkuth has taken up much space and could easily take up far more, for we are beings immersed within that sphere whether we like it or not, and it is one of the most important of the whole Tree for it is the Gateway to all further spiritual development, and until the lessons of Malkuth are well and truly learnt, the paths of the higher spheres must be closed to us.

52. It is a very human tendency to take a greater interest in what is remote, but in occultism as in all things, it is the next step which counts. And that step, for all of us, is right before us, in the physical world, Malkuth.

Part   III

Chapter XVII

THE FLEXIBILITY OF THE TREE

1. We have now covered the individual Sephiroth of the Tree of Life by means of a general analysis of certain of the potencies that come under the heading of each one. Basically a Sephirah is a Divine Emanation and this is the real core of the whole matter. All the attributions besides the Divine Names are really applications of the abstract formulae of the Sephiroth in various contexts. Thus any particular attribution should not be regarded as a hard and fast ruling, for much depends upon the manner in which the Tree of Life is applied to various factors of manifestation. Flexibility of mind must always be striven for if the Tree of Life is to be used to its full potential.

2. Generally speaking, we have in our analysis applied the Tree of Life to the manifestation of our own spiritual Universe, that is, with the Solar Logos in Kether and the material world of the Solar System in Malkuth. However, Malkuth could also be applied to the whole physical plane in general, whether in the Solar System or out of it, and in this way Kether would be the sphere of the Supreme God over all Logoi. Or, if the Sephirah Malkuth is applied to the planet Earth only, then Kether could be the Sephirah of the Planetary Logos. In the microcosm, which is man, Malkuth could be taken to be the physical body and then Kether would be man's Spirit or Divine Spark.

3. Thus it will be seen that there is a Tree of Life in every Sephirah. For if Kether be taken to represent the high spiritual being who is the fount of all Creation or of a System of Solar Systems, the Atziluthic level of Tiphareth

could then be ascribed to a Solar Logos and the Atziluthic level of Malkuth to a Planetary Ruler. But as a Planetary Ruler has a whole spiritual hierarchy dependent upon it then it demands a whole Tree to categorise that hierarchy, which Tree would be entirely in the Malkuth of the greater Tree.

4. The number of ways in which the Tree can be applied then is almost infinite and one could say that cosmically speaking, the whole Tree of Life we use as a system of mystical development is but the Malkuth of a Cosmic Tree. When one has attained the infinitely high state of consciousness known as Union with God, one has only obtained the freedom of the lowest Cosmic plane, and thus one starts off on higher Cosmic evolution in the Cosmic Malkuth.

5. All this is really of consequence only to the advanced esoteric student, and even then the interest can be largely only academic, for the Solar Logos is the Conditioner and Sustainer of our spiritual Universe and we can know directly nothing which is outside our Logos' jurisdiction. All outside is mediated to us via the Solar Logos, and our prime task is evolution within this system. There will be all eternity to get to grips with the extra-Logoidal aspects of the Cosmos when we have finally achieved our goal within this Logoidal system.

6. However, speculation in these matters is not entirely useless for some idea, however vague, of our Cosmic destiny can act as a balancing sense of spiritual proportion when 'the world is too much with us'.

7. The lower aspects of the means by which changes may be rung on the significances of the Sephiroth can, however, be of more immediate use to us.

8. If the four functions of the Jungian psychology are applied to the lower Sephiroth, they fit in well as follows: Intuition to Tiphareth, Feeling to Netzach, Intellect to Hod and Sensation to Malkuth. Alternatively, they could be aligned with the Elements in Malkuth, Intuition to Air, Feeling to Water, Intellect to Fire and Sensation to Earth.

In this case there is a useful line of speculation in the Cardinal, Fixed and Mutable aspects of the Four Elemental Quadrants as applied to the Jungian psychic functions.

9. On the other hand, the Jungian archetypes could be experimentally aligned with various Sephiroth. The anima to Netzach and the animus to Hod for example. Here there is an interesting hint that the projectors of each archetype are of different sexual polarity, for Netzach is on the Masculine Pillar and Hod on the Feminine when the glyph of the Pillars is applied to the Tree.

10. The Miraculous Child would probably best be aligned with Tiphareth, the Wise Old Man possibly with Chesed and the Shadow with Geburah. The Friend could be an aspect of the Holy Guardian Angel of Malkuth.

11. The Mandala, as an integration symbol is pretty obviously a Tiphareth symbol, and using the implications of the Tree, it can be visualised as a reflection of the true being in Kether, and it is found of course reflected in the 'Magic Mirror' of the subconsciousness in Yesod.

12. When mythological figures crop up in Jungian analysis they can of course be aligned Sephirothically as has already been tentatively suggested in our examination of the Sephiroth.

13. To illustrate a further method of applying the Tree we can turn to the Eastern system of etheric chakras. These all apply to the etheric body and thus could be described as a delineation of the Tree in Yesod, or, as they have relationships with the endocrine glands, in Malkuth.

14. The Muladhara Chakra, a 'lotus' of four petals situated at the base of the spine can be assigned to Malkuth; the Svadisthana Chakra situated at the generative organs would then be in Yesod. The Manipura and Anahata Chakras, having their correspondence in solar plexus and heart, would be applied to Tiphareth, although there is a good case to be made for assigning the former to the upper ranges of Yesod. The Visuddhu Chakra of the larynx and the Ajna Chakra between the eyes have been assigned to

Binah and Chokmah respectively, but it is perhaps best to keep these attributions to the Central Sephiroth, which correspond to the upright line of the spine—they would thus unite their function, as do Binah and Chokmah, in Daath. Finally, the Sahasrara Chakra, the Thousand-petalled Lotus above the head obviously corresponds to Kether, the Crown.

15. In all these methods of application there are no hard and fast rules, for much depends upon the individual understanding of the person making the attributions. The suggestions put forward here are not meant to be in any way authoritative but are mentioned merely to suggest the method by which the Tree of Life can be applied to non-Hebraic systems.

16. Also, once a good conception of the Tree has been grasped, by formulating what would be the mode of action of a Sephirah within a Sephirah, further subtleties can be deduced. Indeed, the Sephiroth could be conceived like Chinese boxes, each one having a whole Tree in it, and each Sephirah of that Tree having a further Tree within it, and so on ad infinitum.

17. Too great refinement of course defeats its own purpose but it can be a good exercise to take this process one stage at any rate and consider all the Sephiroth in each Sephirah. This will give over one hundred different categories if applied to the whole Tree and it is unlikely that there would be much use in going onto the second stage and producing over a thousand of them, though the skilled numerologist might find interesting data.

18. As a start one could try to conceive the action of the Three Pillars in each Sephirah, that is, the active, passive and equilibrated mode of function of the Sephirah. One could then proceed to analyse each one according to its four levels; and from this the next stage of formulating the different Sephiroth in a Sephirah is not such a formidable step.

19. Biblical numerical symbolism derives very much from the Qabalah, though one must remember that the

early Qabalists considered there to be ten Sephiroth only, as Daath was not then considered a Sephirah in its own right. Thus the number forty, which appears in the context of the Deluge, the Exodus of the Jews from Egypt, and the time Our Lord spent in the Wilderness, has relevance to the four levels of each of the ten Sephiroth. The numbers four, seven, ten, twelve and the result of multiplying these numbers, as in forty, onehundred, onehundred and twenty, onehundred and fortyfour, onethousand, onehundred and fortyfour thousand, etc. occur most frequently in Biblical literature. All this is really a specialist study but it can be interesting to do a little speculative meditation, bearing in mind the four Qabalistic worlds, the four Holy Living Creatures and Elements, the seven planes and the seven Sephiroth of the 'magical circuit', the ten Sephiroth, the twelve signs of the Zodiac and so on.

20. In relation to the reference to the magical circuit of seven Sephiroth—i.e. Daath, Chesed, Netzach, Yesod, Hod, Geburah and Tiphareth.—it may be objected that Daath was not one of the original Sephiroth. However, there was a well known seven-fold division of the Tree of Life which was used by the early Qabalists, known as the Seven Palaces. In this the Supernal Triad is counted as one, Yesod and Malkuth as one, and the remaining Sephiroth, excluding Daath of course, one each. We have seen that Daath is really the point of contact with form of the Supernal forces, and also that Yesod and Malkuth, etheric and physical, are very intimately related; thus for practical purposes it is quite in order to use Daath as a Sephirah in this manner, and indeed it is very useful to do so, provided one remembers to keep to the middle way between inaccuracy and pedantry.

21. It cannot be stated too often that the Tree of Life is a living system, and life depends upon use and efficient function. And anyone who reads much in old books on the Qabalah will find a considerable amount of dead wood. Whilst having the sense to discard this it is also essential

to put one's creative energy into developing new branches on the Qabalistic Tree—as long as the new growth is not of a parasitic and fungoid nature which will have to be lopped off by subsequent generations.

22. It can be useful to play about with the concepts of the Tree as a kind of parlour game in order to gain flexibility in its use. Thus one could try applying it to the governmental system of a country. Kether—the Head of State, Chokmah—the national ideals, Binah—the Constitution, Daath—the religious hierarchy, Chesed—the legislature, Geburah—the judicature, Tiphareth—the civil service, Netzach—the arts, Hod—the sciences, Yesod—the manufacturies, Malkuth—the land.

23. This kind of thing can lead to shallowness, for the deeper implications of the Sephiroth are stages of spiritual being, but nevertheless such an exercise is useful, and valid even as a representation of the Tree in Malkuth applied on a sociological basis. It is when one has acquired the facility to throw around the Sephiroth like a juggler playing with coloured balls, *plus* a good knowledge of their deeper aspects, that one really begins to appreciate the value of the system as a groundwork on which to base the whole of one's mentation.

Chapter XVIII

RELATIONSHIPS OF THE SEPHIROTH

1. From a cursory glance at the Yetziratic Texts of the Sephiroth it can be seen that certain Sephiroth are particularly related to others and indeed in the last analysis they are all interconnected for the Tree of Life is a composite glyph of the relationships which go to make up a complete whole, whether that whole be a Universe, or Man or even a Sephirah in itself. It is as a guide to certain of these relationships that other subsidiary glyphs are applied to the Tree of Life, such as the Lightning Flash, the Pillars of Manifestation, the Caduceus etc.

2. The Lightning Flash gives the order of manifestation of the Sephiroth from Kether, through Chokmah, Binah, Daath, Chesed, Geburah, Tiphareth, Netzach, Hod, Yesod, to Malkuth. And in this order of things a Sephirah can be considered positive to the one which succeeds it and negative to the one that precedes it. Thus Hod, for example, depends for the forces which go to make up its forms on Netzach, and is the source of formative influence for the Treasure House of Images in Yesod. Also it will be seen that Kether is the supremely positive Sephirah and Malkuth the supremely negative, so that there is a strong polarity between these two Sephiroth.

3. The Pillars of Manifestation when applied to the Tree divide the Sephiroth into three categories. Aligned with the Active Pillar are Chokmah, Chesed and Netzach; aligned with the Passive Pillar are Binah, Geburah and Hod; and aligned with the Middle Pillar of Equilibrium are Kether, Daath, Tiphareth, Yesod and Malkuth. In the same

211

way that one Sephirah is positive or negative to its neighbour when the glyph of the Lightning Flash is applied, a similar relationship can be conceived up and down each Pillar. Thus Chesed, for example, is passive to Chokmah and positive to Netzach; and Geburah is passive to Binah and positive to Hod; whilst on the Central Pillar, which could also be called the Pillar of Consciousness, the states of consciousness should each influence the one below it and be receptive to the one above. This clear run-through of power from Kether to Malkuth would indicate the spiritually enlightened man, but unfortunately there are blockages for most of us on the way down, which are symbolised by the Abyss at the Daath level, the Veil of Paroketh above Tiphareth and the Gulf below Tiphareth, to say nothing of the noxious influences arising from the Qliphothic Pit below Malkuth.

4. The relationship between the Sephiroth of the Central Pillar is also stressed in that each one is assigned to the Element of Air, with the exception of Malkuth, which is Earth. Air is a symbol for consciousness and Earth is the final dense concretion which is implied by Malkuth. The Sephiroth of the Side Pillars are assigned to the Elements of Fire and Water, according to their activity or passivity. Thus Chokmah is assigned to Fire and Binah to Water. It is interesting to note that the assignation of Fire and Water does not apply all the way down each Pillar of Activity or Passivity. The Fire Sephiroth are Chokmah, Geburah and Netzach. This introduces the relationship, and positivity and negativity, between the diagonally opposite Sephiroth. Thus the organising powers of Chesed are reflected from the ideas of form in Binah, and influence the lower forms of Hod; and the fiery motivating quality of Geburah is reflected from the primal force of Chokmah, and influences the vitality of the diverse forces of Netzach.

5. Most of these relationships are covered by the interlinking Paths of the Tree and the correct understanding of these Paths depends much on an understanding of the

Sephiroth they join, just as a full understanding of a Sephirah depends much on an understanding of the Paths leading to and from it and the Sephiroth at the further end of these Paths.

6. The ideas of the polarity of the Pillars is also implicit in the division of the Tree into Triads. The unity of Kether is divided in the next lower plane into the opposites of Chokmah and Binah, which are resumed into unity on the next lower plane in Daath. Still descending the planes, the unity of Daath divides into the polar opposites of Chesed and Geburah, resumed again into unity in Tiphareth, to divide again into the lower polar opposites of Netzach and Hod, finally to assume unity again in Yesod and Malkuth. In this lies much teaching on the degradation or sublimation of force to and from each of the seven planes. The term 'degradation' is not used pejoratively of course, but in the technical sense of 'stepping down'.

7. The Caduceus shows this principle in another manner. At the head is the symbol of fertility, the pine cone, in Kether—and at the bottom, the lower symbol of fertility, the sign of Scorpio, the Scorpion. The special spiritual nature of Chokmah and Binah is shown by the outspread wings which cover them, and the lower Sephiroth are shown to be in polarity by the intertwined snakes, whose tails join in Malkuth and whose heads meet in Daath, whilst they also overlap at Yesod and Tiphareth. The coils of the dark snake pass through the diagonal opposites of Chesed and Hod and the coils of the bright snake through Geburah and Netzach. The bright and dark colours of the snakes indicate force and form potencies respectively, which is confirmed by the nature of the side Sephiroth which each passes through.

8. There are also threefold, fourfold and sevenfold Qabalistic groupings of the Sephiroth on the Tree, which have been previously mentioned.

9. The threefold grouping consists of the Vast Countenance, the Lesser Countenance, and the Bride. The Vast

Countenance, Arik Anpin, or Macroprosopos consists of Kether essentially, but also includes Chokmah and Binah as the Supernal Father and Supernal Mother aspects of this Vast Countenance. The Lesser Countenance, Zaur Anpin, or Microprosopos is centred in Tiphareth but includes the Sephiroth which encircle it. The Bride of Microprosopos is the remaining Sephirah, Malkuth. Applied to the microcosm, which is man, this division gives the alignment of the Sephiroth with the Spirit, the psyche, and the physical body and environment. In this system Zaur Anpin is sometimes called the King, and Malkuth therefore the Queen. Malkuth may also be called the Terrestrial Eve or the Lesser Mother to distinguish it from the Supernal Mother, Binah.

10. The fourfold grouping is the system of the Four Worlds, Atziluth, Briah, Yetzirah and Assiah. These are usually translated as the Archetypal World, the Creative World, the Formative World and the Material World respectively. Atziluth consists of Kether; Briah, of Chokmah and Binah; Yetzirah, the central group of Sephiroth; and Assiah, Malkuth. This is basically similar to the threefold division except that a differentiation is made within the spiritual realms of Kether, Chokmah and Binah.

11. The sevenfold system is called 'The Seven Palaces' and includes the three Supernals in one palace, Yesod and Malkuth also together in one, and assigns one palace to each of the other Sephiroth, with the exception of Daath, which is not considered as a Sephirah in this classification.

12. We have already mentioned dividing the Tree into Triads by considering the alternate unity and division into polar opposites on alternate planes. However there are three main Qabalistic Triads, consisting of one upward pointing triangle, Kether, Chokmah, Binah, and two downward pointing ones, Chesed, Geburah, Tiphareth, and Netzach, Hod, Yesod. These were originally translated by Mathers as the Intellectual World, the Moral World and the Material World. With the possible exception of the

Moral World, these terms can be very misleading. Mathers' Intellectual World could better be called the Archetypal, Supernal or Spiritual World, and the Material World is unsatisfactory as a title for the Material World is essentially Malkuth. Dion Fortune has suggested calling the lowest triad the Astral World, though this is by no means an ideal title. One could suggest calling it the Form or the Psychological World, but the important factor is not really the name, but what one understands by the triad—and there does not seem to be any one word which covers all the implications of these three Sephiroth.

13. Another method of conjoining the Sephiroth is to describe the Star of David or interlaced triangles about Tiphareth. Thus Chesed, Geburah, and Yesod form one triangle, and Daath, Netzach, and Hod form the other. The principle of the Interlaced Triangles is an important one in spiritual progress. The soul or Higher Self or Individuality is symbolised by a downward pointing triangle which projects into incarnation its Lower Self or Personality, symbolised by the upward pointing triangle. In the unevolved man there is no contact between lower and higher consciousness and so the triangles are drawn separately, one above the other. During the process of uniting higher and lower consciousness however, the process is symbolised by the two triangles gradually overlapping until eventually, in the fully illuminated man, they form the Star of David. This signifies the lower consciousness striving to reach up to the levels of Daath awareness, and the higher consciousness striving to make itself effective and functional in the lower worlds.

14. It would also be possible of course to describe a six rayed star centred about Daath or to construct five pointed stars depending from Kether or Daath. Furthermore one can attempt to fit all manner of symbols graphically to the Tree, such as the planetary signs for example. This practice may give some interesting hints or may prove in many cases abortive, but it makes quite an interesting diversion,

and whilst the parlour game attitude is not a good one to maintain in occultism, such intellectual diversions do make for familiarity and flexibility in using the aspects of the Tree, and this is all very much to the good.

Chapter XIX

THE ESOTERIC GRADES

1. The subject of Esoteric Grades has probably caused more foolishness and misunderstanding than any other branch of esoteric learning.

2. In any esoteric group which uses the graded system it must be remembered that all the grades are largely arbitrary, in the lower stages at any rate. Thus an occult fraternity may have a hierarchical system of grades adequately functioning, but another fraternity, perhaps working at a higher or deeper level, would have similar grades but they would all be correspondingly higher, in function if not in name, than those of the first fraternity. Consequently, if a fraternity suddenly breaks new ground, and winds up successfully the previous phase of its group development, it is often necessary for the whole group to be dropped down to the lowest grade and then, having established foundations on the new higher level, to commence building the structure of a new graded hierarchy.

3. From these considerations it will be seen that a neophyte in one fraternity might well be much more spiritually advanced than a neophyte in another. Also, in any genuine group it is necessary for all newcomers to start from the lowest grade and work their way up, eventually finding their own level. In this way a very advanced person may be in the lower grades for some time. So a distinction must be made also between the inner grade, which is the true capability of that person, and the outer grade, which often depends mainly on the date on which they entered a fraternity, it usually taking at

least a year to get through each of the lower grades.

4. With regard to the inner grade there will also be differences of grade within the psychological aspects of one person. Thus he might be able to function at a high spiritual level in some directions and be quite unregenerate in others. An esoteric student, like a chain, is as strong as his weakest link and his advancement should be according to how he masters his weaknesses rather than how great he can be in his strengths. Occasionally though it may benefit a person to be put up to a higher grade, even though his weaknesses do not justify it, because the stimulus of the higher grade may help him to overcome those weaknesses. Likewise, a person who has a very inadequate personality, may, for his own protection, be taken into a higher grade where the emphasis is on the higher consciousness rather than the lower. If he were left in a low grade which brought forces to bear mainly upon the lower levels, the personality might suffer injury. Such a case as this would be rare and only applied where a high grade soul had a low grade personality for an incarnation for karmic reasons. Also only a well established fraternity would dare to advance unfit people in this way, and such people would not be put in the highest grade where pioneering work was going on, for the sake of themselves and the sake of the fraternity.

5. This is an extreme case but it applies in lesser ways to most people. For example, except in very rare individuals, there are certain aspects of the personality which cannot be perfected, however long they may be kept in the lower grades, and so people are usually advanced to higher grades in spite of certain more or less permanent inadequacies they may have. These inadequacies will always constitute a weakness to the group of course, but in physical existence at the present time, perfection is impossible. If anyone were perfect he would not need to incarnate.

6. These weaknesses may affect the group in certain ways. In practical work they can be minimised by intelligent

organisation by the head of the fraternity but the results which cannot be avoided entirely are the reactions of the members of lesser grade, who, when they first enter a fraternity, expect to see absolute perfection manifested by the senior members and are consequently disillusioned—though this may be no bad thing for it is an appreciation of realities that is required of any occult aspirant. The other way in which weakness in senior members may damage the group is that it can serve as a channel for evil forces which always act to disrupt a group. Usually these forces will manifest through a member whose inadequacy is that he is an individualist and a perfectionist and who loses no opportunity to ferret out and criticise the faults of others. Evil generally poses as the good.

7. What is really needed in an esoteric group is group-mindedness and a willingness to turn a blind eye to the defects of others and look after the state of one's own soul. This is no defence of laxity in esoteric matters but is an assessment of factors as they are in reality. Individual members of an esoteric group should not indulge in criticism, in thought, emotion or word, for the responsibility for the assessment of the members of the group rests with the head of the group alone. If the head of the group is gravely deficient in any way then there is little the group can do about it. Criticism will not help matters at all but merely serve to speed the break-up of the group caused by the inadequacy of the head.

8. Finally there is the cyclic factor to take into consideration. A person may be able to function at a high spiritual level for a time and then will drop back to a low level. This is quite a normal occurrence, in the earlier stages especially, and it could be said that the person is of a high grade at his peak points and of a low grade at his low points. Generally speaking, the tendency is an upward one however, and as time goes on the peaks and troughs get progressively higher so that what was a peak of achievement for a person, may, several years later, be a normal

level of functioning, or even a comparatively low level, experienced only when he is spiritually 'off form.' Taking into account this cyclic or spiral factor it can be seen that a high grade person experiencing a low point may well act on a lower level than a low grade person experiencing a peak period. An observer, watching the two together in an environment would not be able to assess their relative merits properly unless he could observe them over a fairly long period of time—even assuming his own spiritual standing was high enough not to distort his powers of observation and assessment.

9. It will thus be seen that the whole conception of grade is a complicated one, but there are definite grades which are aligned with the Sephiroth of the Tree of Life. For practical purposes these grades may often be ideal rather than real, but they have to be real eventually for any real spiritual progress to be made. By means of the grades assigned to the Sephiroth one could judge the standing of any group, for its real standing is based on reality. A head of a group might call himself an Ipsissimus, but if he had not got control of the elements within himself then he would, in reality, not even be an Adeptus Minor, whatever he called himself; and he would not be able to initiate anyone to a higher level than he was himself. Thus the quality of a group depends upon the quality of its leader.

10. Incidentally, a functioning Adeptus Minor would hardly have the lack of reality to call himself an Ipsissimus. As a general rule, the higher a professed occultist claims to be, the lower he usually is in reality. There is nothing to stop anyone from claiming to be an Ipsissimus or Magus or what-have-you and 'initiating' people through as many grades as they like to pay money for, but there will have been no initiation in reality. No genuine Adept, (and only an Adept can initiate), will demand money, simply because initiation cannot be bought, it has to be striven for. As a proviso, it should be said that most esoteric schools charge fees for their initial lessons or cor-

respondence courses in preparation for initiation simply to recover their expenses. After initiation, and consequently membership of a group, all that is asked for is voluntary donations, as with any church, and lack of money is never allowed to be a bar to initiation.

11. The esoteric grades according to the Qabalistic system are as follows: Malkuth—Zelator; Yesod—Theoricus; Hod—Practicus; Netzach—Philosophus; Tiphareth—Adeptus Minor; Geburah—Adeptus Major; Chesed—Adeptus Exemptus; Binah—Magister Templi; Chokmah—Magus; Kether—Ipsissimus. The term Neophyte is used to denote anyone who has just entered a higher grade, whatever that grade may be.

12. This allocation of Sephiroth to grades is misleading to some extent for the real progress is along the Paths.

13. Malkuth represents, in that it is the sphere of physical life, the Seeker, who has realised that there is perhaps much of significance behind the world of physical appearances and who has a sense of looking for a quest to follow out. This could be likened to a faint shadowing forth of the Spiritual Experience of Malkuth, the Knowledge and Conversation of the Holy Guardian Angel, and in his search for an esoteric group to study with, he will need every ounce of Discrimination—the Virtue of Malkuth—that he can muster.

14. On contacting a group and pursuing a definite scheme of esoteric training he can be said to be treading the 32nd and 25th Paths of the Tree of Life, from Malkuth through Yesod to the outer aspects of Tiphareth. During this process, which is essentially one of training the personality, his task is to tread the middle way through the conflicting pulls of the forces of Netzach and Hod.

15. In Malkuth, the tests are mainly those of good character as should be expected of anyone in the world—though good character is particularly essential as a basis on which to build the conscious use of the higher powers of the soul. Also, of course, no-one ever leaves the lowest grade, one

222

builds the higher grades onto it. However spiritually advanced a person may be he still needs the good character and mundane efficiency and common sense of Malkuth. Also, it will be seen that the full initiation of Malkuth, the Knowledge and Conversation of the Holy Guardian Angel, which is a complete grasp of the way of one's destiny, is not likely to be attained until a high degree of development is reached.

16. At the phase of development corresponding to Yesod the subconscious mind should be opened up and so at this stage, ideally speaking, a complete course of psychological analysis should be undergone, for to proceed to higher occult knowledge whilst suffering from any concealed pathology or neurosis is asking for trouble. This process is not necessarily what is known as psychoanalysis—but the gaining of a deeper knowledge of oneself through techniques of spiritual psychology.

17. From Yesod the soul undergoes a subjective experience of great isolation, and there may be a sharp crisis corresponding to the point where the soul passes, symbolically, across the lateral 27th Path. This crisis having been successfully passed, the mystical contacts begin to open up, so that the initiate is able to function in vertical polarity with the inner forces as well as in horizontal polarity with the forces of his acquaintances, friends and relations in the outer world. Should the soul succumb to the crisis point he usually leaves the group, returning quite rapidly to the psychological condition he was in before he joined.

18. During this whole process from Malkuth to below Tiphareth, the training is done largely on a group basis, and any defects that have been left untouched are balanced up after, or in, Tiphareth when the training is more individual. Ideally, the initiate who has reached this stage should be of sound mind and healthy body, with no repressed unconscious complexes and with a functioning area of mystical consciousness. He should be neither dominated

by the environment of Malkuth, the instincts and passions of Yesod, the concrete mind of Hod, or the over-emotionalism of the unbalanced Netzach. This, of course, is a counsel of perfection and rarely manifest in practice, though it is the goal which must be most ardently striven for. According to how its members measure up to this ideal state—or the archetypal grades of the Sephiroth—so is the power and effectiveness of the fraternity.

19. Together with this inner process, of course, goes the training in elementary magical technique according to the system used by the particular group. It is proficiency in this which is often confused with esoteric grades in published works.

20. The opening up of the mystical consciousness has its correspondence with piercing the Veil of Qesheth between Yesod and Tiphareth. This Veil is symbolised in rainbow colours and indicates the light of Tiphareth being refracted through the astral or emotional sphere. On the Yesod side it is as a Bow of Promise which yet veils the direct vision of the mystical consciousness of Tiphareth, which is seen in direct vision as soon as the Veil is passed.

21. The next step is an important one and is called the 'Crossing of the Gulf' and it is of the nature of an Unreserved Dedication. It is said that it takes three incarnations of steady effort to attain this point. It is really a leap of Faith, for it means that the values of the soul have to be changed from those of the outer world of expediency, to those of the inner world of principle. After this step has been taken the initiate has dedicated his life to the service of the Hierarchy and he becomes the 'accepted disciple' of an Inner Plane Adept. This involves first, dedication by the initiate, secondly, a period of probation in which his dedication is tested, and thirdly, possible acceptance by the Inner Plane Adept concerned. It should be stressed that the tests are not artificial ones but come about quite naturally in the circumstances of life of the initiate. Also, the dedication at this stage is a Lesser one, for it is recog-

nised that certain very important duties, such as the welfare of children for example, will have precedence over the Work of the Mysteries should the two happen to conflict.

22. The Gulf having been leaped, and it really implies the power to act as an individual without reliance on others, rather than an eschewing of the things of this world, the processes of Tiphareth are undergone—the Child, the King, the Sacrificed God. These processes are the growth and development of spiritual awareness and action until eventually the personality is 'sacrificed' and the initiate works entirely according to spiritual principle, in so far as his karma allows him. Another way of looking at this would be to say that the initiate has a clear channel of communication between his Higher Self and Lower Self, Individuality and Personality, Soul and lower vehicles, Krishna and Arjuna, Evolutionary Personality and Incarnationary Personality, according to the terminology preferred.

23. The soul then proceeds, symbolically speaking, up the 22nd Path of Karmic Adjustment to Geburah. This is a process of facing and abreacting most of the karma accrued within, roughly, the period of historical time. From Geburah the lateral Path to Chesed is trodden which involves the complete facing of karma throughout the whole evolutionary past of the soul so that when the initiate is firmly established in Chesed he is karma free, has accepted responsibility for all his actions, and is in a position to carry out his work of destiny in complete freedom from the results of past errors. This is the grade of Exempt Adept and such a one would have no need to reincarnate and being exempt from his own karma would be in a position to take on and work out aspects of group karma as was exemplified by Our Lord. Generally speaking, this task is better done on the inner planes at the present time, conditions of physical existence being too degenerate for such a being to work to full efficiency, and high grade workers on the inner planes being so few.

24. From Chesed lies the 'Secret Path' to Daath which is

symbolised by the term, 'the Empty Room'. This implies the facing of absolute reality without the veils of symbols or indeed form of any nature. It is an approach towards the formless verities of the spiritual worlds and involves a complete breaking clear of any previous conceptions and form-ties. It is said to be a higher and supreme form of the approach towards Tiphareth, and in the process terrible spiritual loneliness can be experienced for all previous conceptions even of God have to be dissolved until nothing is left, and the soul feels it is on the point of destruction through isolation.

25. Such an account will be of academic interest only to anyone likely to need the services of this book, but it can be imagined that the soul's seeming destruction before assuming the direct powers of the Spirit are a higher analogue of the fears of the personality approaching the leap across the Gulf and the assumption of the powers of the soul, which cannot be completely believed in until they are experienced.

26. The Grade across the Abyss is the Magister Templi of Binah and such a one is complete master of all the aspects of form at every level. Such a grade is, of course, of immediate interest only to an Inner Plane Adept, for such a grade is not likely to be attained by anyone in incarnation. Similarly, it would be of little point to speculate upon the capacities necessary to attain the much higher grades of Magus or Ipsissimus.

27. However, for those interested in getting a sense of proportion with regard to the real significance of grades, 'The Rays and the Initiations' by Alice A. Bailey gives the Tibetan Master's very full account of the higher grades of initiation.

28. For practical purposes however, it must always be remembered that the lower grades are very much matters of function. Also a grade is only attained when the full powers of a Sephirah have been assimilated. Thus although Geburah is assigned the grade of Adeptus Major, an initiate

in Geburah is only an Adeptus Minor until he 'leaves' the sphere of Geburah and is well on the way to the Chesed initiations. Also there is much overlapping, for initiates will have balancings of karma to face, which relates primarily to the Path between Tiphareth and Geburaḥ, long before they have approached even the Tiphareth level.

29. It might well be a good thing if all speculations as regards Grade were dropped, for there is the very human and erroneous tendency to regard them as badges of rank —which is a complete travesty of the whole purpose and processes of initiation. However, it was thought well to include a chapter upon this subject, for the Sephirothic grades have been quite widely published in the past, leading to much ill-informed guesswork which has tended to be all the more rife simply because any genuine occultist, knowing the complexities and pitfalls involved, usually steers clear of the subject. As a result, an element of mystery has grown up quite needlessly, and mystery is one thing that ought to be dispelled once and for all from the perfectly natural process of spiritual development.

Chapter XX

MISCELLANEOUS ATTRIBUTIONS

1. Under the title of miscellaneous attributions we include all references to precious stones, plants, animals real and imaginary, drugs and perfumes, alchemical symbolism, the organs of the human body and so on.

2. Much of these attributions are taken from old books and generally speaking they are not only arbitrary but chaotic. Before giving credence to any ancient texts it would be well to recall the words of Thomas Vaughan, one of the few spiritually well-informed early Qabalists: "There are many Platonics—and this last century hath afforded them some apish disciples—who discourse very boldly of the similitudes of inferiors and superiors; but if we thoroughly search their trash it is a pack of small conspiracies— namely, of the heliotrope and the sun, iron and the lodestone, the wound and the weapon. It is excellent sport to hear how they crow, being roosted on these pitiful particulars, as if they knew the universal magnet which binds this great frame and moves all the members of it to a mutual compassion. This is an humor much like that of Don Quixote, who knew Dulcinea but never saw her." (Coelum Terrae, 1650).

3. The kind of thing which Vaughan had in mind, in his reference to heliotrope and the sun, for example, can be seen by opening at random any of the old grimoires and magical recipe books which, besides being treasured by collectors, are reproduced ad nauseam in modern books on the subject. The heliotrope for example, or marigold, was associated with the sun because of the superstition that

it always turned to face the sun. Leading by some strange logic from this, Albertus Magnus solemnly declared that if any were produced in a church, no adulterous woman would be able to leave the building while it remained exposed. This divine aid to morality may have come about from the notion that as the sun produced life, so any plant connected with the sun, as regards colour, shape, legend and so on, would have similar attributes and so could be used either as a sexual stimulant or perhaps as a moral antidote to this wholesale sexual rejuvenation in the more subtle ways mentioned above.

4. Correspondences can be made between the Sephiroth and various plants, animals etc. but it must be remembered that the correspondences are only psychological devices which can be used either as a technical exercise in playing about with the concepts of the Tree, or as a means of concentrating the focus of the conscious mind in meditation or ritual magic.

5. Crowley, for example, has made exhaustive lists of correspondences in '777' but they are really of no use to anyone except to Crowley himself, and he is dead. The best that can be made of them is by the technical exercise of going through them and trying to think out why they were so attributed, and even so one will be learning less about the Qabalah than about how Crowley's mind worked. In his list of animals, real and imaginary, for example, one can see that God, Man and Woman relate to Kether, Chokmah and Binah. The attribution of the Unicorn to Chesed is less obvious, but the Basilisk is related to Geburah no doubt because its glance turned people to stone. Though in this case there is an obvious parallel with the Medusa, which is part of the Perseus myth and thus perhaps better related to Daath. To Tiphareth he relates the Phoenix, the Lion and the Child. The Child is one of the Magical Images and the Lion is there because Leo is a Solar astrological sign and also 'King of the Beasts', while the Phoenix, in that it rises from its own ashes, corresponds

to the Sacrificed and Resurrected God of Tiphareth. Crowley could also have included the Pelican, an obvious Tiphareth bird because of its associations with sacrifice; it was said to pierce its own breast with its beak in order to feed its young and was often likened to Christ. The Lynx Crowley applies to Netzach because it is an animal sacred to Venus, whilst the Hermaphrodite is the Magical Image of Hod. The Jackal's relation to Hod may have a Qliphothic basis. The Elephant is one of the classical creatures said to support the world and thus is related to The Foundation, Yesod, whilst the Sphinx is placed in Malkuth either because it contains beasts related to the Four Elements or because it was traditionally at the portal of the Egyptian Mystery Temple below the Pyramids.

6. Whilst one can see the reason for most of the attributions there are many others that could be made with equal validity, and frankly, with equal little point. Some of Crowley's attributions are taken from visions he had whilst working on certain parts of the Tree but that means only that they were significant for Crowley in that context at that time. Arbitrary symbols are not made universal by the simple process of putting them in print. Writers on occultism seem to love to fly to tabular information but in so doing they do more harm than service, for tabular information does nothing but appeal to the type of mind that delights in making imaginary journeys with the use of old railway timetables. And though much of the spiritual journeys of the Qabalah are done in the imagination, it is the creative imagination that is needed to gain any benefit, not the second-hand imagination of juggling about with someone else's data.

7. The whole purpose of symbolism is that, like coinage, it stands for something real. Symbolism, like money, is meant to be used, and cashed in for something of value. Many make the mistake of being esoteric numismatists—mere collectors of symbols.

8. Certain precious stones and incenses are used in cere-

monial magic, but apart from the difficulty of organising it, ceremonial is best left alone by the tyro. Here again, the incenses are largely arbitrary and are best left to the choice of the operator who has some practical experience of their effect on his own consciousness. For general group work, ordinary church incense is perhaps the best thing to use.

9. Regarding stones, for general purposes it is the colour only which is important and so any cheap costume jewelery will do. It is only for advanced work of a talismanic nature that the traditional materials need be used, that is, the metal and precious stone associated with a particular planet. The planetary attributions of the metals are Saturn —lead, Jupiter—tin, Mars—iron, the Sun—gold, Venus— copper or brass, Mercury—quicksilver, the Moon—silver. The precious stones are allocated generally according to colour, their superiority to coloured glass being that the pigmentation is in the atomic and crystalline structure.

10. As regards the symbols of alchemy, the various writings are so full of intentional blinds and accidental corruptions that a high degree of insight and knowledge is required in order to take advantage of whatever teachings may be concealed in them. The position as it stands at present is that if one has the requisite insight to sift the wheat of spiritual instruction from the chaff of elaborate coding, medieval superstition and primitive chemical science, then one has no real need of it, for one will have already passed through the alchemical process. Thus the whole interest becomes purely academic.

11. It is impossible to make a cut and dried catalogue of the various alchemical terms because they vary in meaning from writer to writer. While, as a general rule, the three principles of sulphur, mercury, and salt can be equated with the positive, middle and negative Pillars of Manifestation, the metals with the Sephiroth according to planetary attribution, and so on, this is by no means a universal terminology. Vaughan, for example, who defines

his terms quite well, calls the astral plane Mercury—the 'middle kingdom' of Air; Fire he relates to Spirit; and the material world he considers to consist of two elements only —Earth and Water. It is usually necessary to follow the writings of a particular alchemist right through from beginning to end in order to understand much of what he means. Although it can be a fascinating alternative to reading detective stories or solving crossword puzzles, the general study of alchemy involves so much intellectual effort in return for so little practical knowledge that it is best left either to the expert of the dilettante. The expert can gain some interesting philosophical insights from some of the more spiritually orientated alchemists, whilst the dilettante is best employed playing about with the vast mass of harmless alchemistic literature than dabbling with ceremonial magic, hypnotic trances, Yoga postures and breathing exercises and so on, where he can run into hot water far exceeding the unpleasantness of any alchemist's Balneum Mariae.

Chapter XXI

THE QLIPHOTH

1. The word Qliphoth means 'harlots' or 'shells' and as a philosophical Qabalistic concept need not keep us long. Anyone who wishes to see the Qliphothic demons at work has no need to undertake the mighty conjurations of Abramelin the Mage, he has only to take a look around the nearest hospital, lunatic asylum, prison, brothel, or slum. When compared to such depravities as Belsen and Auschwitz, or the general by-products of modern politics such as nerve gas, napalm bombs, total warfare, atomic fall-out, brainwashing etc., the old fashioned witch or black magician out on a sex-kick seems very small fry.

2. The Orders of Demons of the Qabalah are generally personifications of the Vice of a Sephirah, or a principle opposite to that for which the Sephirah stands. Thus the Contending Heads of Thaumiel are applied to Kether as a denial of Divine Unity; Chokmah is given to Ghagiel—the Hinderers in like manner, and the Silence of Binah is perverted into Satariel—meaning 'Hiding'. The benevolent ruling sphere of Chesed has the Smiters, and Geburah, the Flaming ones, while the Harmony of Tiphareth is shattered by Thagirion—the Litigation. The forces of Netzach are scattered by the Raven of Dispersion, and Falsity, the Vice of Hod, is exemplified by Samael, the False Accuser. The Foundation of Yesod is the Obscene Ass and the overpowering lust of material values is the domain of Lilith—the Woman of Night.

3. Whatever evil is, and it is probably impossible of complete definition, its manifestations generally appear as a

denial of unity—the Dual Contending Forces, the Litigation, the Hinderers, the Raven of Dispersion and so on, or the Crowd of Gods, Worthlessness and Uncertainty applied to the Veils of Negative Existence. The one persistent claim of the mystics is the sense of synthesis and unity and the fact that separation is an illusion. It can be seen then that the words of Christ giving the two new Commandments were a direct attempt to seal the door of evil: "The first of all the commandments is, Hear, O Israel; The Lord our God is one Lord: and thou shalt love the Lord thy God with all thy heart, and with all thy soul, and with all thy mind, and with all thy strength; this is the first commandment. And the second is like, namely this, Thou shalt love thy neighbour as thyself. There is none other commandment greater than these." These sentences contain the complete answer to all the world's problems—so much so, that any other writing on morals, ethics, sociology etc. seems not only an impertinence, but superfluous.

4. It is obvious that these simple spiritual rules are no more considered today as a basis for action than they were on the day they were uttered. Perhaps they are too simple to be taken seriously by the involved pride of men's minds, or the tangled confusion of their emotions—for the more spiritual a thing, the simpler it is.

5. It has been stated that the Qliphothic forces were generated quite naturally by the period of unbalance between the establishment of one Sephirah and another. The Tree of Life is, however, a glyph of the Plan of God and thus there can be no evil in it. The evil arose from deviations, by man and other beings, from this Divine Plan and so any Sephirothic attributions are purely secondary considerations.

6. The Judaic mind liked to systematise all the forces of evil as well as the forces of good, but meditation work upon the Orders of Devils, Demons, Arch-demons and so on is better left alone. Man already has much evil within him without concentrating its potency by occult work thereon.

Such work is best left to the advanced adept. For the ordinary esoteric aspirant the best approach to the evil within is, after having recognised and faced it, to starve it, working only upon the development of the good and spiritual qualities. By developing the contact of the Spirit the psyche will eventually be so transformed that there is no room for evil within it. Direct work upon evil forces will tend to set up a polarity and occult link with these forces and this is one thing which must be sedulously avoided.

7. To attempt to do banishing work upon evil forces often does more harm than good. Thus there is the case in the Bible of the man who was purged of one devil only to be obsessed by seven others who flew into the void so created. Spiritual pathology, like medical pathology, is no matter to be trifled with.

8. Occult fiction makes much of Black Magicians but this is but a result of dramatic fictional necessity. The occultist's work is as similar to the descriptions of most occult novels as a policeman's is to most detective stories. The small fry of Black occultism are not to be worried about for they are only out for their own welfare and usually come to grief before they have advanced very far. Usually they fall into three categories: i) those seeking to make money out of credulous fools; ii) those seeking self-aggrandisement from the adulation of ditto; and iii) those after a drug or sex kick. Of these the last are the most obnoxious of the species in that they corrupt the young and also have good opportunities for extorting blackmail.

9. As regards the big fish of Black occultism, they need not worry the ordinary aspirant. If an aspirant enters a high grade esoteric fraternity he may come up against them if he reaches the highest grades but in the earlier years of his training he is well protected by the forces behind his group. Usually, when someone complains of occult attack, it is found that the real trouble is over-imagination or various levels of persecution complex, and scientological processing usually clears them up.

10. If one really feels oneself to be up against any Black occultism, or even any evil arising up within oneself, the best defence lies in calling upon the regenerative power of Christ. However, evil is not usually so unsubtle as to appear as a horrific nightmare vision—the usual method is to masquerade as good. The politicians have discovered this and one can credit the Powers of Darkness with at least an equal amount of intelligence.

11. The evil within oneself usually poses as the good as well. It has truly been said that 'the road to hell is paved with good intentions'—the paving stones are more often the good intentions we carry out than those we do not.

12. The human mind is capable of incredible subtlety in the dodging of the facing of its own iniquity, though if one is very self-observant one can sometimes detect the Qliphoth within through the manifestation within oneself of any strong irrational dislike. The hidden maggots of one's own soul are usually projected in righteous indignation upon others. The beam in another's eye is usually the reflection of the mote in one's own—as has been hinted in another context.

13. The hypocritical way in which the mind works can well be gathered from reading comparatively modern French literature which tends to go deeply into this way of mind-working. Particularly recommended are Mauriac, Marcel, Gide, Sartre, Camus and also such playwrights as Duerenmatt, and the existentialist writers generally, from Kierkegaarde onwards. This, however, may prove a formidable obstacle to anyone who is not already inclined towards modern literature; and those who do not feel inclined to wade through many pages of philosophy and psychological analysis—fictional or non-fictional—with subsequent lengthy introspection upon themselves, are better advised to study the work of L. Ron Hubbard. Scientology is not a panacea; however, it can clear the decks for action quicker than most other therapies, but a person who is 'clear' is not automatically an Ipsissimus—he is merely

236

an unaberrated human being, and this is so rare in these days that it does seem something rather special.

14. The whole structure of man, and the direction of man's growth, is on a spiritual basis—that is, any course of action must be of a religious significance, for spirit is higher than mind or emotion, though the two latter are the usual human criteria of what is of value and what is not.

15. It is difficult to imagine the scientific or academic types of mind swallowing this truth but it will have to be accepted in the end, later if not sooner. Meanwhile one can only set one's heart on spiritual things and maintain eternal vigilance over oneself. No doubt even Judas thought himself to be in the right, he being obviously not the music hall villain of popular medieval concept, but a very intelligent and enlightened man who perhaps thought that Christ was come to be King of the World and that bringing him face to face with the Authorities would cause him to sieze worldly power and institute the Kingdom of Heaven on Earth there and then. There can be a great lesson in this tragic figure.

Chapter XXII

PRACTICAL APPLICATIONS

1. Enough has now been given in the text of this book for anyone to seek out the keys of esoteric wisdom for himself by means of meditation upon the Tree of Life.

2. For the maximum effect to be gained, meditation should be made a regular practice, daily if possible. In fact, one who does regular daily meditation, even if for no more than ten minutes, will make greater progress than one who spends long periods in meditation at irregular intervals. The great enemy in this connection is inertia, but as in all things the secret of success lies in inflexibility of will and purpose—and the fainthearted do better to leave occultism alone.

3. The time and place of meditation are important, for it is wise to let habit work for one, and it is easier to meditate at a regular time and place each day. The morning is generally recommended for meditation, when the mind is fresh, but each person should experiment and pick out a time which suits him best. It is not a good thing to meditate when cold or tired.

4. A good attitude for meditation is sitting upright in a straight-backed chair with the feet on a foot-rest of such height that there shall be no sense of strain. The attitude should be neither tense nor reclining, but poised. This is achieved by adjusting the height of the foot-rest to the length of the leg. A foot-rest is readily improvised from books or a small box.

5. Freedom from bodily strain obtained by poise is to be preferred, in meditation attitude, to freedom from bodily

strain obtained by relaxation, because when complete relaxation is attained meditation is apt to end in sleep; whereas, if sleep supervenes in a poised meditation attitude, the poise is lost and the student awakened at once.

6. Meditation should not be done in a glaring light, as this tends to make concentration difficult. Noise can be overcome by the use of ear-plugs, though, with practice, noise will tend to have little power of distraction. After long practice, one should be able to meditate anywhere.

7. It is important to write down the results of meditation immediately afterwards, for this serves to 'earth' the realisations obtained.

8. Practical occult work depends for its successful accomplishment primarily upon the power of concentration. The student must be able, without effort, to maintain steady clear-cut concentration over considerable periods before he can attempt any advanced working, and meditation will help to develop this.

9. The picturing of composite symbols and the undertaking of 'journeys' in the imagination such as can be done on the Paths of the Tree to be described in the next volume constitute the more advanced work. Clairvoyance, or the seeing of visions, and clairaudience, or the hearing of voices should be the result of tapping the subconscious mind, and they are as a dream produced at will. It must be clearly understood that whatever is seen or heard is going on within one's own mind. If it seems that visions are appearing to the physical eyes or sounds are heard with the physical ears it may mean that a portion of consciousness has been split off. It is unwise to attempt any practical work until this dissociated portion has been reabsorbed.

10. This splitting off is sometimes due to an over-sensitive temperament and sometimes to wrong methods of development, but in any case it is very harmful. If persisted in, the dissociation spreads further through the mind and the whole personality can become disorganised.

11. It is essential to be able to close the psychic faculties at will and return to normal consciousness. If this cannot be done and if psychic consciousness overflows into everyday life, the student is unfitted for the tasks that life imposes and is obliged to live the life of a hermit to maintain his mental and physical health. High grade initiates sometimes undertake such retreats for the purpose of accomplishing special work but in no case can such experiments be recommended for the beginner.

12. Also, while much has been said about astral symbols and forms it must be realised that these are but means to an end and that the highest form of superconsciousness and the most reliable form of psychism is of the nature of hyper-developed intuition.

13. Given below are three other occult exercises which can be used to advantage in addition to meditation discipline.

i) An evening review of the day's events, *from evening to morning*, on retiring to bed. The events should be run through backwards like a cinematograph film with an accompaniment of comment, judgment, resolution and aspiration. If one goes to sleep in the process—and this exercise is a good cure for insomnia—then so much the better, for the mind will carry on the process during the hours of sleep and may yield remarkable results.

ii) A mid-day salutation to the Inner Plane Adepti, or to the Lord Jesus, who is the Head of the Hierarchy of Masters. One should turn the eyes in the direction of the sun at noon, if circumstances permit, and mentally salute the sun as the visible manifestation of the source of all life. Think of God as made manifest in nature; listen in imagination to the rhythm and swing of the solar system as it circles round the sun; think of yourself as a part of nature—as holding your own position in this vast machine and feel your relationship to all the other parts. Then greet the Inner Plane Adepti, or Masters, as your guides and friends. A brief mental salutation is all that is required

240

and this can be given in almost any circumstances. By thinking of the Inner Plane Adepti in this way an initial contact can be made with them and this contact is capable of development as one advances. Think of them as elder brethren, the 'Company of Just Men Made Perfect', organised into a graded hierarchy in the service of God and Man and Earth.

iii) Contemplation, or communion with the Absolute. This is not the same as meditation nor a substitute for it. It is a stilling of the mind, at any convenient time, and opening oneself to the influences of the inner planes. Realise the presence and power of the invisible realities and the goodness and perfection of God the Creator and Sustainer of this Universe into which that Great Being is ever coming into manifestation. Try to see yourself from the standpoint of your own Spirit and then feel the infinity flowing into you, for the sun of spiritual reality is always there and is obscured only by one's own mental and emotional clouds.

14. Finally there is the question of opening and closing the psychic faculties and this is best done by some simple ritual gesture. A circle described about oneself in the imagination together with the sign of the cross is adequate for routine purposes. On closing it is a good idea also to stamp the foot on the ground as an indication of returning to things of the world.

15. For special occasions, or even as a habit, for it is an excellent exercise in itself, one could use the ritual of the Pentagram. This is performed as follows:

16. Stand facing East. Raise the right hand and say, out loud or mentally, "In Thy hands is the Kingdom, the Power and the Glory"—as you do so making the sign of the cross with the right hand, ('The Kingdom' will come at the bottom of the vertical, 'the Power' on the right shoulder, 'the Glory' on the left.), "for ever and ever, Amen." clasping the hands together. Keeping the right arm straight, first and second fingers extended in line with it, lift it somewhat above the horizontal, and draw in the air before you the sign of the

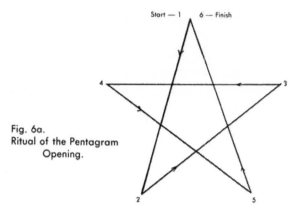

Start — 1   6 — Finish

4   3

2   5

Fig. 6a.
Ritual of the Pentagram
Opening.

Pentagram or five pointed star. (Fig. 6a) The last movement
will bring the right hand back to its starting point. Then
bring it down so that the fingers are pointing at the centre
of the star and say, "In the Name of . . . (God Name of
Sephirah) . . ., I open the East."

17. Now move round to the South, keeping the arm extended so that the fingers describe a quarter circle and
there repeat the Pentagram, but this time say, "In the
Name of . . ., I open the South." In the same way, move
round to the West and North, repeating the Pentagram at
each of these points. Complete the circle by returning to
the East. The Circle and Pentagrams should be visualised
as blazing in the air with a golden light.

18. Open the arms wide, parallel to the floor, and say,
"In the East, Raphael; in the West, Gabriel; in the South,
Michael; in the North, Uriel. About me flame the Pentagrams, behind me shines the Six-rayed Star, (Drop the
left hand and raise the right to make sign of the cross as
before), and above my head is the Glory of God, in whose
hands is the Kingdom, the Power and the Glory, for ever
and ever, Amen."

19. The Archangels should be strongly visualised at each
Quarter in the form most acceptable to the student. The
entire operation can be performed in the imagination if
desired and this is an excellent exercise for the develop-

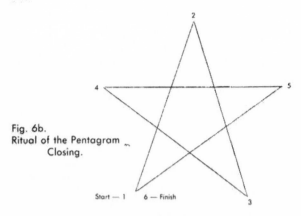

Fig. 6b.
Ritual of the Pentagram
Closing.

Start — 1   6 — Finish

ment of the visual imagination. The phrase, 'behind me shines the Six-rayed Star' is an aspirational one, for it applies in fact only to the Adept beyond the Tiphareth grade.

20. The Closing Ritual is the same, except that the Pentagram is drawn from the left-hand corner in each case (Fig. 6b) and the Archangels are visualised facing out of the Circle instead of facing inwards. For general purposes when the work is not on a specific Sephirah the abbreviated Malkuth Name can be used—Adonai.

21. The exercise of drawing the Tree is a most valuable one, for it helps to establish the Tree of Life firmly in the mind. It can best be constructed by drawing a vertical line and marking off equal lengths along it—say 2 inches. This will give the centre points of Kether, Daath, Tiphareth, Yesod and Malkuth. Then, using a pair of compasses, set to the same distance, (i.e. e.g. 2 ins.) the centre points of the side Sephiroth can be found. Once you have all the centre points of the Sephiroth it is a simple matter to complete the Tree according to Fig. 1. The ability to build the Tree—and hold it—in the imagination is of course also valuable.

22. In the text of this book there is ample material for meditation on the Sephiroth to keep the student occupied for a very long time. Nothing of course can better supervised instruction by a good esoteric school or teacher, but

these are rare and where reasons of geography and so on make this impossible a fair degree of advancement can be made under one's own efforts. And one's own efforts may make the contacts which lead the way towards a particular school.

23. "Ask and ye shall receive, seek and ye shall find, knock and it shall be opened unto you."

TABLE I — THE HEBREW LETTERS 245

a	b	c	d	e	f
Aleph	Ox	א	A, Ē	ALP	1
Beth	House	ב	B	BITh	2
Gimel	Camel	ג	G	GML	3
Daleth	Door	ד	D	DLTh	4
Heh	Window	ה	H	HH	5
Vau	Nail	ו	V, U	VIV	6
Zain	Sword	ז	Z	ZIN	7
Cheth	Fence	ח	Ch	ChITh	8
Teth	Serpent	ט	T	TITh	9
Yod	Hand	י	J, I, Y	YUD	10
Kaph	Palm of hand	ך כ	K	KP	20 (500)
Lamed	Ox-goad	ל	L	LMD	30
Mem	Water	ם מ	M	MIM	40 (600)
Nun	Fish	ן נ	N	NUN	50 (700)
Samekh	Prop	ס	S	SMK	60
Ayin	Eye	ע	O	OIN	70
Peh	Mouth	ף פ	P	PH	80 (800)
Tzaddi	Fish-hook	ץ צ	Tz	TzDI	90 (900)
Qoph	Back of head	ק	Q	QUP	100
Resh	Head	ר	R	RISh	200
Shin	Tooth	ש	Sh	ShIN	300
Tau	Tau-cross	ת	Th	ThU	400

Column (a) gives the name of the Hebrew letter as usually rendered into English.

Column (b) gives the meaning of the name of each letter.

Column (c) gives the form of the Hebrew letter. Some of them have an alternative form when placed at the end of a word. These 'final' forms are given in brackets. There is said to be much esoteric meaning in the shapes of the letters and they are recommended for meditation, though their full significance relates to the Paths on the Tree.

Column (d) gives the usual transliteration into the Roman alphabet.

Column (e) gives the transliteration of the name of each letter.

Column (f) gives the numerological signification. The numbers in brackets refer to the 'finals'. Certain letters when printed large in Hebrew texts take their value x 1000. The whole subject of numerology is a complex and specialised one. There is, for example, the question of the 'dôgish' in connection with certain letters, an accent mark in the form of a dot. This, says Israel Regardie in 'A Garden of Pomegranates', changes the pronunciation of the letter concerned. Thus, he states, the word 'Sephiroth' should be transliterated and pronounced as 'Sephiros'. He also claims that omission of this fact has hampered much Qabalistic research. The crux of the matter seems to lie in the particular Hebrew dialect used. As the Qabalah arose to prominence in Spain, Qabalists tend to use the Spanish dialect. Regardie suggests in 'The Golden Dawn' that serious students might find helpful pointers in investigation of different dialects. These considerations apply mainly to numerological work. In magical work pronunciation has been found to be unimportant — correct and clear-cut *intention* being the main factor. The use of the word 'Sephiroth' is retained in this book as it has become common usage in Qabalistic writings.

TABLE IIa THE SEPHIROTH   Hebrew Spelling

	Title	God Name	Archangel	Order of Angels	Mundane Chakra
1	KThR	EHIH	MTTRUN	ChIUThHQDSh	RAShITh HGLGLIM
2	ChKMH	JH or JHVH	RTziEL	AUPNIM	MSLUTh
3	BINH	JHVH ELHIM	TzPQIEL	ARALIM	ShBThAI
4	ChSD	EL	TzDQIEL	ChShMLIM	TzDQ
5	GBURH	ELHIM GBUR	KMEL	ShRPIM	MADIM
6	ThPARTh	JHVH ALUH VDOTh	RPEL	MLKIM	ShMSh
7	NTzCh	JHVH TzBAUTh	HANIEL	ELHIM	NUGH
8	HUD	ELHIM TzBAUTh	MIKEL	BNI ELHIM	KUKB
9	YSUD	ShDI EL HI	GBRIEL	KRBIM	LBNH
10	MLKUTh	ADNI MLK	SNDLPUN	AShIM	ChLM YSUDUTh

TABLE IIb THE SEPHIROTH English Version

	Title	God Name	Archangel	Order of Angels	Mundane Chakra
1	Kether	Eheieh	Metatron	Chaioth ha Qadesh	Rashith ha Gilgalim
2	Chokmah	Jah or Jehovah	Ratziel	Auphanim	Masloth
3	Binah	Jehovah Elohim	Tzaphkiel	Aralim	Shabathai
4	Chesed	El	Tzadkiel	Chasmalim	Tzadekh
5	Geburah	Elohim Gebor	Khamael	Seraphim	Madim
6	Tiphareth	Jehovah Aloah va Daath	Raphael	Malachim	Shemesh
7	Netzach	Jehovah Tzabaoth	Haniel	Elohim	Nogah
8	Hod	Elohim Tzabaoth	Michael	Beni Elohim	Kokab
9	Yesod	Shaddai el Chai	Gabriel	Cherubim	Levanah
10	Malkuth	Adonai Malekh	Sandalphon	Ashim	Cholem Yesodoth

TABLE IIc THE SEPHIROTH Usual Translation

	Title	God Name	Archangel	Order of Angels	Mundane Chakra
1	The Crown	I am or I become	—	Holy Living Creatures	First Swirlings. Primum Mobile
2	Wisdom	The Lord	—	Wheels	The Sphere of the Zodiac
3	Understanding	The Lord God	—	Thrones	Rest — Saturn
4	Mercy	God. The Mighty One	—	Shining Ones	Righteousness — Jupiter
5	Severity	God of Battles. God Almighty	—	Fiery Serpents	Vehement strength — Mars
6	Beauty	God Made Manifest in the Sphere of Mind	—	Kings	The Solar Light — the Sun
7	Victory	Lord of Hosts	—	Gods	Glittering splendour — Venus
8	Glory	God of Hosts	—	Sons of God	The Stellar Light — Mercury
9	The Foundation	The Almighty Living God	—	The Strong	The Lunar Flame — the Moon
10	The Kingdom	The Lord and King	—	Souls of Fire	The Breaker of the Foundations. The Elements — the Earth.

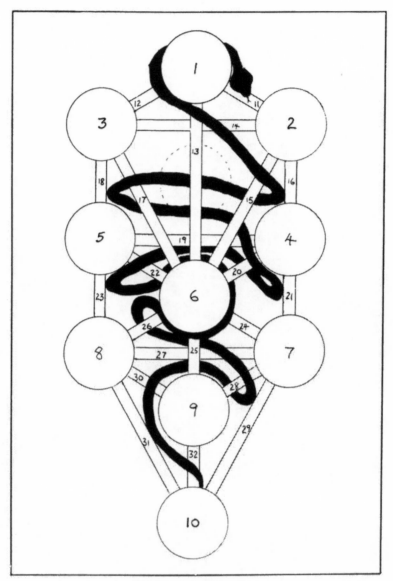

The Serpent of Wisdom

'Let the disciple seize hold of the tail of the serpent of wisdom, and having with firmness grasped it, let him follow it into the deepest centre of the Hall of Wisdom.'

—"THE OLD COMMENTARY"

A PRACTICAL GUIDE TO QABALISTIC SYMBOLISM

Volume II
ON THE PATHS AND THE TAROT

by
Gareth Knight

CONTENTS

PROLOGUE

The Nature of the Paths

THE NATURE OF THE PATHS

In our first volume we considered the ten Sephiroth of the Tree of Life; our present study is the twentytwo Paths that interconnect them. In the Sepher Yetzirah all the aspects of the Tree of Life are called Paths 'the 32 Paths of Concealed Glory' but it is the connecting links between the Sephiroth that are the Paths proper. These are twentytwo in number though their numeration runs from 11 to 32, the Sephiroth representing 'paths' 1 to 10.

Now what do these interconnecting Paths represent? Well, as with the Sephiroth, they represent many things, but the fundamental difference between a Sephirah and a Path is that while a Sephirah stands primarily for an objective state, a Path is the subjective experience one undergoes in transferring consciousness from one Sephirah, or state, to another. Thus the 32nd Path symbolises the experience of consciousness that will be undergone on the transference of consciousness from the physical world of Malkuth to the psychic, subconscious, etheric or lower astral world (according to interpretation) of Yesod. This 'journey' in consciousness can be effected in two ways from Malkuth to Yesod or vice versa and the same applies to all the Paths.

The main symbolism of the Paths is threefold. There is firstly the Hebrew letter, which can be called the Key to the Path for it represents the essence of it in its Qabalistic purity. All other symbolism is of later attribution. The Hebrew letters are extremely potent symbols and it is a definite advantage to commit their shapes to memory, for meditation on their shapes can elucidate much. The order in which they are assigned to the Paths is revealed in the glyph of the Serpent of Wisdom upon the Tree of Life.

i

(frontispiece.) The Serpent trails its way from Malkuth to the Unmanifest and on the way it touches or passes over every Path. The order in which it does so reveals the order of numbering of the Paths, in reverse, and the Hebrew letters follow that numbering.

Secondly there are the astrological signs: three Elemental signs, Air, Water and Fire; seven Planetary signs, Sun, Moon, Mercury, Venus, Mars, Jupiter, Saturn; and the twelve Zodiacal signs, twentytwo in all. The twentytwo letters of the Hebrew alphabet are similarly divided into three Mother letters, seven Double letters, and twelve Single letters for reasons of pronunciation and the astrological signs are attributed to them accordingly. The Elemental signs go with the Mother letters, the Planetary signs with the Double letters and the Zodiacal signs with the Single letters. Early authorities are at variance in precise details of attribution but there is little controversy in modern times, the system used by the Order of the Golden Dawn is accepted by the few modern commentators on the Paths.

The Astrological sign tells us the Spiritual Significance of a Path, a hint of the cosmic factors operating in that particular sphere of consciousness. Again, this is deduced as much from the shape of the sign as from the usual astrological signification. The shapes of these signs are of immemorial antiquity and are said to have been laid down when man used mainly a subconscious type of mentation, so meditation on the actual shapes can again be productive of much.

The Element Earth is not included as this is part of Malkuth. Crowley has legislated for two extra Paths, 31 bis and 32 bis, using the sign for Spirit and Earth respectively instead of Fire and Saturn. This seems, in our view, to be an unnecessary complication. Nor is it necessary to bother about the planets beyond Saturn, comparatively recently discovered. We make no attempt to fit them in because to try to do so shows a misunderstanding of the nature of the factors involved. We are not dealing with things from an astrological point of view, and the seven traditional 'planetary' signs (though including Sol and Luna) are not directly representative of astronomical bodies but are convenient labels for seven types of subtle force which play upon the Earth. As such, an analysis of what Uranus or Pluto might stand for is not germane to our treatise. Whatever the astrological factors involved, they have little bearing on the Qabalistic system, which is a magical rather than an astrological tradition. It may well be, for example, that part of that force we call 'Martian' derives actually from Pluto, but it is accounted for in our magical consideration of Mars; we do not have to have a minutely accurate diagnosis of the actual effects of specific heavenly bodies as does the astrologer.

Thirdly there is the Tarot Trump assigned to the Path. The true attributions have long been a source of controversy and we shall investigate the various claims in Section IV. For the time being, however, we would prefer to draw on no external authorities. If the attributions we use are correct they should be self-evident in our detailed analysis of the Paths, so we suggest that readers reserve judgment until they have studied the first three sections of this book which deal with the meaning of the Paths. They will then be in a position to form their own opinions from a knowledge of the Qabalah itself rather than from a necessarily superficial estimation of the status and knowledgeability, real or imaginary, of the various pundits, whether they be Eliphas Levi, Papus, Wirth, Mathers, Crowley, Waite, Hall, Knapp, Regardie, Case or even Gareth Knight.

This accounts for the major symbolism and our investigations will be based on this entirely, plus the Yetziratic Texts which, though highly cryptic, were of great use in our investigations of the Sephiroth. We also include with the other symbolism at the heading of each Path a list of the Flashing Colours. The same considerations apply here as with the Sephiroth, that is, they can be quite arbitrary. They seem derived primarily from the astrological sign of

the Path thus the King Scale colours of the Planetary
Paths are the seven colours of the spectrum from Mars red
to Saturn indigo. The Zodiacal signs have similar colours
for in their case the spectrum is divided into twelve divisions
from the red of Aries.

But before commencing a study of the first three sections
of our text it is necessary to consider the way we have laid
out the teaching. We managed to get through the first volume
of this work without undue references to such terms as
Spiritual Atom, Individuality, Personality and so on, and
this was done purposely in order to avoid confusion, various
schools having varying terminology.

However, this is no longer possible now that we come to
an analysis of the subjective being of man, though we will
try to keep the esoteric jargon to a minimum.

Briefly, the human being can be divided for purposes of
analysis into three vehicles: the part of him which is
eternal, the part of him that lasts as long as an evolution,
and the part of him that lasts only a human lifetime in
Earth. The first we will call the Spirit, the second the Individuality, and the third the Personality. The Spirit, when
it enters the manifest Universe, has its own spiritual vehicle
which projects into denser manifestation an evolving unit
which we call the Individuality. This in turn projects into
even denser manifestation a series of Personalities with
which it gains experience of dense, worldly life.

Qabalistically, the Spirit can be assigned to the Sephirothic triangle of Kether, Chokmah and Binah; the Individuality
to Chesed, Geburah and Tiphareth; and the Personality to
Netzach, Hod and Yesod, the actual physical body being
represented by Malkuth. There is also a certain amount of
overlap in the linking Sephiroth of Daath and Tiphareth.
The Personality can aspire to and touch Tiphareth in its
higher moments as the Individuality can with Daath. Similarly the Spirit can reach down to Daath.

These vehicles go by other names in other contexts according to the esoteric school from which they emanate.

iv

For example, the Spirit can also be called, or be associated with, the Essential Self, the Monad, or Electric Fire; the Individuality with the Evolutionary Personality, the Higher Self, Krishna, the Soul, the Solar Angel or Solar Fire; the Personality with the Incarnationary Personality, the Lower Self, Arjuna, the Lunar Lords, the Body Nature or Fire by Friction. This list is by no means complete but should give an adequate indication to students familiar with terminologies other than the Qabalistic. We should add also, that in these pages the word 'soul' is used in a non-technical sense, as a general term covering the whole psyche.

In function, the Spirit is, by its very nature, perfect; but on account of what is generally called Original Sin, or more occultly, the Fall, or Prime Deviation, the Individuality is to some extent aberrated. That is to say, it is not a true reflection of the Spirit and thus though the author of apparently the highest motives, these motives may be wrong. As the Personality is a projection of the imperfect Individuality then it follows that the Personality is also aberrated and this should be obvious from common sense observation of the state of the world we live in. Thus the Prime Deviation is the cause of the Abyss and the Gulf on the Tree of Life, those obstructions to the free flow of force from Kether to Malkuth which cause the gaps in man's knowledge of himself. So it is a great struggle for man to link up his Personality consciously with his Individuality, yet this is the first requisite of occult knowledge and power and should have been a natural phenomenon. The same applies with the conformity of the Individuality with the Will of the Spirit which marks the difference between White and Black Magic.

This consideration of the imperfection of the Individuality is an important one with many far-reaching effects. And it must be borne in mind that whilst the Tree of Life is a blueprint of the perfection of manifestation, the True Plan, the actual working out of its factors in terms of human life experience may not be at all perfect. Thus while Chesed should

v

contain a True Imprint of the Spirit as projected from Binah, in actual practice it may not. Needless to say, it will in the end, for there is no doubt about the True Divine Plan coming into objective manifestation on Earth, it is only the time factor which is in doubt, this being dependent upon the rate of human redemption and realisation. Thus we have not only the normal evolutionary path to take into consideration but also the return to the true path of evolution from the false path trodden out as a result of human deviation. This complicates matters a little but we shall deal with it step by step in our consideration of the Paths. It is partly because of this additional complicating factor that the present wave of Western occult teaching, since about 1875, has not stressed the deviationary side of the pattern. The important thing was to get the main simple broad lines of esoteric teaching across. It has led to an apparent contra- diction or division however. On the one hand the esoteric schools teaching that all is in conformity with the Law, the Individuality perfect, (and some even seeming to think their Personalities perfect as well); and on the other hand the exoteric churches stressing the sinful state of man without much rational basis apart from Biblical authority, and in some difficulties about accounting for the obvious pain and suffering in the world. Actually both these standpoints are different sides of the same coin and in order to gain a true perspective we must consider both of them.

In our examination of the Paths we have not followed the numerical order. There is no special esoteric significance in the order we have followed, the order being dictated only by considerations of the easiest way to arrive at a logical, easy to follow, sequence of the meaning of the Paths in terms of human psychology. Reference to the table of contents will explain the reason behind the non-numerical order, and for subsequent ease of reference a numerical index is also provided of the Paths and the Tarot Trumps. Newcomers to the subject are advised to follow the text in the order in which it is written.

Finally, it should be stressed that the divisions of the soul into three separate categories is for ease of elucidation. If there had been no Original Deviation there would be no Abyss or Gulf, no watertight divisions, the true spiritual human being is a Unity. Similarly, the division of the teaching into grades of study, Lesser, Greater and Supreme Mysteries is mainly a traditional expedient. Truth is also a Unity.

SECTION ONE

THE LESSER MYSTERIES
The Paths of the Personality

Part I

The Ways to and from Physical Being

The 32nd Path

Malkuth—Yesod

KEY: ת Tau. Tau or Cross.

SPIRITUAL SIGNIFICANCE: ♄ Saturn.

THEORY: Great One of the Night of Time. (XXI—The Universe.)

COLOURS: Indigo. Black. Blue-black. Black rayed blue.

TEXT: "The Thirty-second Path is the Administrative Intelligence, and it is so called because it directs and associates the motions of the seven planets, directing all of them in their proper courses."

1. This Path joins Malkuth, the physical world, and Yesod, the universal unconscious and etheric web which forms the foundation of physical existence. It is therefore a Path of introversion from the sensory consciousness to the consciousness of the deeps of the inner world. When one treads it one is boring down into the unconscious mind and many and strange are the things that one may meet there.

2. It is like the hole in the earth into which Alice fell, leading to her strange adventures in Wonderland. It is also, on a mythological level, the way down to the Underworld, trod by Oedipus at Colonos, Orpheus in search of Eurydice and many others; but primarily it is Persephone's descent into the world of Pluto, the King of the Underworld. Alice, indeed, might be said to be a modern version of Persephone, for Carroll was a writer who wrote of the deeps of the unconscious mind.

3. The Path is also the way of psycho-analysis and shows the difference between the Freudian and Jungian techniques, for when the unconscious images of Yesod are met with the Freudian tries to analyse them with reference to life history in Malkuth, daily living, but the Jungian process follows the images through until they become symbols of transformation leading to the psychic harmony of Tiphareth. In other

1

2

words, the Jungian technique is, or should be, a pressing on to the 25th Path, Yesod-Tiphareth, after the way-in, the 32nd Path, Malkuth-Yesod, has been trodden.

4. The importance of Persephone is that she was the daughter of the Earth Mother, Demeter, and the whole of this Path is intimately connected with Earth through the Sephirah Malkuth. It is also linked to Yesod, which means the Foundation, the foundation not only of physical existence but of the whole of the higher worlds whose emanations are reflected in Yesod

5. Yesod is the Moon Sephirah reflective, magnetic, of hidden power. In the earliest known version of the myth, the Homeric hymn to Demeter, the nearest witness to the rape, apart from the Sun, who sees all, was Hecate, who, seated in her cave, heard the cries of the virgin victim. Hecate is of course a goddess of the Moon.

6. There is, therefore, a strong connection between this myth and the 32nd Path, and it is significant that this myth was the foundation of the teaching of the famous Eleusinian Mysteries, for as this Path is the way to the inner life it is also the Path of Initiation.

7. This does not mean that psycho-analysis, or the study of Alice in Wonderland, are equivalents of initiation; but they have their parallels, for a Path has many different levels and each Path has to be gone over many, many, times before its full significance is gained. Like the Sephiroth, each, in the end has to be fully understood *and* experienced; and understanding is not a substitute for experience nor is experience a substitute for understanding.

8. The aim of evolution is that each Spirit shall experience and understand the implications of manifest existence. A knowledge of the Qabalah is not essential for this but the Qabalah is a great aid in that it is a ground-plan of all existence and so can be used as a tool in the gaining of experience and understanding. Thus is it said that treading the Paths of the Tree enables an initiate to undertake the work of many average lives in the course of one. And this speeding-up

process is by no means an evasion or easy way out. One can climb the mountain by the slow broad easier way or take the very difficult shorter but precipitous ascent. What is gained in time is paid for with greater danger and greater effort and all reach the summit in the end.

9. Precise details of the Eleusinian Mysteries have never been divulged for the practical methods of all Mysteries of Initiation are secret. However, the aim of all Initiation can be summed up in one word, Regeneration.

10. Regeneration is the bringing to birth of new life and so the initiate is often referred to as the Twice-Born as opposed to the non-initiate Once-Born. This rebirth is the contacting of the Personality consciously to the Individuality and ultimately to the Spirit. The initiate who has the powers of the Spirit manifesting consciously is known as the Thrice-Born, but this process refers more to the higher levels of the Tree of Life beyond Tiphareth for that is where the link in consciousness is made, though of course the results must be demonstrated in Earth. The processes of the Second Birth are summed up in the upward line of the 32nd and 25th Paths from Malkuth to Tiphareth, their main colours being the blues of aspiration. The First Birth is of course physical birth and could be represented by the downward journey of these Paths, daily life being the nadir of these two journeys, in Malkuth.

11. The process of initiation can be taught under the guise of various symbol systems and the symbolism of the Eleusinian Mysteries was that of the growth of wheat. Wheat, together with the honey-bee and asbestos are things said to have been brought to Earth from Venus by the great Melchisedek, and the Mysteries of its symbolism are profound. The symbol of wheat applies to the 32nd Path as the other two symbols apply to the other two Paths leading from Malkuth, the honey-bee to the 29th Path to Netzach, and asbestos to the 31st Path to Hod. Each symbolises a Way, but all, in the end, resolve into synthesis.

12. The wheat grows and is then cut down, the sacrifice,

in more modern terms, of John Barleycorn, or even Christ. Again, part of the grain that is not made into food for man is sacrificed by burying it in the earth, but it springs up again in the Spring, each grain producing yet more grains. It is cut down again and the cycle repeats itself with the Solar year. This process figures in dramatic form in many Earth fertility rites of early and primitive man, but it holds teaching within it of much more than the surface apparencies of sympathetic magic. In the cycle of nature death leads to birth and birth to death and in accordance with the Hermetic axiom 'As above, so below' the same process occurs in the psyche of man.

13. To demonstrate this fact, and the methodology of the Qabalah, it may help us to examine the myth in some detail. The more apparent meaning of the symbolism is that Demeter represents the Earth, as Earth Mother, and Persephone the corn, planted, remaining under the Earth, apparently dead, until it springs up anew and Demeter rejoices, covering the Earth with growth.

14. There are aspects of the myth, however, which are not so easily accounted for by reference only to the processes of vegetable life.

15. Persephone was carried off by Pluto when she was gathering flowers in a water-meadow near the cave of Hecate. There is much Yesodic symbolism in this picture, and this is to be expected, for the Underworld lies in the subconscious and the 32nd Path leads to Yesod.

16. Yesod is the Sephirah whose Mundane Chakra is the Moon, that is to say the Moon is the heavenly body which most nearly symbolises the powers of the Sephirah. The Moon goddess, Hecate, sitting in her cave nearby is an evocative symbol of the elements of the unconscious lying in wait. Also, in some accounts, the companions of Persephone were Artemis and Aphrodite. Artemis is again a Moon goddess, while Aphrodite, though associated with Venus rather than the Moon, is strongly connected with Water, being born of the sea-foam. There is of course an

intimate connection between the Moon and Water, and Water plays a prominent part in this myth for in a probably purer version of it Persephone's companions in the lush, damp, water-meadow were the daughters of Oceanus. Oceanus was a very ancient Greek deity; he was a river who girdled the Universe and gave birth not only to the Oceanids but to all rivers and all stars with the exception of those of the Great Bear. Here we are lifted into the supernal regions, the Great Starry River of the Milky Way, the Waters of Cosmic Space, the Great Sea, Marah, of Binah and so on. Oceanus is a cosmic symbol, the strange lands about his outer shores can, on a lower level, be interpreted as the strange worlds of the subconscious, but they refer ultimately to the outer verges of the Ring-Pass-Not of the Universe and the subconsciousness of the Logos.

17. The flowers that Persephone is picking are roses, lilies, crocuses, violets, hyacinths, narcissi, for the most part sweet smelling flowers reminiscent of the attribution of Perfumes to Yesod. The flower she pulls when the Underworld opens is a narcissus, and there is a parallel between the mythological origin of this flower, the youth Narcissus who peered in the pool, (the Magic Mirror of Yesod?) to gaze at himself, and one of the entrance phrases of the Delphic Oracle, KNOW THYSELF.

18. The God of the Underworld, Pluto, then seizes her and drags her down to his kingdom in a golden car. The Greek conception of the Underworld, a world of shadowy figures, gives a good image of the shadowy world of the etheric place represented by Yesod. However, some hint of the potentialities of death is given in the very name of Pluto, which means 'riches'.

19. Meanwhile Demeter, the mother, sorrows for her daughter and even appeals, unsuccessfully, to the Sun, who has seen all. The Sun is a symbol of the Individuality, the consciousness of Tiphareth, which sees all that occurs to the Personality although it may not have complete or indeed very much control over it. Demeter finally sits in

sorrow and mourning by the Maiden's Well under the shadow of an olive tree. Again there is much symbolism in this image, recalling the Binah symbolism of the Mater Dolorosa; and the olive tree is sacred to Pallas Athene, the goddess of Wisdom, a Chokmah figure. Thus we have a profound illustration of the workings of the Feminine-Side of God.

20. The well by which Demeter sits is a symbol of the 32nd Path and the way into the Underworld and here also we have the water symbolism. The Divine Sorrow under the olive tree calls to mind too another vast complex of religious teaching in that Christ's Agony in the Garden took place on the Mount of Olives.

21. In the Underworld Pluto gives Persephone a pomegranate of which she eats, a symbol of femininity and fructification. By eating of the pomegranate, or taking the principle of fructification within herself, she binds herself automatically to return to the Underworld every year, for only in the descent into the Underworld is new life possible, it requires death to gain rebirth. It is interesting that grief is the experience undergone by Demeter at this time, for grief is also a species of death, a process of fallowing which leads to new life. The pomegranate, a fruit full of seeds, is strongly connected with Yesod. It figured on the tops of the pillars of the Temple of Solomon together with images of the Kerubim and other Lunar symbolism. There is a link here also, of course, with Artemis, the Divine Huntress, a Moon goddess who protected all pregnant beasts.

22. The symbolism of pregnancy and new life was also carried into the Eleusinian Mystery symbolism in that pregnant sows were sacrificed to Demeter as well as fragments of decaying pork, which were later dug into the ground. Decaying matter is the basis for new growth.

23. Death and decay are under the presidency of the Fourth Aspect of God, God the Disintegrator, the other Aspects being God the Father, God the Son and God the Holy Spirit. On this 32nd Path the symbolism is very predominantly

feminine, thus the Feminine Side of God predominates and instead of Father, Son and Holy Spirit we have Mother, Daughter and Virgin Wisdom.

24. In feminine terms, the Fourth Aspect is best symbolised by the Medusa, who had a wild, cold beauty that no man could bear to look upon without the shield of the Divine Wisdom of Pallas Athene. Lacking the ability to look calmly and clearly at the beautiful and terrible face, men were turned to stone; that is to say, they fell into the mortal idea of death.

25. As all the gods are aspects of one God so are all the goddesses aspects of one Goddess, and the one God and the one Goddess are of course the two Sides of the One God, the androgynous Elohim of Genesis.

26. In the fragments of a rite of Isis given in Dion Fortune's novels 'The Sea Priestess' and 'Moon Magic' (Aquarian Press, London) the all-inclusiveness of the Feminine Side of the Deity is given as follows:

I am she who ere the earth was formed
Was Rhea, Binah, Ge.
I am that soundless, boundless, bitter sea
Out of whose deeps life wells eternally.
Astarte, Aphrodite, Ashtoreth
Giver of life and bringer-in of death;
Hera in heaven, on earth Persephone;
Diana of the Ways and Hecate
All these am I and they are seen in me.

And the same source also gives a version of the entrance to the 32nd Path:

Sink down, sink down, sink deeper and more deep
Into eternal and primordial sleep.
Sink down, be still, forget and draw apart
Into the inner earth's most secret heart.
Drink of the waters of Persephone,
The secret well beside the sacred tree . . . .

8

Who drinks the waters of that hidden well
Shall see the things whereof he dare not tell —
Shall tread the shadowy path that leads to me —
Diana of the Ways and Hecate,
Selene of the Moon, Persephone.

27. In the novels of Dion Fortune this teaching is given on its more surface levels of sexual polarity. At the time these novels were written Dion Fortune was concerned with bringing a more open and reverent attitude towards sex as opposed to the cloistered and sanctimonious attitudes left over from the nineteenth century. The Hermetic axiom—'As above, so below'—applies here as everywhere though, and what is written about sexual polarity in these books applies also to the polarity between higher and lower aspects of the psyche and between God and man—which latter includes Goddess and woman, though English grammar obscures the fact.

28. However, while spiritual factors do operate behind the functions of the lower worlds they should not cause the latter in themselves to be neglected as 'improper' or 'beneath consideration'. It is the etheric polarity of sex which has the directest relevance to the 32nd Path and while a knowledge of the spiritual factors is necessary for an understanding of a Path this is no substitute for experience, which, when on the lower levels of the Tree, must and should be of Earth earthy.

29. But the sensory world applies in the main to Malkuth and the 32nd Path is an Inner Way, although still very much connected with Earth. On the personal level Demeter is a part of the self, as is Persephone and indeed all the gods. Categorising crudely, one could say that in the myth the Sun was the Individuality looking down upon all that happens as a portion of the Personality, (Persephone), is drawn into the unconscious depths to be apparently destroyed, to the grief of the rest of the Personality, (Demeter); only to re-emerge later, like the Spring corn, bearing life even more

abundantly. In Christian terms the myth is expressed in terms of the Agony, Trial, Crucifixion and Descent into Hell followed by the Resurrection and Ascension.

30. The teaching is basic to eternal principles and so appears again and again in different guises in accordance with the imaginative needs of the times and the nations. It is a process of withdrawal and return and is dealt with at some length in P. W. Martin's 'Experiment in Depth' (Routledge & Kegan Paul, London) which outlines a method of following the process with reference to the Jungian psychology, the poetry of T. S. Eliot and the historical work of A. J. Toynbee. Toynbee's thesis is that at a time of crisis in any civilisation certain individuals turn from the outer world to the inner life of the psyche and discovering there a new way of life return to the outer world to form a creative minority which acts as a leaven for the renewal of that civilisation.

31. The process is also summarised in a portion of the rite of Isis: "In death men go to her (Persephone) across the shadowy river, for she is the keeper of their souls until the dawn. But there is also a death in life, and this likewise leadeth on to rebirth. Why fear ye the Dark Queen, O men? She is the Renewer. From sleep we arise refreshed; from death we arise reborn; by the embraces of Persephone are men made powerful.

32. "For there is a turning-within of the soul whereby men come to Persephone; they sink back into the womb of time; they become as the unborn; they enter into the kingdom where she rules as queen; they are made negative and await the coming of life.

33. "And the Queen of Hades cometh unto them as a bridegroom, and they are made fertile for life and go forth rejoicing, for the touch of the Queen of the Kingdoms of Sleep hath made them potent."

34. It is obvious from this that the Path of Return is as important as the Path of Withdrawal. In other words, the 32nd Path has to be trodden both ways—the Withdrawal

from Malkuth to Yesod and the Return from Yesod to Malkuth. This can hardly be stressed enough for it is the refusal to come down to Earth, literally, that is the cause of the bulk of spiritual pathology—the root of sin, disease, ignorance. It is the real blasphemy, a rejection of the work of the Father in Heaven, a rejection of the Universe. (The Universe, let it be noted, is the Tarot Trump of this Path.) Until physical existence in the Universe is willingly accepted by the Spirit the Initiation of the Nadir cannot take place. Malkuth is the Gate, the door to evolution and the work of destiny. Evolution cannot take place until Involution is complete.

35. Hubbard has stated that one of the marks of an unaberrated human being is the ability to face chaos or disorder and stick with it; in other words, not to escape into apathy, grief, anger, facetiousness, intellectualising, sanctimony, false mysticism or any other of the myriad methods of running away. As a result of Original Sin this planet is in a state of chaos and disorder. It need not have been, but it is, and this fact must be accepted. The Initiation of the Nadir is the ability to face things as they are, to accept oneself and one's sins and distortions, to accept others and their sins and distortions, realising that the way each has come is the way each has come, and that mutual recriminations or flattering falsifications will not help matters one hairsbreadth.

36. This attitude has been put forward by writers such as Nietzsche and Whitman amongst others, together with a certain amount of varying personal distortion, and it has of recent years even become something of an intellectual catchword—Acceptance. This is laudable in its way but the acceptance has to be a complete and true one, (an attitude of the whole being, not a posture of the mind), for the Initiation to be a real one.

37. The Exemplary Way was shown of course by Our Lord in the Garden of Gethsemane: "And he said, Abba, Father, all things are possible unto thee; take away this cup from

me: nevertheless not what I will, but what thou wilt."
(Mark. xiv. 36) In other words, one must be willing to face,
and go through with, one's own Crucifixion before the subsequent Resurrection and Ascension can be achieved—and
all without fear or attempts to propitiate one's own particular Herod, Pilate, Caiaphas, or mob—objective or subjective.

38. The symbols attributed to the 32nd Path confirm this
process. The Key to the Path is the letter Tau, meaning a
Cross. The Cross is not only the Cross of Calvary but the
Equal-Armed Cross and the Tau Cross. The simple cross of
equal arms is the Point, a symbol of Spirit and Light, ex-
tended in four directions—Light in Extension. It is also the
Cross of the Elements, the Elements being a reflection in
Malkuth of the Four Holy Living Creatures in Kether which
appear at the corners of the Tarot Trump of The Universe.
This card is called The Great One of the Night of Time and
one of the contacts of this Path is the contact with this Great
One, who can be considered Godhead Itself. The small fragment of God-consciousness assigned to each man is the Holy
Guardian Angel, the Knowledge and Conversation of which
is the Spiritual Experience of Malkuth.

39. The Tau Cross is a three-armed cross, that is, a cross
without the upper bar, and besides being the male or virile
part of the Egyptian ankh, symbol of life, it also signifies
two forces impacting on a higher level and producing a
form on a denser level. All form is built up of opposing
higher forces locked together. The shape of the letter Tau
suggests the letter Resh, meaning a Head, but with a downward extension ending with the virile Yod. Thus it can
signify the Spirit, or Head, (a Kether symbol), sending its
force downward into densest manifestation. The downward
projection could also be likened to an inverted letter Vau,
meaning a Nail. This suggests the Spirit nailed to the Cross
of Matter to put it in rather grim terms, but terms which
serve to show the parallel between Cosmic and Christian
symbolism. Being upside down, as the Vau is, is a symbol

12

of sacrifice or reflection—exemplified for example in the Tarot Trump of the Hanged Man—and it is also a visual representation of the Hermetic axiom 'As above, so below'.

40. The astrological sign of the Path is Saturn, a sign composed of the Cross and the Moon, and thus apt for the linking of Malkuth and Yesod. Saturn is considered to be the planet of restriction and limitation and therefore implies Form. It is also a planet of Supernal contacts however and so, as with Malkuth, there is an intimate connection between this Path and the Sephirah Binah, the Mother of Form.

41. The Sickle is also a symbol of Saturn, as implied by the shape of the astrological sign, and this was the weapon with which Cronos (Time) castrated his father Uranus (Space). Here again in symbolic guise is the limitation and constriction of Spirit into Time and Form. The Sickle is also the reaping instrument, recalling the wheat and grain Mysteries.

42. The fact that one's final journey up the 32nd Path will be in the processes of physical death is emphasised in the fact that the popular figure of Death is a skeleton holding a reaping hook. Father Time is another popular figure similarly equipped.

43. The Tarot Trump of The Universe shows a maiden dancing within a framing wreath, usually holding a rod in each hand, and with images of the Four Holy Living Creatures at the corners of the card. There is a scarf about the maiden in the shape of a letter Kaph, said to conceal the fact that she has male genitals and is thus really hermaphroditic. Traditionally, the letter Kaph means the Palm of the Hand, which, according to cheiromancers, reveals character as well as past and future. Its full implications are perhaps best elicited by meditation upon the 21st Path and its other attributions, of which Kaph is the Hebrew letter.

44. The figure on Trump XXI can be considered to be a symbol of the soul, as feminine, or the Spirit, as androgyne. The Androgyne can be referred to the Machinery of the Universe of Yesod. The rods, often spirals, may be either

the positive and negative modes of force which make up manifestation or the principles of involution and evolution. In brief, the card may be said to represent the Spirit, taken on Form, in the frame of the manifest Universe. In Eastern terms, Shiva dancing.

45. The Yetziratic Text of the 32nd Path, which describes it as the Administrative Intelligence, indicates that the Spirit should be in control of the whole of the seven vehicles of man, represented by the planets. In etheric and physical terms these have their analogues in the Chakras and the endocrine glands.

46. We have analysed the Path at some length with reference to Greek mythology but there are parallels in other pantheons which could equally well be explored. Demeter has some very obvious links with the Egyptian Isis—the putting of a king's son in the fire at night to give him immortality, for example. Isis, of course, also searched for her lost husband, Osiris, just as Ishtar descended into Hell to find her lover, but the mythological threads are so numerous that it is impossible to follow up each one in detail. This must be left to the initiative of the student. But once the general principles of the Path are realised it becomes relatively easy to follow out the traditions of mythology and folklore that relate to it. The Qabalistic correspondences often appear in the most unexpected places.

47. There is, for instance, the great Maro dance of the Indonesian archipelago where the divine maiden, Hainuwele, is depicted descending into the earth at the ninth of nine sacred dancing places. The dancers form up in a ninefold spiral about a maiden standing by a deep hole in the ground. The dance commences and the dancers perform a labyrinthine dance about her, getting closer and closer until she is pushed into the pit. Then with loud sacred chanting that drowns the maiden's cries, the earth is heaped upon her and stamped down firmly with the dancing feet.

48. A full account of this dance and its attendant symbolism is given in Jung and Kerenyi's 'Introduction to a Science

of Mythology' (Routledge & Kegan Paul, London; Pantheon, New York) together with an analysis of the whole Greek Kore tradition, which is of course very germane to this Path. The symbolism of the nine is interesting as the 32nd Path is intimately related to Yesod, the Ninth Sephirah of the Tree of Life.

49. The Saturn/Binah symbolism of this Path relates closely to the Divine Mother, the Feminine-Side of God, which in pre-Christian times was the vehicle for worship of the Second or Love Aspect of the Deity, now known more generally as the Second Person of the Trinity, the Son. The full descent of the Spirit into Matter is exemplified by the Crucifixion, the Beautiful Naked Man of Yesod on the Tau or Cross of the 32nd Path. The Path represents therefore the first stages of Devotional Mysticism as well as a Way-in to the inner planes and the unconscious mind. Its main lessons are, ascending, the existence of the causality of things on a higher or deeper level than the physical world; and descending, the acceptance of densest Form limitation by the Spirit, summed up well in Thomas a Kempis' 'Imitation of Christ': "If it be Thy will I should be in darkness blessed be Thou; and if it be Thy will I should be in light: be Thou again blessed. If Thou vouchsafe to comfort me be Thou blessed; and if Thou wilt have me afflicted: be Thou ever equally blessed." (Book 4. Chapter 17.)

NOTES ON THE DESIGN OF TRUMP XXI

The Marseilles Tarot shows a female figure, naked except for a Kaph-shaped scarf, dancing within a wreathed oval. Her attitude, with arms extended downwards and outwards, and her legs forming a cross, suggests the triangle over a cross, the sign of Alchemical Sulphur, and in her left hand she holds a wand. The surrounding wreath is bound at top and bottom with X-shaped bands and in the corners of the card are the Four Holy Living Creatures.

All versions of the card agree in general principle. Levi and Christian are alone in preferring a circle of flowers to the oval wreath, and Christian places the Kerubic emblems at the cardinal points and not at the corners. In Levi's view the circle is the 'Crown of Truth' of Kether. The Golden Dawn have gone on record as considering the central figure to be a misty representation of Aima Elohim in the midst of the colours of the spectrum and the elements placed against the dark yet starry night sky.

Traditions vary in the way the wand or wands carried by the figure is or are held. The Marseilles card shows one, the Italian Tarots generally have one in each hand, while the Besancon Tarot has two in one hand. Wirth and Knapp follow the Besancon tradition and Waite and Case the Italian. Case additionally makes the wands into spirals.

The latter point is endorsed by the early Crowley and they both stipulate that the spirals should rotate in opposite ways. Furthermore they agree that the oval should be a demonstration of the quadrature of the circle, that is, approximately 8 units in height by 5 in breadth, and that the scarf conceals male genitals. Crowley also said originally that the ellipse should be composed of 400 lesser figures and that the central figure should be shining and in the sign of Earth — right hand forward and up, left hand lowered and back, and right foot forward. On the Lady Harris card the figure is shown dancing within the coils of a great spiral serpent, holding the Moon in her hand, and with the Sun above, in the centre of which is the Eye of God. The wreath is made up of the Zodiac and has 72 lines all round it indicative of the quinaries. Behind are a map of the elements and a geometrical solid.

The card is generally recognised to be a universal sign, particularly of the physical universe or terrestrial world. Hall, for example, considers the symbol of a cross within a circle within a blue background to epitomise it. There is some small difference about the arrangement of the leaves of the wreath. They are generally shown in threes, with the exception of Waite, who does not seem to bother too much over details. Wirth and Knapp have them pointing upward, and Case and Waite downwards, as on the Marseilles card. Case and Wirth give 22 sets of leaves, Knapp 24. Knapp also puts the Lesser Arcana symbols about the corners of the card as well as the Kerubic emblems.

The 'Egyptian' Tarot differs in some degree from tradition. It shows a girl playing a three-stringed harp on which is carved a man's head, with uraeus and double crown. Above her is a circle of twelve triple flowers surrounded at the corners by the Kerubic signs, and in the centre a winged lingam.

The 29th Path

Malkuth — Netzach

KEY:	꩜ Qoph. Back of the Head.
SPIRITUAL SIGNIFICANCE:	♓ Pisces. The Fishes.
THEORY:	Ruler of Flux and Reflux. Child of the Sons of the Mighty. (XVIII — The Moon.)
COLOURS:	Crimson. Buff flecked silver-white. Light translucent pinkish-brown. Stone.
TEXT:	"The Twenty-ninth Path is the Corporeal Intelligence, so called because it forms every body which is formed in all the worlds, and the reproduction of them."

1. As is plainly stated in the Yetziratic Text, this Path has much to do with the physical body, the great complex of blood, flesh, bone and sinew that the Spirit uses to manifest in Earth. It is also concerned with the basic instincts, particularly sex, the reproduction of further physical bodies. It is thus a Path in which mind plays little part and so may cause a certain feeling of repugnance in any who operate more or less exclusively in the sphere of the mind, or who, for reasons of what they would probably call 'good taste', do not care to dwell upon the facts of physical life and the chemical and biological factors of their own being in Earth.

2. The mind quite often feels repelled when trying to face the fact that a large part of its functioning is conditioned by factors of brute physical existence — the driving basic instincts of sex and power as postulated by Freud and Adler, and the secretions of the ductless glands which to a large extent regulate personality. The fact of our biological physical roots is one of the things which has to be faced on the 29th Path.

3. This does not mean though that we are entirely conditioned by them, or a mere product of them, as some advocates of Freudian and Adlerian psychology, Endocrinology, Behaviourism and so on would have us believe. The

16

Spirit and Individuality are, or should be, quite capable of controlling the instrument of the Personality in spite of the more animal and more automatically reflex parts of man. We are rooted in instinct and in the mindless protoplasmic regions of physical existence — and necessarily so — but this does not mean that we have no responsibility for our actions. And of course our standards must always change; one does not expect the savage to have quite the fine sense of individual ethics that one should expect from the highly civilised man.

4. The trend of civilisation is increasing control over the instinctual man — 'the old Adam' — but civilised man ignores the instincts at his peril. There is of course an ethic of the instincts shown in wild animal life and very primitive man, and this is to be expected, for the Path connects with Netzach — a Sephirah as holy as any other — from which are projected the forces of God that we might call the Laws of Nature. Man, however, has other contacts with the Divine, represented by the 32nd and 31st Paths immediately, and indeed by all the other higher Paths of the Tree. The influences of these force him forward on the way of psychological evolution, take him from the mere blind observance of the Laws of Nature, of natural man, of the animals, and give him the impulse to formulate and implement the Laws of Civilisation or Humanity. In other terms, this long evolutionary pioneering journey could be called, on the physical level, the Way-in-between — leading from the Garden of Eden, the perfect beginning, to the New Jerusalem, the perfect ending.

5. However, man never escapes from the primitive. He can control it and even transcend it but in physical life it is always with him. The acceptance of this is perhaps the main lesson of the 29th Path. It is a Path of physical evolution, a going back into the primitive past of brontosauri, sabre-tooth tigers, savagery, Nature red in tooth and claw, concealed behind which is the beautiful Isis of Nature in Netzach.

6. The Tarot card assigned to this Path is The Moon—Ruler of Flux and Reflux, Child of the Sons of the Mighty. This card shows a crayfish emerging from a stream or pond onto a path which leads between two towers into a wild range of hills lit by the light of the Moon. On either side of the path are a dog and a wolf and drops of blood fall from the Moon.

7. This is a good composite symbol of the processes of physical evolution, the primitive amphibious forms emerging from the brackish water onto land and essaying a long journey of evolution. The towers can be said to represent the opposite poles of manifestation and the dog and the wolf show the wild and domesticated versions of a same general species. The dog is an animal sacred to Hecate, goddess of the Moon, and the primitive sexual side of the card is also apparent when one considers that to the Greeks the sound of a dog howling at the moon was the apotheosis of obscenity. The blood dripping from the Moon is a reminder of the 'red in tooth and claw' aspect of nature and they are sometimes shown in the form of letter Yods, signifying spermatazoa, the basic simplicity and root of animal life. The Moon is associated with the great cyclic movements of tides on the Earth's surface and also with the growth of vegetation and with the menstrual cycle of woman. This cyclic activity no doubt accounts for the title of the Trump, Ruler of Flux and Reflux. The alternative title, Child of the Sons of the Mighty, seems to signify the primitive Elemental aspects of the Path, the Elemental Kingdoms being 'creations of the created', that is, creations of the Sons of God, not of God, the Mighty Logos Itself.

8. The Key to the Path, the Hebrew letter Qoph, bears with it the symbolism of the Back of the Head. This attribution is strongly suggested by the shape of the letter, which is like the hind part of the cranium with the top of the spinal column attached. The spinal cord is the centre for many automatic responses and reflexes. The hindbrain contains the medulla oblongata, through which pass nerve

fibre tracts uniting the spinal cord and brain, also the cerebellum, which receives impulses from muscles, tendons and joints via the spinal tracts and thus regulates postural activity. One of the marks of advancing stages of evolution is the change of posture from horizontal to the vertical carriage of the spine. In esoteric terminology the medulla oblongata is often referred to as the alta major psychic centre. The intimate connection of the Back of the Head with the physical coordination of the body recalls the description of the Path in the Yetziratic Text — the Corporeal Intelligence.

9. The astrological attribution of the Path is Pisces, the Fishes. In the heavens the two fish are spaced quite widely apart and joined by a long ribbon or string — a kind of umbilical cord perhaps. At one level of interpretation this could be taken to be the Individuality and Personality linked together in the worlds of Form. In early Form experience the Individuality is held captive in Form by the Personality, but as evolution progresses the situation is reversed so that the Personality is held under the control of the Individuality. This is the long-term view of the principle of Flux and Reflux, the ebb and flow of the direction of growth of the Spirit's vehicles into and out of form, and this, of course, is a principle which applies to the highest Cosmic levels as well, giving an insight to the higher significances and possibilities of these psychological Paths.

10. The conventional symbol for the constellation Pisces shows two crescents facing opposite ways and connected — again an indication of the Moon and Flux and Reflux. There is also the more physical interpretation of the symbolism and this is the physical sexual aspect of the Path shown by two labia parted by a shaft. These labia, the feminine sexual organs, are the gates of conception and also of birth. Ascending the Path can be considered a species of psychic fecundation therefore, and descending it, a process of birth to the physical. The source of the power of fecundation and birth is the vibrant Sephirah Netzach, one of whose goddesses is Aphrodite — the Awakener. The sexual aspects of this

Path though are more the physical and etheric sides of sex than the emotional polarity of it, which refers more to the 28th Path from Yesod to Netzach. Aphrodite was said to have been born of the sea-foam, and the sea is the most obvious physical example of the principle of Flux and Reflux. She was carried to land in a mussel shell, again a link with the primitive crustacean forms of life. The use of the crustacean as an example of primitive life-forms emphasises the mechanics of building up Form vehicles about the Spirit, just as the shell builds about the simple living creature.

11. Response to stimuli, the awareness of and reaction to an objective world, has various grades of development. The most primitive form is the reflex action, an automatic movement of nerve cells and the associated muscles which we have already considered under the symbolism of the Hebrew letter Qoph. The next stage consists of tropisms, obligatory movements of the whole animal which becomes common to groups of animals of the same kind. Thus the Group Angels of species could perhaps be assigned to the Sephirah Netzach —the archetypal patterns of every bird and beast. Then comes instinctive behaviour, which is seen at its most organised form in ants, wasps and bees. The beehive is a profound esoteric symbol, traditionally brought to Earth from Venus as a pattern for early man of the goal of civilisation, the co-operation of all for the common good, which is by no means incompatible with the full development of human free-will. The highest form of civilisation will necessarily be composed of highly evolved and spiritually directed men and women and so the improvement of world organisation lies in religion and not politics. And by organisation is not meant the stereotyping of habits of small uncreative cogs in a social machine but willing co-operation in a corporate adventure. Many are perfect organisation men and women, their lives stereotyped by habit from morning til night, but such are almost dead souls, for habit is a killer unless used creatively, that is, in order to release the mind for other activities.

12. There is, however, much of the habitual and the instinctual upon this Path, for it is also a segment of the
etheric plane as will be gathered by the Tarot card attribution of The Moon. In her novel 'The Sea Priestess' Dion
Fortune's hero, communing with the Moon whilst convales-
cent, describes very well this level of existence: "Now I
cannot tell what I said to the Moon, or what the Moon said
to me, but all the same, I got to know her very well. And
this was the impression I got of her—that she ruled over a
kingdom that was neither material nor spiritual, but a
strange moon-kingdom of her own. In it moved tides—
ebbing, flowing, slack water, high water, never ceasing,
always on the move; up and down, backwards and forwards,
rising and receding; coming past on the flood, flowing back
on the ebb; and these tides affected our lives. They affected
birth and death and all the processes of the body. They
affected the mating of animals, and the growth of vegetation, and the insidious workings of disease. They also affected the reactions of drugs, and there was a lore of herbs
belonging to them. All these things I got by communing
with the Moon, and I felt certain that if I could only learn
the rhythm and periodicity of her tides I should know a
very great deal. But this I did not learn; for she could only
teach me abstract things, and the details I was unable to
receive from her because *they eluded my mind.*"

13. The italics are our own and they emphasise an important point, for the things here described cannot be
formulated and categorised at all readily by the mind. This
is the sphere where the natural psychic and the natural
healer are at home—and such are not usually intellectually
minded but work by 'feel' and intuition. There is unfortunately still a large gap between the scientists and the intui-
tives—often the former are all too mind-bound and the latter
all too unscientific. So we tend to get pedants and academics
on the one hand and quacks and faddists on the other—both
types superstitious and narrow minded, each in their own
fashion.

14. The natural world and its etheric counterpart corresponding to the potencies of the 29th Path do represent a barrier and even a frightening illogical horror to the mind, for the mind does not operate in these regions except at a primitive instinctual level. Thus this Path represents a confrontation on one level with Nature, red in tooth and claw.

15. In his early novel 'Watt' (Olympia Press, Paris; Grove Press, New York) Samuel Beckett gives an horrific example of the recoil of the human mind from the natural world. Watt and his friend, alone in a strange garden in an alien universe are in the habit of going down to the stream to look at the rats: "And then we would sit down in the midst of them," Watt says, "and give them to eat, out of our hands, of a nice fat frog, or a baby thrush. Or seizing suddenly a plump young rat, resting in our bosom after its repast, we would feed it to its mother, or its father, or its brother, or its sister, or to some less fortunate relative. It was on these occasions, we agreed, after an exchange of views, that we came nearest to God."

16. It is this savage aspect of Nature, and in man the whole history of tabu, superstition, blood sacrifice, the primitive magic of urine and entrails, that is the make-up of the hideous Black Isis which could be said to sit at the threshold of this Path — a kind of malignant sphinx. The answer to the terrible riddle of the sphinx is, however, "Man.", the highest form of physical existence, who goes through the travails of physical evolution, veritable labours of Hercules, to become eventually a God. And at the end of this terrible 29th Path is the shining image of Netzach, the Beautiful Naked Woman, the White Isis, the Vision of Beauty Triumphant. This is not a thing that can be intellectually demonstrated for it is a mystical experience, the transformation of the dark, hideous goddess to the bright shining beautiful one.

17. In Arthurian legend the Path has much to do with Gawain. Gawain was himself a scion of the brute forces represented by Lot and Morgawse of Orkney and he was

one who had to overcome within himself the primal urges of the 'old law' of revenge. He was indeed one of the bloodiest of knights, who had great difficulty in learning the laws of chivalry. Even at his best he appears uncouth and barbarous when compared to such chivalrous and courtly French knights as Lancelot and his kindred. It was Gawain, in fact, whose spirit of revenge was a major factor in the break-up of the Fellowship of the Round Table.

18. He was also often aligned with the forces of Nature, as not only did his strength rise and decline with, the rising and setting of the Sun, but an early poem, 'Sir Gawain and the Green Knight' describes his shield as bearing the Pentagram—a sigil connected with the Elements. In this story he is challenged to smite off the head of a green giant on condition that if the giant survives he will return the compliment a year and a day later. Thinking such an eventuality unlikely, Gawain does so but the giant replaces his head on his shoulders and gallops off. A year and a day later Gawain fulfills his pledge and submits his head to be struck off by the green giant, but by being willing to undergo this certain death in order to preserve his integrity and the honour of knighthood, he is spared. The green giant is obviously a force of brute nature and the test is akin to the full implications of the answer to the riddle of the sphinx. The Laws of Humanity must be made to transcend the Laws of Nature.

19. Another Gawain story is his marriage to Lady Ragnell, a woman of hideous aspect, but who, *when Gawain accepts her as she is without thought for himself*, becomes transformed into a beautiful maiden. Ragnell is thus another form of the Dark and Bright Isis—and she lives with him seven years, the number of the Sephirah Netzach.

20. A more modern parallel to this myth is the belief that in the centre of darkest Africa—until recently a strange unknown continent very aptly symbolic of rife, primitive and barbaric life—there lives a White Queen, beautiful and ageless. This legend still persists even though it is now known that no such Queen does exist or probably ever did

exist. It has also appeared in literary form in Rider Haggard's 'She' — and though 'She' could be considered one of the Jungian archetypes and thus more relevant to the 28th Path, there are interconnections and overtones between all the Paths of the Tree as with all the Sephiroth, and the White Queen hidden in the Dark Continent is not so much an image of the anima as the Luminous Image of the Creator, concealed and yet, to the 'wise', revealed in Nature.

21. The 29th Path is thus a Path of pantheism and the early and more down-to-earth stages of the Green Ray, the Way of Nature Mysticism. This is by no means the townsman's superficial and sentimental 'love' of the country but the ambivalent love/hate attitude of the countryman who has to wrest his living from it. Real love of Nature, like real love between humans, is not a thing of refined ethereal appreciation, but a confrontation and willing acceptance of reality.

22. The nature of this Path is really below aesthetics in spite of being a channel for the pure creative forces of Netzach. There is, however, a certain connection with art. On its lowest level it is the frenzy of primitive dance, and on a higher level, what the poet Lorca has described as the 'duende'.

23. This is a concept which is by no means easy to describe and one can only recommend study of Lorca's original lecture 'Theory and Function of the Duende' which is now quite famous and should be easily available. Lorca describes the 'duende' as something which is not the muse, nor the angel of artistic creation, but a thing that "surges up from the soles of the feet." Goethe described it in reference to Paganini as "a mysterious power that everyone feels but that no philosopher has explained," and Lorca calls it 'the spirit of the earth'. It is something which is most frequently met with in Spanish culture, in certain gypsy and flamenco singers and dancers, in the bitumen blacks ground in with fist and knee in the paintings of Goya, in the 'Pythagorean

music' of the cape-work of bullfighters of the calibre of Joselito or Belmonte.

24. Its relationship with the 29th Path is perhaps best intuited from Lorca's poetic definition, "an air of the mind that blows insistently over the heads of the dead, in search of new landscapes and unsuspected accents; an air smelling of a child's saliva, of pounded grass, and medusal veil announcing the constant baptism of newly created things." Another aspect of this Path may be gained from the description of 'the smell of death' said to hang about a bullfighter before his last cornada and described by Pilar in Hemingway's 'For Whom the Bell Tolls'. The description is by no means suitable for the drawing room but the cruder facts of physical life seldom penetrate such a sanctum, and for the peace of mind of most of us, probably a good thing too.

25. The Mysteries of this Path correspond closely with the pre-Eleusinian Kabyric Mysteries. Even less is known of these Mysteries than those of Eleusis, but their depiction in early paintings is of pigmy-like men, very phallic, in contact with the Feminine principle in the form of beautiful crane-like birds. The deity worshipped was a form of Demeter, called Pelarge, in conjunction with Isthmaides, a form of Poseidon, God of the Sea. Pelarge came originally from Potniai, a city dedicated to Demeter as Potnia, the mistress. Like Demeter, pregnant sows were sacrificed to her, the pig being the 'uterine animal' of the earth as the dolphin is of the sea.

26. The Kabyric Mysteries are probably the foundation of the later Eleusinian Mysteries. It was Demeter who brought the Mysteries to the city of the Kabyroi and gave them to Prometheus and his son Aitnaios, the Etnean, in other words, Hephaestos. The Kabyroi were in fact sometimes called Hephaestoi. It was an Underworld cult and its connection with Hephaestos, the smith of the gods, shows a link with those early evolutionary Swarms of Divine Sparks known as the Lords of Form in 'The Cosmic Doctrine' who formulated the Laws of Geology and the 'Corporeal Intelligence'

of the planetary spherés. Thus the Flashing Colours of the Path, Crimson, Buff flecked silver-white, Light translucent pinkish-brown, and Stone suggest fire and stone as well as blood and the more colourless secretions of biological life.

27. The crane/swan identity of the higher feminine principle suggests the powers of Netzach and the stork is still popularly associated with birth. Furthermore, the swan-maiden legends have come down in various mythologies though not all have relevance to the somewhat primitive aspects of the 29th Path. The large crop of swan transformation legends in Ireland, a land renowned for Elemental beings and fairies, may have a certain reference to the faery kingdom of Tier nan Og, the Land of Eternal Youth, a Netzach condition behind the Elemental aspects of the natural physical world. Generally speaking though, they have more relevance to the 28th Path, which might be called the 29th Path on a higher arc.

28. One bird maiden which corresponds well with the 29th Path however, is that depicted on a Sumerian baked clay plaque some four thousand years old, whose Earthy and Lunar aspects are shown by her head-dress of bull's horns and the measuring instrument she holds. She is winged but has clawed feet. Both these are bird attributions, but wings, in that they can lift to great heights, are Cosmic spiritual symbols, while claws convey ideas of the primitive and even demonic. She is said to be Lilith, that strange woman who was said to be before Eve.

29. In Isaiah xxxiv her name is rendered in translation as a screech-owl and the whole passage from the 11th to the 15th verse gives some idea of the wilder aspects of the 29th Path: "But the cormorant and the bittern shall possess it; the owl also and the raven shall dwell in it: and He shall stretch out upon it the line of confusion, and the stones of emptiness. They shall call the nobles thereof to the kingdom, but none shall be there, and all her princes shall be nothing. And thorns shall come up in her palaces, nettles and brambles in the fortresses thereof: and it shall be an habita-

tion of dragons, and a court for owls. The wild beasts of the desert shall also meet with the wild beasts of the island, and the satyr shall cry to his fellow; the screech owl also shall rest there, and find for herself a place of rest. There shall the great owl make her nest, and lay, and hatch, and gather under her shadow: there shall the vultures also be gathered, every one with her mate."

30. These are the pronouncements of the prophet Isaiah on the desolation which shall be wrought on God's enemies but it is a fallowing back to first principles of nature, and thus akin to the 29th Path. Primitive life is not evil—it may appear unpleasant to civilised man—but that is by no means necessarily the same thing. Thus the naked form of Lilith is not demonic. Really she is an aspect of the Beautiful Naked Woman of Netzach who descends the 29th Path, putting on the vestments of corporeal nature to become the Young Woman, Crowned and Throned, in Malkuth.

31. It is true of course that the Order of Demons, or Qliphoth, in Malkuth is known as Lilith — the Evil Woman — and confusion must be avoided between the two concepts, but the attribution of the owl, sometimes thought to be a bird of evil, also shows a link with the Supernal Wisdom of Pallas Athene.

32. In conclusion, the swan legend that, because of the astrological sign, has close relation to this Path, is that of Leda, who gave birth to Castor and Pollux, the Heavenly Twins. These twins, if one studies the legend, are excellent representations of the Individuality and Personality, like the two fish of the sign Pisces. An intuitive examination of the myths and legends of beings who have stellar representation and reference to a treatise on the deeper sides of astrology, such as 'Esoteric Astrology' by Alice Bailey (Lucis Trust, London & New York), can lead to some very illuminating insights. There is deep esoteric implication in the fact that the Tarot Trump is sometimes called The Twilight. It shows a link with the transition from one phase to another. Pisces, the astrological sign of this Path, is at the beginning

and the end of the Zodiac according to the way of working the wheel. Similarly, the Cosmic Twilight comes at the beginning and end of a Cosmic Day (or Night), just as the terrestrial twilight marks the division between Earthly nights and days.

NOTES ON THE DESIGN OF TRUMP XVIII

The Marseilles card shows two dogs howling at the Moon, from which drops seem to be falling. In the background are two towers, one each side of the card, and in the foreground a crayfish is seen in a pool, possibly crawling out between the dogs.

Papus says that it is blood falling from the moon and that the path is sprinkled with it. Wirth, like Levi, however, prefers to consider the drops to be dew. Levi also mentions that the animals should be a dog and a wolf, chained to the towers, with a path leading between them towards the horizon. He thought this path should be sprinkled with blood though. Subsequent designs agree with the dog and wolf interpretation with the exception of Wirth and Zain, though the latter makes one dog white and the other black. None, however, have the animals chained.

Waite differs from Crowley in that he thinks the Moon is waxing and not waning—all versions, however, show the same profile head. On the Harris card Crowley considers the drops from the moon to be impure blood and shaped like Yods. The towers each side are black and each contains a figure of Anubis with an attendant jackal.

Knapp also gives blood dropping from the moon and to accentuate the polarity, makes his wolf black and dog white, countercharged by white and black towers behind. Case and Waite both think it dew. All agree that it is a dismal landscape, in Crowley's word, sinister. Wirth has described it as a steppe land behind the towers, behind which is a forest full of ghosts, and beyond that a mountain and precipice bordering a stream of purifying water. Case and Waite show mountains in the distance on their cards.

A count of the moon rays shows Waite and Knapp to have 32 in all. On all the others a full count is difficult owing to their going off the top of the card. Of the falling drops the Marseilles card gives 19, Wirth 18, Waite 15, Knapp 15, Case 18, Crowley 9. Waite's, Case's and Crowley's are definitely Yods. The 'Egyptian' Tarot has neither of these conventions and shows the towers as a black and a white pyramid.

All cards agree on the crayfish except the Crowley/Harris, which shows Khephera, the scarab, with a sun disk. Case draws attention to stones and plants by the water, representative of the mineral and vegetable kingdoms. These appear also on Waite's card.

One old Tarot card has an alternative design of a harpist serenading by moonlight a young girl loosing her hair at a window. Manly P. Hall's suggested symbol for the card is a flame in a cup.

The 31st Path

Malkuth — Hod

KEY:	Ϣ Shin. Tooth.
SPIRITUAL SIGNIFICANCE:	△ Fire.
THEORY:	Spirit of the Primal Fire. (XX—The Last Judgment.)
COLOURS:	Glowing orange scarlet. Vermilion, Scarlet flecked gold. Vermilion flecked crimson and emerald.
TEXT:	"The Thirty-first Path is the Perpetual Intelligence, but why is it so called? Because it regulates the motions of the Sun and Moon in their proper order, each in an orbit convenient for it."

1. This Path, we may say, is the polar opposite of the 29th Path; its symbolism is primarily Fiery as opposed to the Watery nature of the 29th Path. The 29th Path is the Corporeal Intelligence and is much concerned with the biological foundation of man's existence. The 31st Path imparts direction, or the revelation of mental factors, which, developed to greater and greater degree, cause the ultimate vast difference between man and the beasts. That it is a Path of instruction on mental levels is implied by the form in which the Yetziratic Text is set out — as question and answer — the only Text so expressed.

2. The title of Perpetual Intelligence indicates the spiritual factor behind this psychological evolution, for although Hod is very much the Sephirah of mentality, its own Yetziratic Text states that it "has no root by which it can cleave, nor rest, except in the hidden places of Gedulah, Magnificence, from which emanates its own proper essence." The Sephirah Gedulah, or Chesed, represents that sphere where the greater Intelligences that guide evolution abide, and is itself representative of the principle of law and order in the Universe. Thus the mind of Hod is of little evolutionary use

without the in-forming ethical principles of Chesed.

3. Hence this Path is said to regulate the motions of the Sun and Moon, the supreme symbols of radiation and receptivity. In man this is the relationship between Individuality and Personality, and also, particularly on this Path, the relationship between leader and led, for on this Path are the analogues of the first struggles towards civilisation by man and the formation of the family, the tribe and eventually the nation.

4. Esoteric tradition says that primitive man was guided by inner plane beings, or Manus, examples of such being Narada, Hermes, Merlin and so on. One of the keys to this Path then is an understanding of anthropology, just as keys to the 29th and 32nd Paths are a study of biology and primitive religion.

5. The beginnings of civilisation one equates with the discovery of the making of fire and its use for the preparation of food, making of tools, protection from wild beasts, and as a centre for communal life. The astrological symbol for this Path is thus aptly the Element of Fire; and the revelation of the way towards higher levels of physical existence is shown on the Tarot card with an Angel awakening the dead. This need not be confused with the orthodox Christian belief in the one final assumption of humanity in physical bodies to heaven — the principle behind the Tarot Trump is the awakening to new and higher levels of life.

6. The juxtaposition of the ideas of fire and of revelation call to mind the myth of Prometheus, which like the significances of the Path, can be interpreted at different levels, though all levels are reflections and patterns one of another. Thus Prometheus could be considered to have brought fire to man so that man could develop the arts of civilisation, but on a higher level the fire could be considered an awakening of the Spiritual Will in man.

7. This higher interpretation is borne out by the esoteric title of the Tarot Trump — Spirit of the Primal Fire. When the word 'Primal' is used in mystical symbolism it usually

refers to spiritual factors, because spiritual being *was* before anything *is*. The awakening of the Spiritual Will implies the sense of individual identity in man, the realisation of himself as a separate immortal being so that civilisation becomes the co-operation of individuals rather than the natural aggregation by instinct into herds.

8. Thus the gift of Melchisedek which relates to this Path is asbestos, the strange mineral that resists the all-conquering fire and thus symbolises immortality and powers of existence transcending Elemental life. This symbol stresses the factor of individualisation just as the beehive stresses corporate existence, and the Way of Evolution is the way inbetween — the Path of Equilibrium, the straight and narrow way like the edge of a sword. Ultimately there is no contradiction between individual and corporate free-will, which does not imply the entire subjugation of one by the other, but simply a true appreciation of unity.

9. Whilst the Path has high spiritual principles behind it, it is very much a down to earth one so there are great opportunities to be found upon it. It is a Path of living out Spiritual principles rather than the application of the mind to them of the 26th Path or the more purely mental bias of the 30th. As the 29th Path could be pictorially summarised as a lush wilderness teeming with wild life, so the 31st Path could well be imagined in the form of the fires of a semi-nomadic tribe seen in the desert darkness.

10. Apart from Prometheus — whose name means 'forethought' — which is the main thing that distinguishes men from beasts, the most appropriate god-form for this Path would be the Greek Hestia or the Roman Vesta. Hestia was the oldest of the Olympians, and like Athena and Artemis, was ever virgin. Her name means 'the hearth' and she presided over domesticated fire, from the household fires of every family to the prytaneum, or Public Hearth, of every town, and also the priestly sacrificial fires. She is therefore at the very hub of civilisation and this perhaps accounts for her dignified position among the other Olympians, many of

whom were notorious in Greek legend for their somewhat questionable escapades. In Rome, Vesta was similarly the goddess of fire in its domestic and religious ceremonial use, and her rites were simple and un-bloody in nature, the objects of reverence being the hearth fire and a clay vase of water, narrow at the base so that it had to be held and not laid aside. Thus one level of the 31st Path, esoterically speaking, is the Path of the Hearth Fire, that is the building of a home and raising a family according to spiritual principle. The hearth is the altar of family life and the focus of the home; the home exists not for the happiness or even the well-being of the two adults who built it, but for the children that are reared therein — though of course the true home implies by its very purpose and nature the happiness of all within it.

11. The psychological factors of the 31st Path could be said to include therefore, the higher instincts, that is, the more tender feelings of parenthood and mating as opposed to the more selfish self-preservation and procreative instincts of the 29th Path. Vesta was also originally the protectress of sown fields, thus implying the first steps of civilisation from hunters of wild flora and fauna to the tending of crops and herds. Really an extension of the family principle.

12. Hephaestos is another fire god who has relevance to this Path. Originally he may have been a god of the celestial fire, lightning, and he was sometimes referred to as 'the Etnean' and thus was in this aspect a god of the volcanic inner fires of the Earth. Celestial fire has reference to the Divine Wisdom and Will and to the higher powers of the mind and thus is more under the province of higher Paths of the Tree and such mythological figures as Prometheus and Pallas Athene, though these do have certain relevance to the 31st Path in that they are higher analogues of it. The volcanic fire also has relation to the intelligent formation of the planetary spheres, but such aspects are pre-human, though they bear out Hephaestos' attribution of Divine

Blacksmith. As far as humanity is directly concerned he was patron of fire in its use in the forging of tools and weapons which were essential for the beginnings of human civilisation.

13. Thus we see that the Spiritual Significance of the Path is aptly summed up by the attribution of the Element of Fire, for Fire implies the development in animal life of individualised will, the fore-thinking of the higher brain, with the consequent formation of social units in conscious intelligent co-operation, and the development of technology in order to gain dominance over the natural world.

14. The Hebrew letter for the Path, Shin, meaning Tooth, also has the appearance in its shape of a flickering fire, terminating at the upper points in three creative Yods. Its shape also suggests the development of individual facets from a common sub-stratum. The tooth is the hardest part of the body just as the Spirit is the most enduring part of the whole of man. Spirit has considerable relevance to this lowly placed Path, for man's whole evolution is in accordance with the will of the Spirit, and for the benefit of the Spirit. The tooth is a cutting and grinding implement, that which prepares food for subsequent digestion, just as the Personality of man has to cut and grind its way through life after life to provide the experience of manifestation which is digested and transmuted into spiritual sustenance and life by the Individuality. The tooth is also a symbol of creativeness; according to Freud dreams of losing the teeth usually conceal fears of impotence. Thus we can say that the Hebrew letter indicates that the Path is concerned with individualisation — spiritual evolution through the discipline of experience and the development of powers of creation. The evolutionary aspect of the Path is also shown in that it leads to Hod — 'the mean of the primordial' — that is, the Way of Evolution is a process of harmonisation of the contending forces arising from the most primitive levels. The middle way between two opposites is suggested by the shape of the letter Shin.

15. This Middle Way is shown also on the Tarot Trump, for the true design seems to have been a child rising from a tomb and the man and woman each side rising from the ground, not as persons, but as principles of positive and negative in Nature. The child is the growing point in the evolving man.

16. A tradition suggested by this card is the Raising of Lazarus, the bringing back to life of man rendered corrupt by his own sin. There is so much automatic living nowadays, lives lived by habit and narrow convention, that Lazarus could almost be a symbol of modern man. In this context the figure on the card raising the dead would be Our Lord — the Way, the Truth and the Life. And not so much the 'pale Galilean' of many 'Christian' dead, but the Risen Christ — in Glory, and Triumphant.

17. As this Path leads to Hod there is an influence upon it of the civilising aspects of number and speech, the one allowing calculation and measurement and the other allowing a higher degree of communication than brute noises. There are many of course who use the power of speech to corrupt or even prevent communication but this is a Qliphothic abuse of the Divine Powers of this Path.

18. Speech is of profound occult significance as is hinted at in the term Logos for God, and the Bible is by no means the only religious book which reveals the profound higher import of speech in "In the beginning was the Word." There is a traditional belief that to discover the real name of a thing is to gain power over it, as is shown forth in the legend of Isis obtaining the real name of Ra. The giving of a name is a sacrament in the Church and a novitiate of Holy Orders or an initiate in an Esoteric Fraternity always takes a new name. The original purpose in baptism was the giving of a *Christian* name, that is, the taking on of a name from Christian history or tradition as a token of intention and aspiration. There are many today who would more appropriately have been baptised 'Thomas' — for they doubt very much.

19. H. P. Blavatsky in 'The Secret Doctrine' also stresses the significance of the powers of speech and says that a person's use of language is of greater import than they might dare to think. It seems therefore, that many might do far better by themselves to cultivate silence— a Binah virtue — for compulsive garrulousness, on all levels, drowns out the sound of the Spirit, the still small voice. It is not out of mere penitential caprice that some religious Orders impose vows of silence.

20. Number, like speech, represents actual potencies, and is not merely symbolism. The difference between chemical elements, for example, is purely one of number, as is also the difference between different colours, the notes of the musical scale, the temperature of a substance and also its different states as solid, liquid or gas, and so on. Any of this can be verified from an elementary textbook on science.

21. As an example, the atom of the element Krypton has orbital tracks of 2, 8, 18 and 8 electrons about its nucleus, (the number of electrons in a particular orbit corresponding to the mathematical series $2(1)^2$, $2(2)^2$, $2(3)^2$, and the outer ring of the most stable elements such as Krypton, the 'inert' gases, always being 8), and differs from its neighbour, Bromine, in that Bromine has only 7 electrons in the outer ring. This difference of number accounts for the widely different physical properties that the elements display in the world of appearances— Malkuth. On the other hand the nucleus of any element contains charges of a different polarity, which are held packed in together with tremendous force, a force which, when released, gives us such necessities of modern life as atomic and hydrogen warheads and bombs. The factor of number could be attributed to the 31st Path and the factor of the latent power to the 29th Path and the differences of chemical properties, colour, density and so on, to the Sephirah Malkuth, the physical world. Thus we can see how the 29th and 31st Paths complement each other in their convergence on Malkuth.

22. This is all in the realms of chemistry and physics but

there are the psychological analogues in man. The 29th Path represents the hereditary factors which make up man in the world, the power of his instincts, the forces of his body; the 31st Path holds the key to temperament, that is, not hereditary factors of physique and nervous system, but the projection of a Personality from an Individuality; and the important keys to character here are not in physical ancestry but the ancestry of former projections or incarnations. Thus, as a treading of the 29th Path is a confrontation with the whole gamut of the biological past, which has been recapitulated in the womb of the mother, so a treading of the 31st Path can be revealing of past lives, or at any rate the factors in past lives which play an important part in the temperamental make-up in the present life, for all cannot be revealed until the consciousness of Tiphareth is attained, the focussing point of the Individuality.

23. To sum up, the ascent of the 31st Path is an appreciation of the inner forces that make up the physical appearances of Malkuth, objectively or subjectively. The descent of it is the bringing down of the factors of the soul which are important for the present incarnation. These will be largely karmic, otherwise one would not, in conditions of the present, be incarnate. They can reveal destiny however, and the nature of karma often points to the nature of the destiny. In one way, the Path may be seen to be a lower reflection of the 22nd Path, which is the Path, par excellence, of Karmic Adjustment, for all the Paths, particularly those on the same side of the Tree, interlink and are analagous on lower or higher arcs one with another.

NOTES ON THE DESIGN OF TRUMP XX

The Marseilles card shows a winged angel with trumpet and banner, and below, a figure rising from a tomb, naked, and on each side, a naked man and woman also rising, either from other tombs or from the ground.

Wirth has these two figures definitely rising out of the ground, a point also mentioned by Westcott, which would suggest that they are principles—positive and negative—of natural life and that only the central figure is human as such. With this card attributed to Shin it would represent the first stirrings of the interred Spirit from the natural world. As with the Marseilles card, Wirth shows rays proceeding from the angel and he makes them 12 in number, a point followed by Case. Knapp makes these a general fiery radiance and agrees with Wirth in putting in falling drops, though 16 in number as opposed to Wirth's 20.

On Knapp's card all the figures arise from one tomb and have clothes, or at any rate coloured shrouds, the central one being a small child. Manley P. Hall's symbolic interpretation is that of a skull on a black field surmounted by a rose on a white. There are also flowers growing all about on Knapp's card, and as with Wirth, the angel bears a solar disk on the brow.

Waite and Case follow in making the central figure a child but cause it to face into the card in the traditional way rather than out, as Knapp has it. They also have the trio naked, and rising from three separate tombs, which are apparently floating on water. In the background they have mountains, but Waite is alone in showing other figures rising from other tombs. Case mentions that the banner should measure five units by five so that the cross upon it this covers nine out of a total of twentyfive imaginary squares; and he also causes the position of the arms of the man, child and woman to suggest the word LVX.

Crowley had originally agreed along these lines. He saw the central figure as a fair youth rising from a tomb in the attitude of the god Shu supporting the firmament and flanked by a dark woman making the downward pointing triangular sign for Water on her breast, and a man making the upward pointing triangular sign for Fire on his forehead. Subsequently, when he came to collaborate with Lady Frieda Harris on a new set of cards, he chose to call this one The Aeon and emblematic of the New Age. Thus he set a figure of Horus in the centre of the conjunction of Nuit above and Hadit below. Briefly, Nuit, whose symbol is the night sky, could be called 'the circumference which is nowhere', the unlimited possibility; and Hadit, the winged disk, 'the central point which is everywhere', the ubiquitous point of view. At the bottom of the card is shown a flower-like letter Shin with human figures in each petal, and behind it a suggestion of the sign Libra, an indication of the Aeon after this one of Horus; the fact that the Age of Horus is only just beginning is shown by Horus having one hand empty, as yet undeveloped of attributes.

The 'Egyptian' Tarot shows three mummies, of a man, woman and child, emerging from a sarcophagus on which is depicted the Scarab, a sign of immortality and rebirth. Above is a winged genie, blowing a trumpet, in the Sun.

It was Count de Gébelin's opinion that the coffin on the traditional card was a later interpolation and that originally the card represented the Primal Creation. Waite has scorned this idea, but as Manly P. Hall points out, there is little difference esoterically between birth and rebirth, so the inner meaning of the card would remain unchanged.

LE · MAT

LE · BATELEUR

LA · PAPESSE

L'IMPÉRATRICE

Part II
The Structures of the Personality

The 28th Path

Yesod — Netzach

KEY: ꙍ Tzaddi. Fish-hook.

SPIRITUAL SIGNIFICANCE: ≈ Aquarius. The Water Bearer.

THEORY: Son of the Morning. Chief among the Mighty. (IV — The Emperor.)

COLOURS: Violet. Sky-blue. Bluish-mauve. White tinged purple.

TEXT: "The Twenty-eighth Path is called the Natural Intelligence; by it is completed and perfected the nature of all that exists beneath the Sun."

1. The Twentyeighth Path, in that it joins Netzach and Yesod, will be a Path of great power and force, for by it the pure forces of the creative imagination pour into the subconscious mind. This power is well symbolised by The Emperor, for this inflow of force is one of the prime factors in the make-up of the Personality of man.

2. The Personality should be a simulacrum of the Individuality in the developed person; in other words, that which is below should be as that which is above — in accordance with the Hermetic axiom. This factor is shown in the sign of Aquarius, which shows a zig-zag line, recalling to mind the Lightning Flash, reflected in a similar zig-zag line below it. The upper line represents the Individuality and the lower line the Personality. In this manner "is completed and perfected the nature of all things beneath the Sun" — the Sun being, of course, Tiphareth.

3. It is perhaps as well that this Path is called the Natural Intelligence for its powers and potencies can have an appearance which seem to belie this. Yet it is by no means a Path of 'supernatural forces'. In any case, there can be no such thing as the *super*natural; the Laws of a Universe are supreme in that Universe, just as the Laws of any Plane are supreme on that Plane. If one falls over a cliff, for in-

stance, waving a magic wand—assuming one has one at the time and the presence of mind to use it—will not in any way lessen one's impact with the ground. A parachute is the magical weapon needed in such a case. The physical outcome of any magical operation does not come about in any miraculous manner unless one happens to be the magical calibre of a Christ—and even here it appears obvious that the miracles only seem to be such, just as a cigarette lighter might seem miraculous to a savage.

4. All the 'magic' of this Path is but an appearance, and the glamour of it is entirely Qliphothic—unbalanced force. This being a Path of considerable power it is quite easy for forces to be unbalanced, but such unbalance, resulting in compulsive behaviour and superstition, is no part of the Path, which being of the Tree of Life is part of the Divine Plan and therefore perfect, but unevolved man's uncontrolled reaction to it.

5. The power of the Path could be said, symbolically, to be a result of the tremendous polarity between the Beautiful Naked Woman of Netzach and the Beautiful Naked Man of Yesod. In Netzach is the *image* of the Individuality shining direct into the subconscious mind of the Personality and attracting and influencing it as a fisherman plays a fish—hence the Hebrew letter of the Path, Tzaddi, a Fish-hook. The correct discernment of this force within the Personality, and intelligent co-operation with it, leads to the perfectly natural process of spiritual growth as the term, Natural Intelligence, implies. Owing to factors resulting from the Primary Deviation however, the links between levels of consciousness are occluded, producing the frequent aberrations that are found on this Path.

6. In psychological terms, the forces of this Path correspond closely to the Jungian archetypes, though there is rather more to it than just this. The Order of Angels of Netzach, for example, the Elohim, are the forces behind all the gods and supernatural powers conceived by the mind of man. The powers from the relatively formless Netzach are

basically the same, however, whatever the theories and nomenclature that man may care to attribute to them, scientific or religious.

7. Whether Jung realised it or not, and it is possible he suspected more than he cared to admit, the archetypes of the unconscious, particularly the contra-sexual image, are images of the Individuality of man. The tremendous power of the anima image over man is a frequent motif in literature, perhaps as well as anywhere in Marlowe's 'Dr. Faustus':

> "Was this the face that launched a thousand ships
> And burnt the topless towers of Ilium?·
> Sweet Helen, make me immortal with a kiss.
> Her lips suck forth my soul; see where it flies!—
> Come Helen, come, give me my soul again.
> Here will I dwell, for Heaven is in these lips,
> And all is dross that is not Helena."

8. In this passage, Marlowe, with great poetic insight— and artistic inspiration is also a factor on this Path—shows the ease of confusion between the image of the Individuality, which is subjective, and the objective projection of that image upon another person of the opposite sex.

9. The Individuality, whose life-span is a Cosmic Day, is relatively immortal from the point of view of the Personality; so the words "make me immortal with a kiss." show well the experience of consciousness achieved when a functional union between Personality and Individuality is made. This experience can well seem like a loss of identity to the Personality and yet be, at the same time, a transcendent experience, hence "Her lips suck forth my soul . . . give me my soul again . . . Heaven is in these lips . . . all is dross that is not Helena."

10. When, however, the contact with the Individuality, essentially an inner experience, is confused with objective reality by its projection upon another, then obviously there is going to be trouble, whether in more modern times as a

bad marriage or tragic love affair or in Homeric legend as the launching of a thousand ships and the ten year siege and burning of a city. These are the lengths to which glamour can lead man and glamour is still very much with us. The wider aspects of the subject are well dealt with by the Tibetan in Alice Bailey's 'Glamour—A World Problem' (Lucis Trust. London & New York.)

11. It is only in comparatively recent times that passion has been considered an enobling thing and this attitude is erroneous. The great romances of Western literature, Lancelot and Guinevere, Romeo and Juliet, Heloise and Abelard, (an actual case), and so on, are all examples of an abuse or lack of control of sexual, or horizontal, polarity. This kind of situation may be caused by a restimulation of factors in past lives when the *vertical* polarity (i.e. devotion to the god-head) of such cults as those of Ishtar or Astarte was abused by confusing it with horizontal (i.e. sexual) polarity. In such cases the Temple sexual sacrament became divorced from its sacramental aspect through confusion of the goddess with the priestess and/or all mankind with the priest or male worshipper.

12. The modern regard for romance—which is essentially escapism, a denial of life-as-it-is-in-Earth, and hence a blasphemy against Adonai—stems largely from the outer aspects of the Venus cult of the Mediterranean which was stamped out in the Albigensian persecution. The Trouveres and the Troubadours represent the esoteric and exoteric aspects of this brief efflorescence, which drew its inspiration from the remains of Roman culture, in turn derived from the Greeks, with secondary tributaries from Mithraic and Persian sources. The Greek tradition owed much to the Egyptian; and the Egyptian, in its later debased form, also affected the Roman directly. Later, in Arthurian legend, the Mediterranean Venus cult combined with the northern Druidic Nature and Sun worship and also the Celtic Christianity, which was non-monastic, non-ascetic, and linked Christianity with love of Nature. Thus the Arthurian cycle

is a mine of mystical knowledge though somewhat distorted by later orthodox Christian glosses.

13. Nature worship, whether Druidic, Celtie Christian, or any other, aligns well with this 28th Path. Nature is under the Divine Aspect of God the Father, and the Emperor of the Tarot Trump can be considered an anthropomorphic representation of this Aspect, the higher analogue of which is in Chokmah. There is also a link here with the Jungian Wise Old Man archetype and also with the animus, the contra-sexual image of woman. This former archetype can also be obsessive as is exemplified in the case of the German philosopher Friedrich Nietzsche, in his case under a Dionysiac form.

14. The Feminine-Side of the worship of Nature, Queen Venus, or Isis of Nature, is shown forth by the Magical Image of Netzach, the Beautiful Naked Woman, and its deeper aspects stem from Binah. If the spiritual aspects of this Path are not kept well to the fore, (the roots in Chokmah and Binah), it is quite easy for its potencies to overspill into the degeneracies of orgy, witchcraft and obsessive passion. In such a case it is almost as if there were a fall from the higher aspects of the 28th Path to the lower aspects of the 29th. Heloise and Abelard, for example, should have helped each other towards the vertical polarity of mystical consciousness as symbolised by the astrological sign of the Path, Aquarius. Their relationship became obsessive and exaggerated however, and so they became two people forcibly tied together by a horizontal link as symbolised by the astrological sign of Pisces—two poor fish indeed. He, in fact, was castrated, a strange karmic effect which may point back to some sin against an ancient Temple of Isis, where, in some cults, the priests castrated themselves in their fervour. There is a grim and terrible lesson in this story as indeed there is also in Lancelot and Guinevere or Romeo and Juliet, to name but two examples of what is now almost a commodity in a wish-fulfillment industry. Perhaps it was with some mystic fore-knowledge of Hollywood and the tele-

44

vision cults that Shakespeare wrote, so truly, "The fault, dear Brutus, is not in our stars, but in ourselves."

15. The 28th Path, however, is the channel of artistic inspiration, whatever the medium of expression, and also of any creative work in the sciences, pure or applied. The creative aspect of the human mind, which always has to fight against established order, not only in the world but within the psyche of the creator himself, recalls to mind the goddess aspect of Netzach—Aphrodite the Awakener. The Esoteric Title of the Tarot Card— Son of the Morning, Chief among the Mighty—likewise has reference to Venus, the most powerfully occult planet according to 'The Secret Doctrine'.

16. More especially it refers to Lucifer, who is by no means the devil that popular thought of the middle ages believed him to be, but a great awakening light-bearing Angelic being, intimately connected with Venus — and of course all too many are ready to consign even the works of Venus to the Devil. Lucifer's higher aspects are indicated in the legend that the Holy Grail was made from an emerald that fell from his crown. The emerald is the precious stone sacred to Venus and also occurs in the legend of Hermes, for it was upon an emerald tablet, laid upon the breast of the corpse of the great Arch-Hierophant, that the Hermetic axiom 'As above, so below' was said to be engraved. This legend of the tomb of Hermes gives a further link with the similar legend of the great Western occult figure, Christian Rosencreutz.

17. The figure of the Emperor on the traditional Tarot Card holds a sceptre upon which is the orb and cross of Venus. He also has a shield bearing the emblem of an eagle and is himself in a posture indicative of the symbol of Al-chemical Sulphur. Alchemical terms vary from writer to writer but generally speaking Sulphur signifies Divine Force in its more positive aspects. 'The Gluten of the White Eagle' is the etheric substance given off in sexual polarity. It was the production of this that was the aim of the organisers of

the witch cults and similar orgiastic rites. The actual sexual orgy came only at the end, after the magical power given off had been utilised by the Hierophant, for in magic the physical sexual act is useless, except as a safety valve, for it 'earths' the power. Thus, though the main attraction of such dark rites may have been a sexual romp for the more ignorant celebrants, the organisers of the rites were interested in the preliminaries leading up to the final debauch, which, like modern striptease and cabaret, were designed to excite but not fulfill. Thus one reads in confessions of witches who have had sexual intercourse with the Devil (i.e. with the masked hierophant) that the union felt cold. This was no doubt because the man, not being interested in the physical earthing of the powers of lust let loose, used a stick. The less debased form of sexual polarity working is illustrated in Dion Fortune's novels 'The Sea Priestess', 'Moon Magic', 'Goat-foot God' and 'The Winged Bull' and this is a working relating to the 28th Path. The more debased form of the witch cults verges closer to the lower 29th Path.

18. The legends which relate to the 28th Path are much akin to the wish-fulfillment dreams of men and of women. The prime wish-fulfillment dream of woman is perhaps the fairy story of Cinderella. This is really the ordinary woman being transformed into the goddess and finding the Prince — the idealised human male figure. The wish-fulfillment dreams of men are perhaps best found in the legends of the swan maidens, fairy creatures, lesser forms of the goddess. Such is to be found in the Irish legend of Angus Og, who, stricken almost to death with the love of a maiden he had seen in a dream, finally finds her, a swan maiden, and changes into a swan himself to join her.

19. There is a direct link here with Tier nan Og, the Land of the Ever Young, that mythical place in Irish legend which is really the kingdom of faery, or, in esoteric terms, a certain level of the astral plane. There are many legends which relate to it, usually in the form of a moral man being lured

into underground or fairy regions, there to mate with a maiden not of the human race. The best known is perhaps the story of Tannhäuser, who spent seven years in the Venusberg, the Mountain of Venus.

20. Tier nan Og also exists, as might be expected, in many other forms according to the race in whose subconscious mind the potencies of the astral plane impinge. Thus there are the stories of the Fortunate Isles, the Isles of the Blessed, the Hesperides, and the Arthurian Avalon:

"Where falls not hail, or rain, or any snow,
Nor ever wind blows loudly; but—lies
Deep-meadowed, happy, fair with orchard lawns
And bowery hollows crown'd with summer sea."

In Biblical terms it has aspects in common with the Garden of Eden, and in classical myth there is the remote Ogygia where Cronos sleeps, and there is also the island where Circe held Ulysses.

21. There is also an interesting link between the Grail and the Swan legends in the story of Lohengrin, son of Percivale, who, a knight of the Chapel of the Grail at Montsalvatch, answered the summons for help that was indicated by the tolling of a magic bell, untouched by hand, in the Chapel. Going forth, he came upon a silver swan drawing a boat along the river which took him to be a champion of a lady, whom he married after conquering her oppressor, on condition that she did not ask his lineage. Eventually curiosity overcame her and as a result he returned to the Grail Chapel in the little boat drawn by the swan.

22. There is therefore great ramification of meaning in the 28th Path, ranging from sexual polarity, the contact with non-human kingdoms, to the forming of a vessel within consciousness for the image of the higher aspects of the soul. This latter pertains to the Quest of the Holy Grail, for the Grail occurs at a junction point between planes of consciousness and really means the making oneself into a cup or chalice for the entry of higher forces. Ascending the Path

is thus a Quest of the Holy Grail; it can also be an awakening of consciousness to the perfect world of Elemental and lesser Angelic beings, with the attendant risk of unbalance or even, if one is very foolish, obsession. It is also a link with the creative aspects of the self, and thus the mythical figure of Pegasus has relevance to the Path, for the winged horse represents the flights of creative fancy.

23. Descending the Path is a process of bringing these powers into the mind, and this refers more to the subconscious than to the work-a-day conscious mind, though as the subconscious affects the conscious mind profoundly it is a way to expansion of consciousness, and the living of life more abundantly.

NOTES ON THE DESIGN OF TRUMP IV

The Marseilles Tarot Emperor sits on a throne, out of doors, in the sign of Alchemical Sulphur, a triangle over a cross. He has a shield showing an eagle, a Venus sceptre and a strangely shaped crown with six points. About his neck is a wreath.

Oswald Wirth gave him an orb to hold surmounted by a cross similar to the sceptre held by the Marseilles Empress. The sceptre he changed from a Venus one to a fleur-de-lys. He introduced his usual single flower in the background and also a Sun and Moon on the Emperor's breastplate, who, in this card, sits on a cubic stone which has an eagle engraved on its side, the Emperor having no shield. He also abandoned the six points of the crown (which Papus took care to mention in his book — six each side of the crown, making a zodiacal twelve) and introduced four spikes on the top of the headdress.

Westcott, who derives most of his Tarot information from Eliphas Levi, suggested a lotus topped sceptre and favoured a thone which, he says, in 'modern Tarots' is decorated with a black eagle. He also says that in 'older designs' the triangle over cross was indicated in the posture, suggesting the Athanor of the alchemists. As all designs except Waite's show this posture (and Waite's was published some 15 years after Westcott wrote this) it would seem that the 'modern Tarot' referred to might well be the Golden Dawn version, of which Society both Westcott, and later, Waite, were members.

Waite's design shows the Emperor facing straight out of the card, sitting foursquare. He has mountains and a river in the background and the sceptre is made into a T-shape surmounted with a circle — a kind of extended ankh or lingam sign. The orb is undecorated. Waite is the first to introduce Aries symbolism to the card, shown by an Aries sign on top of the Emperor's crown and four ram's heads on the throne. This is almost conclusive proof that at this time Waite accepted the Golden Dawn attributions which place the Emperor on the 15th Path, whose astrological sign is Aries. It would also seem that the Aries symbolism of this card is really a Golden Dawn innovation, though the Golden Dawn cards have never been published.

Case prefers the traditional posture but includes mountains, the river, and rams heads — in this case on the Emperor's shoulder-piece and on the side of the cubical stone. He restores the six-pointed helmet, follows Waite in sceptre design, and has an orb like Wirth's.

Crowley early considered the Emperor to be a flame clad god with fiery symbols, attitude showing the triangle and cross and seated on a cubical stone marked with the alchemical Green Lion and White Eagle. The figure on the subsequent card is more like an Emperor and the allocation to the 15th Path is shown by a beam of light shining from the top right of the card, according to Crowley's text in the Book of Thoth, emanating from Chokmah. This would indicate that at the time of designing the card, despite Liber Legis, Crowley was undecided about the transposition of The Star and The Emperor — or else that he designed the card first and then after it was painted changed his ideas of Path attribution when he came to write the text. The transposition of the zodiacal sign as well as the Trumps (cf. Section IV. Part I for greater details of all this problem.) between the 15th and 28th Paths would therefore be, possibly, an attempt to cover up the error, to brazen things out—for though he admits to being lazy, he was far from stupid, and thus the possibility of him making an oversight of such a magnitude seems unlikely. The Aries symbolism of the card would appear then to be a 'deliberate' mistake — brought about at first by vaccilation and then awkwardly covered up in order not to cause himself too much trouble. The Aries symbolism is a ram-headed sceptre and two Himalayan goats standing behind, like pillars. Also shown are bees on his costume, an orb with Maltese cross, a lamb with flag, fleur-de-lys, and a shield with a double eagle of Sulphur crowned with a crimson disk.

In the Egyptian styled Tarot the Emperor wears a triangular masonic apron which forms the symbol of Sulphur with his crossed legs. On his breast there is a hawk and on the cubic stone on which he is seated is depicted a cat. He wears a uraeus and bears a serpent sceptre surmounted by a circle.

It may be as well to mention an early Venetian design of about 1475 wherein the Emperor has a three-pointed trifoliate crown surmounted by a trefoil and bears a simple orb and fleur-de-lys sceptre. By his side kneel two children, their hands crossed on their breasts. This is said to refer to Charlemagne and his two sons.

The hieroglyph by Manly P. Hall on Knapp's card shows four eyes, each at a quadrant point.

The 30th Path

Yesod — Hod

KEY:	ꓶResh. Head.
SPIRITUAL SIGNIFICANCE:	☉ The Sun.
THEORY:	Lord of the Fire of the World. (XIX—The Sun.)
COLOURS:	Orange. Gold yellow. Rich amber. Amber rayed red.
TEXT:	"The Thirtieth Path is the Collective Intelligence and astrologers deduce from it the judgment of the stars and celestial signs, and perfect their science according to the rules of the motions of the stars."

1. The Flashing Colours and the emphasis on the Sun show this to be a Path of enlightenment. The Hebrew letter means the Head and so implies intelligence, while the Yetziratic Text emphasises the perfection of science. In this text, astrology may be taken to represent all science, for the aim of all sciences, as with astrology, is the formulation of laws by which predictions of future occurrences may be made. Thus, for example, Newton's Third Law of Motion, that every action has an equal and opposite reaction, allowed man to predict effects from specific causes in the realms of mechanics and to adapt his inventive genius to the design of machinery to make use of this law of nature, eventually resulting in the jet aircraft and the space rocket. This is the means of man's technological evolution — the formulation of laws in order to predict the operation of cause and effect on the physical plane.

2. There is also, of course, the operation of causes on higher planes, as yet little understood by science, which results in effects on the lower planes. Thus the reference to astrology is apposite; it refers not so much to the largely superstitious newspaper astrology as the the 'starry wisdom' of the spiritual realms, the interaction of the great Logoi

49

50

or Gods whose vehicles of physical manifestation are shown forth in the heavenly bodies. The Sun represents our own Solar Logos, who is omnipotent as far as this solar system is concerned. Thus the forces attributed to the Zodiacal signs are not so much emanations to Earth of the constellations themselves, but are the markers on a great clock which serve to indicate the type of force emanating from the Solar Logos at any particular time. Generally speaking, however, there are so many variable factors in astrology that its use as a system of prognostication is unreliable. The birth chart can give a rough indication of character but the effect of the higher forces and of Earth experience varies so much from person to person that 'progressed charts' are, on the whole, unreliable unless the person is of almost vegetable-like character and the astrologer highly skilled.

3. The term Collective Intelligence is a useful indicator to the factors of this Path for in its ultimate sense it implies knowledge of the whole gamut of forces on every level synthesised into a centre of knowledge. Such exists though only in the most Central Sun of all, and it is doubtful if man would ever attain to such a comprehensive Collective Intelligence. He would certainly not whilst in incarnation because of the limitations of the physical brain, notwithstanding the fact that the human brain contains vast potential which is untapped by humanity at present. Even the limited Collective Intelligence of 'the essential unity of mankind on this planet' would, however, completely transform the present state of world affairs.

4. The Path leads from Yesod to Hod, connecting the Vision of the Machinery of the Universe with the Vision of Splendour. Hod, of course, has, according to its Yetziratic Text, its roots in Chesed, the Sephirah of the Vision of Love. Thus the sunny aspect of this Path stems largely from the realisation of the Divine Love and Splendour which motivates the lower planes of manifestation which in themselves are

known as the Machinery of the Universe, the etheric structures of Yesod.

5. Hod is the Sephirah of the Divine Messenger and of the Lord of Books and of Learning, and also of the Archangel Michael who disperses the forces of darkness. All this is implicit in the gift of mind to the human race; and the flowering of rational thought after the ages of barbarity and medieval superstition has been well called the Age of Enlightenment. In the words of Pope:

"Nature and Nature's laws lay hid in night:
God said, 'Let Newton be!' and all was light."

6. The Age of Enlightenment heralded also those political manifestations of the Collective Intelligence such as the American War of Independence and the French Revolution. And there is to this day a great feeling of light and clarity in the prose of such men of the period as Thomas Paine; and the darkness and superstition such men as he were up against can be gauged from the practice in his day of selling hob-nails for boots engraved with his image so that the more conservative of the labouring classes could trample on his effigy all day without effort.

7. One can have too much of a good thing however. The Sun shining unremittingly causes life to wither and die, and Reason unremitting and unbalanced has a similar effect. The pendulum swings to and fro just as night and day, or summer and winter alternate and the gross materialism of the nineteenth century, the effects of which persist to this day, represents Reason gone beyond its due limits. When such is the case, no longer do we have the life giving Sun of the 30th Path but the life enchaining Devil of the 26th, when it is forgotten that "Le coeur a ses raisons que la raison ne connait point." — and one could with equal validity and with more profound import substitute the word 'Spirit' for 'heart' in this quotation from Pascal.

8. Reason is not without beauty however, if perhaps accessible only to the mathematician in its higher aspects,

though available to all in the design of a functional scientific instrument or a highly developed machine such as an aeroplane or even a bomb. Anything that has perfect function must have perfect design, and Hod is the Sephirah behind physical forms.

9. This Path is also the polar opposite of the 28th Path from Yesod to Netzach and it has its great potentialities and also its weaknesses brought about by human misuse, just as has the 28th Path. The Person enmeshed emotionally in an unbalance of the 28th Path is usually appealed to to 'use his reason', which is, in effect, an appeal to get his subjective Tree of Life balanced up within himself. In Jungian terms the effect of the two Paths relates to the 'thinking' and 'feeling' types respectively—two opposite functions in the Jungian scheme of things as on the Tree of Life. Thus, concentrated working upon one or other of the Paths should, in a normal person, effect a balancing up of the psyche, or an integration process.

10. Just as an unbalance of the forces of the 28th Path leads to 'glamour' so does an unbalance of the 30th Path lead to aridity. The Tarot Trump, Lord of the Fire of the World, (Divine Reason), shows however, the true powers of the Path, the Sun showering golden rain upon two near-naked children. This is the outpouring of the forces of Life, Light and Love upon the young human race. The wall signifies an enclosure, the limitation which is a protection, the cultivated growth within a garden which is sealed off from wild nature. This has its higher implications on a Cosmic level, for it is by limitation only that growth can be attained. The mind of man is limited; it is not omniscient and cannot be during his early growth. This is perhaps just as well, as was hinted by Our Lord when He said: "I have yet many things to say unto you, but ye cannot bear them now." (John. xvi. 12)

11. The 30th Path, moreover, in that it is the Path from Yesod, the unconscious mind, to Hod, is a Path on which great wisdom can be attained, for Hod is the means of

contact with the Greater Beings of evolution concerned with teaching — Socrates, Hermes, Merlin, Buddha and the like, whose main sphere of influence is in Chesed. There being a strong link between Chesed and Hod means that teaching from these high sources is projected down the planes to form a pool of teaching, as it were, in Hod. Hod is often called 'the Water Temple', referring to its symbolical use as a pool in which the higher wisdom may be seen reflected.

12. Thus the 30th Path from Yesod to Hod is the beginnings of the great Hermetic Ray, the Path of Wisdom, which leads via the 26th Path to Tiphareth. Similarly, the 28th and 24th Paths relate to the Power Ray or Green Ray as it is sometimes called. The way of the 25th Path represents the Purple Ray of Devotion. All these Paths meet in Tiphareth, that is, in the fusion of the Individuality and Personality, which means that the principle of sacrifice is implicit in all of them, that being the only way to the Higher Life, through the Mysteries of the Crucifixion to the Vision of the Harmony of Things in the central Sephirah of the Tree.

13. But Hod is no more a Sephirah only of barren reason then Netzach is of weak sentimentality — it is only perverted human nature that makes it sometimes appear so. So just as there is the lithe, hard splendour and the power of the 28th Path so is there the expanding of consciousness in the light of Pure Reason on the 30th Path. It is essentially a Path of Light — Sun Light — the Light of the whole concourse of Solar Logoi throughout Cosmic Space — hence, Light in Extension.

14. There is a further range of powers upon this Path of vast implication which is suggested by the Magical Image of Hod — the Hermaphrodite. The Path from Hod to Yesod is on a direct line with the course of the Lightning Flash upon the Tree, the glyph which shows the order of the increasingly denser manifestation of the Spirit. The Path represents the stage where the differentiation of the sexes came about.

15. Spirit is, of course, androgynous, and according to

'The Secret Doctrine', procreation was originally asexual — thus we have the teachings about the Sweat-born, the Egg-born and so on. The present swarm of humanity, however, developed orginally the sexual means of reproduction and the manifestation upon Earth as primarily male or female. Varying teachings have been given about cycles of sexuality in incarnations but it now appears that there is no definite periodic law, but that a Spirit will manifest predominantly as male or female, though with occasional minor incarnations as the opposite sex. Generally speaking, womankind represents Spirits at that time indigenous to Earth, and mankind Spirits which then came from other planets. There are various hints of all this in Genesis and the esoteric theories are treated at some length in H. P. Blavatsky's 'The Secret Doctrine' etc.

16. The basic thing is, though, that Original Sin, to use the ecclesiastical term, lay not in the differentiation of the sexes but in the human reactions to the unfoldment of this part of the Divine Plan. Thus the driving of Adam and Eve from the Garden of Eden was because humanity abused the Mysteries of human creation, not because they discovered the use of them. It was they, after all, who reacted with shame after the acquisition of the knowledge. As a result, the Curse was pronounced, or in other words, it was the inexorable working of Cosmic Law that there should become enmity between the woman's seed and the serpent's seed. (cf. Gen. iii. 15) In other words, mankind 'bruised the head' of the fruits of wisdom and knowledge because of its profanation of those powers, and karma 'bruised the heel' of man by causing him to be no longer the king of creation but merely a puny but intelligent animal, the prey to weaknesses and disease of his own generation.

17. The main cause of suffering within man is the gulf within himself, "the temple is unworthy of the indwelling god", and the consequent gap between vision and reality gives the ever unsatisfied nameless desire within man that is symbolised by the eagle or vulture constantly gnawing

at the liver of Prometheus. Prometheus, it will be remembered, is doomed to remain in chains until Hercules releases him. This is the law decreed by Zeus, who represents the creator of the natural animal world in which the early vehicles of man existed in a state of beatific ignorance. Prometheus represents the coming down into those vehicles of Divine Wisdom — creative forethought and all that that implies. The result of this is the chaining of 'Prometheus' into these animal vehicles of dense manifestation, in spite of his higher origin. The timing was not right and hence the suffering, but the default in timing was due to previous karma necessitating a considerable redeeming sacrifice of some sort. The original refusal to manifest, and the subsequent abuse of creative powers prematurely received, constitutes the bulk of Original Sin and its consequent karma brought about largely through the lack of correlation thus caused between physical and spiritual evolution. When man on Earth, Hercules, has accomplished his twelve labours of evolutionary progress, symbolised by the Zodiac, then Prometheus is released. But it will also be remembered that the condition of Prometheus' release is that one should die in his place, and this volunteer is Cheiron, the centaur, animal man who willingly dies for the sake of the immortality of Prometheus.

18. The above, at best, can be but an approximation of the factors involved and the allegories mentioned can also be interpreted in other ways. Actually, the details of theory are not of prime importance; the effects of these original deviations operate and can be studied more accurately in the present life. Thus there are many still refusing to incarnate fully by hedging themselves behind a protective barrier of mind and dodging experience as human beings. As many of these are naturally attracted to science, and the scientist has become a figure of power these days, there is some cause for concern. Such are quite capable of destroying or experimenting with life for the sake of a theory and are quite able to do it owing to the self-imposed deadness of

56

their own feelings. And when such Spirits choose for their sphere of interest politics or warfare then, with the means of destruction now available, humanity had better beware.

19. Another common form of deviation is linked with the differentiation of the sexes. One sees men refusing to be men and women refusing to be women. This does not refer only to the more obvious forms of perversion such as homosexuality, but also to the quite common manifestation of 'cocksure women and hen-sure men' as D. H. Lawrence described it. This is not to advocate a return to the social conditions where men are lords of all they survey and women their pets or chattels. All Spirits, and therefore the sexes, are equal. It has a broader reference: men being men and not tycoons, clerks, labourers, bores; women being women and not socialites, drudges, or empty headed gossips. Life is meant to be lived and the original reluctance or refusal to incarnate or to differentiate into sexes has its results in people trying to be 'things' and not living beings. The all-human deviation can be seen in the twisting of the teaching of the one who came to Earth and was crucified in order that humanity "might have life, and that they might have it more abundantly." (John. x. 10.) into a promulgation of 'slave morality'. Humility and meekness are the 'noblesse oblige' of the Spirit, and are paid to God, not to man. There is nothing holy nor Christian about denial of life, but this attitude has come to be associated with Christianity and thus there is much truth in Nietzsche's jibe that "the last Christian died on the Cross." The hero of Gethsemane and Golgotha was no "gentle Jesus meek and mild" and it is a great irony that many of the professed followers of Christ have all but succeeded in doing what the Jewish High Priests and the Romans failed to do—effectively silence the real Christian message.

20. The Sun on the 30th Path then, can throw a glaring light on the deviations within the self as they manifest in the Personality, and thus it can well be seen that the Archangel Michael's sword and spear are not merely symbolic

weapons for use against medieval pantomime demons, but are points of accusation and cauterisation directed at the inmost heart of whoever treads this Path on its deeper levels. The Qliphoth need no mighty conjurations, they are embedded deeply and inextricably entwined within ourselves, and so from this it will also be obvious why Hod should be at the base of the Pillar of Severity when the Pillars are applied to the Tree. The 30th Path is a Path of great light but this Divine Light may be uncomfortably self-revelatory, for the Path corresponds in the Personality to the 22nd Path of Karmic Adjustment in the Individuality.

21. However, the Paths of the Tree of Life are great journeys and experiences of the soul and he who seeks the quest of the Holy Grail in Kether will welcome the purificatory processes on the way. He who dares to stand naked in the glaring sunlight of Truth as the children do on the Tarot Trump will realise that he is embarked upon a true and testing Quest and no medievally englamoured romance or esoteric parlour game.

22. The ascent of the 30th Path is a way of attainment of Wisdom, and that wisdom may not be flattering to one's self-esteem. The descent of the Path is the bringing of that wisdom down into the core of one's consciousness that it may be lived out in the world, in Malkuth.

NOTES ON THE DESIGN OF TRUMP XIX

The Marseilles version shows two children embracing before a wall, behind which is a huge Sun, complete with face and with drops falling from it.

There is some difference of opinion on whether the children should be naked or not. Levi and Papus have described them so, and they appear so on Case's card. However, on the Marseilles version they are shown wearing loin cloths, and this has been followed by Wirth and Knapp. It is by no means necessarily prudery which provides these garments on the old exoteric card for on other Trumps, such as The Star or The Devil, complete nudity is shown — though with the concession to Mrs. Grundy that the sexual organs are obscured by the interposition of an element in the picture, such as the ropes or chains in the case of The Devil, or one of the vases in The Star. A similar arrangement by use of contrived arrangement of hands or legs could have been used quite easily here, so it would seem that, like the scarf on the naked figure of The Universe, the loin cloths here serve a symbolic purpose. As we have considered the Path from Yesod to Hod to be concerned with, amongst other things, the differentiation of the sexes, the loin cloths may well originally have been Edenic fig leaves, and these two children or adolescents representative of Adam and Eve and the young humanity of antedeluvian times. The inclusion of flowers garlanding the wall on some old packs would confirm an interpretation of the wall being that bounding the Garden of Eden. These flowers, in the form of sunflowers, are reintroduced by Waite and Case; four in number, with Case showing an additional one in bud, turning towards the Sun. Knapp shows the pair standing within a ring of flowers, which ring is a double 'fairy ring' of darker coloured grass in the version of Wirth and Case.

Waite follows a different tradition of design, one which was mentioned by Eliphas Levi. This shows a naked child upon a white horse and holding a scarlet standard before the usual wall and Sun. According to Waite, this represents the unfoldment of spiritual consciousness, represented by the child, horse and standard, as opposed to the natural consciousness of the Sun and flowers on the other side of the wall. This is quite valid as an interpretation but taking into account the position of the card on the Tree of Life the unfoldment is more that of the androgynous state from the sexual, or vice versa, according to the direction in which the Path is traversed. In this case, the two children seems the better symbolism, who are becoming more sexually polarised as they approach Yesod, or more androgynous, as little children, as they approach Hod. The giving of loin cloths to them is thus to conceal a great Mystery.

Crowley always favoured the two children version, who, he early said, should be "wantonly and shamelessly embracing". On the Harris card the Sun is charged with a rose and is shining upon a wall encircled green mount. The children have butterfly wings and Rose-crosses at their feet, whilst around the card are the signs of the Zodiac.

Case, as usual, makes much of the numeration of the symbols on the card—the courses of bricks in the wall, the rays of the Sun, the drops falling from it. He gives an 8 pointed Sun, with 8 wavy secondary rays, and 48 tertiary rays. In this he follows the Marseilles card. Wirth has 12 main rays and 12 wavy secondaries and is followed by Waite—though the numeration is indistinct on the latter's design. Knapp has 32 identical wavy rays interspersed with gold drops. Of these falling drops Waite has none, the Marseilles card 13, Wirth 19, Case 13, (six each side and one between the couple), Knapp 66, (32 round the Sun, 34 falling), and Manly P. Hall, whose symbol for the card is a sphere surmounted tau-cross, favours 13. It is generally agreed that the wall is of stone, not brick, and Case, Wirth and the Marseilles card (a little confusedly) show five courses, Knapp six, and Waite at least eight, the actual number being undetermined.

The Zain version shows no wall and the near-naked children are replaced by a mature couple fully clothed. The Sun above them is described in the text as having 21 rays but has only 15 on the card, five triads, each with ankh, disk and serpent symbolism. They are surrounded by a circle of 24 flowers but with only 20 visible.

Levi has mentioned in passing an old version of this card which showed a spinner weaving destinies.

The 27th Path

Hod — Netzach

KEY: פ Peh. Mouth.

SPIRITUAL SIGNIFICANCE: ♂ Mars.

THEORY: Lord of the Hosts of the Mighty. (XVI—The House of God.)

COLOURS: Scarlet. Red. Venetian red. Bright red rayed azure and emerald.

TEXT: "The Twenty-seventh Path is the Active or Exciting Intelligence and it is so called because through it every existent being receives its spirit and motion."

1. This Path, a lateral one, is the main girder of the Personality, linking the centre of creative power in Netzach and the centre of concrete ideation in Hod. It is a Path, therefore, which holds tremendous dynamics; it links directly the basal Sephiroth which are aligned with the opposite poles of the Principles of Manifestation, the Positive and Negative Pillars.

2. It is rather like the principles in the structure of the physical atom, which is a complex of forces of differing polarity held in together as a unit with tremendous force, and as the splitting of the atoms of one gram of helium releases 200,000 kilowatt-hours of energy, enough power to light 200,000 lamps of 100 watts for ten hours, so the psychic energy bound up within a unit of human life may be considered to be a similarly astronomical figure. It is energy on this scale that may account for certain types of hauntings, particularly those of a violent or long lasting type. Great shock such as murder or sudden death may cause a splitting off of certain aspects of a Personality, resulting in the great force that must be present for entities to build up etherically without prepared conditions and to throw heavy physical objects about.

3. This kind of thing relates to rare types of spiritual pathology and need not detain us, but it does give a concrete example of the high potencies involved in the make-up of the lower vehicles of a human being. It is this force—again in direct line on this Path with the Lightning Flash—through which "every existent being receives its spirit and motion." The Yetziratic Text also calls the powers of this Path the Active or Exciting Intelligence, for it is the manifestation of life-force in the lower worlds.

4. For this reason the planet Mars is well attributed to this Path, for Mars is essentially the planet of activity and excitation and is indeed the Mundane Chakra of Geburah, the great Sephirah of Force in Activity. This fundamental aspect of Mars is shown by the shape of its sign, the disk of spiritual being surmounted by an arrow. The colours of the Path are also varieties of red, essentially the Mars colour.

4. The Hebrew letter of the Path is Peh, signifying the Mouth. The mouth is that part of the organism that takes in nourishment and utters speech. The receptive aspect can be regarded as the receiving of the downflow of life-force from Netzach via the Path of the Lightning Flash. By this means the lower being is kept in existence. Again, as this Path represents the structure of the Personality, the attribution of the Mouth reminds us that the purpose of incarnation is the seeking of the food of experience in Form for the benefit of the Individuality and the Spirit.

6. Considered in its positive aspect, as an organ of speech, objective communication, it is obvious that the Personality also serves this purpose. There is, however, the deeper significance of the symbol in that the mouth is that which acts as a vehicle for the Word. The Word, in its metaphysical sense, stands for the first manifestation of Spirit itself. "In the beginning was the word, and the Word was with God, and the Word was God." (John i. 1.) In the case of the 27th Path the Word has reverberated down to the astro-mental levels of being and formed a vehicle for

itself—the Personality. It is through this Personality that the Word is uttered in the densest level of existence, Malkuth, the physical world.

7. The shape of the letter Peh suggests a mouth and the Yod like. shape inside may be considered as the tongue, which formulates the Word in action, or else as the Word itself. The shell of the mouth is represented by a shape like the letter Kaph, which also appeared on the 32nd Path as the scarf enwrapping the figure of the soul or Spirit on the Tarot Trump, The Universe. The higher meanings of the letter Kaph are a part of the 21st Path which joins Chesed to Netzach, that channel between Individuality and Personality where the purity of the Spirit first in Form imprints its image on the as yet formless levels of the lower self.

8. The idea of a vehicle for the Spirit is also given in the Tarot Trump, in this case in the form of a building, called The House of God, a fitting name for what the Personality should be. Its esoteric title is Lord of the Hosts of the Mighty, implying a conjunction of the forces of Netzach and Hod whose God-Names are Jehovah Tzabaoth and Elohim Tzabaoth, Lord of Hosts and God of Hosts respectively.

9. At first sight the design of the Tarot Trump calls to mind the Biblical story of the Tower of Babel by which men attempted to build an edifice reaching the Heavens; and the resulting confusion of tongues after the failure of this project is confirmed by the letter Peh attributed to this Path—the Mouth.

10. The Bible states that the Tower of Babel was struck down by a wrathful Jehovah, who would not tolerate men achieving such heights. However, the wrathful Jehovah is a minor tribal deity and there is an obvious distortion of motives here. It is man's ultimate destiny to become a God, and so the Solar Logos would obviously not thwart the achievement of this aspiration.

11. It is probably quite true that Babel fell and tongues were confused because of man's pride, but in the sense

that the pride of man, (the sin of separation), caused men to build wrongly, or prematurely, and thus, by operation of Cosmic Law, to bring confusion and defeat upon themselves. It is indeed typical of man to put the cause of the failure upon the jealous pride of God. "And the Lord said, Behold, the people is one, and they have all one language; and this they begin to do: and now nothing will be restrained from them, which they have imagined to do. Go to, let us go down, and there confound their language, that they may not understand one anothers speech." A priesthood, of whatever religion, once it has attained earthly power, is very prone to find divine reasons to keep men humble and preserve the status quo. But there is pride and pride, and man gains little by that false humility—(really spiritual laziness or even cowardice)—that is content to leave everything to the priesthood, or to Jesus, or to God. Christ's parable of the talents has relevance here, the man who buried his talent received short shrift.

12. The story of Babel in connection with this Path and Tarot Trump then is a reminder to build one's foundations true—(on the rock of Faith, to quote another parable)—and true Faith at that, certainly not the prideful Faith of the Pharisee which sets one up supposedly as better than other men. The modern occult movement has tended to go very much in this direction but such an attitude is again the sin of separation, and an illusion, for all paths to God are ways of synthesis, as ways to the One must be.

13. There is another meaning to this Trump which is revealed by close examination of the traditional design. It will be noted that the Tower is not struck down. On the contrary, the bodywork of the Tower is unscathed and the crown-like roof merely lifts up to receive the bolt of fire or lightning. The falling pieces are not bricks or stones but radiations from the sky and it may be interesting to numerologists that their number in the old Marseilles Tarot is 37, the mystic number—"the unity itself in balanced trinitarian manifestation" according to Crowley—which,

multiplied by any multiple of three, gives the numbers 111, 222, 333, 444, etc. Similarly, the number of courses of bricks in the Tower is 22, the number of the Hebrew letters and Paths upon the Tree. The top of the Tower is a Crown, symbol of Kether, with four battlements, aligning with the Four Aspects of God, and there are three windows, one above two, showing the means of manifestation of force and again emphasising "trinitarian manifestation."

14. The two figures falling from the Tower, though their sex is not plain on the old cards, are generally considered to be a man and a woman. All these considerations call to mind the alchemical symbolism given in that greatly underrated mystical treatise in the guise of a romance, 'The Chymical Marriage of Christian Rosencreutz.', first published in English in 1690 and apparently not at all since then apart from an abridged version in A. E. Waite's 'Real History of the Rosicrucians' (Redway, London. 1887)

15. The story tells of the summoning of Christian Rosencreutz to go on a quest on Easter Day which lasts for seven days. His adventures are a summary of the initiation process. The first day he is summoned to a strange marriage of a King and Queen. The second day he sets out and chooses one of three ways—the hard stony way of initiation is the one he chooses, almost inadvertently, from the broad easy way of normal evolution and the fantastically difficult way endurable only to one in a thousand, presumably saintship. The third day he is tested along with his other pilgrims by being weighed in a balance when all the unworthy are chastised and sent away. The fourth day he is presented to the King and Queen and is initiated into the secret knowledge of a strange temple, and shown a play in seven acts depicting symbolically the history of the relationship between God, his Son the Christ, and Earth the Bride. After this, the King and Queen submit themselves to be mysteriously beheaded. The fifth day he steals a glimpse of 'the naked Venus'—Isis unveiled, which act subsequently causes him to be sent back to the world, no

doubt as a teacher, instead of remaining in bliss in the eternal company of the mysterious Order and the resurrected King and Queen. There is a mock burial of the King and Queen, their real bodies having been secretly sent to a strange Tower in the night, followed by them all journeying to the Tower. The sixth day they all take part in the alchemical process of transmuting the dead bodies of the King and Queen into new life in the strange Tower of seven storeys. On the seventh and last day they return with the resurrected King and Queen to the original castle and are invested with the Knighthood of the Order of the Golden Stone and in view of his having seen Isis unveiled, Christian Rosencreutz is returned to the outer world.

16. The sevenfold alchemical process in the Tower is of great interest, for this Tower may be aligned with the Tower of the Tarot Trump. In the ground floor of the Tower they are set to work extracting essences from plants and gems to be used in the subsequent regenerating process. On the second level the bodies are distilled in a retort and the liquor obtained run off into a golden globe. On the third level the globe is heated by means of sunlight reflected in many mirrors, and when the globe is finally cut open by means of a diamond, a large white egg is revealed. On the fourth level the egg is incubated in a square sand-bath and a bird hatched out which is at first black and wild but which, on being fed on some of the liquor distilled from the bodies, becomes tame, its feathers turning to white. On the fifth level the bird is put in a water-bath of a milk-like liquid and all its feathers are boiled off, revealing the bird naked and shining, which process turns the bath blue. The bath itself is heated strongly and ground to a blue powder which is used to paint the bird, all but its head. On the sixth level the bird is placed on a strange altar which was in the Temple on the fourth day of the adventure, and there pecks and drinks the blood of a white serpent in a skull. The serpent is revived and the bird then becomes a willing sacrifice, suffering its head to be chopped off. There is

no blood until the breast of the bird is opened, which blood is then caught in a receptacle. The body is then burned and the ashes saved. On the seventh level only certain of the pilgrims are allowed, the others being told that the sixth level is the highest and being put to making gold from some of the bird's ashes. The four who are allowed on the seventh level are put to mixing the ashes with water and moulding a little man and woman, which are then heated and become of a most beauteous aspect. These beautiful homonculi are then fed with the blood of the bird—which after all was made from the original bodies—and grow to life size. Then trumpets are placed in the mouths and fire enters through a hole in the roof, ensouling them, the now regenerated and resurrected King and Queen.

17. The whole process is a résumé of higher initiation. The King and Queen before regeneration may be considered to be the two aspects of the Personality represented by Netzach and Hod, and the initial engagement to marry is well placed on the 27th Path, for this Path directly unites these two Sephiroth. The aim is, however, a higher synthesis, so the Personality is sacrificed, that is, its interests are no longer paramount and its forces are turned in upon itself in a kind of 'distillation' representing the early initiatory process which results in an egg, the germ of contact with the Individuality. This egg is hatched out, that is, the Individuality takes over, at first crudely and in an unbalanced way, but eventually in harmonious control of its lower vehicles. This is symbolised by the bird being at first wild and black and then tame and white. Its Qabalistic analogue is in the Tiphareth stages of the Child, the first stumbling efforts of the Individuality to gain control, and the King, the Individuality in full control. The bird has its feathers boiled off and is painted with the blue tincture obtained from the liquid and the bath. This may be said to represent the processes of the soul on the 22nd and 19th Paths, Tiphareth-Geburah-Chesed, where all past karma is worked out and the Individuality/Personality realises

itself for what it is, all its outer vehicles accounted for and all evolutionary experience distilled to make the general 'colour' of the Spirit in Form. In this archetypal example it is blue, the colour of Chesed and aspiration. There then comes the high Daath initiation which is part of the Qabalistic Sacrificed God formula of Tiphareth. The pecking of the serpent in the skull is a breakthrough to the Supernal Worlds, after which the Spirit ceases existence, voluntarily, as a separate being in Form. The results of this very high Daath contact are all that most can attain and it is indeed an achievement, symbolised by the ability to make gold. But this is a material achievement, that is to say, the worlds of Form are not completely transcended. The highest initiation is that of the Supernals where new vehicles of a spiritual nature are made and ensouled with the Divine Fire from the Unmanifest—that is, a contact is made with the Cosmic Atom of the self, which originally projected the Divine Spark into manifestation. (cf. 'The Cosmic Doctrine.')

18. (In passing, it is interesting to note that the Divine Fire was directed into the new bodies through the mouth, the signification of the Hebrew letter Peh.)

19. In this process we have a completely new line of interpretation for the apparently downthrown King and Queen on the Tarot Trump and for the Fire of Heaven entering through the Crown-like roof. The implications lead us right into the Unmanifest beyond Kether, but the beginnings of the process are in the Personality and the 'engagement' is the intention to unify the opposite poles of the self to the very highest level.

20. On a lower level of interpretation the descending Fire may be considered to come down the 25th Path. Wherever Paths cross is an important point upon the Tree of Life. Thus, applied to the etheric vehicle of man, the junction of the 27th and 25th Paths may be aligned with the Spleen Centre, the centre which takes in force from the environment. Thus the Tower, the House of God, in this instance symbolises the body, and the Fire of Heaven the inflow of

pranic force. In line with this attribution is one of the titles of the Tarot Trump of the 25th Path, the Bringer Forth of Life, and also Daughter of the Reconcilers.

21. The treading of this Path, then, may be rough going unless the Personality is well balanced and open to the descending Fire. It is a Path of the simultaneous use of vertical and horizontal polarity in the vehicles of the Personality. It is also on the line of the Lightning Flash, and the higher pole, or source of power, is Netzach, which power is received into the form consciousness of Hod. If the Personality has built itself too rigid a form the downcoming Fire from Tiphareth may prove very disrupting because it has to blast through the rigid blockages—if it can get through at all. On the other hand, too much 'Netzach' in the build-up of the Personality may cause the Tower to be unstable, the mortar binding its bricks having too little binding force—thus diffusion of consciousness would probably result.

22. It will be obvious then that the first essential of occult work is a balanced Personality, for without that, the Interior Castle, to use St. Teresa's term, ("I thought of the soul as resembling a castle, formed of a single diamond or a very transparent crystal, and containing many rooms, just as in heaven there are many mansions."), will be built on insecure foundations.

NOTES ON THE DESIGN OF TRUMP XVI

This card is variously called The Fire of Heaven, The House of God, The Hospital, The Tower of Babel, The Tower, The Lightning Struck Tower, etc. The Marseilles card shows the top of the tower being struck off though the tower itself remains intact. Two figures are falling to the ground and there are many small circles falling also. The top of the tower is like a crown, with four castellations, and the tower has three windows, one over two.

Wirth shows one of the figures crowned and the actual tower being shattered; he also adds a door to the tower. Knapp follows suit and Hall's symbol is a hand grasping a bunch of thunderbolts. On Wirth's card the flash is seen coming from the Sun, and Knapp shows money falling as well as masonry.

Levi likened the tower to Babel and suggested the figures might be Nimrod and his minister, possibly facetiously. He said one of the figures should be in the form of a letter Ayin, a point agreed by Crowley.

Waite places the tower on a high pinnacle and makes the top a rather fancy crown. He makes the falling figures an uncrowned man and a crowned woman and has flames appearing out of the windows, he to the left, she to the right. On the man's side are twelve Yods and on the woman's side, ten. The introduction of

Yods into Tarot symbolism was a favourite Golden Dawn device. Case follows Waite closely though he restores the crown to its original simplicity and shows the lightning flash coming from the Sun, and also closely resembling the form of the Qabalistic Lightning Flash. He also gives 22 courses of masonry, emblematic of the 22 Hebrew letters etc. The Marseilles tower also has 22 courses, which is remarkable for an exoteric pack; the number of falling Yods is also 37, which is a number of considerable numerological significance.

Crowley's card shows the tower completely shattered; he also shows a huge Eye of Horus at the top and the Mouth of Hell at the bottom, belching flames. Near the Eye are a dove, bearing an olive branch, and a lion headed serpent. The falling figures are geometric abstractions.

The 'Egyptian' card shows two falling figures before a pyramid, the top of which has been struck off by lightning. There is a door in the pyramid showing various god forms and figures difficult to distinguish.

Part III

The Links With The Individuality

The 25th Path

Yesod — Tiphareth

KEY: ☐ Samech. Prop.
SPIRITUAL SIGNIFICANCE: ♐ Sagittarius. The Archer.
THEORY: Daughter of the Reconcilers. Bringer Forth of Life. (XIV — Temperance.)
COLOURS: Blue. Yellow. Green. Dark vivid blue.
TEXT: "The Twenty-fifth Path is the Intelligence of Probation or Temptation, and is so called because it is the primary temptation, by which the Creator trieth all righteous persons."

1. This Path, leading from Yesod to Tiphareth, is the direct line of contact between the Individuality and Personality and on it are developed the first glimmerings of mystical or higher consciousness. Before mystical consciousness can gain a hold in the lower vehicles however, these vehicles have to be quietened and this process is symbolised by likening the process of development to a journey through a desert or wilderness, when the soul is thrown entirely upon its own resources, assisted only by Faith. In this way the Yetziratic Text can be seen to be relevant, for those whose courage or Faith fails them will scurry back to the apparent security of consciousness in the lower worlds. All three ways to Tiphareth, the 24th, 25th and 26th Paths, contain that experience known as the Dark Night of the Soul, and in the symbolism of the 25th Path the soul has to advance on the Desert Way, leaving behind the life of the outer and lower worlds, not yet conscious of the life of the inner and higher worlds, invoking the inner light that will become a golden dawn in the darkness.

2. This experience is a well-known one in the annals of Devotional Mysticism and so some idea of it may best be conveyed by some quotations at length from 'The Dark

69

Night of the Soul' by St. John of the Cross. The translation
used is G. C. Graham's. (Watkins. London.)

3. "Souls begin to enter this dark night when God proceeds
to lead them from the state of beginners, proper to those
who meditate on the spiritual road, and begins to set them
in that of the progressives, which is, at length, that of the
contemplatives, to the end, that passing through this state,
they may reach that of the perfect, which is the Divine
union of the Soul with God. Therefore, so that we may the
better understand and set forth what night this is where
through the soul passes, and for what cause God places her
therein, we must here first touch upon some propensities of
beginners, so that they may know the weakness of their
state, and pluck up courage, and desire that God may set
them in this night, wherein the soul is strengthened and
confirmed in virtue and made ready for the inestimable
delights of the love of God. And even though we dwell somewhat thereon, it will not be more than suffices in order
adequately to treat, further on, of this dark night. We must
then know that, after the soul resolutely converts herself to
God, God generally sets to work to educate her spiritually
and to regale her, as does a loving mother her tender child,
who she warms at the heat of her breast, and rears with
sweet milk and soft and delicate food and bears about in her
arms and cherishes; but, by degrees, as it waxes in growth,
the mother begins to wean it and hiding from it her soft
breast, anoints it with bitter aloes, and putting the infant
from her arms, teaches it to walk with its feet, to the end
that, losing its childish ways, it may become used to greater
and more real things . . .

4. "This night, whereby we mean contemplation, produces
in the spiritually minded two sorts of darkness or purgations,
answering to the two parts of man, that is to say, the sensitive and spiritual. And thus, the first night or sensitive purgation is that wherein the soul purges and strips herself naked
of all things of sense, by conforming the senses to the spirit;
and the next is, the spiritual night or purgation, wherein

the soul purges and denudes herself of all mental activity, by conforming and disposing the intellect for the union of love with God. The sensitive is usual and happens to many, and it is of these beginners, that we shall treat first. The spiritual purgation is gone through by very few, and those only who have been proved and tried, and of these we shall treat afterwards.

5. "The first night or purgation is bitter and terrible to the sense. The second transcends all description, because it is exceeding fearsome for the spirit, as we shall presently shew: and as the sensitive comes first in order and takes place first, we shall briefly say somewhat thereof; so that we may proceed more especially to treat of the spiritual night, whereof very little has been said, either by word of mouth or writing, and moreover, because the experience thereof is extremely rare. Now, since the method these beginners pursue on the journey towards God is slavish and bears a strong resemblance to their own desires and delights, as was above set forth; since God wills to lead them higher, and deliver them from this base fashion of love to a loftier degree of love of God, and free them from the inadequate and mechanical exercise of the sense (the imagination) and mental activity which go agroping after God in such a feeble sort and with so much difficulty, as we have said, and places them in the exercise of the spirit, wherein they can communicate with God more abundantly and freer from imperfections; when, at length, they have practised themselves for some time in the journey of virtue, persevering in meditation and prayer, wherein, with the suavity and relish they have found, they have become detached from worldly things, and aquired some spiritual strength in God, so as to be able to curb the creature appetites and in some small degree suffer for God some slight load and dryness, without turning back at the crucial moment; when, to their thinking, they are proceeding in these spiritual exercises to their entire satisfaction and delight; and when the Sun of Divine favours seems to them to shine most radiantly upon them,

God darkens all this light, and shuts the door and fountain of the sweet spiritual water, which they were wont to drink in God as often and as long as they chose . . . and thus, he leaves them in darkness so profound that they know not whither to direct the sense of the imagination and speculations of the mind. For they cannot take a single step towards meditation, as before they were wont, the interior sense being now submerged in this night, and made so barren, that not only find they no substance and delight in spiritual matters and good practices wherein they were wont to rejoice and find relish, but, on the contrary, in its place a nauseous savour and bitterness. For, as I have said, as God knows them to have, at length, increased somewhat in growth; in order that they may acquire strength and escape from their swaddling clothes, He severs them His sweet breast, and putting them from His arms, teaches them to walk alone, the which, to them, is passing strange, as everything seems topsy-turvy."

6. The experience of the 25th Path is that of the first or 'sensitive' Night of the Soul, to use the term of St. John of the Cross. The second or 'spiritual' Night is that of the approaches to the Abyss and Daath, so it is not surprising that it "is gone through by very few, and those only who have been proved and tried", for, as the blueprint of the Tree of Life shows, it is a very advanced mystical state. Only the first, lesser Night need concern us at the moment and anyone who reaches it, and gets through it, has achieved a fair degree of mystical enlightenment—at least to the verges of 'Soul consciousness' as some schools call it, or the conscious contact of the Individuality with the Personality. To get through the Dark Night of the Soul unaided would be an achievement indeed and this is another reason why self-tuition is not recommended for any course of occult or spiritual training, for only a person exceptionally strong in Faith would be able to keep going in the face of such spiritual aridity. For any who do have to go it alone however, the whole book by St. John of the Cross is well worth study.

7. It is interesting to equate the terms of St. John of the Cross with the Qabalistic system, for they do align one with another very well. According to him, the soul — in this context, the Personality, — has three aspects, Will, Intellect and Memory, and these may be aligned with Netzach, Hod and Yesod respectively. Furthermore, he says elsewhere that it is St. Paul's well known categories of Faith, Hope and Charity which are at the same time a cause of the spiritual darkness and the means to go through it. "For Faith voids and darkens the intellect of all its human knowledge, and, by so doing, prepares it for union with the Divine Wisdom. And Hope empties and alienates the memory from all creature possessions . . . and sets it upon what it hopes to enjoy in the future. And this is why the hope of God alone, can absolutely dispose the memory because of the vacuum it causes therein, to be united with him. Just in the same way doth Charity void and empty the affections and appetites of the will of whatsoever thing is not God, and sets them on Him alone; and so this virtue prepares this faculty and unites it with God through love."

8. The phrase in the earlier passage that the Night of the Soul is a test to see whether the soul will turn back "at the crucial moment" may be accepted more literally than was perhaps intended, for the word 'crucial' comes from the Latin 'crux' — a cross, and the point of greatest difficulty on the 25th Path — the greatest darkness before dawn — is at the point where a cross is formed between it and the transverse 27th Path of Mars and the Lightning Struck Tower, or House of God.

9. The fact that the three virtues outlined by St. Paul in his Epistle to the Corinthians are both the cause and the means of ending the Dark Night of the Soul gives a reason for the allocation of the Hebrew letter Samekh to the Path — this letter meaning a Prop or Crutch. To speak symbolically, the soul needs the Prop or Crutch of Faith, Hope and Love of God in its weak state at this point, though of course these were the means of wounding also and according to the

strength of these qualities so is the severity of the test. (Incidentally, we might note here the alternative title of the Trump of the 27th Path — The Hospital!) Those of weak Faith, Hope and Charity have little great Darkness to go through at a time, though the process may be extended over many, many years intermittently. Similarly, those of great spiritual virtue are likely to have a comparatively short but very severe testing. This follows logically from the fact that it is the spiritual virtues that cause the 'wound' that only they themselves can remedy. There is a profound occult hint here for it signifies a) that all the tests of the soul are within the soul itself, and b) they are automatically governed by the strength and speed of progress of the soul, so that no soul is broken through spiritual aspiration and progress. Not all are expected to take up the Cross of a World Saviour. Yet even so, one's own Cross will test one searchingly enough. This may be seen not only in the personal testimony of the mystics but also in the record of the process on a group level in the Biblical story of the Jewish Exodus from Egypt into the forty years in the Wilderness.

10. From this it is obvious why the forty day journey of Our Lord through the Wilderness was of a more testing character than is the lot of most. Most souls have only their Faith, Hope and Charity to be tested but Our Lord, one who had real and potent occult power, also had to face the temptations of firstly, his own self-preservation, which was not only a question of commanding the stones of the wilderness to become bread but an avoidance of the Crucifixion; secondly, the use of his own power to lead the rebellious Jewish nation, which was ripe for it, to a rebellion against Rome and the establishment of an empire of its own with Jesus ben Joseph as Emperor; thirdly, the direct defiance of God by using his great powers to set up a spiritual kingdom in Earth divorced from the rule of the Solar Logos — to become, in fact, an anti-Christ. Again, as with Faith, Hope and Charity, it is the very divine powers themselves that cause the temptation, and Satan is a personification of these as-

pects, and thus, like them, within the soul and not an external adversary. This is the rationale behind the Rosicrucian phrase "Demon Est Deus Inversus."

11. Another link with the Prop or Crutch symbolised by the Hebrew letter is the crutch of the great god of healing, Asclepios, whose influence, together with the healing radiations of the Archangel Raphael, the Archangel "who standeth in the Sun", flows down the 25th Path from the Sephirah Tiphareth. This is the brighter side of this Path of Probation and Temptation, and, it is said, when all sin and its effect, disease, are wiped from the face of the Universe, then Asclepios will no longer be lame and will throw away his crutch. Thus this great god-form has implications beyond that of a god of healing, for the same might be said of the Solar Logos, whose symbol, and to some extent Its very being, lies in the Sun.

12. The Tarot Trump of the Path, Temperance, shows both aspects of the Path—an angel, presumably Raphael, standing in a wilderness and pouring the waters of life from a golden vase into a silver one—two obvious symbols of the Sun Sephirah, Tiphareth, and the Moon Sephirah, Yesod, which this Path conjoins. The title of the card, Temperance, may also be considered in the sense of the tempering of souls, as with metals, to make them fit to be used as tools in the Great Works of God.

13. The astrological sign, Sagittarius, is the sign of aspiration, and well fitted to this Path as is the colour blue, the Atziluthic Colour of the Path. This colour of aspiration extends the whole length of the centre of the Tree from Malkuth to Kether, though of a darker colour, indigo, at the more material end. Sagittarius is associated with the Centaur, a creature symbolising the state of half god, half beast, which man is; and it was one of these creatures, Cheiron, who consented to die that Prometheus might have eternal life. In other words, this is the transition of human existence from terrestrial humanity to Divine Lords of Humanity.

14. Sagittarius is also the Archer and in this context may

be considered as the Individuality marking out its prey, the Personality, and speeding the arrow into it. This causes Divine Love just as the arrow of the popular Cupid causes human love.

15. Another symbol associated with this Path is Qesheth, the rainbow which appears behind Yesod. The rainbow, according to the Bible is a covenant to man of God's Love and so we may consider it to be caused by the dawning light from the Sun of Tiphareth shining through the mists of illusion. In actuality it is the first dawnings of mystical consciousness to the soul in its state of spiritual dryness halfway between the states of Incarnationary and Evolutionary consciousness.

16. Thus, ascending, the Path is one of apparent darkness and aridity, the soul aspiring to the light of higher consciousness, sustained only by its own resources; and descending, it is the downflow of Life, Light and Love—three exact terms, not misty generalisations—from the Individuality, seeking to make and establish contact with its projection in incarnation. Thus does the Archer hunt his quarry, for as the huntsman seeks to kill his prey for food, so does the Individuality seek out conscious contact with its projection for similar reasons, for the fully illuminated man is he who is dead to the domination of the lower worlds, using his vehicles in the lower worlds for the ends of his higher nature.

17. To this end is the Tarot Trump called Daughter of the Reconcilers, for the Path reconciles the Evolutionary and Incarnationary vehicles of man, the Individuality and Personality. It is also called the Bringer Forth of Life, for in this manner is new life brought to birth, the higher life into the outer world, and the life of experience in dense manifestation to the higher worlds.

NOTES ON THE DESIGN OF TRUMP XIV

The Marseilles card shows an angel pouring liquid from one vessel to another, the top one is usually considered to be gold and the lower one silver. Wirth follows this but substitutes a single flower for the conventional shrubbery of the exoteric card. Knapp is again similar but has many flowers growing in the background. Like Wirth, Waite and Case he puts a solar disk on the angel's brow.

Waite puts a triangle in a square on the angel's breast and also has it standing with one foot on earth and the other in water. From the pool a path leads across undulating country to a line of mountains over which is the Sun in which can be discerned a crown. Irises grow by the pool and the figure's head is radiant.

Case follows this generally but omits the flowers and has a seven pointed star on the breast — which is, of course, another form of Waite's septenary figure. The idea originated, it seems, from Levi. Case makes a radical contribution in having the angel bear a torch in the left hand and a vase in the right from which are poured fiery Yods and water onto an eagle and a lion. Behind the figure he puts a rainbow; this is an alternative to Waite's irises. Case suggests that the figure could well be Iris and there is much to be said for this view — Iris was a privileged messenger of the gods. Alternatively he suggests the Archangel Michael, though from a Qabalistic point of view Raphael might be more appropriate.

Crowley seems to be the first to have published the ideas depicted on Case's card, and he also suggested a moon-shaped cauldron at the angel's feet giving off silver smoke of perfume — obviously a symbol for Yesod. He also saw the figure as Diana the Huntress: there is a link of course between this goddess, Sagittarius, the hunter's bow and the Bow of Promise.

When it came to designing the Harris card though, he made many innovations, though all on the lines already laid down. He preferred to call the card Art, and considered it a consummation of the dual figures of his Trump VI, the Lovers, (q.v.) based on alchemical symbolism. This card shows a single androgyne figure in place of the two figures on Trump VI. This figure has two heads, one a black woman with gold crown and silver bands, and the other a white man with silver crown and gold fillet. A white arm on the black head's side pours from a cup the Gluten of the White Eagle, and a dark arm on the white head's side pours flames — the Blood of the Lion, from a torch, into a central golden cauldron. The figure's robe is vegetable green with unified serpents and bees and there are moon bows by each head. From the cauldron rises a stream of light which forms two rainbows and becomes the cape of the figure. Attendant are the Red Lion, now become white; and the White Eagle, now become red. Fire and water mingle harmoniously at the bottom of the card.

In the centre an arrow shoots up, that of Sagittarius. The alchemical symbolism is reinforced by the writing on an aureole behind the figure which reads: "Visita Interiora Terrae Rectificando Invenies Occultum Lapidem", which means, "Visit the interior parts of the Earth: by rectification thou shalt find the hidden stone". The initials of the Latin text spell VITRIOL — the Universal Solvent. Alchemically, the Philosophers' Stone is a balanced combination of Salt, Mercury and Sulphur: the gold and the silver, the red and the white. The mystical interpretation should be obvious and is further hinted at in Manly P. Hall's symbol for the card, which is a modified form of the t'ai chi t'u sign, signifying the Union of Opposites — or what might be a happier term, Union of Complements.

The 'Egyptian' form of the card generally follows tradition, a winged being, with Sun behind, (of eight points) and additionally, with winged feet and a flame over the head; a design of flowers below.

The Golden Dawn card had a volcano in the background.

The 26th Path

Hod — Tiphareth

KEY: ע Ayin. Eye.

SPIRITUAL SIGNIFICANCE: ♑ Capricorn. The Goat.

THEORY: Lord of the Gates of Matter. Child of the Forces of Time. (XV—The Devil.)

COLOURS: Indigo. Black. Blue-black. Cold very dark grey.

TEXT: "The Twenty-sixth Path is called the Renewing Intelligence, because the Holy God renews by it all the changing things which are renewed by the creation of the world."

1. As the 25th Path is a Dark Night of the Soul on the Way of Love, or Devotional Mysticism, so may the 26th Path be considered a similar test on the Way of Wisdom, the Hermetic Path; and the 24th Path on the Way of Power or Nature Mysticism and art. This three-fold division does not mean that one person will only have one or the other experience according to his 'Path'. On the contrary, everyone gets the lot—for the three-fold division is merely for convenience of study and is by no means a system of watertight barriers.

2. Some may feel the tests of one Path more than the others according to personal bias but the balanced soul will feel the tests more equally. And it is well to work subjectively over all these Paths on the Tree of Life for all must in the end be assimilated—by experience and understanding. Perhaps it would be truer to say that the 24th Path tests the driving emotions, the 25th Path the devotional aspirations, and the 26th Path the intellect as the soul makes its journey from consciousness centred in Yesod to consciousness centred in Tiphareth; thus, according to the bias will either of the three Paths be experienced the more. And the Tree is useful here for it enables the other Paths to be sought

78

after and worked upon in meditation so that more balanced progress is made.

3. The Yetziratic Text gives a clue to the problem the mind faces in coming to a mental conception of what God is, for as man changes so does his idea of God change. For man's mind, God is, and can only be, the ideal of man. Thus we get in the many races of man the many ideas of what God is: a ferocious tribal deity among savages, ruler of a Divine city-state with the ancient Greeks, a stiff formal hieratic figure with the ancient Egyptians, an Oriental despot with the Old Testament Jews, and so on up to modern times. And just as the religion and mythology of a race reflects that race's psychology so does the religion and faith of an individual reflect that individual's psychology.

4. This of course does not disprove the existence of God, but recognises that all ideas of God are the creation of man's mind. Mind cannot come to grips with that which transcends it — the spiritual levels of being. Thus the attribution of The Devil to this Path is apposite, for the Devil is an illusion, just as are all men's formulated ideas of God. The mind just does not have the means to get reality on the matter. This is inferred, amongst other things, by the Trump of the man hanged upside down on the Path that leads from Geburah down to Hod. To the mind, spiritual reality seems topsy turvy — and the closer the mind gets to truth, the more it is led into paradox.

5. Yet this inability of the mind does not mean that all religions are deluded and worthless; they all lead towards the one light. And anyone who throws over orthodox religion misses a lot. If one has the spiritual insight to see the essential unity of all religions then one ought to have the ability to get the most out of, and to contribute one's share to, any one religion. The best religion is that which makes the greatest appeal to one.

6. Also, while the appreciation of the universal validity of all religions is the best means of approaching spiritual reality by means of the mind, it must be borne in mind that

the rationale of a religion is to be irrational. Ultimately, in its gropings towards an understanding of the Godhead, the mind is faced with the conception of 'the infinite'. In the words of the nineteenth century French occultist, Eliphas Levi, "The Infinite is the inevitable absurdity which imposes itself on science. God is the paradoxical explanation of the absurdity which imposes itself on faith. Science and faith can and ought mutually to counterbalance each other and produce equilibrium, they can never amalgamate." (Paradoxes of the Highest Science'. Theosophical Publishing House translation.)

7. Here is another aspect, and it is shown on the Tarot Trump, one can be voluntarily enslaved by science or by faith if either is unsustained by the other and it will be seen on the card that the figures chained to the Devil are not themselves devils, but human beings wearing devil's caps and holding their tails on behind them. Putting the Devil 'up on a pedestal' in the latter packs is a nice touch and on the Marseilles version he is also raised up — but on two stones. This duality is further resumed in the Devil's horns and the two forks of the Hebrew letter Ayin — signifying one can be spiked on either one of the Devil's horns, rational science or irrational dogma. It will be noted that the Devil holds a sceptre in the left hand instead of the right — thus it is as an image reflected in a mirror — the noumenal appears inverted in the phenomenal worlds — again as hinted by the inverted Hanged Man of the 23rd Path.

8. The astrological sign Capricorn is also attributed to this Path and this sign is said to govern all things of authority, limitation and concretion, as may be gathered from its planetary ruler, Saturn, and the Atziluthic colour of this Path, indigo, the same as the 32nd Path, which is directly attributed to Saturn.

9. Some may feel that no criticism can be made of real religious Faith, and this is true, it is the folly of the faith in dogmatic authority that is at issue really, and needs only the memory of Galileo to serve as an example, though there

are countless other examples particularly in modern political faiths from Liberal laissez-faire to Marxist determinism. In our day it is more the authority of science and reason that has replaced the ecclesiastic authority, though the pendulum is beginning now, in the middle of the twentieth century, to move back towards the equilibrium point, and doubtless, human nature being what it is, will eventually swing to the irrational side, and then back again, and back again, and back again, and back again, until humanity achieves some semblance of permanent balance in its outlook — or even stops being the dupe of external authority.

10. The abuses of authority, whether rational or irrational, are, of course, based on one cause, and that cause is ironically appropriate to this Path of Knowledge. It is Ignorance. As Levi went on to say in the work quoted above:

11. "It is through Ignorance that a man is proud since he then fancies to make himself honoured by rendering himself ridiculous and contemptible.

12. "It is through Ignorance that a man is avaricious since he thus makes *himself* the slave of what is made to serve *us*. It is through Ignorance that a man becomes a debauchee, since he thus makes a *deadly* abuse of what should relate to and propagate *Life*.

13. "Through Ignorance men mutually hate in lieu of loving, isolate themselves instead of helping one the other, separate instead of associating, corrupt instead of improving each other, destroy in place of preserving and weaken themselves in egoism in lieu of strengthening themselves in universal charity.

14. "Man naturally seeks that which he believes to be good, and if he almost always deceives himself, foolishly and cruelly, it is that he does not *know*. The Despots of the old world did not know that the abuse of Power involves the fall of Power, and that in digging the earth to hide their victims they were digging their own graves. The Revolutionists of all times have not known that anarchy being the conflict of Lusts and the fatal reign of Violence, substitutes

82

might for right, and paves the way ever for the rule of the most audaciously criminal.

15. "The Inquisitors did not know that in the name of the Church they were burning Jesus Christ, that in the name of the Holy Office they were burning the Gospel, and that the ashes of their autos-da-fé would brand indelibly on their foreheads the mark of Cain.

16. "Voltaire, in preaching God and Liberty, did not know that in the narrow minds of the vulgar Liberty destroyed God; he did not know that in the dark foundations of symbols hides a light sublime; that the Bible is a Babel on the summit of which rests the Holy Ark; and he never thought he was preparing the materials for the impious farces of Chaumette and the paradoxes of Proudhon.

17. "Rousseau did not know that amongst the bastard children of his proud and fretful genius he would have one day to reckon Robespierre and Marat."

18. What then are the means of overcoming such Ignorance—the Ignorance of the real, spiritual basis of life? Theology does not seem to be the answer. Levi, in fact, took a very poor view of it:

19. "The most dangerous and the saddest of sciences is Theology, for it constitutes itself wrongly a science of God. Rather is it a science of the foolishness of man when it seeks to explain the inscrutable mystery of the Divine."

20. His reason for this view is that: "It is through blackened glasses that we can alone gaze on the sun; looked at through a clear glass, it seems to us black, and blinds us. God is for us as a sun; we must walk by his light with lowered eyes: if one tries to gaze fixedly on Him our sight fails."

21. Most theologians would have reservations to make on these statements, and no doubt rightly so, but nonetheless Levi here puts his finger straight to the crux of the matter and the secrets of the Path, which, being a Hermetic student of no mean ability, he knew well. It may be that, as St. Paul said, in our present life we can see but as "through

a glass darkly" but the apparent difficulties to the mind are insurmountable only if the concrete mind remains fixed as concrete mind—that is, remains in Hod content merely to gaze up towards the Sun of Tiphareth. But the Path is meant to be trod, and the attribution of Capricorn, the Goat, signifies that by treading it nimbly, leaping from crag to crag, we can attain great heights. And in the process the mind will be changed, for this Path is, after all, called the Renewing Intelligence, and as the mental air becomes more rarified, so will the mental processes be transformed from intellect to intuition. The Path is a transformation process of intellectual Hod consciousness to illuminated Tiphareth consciousness. The Goat, supremely creative but with its legs shackled, once released, can leap higher and higher until eventually it can sail off the highest pinnacle and become the winged All-seeing Eye of the Egyptians — the Eye being the signification of the Hebrew letter Ayin, the Key to this Path.

22. There is also, in connection with the Goat, the whole body of religious doctrine centred about the Scape-goat. This animal was driven off into the desert supposedly carrying all the sins of the tribe with it—and the Lord Jesus is considered by the Churches to be the scapegoat for all humanity, all our sins washed away with his blood. In fact, it is doubtful if things are quite as easy as this. Our Lord, according to esoteric teaching, lifted a great load of world-karma by his sacrificial death, but his Exemplary Way was trodden for others, not in the sense that all was now done for us, but in the sense that the True Pattern was now laid down for us to tread if we have the faith and belief to tread it. Were it otherwise then the end of the world could have been delcared on the day of Christ's Ascension and there would be no need for any Acts of the Apostles, Christian Church or eventual Revelation. Christ—literally a deus ex machina — would have cleared up all our rotten mess without any further bother to us. And for all we know, this may have been part of his third and most grave temptation, an over-

throw of Divine Law by an illconsidered act of 'mercy'.

23. So the Scapegoat is not a religious device for doing our dirty laundry for us—it is an example of the principle that each must base his life on if peace is ever to come to this world. This principle is the *willingness* to take on the faults, errors, sins, of others and to accept them and all the effects consequent upon this acceptance. It is the opposite of the usual attempt to try to load blame and condemnation onto others, that is, to make *them* scapegoats.

24. No-one, of course, can tread the Way of any other for him. But at the same time, the living of the right life, and the taking of the right attitudes, does help to make the way easier for others, both by talismanic action and example, so one is at the same time being a scapegoat by bearing some part of others' sins. And here it will be seen how close we are verging on paradox, with a great temptation, (which must be resisted, for its fruits are worthless), to start splitting hairs of definition about sin, redemption, forgiveness, and so on. The truth of the matter has to be reached by an intuitive leap, not by means of formal logic. Little help will be gained from studying professors of theology unless one is already one of the converted; it was, after all, without their aid that Christ came into the world and the early Christian church started. Perhaps the closest that the intellect, as intellect, can come to grips with religious truth is in the writings of some existentialists but it is a treacherous and vertiginous way, as the Jesuit poet Gerald Manley Hopkins, by no means an existentialist, knew nonetheless from his own intellectual experience:

> "O the mind, mind has mountains; cliffs of fall
> Frightful, sheer, no-man-fathomed.
> Hold them cheap
> May who ne'er hung there."

25. This Path is perhaps the most difficult of all the Paths to elucidate, concerned as it is with apparent contradiction and paradox. It is a Way to God by the symbolism of the

Devil, it teaches of the scapegoat that is not a scapegoat, it holds the limitation of Saturn and the spiritual clarity and universality of the All-seeing Eye which knows no limitation, and so on. The Tibetan Master says that Capricorn is the most difficult astrological sign to write about, that it is the most mysterious sign of the twelve. He even goes so far as to say in A. A. Bailey's 'Esoteric Astrology' (Lucis Trust, London & New York): "The symbol of this sign is undecipherable and intentionally so. It is sometimes called the 'signature of God'. I must not attempt to interpret it for you, partly because it has never yet been correctly drawn and partly because its correct delineation and the ability of the initiate to depict it produces an inflow of force which would not be desirable except after due preparation and understanding."

26. It would be foolish for us to rush in where Masters fear to tread! Nevertheless, the outer significances of the Path are by no means undecipherable and for general purpose it may be said to be the way of the mind from intellect to intuition. This process is best attained by the technique of meditation and also by the study of, (and meditation upon), those types of esoteric writing which are designed "to train the mind rather than to inform it". Of such writings are Dion Fortune's mediumistically received 'The Cosmic Doctrine', also 'The Stanzas of Dzyan' which appear in H. P. Blavatsky's 'The Secret Doctrine', and the many fragments of archaic scripts which appear frequently in the Tibetan's books given through Alice Bailey. Again, more familiar texts such as the Book of Genesis or The Revelation of St. John the Divine could be included in this category. They are texts which do not allow the concrete mind to become over-dominant.

27. Thus the system of Zen Buddhism might be aligned with this Path, for it is a system which deals with the intellect by frustrating it with commands or 'Koans' such as "A sound is made by the clapping of two hands. What sound is made by the clapping of one hand?" or "When the Many

are reduced to the One, to what is the One to be reduced?" The struggle to answer questions like these should lead to a state of 'satori', which is indefinable except perhaps as "a sudden realisation of the truth". This system may be a bit too drastic for most mind orientated Westerners however.

28. Tradition says that The Devil of the Tarot Trump was the 'idol' which was 'worshipped' by the ill-fated Knights Templar, who had brought back much mystic knowledge from the Near East. If this is true it might explain the more material aspects of this Path, and some of the accusations levelled against the Order, which suggest a Way of Enlightenment by means of a surfeit of sensuality and materiality until the soul revolted against it — a process of killing the cat by stuffing it with cream in other words. It would, however, be a system of development requiring the strictest supervision — though this would, of course, be possible in an Order not only religious but military. Even so, it could easily fall into degeneration, which may or may not have happened in the case of the Templars.

29. It is certainly not a method one could recommend to all and sundry any more than Zen, self-taught. The way of meditation is by far the most foolproof system though one could, if one is cursed with an over-voracious mind that must have everything logically labelled and explained, try feeding it to vomiting point with tomes of philosophy or comparative theology or metaphysics. But there are many minds capable of swallowing all that and still coming back for more.

30. The ascent of this Path is a process of transferring from the concrete to the abstract mind — from intellect to intuition — and the descending way is perhaps of even greater use, for it is an occult maxim that to understand anything it is best to aim at the highest point of understanding and work downwards. Thus one makes an intuitive leap and then comes down to logic and observation to see if the facts fall into the right place. It is a way that works, for it is the method of scientific discovery, and also, for that matter, the

way in which this book is written. In this way are the forces of the Lord of the Gates of Matter, Child of the Forces of Time, transcended, and, to paraphrase the Yetziratic Text, all things renewed which can be renewed by the construction of a new creative orientation upon them.

31. The fact that The Devil is called Lord of the Gates of Matter and Child of the Forces of Time does not mean that matter and the phenomenal worlds are evil, it means that our mental conceptions of matter and time are, like the Devil, illusory; and the only way to see things correctly is with the Spiritual Eye, beyond time and space. The development of that type of Pure Reason which makes such perception possible is an aspect of the Renewing Intelligence, or, if one prefers, a ray of light from the One in Revelations who spake from the throne, saying, "Behold, I make all things new."

32. This Path is a difficult one, for it is the intellect's approach to God, which, if it is not prepared to be transformed or renewed, but attempts to 'define' God on its own terms, meets only with the monstrous image of itself — a Caliban-like figure — reflected in the glass of its own illusions.

NOTES ON THE DESIGN OF TRUMP XV

The Marseilles card shows a horned bat-winged figure holding a torch and elevated on a split pedestal, possibly in a quagmire. Two human figures holding tails behind their backs and with horned head-dress are tied by their necks to a ringbolt in a stone.

This is one of the Trumps fully illustrated by Eliphas Levi, and his version depicts a goat-headed creature throned on an altar surmounting a sphere. It is winged and has a flaming torch-mitre between its horns and a pentagram on its brow. Above left is a white horned moon and below right, a black. It points, making the sign of esotericism, with each hand at each moon. Levi describes it as a monster with woman's breasts, scaled belly, feathered torso and male genitals, (shown as a caduceus), a chimera, a malformed sphinx, a synthesis of deformities. The right arm is marked SOLVE, the left, COAGULA.

Wirth gives the figure a goat's head but reverses the arms. The left, marked SOLVE, holds up a lingam, and the right, extended downwards and marked COAGULA, holds an upright torch. The two small figures, not shown on Levi's version, appear as demons chained to the Devil's pedestal. Papus remarks that the arms are used oppositely to those of Trump I, the Magician. He says the cubic pedestal should rest on a sphere. There is no pentagram on Wirth's figure, but the astrological sign of Mercury is shown on its apron.

Waite inverts the pentagram on the Devil's brow and also gives a goat head. The supporting figures are completely human save that the woman has a pomegranate — and the man a flame-ended tail. Each also bears horns. The chains by which they are fixed to the pedestal could easily be removed by them. The Devil lifts his right hand in a sign of duality and in his left holds down an inverted torch. The feet of the Devil are talons. Case's version follows Waite closely, but introduces the sign of Mercury above the genitals. Also, the figure has one male breast, the other female, and its legs are feathered rather than hairy. It has asses ears.

Crowley originally supported Levi's picture but warned against the commentary in the text. In his own version of the card he shows a goat with spiral horns, the Eye of God in the centre of its forehead and Bacchanalian grapes. He calls it the All-Begetter — a Pan figure. It is supported on a caduceus and its devotees are shown below divided into two spheres or cells. A tree trunk rises right through the centre of the card, its roots transparent to show the leaping of the sap, and its top piercing the heavens; a ring surrounding it at the top is emblematic of Saturn and the body of Nuit. The background is one of fantastic, tenuous and complex forms.

The 'Egyptian' card shows Typhon standing on the ruins of a temple. He holds in the right hand a sceptre surmounted by a circle between divergent bars and in the left hand an inverted torch. He has a flame above his head, a horn on his nose, woman's breasts, hog's body, goat's feet, crocodile head and a snake appearing from the navel. Two men with goat heads are chained to his feet. What seem to be blighted plants decorate the bottom of the card.

Manly P. Hall suggests that the Divine Name, JHVH, is representative of the card, and considers that the figure represents the magic powers of the Astral Light, in which the Divine Powers are reflected in an inverted or infernal state.

An old version of this card shows the Devil as Argus, with eyes all over his body — an interesting exoteric confirmation of the link between this Trump and the Hebrew letter Ayin which means an eye.

The 24th Path

Netzach — Tiphareth

KEY: ♋ Nun. Fish.
SPIRITUAL SIGNIFICANCE: ♏ Scorpio. The Scorpion.
THEORY: Child of the Great Transformers. Lord of the Gates of Death. (XIII — Death.)
COLOURS: Green blue. Dull brown. Very dark brown. Livid indigo brown.
TEXT: "The Twenty-fourth Path is the Imaginative Intelligence and it is so called because it gives a likeness to all the similitudes which are created in like manner similar to its harmonious elegancies."

1. The Tarot Trump of this Path is Death and one of the esoteric titles of this card is Lord of the Gates of Death. It may be noted that there is no reference to birth throughout the symbolism of the Trumps and this is because birth is death and death is birth, each being opposing sides of the same coin. Whenever there is change there is death to the former condition and birth to the new condition and this is shown in the other title of the Tarot Trump, Child of the Great Transformers.

2. 'The Cosmic Doctrine' lists seven types of death. The First Death is, abstractly stated, the interlinking of two forces so that a vortex is set up, the two forces ceasing to exist as independent movement but becoming a centre of stability manifesting on a lower plane. This principle may apply at any level of the Tree, for it is a prime principle of manifestation and holds good from the spiritual heights of the creation of a Divine Spark to the structure of the minutest physical atom. The two movements can be said to die to give birth to a unit on a lower plane. Similarly, when this form eventually breaks up, or dies, it releases the two forces on the higher plane, which thus are born again. So birth and

89

death are terms for the one and the same transformation process, but viewed as a beginning or an ending according to the plane of observation.

3. The Second Death has to do with evolutionary change. Life, having evolved in a lowly form, has to pass to a higher form to continue its evolution. Thus prehistoric forms of life are now extinct. To a consciousness ensouling a primitive form, the dying out of its race will seem a death and a tragedy, but to a consciousness in the higher form, the new form is seen as a birth giving new opportunities, and thus an occasion for rejoicing. Applied to biological evolution, this process may be applied to the 29th Path; applied to psychological evolution, the rise and fall of races and civilisations, it may be applied to the 31st Path.

4. The Third Death is the death of the physical body and may be considered a part of the 32nd Path. When one dies physically one is treading this Path. This is perhaps why it is sometimes referred to as "the terrible 32nd Path". However, although the circumstances of death may be unpleasant or uncomfortable, physical death is a necessary thing for it enables the soul to meditate upon its experiences of the last life, and then to come back to Earth again freed from the limitations of physical age and the restricted outlook of the last Personality.

5. The Fourth Death is sleep and is a lesser Third Death. The uses that are made of sleep are of very important practical application. 'The Cosmic Doctrine' says: "During the waking life of the body the Individuality is intent upon translating into its own terms of abstraction the concrete impressions flowing into the lower soul. When it is no longer thus in-turned it becomes objective upon its own plane and beholds the 'face of the Father'. It then measures itself by the Divine standard and makes such adjustments as are within its power; but the adjustments of the spirit are aeonial and are measured by the span of Heaven.

6. "During sleep the little-evolved soul may not, however, sink into oblivion, but, being much concerned with the

unsatisfied desires of the flesh, may continue to function in relation to the thought-forms begotten of these desires. It dreams the dreams derived from unsatisfied passions and the urges of the instincts. The Individuality is not freed, and instead of beholding the 'face of the Father which is in Heaven' beholds the reversed image of the human form and thereby develops in its likeness. The Individuality, being unable to function on its own plane, makes no growth and remains unevolved; and the Personality becomes an exaggerated caricature of itself. From this it can be freed only by the Third Death, thereby enabling the Individuality to assert itself, but if the Third Death be incomplete the lower soul will continue to dream upon the astral plane. This leads us to the question of the Fifth Death."

7. This is the reason for the widespread occult practice of making a review of the day's affairs on falling asleep—as outlined in Chapter 22 of Volume I of this book. This exercise puts the mental processes into the way of mentation of the Individuality and also breaks up the Personality thought patterns that have built up during the day. In this way the occultist makes as much progress during his sleep as in his waking hours, and possibly much more, for Personality-dominated sleep can be retrogressive. Truly is it said that occultism is a twentyfour hours a day business.

8. A similar situation occurs with physical death and so there is much to be said for the Roman Catholic practice of preparing the mind for the way it will eventually receive death, and also for the Sacrament of the Last Rites or Extreme Unction. The astral plane dreams of incomplete physical death mentioned in the passage last quoted may be examined at leisure in many books of spiritualist communications—though this does not imply that all spiritualist communicators are in this 'fools' paradise.'

9. Physical death, the Third Death, should lead on into the Fifth Death, the death of the Personality; and here it may be as well to stress the point that the numeration of these deaths is for ease of reference only and is not an indication

of sequence. Similarly, there is no correlating order when they are applied to the Tree of Life. Like the physical Third Death, the Fourth Death of sleep may be aligned with the 32nd Path, extending into the 25th; while the Fifth Death, the death of the Personality, is wholly relevant to the present section in that it is a process of the 24th Path.

10. 'The Cosmic Doctrine' describes it as follows: "The Fifth Death is the death of the Personality. The Personality, when withdrawn by death from the body, yet continues to live and to function as a Personality, and the man is in no wise changed and still 'answers to the name he bore in the flesh'. In the Lower Hells he burns with desire until the possibilities of desire are burnt out. Desire then remains only as an abstract idea and is part of the Individuality. He then dies to the lower desires but continues to live in the higher desires.

11. "These in their turn he learns to be finite and mortal; he finds them to constitute barriers between himself and his Father Whose face he would behold, and he desires to escape from them. He would no longer love with the personal love which loves a person, but with the higher manifestation of love which itself is Love and loves no person or thing but is a state of consciousness in which all is embraced. He then seeks freedom from the lesser love, and it is this desire for release from that which though good is finite in order to realise the good that is infinite which causes the Fifth Death, and he is born into consciousness of the Individuality, and lives upon the plane of the Individuality perceiving the 'face of his Father Which is in Heaven'.

12. "But with the waking of desire come again the dreams, and with the dreams comes the recall into matter. The Spirit, beholding the face of its Father until consciousness is weary with Its brightness, closes its eyes and sleeps; and sleeping, it dreams of the unfulfilled desires and so it is born again, for upon the plane of desire a state of consciousness is a place, and as we desire, so are we reborn. Thus each man makes his own Karma.

13. "It may be asked, how then is it that men make for themselves suffering and limitations which they could not desire? It is because they reap not the fruits of fantasy, but the fruits of actuality. They are given *the results of that which they have permitted themselves to desire, not the thing they desire.* To exemplify—the man who desired power would obtain vanity. To obtain power he would have to desire the qualities which confer power, namely strength, foresight and wisdom. The man who desires power builds for himself the consciousness of the vain egotist. The man who desires strength, foresight and wisdom, builds for himself the consciousness of power."

14. The Sixth Death is trance which is akin to physical death and sleep and thus can be related to the line of the 32nd and 25th Paths. The Seventh Death is Illumination, which, in that it is a death of the Personality, (though a living death), is also apposite to the 24th Path, but with the difference that the Personality lives within the physical world, so that all the Paths below Tiphareth are still functional but controlled from the higher instead of the lower levels, by the Individuality rather than the Personality itself. The remarks in 'The Cosmic Doctrine' about this condition are quoted at length in Chapter 16 of Volume I of this book, the chapter on Malkuth, for Illumination is a manifestation of a small part of the Kingdom to come—in Earth.

15. The ascent of the 24th Path, then, is the process of the Fifth Death, the death of the Personality, whether this be consequent upon physical death or whether it be a part of that greater death—the death of Initiation. In the former case the Personality ceases to exist, and in the latter case the Personality still exists and functions in the world, though not for its own ends, but for the ends of the Individuality wherein the centre of consciousness is now situated. The centre of Individuality consciousness, Qabalistically speaking, is in Tiphareth; and the 'face of the Father' which is referred to is, in one sense, the image of the Spirit, in Heaven, that is, Kether and the Supernal Triangle. There is,

of course, the Abyss dividing the Archetypal and Creative Worlds of Spiritual consciousness from the Formative World of Individuality consciousness—so it might be truer to say that the image gazed upon is really the Individuality's higher ideas of what its Spirit is. We should place this image, in our symbological analysis, in Chesed, or perhaps Daath, though this level, astride the Abyss, is relatively formless.

16. It must be borne in mind, of course, that at these levels there is no 'image' as we understand the term, for any level above Hod has neither shapes nor forms in the sense that we, with our time and space conditioned consciousness, usually understand the terms. The 'image' is therefore more a kind of 'intuition' of what is right or wrong for that Individuality. If the 'image' is wrong or distorted the Individuality will of course be attempting to mould itself on a pattern not in conformity with the Spirit which originally projected, and still projects, it. This false 'image', or Eidolon as it is more usually called in this context, is at the root of Original Sin. The Spirit is perfect, but when the Eidolon is projected, the image of itself that will be used as a pattern for the vehicles of denser manifestation, if that Eidolon is distorted then the inevitable results are sin, evil and disease. And the cause of distortion of the Eidolon in almost all cases is reluctance to manifest, or in other words, fear of pain.

17. An analogy may make this clearer. It is as if the Spirit originally coming into manifestation were like a gymnast about to do a double somersault, say, over a vaulting horse. There is negligible danger involved, given self-confidence. But on the run-up, our gymnast loses confidence, suddenly imagining what might happen to him if his foot slipped, or someone had removed the mat from the other side, or if he caught his head on the top of the horse, or if the springboard did not work, and as a result of this mis-use of the imagination, which should be concentrated on the task in hand in an assertive and creative way, he leaps half-heartedly. This produces the inevitable result— he does not clear the horse

and maybe dislocates his neck, or breaks a wrist or an ankle, and perhaps sundry ribs into the bargain.

18. This is, more or less, the reason for chaos in the world today, for, to pursue our athletic analogy, it is not as if each Spirit in its fall injured itself alone, but all humanity being interlinked, the fall of one involves the fall of all, much as if a group of athletes formed a human pyramid on a tight-rope—if one should lose his nerve and fall, all would fall. Though in the case of the Human Fall, none were blame-less. Some may have fallen first, but all the others followed, and needlessly so. So confusion became worse and worse confounded.

19. The solution does not lie in seeking scapegoats. One who led others astray is not more to blame than those who followed. Had they not followed he could not have led. Similarly it takes more than one to make a tyrant, a tyrant could not exist did not others bow themselves to his tyranny. So, in the words of John Donne, "Never send to know for whom the bell tolls; It tolls for thee." One cannot set others to rights without first restoring the true pattern or Eidolon within oneself.

20 The way that each has come, on the Way of Evolution, is different from the way that each should have come. There is the True Way, of Destiny, and the Deviated Way, of Karma. Fortunately, one does not have to retrace one's steps back to primal beginnings and start all over again. The way each has come is the way each has come and as the original deviation was brought about by a refusal to accept the Way, the way back to the Path of Destiny of each one is achieved by making that acceptance now. Accepting the way that one has come, and everyone else has come, and accepting what one is and what everyone else is, and accept-ing the way one has to go and the way everyone else has to go, without fear of pain, or attempts to dodge pain, or at-tempted propitiation to avoid pain, one's own or others.

21. Now this does not mean scorning anaesthetics or

lacerating oneself in a frenzy of masochistic remorse. It means that one must seek out what one's True Will is, and do it—irrespective of whether it is convenient or not. Once one's true will is found, to implement it will require change, and change is always painful—or always appears so. But by accepting change, in oneself, or in others, and accepting the pain that might come with it, one is taking steps to do what one refused to do in the beginning of manifestation— to accept fully the conditions of the Universe of the Father, which is based upon change, and upon the bringing of spiritual principles right down to solid Earth—without compromise, without regard for convenience, without the dishonesty of supressing one's own ideas for fear of offending others.

22. All this is, of course, by no means new, as may be seen by reference to the Gospels: "Take therefore no thought for the morrow; for the morrow shall take thought for the things of itself. Sufficient unto the day is the evil thereof." "Ye are the salt of the earth: but if the salt have lost its savour, wherewith shall it be salted?" "Let your light so shine before men, that they may see your good works, and glorify your Father which is in heaven." "Except ye be converted, and become as little children, ye shall not enter into the kingdom of heaven." "If thine eye offend thee, pluck it out, and cast it from thee: it is better for thee to enter into life with one eye, rather than having two eyes to be cast into hell fire." "Unto every man that hath shall be given, and he shall have abundance: but from him that hath not shall be taken away even that which he hath." These examples, taken at random from the Gospel of St. Matthew alone, show the stirring message of the Christ, which now, after nearly twothousand years, has become somewhat obscured by the establishment and respectability of the Christian religion. The problem of the twentieth century Church seems not to be a question of getting the money changers out of the temple, but getting the spring-cleaners in, and the moth and the dust out, some living green growth and

rising sap in, and the dead wax immortelles of convention rather than conviction out.

23. Again this does not mean that selfishness and unconventionality for unconventionality's sake are to be rules of conduct. The aim is to elicit one's true Spiritual Will and to have the courage to act by it, and one's true Spiritual Will cannot possibly be of a selfish or mere 'trying to be different' nature. Thus is this slight digression of relevance to the 24th Path, for, in that the Path represents Death and Birth of the Personality, it has much to do with willingness to change. The other two Paths up to Tiphareth have similar functions, of course: the transformation of intellect to intuition on the 26th Path; and the transformation from Personality Will, Intellect and Memory to Charity, Faith and Hope on the 25th Path. All these Paths to Tiphareth are Paths of Sacrifice—which means really the exchange of something for something better.

24. Furthermore, it is necessary to realise at this point of transference from Personality to Individuality orientation, that the Individuality is by no means perfect, even though its imperfections may have come about through, or may manifest as, good intentions. In so far as the Individuality differs from the true pattern of its Spirit so is it aberrated, and this must be borne in mind in all considerations of the Individuality which we shall pass onto in our analysis of the higher Paths.

25. Although all three Paths to Tiphareth, the 24th, 25th, and 26th, are of equal importance, being ways to union between Individuality and Personality, the 24th Path carries additional significance in that it is on the Path of the Lightning Flash and thus represents the fundamental birth and death of the Personality. And as it is thus analagous to the birth and death of the Individuality over the Abyss, so these higher considerations are relevant, for attitudes held by the Individuality on its first manifestation will tend to show up in the Personality at its first manifestation, by the Law of

Correspondences. In this manner do cycles of karma appear in life after life after life.

26. This is why the Path is called the Imaginative Intel--ligence. It "gives a likeness to all the similitudes which are created in like manner similar to its harmonious elegancies." A loose use of pronouns often makes these Yetziratic Texts seem obscure but the meaning should be plain on close examination. In this phrase, "its" refers to the Individuality, whose "harmonious elegancies" are the "similitudes of the Spirit." These were projected from the Spirit to the Individuality in 'like manner similar' to the projection of the 'similitudes' of the Individuality to form a Personality.

27. Generally speaking, there is no reference to Deviation in the Tree of Life symbolism, for it is a Plan of what manifestation should be, and therefore acts as a blueprint against which actual deviated human manifestation may be measured. In actual fact of course, the "harmonious elegancies" may not be so harmonious or elegant as one might like to think, for they are false imprints or similitudes—strictly speaking, not similitudes at all, but substitutes.

28. There is one aspect of the Tree which is concerned with the Fall and that is the Abyss, bridging which is the Sephirah Daath. The Abyss has an analogue which is met with on all three Paths before Tiphareth, and this is known as the Gulf. The Gulf is something that has to be leaped, and leaped alone, stripped of all hindering burdens, in faith. It could be called the dead-point between Personality orientation and Individuality orientation. On the 26th Path the intellect has to be laid aside before the powers of the intuition can take over. On the 25th Path, the will, memory and intellect have to be set aside before the powers of charity, faith and hope can take over. And on the 24th Path, death has to be accepted before rebirth into higher consciousness can be achieved. It is thus one of the crisis points of spiritual progress because of the great temptation to turn back from the unknown to the apparent safety of known things, and to succumb to this temptation is to lose all the

fruits of past endeavour. The only aid at this point is perhaps an invocation of the 'unmanifest knowledge' of the invisible but ubiquitous Sephirah Daath, which will give courage to the soul even where there seems to be no justification for courage, every path seeming to be one of defeat, but it will be remembered that one of the Virtues of the Sephirah Daath is Confidence in the Future, and its Vices include Apathy, Inertia, Cowardice — in short, Fear of the Future.

29. Death and Rebirth are concepts at the base of all true occultism and all true religions and one comes upon the symbolism again and again:- in the symbolic tombs of Hermes and Christian Rosencreutz, in the tearing to pieces of Orpheus — a particularly relevant figure for this Path in that the Path is also that of the Green Ray, as it comes from Netzach — and of course, in the supreme religion of the West, the Crucifixion and Resurrection of Our Lord.

30. The symbolism of the 24th Path not unnaturally is concerned with the same motif. The Tarot Trump is Death, or The Skeleton Mower, wielding a scythe. The scythe may be considered a symbol of time and it was also the weapon of the castration of Uranus by Cronos. Conception as well as birth and death has its place on this Path — and sexual intercourse has ever been closely associated with death as even a cursory familiarity with Elizabethan literature will show. There are the allusions to lovers dying in their mistresses laps and so on. And although it may, more often than not, have been the excuse merely for a perennial literary dirty joke it does in fact have profound relevance to this Path, for the beginnings of the approach to Individuality consciousness is an act of Divine Love, and also the fertilisation of the seed of higher consciousness which will gestate and eventually come to birth. The initiate who has attained Tiphareth consciousness is, after all, called the Twice-Born. The heads and hands lying about the field on the Tarot card are often considered to be new life growing, but the significance of the skeleton is often missed. The skeleton is the basic structure of the body upon which all else is built and

so may well be regarded as a symbol for the Individuality or even the Spirit upon which the outer vehicles are built

31. There may be a deeper significance in the fact that this card is not named in the old packs, though it is more probably due to superstition, like the number thirteen being considered unlucky, which may well stem from the number of this card.

32. So much for the theory of the card. The Spiritual Significance of the Path is shown in the astrological sign Scorpio—a Water sign which gives a link with the Hebrew letter Nun, which means a Fish. The sign is considered by astrologers to have much to do with death and regeneration, which, of course, aligns well with this Path. The shape of the sign indicates the injection of force onto a lower level and is also suggestive of the male sexual organ. The impregnation of matter with life force is one of the powers of this Path when considered in a descending direction. The sign of Scorpio also often appears at the base of the glyph of the Caduceus, which again confirms the sign as a symbol of higher force into lower levels. Likewise, the Seven Scorpions of Isis are emblematical of the force of the Ain Soph, the root of the Isis powers, the Feminine-Side of God, manifesting in the seven planes of the Universe.

33. Finally, the key of the Path is the Hebrew letter Nun, the Fish. Again there is a level of sexual symbolism in that the Fish is a symbol of the male sperm and it is of interest that this should appear on the Path connecting the central Sephirah of the Tree with the Sephirah that appears at the base of the Male Pillar, whereas the corresponding 26th Path connecting with the Sephirah which appears at the base of the Female Pillar should have a letter closely resembling the Fallopian tubes and uterus. It may or may not be stretching symbolism too far to draw attention to the letter Samekh on the Path down to Yesod, the sexual centre on the etheric Tree, which means a crutch. However, the suggestion is made for what it is worth.

34. On another line of interpretation the Fish is an animal

which has its being in water. Water is a symbol of the astral levels on which the Personality usually and mainly operates.

35. The more important aspect of the Fish though, is that it is a symbol of the Christ and thus indicates that the way of death and subsequent regeneration is to be found in the Exemplary Way of Our Lord. For this Path is the culmination of the experiences of the Personality making its way to Individuality consciousness in pursuit of the quest back to the Father. And, as can be stressed hardly too strongly, the key to the whole process of redemption and regeneration is summed up in the words of Our Lord, who has sometimes been called 'The Lord of the Personality': "No man cometh to the Father but by me."

NOTES ON THE DESIGN OF TRUMP XIII

In common with many exoteric packs, the Marseilles version of this Trump bears no name. It shows a skeleton mowing with a scythe a field in which there are human hands and feet, and two heads, a man's and a woman's, the man's head crowned.

In the esoteric versions under review the skeleton faces the other way, that is, to the left, with the exception of Crowley and Case. Waite uses a different symbolism. Crowley early remarked that the scythe handle should be a Tau-cross and this is the case in Wirth's and Case's but not in Crowley's subsequently designed card. Making a count of the human bits and pieces, Wirth gives three hands, one foot, woman's head, and man's crowned head as in the Marseilles card; Knapp gives the two usual heads plus three more, uncrowned, two hands and no feet; Case gives the same as Wirth; and Zain three heads, (two male, one female), three hands and three feet. Additionally, Case provides a bush with a single rose in the foreground, cypress trees in the background, and a rising sun from which a river flows.

Waite gives what he considers to be a better image and there is much to be said for his claim. He shows an armoured skeleton on horseback holding a banner on which is the Mystic Rose. A king lies dead beneath the horse's hooves and a woman and child kneel helpless before the figure, while a figure in priestly garments vainly stands in its path. It is a conception often seen in medieval paintings. In the background is a river with a boat on it — no doubt a form of the River Styx and its ferry — and beyond it a steep precipice. On the top of these high cliffs is a fair land, mountain peaks in the distance, with the sun rising between two pillar-like towers.

The ancillary symbolism of this picture, as well as that of Case's, draws attention to the other side of death, which is birth. To die to one thing is to be born to another. This, in the Brotherhood of Light 'Egyptian' version is signified by a rainbow — the Bow of Promise. Below are lotuses growing, each bearing a uraeus. On the Harris card it is shown by the skeleton wearing an Osiris headdress and bubbles of life rising from his side. At the bottom of the card are embryonic and marine forms of life and at the top, an eagle.

Hall's symbol is a triangle rising out of a square, and he also remarks that in some old versions the skeleton has cut off its own foot. It is difficult to see any esoteric reason for this. It may have been medieval humour or possibly a cautionary picture, for a scythe is a notorious tool for inadvertently bringing off this feat — or should one say foot?

L'EMPEREUR

LE·PAPE

L'AMOVREVX

LE CHARIOT

SECTION TWO
THE GREATER MYSTERIES
The Paths of the Individuality

Part 1

The Structures of the Individuality

The 20th Path

Tiphareth — Chesed

KEY: ' Yod. Hand.

SPIRITUAL SIGNIFICANCE: ♍ Virgo. The Virgin.

THEORY: Prophet of the Eternal. Magus of the Voice of Power. (IX—The Hermit.)

COLOURS: Yellowish green. Slate grey. Green grey. Plum.

TEXT: "The Twentieth Path is the Intelligence of Will and is so called because it is the means of preparation of all and each created being, and by this intelligence the existence of the Primordial Wisdom becomes known."

1. Tiphareth is the central Sephirah on the Tree of Life and so represents the focussing point of the whole being of man in manifestation. It is the balancing point between the two aspects of force and form in the Individuality, (Geburah and Chesed). It is also the link between Individuality and Personality, the central point of the Daath-Yesod magical circuit— Daath, Chesed, Geburah, Tiphareth being the Individuality half of the circuit and Tiphareth, Netzach, Hod and Yesod being the Personality half; Tiphareth is the linking Sephirah. Excluding the physical body, (Malkuth), and the spiritual vehicles, (the Supernal Sephiroth), these seven Sephiroth comprise the complete psyche. Tiphareth is also the mid-point between the spiritual levels and dense manifestation in Earth. In view of all these factors it is well called the Mediating Intelligence.

2. Chesed represents the first manifestation of the being in sub-spiritual existence and thus holds within itself the purest image of what the Spirit should be in its manifestation as a human being in Earth. In view of this, the Yetziratic Text calls it the Receptive Intelligence, "so called because it contains all the holy powers, and from it emanate all the spiritual virtues with the most exalted essences."

103

3. The 20th Path, joining Tiphareth and Chesed, is therefore the link within the Individuality giving the vision of what the pattern of destiny is, which pattern stems ultimately, of course, from the spiritual levels. This pattern is the Individuality's own idea of itself and is the pattern upon which the Individuality strives to mould its succession of Personalities, which in turn give the experience of dense manifestation upon which the Individuality itself is built. Thus this image is a kind of alpha and omega, a beginning and an ending, at the same time. The alpha image is the image of the Spirit itself, inexperienced and unevolved. The Individuality tries to project a Personality based upon this image, unsuccessfully at first, owing to inexperience, but gradually, in life after life, with greater accuracy, (and sometimes with different types of Personality altogether to redress unbalances of development.) Eventually it can project a Personality just as it wants, which means, of course, that it has conquered or gained functional control of dense manifestation. But all the hundreds of Personalities built up through the evolution go to enrich the make-up of the Individuality, and so the Individuality can now hardly be limited to the simple image of itself that the Spirit laid down at the beginning of time in this evolution. The image itself could be said to have evolved also to that of what the Individuality should be at the end of an evolution — which we might call the omega image. Thus there is the image of the beginning and the image of the ending and the way inbetween is the way of individual destiny. In terms of Biblical symbolism the image of the beginning is The Garden of Eden and the image of the ending is The Heavenly Jerusalem, the way inbetween being the history of man.

4. In view of these factors, the meaning of the Yetziratic Text should be plain. The Path is called the Intelligence of Will, that is, the Spiritual Will. (The relevance and true meaning of the axiom of Crowley, "Do what thou wilt shall be the whole of the Law", as applied to Chesed, was discussed in Chapter 10 of Volume I.) As the Yetziratic Text

goes on to say, by this Intelligence, or action of the Spiritual Will, "the existence of the Primordial Wisdom becomes known." The Primordial Wisdom is, of course, the knowledge of the spiritual realities of the supernal levels, and the continual contemplation of the true image is also obviously "the means of preparation of all and each created being," for it acts as a guide to the individual way of evolution and the types of vehicle that need to be built up to follow it.

5. Thus the Tarot card presents a Hermit, a holy man, bearing a lantern to guide one along the Path. This image is a particularly evocative one and well repays meditation. It recalls to mind the picture of Christ as Light of the World and this Light-bearer of the Tarot may be equated with the hidden, or unrevealed cosmic mind of man, which serves to guide and inspire the soul in all its ways. It is in some respects a Daath figure, for this Path, although joining two Sephiroth lower on the Tree than Daath, has definite Daath characteristics in that it acts as a link between the Spirit and the Individuality. In some versions of the card the Hermit is preceded by a serpent, which is a symbol of Divine Wisdom, and in this context is in the shape of the traditional Egyptian uraeus worn on the headdress of royalty, priesthood and gods, and also suggesting by its shape the Hebrew letter Yod.

6. The Hermit bears a staff usually said to be the staff of Faith, or that mentioned in the 23rd Psalm: "Thy rod and thy staff they comfort me." This psalm also gives another level of significance of the Path in the words "Thou preparest a table before me." The preparation of a banquet is a profound mystical symbol occurring in Rosicrucian, Christian and pagan literature. The main Christian example is the Last Supper where the Christian sacrament was first given. Again we have an emphasis on a beginning and an ending. The prime legendary instance is that of the Round Table of King Arthur, which is a great Cosmic glyph in its deeper sense and is well aligned with Chesed as well as Chokmah. The aim of human evolution is the assembly of

kings in equality and diversity about a common centre.

7. The esoteric titles of the Tarot Trump again reveal reference to the beginning and the ending of evolution. Prophet of the Eternal indicates the seeing into the future state to the point where time no longer exists but becomes eternity. Magus of the Voice of Power reminds one of the beginnings of evolution when the Word came forth, not only macrocosmically, but microcosmically in the individual Words of all the Divine Sparks that make up the human swarm.

8. The Key to the Path is the Hebrew letter Yod, the first letter of the supreme Divine Name JHVH, which signifies the first beginning of things. Its signification is the Hand and this Path represents the Hand of God or the Hand of the Spirit guiding the soul on its evolutionary way. An alternative meaning is the male sperm, once again signifying the prime beginnings of things, the seed from which all future development arises. In this case it is the impregnation of the lower vehicles with the Divine Will of the Spirit.

9. It is interesting that the Spiritual Significance of the Path is the astrological sign Virgo, the Virgin, and the association of this sign with the Divine Seed of Yod recalls to mind the doctrine of the Immaculate Conception. It is well known that Virgin Birth has been attributed to many others besides Christ; in fact almost every great world teacher has been credited with this miraculous beginning.

10. Applying this frequently recurring doctrine psychologically, we may consider the soul as the Divine Mother, (the soul, or Ruach, traditionally being considered feminine), and giving birth to the Christ within. The inner birth of the Christ child, (Christ-consciousness), and its development to Kingship and Sacrificed-Godship, is a process which is applied Qabalistically to Tiphareth, the focussing point of the Individuality.

11. Christ-consciousness may be called the realisation of the Will of the Father Which is in Heaven, or the Will of the Spirit, whose Will is the same, axiomatically, as that of

God the Father. The first spark of this Christ-consciousness may thus be seen to be the influence of this 20th Path, which is the link between Tiphareth, (the lowest point of Individuality and the highest of Personality,) and Chesed, (the area of being, in manifestation, where the True Will of God and the Spirit is known.) By following in the steps of the Light-bearer, symbolically speaking, the way of destiny may be trodden from that of the Christ child in the manger among the beasts to that of the Sacrificed and Risen Saviour. This is again an indication of the beginning and the ending for any particular Spirit's way of evolving destiny.

12. Unfortunately, owing to the Prime Deviation, the actual situation is hardly as simple as this. This Deviation, which has come down to us as the Christian doctrine of Original Sin, was a refusal on the part of the Individuality to carry out the original Will of the Spirit when it entered the Universe of God the Father. Consequently, the false pattern was made. In Qabalistic terms this means that the image in Chesed is not the same as the image in the Supernal Triangle of the Spirit. There is a rift between Spirit and Individuality which has been reproduced on a lower arc in the rift between Individuality and Personality. Thus the Abyss and the Gulf are man made, the fruits of sin. The evolutionary process should, according to the Divine Plan, have been one of struggle, but not the wallowing in spiritual darkness beset by war, poverty and disease that the human condition has subsequently become.

13. These gaps in the chain of being from Spirit to Matter cause most of mankind to be dominated by selfish urges of the Personality, or else by unbalanced unhuman urges — twisted idealism — from the Individuality. It is the primary aim of all systems of spiritual development to re-form the link between Individuality and Personality and this is also the aim behind religious observances. In exoteric religion, however, the process is not usually recognised as such. Many of the mystics of the Church call 'communion with God' what is in reality communion with their own Individuality.

14. Now the Individuality, although appearing to the Personality to be a superior and more ethical part of the self is not perfect. In the early days of the modern Western esoteric revival it was usually considered to be so as a matter of expediency. Those who were in a position to know that it was not so did not reveal the true situation because a) it was necessary first to establish a large number of esoteric students with Individuality orientation without over-complicating the issue; and b) a premature revelation of the imperfection of the Individuality to an esoteric group would cause an unwelcome inrush of unbalanced force due to a restimulation of old deviated patterns stemming from Lemurian times. A group has to be very firmly established before it can stand psychic unbalance of this potency. Restimulation of currents of Lemurian black magic is no light matter.

15. Sufficient general progress has now been made, however, to allow a truer picture of the situation to be revealed. Indeed, the true situation gradually revealed itself. It was evident in the manifest unbalanced nature of many leading occultists who had made good Individuality contact, but spent much of their energies in disruptions and small squabbles — all from the best of motives — within their organisations. This was certainly no good advertisement for the claims of the occult movement.

16. It was no redeeming feature, either, that the errors inherent in the Individuality should manifest in the guise of high ethical intentions. In practice they usually resulted in a demonstration of the Vices of the Individuality Sephiroth —Pride, Contentiousness, Cruelty, Bigotry, Hypocrisy, Tyranny. These 'higher vices' have, of course, been plainly evident in the history of the Church as well as that of occultism. In the Church there have been the cruelties of the Inquisition, burning people at the stake for the high ethical motive of 'the good of their souls'. In occultism there has been the ridiculous pride of jockeying for position, measuring up one person's 'degree of advancement' over another's, and

so on—examples in both fields, exoteric or esoteric, are legion. Naturally, all such attitudes are travesties of the True Will of the Spirit and of God, in whose name most of these well intentioned blasphemies were perpetrated.

17. All this does not mean that Individuality contact should be eschewed. On the contrary, the appalling gap between Individuality and Personality must be bridged. But it does sound a word of caution that the high intentions of the Individuality, often appearing as stirrings of conscience, may not be all that they seem. And even an apparently perfect Individuality may be in error because it is not in alignment with the mode of being and destiny of the Spirit which projected and still projects it.

18. The lesson to be learned here is that the Quest of the Holy Grail does not end in Tiphareth or even Chesed, but in Kether; and personal destiny and complete evolution can only be achieved when *all* the broken links are restored and the True Will of the *Spirit*, not just of the Individuality, is manifested in complete control—in Earth.

NOTES ON THE DESIGN OF TRUMP IX

The Marseilles card shows an old man, apparently *not* hooded, but in a voluminous cloak, holding up a lantern, which is partly shrouded by the cloak, and walking with a staff.

Wirth divides the staff into eight segments and has him preceded by a serpent, a point which is supported by the early Crowley and Knapp. The latter makes the staff a shepherd's crook. With both Wirth and Knapp the Hermit is hooded. Waite and Case have him standing still on a mountain pinnacle, also hooded, and Case makes the hood into a definite Hebrew letter Yod. The two latter also show a sixpointed star in the lantern, and the lantern is less obscured by the cloak than in other versions.

The 'Egyptian' Hermit has the traditional attributes, though the staff is a serpent staff. He is preceded by two serpents and he faces straight out of the card.

In the Crowley/Harris card the Hermit suggests by his shape a Yod, his lamp contains the Sun, and he is looking at a serpent entwined egg. The three-headed Hound of Hell follows, whom he has tamed.

Manly P. Hall, who gives the symbol of a pentagram, its internal planes coloured in white and straddling a red square on a blue field, says that exoterically the Hermit was often thought to be Diogenes on his quest for an honest man. He also says that sometimes the staff is in seven sections. Eliphas Levi thought the card might be called Prudence.

The 22nd Path

Tiphareth — Geburah

KEY: ל Lamed. Ox-goad.

SPIRITUAL SIGNIFICANCE: ♎ Libra. The Scales.

THEORY: Daughter of the Lords of Truth. Ruler of the Balance. (VIII—Justice.)

COLOURS: Emerald. Blue. Deep blue-green. Pale green.

TEXT: "The Twenty-second Path is the Faithful Intelligence and is so called because by it spiritual virtues are increased, and all dwellers on earth are nearly under its shadow."

1. This Path is viewed with some trepidation by many neophytes of the Western Esoteric Tradition because it is generally known as the Path of Karmic Adjustment. However, all the higher Paths can be equally disturbing in their effects upon the Personality, for the higher up the Tree one goes, the closer one gets to fundamentals. A change in one's state of being in Kether, for instance, would affect one's whole being right down to the physical plane. A change in Yesod, on the other hand, though having its physical effects, (and the passions bring about physiological changes just as does the etheric vehicle,) would not have any direct effect upon the higher areas of one's being. There would be an indirect effect of course, a physical hangover after a party is not conducive to mental work, so in such a case Malkuth could be said to affect Hod. But it is the effects in Malkuth that are affected; Hod appears to be affected because the physical vehicle cannot take its mental currents. In reality the intellect is as keen as ever, but just not functioning in Earth because the lower communication channels are blocked. The main chain of cause and effect always works downward, from higher plane to lower.

2. Also, of course, one may come up against karma anywhere on the Tree. This is only to be expected. The original

Deviation took place at the Daath level so all factors of existence below Daath are bound to be riddled with sin and error. This requires the action of karma to rectify it. Karma is not a popular word among esoteric students — the conception of its workings do not fill many with enthusiasm. This is typical of human nature, for the cure is often disliked more than the disease, dentists are often disliked more than tooth decay until perhaps the excruciating pain of toothache restores a sense of values. The Lords of Karma may be likened to physical surgeons, though more properly they are Restorers of Cosmic Balance or Lords of Truth.

3. These terms, which are the esoteric titles of the Tarot Trump, give the whole theory of the Path very well. The implications of the figure of Justice on the card, with sword and scales, are resumed in the astrological sign of the Path, Libra — the Scales. The Path leads towards Geburah, which, as explained in Volume I, has aspects which may be likened to a Judgment Hall. Like its opposite number, the 20th Path, this Path has affinities with Daath, for Daath is also a sphere of Cosmic Balance.

4. Perhaps the most complete analysis of the 22nd Path is to be found in the Egyptian Book of the Dead, particularly the Judgment scene. It was the Egyptian belief that each individual was judged after death and, according to the result, either went to a life of everlasting bliss or was instantly annihilated.

5. This is interesting from the point of view of modern esoteric teaching, for although it is not widely believed that any souls are completely annihilated, (with certain rare exceptions, cf. 'The Cosmic Doctrine' on the function of comets as Cosmic Scavengers), the general Egyptian idea is in accord with esoteric tenets. When the Personality is judged in accordance with Spiritual Principle, that part which measures up favourably will be assimilated by the Individuality as part of its fund of manifest experience; so the Individuality becomes enriched. Evil traits, however, will be completely rejected, not through any policy of sep-

aration of sheep from goats or wheat from tares, but because that which does not conform with Spiritual Truth cannot, by that very fact, have any reality. It may have phenomenal existence but it cannot have noumenal being.

6. Non-existence of evil from a Spiritual viewpoint does not mean that it may just be written off—ignored. Christian Scientists might dispute the point, but while Spirit itself must be perfect and free from evil on noumenal levels, we live and move and have most of our being in phenomenal existence, and on these levels evil is certainly very real. So evil which is not absorbed into the Individuality remains to be accounted for, for it must be absorbed in the end, though after transmutation or sublimation. This task the Individuality often does not care to face, but puts the matter off. The principle is much like that of the Personality not being able to face up to certain home truths about itself. The scientific term for this almost universal situation is dissociation or repression, and the symptoms are the varying degrees of neurosis, or even psychosis, which are so common.

7. We have here, then, the elements of a psychiatry of the Individuality in addition to the more familiar orthodox psychiatry of the Personality. Those aspects of former incarnations which are not absorbed remain linked to the Individuality with a certain autonomous life of their own. This accounts for the phenomenon of 'magical bodies'.

8. Magical bodies are met with chiefly by occultists though they are indeed very common. They tend to be more defined with occultists however, for such have to some extent formed a conscious link between Personality and Individuality. As a result of this link, any magical bodies remaining in connection with the Individuality will more easily manifest through the Personality than is the case with most people.

9. Magical bodies reveal themselves in much the same way as do the Jungian archetypes of the unconscious; that is, they may have a temporary obsessing effect. Usually they stem from incarnations when great power was possessed and abused. They sometimes crop up in ritual and may be

visible to clairvoyant sight. Even without clairvoyant sight a change will become obvious with the officer concerned; his voice may take on a hard and domineering quality and of course the psychic stresses of the magical operation will be considerably altered. Quite often, too, the officer concerned will think that he is being very successful when such a thing happens, for it brings on a feeling of power and expanded awareness, but such is not the case, for it is not the manifestation through him of any divine force, but a restimulation of his own past misdoings.

10. Such ritual magical bodies are of the ancient Egyptian priesthood more often than not, that priesthood being one which combined a great knowledge and practice of ritual magic with a rigid political dictatorship—and dictatorships by the priesthood are, by their very nature, far more domineering and insidious than dictatorships by politicians or the military. Thus there was, during the thousands of years of Egyptian civilisation, much opportunity for the abuse of power.

11. Another common source of magical bodies is the military of past ages though these do not tend to come up in ritual. Restimulation seems to be sparked off more often than not by similarity of conditions or surroundings. Thus one might be walking one day out of a building, whether it be department store or whatever, that is built with pillars and wide steps in the classical style, and suddenly one has an upsurge of feeling of power. One stops, looking round, expecting to see, and in fact actually seeing and hearing in the imagination, the roaring of a Roman crowd and oneself dressed as a Roman officer or dignitary.

12. Normally one would shake one's head and pull oneself together and pass on one's way. It is only if such a thing became really obsessive that there would be trouble, in fact such might be the cause of some insanity, not that all who call themselves Napoleon are to be taken too literally.

13. Such a consideration may serve to knock some of the glamour off these vestiges of former incarnations, which is

all to the good. They are not really glamorous, manifesting usually as bursts of apparently unaccountable bad temper, irritability or frustration. The latter particularly so as in the twentieth century one cannot carry out the impulses of one's evolutionary youth and have someone flogged or flayed for knocking into one in the street. The past does have a romantic glow for many people though and to such we must give the reminder that an upstart bully of a Roman officer is no more glamorous than his modern West Point or Sandhurst counterpart; similarly, a scheming Egyptian priest of Amon-Ra or Osiris is little different from his modern counterpart jockeying for a sinecure in the church. Not that all military officers are vain bullies or all priests ambitious schemers of course — far from it — but the point is that ancient folly is no more commendable or exciting than modern folly.

14. While most magical bodies seem to build up round instances of abuse of power, this is not necessarily always so. They could equally involve an abuse of wisdom or love. Such might be very fair seeming, and thus they may be the more insidious. We might have one so filled with the 'love' of his brother's soul that he cheerfully has him stretched on the rack and burned at the stake to preserve him from heresy. One can well imagine the difficulty that might be encountered by an Individuality trying to absorb the acts of one of its Personalities that, for instance, in a travesty of 'love' hammered a wooden wedge into Giordano Bruno's mouth so that he could not put his soul in jeopardy by uttering heresies or blasphemies while he was being burned alive.

15. Such magical bodies, then, may be met with, and they may be considered as elements in one's past experience rejected from the Judgment Hall of Osiris, or, in other words, not assimilated by the Individuality. Obviously, their continued existence in the manner outlined above is a pathology, albeit a common one. What then to do about it?

16. The answer lies in one word — Redemption. As a word, Redemption has almost lost its meaning through over-

familiarity. It means the ability to face up to the true situation within oneself coupled with the willingness to change it. This is a lot easier to say than it is to do, for it requires ruthless honesty, considerable powers of discernment, and not a little courage, but prolonged intention and aspiration, which can be easier achieved by dedication to some religious organisation, esoteric or exoteric, will help to attain it. With a magical body, the aim is to face up to it, see exactly what it is, what it has done, accepting this however hideous or disgusting it may be, and once this confrontation has been fully achieved then one has power over that magical body instead of being the passive victim of its arbitrary and unpredictable restimulation.

17. The controlled use of a magical body is of practical concern only to a ceremonial magician; there are not many other circumstances where the ability to take on the mentation of an earlier epoch would be much use, unless perhaps one is an historical novelist. It may be of general interest though that such is the means of communication used by the Inner Plane Adepti. A Master has no vehicle of Personality, for his last Personality will have been absorbed into his Individuality like all the others. His usual mode of being is as a centre of abstract mental force, which could be equated on the Tree with Chesed. Naturally a human being existing at such a level would be hard put to communicate with human beings on Earth, most of whom do not operate consciously even as high as Tiphareth. The Master therefore takes on a magical body, that is, he regenerates the abstract stresses of an old Personality of his, and uses this as a vehicle of communication. It is because of this that Masters do not like their 'identities' to be widely publicised, for it naturally tends to lead outsiders to identify the Master as he is now, with the Personality he was at some time in the past. There is naturally a vast difference, for all Personalities are of limited experience and capacity, and because of this some Masters use more than one 'identity' with which to communicate. They select the Personality most able to

transmit the teaching they want to give, much as one might pick a different suit of clothes from the wardrobe according to the kind of place one was going out to.

18. Reverting to the Judgment scene of the Egyptian Book of the Dead, we may say that the ultimate Devourer of the Unjustified, depicted on the papyri as a fearsome crocodile headed monster, is a part of ourselves. Like most fearsome bugaboos in religous myth or legend, the supposedly evil monstrosity is, in reality, a cloak for something which we cannot face within ourselves, namely, in this case, the redemption and assimilation of all our past. Much of this confrontation is done of the lateral 19th Path but the initial weighing-up of all factors, leaving nothing out of account, is on the 22nd Path.

19. All pictures of the Egyptian Judgment Hall show a balance; and alternative title for the place, or subjective condition, is the Hall of the Double Maat. Maat is the Egyptian goddess who, besides being the feminine counterpart of the recording god Thoth, is the goddess of Absolute Law, and the heart of the dead is weighed in the balance against the symbol of Maat, which is a feather, emblematical of Right and Truth. The fact that it is the heart that is weighed is interesting in that the heart centre corresponds to Tiphareth, and Tiphareth is the lower focussing point of the Individuality where contact with the Personality is made.

21. Minor details vary from papyrus to papyrus but the weighing is usually performed by Anubis, the Opener of the Ways, who also leads the soul to the Judgment Hall. In other papyri, the weighing is done by Maat herself, in which case, as in the Papyrus of Qenna, the head of Anubis appears on the upright of the balance. Thoth records the result of the weighing and the justified soul is led by Horus from thence to the presence of Osiris, who is accompanied by his consorts Isis and Nephthys.

21. The point to remember in all this is that all the godforms are aspects of the soul itself and not external agencies. Thus the process may be considered psychologically as a

condition of self-assessment, where the Personality is absorbed by the Individuality, (Osiris), with the exception of any aspects which cannot be absorbed, or confronted, at that time. These latter aspects are 'devoured' by the strange beast mentioned hitherto, which means that they have no existence as far as the Individuality is concerned, though they do remain to be accounted for later. The Devouring Beast thus becomes a repository or vast complex of repressed material and so is The Dweller on the Threshold, that hideous form that has to be faced before leaving one state of existence for another. The form is all of the adverse aspects of oneself that one has not faced up to and it is met in its final form on the 19th Path. In the context of that Path it is sometimes referred to, by esotericists, as the Hunchback. The hump of its back is the weight of unresolved sin and it appears in the popular imagination as Punch or Punchinello, the hero of the children's puppet theatre and originally of the Italian Commedia dell' arte.

22. There are ideas of a Judgment in most religious doctrines, though the Christian belief prefers to consider the Judgment to be that of all humanity at one fell swoop at the end of the world. From an esoteric standpoint this is a misinterpretation. There may well be a final form of general assessment made then, but the whole doctrine of reincarnation makes the belief in a personal subjective assessment after each life almost a logical necessity. Some of the more hideous forms of the Revelation of St. John the Divine might be considered, however, as aspects of the Dweller on the Threshold of the whole human race—the Dweller on a group level.

23. Whilst on the subject of death, whether of an epoch, an evolution, or an individual, we should also mention the death of Initiation. In our present context we are concerned with Initiation at the Tiphareth level. This also brings in its wake a subjective judgment or assessment and the process is described symbolically and not without humour in 'The Chymical Marriage of Christian Rosencreutz'. In this story,

all the candidates for knowledge of the higher Mysteries are weighed in a golden balance, and those who fail the test are rejected. As the book says: "After the inquisition had passed over the gentry, the learned, and unlearned, in each condition one, it may be, two, but mostly none, being found perfect, it came to those vagabond cheaters and rascally Lapidem Spitalem ficum makers, who were set upon the scale with such scorn, that for all my grief I was ready to burst my belly with laughing, neither could the prisoners themselves refrain, for the most part could not abide that severe trial, but with whips and scourges were jerked out of the scale".

24. This passage is particularly interesting in that the description of the Mistress of these Ceremonies may well be a description of the appropriate Tarot Trump as it was in 1616, or possible 1601-2, or even, if we are to believe the claims of the manuscript itself, 1459. This personage is described as a "Virgin, who had arrayed herself all in red velvet, and girded herself with a white scarf. Upon her head she had a green wreath of laurel, which much became her."

25. The 22nd Path has an additional importance in that it is on the line of The Lightning Flash representing the line of the descent of involution of the Sephiroth. The Hebrew letter of the Path, Lamed, has reference to this. Geburah represents the condition of the Spirit in action in the higher levels of Form and the subsequent descent to Tiphareth via the 22nd Path is the establishment of the Spirit as a unit of Individuality at these sub-Supernal levels, from which levels the further projection of a Personality into Earth is made. The highest Path on the Tree, the 11th, represents the first coming forth of the Spirit into manifestation and is assigned the letter Aleph, meaning an Ox. The ox is one of the earthiest of symbolic animals and so we see that manifestation in Earth is implicit in the Spirit's purpose from the very beginning of things. Thus, the process of the Spirit, active in Geburah, driving its own projection down to the

relative stability of Tiphareth, is well symbolised under the form of an Ox-goad.

26. The shape of the letter itself, suggestive of two Yods, (one above and one below a lateral dividing line), suggests the Hermetic axiom "As above, so below" — a reference to the aim of producing a Personality which is a true reflection of the Individuality, just as the Individuality should be a true reflection of the Spirit.

27. The symbol of the Ox-goad, like the symbols of Geburah, may evoke suggestions of punishment, but this is not strictly accurate. The drive to fulfill destiny or the need to work out karma are not in themselves punishments, though they may appear so to a deviated Personality which insists on "kicking against the pricks". In a similar way, it is by no means certain that the flail of Osiris is a weapon of chastisement — perfect law and order should have no need of such recourse. Modern scholarship suggests that the flail was an instrument for flicking at bushes to obtain fragments of gum for incense. Thus, although man tends to make God in his own image, (and this is usually well enough, though the converse is a more accurate statement), man has distorted his own image by his Prime Deviation, so we should not think God's works to be too close a reflection of man's works. Divine Justice is a very different thing from human justice' and one can hardly visualise Christ functioning as governor or a warder in Dartmoor or Alcatraz. In terms of human suffering it would be interesting to know which caused the most in the history of mankind— criminality, or the punishments for it inflicted by society.

28. A truer approach to the potencies of this Path might be gained by considering the Hebrew letter under its lesser known, somewhat apocryphal symbolism of a Wing, for it is by the Wings of Faith that the soul can best achieve its destiny and escape from the shadow of karma. Faith emanates primarily from Binah, and flows into Geburah via the 18th Path, known as the Intelligence of the House of Influence. Binah is, of course, according to its Yetziratic Text, "the

Creator of Faith" and "the parent of Faith from which doth Faith emanate."

29. So we have a link shown to us by the Yetziratic Texts, which also describe the 22nd Path as the Faithful Intelligence, by which "spiritual virtues are increased." "All dwellers on earth are nearly under its shadow" and we may well assume that by striving to become completely under the protection and shadow of the Wings of Faith we shall attain to the realisation that the Divine Justice of Absolute Balance is not a system of remorseless punishment, but our protection against Cosmic Darkness, "Spiritual wickedness in High Places", and complete annihilation.

30. As Jesus said: "If ye have faith as a grain of mustard seed, ye shall say unto this mountain, Remove hence to yonder place; and it shall remove; and nothing shall be impossible unto you." (Matthew. xvii. 20) This has particular relevance to the man-made mountains of sin, corruption and ignorance, which the astringent tests of this Path serve to remove.

NOTES ON THE DESIGN OF TRUMP VIII

This card is numbered XI by the Golden Dawn, Waite, Case and Crowley. The Marseilles version shows a conventional figure of Justice, with sword in right hand and scales in left. A conventional shrub nearby shows it to be out of doors. The back of the throne could possibly be two pillars with a veil between.

Oswald Wirth makes no change except that there is no indication that the scene is out of doors, and in fact all later designs seem to indicate that it is indoors. Papus says that she sits between the columns of a temple, and mentions that her coronet is of iron; he also sees a solar cross on her breast. Waite follows this in making the background definitely two large pillars with a veil between. He also makes her crown of three square castellations with a square jewel instead of a circular one, in a round setting. Case is more traditional and makes the pillars and veil definitely part of the throne. Behind are heavy draperies. He also uses the old pattern for her headdress but makes the indeterminate pattern on its top in the Marseilles version into three points. Wirth did similarly but added two thinner points between the main three—this does give the Geburic five. Case also introduces a Tau-cross symbolism into her neckpiece and makes the crown jewel a circle within a square. Knapp places an ornate throne, carved with lion and sphinx, at the top of three steps. In this case the back of the throne is not a veil but the two pillars are accentuated. At the top of each one is a burning lamp. Manly P. Hall's symbol is an hourglass and he has also pointed out that some figures have a braid of hair wound round the neck, which he thinks indicative of a hangman's knot. This is so on the Marseilles card.

The 'Egyptian' Justice is blindfolded and on a throne elevated on three stops. She has a headdress of lance-heads as well as the usual nemys and uraeus, and is supported by a sphinx standing on a lion, a winged Isis standing behind her, and a winged turtle overhead. Above all is a strange device like a half-sun on top of a lotus stalk which may represent a canopy.

In the Crowley/Harris version the card is called Adjustment and shows a masked woman poised on tip-toe before a throne, crowned with Maat feathers and uraeus, and wearing a harlequin robe with diaphanous cloak. She holds a great sword point downwards and from her headdress depend huge scales in which are bubbles of Illusion. The throne behind her is made of four spheres and pyramids, the whole figure suggesting a diamond shape and with balanced spheres of lightness and darkness about it.

The 19th Path

Geburah — Chesed

KEY: ♉ Teth. Serpent.
SPIRITUAL SIGNIFICANCE: ♌ Leo. The Lion.
THEORY: Daughter of the Flaming Sword. Leader of the Lion. (XI —Strength.)
COLOURS: Greenish yellow. Deep purple. Grey. Reddish yellow.
TEXT: "The Nineteenth Path is the Intelligence of the secret of all the activities of the spiritual beings, and is so called because of the influence diffused by it from the most high and exalted sublime glory."

1. As the 27th Path, (a Path of great dynamic power), is the main girder of the Personality, so is the 19th Path, (also one of great force), the main girder of the Individuality. As the Spiritual Significance of the 27th Path was shown by the strong, fiery planet Mars, so is the Spiritual Significance of the 19th Path shown by the equally strong and fiery sign of Leo. The 'packing force' of the 27th Path is that which holds the diverse aspects of the unit of incarnation, the Personality, together; the 'packing force' of the 19th Path holds the unit of evolution, the Individuality, together. So the Tarot Trump of this Path is, not unnaturally, Strength — a woman holding apart, without effort, the jaws of a lion.

2. The lion is a common alchemical symbol representing the uncontrolled forces of nature in the subjective world apart from the complex of symbolism which surrounds it in its function as a Kerubic sign of Fire, or the Root of Fire. The woman may be considered an aspect of the throned woman of the 14th Path, The Empress. The 14th Path is the Path within the Spirit itself which corresponds with what the 19th Path is to the Individuality and the 27th Path is to the Personality. The link between these Paths is further pronounced in that the lion is held by the mouth, which is

the signification of the Hebrew letter Peh on the 27th Path.

3. The lion symbolism is also found in the Spiritual Significance of the Path, Leo, the Lion. This constellation has been regarded as of fundamental importance in many esoteric systems, notably in that of the Golden Dawn, which revived the astronomical system of Ptolemy of Alexandria. This system, instead of the now usual method of measuring Right Ascension and Longitude from a suppositious point divided by the Equinox and called 0° of Aries, considers the start of the Zodiac to be the star Regulus Calculation by this method avoids the gradual discrepancy through the years between the signs of the Zodiac and the actual constellations caused by the Precession of the Equinoxes.

4. Regulus, (the name means 'Star of the Prince'), is in the constellation of Leo, and has the significant alternative title of Cor Leonis — 'The Heart of the Lion'. So we have the constellation of the Lion as the starting point of the Zodiac just as, on the Tree of Life, the Lion represents the first formation of the Individuality from Chesed. The Individuality is the projected unit in the worlds of Form and it performs "all activities of the spiritual being". This explains the gist of the Yetziratic Text and the Spiritual Being itself is, of course, represented by the woman on the Tarot card, whose figure of eight hat emphasises her link with eternity. The activities themselves could be called a lesser, subjective Zodiac, representative of the twelve tasks of Hercules, that mythological representative of humanity who, incidentally, wore a lion-skin on his back.

5. The symbols of this Path — the Lion, the Serpent of the Hebrew letter, the Flaming Sword of the esoteric title of the Tarot card, — suggest many other traditions. There is the Biblical story of Adam and Eve and the Serpent in the Garden of Eden, which is an allegory of the Fall of the human race into the worlds of Form. This primordial event — not to be confused with the Prime Deviation — has analogues with the 19th Path in that this Path is the way of coming forth into activity of the human soul after its initial

projection into Form in Chesed. It will be remembered that Adam and Eve were prevented from returning immediately to Eden by an angel with a flaming sword. The latter symbol gives a link with our Tarot Trump and the angel may be considered a personalisation of the forces of this Path, for this Path holds the pattern of "all the activities of the spiritual beings" and the destiny of these activities is not an immediate return to Spirit, but a rounding of the nadir in Earth first.

6. Cor Leonis reminds us of Richard I of England, who, although by no means an ideal king, captured the popular imagination with his nick-name of 'The Lion Heart.' Had it not been for the deeper mythological implications of King Arthur and his Knights of the Round Table, this king might well have been the nucleus of an even greater legend cycle. He is intimately associated with Robin Hood and his Merry Men of Sherwood Forest, who, like the Round Table Knights, were up-holders of a new law and had their eyes fixed upon a set of ideals by which to live their lives. This attitude of living out a principle is in truth an "activity of the spiritual being" in Earth;

7. Whereas, (apart from the more esoteric implications,) the Arthurian Knights were striving to replace the old law of revenge with the new law of chivalry, the Outlaws of Sherwood Forest were, in a way, fore-runners of the Aquarian Age. Their policy of robbing the rich to give to the poor was a crude attempt at the more enlightened social justice and equality of persons of our own day. The fact that they numbered a man of religion, Friar Tuck, and a woman, Maid Marion, in their midst, also gives some esoteric hints as to what lay behind their brand of idealism. There seems to be, as in the Arthurian cycle, a combination of the Nature loving Celtic Christianity and the Queen Venus cult of Southern France. The story of Blondel finding his master, King Richard, by singing outside all the prisons of Europe, gives a link with the Trouvere and Troubadour tradition. Richard was himself the son of Eleanor of Aquitaine who,

a leading patron of Courtly Love, greatly influenced the English group soul after her marriage to Henry II.

8. The whole of this cycle is predominantly upon the Green Ray, but the relevance to the 19th Path stems from the attitude of living out an ideal—a difficult but an ennobling task. The hazards of bringing spiritual principles down to earth and living them out is particularly obvious in another story connected with this Path—Daniel and the Lions' Den.

9. Daniel and his companions, like many others before and since the Exemplary Life of the Christ, put the values of their own Spirits before the expediencies of the world of unregenerate men. Such was their Faith that neither flame nor wild beast could harm them.

10. Daniel is credited with being a master magician, as one might expect from one who could bring down the powers of the Spirit so strongly that they could directly control the forces of Earth. There are few who could conquer the lions and fires of their own subjective passions in this way, let alone their counterparts in the objective world. Needless to say, complete mastery of subjective work should always precede any objective experiments. Failure to realise this has led many would-be magicians astray. The Order of the Golden Dawn was a case in point as may be seen from some of their published rituals. They tried to control the Elements without, before having gained control of the Elements within. This is asking for trouble for anyone of less than Adeptus Minor grade, that is, one who has attained Tiphareth or Individuality consciousness and control.

11. A similar legend is that of Androcles and the Lion. This story has come down to us much like a cautionary tale with the moral of always being kind to animals. While one cannot quarrel with such sentiments, there is much more to it than this, and the same could be said of most stories that have caught the popular imagination generation after generation. In all cases there is a certain amount of distortion of the original, but beneath this overlay is always a deep esoteric teaching.

12. The 19th Path, like the 22nd Path, is one which lies on the course of the Lightning Flash and so has additional significance. After the image of the Spirit has been projected from Binah, though Daath, to Chesed, it begins to build up a dynamic round of activity. This process is represented by the 19th Path from Chesed to Geburah. The Path is naturally one of great dynamism and purity as it is so close to the first manifestation of the Spirit in the worlds of Form — subject, of course, to the proviso that, owing to the Deviation, the image in Chesed may not be the true image of the Spirit.

13. Treading the Path the other way, from Geburah to Chesed, is the initiatory path of the Adeptus Major to the Exempt Adepthood of Chesed — a state of being where further incarnation in Earth is unnecessary. The realisations of this Path are therefore particularly profound, for they are the end-result of the experience and understanding of a complete cycle of evolution.

14. Basically, the test of this Path is the ability to face up to everything that has happened during the complete span of personal evolution, accepting it all for what it is, without evasions or repressions. It is a final reckoning up and so has similarities with the 22nd Path of karmic adjustment. In this case, however, there can be no putting off of matters til a later date. Here, whatever cannot be confronted remains as an immediate barrier to any further progress.

15. This is also a Path, therefore, which tends to be viewed with some trepidation. It is not merely a case of being weighed in the balance and the worst excrescences of the soul being rejected. On this Path there can be no more rejection, for rejection is against the Law of Love, or Synthesis, which is the Ray upon which our Solar Logos' Universe is based. There are, of course, none so blind as those who will not see, but on this Path all are *made* to see. Any excrescences are not merely entered in the book of Thoth, as on the 22nd Path, they are clawed and ripped away

forcibly. Thus the Egyptian cat and lion-headed goddesses, Bast and Sekhmet, are relevant to this Path.

16. So the Path is not a pleasant one — but only for the reason that we who tread it are not pleasant people. The pure in soul could, like Daniel, Androcles and the rest, tread it without fear of hurt — and the word 'hurt' is used advisedly. One may be hurt by the corrosive action of karma but one cannot come to harm by it, unless of course, one should venture too far too soon, or try to avoid issues when their time is ripe.

17. The confrontation of all past experience also entails taking responsibility for it. This may seem difficult to understand for the immediate usual reaction is to put blame upon others for all misfortunes, (though personal credit is usually taken for successful circumstances). It may seem difficult to see why one is responsible for everything that happens to one, but, given a belief in reincarnation, it should not be too difficult to realise that even the things one would apparently be least responsible for, one's childhood circumstances for example, are in fact the result of one's own inter-incarnationary desires — we make our own karma to a large extent. And if one is of the turn of mind that considers the Laws of the Universe to be harsh, or even unjust or tyrannous, there is the fact that originally no Spirit was forced to enter the manifest Universe. All ate of the Tree of the Knowledge of Good and of Evil of their own free will. That is to say, that all entered into a co-operation with the Solar Logos voluntarily, giving their aid in building an evolving Universe in return for the evolutionary experience that this would bring, thus equipping each human being with the means to become a God or any other of the high alternatives of Cosmic Evolution.

18. Most, of course, subsequently took their hands away from the plough, or tried to. The results are over-familiar. The goal for humanity remains, however, for all who press on to the uttermost — as all eventually will. Some hints of the glories of the Cosmic future then in store are contained

128

in the Tibetan Master's book 'The Rays and Initiations', written by Alice Bailey. (Lucis Trust. London & New York.) In the meantime, the way inbetween remains, and the key to that way is acceptance—acceptance of fact, and acceptance of responsibility for it.

19. It was attempted avoidance of fact and responsibility that led to all the trouble in the first place. Continued avoidance only makes matters worse. The reason for this avoidance was, in the first place, fear of pain — and this fear remains to this day. This is the reason why responsibility for error cannot be faced, why it has to be pushed, compulsively and automatically, onto another. To accept the truth about one's own deep-seated faults is painful.

20. There is only one way finally to overcome this fear and pain, and that is to accept it. The symbolism of drinking from the Cup is a wellknown one in esoteric writings, but what does it mean in terms of actual fact?

21. It means the realisation and full acceptance within ourselves of the way we have departed from our true Path of Spiritual Destiny. The drinking of the Cup is the complete acceptance of the way we have erred; and the way each has erred is the way each has erred and cannot be altered by one hairsbreadth. So there is no point in wasting time rejecting what we have done. If we spend our time crying about the past, or refusing to acknowledge it, we are rejecting the way we have come, we are rejecting our sin, our responsibility. And in the degree that we reject the sin, or the imperfections of each one of us, in that degree do we fail to understand how resurrected life may be achieved.

NOTES ON THE DESIGN OF TRUMP XI

This card is numbered VIII by the Golden Dawn, Waite, Case and Crowley. The Marseilles card shows a woman in a lemniscate hat holding the jaws of a lion. Opinion of commentators is divided between whether she is opening its mouth, closing its mouth, or holding its head to her breast after having stunned it. Levi and Papus considered she was closing its jaws, but of the versions we are here reviewing, all show her to be opening them except Waite and Zain. In no case does the lion seem stunned or held to her breast.

The basic symbolism is the same on all cards. The Golden Dawn thought a dark veil should float about her head and cling round her. Knapp puts a few well gnawed bones about in the foreground—Manly P. Hall's symbol this time being a swan. Waite and Case dispense with the lemniscate hat and substitute a similar shaped nimbus and a floral wreath. They also show the lion being led by a chain of flowers, obviously roses. On Case's card and possibly on Waite's, the chain forms a figure of eight about the lion's neck and her waist. Waite and Case show trees in the background and a conical hill, which is also suggested in Knapp's. The Egyptian version shows the woman in a vulture headdress with uraeus, surmounted by a vase and crowned eagles. Above is a simple frieze and below, paintings of nature in something after the style of the Akhnaton period.

The Crowley/Harris card shows a naked woman holding a flaming Holy Grail, riding upon a lion. The lion has seven heads, those of an angel, saint, poet, warrior, bacchante and satyr sharing the neck, and the tail being a lion-serpent. The reins with which the lion is harnessed are said to represent passion and there are dim martyr's heads under the lion's feet. Ten luminous rayed circles represent the Sephiroth and there are ten snake-like horns of a destroying/creating beast at the top of the card round an emblem of New Light.

Crowley preferred to call this card Lust—somewhat in the sense of Lust for Life. In the past it has been known as either Force or Fortitude. An early design of a card called Force shows a woman, haloed, in a dress embroidered with trifoliate crosses, effortlessly breaking a stone pillar.

VIII

LA · JUSTICE

VIIII

L'HERMITE

X

LA · ROUE · DE · FORTUNE

XI

LA FORCE

Part II
Influences Upon the Personality

The 21st Path

Netzach — Chesed

KEY:	⊐ Kaph. Palm of the hand.
SPIRITUAL SIGNIFICANCE:	♃ Jupiter.
THEORY:	Lord of the Forces of Life. (X — The Wheel of Fortune.)
COLOURS:	Violet. Blue. Rich purple. Bright blue, rayed yellow.
TEXT:	"The Twenty-first Path is the Intelligence of Conciliation and Reward, and is so called because it receives the divine influence which flows into it from its benediction upon all and each existence."

1. This is a Path which connects Individuality and Personality—apart from the organic fusion of the two in the Sephirah Tiphareth. Chesed represents that part of the Individuality where the pure image of what the Individuality intends to be is held. This image should be a true reflection of the Will of the Spirit. The Sephirah into which the influences of Chesed flow, via the 21st Path, is Netzach, representing the creative imagination and higher emotions within the Personality. Thus the potencies of this Path are responsible for the ideals and aspirations which capture the imagination of man.

2. Foremost of these, perhaps, in Western European man is the ideal of the Quest of the Holy Grail. This ideal can affect a man in many ways and may even be viewed under entirely different symbolism. A literary example is Harry Street in Hemingway's 'The Snows of Kilimanjaro', who, reviewing his past life as he is dying, is haunted by the story of a leopard, found dead on the slopes of Kilimanjaro. No-one knew why the leopard should have been at such a height nor what it could have been seeking.

3. The influence acts primarily upon the emotions, and is that undefined yearning which impels men or women to set

131

132

out on a quest. What the search is for may not clearly be
known, nor yet whether the thing sought for even exists. It
is this that impels the man or woman to enter upon that
stage of the Path known as 'the Seeker' and of course the
quest is an inner one. Yet this urge may be the reason that
impels certain souls to embark on lives of physical adventure, to be willing victims of that wanderlust so well presented in Kipling's 'The Long Trail':

> "You have heard the beat of the off-shore wind
> And the thresh of the deep-sea rain.
> You have heard the song—how long? how long?
> Pull out on the trail again!"

4. Also, the fact that it is the emotions that are stirred by
this impulse from the Individuality, causes some to mistake
the call of their own higher nature for the magnetic attraction of another human being. Such fall under the spell of
the contra-sexual image. Another interesting factor is that
the desire for change that this impulse brings—and which,
with most, results in daydreams of Elysian life on remote
desert islands, or, more practically, the post-Christmas
plans for a summer holiday—is, on its deeper levels, a wish
for death. The Path of Death of the Personality, the 24th,
also leads from Netzach.

5. The influences of this Path, coming in at this time more
strongly, due to the Law of Cycles, may also account for that
post-war phenomenon 'the Beat generation'. There is much
in their general outlook which suggests this—the urge to
wander, a preoccupation with mysticism and, unfortunately,
(what may be a restimulation of ancient factors of Black
Magic), a tendency to drug addiction and sexual experimentation as a means of 'getting out of this world'. Unfortunately this approach to life solves few problems, material
or spiritual, for the only way to improve the mess of modern
civilisation is to get down to Earth and to grips with it. And
although narcotics may be the quickest way of 'getting out
of this world' it is also the most expensive—exorbitantly so

in the coin of spiritual, mental and moral health. The truth is, however trite or grisly it may appear to some, the qualifications for full mystical development are the same as those needed for success in the world — balance and control. Drugs achieve neither. Also, compulsive unconventionality is as deadening and weak as compulsive conventionality, one being the reflection of the other. Furthermore, no problems are solved by turning one's back on them, however picturesque a posture one may strike in so doing.

6. The emotional urge of 'the Quest' may come to any, young or old, though — with the exception of those who have led the mystic or occult life in previous incarnations — it is more usual for the urge to manifest in middle age. This period is one where one has passed the mid-point of the physical life, dissolution begins to set in, however slowly, and the Personality is more naturally disposed to think upon the subjective worlds and the state of existence after death. After middle age the direction of life is, after all, broadly speaking, towards death rather than to the conquest of material life. Thus the impulses of the Individuality are more likely to gain a hearing with the Personality now less distracted by ambitions and desires.

7. However, without necessarily taking on the more startling effects of a sudden conversion, the impulsion may be a sudden, strong one and not the result of a gradual change of viewpoint lasting several years. It may impel the Personality to an interest in the metaphysical even if that Personality's mind is hardened into a strongly materialist mould. If such is the case, then the person concerned would probably start off on a scientific approach, going to spiritualist meetings and so on, in order to see if there is any truth in the spiritualist claims. Such an attitude of suspended disbelief in the cause of searching for not-so-obvious truths is all to the good, particularly in the outer realms of mysticism and occultism where there is much charlatanry and self-deception. The main dangers to avoid here are, first, a shying away from the whole business because of the para-

mount false claims, glamour, and emotional exaggeration which are rife, not so much in the Spiritualist Movement itself, (though here it does exist to some extent), but in the blind followers of the more vocal exponents of professional 'occultism'; and secondly, a preoccupation with the phenomena of communication itself or other parlour tricks of the less spiritually enlightened séance room. The first requirement on the early stages of the Quest is, of course, the Virtue of Malkuth, Discrimination, but all the Virtues of the lower Personality Sephiroth will soon be called into play — the Independence of Yesod, for a staunch openmindedness will have to be maintained, (neither following blindly any who cry "Lord, Lord!", nor, on the other hand, being bludgeoned into apathy from fear of what friends and relations might think of one's new 'peculiar' interests); the consequent sifting of evidence, subjective and objective, that is implied in the Truthfulness of Hod; the ability to admit one's ignorance, to 'become as a little child' implied in the Unselfishness of Netzach; and above all, that virtue which will carry the soul through any difficulties on the Path, the Devotion to the Great Work of Tiphareth.

8. Eventually the Path may lead to one of the esoteric schools, though not necessarily so, for some work best unaffiliated to any particular organisation. But in all cases, as the Tibetan stresses in Alice Bailey's "A Treatise on White Magic" the aim is contact with the Individuality — or with the Soul, to use the Tibetan's terminology. This may lead to selfless service in any sphere of human endeavour whether political, financial, scientific, social, artistic, or any other field in which the work of destiny lies.

9. Some remarks by the Tibetan in this same book lead us on to a consideration of the deeper aspects of the symbolism of this Path. There is a link between this Path of Desire and Vision and the 32nd Path of the Coming and Going into and out of physical form in Malkuth. It will be remembered that the scarf about the dancing figure of The Universe was in the shape of a letter Kaph. This letter is the Key to the

21st Path. The Key to the 32nd Path on the other hand is Tau, which, the Tibetan says, is "the symbol of reincarnation. It is desire for form which produces the use of form and causes cyclic and constant rebirth in form."

10. This cyclic and constant rebirth in Form is obviously of immediate relevance to the 32nd Path, in fact the ovoid shape in which the figure on Trump XXI appears can be considered as the opening of a Cosmic Womb. Rebirth is, however, brought about by desire, as the passage from 'The Cosmic Doctrine' already quoted at length in connection with the 24th Path says. "The Spirit, beholding the face of its Father until consciousness is weary with Its brightness, closes its eyes and sleeps; and sleeping, it dreams of the unfulfilled desires and so it is born again, for upon the plane of desire a state of consciousness is a place, and as we desire, so are we reborn. Thus each man makes his own karma."

11. Now it is obviously not the Personality that has this desire, for the Personality does not exist at this stage except in a seed state. The last Personality has been absorbed before, when, as the previous paragraph in 'The Cosmic Doctrine' stated, man undergoes the Fifth Death and "is born into consciousness of the Individuality, and lives upon the plane of Individuality perceiving the 'face of his Father Which is in Heaven.' "

12. The 'face of his Father Which is in Heaven' may be considered the image of the Spirit itself, and it is a vision across the Abyss, provided that the Individuality can function consciously at this level. The Spirit beholding the face of its Father, would more properly be termed the Spirit-functioning-as-Individuality, or, more simply, the Individuality. This is clear from the context. So it is the Individuality which has the dreams of unfulfilled desires and manufactures its own karma. Here is the rationale why the Individuality cannot be perfect in itself, a fact which has already been mentioned in our consideration of the 20th Path, (Tiphareth — Chesed.) As this Path, so closely linked with the 32nd, also leads from Chesed, it may be inferred that the root of any

karma will lie in Chesed, precisely where the true image of
the Spirit in the Supernals is distorted when it comes down
to Individuality manifestation.

13. The emphasis on cyclic rebirth is resumed in the Tarot
card, The Wheel of Fortune — no great symbolic remove from
the Wheel of Birth and Death. But we must not fall into the
trap of equating physical rebirth with karma. It is true that
in so far as the image in Chesed does not correspond with
the reality in the Supernals then the 'desires' of the Individuality will have karmic effects, but it is the *destiny* of
the Spirit to achieve experience in Earth by cyclic rebirth,
so the 'desire' of the Individuality is in line with the True
Plan. It is only false in so far as it may lead to incorrect
action in Earth and thus prolong the evolutionary process
needlessly, through karma displacing destiny. As a matter
of fact, most deviations concern an attempt to avoid this
process of cyclic rebirth through fear of physical life.

14. The Wheel of Fortune, then, is a symbol of the pattern
of evolving destiny held within the Individuality. The same
could be said for the symbol for Kaph, the Palm of the
Hand, which not only is, traditionally, a chart of destiny,
but also the part of the Divine Anatomy whereby the Spirit
is nailed to the Cross of Matter.

15. When the soul is discarnate the trend of evolving
destiny impels towards incarnation; and when the soul is
incarnate it manifests in the emotions as the desire for the
life and realities of the higher worlds. The circular shape of
the Wheel of Fortune, which symbolises this, is reminiscent
of the Table Round, and though a more popular round table
in modern life might be the roulette wheel, the real wheel
is a reflection of the great image of Chokmah, the Wheel of
the Zodiac, of which the Round Table of Arthur is a representation.

16. The goal of human beings is to become as kings, equal
in diversity, seated about this table. When such occurs there
will be the perfect manifestation of divine law and order,
and so the Spiritual Significance of this Path is aptly the

planet Jupiter, the Mundane Chakra of Chesed, essentially the Sephirah of Divine Rule.

17. This is summed up in the Yetziratic Text, which describes the Path as the Intelligence of Conciliation and Reward. In view of the deviation of the human race, Reconciliation might be a better word, for once the true destiny is realised the true image of what the Spirit is will be sensed in Chesed, via this Path. Then is a man reconciled to God and his own True Being, so the Quest might be considered in one aspect as the Return of the Prodigal Son.

18. The last phrase of the Yetziratic Text reads a little strangely perhaps: "It receives the divine influence which flows into it from its benediction upon all and each existence." One may ask how it can receive something which stems from itself. However, it is a fundamental occult law that whatever one gives so will one receive. Thus the benediction which flows from this Path, (that is, the work of destiny, or Love under Will, which 'makes all things new' and helps to bring the Kingdom to Earth), in turn draws down by its own downward outflowing the cosmic resources of the Spiritual realms. Thus is the initiate called one who owns nothing but has the use of all things. To own something for the sake of ownership is to block the flow. To use all one's talents and possessions in the service of others is to act as a channel for cosmic resources. This is the aim of all magic and the true meaning of priesthood.

NOTES ON THE DESIGN OF TRUMP X

The Marseilles card shows a six-spoked wheel upon which are crude images of a monkey descending on the left side, an indeterminate creature ascending on the right, and a crowned sphinx with sword seated at the top.

Levi said that the wheel was the wheel of Ezekiel, which he drew, and that the descending figure was Typhon and the ascending one Hermanubis. Wirth gives the wheel eight spokes and has it floating in a boat containing two serpents. The ascending figure he makes dog headed, armed with a caduceus, the descending one he gives a satyr's head and a trefoil double merman's tail, armed with a trident. He puts the sign of Mercury and Salt against each one respectively, and Sulphur against the sphinx. Knapp follows this design but omits the signs and makes the descending figure's head more animal like—a cross between a cow and an alligator in appearance. Papus regarded the ascending creature as Anubis, the descending one as Typhon, whom he regarded as the genius of good and the genius of evil. Manly P. Hall's symbol is a pyramid of ten dots on a yellow ground.

138

The Golden Dawn version of the card showed the wheel with zodiacal spokes in colours of the spectrum, presided over by a Sphinx above and a cynocephalus ape below. The early Crowley favoured a wheel of six shafts with the triad of Hermanubis, Sphinx and Typhon, each representative of Mercury, Sulphur and Salt respectively. On the Harris card he has the wheel going the opposite way to everyone else, Hermanubis climbs up the left side and Typhon, with ankh and crook, descends the right. The wheel is ten spoked.

Waite follows Eliphas Levi's reconstruction and places the Holy Living Creatures at each corner of the card, in clouds, reading from books. Typhon is in snake form and Anubis, unlike the representations of Wirth and Knapp, does look like Anubis. The wheel consists of an outer circle in which are the letters TORA interspersed with the letters of the Holy Name JHVH in Hebrew. Inside this there are eight spokes, four of which are given symbols: the one pointing to the Sphinx to Mercury, the one pointing at Typhon, Salt, the one pointing at Anubis, Sulphur. There is thus a difference of opinion on the attributions of Sulphur or Mercury to the Sphinx or Anubis and a case can be made out for either. Case's design follows Waite's except that the Holy Living Creatures are not reading books.

The 'Egyptian' Tarot shows an eight spoked wheel, a serpent on each spoke and a winged horned disk at the bottom of the shaft. The Sphinx holds a javelin and has a hawk on its back. The figures of Typhon and Hermanubis are quite un-Egyptian.

The man, mouse and monkey seen on some exoteric cards is, according to Levi, a superficial rendering for which Etteila was responsible.

The 23rd Path

Hod — Geburah

KEY:	ꟷ Mem. Water.
SPIRITUAL SIGNIFICANCE:	▽ Water.
THEORY:	Spirit of the Mighty Waters. (XII—The Hanged Man.)
COLOURS:	Deep blue. Sea green. Deep olive green. White flecked purple.
TEXT:	"The Twenty-third Path is the Stable Intelligence, and is so called because it has the virtue of consistency among all numerations."

1. It may seem strange that this Path, which is so obviously one of Water, not the stablest of Elements, should yet be called the Stable Intelligence. But the Path connects Hod and Geburah and herein lies the clue to the matter.

2. The Sephirah Hod, in common with Binah and Chesed, is a 'Water' Sephirah and there is an aspect of the Sephirah sometimes referred to as 'The Water-temple of Hod'. A principle of Water is reflection, and it is in Hod that the reflections of the principles of the higher worlds may be discerned. Hod, of course, refers to mind, and so the reflections of this Sephirah are intimations of pure reason rather than the images of lower psychism which are to be seen in the Magic Mirror of Yesod. Where images occur in Hod they are more in the nature of abstractions, (the geometrical symbols of Pythagorus, for example), rather than the teeming welter of subconscious elements, (dream images, for example), of Yesod. The similarity of function of the two Sephiroth is indicated in the symbols of their Mundane Chakras. The Moon, of Yesod, is shaped like a cup, a receiver, and this same symbol surmounts the symbol for Mercury.

3. Geburah, on the other hand, is not a 'Water' Sephirah but, like Chokmah and Netzach, a 'Fire' one. Yet there is an

139

aspect of it that is much akin to the action of water. It is very easy to regard Geburah solely as a violent, intensely active Sephirah, but it achieves its effects also by the slow wearing away of accretions over a great length of time. This aspect is shown by the symbol of the Chain, but a more accurate example of the process may be found in water, which, dripping on a stone for many years will wear a hole through it, or which will round off a sharp rock into perfect smoothness after long immersion. Thus we have, on this Path, in the one case, the stability necessary to reflect the higher worlds without distortion; and in the other case, stability of effort over countless eons of time.

4. Broadly speaking, Chesed is the Sephirah associated with what the Individuality *is*, Geburah is the Sephirah associated with what the Individuality *does*. Geburah also has a corrective or assessing element in it which implies the ability to see what *is*, the ability to see what *should be*, and then the ability to take action to merge the two kinds of reality so that after the Geburic action everything that *is* is as it *should be*.

5. These principles of action are also available to the Personality and the link in consciousness which causes this to be so is, on the Tree, the 23rd Path. Hod, the sphere of mind in the Personality, is analogous to Geburah in many ways; this is particularly shown in the analytical powers of the mind. This has its dangers at the present time when there is great emphasis placed upon mind; the mind is all too apt to be used in its destructive function instead of constructively. Thus, internationally, we are faced with continual war but the bombs and bullets are ideas. The World War has never really stopped since 1914; all that really happened in 1918 and 1945 was that it ceased to be fought on a physical level, except for occasional skirmishes, and even then through general exhaustion rather than humane principles. Our Lord once asked a crowd of very righteous people who dared to cast the first stone, and after looking into their hearts, none did. We can only hope that a

similar display of self-honesty may prevail today, particularly as we have progressed from throwing stones to throwing bombs. At least jesting Pilate had the choice of stopping for an answer; we may not be so lucky once the gamma-rays get going.

6. However, if centuries of civilisation, let alone eons of evolution, have not served to teach man to use his powers constructively one is tempted to wonder what any religious appeal can do. Viewed in the light of the present context, the symbol on the Tarot Trump has its irony—it shows a hanged man. The powers of this Path should show man how to use his mind in conformity with the True Plan of evolution. When any difficulties have occurred in the past the human reaction has tended to be a great willingness to hang the other man, whether by rope or nails or whatever comes cheapest. The real lesson that this Path has to teach, put in the bluntest vernacular terms, is "Go hang yourself!"

7. Esoterically, the symbol of the man hanged upside down is one of sacrifice. Now self-sacrifice does not mean a morbid search for martydom. It means a) utterly unselfish co-operative effort for the good of the whole and every individual within that whole; and b) the exchange of something for something better. The exchange of money for a whiskey and soda represents the second aspect of sacrifice; the use of that money to buy a starving man a meal would cover both factors. Like all spiritual truths, it is really very simple — though to those who base their ethics, usually through fear basically, on "Me first!", or on a complicated web of plausible reservations, it may appear just simple-minded.

8. Yet this issue of simplicity and simple-mindedness illustrates another lesson of this Tarot card. The Hanged Man is upside down, indicating that the values of the higher worlds are the reverse of the lower. (A similar symbolism occurs in the parallel 21st Path whose Trump is the turning Wheel of Fortune.) The Personality is based on the animal life from whence it stems and, if uninformed by the higher nature, it naturally acts in accordance with the simple phys-

142

cal laws of survival. This leads to an attitude of "Fight for food and shelter first, and philosophise about it afterwards."

9. Spiritual values are different, for they are based on a Cosmic background and the knowledge and certainty that All is One and that Life is indestructible. This essential Unity was stressed by Our Lord.when he said: "Verily I say unto you, Inasmuch as ye have done it unto one of the least of these my brethren, ye have done it unto me." and "Inasmuch as ye did it not to one of the least of these, ye did it not to me." (Matthew xxv. 40 & 45)

10. For any who are not Illuminati, this needs Faith—and a lot of it. Unfortunately, attempts have been made in the past to bolster up Faith with threats. Promise of hell fire is not, however, a particularly apt way of bringing souls back to the God of Love, though of course such teachings are really, though hideous distortions, based upon psychological fact. Esoteric eschatology teaches that the worst that most need expect is the automatic 'burning out' of desire when there is no physical body to satisfy those desires. Thus while lack of functional control can lead to some discomfort after death, this discomfort, which no doubt can be severe, is by no means a punishment. There should be no threats implied in the descriptions of 'the wages of sin', only warnings of the action of cause and effect. "If you put your hand in the fire then you will get burned." is a statement of fact, and blaming God, the fire, the person who told you, the person who did not tell you, or even yourself makes little difference to the outcome—in this case, a painful finger.

11. With this in mind let it be stated that perhaps the most basic Spiritual Law of the Universe is, however much appearances may seem to indicate the contrary, you get out of life exactly what you put into it.

12. Exactly what to put into living each must decide for himself. Qabalistically, this Path should hold the answer. Put into plain terms this means that the first task is to make the mind into a clear receptive vessel, capable of registering

pure reason without being occluded by false opinions or mental taboos.

13. Once the light of pure reason is achieved, one's destiny becomes clear, as the symbolic links of this Path will show. The Water symbolism immediately refers us to Binah, the Great Sea, whose influence passes to Geburah, and thence to this Path and Hod, by the 18th Path. Binah is of the Spirit, the most concrete form of the Spirit qua Spirit, wherein the true image of the Self and Destiny rests. Also, the Spirit of the Mighty Waters, the title of the Tarot Trump, well repays meditation. The Mighty Waters are those of the Anima Mundi, the Universal Soul, wherein is reflected the True Luminous Image of the Creator. This is represented in the diagram known as The Great Symbol of Solomon. (cf. Notes of the Design of Trump XII.) On a yet deeper level the Mighty Waters are those of Ain Soph in the Unmanifest wherein each Spirit's Cosmic Atom lies, projecting the Divine Spark itself into manifestation.

NOTES ON THE DESIGN OF TRUMP XII

The Marseilles card shows a man suspended by one foot from a beam supported by two lopped tree trunks, each with six lopped branches. His head hangs over a pit and his legs are crossed, with his hands behind his back so that the arms form a triangle.

On the Marseilles pack it appears that the man's ankle is bound with a supple branch of the crosspiece, but Wirth substitutes a rope. He also gives the man moon-shaped pockets to his jacket. These are only suggested by the Marseilles version. Following Levi, Wirth attaches a money bag to each armpit. This is an old tradition with this card, which has been commonly associated exoterically with Judas Iscariot.

Surprisingly, Case makes little of the number of lopped off branches though Levi, Papus, Wirth and Knapp take care to make them six each side. Case counts the man's buttons though and makes them ten — for the Sephiroth. Waite's Hanged Man has none, Wirth's six, and Knapp's seven. There are ten on the Marseilles version.

Wirth, Knapp and Case follow the Marseilles form of the gallows. Case however, is the only one who deliberately seems to make it into a letter Tau — for Form. Crowley had long supported a Daleth shape, the letter of Venus, which signifies Grace and Love — essential to the deeper meanings of this card. Waite is another Tau supporter but makes the gallows into the shape of an actual Tau-cross.

The 'Egyptian' card shows the usual form of gallows but the uprights are twined with vines, bunches of grapes, (three each side), hanging at intervals. There are the usual six lopped branches each side but they occur at the top of the uprights as if these were made from palm trees. The man's hands are bound to form a *downward* pointing triangle and coins drop from them. His legs are crossed in the normal way and juice drips from the topmost bunches of grapes which hang over the cross bar. This is probably to signify the connection between wine, blood and sacrifice.

The binding cord always seems to be distinct from the actual wood of the crosspiece except on Waite's card, and on this it is obscure. Crowley's card shows it to be a serpent, which binds the man to an ankh. He is also nailed to a lattice-work with green disks (for Venus) at the termination of his limbs and at his head. His attitude displays a cross over a triangle as in the traditional design.

Westcott and Waite make dark hints about the secret significance of this card. Westcott is of the opinion that none know the real meaning except for some few who have discerned it by clairvoyance or intuition. He says that the key is held only by such as know the Hebrew letter it belongs to and the correspondences of that letter. Westcott was obviously hinting at Mem here, the Golden Dawn attri-bution, whose main attribution is Water— it is thus the most motherly of the Mother letters. The key idea is Reflection, and so we are led to the Hermetic axiom "As above—so below" and the consideration cautiously given by Waite many years later that an alternative for this card could be the well-known Qabalistic picture of Macroprosopos appearing over the horizon, his whole head and shoulders and triangularly held arms reflected in the waters. The waters are the same as those mentioned in the early part of Genesis and the diagram is the Great Symbol of Solomon, it is given in the frontispiece of Eliphas Levi's 'Dogme et Rituel' or 'Transcendental Magic'.

It is thus a question of Spirit and Form and it is a fruitful line for meditation though the reason for all the secrecy of the past is difficult to see. Manly P. Hall not unnaturally gives the figure of a triangle surmounted by a cross as a symbol for meditation — that is, Spirit immersed in Form, hence the higher ideas of Sacrifice. Eliphas Levi has also suggested that the Hanged Man is a form of Prometheus and this idea is certainly well worth consideration.

Part III
The Links with the Spirit

The 13th Path

Tiphareth — Kether

KEY:	☽ Gimel. Camel.
SPIRITUAL SIGNIFICANCE:	☽ The Moon.
THEORY:	Priestess of the Silver Star. (II—The High Priestess.)
COLOURS:	Blue. Silver. Cold pale blue. Silver rayed sky blue.
TEXT:	"The Thirteenth Path is named the Uniting Intelligence, and is so called because it is itself the Essence of Glory; it is the Consummation of Truth of individual spiritual things."

1. The Yetziratic Text of this Path gives the whole basis of spiritual reality in a nutshell — Unity equals the Essence of Glory equals Truth. Also, in so far as one can say that one aspect of spiritual manifestation is more important than another, the 13th Path ranks above all others, for it is on the direct line of contact between Spirit and Individuality. It is part of what might be called the backbone of the Tree of Life, the long Path between Spirit and Earth, Kether and Malkuth, which we split, for purposes of analysis, into three — the 32nd, 25th and 13th Paths. The Atziluthic colours of these Paths are the same, the Blue of Love and aspiration, darkening to indigo in the denser levels of Form.

2. The vertical line up the Tree is the Path of the Arrow, the Way of the Mystic, who seeks not the manipulation of occult powers but Union with God. The blue of the lower levels of this Way is darker but not because it is 'tainted' with matter. This is an error Crowley fell into, revealing an oddly puritan streak, perhaps derived from his Plymouth Brethren childhood. Matter is not impure. The more obvious reason why the 32nd Path is coloured indigo on the Atziluthic Scale is because indigo is the prismatic colour attributed to Saturn, the planet of Form and Limitation. The deeper teaching behind this is that one cannot, must not, embark

145

on the Way of Mysticism until one is completely grounded in Form and has learned all its lessons. To try to fly to the higher realms before the nadir is rounded is not holiness but cowardice, not saintliness but sin, it is a regression along the Path of Involution and thus is the Left Hand Path, whatever the ostensible high intentions. 'Holiness' is being used as a way of escape, as a tool for personal use, as a means of blasphemy against Adonai— God in Earth.

3. The Path of the Mystic ascends the 32nd Path, the Gateway to the inner planes, and passes through the subconscious realms of Yesod. As Yesod is a Sephirah connected with the sexual function we have here Qabalistic evidence that the sexual imagery of some mysticism is not necessarily proof that mysticism is the result of sexual frustration as some psychologists would have us believe. From Yesod the Way leads across the 'wilderness' of the 25th Path, the Intelligence of Probation, which is the first Dark Night of the Soul before the golden dawn of Tiphareth consciousness is reached and the contact with 'the god within'. The Tiphareth contact is, however but the lowest aspect of the 'god within', for the Path leads on as far again right up to the fount of spiritual being in Kether. This latter half of the Way is the 13th Path and its Hebrew letter is Gimel, a Camel, reminding us that here is another Desert, a higher analogue of the 25th Path, and thus the second Dark Night of the Soul.

4. As the first Dark Night of the Soul might be termed symbolically a crossing of the Gulf, so the second indicates the way across the Abyss, and the best available authority on both experiences is St. John of the Cross. We have already studied his book 'The Dark Night of the Soul' in connection with the 25th Path and we can do no better than adopt the same procedure here. St. John's descriptions of the second Dark Night are even more copious than of the first, complete with biblical illustrations and comparisons with his own poetry. Anyone who is interested in the practical reality of mysticism rather than in mere symbolic descriptions of it should read this book. They will at least see that true mysti-

cism is by no means all sweetness and light, or an escape mechanism of muzzy bliss.

5. What then are the experiences of this second Dark Night of the Soul? In a phrase, they could be described as 'a sense of utter desolation'. All the expansion of awareness and feeling of at-one-ment that is possible to the soul with Tiphareth consciousness is suddenly annihilated and the soul feels empty, alone, without God and without the love of fellow men. This is an automatic experience once a certain stage of the Path is reached. In the words of St. John:

6. "This dark night is an influence from God upon the soul, which purges her of ignorance and habitual imperfections, natural and spiritual, and is styled by contemplatives, infused contemplation or mythical theology, wherein God teaches the soul in secret, and instructs her in the perfect love, all act on her part being limited to fixing her attention lovingly on God, listening to His voice and receiving the light He sends, without knowing what manner of thing this infused contemplation is. Inasmuch as it is the benignant Wisdom of God, the which works particular effects upon the soul; for, by purging and illuminating her, it disposes her for the union of love with God, where this most loving Wisdom herself, which purges the spirits of the blessed, by shining on them in their brightness, is she who now purges the soul and illuminates her.

7. "But the doubt presents itself, why does the soul apply such a term as dark night to the Divine light which, as we say, illuminates and purges her of her blindness? Whereto it is answered, that in respect of two considerations, this Divine Wisdom is not only night and darkness for the soul, but also pain and torment. The first by reason of the altitude of the Divine Wisdom, which exceeds the comprehension of the soul, and is therefore dark as night to her. The second, because of her own baseness and impurity, and therefore it is to her noisome and grievous, and also dark."

8. The last sentence indicates that the Individuality is by no means perfect, even in a saint. However, this process in

the mystic produces perfection. In one who has travelled the 'occult' way, developing the powers in action of the Individuality in Earth, most, if not all the excrescence should have been cleared from a soul on the 19th Path. For such a soul, proceeding across the Abyss from Chesed through Daath to Binah, the experience would still be met with, but more "by reason of the altitude of the Divine Wisdom, which exceeds the comprehension of the soul" than because of "baseness and impurity."

9. This Way of experience from Chesed is known as the 'secret silent Path'. It is called secret simply because it does not appear on the Tree of Life and the 'silent' refers to its quality of 'nothingness'. The usual symbolism for this condition is the Empty Room or the Condemned Cell. The Cell contains nothing and the walls are bare save for a small barred window which can be looked through by pulling oneself up by the arms. All to be seen through the window is a gallows but there is a radiant rising Sun in the background which has the strange effect of seeming to pull one into it, through the barred window, to be absorbed by it. This is the usual symbolism and it is intended to imply the complete absence of symbolism. The experience of this Secret Path is one of loneliness and desolation, in short it is the same experience as the Dark Night of the Soul on the 13th Path. Both Paths are Ways across the Abyss and through the environs of Daath so this is perhaps to be expected. A study of the Sephirah Daath will do much to help towards an understanding of these two Paths.

10. To return to the testimony of St. John, there comes to the soul in this experience a "kind of grief, which is the Majesty and Grandeur of God, which gives rise in her to the other extreme therein contained, of her own intimate poverty and wretchedness; the which is one of the chiefest tortures she suffers in this purgation. For, she feels within herself a profound void and utter dearth of the three kinds of wealth which are ordered for her enjoyment, which are: temporal, physical, and spiritual; and she sees herself plunged into

the contrary evils, to wit: miserable trifles of imperfections, aridnesses and emptinesses of the perceptions of the faculties, and desolation of the spirit in darkness. For, inasmuch as God now purges the soul of her spiritual as well as her sensitive substance, of her interior as of her exterior powers, it is necessary that she be placed in emptiness and poverty and desertion on all sides, and be left parched, void and empty and in darkness. For the sensitive part is purified by dryness, and the intellectual powers in the void of their cognitions, and the spirit in thick darkness. All which God effects by means of this obscure contemplation; wherein, not only does the soul suffer the void and suspension of these her usual supports and perceptions, which is a kind of suffering most agonising, (like as if a person were hung or suspended in the air, so that he could not breathe), but he also purges her, destroying or voiding or consuming therein, (like as fire works on the rust and tarnish of metals), from all the affections and imperfect habits she has contracted throughout her life. And, forasmuch as they are deeply rooted in her, she suffers grave restlessness and interior torture, beside the said poverty, and physical and mental void."

11. The imagery of St. John's description of the experience is again Qabalistically interesting; the hanging, "suspended in the air" is a figure of speech which is very close to the symbol chosen by the Qabalists to represent the condition — The Abyss.

12. Such a high level of purification, of course, leads the soul straight on to God, or to Kether. It is, in fact, a final purification. As St. John says: "And so the soul which passes through this purification and is left thoroughly purged, either does not enter Hades, or stays not long there, for, in one hour of this earthly purgatory, she derives more benefit than in many there."

13. After reading the above descriptions of it, and the even more detailed ones in the actual book, this does not seem surprising! It leads however, to the experience of the ap-

proaches to the final Union with God, the Spiritual Experience of Kether. This experience has also been experienced and recorded by St. John: "I went forth from out the converse and scanty exercises related, to the operations of, and converse with, God. That is to say, my understanding escaped from itself, being from human, transmuted into Divine; because, being united with God by means of this purgation, it no longer perceives in the same limited and imperfect way as before, but by the Divine Wisdom wherewith it has been united. And my will escaped from itself, making itself Divine: for, since it has now become one with Divine love, it loves no longer with the cribbed and confined strength and vigour as of yore, but with the passionate strength and purity of the Divine Spirit; and so, the will works no longer in respect of God after human fashion, in exactly the same way as the memory is absolutely changed into eternal reflections and perceptions of glory. And finally, every energy and passion of the Soul by means of this night and the purgation of the old Adam are born afresh into Divine harmonies and delights."

14. This is the testimony of one who achieved this state, that of full spiritual contact whilst living in Earth. To make a fine distinction this is probably not the actual Union with God of Kether, for such would imply a withdrawal into the Unmanifest, but it certainly is an experience of the higher reaches of the 13th Path.

15. In Qabalistic terms this state is the initiation known as 'The Babe of the Abyss'. Naturally such a state cannot be conferred by the means of a simple ritual, it is a condition which is attained only after years of spiritual striving. A so-called 'initiation ceremony' on the physical plane can only be, at best, a trigger mechanism to get a process started within a soul, and a confirmation of what has already been achieved. Real initiation is a subjective realisation which comes about by a natural process of growth and is not a thing that can be bought, sold, given or received.

16. The initiation undergone by St. John of the Cross was

a very high one, and one which Crowley fancied himself to have taken. He makes much of 'The Wastelands' and 'Babe of the Abyss' and one of his groups was called the Order of the Silver Star after the title of the Tarot Trump of this Path. But initiation is not merely a question of knowing the externals of symbolism, it is a state of being, and anyone can judge for themselves the extent of Crowley's real condition by comparing his writings with those of St. John of the Cross, who achieved without any advanced knowledge of symbols, secret or otherwise, but purely by faith and spiritual will. An even more revealing and damning analysis would be to compare their lives. It seems necessary to emphasise this, not so much for the doubtful pleasure of kicking a man who is already down, but in order to act as a warning to the many who tend to injure themselves by trying to follow the Crowley system without sufficient knowledge of its pitfalls—some of which, sad to say, seem deliberately placed, either through malice or a misplaced sense of humour.

17. The High Priestess of the Tarot Trump is usually compared to Isis and there is much to be gained from following up this line of tradition. In this case, the Silver Star is Sothis, the star sacred to Isis and attributed to the Sephirah Daath. Isis is also associated with the Moon, which ties up well with the astrological attribution of the Moon to this Path.

18. This simple fact conceals and reveals much. The Moon is intimately connected with the Earth, and also with the etheric levels, represented by Malkuth and Yesod on the Tree. It is the Ruler of Flux and Reflux, as well as being a symbol of receptivity. Thus Daath is akin to Yesod; in fact it could be called Yesod on a higher arc. In terms of the ascent of the Tree, Daath is a Gateway to Cosmic Space— Sothis or Sirius being the extra-Logoidal heavenly body most closely connected with this Solar System. Descending the Tree however, that is, looking at things entirely from the point of view of the manifestation of the Solar Logoidal Plan, the Lunar aspect of Daath shows the fundamental

working or the Laws of Cyclic Action and Polarity. The close analogy to the etheric plane is also important, for the etheric level has two aspects, it unites all things in Earth and also it holds them in dense physical existence. It is evasion of these two factors that constitutes the bulk of sin and error. The effects are obvious in the chaotic state of the world today; the causes are denial of the unity of all things, (the sin of separateness), and the refusal to face reality in Earth.

19. In Qabalistic terms this wholesale deviation from reality resulted in the formation of the Gulf and the Abyss. It is these two blockages in the line of contact between Spirit and Earth that cause most of the trouble and results in the unpleasant experiences of both the Dark Nights of the Soul. The repercussions of these blockages go further than just giving mystics a bad time though, they also play an important part in all world conditions. Particularly is this so in the field of sexual problems and problems of relationship.

20. The human Spirit is androgynous and thus any attempt to deny the conditions of existence in Earth manifests often as an urge for Independence. This, it is true, is the Virtue of Yesod, but an exaggerated or compulsive manifestation of a Virtue results in a Vice. So we may have the androgynous Daath state of the Spirit attempting to exert itself in the lower analogue of Daath, Yesod. This means an inability to form any satisfactory relationship, particularly sexual.

21. There is no such thing as independence in the physical universe; all are related and complementary to each other, bound together on the one hand by the etheric Machinery of the Universe, and on the other hand unified in Love in Earth to the degree that spiritual redemption is achieved. Where Love is missing, one has only the mechanics of sex, enslaved by the false image of androgynous independence, separated by a very wide gulf indeed from love and a home and children and all that flowers from these basic principles of human life in Earth.

22. These things work out in many different ways of course. It is not the destiny of all to rear a family for example, for the pioneer in any walk of human life such a thing is usually impracticable and unfair to parents and children alike. It is the principle behind that is important, and how this works out in Earth. And even the pioneering Spirit should have incarnations devoted primarily to domesticity and the enjoyment of the fruits that he has laboured for on humanity's behalf. Again, Independence should not be regarded, because of this, as a dirty word. It is often necessary. It is where compulsive automatic action occurs that the deviation must be looked for.

23. Such things may manifest as the highest of motives, aspirations and ideals, but where compulsive, they are deadly. This is particularly so when acting on a group level in the unhuman, dis-personalised bureaucracy of a large organised social unit whose way of function rests on adherence to a book of rules rather than the dynamic initiative of the human personality. This applies to private business corporations as well as government departments — no-one has a monopoly on inhumanity.

24. To revert to the Tarot Trump, a more modern way of interpretation would be to regard the High Priestess as the Virgin Mary. This may give a greater degree of reality on the real meaning of this Path than the formulation of pagan goddesses from the ancient past. The Virgin Mary is called 'Stella Maris' — Star of the Sea, which is not such a far cry from Priestess of the Silver Star. Blue and silver, the colours of this Path, are also traditionally those of Our Lady, and a further interesting factor is the doctrine of the Assumption of the Virgin Mary into Heaven. This doctrine implies a direct link between Heaven and Earth and this direct link is obviously the central Path on the Tree, consisting of the 32nd, 25th and 13th Paths which together join Kether and Malkuth.

25. The Key to the Path, the Hebrew letter Gimel, confirms this. It is made up of two dynamic Yods, one at the

top of a shaft and the other at the bottom, the one meaning life in Heaven and the other, life in Earth. It is, indeed, a simple form of the Caduceus, that shaft of Divine Power with the pine cone at the summit and a scorpion at the base. The scorpion, with all its attendant astrological overtones, is also a symbol sacred to Isis. Scorpio is, of course, the sign of the 24th Path, whose Tarot Trump is Death. It has among its meanings sexuality, and the impactation of life into Form, as well as death, some of the implications of which we have examined in connection with the 24th Path. That they have relevance to the 13th Path as well is corroborated by the Roman Catholic practice of calling upon Our Lady at the hour of death. In this way the discarnating Personality is given a correct orientation from the outer to the inner worlds as it embarks upon the 32nd Path. Like death and birth, the 32nd/25th/13th Path is very much a Path of transition; it is the link between Kether and Malkuth, the human Spirit in Heaven and the human Spirit in Earth.

26. It could be called the most direct Path on the Quest of the Holy Grail. The Grail is the vessel that one can make of one's own being so that it is capable of holding the higher forces — the Blood or Waters of the Spirit. Needless to say, this can take place on many levels, but the most profound is that which results from a clear run-through down the central Paths so that the Grail in Malkuth contains the blood of Kether. Blood is a symbol of the Spirit, it is indeed, more than this, it is the actual carrier of the Spirit's influence in the physical body. In the Grail stories the blood drips from a lance, and the Lance is a Kether symbol, a symbol of manifesting Deity.

27. The Grail stories make interesting reading, bearing the writings of St. John of the Cross in mind. Although a transcendent experience, the Vision of it carried its own purgation. Most of the knights did not find it, while some, such as the vengeful Gawain, could not even work up much interest in its Quest. Of those who did achieve, the most

successful was Galahad, the faultless knight. His father Lancelot, however, had a very rough time because although he was 'the best knight in the world' his life was far from blameless. He did achieve a sight of the Grail but he was warned not to enter the Grail Chapel door. There, according to Malory, "it seemed to Lancelot that above the priest's hands there were three men, whereof the two put the youngest by likeness between the priest's hands, and so he lift it up right high, and it seemed to shew so to the people. And then Lancelot marvelled not a little, for him thought that the priest was so greatly charged of the figure, that him seemed that he should fall to the earth. And when he saw none about him that would help him, then came he to the door a great pace, and said, Fair Father Jesu Christ, ne take it for no sin though I help the good man, which hath great need of help. Right so entered he into the chamber, and came toward the table of silver; and when he came nigh he felt a breath that him thought it was intermeddled with fire, which smote him so sore in the visage that him thought it burnt his visage; and therewith he fell to the earth, and had no power to arise, as he that was so araged that had lost the power of his body, and his hearing, and his saying."

28. This may seem very unjust, for Lancelot had acted upon the best of intentions. But in the higher realms of spiritual reality the sole criterion is truth — falsity is burned up in a flash and good intentions are no protection. A red hot coal will burn the hand that picks it up, however commendable the motives involved. The Laws of any plane are paramount upon that plane.

29. So on the Way of Evolution one should not try to proceed to another plane until the laws of the plane one is on are mastered. There is much exaggeration in many of the warnings about fearful occult forces but there certainly can be danger to the dabbler if he dabbles long enough. No one would try to teach themselves surgery by opening up their own or their friends' guts with a razor blade, but many

seem to think that similar experiments on the psychological level are quite in order. Fortunately most dabblers are like many of the knights on the Quest, their own ignorance or basic lack of interest saves them from harm. But danger can come to the more advanced, as, for instance, with someone sensitised to a high degree from practising the Eastern systems who suddenly starts to play about with the potent ritual methods of the West.

30. The letter Gimel of this Path could be likened to a Cosmic battery, the two Yods being terminals. If the power is suddenly switched through the line in between, the channel has got to be capable of standing up to the voltage. In plain terms, this means that the vertical contacts of higher mystical experience should not be attempted until the Nadir is passed. This means, first and foremost, acceptance and full control of the forces and conditions of the dense physical universe.

NOTES ON THE DESIGN OF TRUMP II

The Marseilles version of this card is particularly crude but there are definite suggestions of pillars and a veil behind the Priestess. She has a triple tiara and an open book. Wirth partly closes the book; gives the Priestess crossed keys, gold and silver, in the other hand; places a moon crescent on the top of her tiara and provides a chequered floor. He has also suggested she should lean against a sphinx. Papus considered that a transparent veil should fall across her face and, like Levi, that a solar cross should be on her breast. Levi, following the tradition of some older Tarots, said she should have a horned moon headdress. He points out that old versions of the card ascribe all the attributes of Isis and cites examples that show her suckling Horus, or with long unbound hair. He also considers that her veil should be thrown back behind her head and that on each side of her throne should be lotuses blooming in the sea. Also, she should be making the sign of esotericism with the hand not holding the book.

Waite went some way towards Levi's last suggestions in having the bottom of the Priestess' robe take on the appearance of water, and in giving the pillars lotus tops. The black pillar to her right has the white letter B (for Boaz) on it, and the white pillar a black letter J (for Jachin); the veil between them is embroidered with palms and pomegranates and at her feet is a crescent moon. He gives no chequered pavement for the scene is in the open air and behind can be seen the sea and a distant shore. (It is possible this might be a desert but the signification is the same. The Hebrew letter Gimel means Camel — 'ship of the desert'.) Case omits the crescent moon at her feet, puts the pillar letters in Hebrew, (Beth and Yod), and makes the bases of the pillars into cubes like the High Priestess' seat, which is also a cube in the Waite version. Waite and Case show a scroll, not a book, inscribed with the word TORA.

In Knapp's version the High Priestess has a gold throne surmounted by owls and on the top of three steps. The rest of the floor is chequered and beyond the veil and pillars is utter darkness. She is veiled, has book and keys, but the sign on her breast is Mercury. (There is a close connection between Isis and Mercury/

/Hermes/Thoth). Manly P. Hall's hieroglyph is a gold crown with a dark crown, reverse, beneath it, as if reflected. Knapp has the book closed.

The early Crowley suggested she should be reading intently in the book, but on the Crowley/ Harris card she is a figure weaving crystals and fruits with a veil of light and carrying a huntress' bow and a sistrum, with a camel at the bottom of the card.

The 'Egyptian' card follows the general pattern, lotus pillars, cubic throne, veiled priestess, partly concealed book, moon crescent on triple headdress, the symbol on her breast being Mercury.

In exoteric packs this card has gone under several names, no doubt in accordance with the religious feelings of the time. She was crudely Christianised as 'The Female Pope', or more jocularly, 'Pope Joan' after the old legend. In Italy however, good taste preferred to restore her to pagan status as 'Juno'.

The 17th Path

Tiphareth — Binah

KEY:	⛢ Zain. Sword.
SPIRITUAL SIGNIFICANCE:	♊ Gemini. The Twins.
THEORY:	Children of the Voice. Oracle of the Mighty Gods. (VI—The Lovers)
COLOURS:	Orange. Pale mauve. New yellow leather. Reddish grey inclined to mauve.
TEXT:	"The Seventeenth Path is the Disposing Intelligence which provides Faith to the Righteous, and they are clothed with the Holy Spirit by it, and it is called the Foundation of Excellence in the state of higher things."

1. Binah is the most 'concrete' of the three Supernal Sephiroth, it contains the image of the Spirit and its destiny in Earth, and this Path is the means by which knowledge of what the Spirit's destiny is, is focussed into the central focus of consciousness in manifestation, the Sephirah Tiphareth.

2. Binah is "the parent of Faith, from which doth Faith emanate" and this phrase from the Yetziratic Text of Binah is confirmed by the Yetziratic Text of this Path "which provides Faith to the Righteous". From this, the relevance of the rest of the Yetziratic Text follows easily; by Faith are the Righteous "clothed with the Holy Spirit", and Faith is "the Foundation of Excellence in the state of higher things."

3. The Holy Spirit is the Third Aspect of God, or Third Person of the Trinity, and is in this context attributed to Binah. This has caused a certain amount of controversy, in the past, between Qabalists. It is argued that the allocation of Father, Son and Holy Spirit to Kether, Chokmah and Binah respectively, is an unsatisfactory arrangement and the work of Christians trying to twist the Jewish Qabalah to their own theology. Now while it is true that a better 'general purpose' attribution might be God the Father in Kether, the

Son in Tiphareth and the Holy Spirit in Yesod, such discussions are hardly worth the effort of argument. They all stem from an attempt to fix definite categories to all aspects of the Tree of Life — to make it a cut and dried, and therefore dead, system. The Tree of Life is of little use to anyone unless they have the flexibility of mind to cope with what is, to all intents and purposes a living entity — or, more accurately, the reflection of a living entity.

4. Students of the Qabalah must be able to apply factors of life to any part of the Tree with an open mind, checking up how all the related factors fit in with different arrangements. A synthetic mind is called for as much as an analytic one — though both are equally important in their place and one should be able to use one or the other aspect freely at will. The twentieth century has been called 'the Age of Analysis' and though this is a necessary general trend it sometimes runs to excess. It is all too easy for the brightly polished intellect to equate analytical ability with perspicacity, and synthetic ability with stupidity; just as a few hundred years ago the picture was reversed and synthesis was considered saintly and analysis of the Devil. It is necessary to work intelligently with the trend of the current cycle.

5. The Holy Spirit may be applied to Yesod or Binah and there is indeed much in common between the two Sephiroth, as meditation along the Moon/Water symbolism of Yesod and the Great Sea of Binah will show.

6. Binah is also closely connected with the Holy Guardian Angel in spite of the fact that the Knowledge and Conversation of the Holy Guardian Angel is the Spiritual Experience of Malkuth. There is, of course, again a close link between Binah and Malkuth, the Superior Mother and the Inferior Mother. The Holy Guardian Angel is not the Individuality, but that aspect of the 'Group Thought-form' of God which impressed the Swarm of Divine Sparks at the beginning of Time. When the Swarm broke up to undergo individual

experience in manifestation the 'Group Thought-form' broke up also, each fragment connected with a particular Divine Spark. The above is, of course, at best crude analogy but the Holy Guardian Angel may be considered to be that part of a human being which reveals his purpose in manifestation to him in accordance with the Divine Plan.

7. In this we have the explanation of the esoteric titles of the Tarot Trump and also of the astrological sign. The intimations of a Holy Guardian Angel is an Oracle of the Mighty Gods, each Holy Guardian Angel being a Child of the Voice, Word or Logos. Such intimations will, of course, be above the levels of mind and so they manifest, as the Yetziratic Text implies, as Faith. This may be not only a general Faith in God but the faith in himself that every dynamic human being has to press on with what he considers to be his true field of endeavour, his true vocation, whatever the opposition.

8. The astrological sign, Gemini, the Twins, indicates the true relation that should exist between the Holy Guardian Angel and the Individuality. They should be a reflection one of the other.

9. This, of course, may apply equally to the Spirit and Individuality, or to the Individuality and Personality. It is to the latter pair that the Heavenly Twins, Castor and Pollux, are more commonly referred in esoteric writings.

10. Castor and Pollux were children of Leda. Pollux and Helen of Troy were sired by Zeus in the form of a swan, and Castor and Clytemnestra were true children by her husband, Tyndareus. Here is a close analogy with the Holy Guardian Angel which, like Pollux, was formed directly by God, and the incarnating Spirit which, like Castor, is essentially human. Castor was mortal, Pollux an immortal. The legend tells that Pollux bought immortality for Castor by consenting to spend half his time in Hades. This could be interpreted as the downward directed meditation of the Holy Guardian Angel, the Spirit, or the Individuality, according to the level

of interpretation, when its lower unit is in incarnation. The final goal is also demonstrated in the myth: Zeus, impressed by this demonstration of brotherly love, placed them both in the sky as a constellation. This shows the Cosmic future of humanity and also its means of attaining it — through Love to the Stars.

11. The Tarot Trump is called The Lovers, and shows three people, one male, two female, over whom hovers a Cupid with bow and arrow. One of the women is crowned and faces the couple, who are obviously The Lovers. It needs no great powers of elucidation to deduce that the couple are the counterparts of the Dioscuroi, the Heavenly Twins; the crowned woman is the principle of Form; and the Cupid is the driving principle behind manifestation, really the primeval Eros of Kether. The mighty Eros, a figure of dynamic Cosmic Love has been popularised down the ages into the sentimental Cupid, just as the true significance of this card was for long considered exoterically to be that of man's choice between Good and Evil, with Evil about to get an earful of arrow from the winged figure of Justice. An even shallower interpretation regarded it as a card upholding the sanctity of marriage. This process of different levels of interpretation is inevitable and of course one has to bear in mind that the significance of symbols will change as one's own understanding matures. If a symbol is a good one, all levels of its interpretation are correct and he is a rash man who thinks that he has reached the ultimate meaning of any esoteric symbol. This fact must always be borne in mind in esoteric investigation.

12. There is an interesting confirmation in the design of this Trump in 'The Chymical Marriage of Christian Rosencreutz' wherein a Virgin is mistress of ceremonies and the young King and Queen about to be married have a Cupid constantly hovering over their heads.

13. The Key to the Path, the Hebrew letter Zain, means a Sword. The shape of the letter suggests a sword and, in another way, the action of the Holy Guardian Angel. The

Holy Guardian Angel is Knowledge and Purpose on its own high level and is indicated by the Yod at the top of the letter. The Holy Guardian Angel projects a 'rod' of Knowledge and Purpose downward into manifestation and this is represented by the vertical line of the letter. There is nothing attached to the lower end of this shaft for the inner opportunity presented has to be seized and acted upon.

14. The attribution of the Sword may seem strange at first in connection with The Lovers and Twins, for the Sword is a symbol of separation. It is, however, in perfect accord with the rest of the symbolism. This Path is essentially one of Separation for the separation of the Sparks of the Human Swarm is essential for individual evolution; similarly there must be a separation between the part of the Self that stays in Heaven and the part that descends into manifestation. This separation is part of the Vision of Sorrow of Binah, one of whose Magical Images is a heart pierced with swords. Furthermore we must bear in mind that the Heavenly Twins, though similar, and united by relationship and love, *are* separate beings. Without separation there could be no demonstration of Love.

15. The Sword is also a weapon of destruction and so we may align it with the Fourth Aspect of Deity—God the Destroyer or Disintegrator. This indicates an aspect of the ascent of this Path when all manifestation is eventually reabsorbed into the Great Sea. This can be regarded as Binah at one level; ultimately it refers to Binah's analogue beyond Kether, Ain Soph, the Limitless.

16. Legends about the Sword are numerous. There are swords which sing and swords which speak, though perhaps the most famous is Arthur's Excalibur. Throughout all Brythonic legend there are accounts of Divine Purpose being revealed by means of a sword cleft in a stone and sometimes found floating in the water. It was by means of such an oracle that Arthur was made king. The association with stone is interesting as it indicates manifestation in dense

matter, and the water in which the stone floats is a reminder of the Waters of Binah or Ain Soph. Excalibur itself came from and was returned to the Lady of the Lake.

17. There is a sexual element in sword symbolism but this is by no means the whole story, it is but a facet of the whole principle of polarity which produces manifestation—hence the relevance of this Path to Binah and the symbolic relationships of this Path shown on the Tarot card and in the myth of the constellation. The Sword may be considered to be the *power* of polarity—on all its levels. Excalibur is a case in point where this obviously applies, and its scabbard, which Merlin said was worth more than the sword itself and which was stolen by the sorceress Morgan Le Fay, represents the *knowledge of the application* of this power. The whole Arthurian cycle is an esoteric treatise on the principles of polarity which would take a complete volume in itself to analyse. However, although this may be put forward in the guise of love affairs between various lords and ladies, the implications are very deep, for polarity is the very principle of manifest existence. When dealing with the higher aspects of the Tree of Life, as we are now doing, we must expect to deal with fundamentals, and the real factors about Excalibur, the Knights and Ladies, the Holy Grail and Table Round, are, at these levels, not merely examples of human behaviour, as they might be validly considered lower on the Tree, but principles of Cosmic Realities.

18. We have said that the Path from Yesod to Hod is one of sexual division and the attendant problems that come about from refusal to recognise this division or accept it. This Path is a parallel one to that Path and so represents the same tendencies but at a higher level. It is a point of some academic nicety where exactly the roots of the Prime Deviation lie. The Spirit is said to have been perfect until it learnt of the Plan of the Manifest Universe; then it took on imperfection. Thus one could put the root of the trouble in Binah, but it is perhaps safer until more is known, to follow the more traditional idea of the Serpent of Confusion

rising only as far as Daath. The fact is that the wrong image was projected into Chesed and the Spirit is responsible, for it is the Spirit which projects, and should act through, all the vehicles of man.

NOTES OF THE DESIGN OF TRUMP VI

Versions of this card differ considerably, as also do its titles — 'Vice and Virtue', 'The Two Paths' etc. The Marseilles card shows a man between two women, one of whom wears a wreath. Above is a winged Cupid, with bow and arrow, in the Sun.

Wirth divides the man's clothing vertically by colour and gives one woman a floral headdress and the other a crown. The Cupid is blindfolded. Papus considers the Cupid figure to be 'the Spirit of Justice' in a radiant halo and thinks one woman should be crowned with a circlet of gold and the other crowned with vine leaves with the rest of her dress dishevelled. Knapp emphasises the difference between the women by making one a winged angel and the other dishevelled almost to the point of indecency. The man is of puritan appearance, arms crossed on breast, and standing at the junction of two paths. The Cupid figure on Wirth's version is blindfolded and directs his arrow straight at the man. These designs seem to follow Levi's view that the women represent Vice and Virtue, though he considers the Cupid figure to be Love, in the Sun of Truth, directing an arrow at Vice.

According to Case, both he and Waite follow an unpublished esoteric Tarot. This can hardly be the Golden Dawn one, which differs radically from all other designs. Waite and Case show an angel in the Sun dominating the top half of the card, arms stretched out in blessing. Below him are a naked woman under a fruit tree in which is entwined a serpent, and a naked man under a tree bearing triple flames. In the centre background is a conical hill.

The Golden Dawn version is of Andromeda manacled to a rock, a dragon rising from the waters at her feet, with Perseus flying through the air to her assistance with drawn sword.

Crowley's early ideas were of the two women as a priestess and a harlot, representative of things sacred and profane. He thought the man should be a boy, in the sign of Osiris risen, inspired to prophecy on these things—'Cupid' being in reality Apollo, who inspires prophecy and is a Sun god.

His card produced in collaboration with Lady Harris is different again, being inspired by alchemical symbolism, notably that of 'The Chymical Marriage of Christian Rosencreutz'. A figure of the Creator blesses the Moorish King and the White Queen, protagonists of the drama described in that important Rosicrucian document. The King, with gold crown and robe embroidered with serpents, holds the Sacred Lance, and the Queen, with silver crown and robe embroidered with bees, holds the Holy Grail. They are countercharged by a fair and dark child standing before them, the one holding roses and the other a club. At the top of the card is a blindfold Cupid, an arch of swords, and a naked Eve and Lilith. At the bottom of the card are the alchemical Red Lion and White Eagle, and also a winged Orphic egg with serpent.

Manly P. Hall describes yet another version of the card wherein a marriage ceremony is shown conducted by a priest. This would seem similar to the design from which the Waite/Case version might be derived. Of the traditional design, Hall considers that it represents a youth at the threshold of maturity—the 'Parting of the Ways'—with, above, his genius of Fate, (which we would call the Holy Guardian Angel, in Binah; the youth being emblematical of the newly manifesting Spirit). Hall's symbol for the card is two interlaced triangles, the Star of David, the downward pointing triangle being printed in heavier line.

The Egyptian Tarot follows the traditional pattern of a man standing at two ways, with two women indicating opposite directions. Above is a winged genie in a twelve rayed aureole of flame pointing a bow and arrow towards 'Vice'.

The 15th Path

Tiphareth — Chokmah

KEY:	ה Heh. Window.
SPIRITUAL SIGNIFICANCE:	♈ Aries. The Ram.
THEORY:	Daughter of the Firmament. Dweller between the Waters. (XVII—The Star)
COLOURS:	Scarlet. Red. Brilliant flame. Glowing red.
TEXT:	"The Fifteenth Path is the Constituting Intelligence, so called because it constitutes the substance of creation in pure darkness, and men have spoken of the contemplations; it is that darkness spoken of in Scripture, Job xxxviii. 9. 'and thick darkness a swaddling band for it.'"

1. The complete passage quoted from in the Yetziratic Text runs as follows: "Or who shut up the sea with doors, when it brake forth, as if it had issued out of the womb? When I made the cloud the garment thereof, and thick darkness a swaddling band for it, and brake up for it my decreed place, and set bars and doors, And said, Hitherto shalt thou come, but no further: and here shall thy proud waves be stayed?"

2. This sea, swaddled in cloud and thick darkness, is no ordinary sea, but the Waters of the Unmanifest pouring into manifestation. This occurs under the presidency of God and all that "becomes" from the Sea of Not-being is ordained its rightful place in the scheme of things that makes a Universe. Here are the Waters and the Firmament of the esoteric titles of the Tarot Card; they are the same as those mentioned in Genesis.

3. The processes of this early creation is put in more detailed terms in 'The Cosmic Doctrine': "It will be recalled that the Great Entity (Solar Logos) gathered about itself atoms of each Cosmic plane, out of which it formed its body. These atoms themselves are entities, though of a lesser degree of development than the Great Entity of which

they form a part. Being of lesser development, the full recapitulatory growth is achieved earlier. Each atom, having realised itself, has created a concept of itself. These concepts, projected by the atoms, are not atoms, but so many units of knowledge of ways in which reaction is possible. They are not, therefore, sorted out into concentric belts, because there is nothing in them upon which gravitation can act. They are merely forms of reaction.

4. "Now, the consciousness of a Great Entity is not aware of the individual reactions of its atoms, any more than the consciousness of man is aware of the individual consciousness of the cells composing his body. Therefore, when it seeks to conceive an image of itself, it has to take the reactions of the different types of atoms in their respective aggregates, and is dependent upon the atomic concepts for the creation of the necessary atomic images. Therefore, the Great Entity has to create its concept of itself in objective substance, and is therefore limited and bound by conditions of the nature of the already created images which it utilises. Thus, the atoms, by conceiving their own images, perform the primal act of creation.

5. "The first act of creation proceeds from the *body* of God, and is but a mass of unorganised units—'Darkness was upon the face of the deep'. These units, having no organisation and consequently no relationship among themselves, could not attain to objective consciousness, but the concept of the Great Entity, based upon its Cosmic experiences, as soon as it became projected organised them into relationships, and they then became conscious of each other, and became affected by each other."

6. These considerations take us into deep waters of esoteric cosmology which cannot be fully investigated here. We are dealing with the Tree of Life in terms of the psychology of man and so our consideration of the Paths is limited to how best they can be used to help man to know himself. In fact, what we may quite legitimately call The Unmanifest in our present examination of the Tree is, in

reality, only the Sixth Cosmic plane. Our complete Tree is on the densest Cosmic plane and so is really only the Tree in the Sephirah Malkuth of the Cosmic Tree. The Cosmic Tree does not concern us now, for man has no existence on these levels, but it is well to bear in mind the possibilities of the Sephiroth and Paths when applied cosmically. They represent areas of Cosmic being and consciousness of which we can at present have no glimmer of understanding.

7. The relevance of the above quoted passage will be obvious however when one considers that the Spiritual Experience of Chokmah, the Sephirah to which this Path leads, is The Vision of God face to face. The Mundane Chakra, furthermore, of this Sephirah is the Zodiac and in connection with this we have the Tarot Trump The Star on this Path. Through this Path the soul may glimpse a spark of the majesty of its Creator as if it were sitting before a narrow unglazed window staring upwards into the darkness of space, there to see suddenly a star shining brightly, indicating the origin whence the soul has come and the goal towards which it must wend on the Way of Evolution.

8. The factor of the beginning and ending of one's evolution is shown by the shape of the astrological sign Aries; the sudden looping down into manifestation and subsequent return to the level of inception. Likewise the Hebrew letter suggests by its shape a Window through which the vision of this Path may be seen. The Window is indeed its meaning.

9. Another quotation from 'The Cosmic Doctrine' is of interest here. It will be gathered that all the 'atoms' mentioned previously are the nuclei of the indwelling lives of a Solar System, human or otherwise. This group of atoms, with their projected consciousness which makes up primal manifestation, is referred to in the following passage as 'a satellite' of the Great Entity—our God.

10. "The Great Entity is aware of Its satellite. Its consciousness conditions Its satellite, and the satellite is aware of the Great Entity; but though the *collective* consciousness of the satellite is influenced by the Great Entity, and there-

fore there is reaction between Entity and satellite, it is not conscious of the Great Entity with its collective consciousness but with innumerable individualised consciousnesses whose collective consciousness is merely aware that they are aware, which is quite a different matter.

11. "There exists then, in the satellite, a collective consciousness which is self-conscious, aware of the conditions in the groups of atoms gathered around the seed-atoms with which they are associated but which are unaware of the conditions of groups of atoms gathered around other seed-atoms, and which are also each and separately aware of the Great Entity.

12. "The consciousness of the Great Entity towards the satellite resembles the sight of the human eye, but the consciousness of the satellite toward the Great Entity resembles the sight of a spider's eye—innumerable facets reflecting innumerable images which have to be focussed within the brain—the brain correlating with 'group-consciousness'.

13. "When all the Divine Sparks are perfectly adjusted to each other so that there is perfect reciprocity of reaction throughout their mass, then there is a collective consciousness which focusses the images of the facets. When this is achieved there is reciprocal consciousness between the satellite and the Great Entity, because they meet on equal terms."

14. Putting this somewhat abstractly expressed teaching into the context which concerns all humanity here and now in Earth, it can be seen that two things are necessary before our present phase of evolution is achieved: a) *perfect adjustment between all human beings*, one with another, (and with the non-human beings that make up the physical and superphysical worlds as well. This means joyful acceptance of the conditions of the natural physical world, and a vital religious and mystical awareness.) b) *the attainment of the Vision of God face to face*, which should never have been lost in the first place. As things are now, the Gulf and the

Abyss between man's different levels of being have to be bridged before this can be fully achieved.

15. The means to this goal of all mankind could be put in even simpler terms, and has already been done so. "Thou shalt love the Lord thy God with all thy heart and with all thy soul, and with all thy strength, and with all thy mind; and thy neighbour as thyself." (Luke. x. 27. and also Mat. xxii. 37. Mark, xii. 30. etc.)

16. It seems superfluous to add anything to this for in it is summed up all the Laws of Evolution and their practical application. We may perhaps draw from one or two other traditions however, to supplement the text, for lip service is all that is usually paid to it these days—particularly on the group level of communities, races and nations.

17. The Mundane Chakra of Chokmah is the Zodiac, and this might be termed the complete image of God, shown forth by twelve types of reaction. These have been called the Twelve Heavenly Men and are all aspects of the One God—Kings, as it were, seated about a Cosmic Round Table. In Alice Bailey's book 'A Treatise on Cosmic Fire', the Tibetan states that the Path of Earth Service involves "twelve cosmic identifications'. This might be considered as a realisation of the whole being of God through a series of realisations of the real meaning of the twelve Zodiacal signs. This is of course quite beyond any appreciation of astrology as we understand it. The Round Table is said to have been brought by Merlin from the constellation of the Great Bear, and as is well known in esoteric teaching, the Seven Rishis of the Great Bear hold the pattern of evolution for seven planets of which our Earth is one. This may serve to indicate something of the tremendous breadth and depth of the realisations required for those who essay this Path.

18. However this is of more concern to the Hierarchy of Masters than to most of us, so it is perhaps sufficient to bear in mind that The Star of this Path is our own perception of God, the facet of the 'spider's eye' of group consciousness by which each contributes his share towards

evolution, and the ultimate goal of reciprocal consciousness between God and his Universe. We cannot expect to perceive, let alone comprehend, the whole of the Majesty of God—our vision is limited by the narrow aperture of The Window of our own consciousness or area of realisation. It should be our goal though to perceive what we should never have shut our eyes to in the beginning—that single star in the spangled heavens of God's existence that is our own particular vision of Divinity.

19. This star might, in another way, be considered as that seed-atom in the Cosmic body of God that projected us as we are into manifestation. Hence the truth of Crowley's maxim "Every man and every woman is a star."

20. It will be seen on the Tarot Trump that the Star is surrounded by seven others. This may be considered to represent the Solar Logos, the Grand Man of the Heavens, with the seven Planetary Logoi, the Seven Heavenly Men. (These should not be confused with the Twelve mentioned earlier.) Or, microcosmically, it can represent our own Cosmic atom, and the seven seed-atoms which form the nucleus of each of our seven bodies of manifestation. On a more remote level it could be considered as the Senior of Seven, or the One About Whom Nought May Be Said, (because no-one knows anything to say) and the Seven Solar Logoi emanated by Him or It, and so on right through the sevenfold Cosmic Hierarchies to the Parabrahm in the Central Stillness of the First Cosmic Plane. Such considerations can only be of academic interest for us, however, as we are limited to the lowest Cosmic plane and the periphery of consciousness or Ring-Pass-Not of our own Solar Logos.

21. The bird on the Tarot Trump is a creature of air, a winged symbol, representing the freedom of Cosmic space. The woman, in that she is between land and water and in view of her attribution to this Path, recalls to mind the Seventh Angel in Revelations: "And I saw another mighty angel come down from heaven, clothed with a cloud: and a rainbow was upon his head, and his face was as it were the

sun, and his feet as pillars of fire: And he had in his hand a little book open: and he set his right foot upon the sea and his left foot on the earth, And cried with a loud voice, as when a lion roareth: and when he had cried, seven thunders uttered their voices. And when the seven thunders had uttered their voices, I was about to write: and I heard a voice from heaven saying unto me, Seal up those things which the seven thunders uttered, and write them not. And the angel which I saw stand upon the sea and upon the earth lifted up his hand to heaven, and sware by him that liveth for ever and ever, who created heaven, and the things that therein are, and the earth, and the things that therein are, and the sea, and the things which are therein, that there should be time no longer: But in the days of the voice of the seventh angel, when he shall begin to sound, the mystery of God should be finished, as he hath declared to his servants the prophets." (Rev. x. 1-7.)

22. This is a visionary prophecy of the end of our present evolution and, like the higher realms of esoteric meta-physics, it need not here concern us in detail. It is of interest, though, for the parallel imagery with the text from Job quoted in the Yetziratic Text, and also for the fact that this Path is that of Aries. Aries is the first sign, representing the beginnings of things, but as the Zodiac is a wheel the cycle is not complete until Aries is commenced again, so Aries is also the ending. This might be inferred from the actual shape of the astrological sign, a line which loops round to end at the level from which it started. Also it provides an additional esoteric meaning to the words "I am the alpha and the omega" and "The last shall be first and the first last."

23. In her higher aspects, the naked woman on the Tarot Trump may be considered to be the Principle of Manifesta-tion which caused the sea of the Unmanifest to "brake forth as if it had issued out of the womb". She is, like the High Priestess of the 13th Path, the wreathed virgin of the 17th Path and the Empress of the 14th Path, a representation of the Feminine Side of God. The Godhead is shown forth in

172

all its aspects in the many mythologies of man. The Feminine-Side is the Goddess behind all goddesses just as the Masculine-Side is the God behind all gods. Yet the two are one God—the Divine Androgyne.

NOTES ON THE DESIGN OF TRUMP XVII

The Marseilles card shows a naked woman kneeling on one knee by a pool, pouring liquid from two vases. In the sky is a huge star surrounded by seven smaller ones. In the background a bird sits upon a bush. On the Marseilles card it is not quite clear where land and water actually meet, so the exact position of the woman cannot be defined. Wirth causes her to be kneeling on the land and pouring one vase onto the earth and the other into the water. Waite, Knapp and Case agree on this except that they place her leading foot *on* (Waite and Case) or *in* (Knapp) the water. Zain puts knee and leading foot on the water, trailing foot on land.

The actual star of the Marseilles card has eight main points with eight secondary ones inbetween them. Seven of the main points have a line down the centre — the exception being the topmost one. The surrounding stars are grouped in two vertical rows of three with a seventh in the centre over the woman's head; they have eight points except the topmost two, which have seven.

Papus described the woman as crowned with the seven stars. Wirth has the main star with eight main and eight secondary points, all with a central line, though the secondary points are very much smaller than the main. The surrounding stars are grouped traditionally, all eight-pointed, but the middle one of each row and the central one of all, (which is smallest of all), are divided into lozenges internally.

Waite breaks up the regular pattern of grouping of the smaller stars and makes all the stars simple eight-pointed geometric figures. Knapp's main star is like Wirth's, his regularly grouped smaller stars all simple eight-pointers. Case follows similarly except that the two midpoint stars have diagonals drawn in and the small central one is divided into lozenges. Zain gives an eight-pointed star with two triangles on a common base inside it, the top one white, the lower black; seven four-pointed stars are grouped evenly about it.

The Golden Dawn considered the large star to be seven-pointed — the star of Venus. Levi agreed it was Venus but gave it eight points. This may indicate that Levi attributed the card to the Tree of Life according to the same system as the Golden Dawn and that his published attributions were blinds. However, on the other hand, he may have arrived at Venus from the number of the surrounding stars and not because Venus is the Mundane Chakra of Netzach to which the 28th Path leads, the Path to which the Golden Dawn attributed this card.

The bird on the bush in the Marseilles card is also variously presented. Levi and Papus say that it is optionally an ibis or a butterfly on either a bush or flower. Wirth, Knapp and Zain have a butterfly on a flower; Westcott, Waite and Case prefer an ibis on a bush. The two latter also place a mountain in the background. The Golden Dawn tradition was that the bird was a dove (of Spirit) hovering above the Tree of Knowledge.

Crowley's early description of the card was that it shows a playful naked water nymph pouring silver waters into a river and golden waters over her head, with butterflies and roses all about. He said that there should be flames above in addition to the star of seven rays and that her attitude should suggest a swastika. The Crowley/Harris card follows these ideas generally. It is built up on a spiral design and also shows a celestial globe, the poles of which coincide with the position of the breast shaped cups. There are crystals at the bottom of the card and the seven-pointed star of Venus rises above, seeming to rotate, with swastika-like rays of fire coming from it.

Manly P. Hall's symbol for the card is a finger to hushed lips.

SECTION THREE
THE SUPREME MYSTERIES
The Paths of the Spirit

Part I

Influences upon the Individuality

The 18th Path

Geburah — Binah

KEY:	⊓ Cheth. Fence.
SPIRITUAL SIGNIFICANCE:	♋ Cancer. The Crab.
THEORY:	Child of the Powers of the Waters. Lord of the Triumph of Light. (VII—The Chariot.)
COLOURS:	Amber. Maroon. Rich bright russet. Dark greenish brown.
TEXT:	"The Eighteenth Path is called the Intelligence of the House of Influence (by the greatness of whose abundance the influx of good things upon created beings is increased), and from its midst the arcana and hidden senses are drawn forth, which dwell in its shade and which cling to it from the Cause of all causes."

1. This Path joins Geburah, the Sephirah of spiritual activity in manifestation, and Binah, the Sephirah of archetypal Form. Thus the Chariot serves as a good symbol for it in that a chariot is a vehicle designed for active movement. The vehicle of the Spirit for its activity in manifestation is a series of bodies or sheaths made up from the material of that manifestation, one body for each level from Spiritual to Physical.

2. Each body builds up around a 'permanent atom' on its corresponding plane and this, sometimes called a seed-atom, remains attached to the Spirit for a series of incarnations. The seed-atoms hold, therefore, the memory of all past incarnations of the Spirit while the atoms of the various planes that gather round them each time to form a vehicle are subsequently dispersed to form the common pool of matter for that plane which is utilised by other manifesting Spirits.

3. It is possible that a portion of, say, astral or mental substance may be utilised by an incarnating entity before it has been completely broken down into its component parts. Thus it will still retain certain aspects of the imprint of the previous entity. This sometimes accounts for strange

affinities and repulsions, often seemingly out of character, in a Personality. Such would not be marked in a Spirit in good control of its vehicles but it can and does happen and is well to bear in mind before jumping to conclusions about former incarnations, pre-terrestrial ties or the doubtful theory of 'soul mates'.

4. The symbols of this Path all stress the aspect of Form —the House of Influence, the Crab with its hard carapace, the Fence, and the Chariot, which, on the Tarot Trump has a square house-like superstructure. Form is again emphasised in the Moon symbolism of the card, moons appearing on the king's sceptre and upon his epaulettes. The Moon is a general symbol of Form, for, like Form, it is predominantly receptive; its great power over the tides of the oceans is a drawing or actively receptive power like all aspects of the Feminine-Side. The polarity of manifestation is shown in the two horses which draw the chariot, in the design of the king's crown, in the two wheels of the chariot and also in the two sets of pillars which support the chariot's canopy. A chariot is a mobile throne which again refers us to Binah, whose Order of Angels is the Aralim, Thrones. The mobility of this throne or chariot is the Geburah aspect of the Path and as the war-horse is attributable to Geburah it is perhaps better to leave the animals drawing the chariot as horses rather than to make them sphinxes as is the usual modern formula. One could also say that the chariot has its basis of mobility in Chokmah, whose Order of Angels is the Auphanim, Wheels.

5. Such a wealth of symbolism should not be allowed to veil from us the reality for which it stands. This is always a danger in a symbol hunt and often causes the symbols to transform themselves from arcana into red-herrings, from which it is but a short step to stinking fish. It would, for example, be of great interest perhaps to thresh out just what animals ought to be depicted drawing the chariot, horses, sphinxes, griffons, lion and unicorn or that strange Daath-like beast, the amphisbaena, with a head at both

ends. Similarly, many could no doubt grind a very pretty axe over the true signification and design of the glyph on the front of the chariot, but they would be in danger of cutting their own throats with it because it does not really matter. As things stand, every Tarot designer puts his own idea of what it ought to be, which does not necessarily mean that any particular one is necessarily right or wrong. It is apposite to mention this here as an over-emphasis of symbolism is an over-emphasis of Form. One must remember that, in the symbolism of this Trump, the chariot has a king in it; that is, any symbol is only a more or less inadequate representation of a spiritual reality and so, particularly in a symbol system as corrupt as the modern Tarot, it is often best to use symbolism only to get the bare outlines fixed and then to use one's own intuition to fill in the minor details. If one worries over minor details of symbolism one is apt to lose the whole of the reality.

6. The Form stress in the symbolism of this Path is not so much the actual forms that the Spirit will use in its manifestation but the aim or purpose of the Spirit within those forms, as well as their action in the worlds of Form. Aim, quality and action are indeed inextricably intertwined, which is part of the Mystery of the Divine Trinity. It often helps us in our elucidation of reality to make a division between the Three Persons or Three Aspects, calling them Father, Son, Holy Spirit, or Will, Love-Wisdom, Active Intelligence, but of course all three are really One—together with the often ignored Destroyer or Disintegrator Aspect. To refer back to the Tarot imagery, the four pillars of the chariot are but parts of one vehicle. This is often forgotten in our analytical investigations and can lead to misunderstandings—for example the Pillars of Opposites would really be better called the Pillars of Complements.

7. In Binah is held the purpose of the Spirit in incarnation and how it proposes to set that purpose in motion in Form. Form is a necessary part of the scheme of things—it gives a thrust block or sphere of limitation for the Spirit to act

against or within. The analogy of the internal combustion engine is a familiar one; if there is no compression the exploding gasses simply dissipate and no motion is possible. So Form is necessary for Evolution.

8. Form acts as a limitation but it is not, because of this, evil, as some pagan cosmologies would suggest. In esoteric terms this limitation is a Ring-Pass-Not, a field of limitation inside which the active force of the Spirit is confined. From this we can see the relevance of such symbols as the House, the Fence and so on, which are attributed to this Path. There are many other symbols which could also have been used, from the womb to the internal combustion engine, all of which show the action of this Feminine, Negative or Form-Side of God.

9. This Path acts as a channel of communication between the Spirit and the Individuality—from the aspect of the Spirit where the Spirit's destiny in Form is archetypally held, (Binah), to the intelligently active part of the Individuality, (Geburah). Thus the Path is called the House of Influence. The parenthesis in the Yetziratic Text, "(by the greatness of whose abundance the influx of good things upon created beings is increased)" indicates how necessary this link is for the destiny of the Spirit to be worked out in manifestation. Where destiny is not being worked out karma is generally accruing and the results of this are rarely welcomed as "good things". From this will be seen part of the results of the Primary Deviation which drove a wedge or Abyss between the two levels of being.

10. Binah is the Parent of Faith from which all higher knowledge of destiny is gained by the Individuality. This knowledge is the "arcane and hidden senses" mentioned in the Yetziratic Text. These stem, the Text says, from the "Cause of all causes", Kether and the Unmanifest. This means our fount of being on Cosmic levels, and as our aim in evolution is to link up this part of our being with the parts of us in manifestation, it is obvious that our first task is to get the channels clear—to bridge the Gulf and the

Abyss. Only then is it possible to get the knowledge of our destiny filtered down to the densest levels and worked out upon the physical plane in daily living.

11. The esoteric titles of the Tarot Trump show two aspects of the Path. The Child of the Powers of the Waters refers to our position in the Waters of Form or Manifestation. The Lord of the Triumph of Light refers to our Cosmic position as Lords of Light. This is another way of expresssing the symbol of the King in the Chariot, the Crab in its Shell, the Influence in the House. The dual quality is suggested also by the dual shape of the astrological sign.

12. All this symbolism emphasises our position in the chain of evolutionary hierarchies. We are Cosmic beings immersed in the Waters of Manifestation and our task is to act as mediators—brightening the waters with our light and at the same time enchancing the power of our light by its immersion in the waters. It is not a necessary fact of Spiritual realities that our lights should fizzle out in a lot of steam and stench on contact with the waters of manifest existence.

13. A light doused, obscured, or 'hid under a bushel' manifests in daily life as a lack of responsibility. Responsibility, true responsibility, for maintaining the right or light can stem only from within oneself. If one acts according to the dictates of even a comparatively high moral ethos and yet does so not by virtue of the truth of one's own light shining within but because one takes one's standard of action from the dictates of another, then one is replacing one's own light with the authority of another. This is not responsibility, it is evasion of it, whatever the outer appearance apparently to the contrary. To substitute another's light for one's own is no way of bridging the Abyss—it merely camouflages it, making a deceptive, deep and very real trap. Hypocrisy is not always as obvious as one might think. In the words of T. S. Eliot's Becket in 'Murder in the Cathedral', it is "the greatest treason: to do the right deed for the wrong reason".

NOTES ON THE DESIGN OF TRUMP VII

The Marseilles Chariot shows a king in a four-posted canopied cubical chariot drawn by two horses. It is possible that the two horses are in fact an amphisbaena — a mythical animal with two heads which, by their position, enables it to move as easily forward or backwards — a kind of Janus figure. The king's crown is strange, having a fleur de lys decoration one side and filled in solidly on the other, a point which is not followed by any of the later designs. It may be a misprint but it fits in well with the other dual symbolism. The figure at the head of the sceptre is best elicited from the actual diagram which appears in the book. His shoulder pieces are in visaged moon form and his cuirass shows three approximately right-angled bands. On the front of the chariot is shown the letters V.T—probably indicating the Hebrew letter Tau, Hebrew being read from right to left, and symbolic of Form.

This card is one fully illustrated by Eliphas Levi. He represents the horses as sphinxes, one black and one white, pulling in different directions but looking the same way. The canopy of the chariot is embroidered with stars and the king's crown consists of three pentagrams. The sceptre is similar to the Marseilles version, which Levi describes as a globe, square and triangle. On the front of the chariot the V.T is replaced by the lingam and a winged disk. The shoulder pieces are as those on the Marseilles card and Levi says they are Urim and Thummim, represented by the two crescents of the Moon in Chesed and Geburah. The Urim and Thummim are part of the sacred accoutrements of the Jewish priesthood. Little is known of their significance. Some consider they were fetish stones carried out of Egypt, others that they were forms of dice used in divination, and others that they were sacred names on talismanic sheets of gold. In Levi's opinion The Chariot is the most beautiful and complete of all the Tarot cards.

Wirth, Papus and Knapp all follow Levi closely, though Knapp introduces a triple flame above the king's head. Waite and Case also follow similarly. Waite says the figure should have a drawn sword but his diagram shows a diamond headed sceptre. He displaces the threefold cuirass pattern by a square jewel. He also adds a background of river, trees and a walled town, giving the idea of Hebrew letter Cheth, a Fence, another indication that at this time he supported the Golden Dawn attributions. The skirt of the king divides into eight segments covered with geomantic signs and complete with a belt of mystic symbols; Case follows suit. He also substitutes for the triple-pentagram crown one with an eight-pointed gold star. Case's only real modification from Waite is to retain the pentagram crown and to add three T shaped figures on the inside of the sides and top of the breast square. He also puts a smile and a frown on the faces of the sphinxes and the Urim and Thummim.

Crowley originally supported Levi's design though he thought the chariot should be driven furiously. In the Harris design the charioteer is completely armoured and holds the Holy Grail made of amethyst and with blood in it. On his armour are the ten stars of Assiah and his crest is a crab. The chariot is drawn by four sphinxes each composed of four Elements, thus representing the sixteen sub-Elements.

The 'Egyptian' card shows the charioteer with drawn sword, which is curved. On his breast are shown two set-squares and a T-square. Otherwise the accoutrements are similar to the traditional except that there is no lingam on the chariot front and his headdress bears the usual uraeus. Uraei with solar disks appear in the ornamentation over the starry canopy together with a figure of Isis stretching her arms over two eyes, also ten female sitting goddesses wearing what seems to be Maat feathers. The sceptre is a clear-cut triangle on circle on square.

Manly P. Hall's symbol for the card is a ring of seven five-pointed stars.

The 16th Path

Chesed — Chokmah

KEY:	ו Vau. Nail.
SPIRITUAL SIGNIFICANCE:	♉ Taurus. The Bull.
THEORY:	Magus of the Eternal. (V—The Hierophant.)
COLOURS:	Red orange. Deep indigo. Deep warm olive. Rich brown.
TEXT:	"The Sixteenth Path is the Triumphal or Eternal Intelligence, so called because it is the pleasure of the Glory, beyond which is no other Glory like to it, and it is called also the Paradise prepared for the Righteous."

1. The 16th Path is parallel to the 18th. They are both links between Spirit and Individuality, and again there is emphasis on Form in the symbolism. In the JHVH formula Vau is active manifestation in Form, the result of the union of opposites of Yod and Heh, a more complete consideration of which belongs to our examination of the Tarot Court cards. From an esoteric Christian standpoint the Nail is a significant symbol, being (in triplicity) that which nails the Spirit to the Cross of Matter.

2. The shape of the letter Vau is similar to Zain, the Sword. We considered Zain to be made up of a Yod, (representing Spiritual reality), extending a line of communication down into manifestation. We might apply a similar line of interpretation to the letter Vau. In the case of Vau though, the Yod is positioned differently. It is not athwart the vertical line of communication but inclined down into it—as if the great dynamic force of Chokmah were driving its spiritual influence down into the pristine form of the Individuality held in Chesed. Thus, whereas the emanations of Binah are known as Faith, the emanations of Chokmah could be called Spiritual Will.

3. As Chesed is that part of the Individuality which beholds, or should behold, the face of its creator, the Spirit,

holding within itself a pattern of the Spirit on which to mould its further manifestation, and as Chokmah is the pure type of Spiritual Being, the direct reflection of the very source of Being itself in Kether, so this Path we can take to be, as the Yetziratic Text says, "the pleasure of the Glory, beyond which is no other Glory like to it." When all the aspects of our manifest existence radiate and reflect truth to and from one another in this way, then will 'the Kingdom come'. So we can think of this Path as a pattern for what is to be, and a promise of what will be; thus is it called also "the Paradise prepared for the Righteous."

4. A Magus is one who mediates power from one level down to another and so the function of this Path is well summarised in the esoteric title of the Tarot Trump—Magus of the Eternal. The Eternal is in Kether and the Unmanifest and is brought into manifestation through Chokmah, (the particular type of the Spirit, corresponding to one of the Zodiacal signs), and thence to the Individuality for transmission to Earth by the everyday life of the Personality. The term "Triumphal or Eternal Intelligence" in the Yetziratic Text endorses this fact. One of the aims of our evolution is the manifestation of Christ-consciousness in Earth, and the birth of this Christ child in each one—in the cave among the animals of Malkuth—is heralded by a star —the radiant essence of the Spirit in Chokmah—rising in the East, the place of greatest symbolic light and revelation.

5. The astrological sign of this Path is Taurus, the Bull, an animal which symbolises densest concretion in Earth, whilst its feminine counterpart, the Cow, has from time immemorial been a sacred beast, symbol of the feminine, sustaining, receptive principle of Form—the matrix in which the jewel of the Spirit is set. The shape of the sign is well related to the powers of this Path, a lunar disk over a solar circle, indicating reception of the powers of the Eternal and their radiation in life-giving light and warmth in the worlds of manifestation.

6. There are some interesting lines of investigation in the

stars and constellations which go to make up the Zodiacal sign of Taurus. Most significant are the Pleiades, which appear at the shoulder of the Bull. The Pleiades, along with the binary Sirius and the Great Bear are among the more important stellar groupings as far as our Solar Logoidal system is concerned. Just as Sirius bears similar relationship to our Solar Logos as the Individuality does to the Personality of man; and the Great Bear holds the patterns for the seven Planetary Logoi of our Solar Logoidal jurisdiction; so do the Seven Sisters of the Pleiades have an important esoteric link with our Planetary Logoi. Not much can be given about the exact nature of the link because the factors involved are too vast for a detailed human understanding, but the Pleiades have been called the 'sisters' or 'wives' of the Seven Rishis of the Great Bear. In other words, they are Feminine or Form-side aspects of the Cosmic Patterns held in the Great Bear that the Planetary Logoi of this Solar system use as guides for their evolution. They have been thus assigned as under the presidency of the Third Aspect of Deity—Active Intelligence.

7. Interesting as this may be, we humans have enough on hand in coping with our own evolution without bothering over-much about the evolution of Cosmic beings. But an occasional consideration of these points does help to give a sense of Cosmic proportion when perhaps we are in danger of becoming a little too vainglorious.

8. The Pleiades are mythologically considered to be doves. These birds are sacred to Venus, which is the ruling planet of the sign Taurus. A dove is also an emblem of the Holy Spirit, an example being the Biblical story of Jesus' baptism in the Jordan. The Holy Spirit is, of course, the Third Aspect of God, so we have an interesting correlation here between mytholigical, Biblical, astrological and esoteric symbolism.

9. Alcyone, the brightest star of the Pleiades, is a particularly important star as far as our Solar system is concerned, and was believed, in ancient times, to be the hub

of the Universe. This point is also put forward in H. P. Blavatsky's 'The Secret Doctrine' and any interested in these Cosmic stellar factors can do little better than to study this work and also the Tibetan's writings through Alice Bailey—'Esoteric Astrology' in particular. (Lucis Trust. London & New York.)

10. Another significant part of Taurus is the constellation Cornucopia—the horn of Taurus—or the Horn of Plenty. This gives us a direct link between the Table Round of Chokmah and the Zodiac via the Holy Grail. The early form of the Grail in Arthurian legend was the Cauldron of Ceridwen from which all men could feast of their favourite food to their hearts' content. One of the mythological Arthur's tasks was to fetch this Cauldron up from Hades, or in other words, to redeem it.

11. In the later Grail books the Grail became a symbol of the highest spiritual significance, so much so that, together with its hero, Galahad, it came to be somewhat emasculated. It is an unhappy tendency of human error, (brought about by a rejection of the earthy), to picture the good as 'too good to be true', which makes the bad seem much more interesting. Thus we have the expression lifted and somewhat twisted from J. M. Barrie, "Heaven for climate— Hell for company." Milton failed to overcome the pitfall —his Satan is much the most interesting character in 'Paradise Lost'. And even the hero of Calvary has barely escaped transformation into 'gentle Jesus, meek and mild'—a kind of ideal Victorian curate.

12. However, be that as it may, the Holy Grail is a symbol of the highest spiritual significance whether it appears in the transcendental guise of the later texts or in the earlier presentation as a communal bowl for hungry, hard-drinking warriors. The latter has many spiritually pertinent points in its favour. It stresses communality, the many obtaining their source of life and enjoyment from a single, central fount which is never exhausted. So this Cauldron is a fine symbol of Kether, the Fount of Spiritual Being. The Ban-

quet too is a symbol that plays an important part in the Mysteries of religion. In Christianity it figures as the Last Supper and is re-enacted whenever Holy Communion or Mass is observed.

13. The Grail, in all its forms, is very relevant to this Path therefore. The Path leads to and from Chokmah, wherein may be envisaged the Zodiacal Table Round with the Cosmic Holy Grail in the centre. This represents the eventual goal of Evolution, when all are as kings seated about this Table, in equality and diversity. This is "the Paradise prepared for the Righteous" which the experience of this Path foreshadows.

NOTES ON THE DESIGN OF TRUMP V

The Marseilles card shows an ecclesiastic figure with three-tiered mitre seated between two pillars surmounted by four-point crowns. He bears a triple-cross sceptre and makes the sign of esotericism with his right hand. Before him are two kneeling acolytes. On the backs of his gloves are crosses.

Wirth follows the symbolism closely and says that the seven rounded points of the triple-cross—which appear to be trefoil on the Marseilles card—represent the seven deadly sins, i.e. Pride, Sloth, Envy, Wrath, Lust, Greed and Avarice, attributable to Sol, Luna, Mercury, Mars, Venus, Jupiter and Saturn respectively. He also places a cross on the top of the mitre. Papus says the men kneeling are crowned, one robed in red, the other in black. Knapp follows in this respect except that the men are not crowned, the one in black has a full head of hair and the other is tonsured. Knapp also introduces trefoils on the back of the throne, a Calvary cross on the Hierophant's breast and mitre, equal-armed crosses on the flaps of his headdress, and also a veil behind him between the pillars. Manly P. Hall's hieroglyph is a pentagram.

The pentagram idea seems to have originated from Eliphas Levi, who says that the Hierophant is at the centre of a quinary figure formed by himself, the heads of the pillars and the heads of his two assistants. By drawing lines between these points, he says, a figure is produced of a square divided by a cross into four triangles, the Hierophant being in the centre. "We might almost say like the garden spider in the centre of his web, were such a comparison becoming to the things of truth, glory and light," he goes on to say. In fact, the image he conveys with such apology, no doubt also with tongue in cheek, is a profound Rosicrucian symbol.

Further, in a letter to Baron Spedalieri he says the triple crown represents Kether, the pillars Chokmah and Hod, the two ministers Binah and Netzach. There is obviously a slip of the pen here and what he meant to say was, no doubt, that the pillar heads represent Chokmah and Binah, and the heads of the priests Netzach and Hod. He also refers the triple cross to the three lower Qabalistic Worlds of Briah, Yetzirah and Assiah.

Waite follows the traditional design but with several introductions: innocent looking but quite definite phallic symbols of union on the top of each pillar, horned circles on the back of the throne, (deliberately disguised), three points on top of the mitre, crosses on the Hierophant's shoes, a carpet with four encircled equal-armed crosses, chequered paving, and crossed keys before the throne. The attendant priests are dressed in robes one of which is embroidered with roses, the other with lilies; both are tonsured. Each wears a Y-shaped pallium, a symbol of yoke or union. The front of the Hierophant's dress bears a similar design, not readily noticeable, down the front of which are four crosses. The top one is like an equal-armed cross except that the transverse arm is slightly shorter; in the next one the transverse arm is moved up the shaft to form a Calvary cross; in the next it is further shifted to show a sword-like cross; and the bottom one is equal armed and partially covered with a central disk to resemble the Cross of Initiation. There are also equal-armed crosses in the key handles.

Case follows most of Waite's innovations, though he has no crosses down the front of the Hierophant's garment. He introduces instead a moon-shaped clasp at the top. The horned circles on the throne he makes more obvious and he substitutes a small sphere on top of the mitre for Waite's three prongs. Like Waite, he has 15 trefoils on the tiara or mitre, 3, 5 and 7. He draws attention to the fact that there is a total of ten crosses.

Crowley early favoured Levi's pentagram arrangement but thought it would be better formed by the Four Holy Living Creatures adoring the Hierophant. The card designed for the Harris Tarot is largely influenced by Crowley's private metaphysics, the main characteristic of which is a lack of humanity or humanness. As he says: "There is a distinctly sadistic aspect to this card." His Hierophant seems to be laughing at a private joke and is in pentagram form, a dancing child in a pentagram is in his heart. He is seated on the bull of Taurus, with an elephant, the Indian equivalent, in the background. The child is equated with Horus—the Ruler of the New Age. There is an aureole, with dove and serpent, behind his head, fixed with nine nails—the nails being symbolic of the Hebrew letter Vau and the nine indicative of the Moon, which is exalted in Taurus. In the background is the starry night sky, emblematic of Nuit. His headdress is phallic and he bears a sceptre surmounted by three interlaced circles indicating three 2000 year aeons. At the four corners of the card are the Holy Living Creatures. His devotee is a woman facing out of the card holding a crescent moon and a downward pointing sword. She is representative of the Scarlet Woman and Venus, ruler of Taurus.

The 'Egyptian' version shows the Hierophant wearing the Egyptian double crown of North and South with uraeus. He is seated between four lotus pillars below which are figures of warriors and above, uraei with solar disks. Horned beasts are shown also each side at the top, and over all a winged sphere with ram's horns. The Hierophant is making the usual esoteric sign and has two men kneeling at his feet. He leans on a triple cross sceptre.

For reasons similar to those pertaining to the High Priestess this card has been called 'The Pope' and 'Jupiter' exoterically.

Part II

The Structures of the Spirit

The 14th Path

Binah — Chokmah

KEY:	ד Daleth. Door.
SPIRITUAL SIGNIFICANCE:	♀ Venus.
THEORY:	Daughter of the Mighty Ones. (III—The Empress.)
COLOURS:	Emerald green. Sky blue. Early spring green. Bright rose or cerise rayed pale green.
TEXT:	"The Fourteenth Path is the Illuminating Intelligence and is so called because it is that Chasmal which is the founder of the concealed and fundamental ideas of holiness and of their stages of preparation."

1. As the lower transverse Paths, the 27th and 19th, are, respectively, the 'girders' of the Personality and Individuality, so is this Path the main girder of the Spirit itself on its own levels of manifestation. The Yetziratic Text calls it "that Chasmal (i.e. Brilliant One) which is the founder of the concealed and fundamental ideas of holiness". It is, indeed, the hidden foundation of all beings in Form. The fount of our being is in Kether, but manifestation as a stable unit requires the functioning of the Principles of Polarity, which at this level are the archetypal principles of Chokmah and Binah — and it is this 14th Path that interconnects them.

2. The Path is thus itself an archetype of all subsequent manifestation. It is a first forming in actuality of the principles inherent in the incoming flow of spiritual power from the Unmanifest. It is thus the Gate to manifestation, or, to coin the symbolism of the Hebrew letter, the Door to it. Likewise could it be called the Door to the world of the Spirit— for this Path is along the Path of the Lightning Flash and when returning upon that Way, this Path is the last channel of consciousness where the Pillars of Manifestation in their action of upholders of Form, hold sway. It is the Door to Illumination as the Yetziratic Text infers, the Complete Illumination of the Vision of God face to face in Chokmah.

3. However, it is on its manifesting aspect that the symbolism of the Tarot Trump lays emphasis. This foundation stone of the building of the Temple of Man in manifest existence is called the Daughter of the Mighty Ones—emphasising in the Daughter symbolism its receptive Form aspect. The Mighty Ones are the Principles of Manifest Existence which are shown forth on the Tree as the Sephiroth Chokmah and Binah, prime force and archetypal form, root potency and root latency, Supernal Fire and Supernal Water, Alchemical Sulphur and Alchemical Salt—and all the vast complex of symbolism and meaning implied by these two great Sephiroth, representatives on the highest causal levels of the two Pillars of Manifestation.

4. On the card the Daughter of the Mighty Ones appears enthroned in an open field, holding a sceptre surmounted with the sign of Venus and having a shield inscribed with an eagle. She can be considered to be another aspect of the great Feminine-Side of God—which also appears in the High Priestess, the Leader of the Lion and so on, and can be equated with any of the goddesses of the pagan pantheons. It is indeed a synthesis of them all.

5. The ramifications of this symbolism are enormous as might be expected. The Feminine-Side tends to be overlooked nonetheless by the orthodox Church except perhaps in the Roman Catholic regard for the Virgin Mary and the female saints. This is unfortunate for it means that we tend to consider only half of what God really is. The limitations of English grammar may contribute something to this. There is, anyway, an element of irony in the fact that the ancient Qabalists called God, after the Magical Image of Kether, "He who is all right side", for in the neglect of the Feminine Divine Principle only one side of God is commonly considered.

6. The Feminine-Side is in one aspect the Form-side of Manifestation, commonly referred to esoterically as Isis of Nature. This name holds a wider implication than Isis as a mere rustic goddess — it embraces all Nature from First Manifestation right through all the planes down to the dense

physical world in which we are anchored. It is this view of Isis that is implied in the title of the well known esoteric textbook, H. P. Blavatsky's 'Isis Unveiled'.

7. That the realisation of this aspect of things is a fundamental point in the progress of the soul is brought out in 'The Chymical Marriage of Christian Rosencreutz'. Here, the narrator of the story, who achieves further in the Mysteries than any other, does so because he was afforded the sight of Isis Unveiled—or in the symbolism of the story, the naked Lady Venus.

8. A quotation from the text is of interest for it is loaded with deep and evocative Rosicrucian symbolism: "the Page led me by the hand through a very dark passage till we came to a little door now only put too, for, as the Page informed me, it was first opened yesterday when the coffins were taken out, (i.e. those of the royal bride and bridegroom. G.K.) and had not since been shut. As soon as we stepped in I espied the most pretious thing that Nature ever created, for this vault had no other light but from certain huge carbuncles, This was the King's Treasury, but the most glorious and principal thing was a sepulchre in the middle, so rich that I wondered it was no better guarded, whereunto the Page answered me, that I had good reason to be thankful to my planet, by whose influence I had now seen certain pieces which no humane eye (except those of the King's family) had ever viewed. This sepulchre was triangular, and had in the middle of it a kettle of polished copper, the rest was of pure gold and pretious stones. In the kettle stood an angel, who held in his arms an unknown tree, whose fruit continually falling into the kettle, turned into water therein, and ran out into three small golden kettles standing by. This little altar was supported by an eagle, an ox, and a lion, which stood on an exceedingly costly base. I asked my Page what this might signifie. "Here," said he, "lies buried Lady Venus, that beauty which hath undone many a great man, both in fourtune, honour, blessing and prosperity"; after which he showed me a copper door in the pavement, saying, "Here,

if you please, we may go further down". We descended the steps, where it was exceeding dark, but the Page immediately opened a little chest in which stood a small ever-burning taper, wherefrom he kindled one of the many torches that lay by. I was mightily terrified and asked how he durst do this. He gave me for answer, "as long as the Royal Persons are still at rest I have nothing to fear." Herewith I espied a rich bed ready made, hung about with curious curtains, one of which he drew, and I saw the Lady Venus stark naked (for he heaved up the coverlets too), lying there in such beauty, and a fashion so surprising, that I was almost beside myself, neither do I yet know whether it was a piece thus carved, or an humane corps that lay dead there, for she was altogether immoveable, and yet I durst not touch her. So she was again covered, yet she was still, as it were, in my eye. But I soon espyed behind the bed a tablet on which it was thus written. (Here follows a short passage in strange script superficially similar to the Enochian or Angelic language used by Dr. Dee and Edward Kelly in their magical experiments of the sixteenth century and revived in MacGregor Mathers 'Golden Dawn' teaching. G.K.) I asked my Page concerning this writing, but he laughed, with promise that I should know it too, and, he putting out the torch, we again ascended. Then I better viewed all the little doors, and found that on every corner there burned a small taper of pyrites of which I had before taken no notice, for the fire was so clear that it looked much liker a stone than a taper. From this heat the tree was forced continually to melt, yet it still produced new fruit. "Now behold," said the Page, "when the tree shall be quite melted down, then shall Lady Venus awake and be the Mother of a King." "

9. An interesting consequence of all this is that the narrator, (who is Christian Rosencreutz himself), on being made, with his companions, a Knight of the Golden Stone, finds that he alone has had the sight of the Lady Venus and that this is a Mystery so high and profound that the very experience of it is almost regarded as a blasphemy. The

only person to have received the experience before was the door-keeper to the castle, who is now to be released from his post as soon as Christian Rosencreutz confesses to his vision. From thenceforth Christian Rosencreutz is to be the doorkeeper.

10. This is a most interesting point when one considers what Christian Rosencreutz really represents. Just as Our Lord is the perfect man entering into the corruption of human life in Earth to show the way through and out of it, so Christian Rosencreutz is the perfect man who, in order that the Divine Plan should be preserved unsullied by corruption, remained out of dense manifestation. The corruption resulting from man's Fall is Qabalistically considered to extend as far as Daath. This 14th Path is immediately above Daath and has the Hebrew letter attribution of a Door—the Door which has corruption on the one side and perfection on the other, and the keeper of the door is Christian Rosencreutz. It is the Rosicrucian Mysteries that come after the Christian Mysteries of Tiphareth, and only after them—which does not say much for the spiritual perspicacity of some organisations that offer to teach the secrets of the Rosicrucians and yet claim they are not religious bodies. Though such organisations may do good work at their own level the two statements are mutually contradictory and suggest a lack of a really deep grasp of the principles involved.

11. However, a full analysis of the Rosicrucian symbolism of 'The Chymical Marriage' is out of place here, as it would take a whole book to itself, but a hint of the tremendous factors involved can be discerned from the last statement of the Page—a character who represents very well an aspect of the Holy Guardian Angel. "When the tree shall be quite melted down," he says, "then shall Lady Venus awake and be the Mother of a King." In other words, (and this is only one interpretation of many possible, and all equally valid each in their own degree), when the Tree of Life, the whole manifested Universe, is withdrawn to the Unmanifest, then

the life locked up within that vast form, which kept it in being in a state of manifest coherence, will be freed. This life which holds Form in being will no longer be the sleeping Venus or Isis of Nature but the living waters of the Ain Soph, the Great Sea of the Unmanifest into which all spiritual beings who have attained their full evolution in Form will withdraw as individual units—as Kings. And the great Form principle will be their Mother.

12. It is difficult to find exact expressions for ideas such as this for inevitably one becomes immersed in complexes of related symbols—womb, Great Mother, amniotic fluid, Primordial Sea, Waters of the Unmanifest or of Binah or of the Astral Light and so on—which merge into one another in a manner which tends to baffle the mind. It becomes something like trying to count the series of infinite images to be seen in two parallel mirrors. But such is inevitable when considering Mysteries whose level of being is so far above the reach of the mind. It is possible to know a thing by intuition and yet be very hard put to explain it. The failure to explain a belief does not indicate its falsity—it implies only an inadequate reasoning faculty. As there is so much stress laid upon reason these days though, it can happen that a person may gain a correct grasp of a situation by intuition and yet feel obliged, because of the current intellectual climate, to find reasons for his attitude. Further, one may have the case of a person intuitionally correct but who gives bad reasons for his standpoint. He may then be judged on his false reasoning and his true assessment be decried on that score. Similarly, one may have a person who fails to grasp a situation intuitionally but yet who is able to advance very good reasons for his incorrect viewpoint—such is liable to get a better hearing.

13. Of course the ideal is to be intuitionally correct and to have the right reasons as well, but such does not always occur. A case in point in legend is the attitude of Mordred and Morgan le Fay. They had very good reasons for attacking King Arthur. He was, in the bluntest terms, a

willing cuckold and also out of touch with the common people, (the commons sided with Mordred in the last great battles), but the attitude of Morgan and Mordred, whatever deeper motives of jealousy or hate may have been at the back of it, was one of reason and extreme perfectionism. Yet it was of the Devil for by it the Fellowship of the Table Round was destroyed. The Illuminating Intelligence of the 14th Path is the Light of the Spirit — not the Light of Reason, which, as the Tarot Trump of the 26th Path implies, can be of the Devil, an imprisoning illusion, even more so than the glamours of the emotions or the astral plane.

14. From all these considerations it may be inferred how vast and potent a figure the Empress of the Tarot Trump, the Daughter of the Mighty Ones, in her deeper implications is. And of course the same applies to the other Tarot figures in the upper reaches of the Tree—the Fool, the Magician, the High Priestess. These are the levels of the spiritual foundations of all manifestation and the vast simplicities of spiritual truth and so they are never likely to be fully elucidated by us in our present condition.

15. The Empress is throned in the midst of Nature, showing her intimate connection with all natural Form existence, and she bears a sceptre of Venus and a shield with an eagle. The sign Venus by its configuration shows its relevance to this 14th Path. It is a solar circle, an emblem of radiant spirit surmounting the cross of manifestation.

16. The eagle is also a profound symbol well fitted to this Path. It is a bird capable of rising to tremendous heights and is considered traditionally to be the only creature able to look directly at the Sun—the symbolic source of spiritual life and light. In Christian symbolism it has been considered as a messenger from Heaven, which ties in well with its association with Ganymede, the cup-bearer of the gods. It appears in alchemical symbolism in much the same terms—its devouring of the lion indicates the volatilisation of the denser aspects of man's nature. It is also a symbol of divine majesty, a meaning somewhat ambitiously taken

192

over by the Roman Empire and by other nations ever since. From a mystical point of view the common variant of a double-headed eagle refers more to Daath, whose most appropriate god-form is Janus—he who looks both ways.

17. So on the 14th Path we have the inherent strength and potentiality of the highest vehicle of man—the Spirit in manifestation. This is in the same way that the 19th and 27th Paths are representative of the lower vehicles of Individuality and Personality. On the 14th Path we have the great might of the Spirit impelling itself down into Form. On the 19th Path we have the effortless control of the Lion, the lower levels of manifestation. On the 27th Path we have the opening up of the densest centres of consciousness and Form to the incoming Fire and Light of the Spirit. Thus the Paths contain not only symbols of mystical and psychological fact but of immediately relevant aspiration.

NOTES ON THE DESIGN OF TRUMP III

The Empress of the Marseilles Tarot is crowned, has a Venus sceptre and a shield bearing an eagle. A small shrub shows that the scene is out of doors. She is seated on a throne but it is difficult to decide whether the promontories behind her are angelic wings or the pillar like tops of the back of the throne.

With Wirth it is difficult to tell whether the scene is indoors or outdoors, but a flower is tucked in by the side of the throne. Wirth gives the Empress wings and places nine stars round her head and a crescent moon at her feet. The sceptre is changed to one bearing the fleur-de-lys. Papus says that the woman can either have wings or else be depicted standing in the Sun. He prefers the Venus sceptre and thinks she should actually hold an eagle, not merely have a representation of one on a shield. He suggests twelve stars about her head or else a twelve pointed crown. Levi agrees that she should be winged and crowned and holding a sceptre with an orb of the world at the end. (This is similar to the Venus sceptre which could be alternatively described as the orb of the world surmounted by a Cross of Manifestation and with an inverted Tau shown on the orb—see the Marseilles Tarot diagram.) Knapp follows these lines and favours nine stars, an eagle, Venus sceptre, crescent moon underfoot, wings and a blazing sun behind. The idea of all these attributions, as Levi points out, is the woman "clothed with the sun, and the moon under her feet, and upon her head a crown of twelve stars: and she being with child..." of the Revelation of St. John. (Ch. xii. v. 1-2.) Additionally, Knapp puts her throne at the top of three steps, each having three, five and seven stars inscribed on them, in descending order. Manly P. Hall considered the bird shown on her shield to be a pheonix. He says she is called Generation and represents the threefold world out of which proceeds the fourfold material world. Levi calls her the 'Quintessence of the Triad' and her sign, the eagle. This corresponds, in our view, with the 14th Path, so again Levi may have had the same ideas about attributions as the Golden Dawn. Hall's hieroglyph is a triangle, apex up, containing three points, on a background light at the top and dark at the bottom.

Waite emphasises the principle of generation by having a cornfield in the foreground, trees behind in a garden, with a river flowing through them terminating in a waterfall. She reclines on cushions, has a flowered robe, a heart shaped shield with the sign for Venus inscribed thereon, and holds up a sceptre with the globe of the world at the top with no cross. Her diadem is a wreath with twelve stars. Case's design is similar but with a Venus sceptre and a dove on the shield. He mentions that her wreath is of myrtle and that she is pregnant. Like Waite, he gives her a necklace, which he says is of seven pearls.

The Crowley/Harris Empress is seated before a door or gate in the traditional posture which, it is said, symbolises Alchemical Salt. She has a zodiacal belt, a Venus symbol on her crown, and bees and spiral surrounded dominoes on her robe. She holds a lotus sceptre and is surrounded by a sparrow and dove, (birds of Venus), a pelican, and her shield bears a white double eagle.

In the Zain card she is in profile, holding a globe-topped sceptre, eagle, and has a crescent moon beneath her feet. A Sun is behind her with 30 rays and she is crowned with twelve stars. Her headdress bears a uraeus. The cube upon which she sits is covered with eyes.

The 12th Path

Binah — Kether

KEY: ב Beth. House.
SPIRITUAL SIGNIFICANCE: ☿ Mercury.
THEORY: Magus of Power. (I—The Magician.)
COLOURS: Yellow. Purple. Grey. Indigo flecked violet.
TEXT: "The Twelfth Path is the Intelligence of Transparency because it is that species of Magnificence called Chazchazit, the place whence issues the vision of those seeing in apparitions."

1. The Yetziratic Text calls this Path the Intelligence of Transparency which implies the ability to see things as they really are. The form no longer conceals the luminous image of the Creator but reveals it. The Veil of the Temple, to speak symbolically, is no longer opaque; one no longer sees as in a glass darkly. This is not surprising as the Path leads from Binah, the principle of Form in Spirit, to Kether, the very source from whence Form and its indwelling force arises.

2. Not unnaturally, this state of consciousness is a "species of Magnificence" and its special title given in the Text, 'Chazchazit', derives from the Hebrew ChZCh, a seer, or seership—'Chazuth' being a vision. This of course is the highest form of seership, spiritual knowledge, a very much more delicate and accurate form of inner perception than the intuition even, which in turn is a very much higher and more accurate form of awareness than clairvoyance, clairaudience or any of the other various forms of lower psychism.

3. Students of the occult when first drawn to the subject usually evince the greatest interest in the techniques of lower psychism and the possibility of wandering about on the etheric or astral planes, and when not doing pitched

194

battle with Black Magicians in occult novel tradition, then hunting up all their past incarnations. This is a very englamoured view of the situation and often leads to disappointment on contacting a real, and not a fictional, esoteric group. The prime aim of an occult group is to get its students to see reality, to break up their false illusions. It is not always realised by those who enter upon such a path that the breaking up of illusions may mean first disillusionment.

4. This does not mean that the astral plane, past incarnations or Black Magicians are an illusion—they are very much realities, but a student needs to be able to recognise reality, to have his own reality, before he can get to grips with them—and also in order that they do not get to grips with him. It is not always realised that a large majority of those living in the physical universe are not really in contact with it at all but are wandering most of the time in a subjective dream world of their own. It is often such people who are drawn to occultism and dreams of flights on the astral plane, little realising that it is in the glamours of the astral plane that they are enmeshed already. And if one such as this should join an esoteric group controlled by one such as themselves, with others like themselves as members, then there is a situation very much like James Thurber's fable of 'The Owl Who Was God'. Because he looked wise all the birds followed him, and being blind by day he led them onto a road where reality soon came along in the shape of a motor vehicle which squashed most of them flat. The real tragedy is that even death may not help a badly astrally englamoured type of person, for once really on the astral they are free of all the vulgar physical distractions to drag them out of their subjective shell. It is only when in physical incarnation that most of such can be helped. Actually few people are entirely free of this type of illusion, hence the importance of life in Earth.

5. Consequently, in any system of occult development which is to be more than superficial the student must first

be well grounded in Earth, capable of efficient functioning in any of the mundane situations in which he may find himself. A person who cannot sweep a floor efficiently is not likely to be much good at dealing with dirt, (misplaced matter), or evil, (misplaced force), on higher levels of existence. Once a good grasp of handling the responsibilities of the physical plane is achieved then the student can undertake the responsibilities of functioning on other planes than the physical. To this end, contact between Personality and Individuality must be achieved and this is not done by astral projection but by direct work upon the level involved. That level is the mental, where the link between intellect and intuition is formed. This is achieved by meditation only, and meditation over a considerable period of time. It is only when a clear run through of spiritual force through all the lower levels is achieved that the student can safely undertake the higher magical work of bringing through archetypal spiritual realities or the lower magical work of astral investigation.

6. So it will be seen that occultism is no easy escape route from the chores of physical life. It will also be realised that the "seeing in apparitions" of the Yetziratic Text of this Path is not, as the awkwardness of the translation suggests, a method of hunting ghosts but, placed as it is on the tree in the Supernal Triangle, a supremely high form of spiritual awareness unlikely in the extreme to be attained by any in physical incarnation—physical conditions being as they are in the present epoch, (even though they may be better than at any previous age within historical memory). As things stand now, as soon as a soul has no longer the absolute necessity to incarnate physically, it is withdrawn to contribute to solving the problems existing on the inner planes. The results of the Deviation went up to Daath so things are by no means all sweetness and light on the inner planes any more than they are here—subjective Spiritualist communications about the 'heaven-worlds' notwithstanding. So that is why we never see a

perfect man, or have not done for nearly two thousand years—and we all know what happened to him. Generally speaking, before any soul completes its evolution and perfection is attained, its services are required elsewhere where only one such as it can operate. Its service can be more potent on the planes of causation than on the plane of effects.

7. We have established then that this Path is a high spiritual mode of consciousness which is aware of things as they are in reality and is able to sense the True Plan in the inscrutable heights of Kether and to bring down this True Plan in the form of a True Imprint into the Form Sephirah Binah. This bringing down of the Plan is a necessary corollary for knowledge is little use without a manifest effect, though the knowledge and effects we are considering here are very much beyond what we generally understand by knowledge and effects. Of course the True Plan and Imprint has to be brought down eventually to the levels of mental knowledge and physical effect but we are here concerned only with its formulation in the concrete part of the Spirit in Binah. The process of bringing force down from this Sephirah has been dealt with previously, i.e. on the 17th, and 18th Paths etc.

8. The Tarot Trump for this Path is thus aptly The Magician, or esoterically, the Magus of Power. A magician or magus is one who brings down higher forces to a lower level—in this context from Kether to Binah. The Magician is shown on the card as wielding the Wand or Rod of Power, standing before the Table of Manifestation—the figure of eight hat he wears indicating his eternal significance—eternity being of the Unmanifest whence Kether arises.

9. The planet Mercury assigned to this Path is the Mundane Chakra of Hod, an essentially magical Sephirah, though the magic of Hod is at a much denser level than that which we are considering now. The shape of the astrological sign gives a true lead to the significance of the

Path. It is the sign for Venus, (a radiant Solar orb over the Cross of Manifestation), surmounted with the receptive Lunar crescent. This conveys the idea not only of Spirit activating all the levels of Matter, but receptive itself to the higher Cosmic forces.

10. The Hebrew letter of the Path means a House. At this level the House is being builded—it is not immediately concerned at this stage with its effect on the Individuality as with The House of Influence of the 18th Path. Esoterically considered, the House is a holy one and might therefore be called a Temple, the Temple of the Spirit, a metaphor coined by our Lord with reference to his Resurrection. The Temple or House of God may be considered as the physical body, or less exclusively, all the bodies used by the Spirit— the whole man in manifestation, who should be a living replica of the blueprint or True Plan in his own Kether.

11. So we could say that the aim of initiation or evolution, for their aims are the same, is the building of a House fit for the Spirit to dwell in, and when this is achieved in physical reality in Earth, then do we have, with all the Houses of all the Spirits built foursquare on sure foundations and finely furbished, the city of the New Jerusalem descended from Heaven to Earth. This is indicated in the shape of the Hebrew letter, a thin transverse line at the top joined by a vertical to a thick transverse line at the bottom, which shows that what is abstract, the True Plan, shall descend and be shadowed exactly as a True Imprint in the dense. The Kingdom shall have come to Earth.

NOTES ON THE DESIGN OF TRUMP I

The Marseilles Tarot shows the Magician, wearing a figure of eight hat, standing before a table on which are his accoutrements. In his left hand he delicately holds a wand, and conventional shrubs show that the scene is out of doors. His arms are bent at the elbows, the left one pointing up and the right pointing down. Levi and Papus consider that his stance indicates the letter Aleph but it could equally indicate a swastika. Knapp abandons this stance by having the right arm pointing straight downward to earth, while the wand in the other hand he makes into a caduceus. Around about he puts roses growing while Wirth has the usual single flower. Most designers make the accoutrements on the table the Suit symbols of the Lesser Arcana. Levi says the Magician should have a wallet in which are more of his magical weapons; he also specifies that the Magician is pointing to heaven with his wand and has the other on his breast—this is a slight variation from the Marseilles position of the hands. Levi, who at one point mentions the large hat at another refers to a figure of eight nimbus about the head. He also mentions an early German version in which the Magician holds his girdle in one hand and a Pentagram in the other. On the table between an open book and a closed purse are 10 deniers or talismans in two lines of three each and a square of four. The feet of the table, he says, form two Hebrew letter Hehs and the Magician's feet are two inverted Vaus.

Waite differs from the traditional in having the Magician bare headed, a figure of eight nimbus over his head, and having his arms in a diagonal straight line, the right hand holding a wand aloft and the left pointing to earth. There is a rose bower over his head and beneath and before the table are more roses and lilies growing. His belt is a serpent swallowing its tail. Case follows this pattern, but has the table placed so that the Magician points more at the table top. He also hints at the square and compasses in the design of the table legs.

Crowley's idea of the card is a winged naked Mercury juggling with the instruments of his art, in a shape suggestive of a swastika or thunderbolt. On the Harris card his instruments are shown as the four Elemental symbols, a papyrus, a pen and a wand. He is attended by the cynocephalus ape of Thoth.

Opinion seems divided on whether he should be dark or fair but it is generally agreed that he should appear confident and intelligent. Manly P. Hall, who attributed no hieroglyph to the Knapp Zero Trump commences his series here by assigning a golden three pointed crown. The 'Egyptian' card shows the Magician in profile before a cubic stone, bearing the usual implements and engraved on the side with the ibis of Thoth. The Magician has a gold sceptre, surmounted with a circle in the right hand and points to earth with the left. Like the Waite and Case versions the Magician has a head-circlet of gold, in this case over a nemyss, and his belt is the uroboric serpent. In the background is a four pointed star.

Papus has suggested that the hands of Tarot personages are held in positions similar to the corresponding alphabetical correspondence of the Barrois system of dactylology or primitive language, particularly Trumps I, II and V. Readers who know anything of this system are invited to check but it seems rather like a combination of coincidence and imagination.

The Magician is often called exoterically 'The Juggler'.

The 11th Path

Chokmah — Kether

KEY:	ℵ Aleph. Ox.
SPIRITUAL SIGNIFICANCE:	△ Air.
THEORY:	Spirit of Aether. (O—The Fool.)
COLOURS:	Bright pale yellow. Sky blue. Blue emerald, Emerald flecked gold.
TEXT:	"The Eleventh Path is the Scintillating Intelligence because it is the essence of that curtain which is placed close to the order of the disposition, and this is a special dignity given to it that it may be able to stand before the Face of the Cause of Causes."

1. The "Face of the Cause of Causes" is the fount of all creation in Kether, which is why the Spiritual Experience of Chokmah is the Vision of God face to face. This path then is that high level of consciousness whereby the illumined soul proceeds from the direct Vision of God face to face, to the even greater transcendental experience of the Spiritual Experience of Kether, actual Union with God. Then the soul knows even as it is known. This Scintillating Intelligence is, as the Yetziratic Text says, "the essence of that curtain which is placed close to the order of the disposition."

2. There is an old proverb "Man proposes, God disposes," and in Kether is the True Plan for manifest evolution and the disposition of all created life. Thus the "order of the disposition" is an adequate title for Kether. The 'curtain' or Veil is that of Form-life. Form is the curtain that hides (though at the same time reveals) the Life-essence, but it is almost pure Force at this point for the 11th Path "is the essence of that curtain". At these supernal levels the form is very attenuated in comparison with the dense level of being to which our Personality consciousnesses are accustomed,—but it is none the less potent for that. An incorrect form or misapplied force at a higher level of manifestation will produce ever increasing distortions as its effects come

down the planes, for each plane controls the one below it.

3. We have, then, the attribution to this Path of the Element of Air, which is a good symbol for the Spirit as it is unconfined and permeates all things as well as extending physically to a great height, (—or more properly its Ring-Pass-Not is of greater extension than that of the liquid and dense forms of planetary matter.) Even more extended is the aether, (and the physical plane is divided esoterically into solid, liquid and gas and four levels of aether), and hence we have the title of the Tarot Trump—Spirit of Aether.

4. Again it should not be thought that, being an analogue of Air, the Spirit is an abstract, tenuous, ineffective thing. Far from it. Like the air of the physical world, it can be taken for granted and even ignored in spite of it being essential to life—but it is capable of making itself felt, just as physical air can become a hurricane or a tornado. Also the air is a great disperser and so we have a link with the Great Unmanifest which attenuates things into non-existence from a manifest point of view. In this effect it is in line with the action of God the Disintegrator, the great Fourth Aspect of God. Earth can confine, Water dissolve, and Fire transform, but it is predominately Air that is the great disperser. This we shall have to consider in the context of the Four Suits of the Lesser Arcana.

5. The 11th Path, like all the Paths, can be trodden two ways. Its ascent is the final approach to Union with God—leading to manifest dissolution. Those who walk with God, like Enoch, are not. Its descent is the first section of the Descent of Power symbolised Qabalistically by the Lightning Flash. It thus represents first beginnings.

6. The Tarot Trump is called The Fool and is perhaps the profoundest symbol of the whole Tarot. The Fool is a great archetype that has always played a major part in folk tradition. It is embedded in the group subconsciousness of almost every race, whether it appears as the medieval Court Jester, the harlequinade of the Commedia dell' Arte, the puppet Punch and Judy, or the clowns of the modern

circus. In the Arthurian cycle there is even a knightly fool, Sir Dagonet, the jester of King Arthur. Again, the Fool and blood, the Fool and tragedy, as for example in Petrushka or the perennial opera I Paggliaci, is something which strikes home deep into the subconscious mind. This is a quality which can be caught by comics of genius such as Charles Chaplin or Jaques Tati. Again, there were the Fool's Days of medieval times when the whole court was turned topsy-turvey, a tradition still carried on in some armed services today at Christmas. The idea even entered the Church, with the boy-bishop, and considerable attendant vulgarities and blasphemies. For such things to be tolerated and submitted to a deep level of unconscious motivation must be in force.

7. The Fool is also an object of some respect—he is a creature of paradox—being at the same time wise as well as a fool. The highest example of this element of paradox and hidden meanings and motivations is in the Third Act of King Lear. Shakespeare certainly created some marvellous fools in his time but here he surpassed himself. In the situation of a foolish King going genuinely mad, accompanied by his Fool, full of double-edged jokes and saws, protected by a disguised Duke of Kent whom he has banished and is posing as a rather uncouth serving man, and meeting in a hut on a heath in a wild storm Edgar, heir to Gloucester, betrayed by his bastard brother on a false charge, and posing as a madman, we have the quintessence of the archetype and probably most of its possible combinations. The implications and undertones of this scene defy all critical analysis—which is perhaps to be expected when great art is coupled with deep archetypal elements.

8. All this may help to show how difficult it is to make an adequate analysis of this Tarot card. True to type it has frequently been misplaced in past elucidations of the Tarot system, throwing out all or most of the other attributions and so reducing the system to varying degrees of chaos. And of course, in another sense, this 11th Path, the Path of

the Fool, does lead to Chaos—the Great Unmanifest, the Vast Paradox, that which is and yet is not.

9. To put the meaning of the card in its simplest terms— which is rather like reducing the play King Lear to the statement "There was once a king who gave away his kingdom"—it signifies the innocence of the Spirit coming forth into manifestation completely inexperienced yet with the wisdom of the Cosmos behind it. This Unmanifest past is symbolised by the bag carried over the shoulder. Also the fact that evolution is cyclic, that the Form Universe has been used before by previous civilisations or Swarms of Divine Sparks, is shown by the broken obelisk—the remains of previous evolutions.

10. There is also emphasis on the transformation of all values in the shape of the dog, wolf or tiger attacking the Fool, to which he pays no attention whatsoever. That is, the values of the Spirit are not the same values of those of the ordinary world. There is a literary treatment of this theme in Dostoevsky's 'The Idiot': Prince Muishkin is an almost Christ-like figure, a man of complete innocence, yet who appears to be an idiot in the context of the ordinary social world. After all, in the myopic values of the mundane world, Christ was a fool to let himself be crucified when he might have averted it by a miracle—or less spectacularly by running away, or simply by keeping his mouth shut in the first place.

11. Finally there is the French title of the card which we ought to consider—Le Mat. This is commonly thought to be derived from the Italian Il Matto, the madman, but the word Le Mat applies also to chess as the mate or checkmate. Checkmate is derived from the Persian, and means "the king is dead". This offers another line of interpretation. On the ascent of the Path, the King of the Round Table of Chokmah, the fully evolved Spirit, now returns to the Un-manifest; in short, as far as manifestation is concerned, he is dead.

12. However, we must also bear in mind the opposite

trend of the Path, into manifestation, the key to which is Aleph—the very first letter of the Hebrew alphabet, the beginning of things as well as the ending. This letter bears the symbol of the Ox, the most earthy of symbolic beasts, which shows us that, however abstract our studies of the nature of the Spirit become, the Spirit's aim is rooted in Earth, the ox is a beast of the plough. It is no coincidence that the highly important constellation of the Great Bear, Arthur's Wain, is also known as The Plough. This again leads us into Cosmic considerations but they are in no way more important for us than the more mundane symbolism of the plough, the tiller of the Earth to make it bring forth fruit. This is our immediate and paramount task, the civilisation of Earth. And he who takes his hand from the plough of his immediate Earthly duty, (which is a Cosmic and Spiritual duty also, however much familiarity may tend to breed contempt), will never by that act attain to his heavenly home in the stars. The furrow awaits his tilling—and until it be tilled, and the seed sown, and the harvest garnered and gathered in—his place remains in Earth, with the added burden of rooting out the weeds and breaking up the clodded sods brought about by his own neglect and spiritual defection.

NOTES ON THE DESIGN OF TRUMP 0

The Marseilles version shows a man in ragged motley, a staff in his right hand, and a pole in his left from which depends a bag over his right shoulder. An indeterminate animal jumps up at him from behind. Wirth has described the animal as a white lynx though Papus calls it a dog, which is the usual interpretation, as is also the fact that the dog is hostile to the Fool. On Wirth's card the Fool is not ragged but in his text Papus describes him so. Wirth also shows a crocodile lying in wait behind a broken obelisk, a belt of zodiacal plaques about the Fool's waist, and a single flower growing nearby instead of the conventional shrubs of the exoteric Tarot. Papus says that the Fool should be walking towards a precipice wherein the crocodile waits to devour him. Paul Christian, a mid-nineteenth century French commentator and supporter of the Egyptian origin of the cards, thinks the Fool ought to be blind but agrees on the crocodile and obelisk. Knapp follows this tradition, the Fool being hood-winked, (and bareheaded), but shows the obelisk with attendant crocodile on the river bank, not at a precipice. Eliphas Levi considered the attacking animal to be a tiger.

Waite broke with this tradition in depicting a young innocent in gorgeous attire walking over a precipice with a domesticated dog bounding joyfully beside him. The Fool holds a rose in his left hand and a curiously embroidered wallet is slung on a pole over his right shoulder and held in his right hand. He walks over a precipice with the Sun shining behind him and there is a vista of mountain peaks in the distance. Case follows Waite, and suggests that the figure is androgynous. Case, who rightly leaves nothing to chance, describes minutely the significance of the design of the Fool's clothing—a system of spoked wheels with trefoils, a star, a crescent, a circle with a triple flame, JHVH traced in the folds of his shirt, and so on. It is impossible to deal at length with such details here but reference is recommended to Case's book 'The Tarot'. Both he and Waite give the Fool a wreath with a feather in it.

The Golden Dawn Fool differed radically from both these versions. It was considered that though the traditional design was very good in its way, it obscured the deeper meaning of the card. In colours suggestive of early dawn on a Spring day they depicted a naked child under a rose tree, at the same time reaching up to the yellow roses and holding a grey wolf in check. A few moments' thought will show that the idea behind is similar to the traditional card in spite of the superficially great difference in symbolism. This way of mind-working must be used in considering all the variations of Tarot design in order to get the best results from one's efforts. It may be also readily deduced that the Waite/Case version is a compromise between the traditional and the Golden Dawn design.

Crowley had originally considered the Fool to be a bearded ancient shown in profile, no doubt with reference to the Magical Image of Kether. He suggested that he should be laughing; that the bag, carried in the traditional manner, should be a sphere containing Illusion; and that his staff should be 463 lines long. He favoured a lion and dragon at the Fool's feet, attacking *or* caressing. When he came to collaborate on the Harris Tarot the result was somewhat different. The Fool, a combination of the Green Man of Spring, Parsifal, Harpocrates and Hercules, straddled the whole card, with horns of Bacchus and the Minor Arcana accoutrements. A crocodile was shown lurking below him and also a tiger, attacking or caressing, while between his legs was the lotus of Harpocrates. Other symbolism shown was the Dionysian pine cone, grapes and ivy, a spiral rainbow, a vulture of Maat, dove of Venus, butterfly, winged globe with twin serpents, twin infants and a radiant Sun. He described the whole picture as "a glyph of radiant light."

The 'Egyptian' version shows a blind man, two bags on a pole balanced over his left shoulder, a Bes-headed black staff, broken obelisk and crocodile. In the background is an eclipse of the Sun and below the main picture two crocodiles surmounted by a head of Bes, the buffoon of the Egyptian gods. The card is numbered XXII.

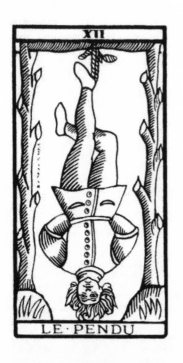

XII

LE·PENDU

XIII

XIIII

TEMPERANCE

XV

LE·DIABLE

SECTION FOUR
THE TAROT

Part I
The Greater Arcana

The Greater Arcana

1. It may seem needless to devote a chapter to the Tarot Trumps when we have already extensively dealt with their symbolism. However, we have seen how far apart ideas of design can be and there is also diversity of opinion over the true attributions. The system used in this book, although in the main line of the Western Tradition, differs in some respects from all previous ones, so it may be well to make a short historical examination of other peoples' ideas.

2. The only justification for any system, of course, lies in internal evidence, the ease with which the attributed symbols fit together. A symbolic key, like a physical one, should fit its lock and open the door without any forcing. With the Qabalah absolute accuracy is difficult, for many keys fit more than one lock and many locks take more than one key, so in sorting out the eighty-eight locks and keys of the Paths, the Hebrew letters, the astrological signs, and the Tarot Trumps, there is plenty of room for variety of opinion.

3. Serious attention was first drawn to the Tarot by the French scholar Court de Gébelin in the eighth volume of his huge work 'Le Monde Primitif' published between 1773 and 1782. In those days Ancient Egypt was regarded in much the same light that the planet Venus is now. It was a place mysterious, too remote to know much about and yet just near enough to excite speculation and curiosity. It was not until 1799 that the Rosetta stone was found. This allowed the hieroglyphics to be translated and opened the way to archeological science and the specialised branch of Egyptology. So Court de Gébelin started more than he realised

when he ventured the opinion that the Tarot was in the
beginning an Ancient Egyptian book of magic. By this somewhat unscientific guess he stimulated an interest in Egypt
and in the Tarot, both of which had been neglected for a
long, long time.

4. As far as Tarot research is concerned he was followed
by a barber by the name of Aliette. In a series of books
between 1783 and 1787, writing under the name of Etteila,
he treated the cards from a mystical point of view. Aliette
became a very fashionable fortune teller and in the words
of a later student of the system, Eliphas Levi, he "possessed a highly trained intuition and great persistence of
will, though his fancy exceeded his judgment." He undertook to restore to their original form the Tarot figures which
had been poorly reproduced in Court de Gébelin's book but
in so doing he added many dubious modifications of his own.
He did sense a link between the Tarot, astrology and the
Qabalah but most of his reforms were subsequently discarded by 19th century occultists.

5. The most important figure of the mid-ninteenth
century is another Frenchman, Alphonse Louis Constant,
who wrote under the pseudonym of Eliphas Levi. His work
which bears most directly on the Tarot was 'Dogme et
Rituel de la Haute Magie' of 1854. Its English translation
is known as 'Transcendental Magic'. In this book he places
the Zero Trump, The Fool, between the Trumps XX and
XXI in the sequence of the Tarot Major Arcana. His list of
attributions between the Trumps and the Hebrew letters
thus runs as follows:

I — Juggler — *Aleph*	XII — Hanged Man — *Lamed*
II — Female Pope — *Beth*	XIII —Death — *Mem*
III — Empress — *Gimel*	XIV — Temperance — *Nun*
IV — Emperor — *Daleth*	XV — Devil — *Samekh*
V — Pope — *Heh*	XVI — Tower — *Ayin*
VI — Vice & Virtue — *Vau*	XVII — Star — *Peh*
VII — Chariot — *Zain*	XVIII — Moon — *Tzaddi*

VIII — Justice — *Cheth*	XIX — Sun — *Qoph*
IX — Hermit — *Teth*	XX — Judgment — *Resh*
X — Wheel of Fortune — *Yod*	O — Fool — *Shin*
XI — Strength — *Caph*	XXI — Universe — *Tau*

Thus all the Tarot Trump/Hebrew letter attributions with the exception of the last—Universe/Tau—are at variance with the system we use in this book.

6. Whether it be right or wrong Levi's published system of attributions has been followed by French occultism down to the present day. The attributions were consolidated in Levi's form by Dr. Gerard Encausse who, under the pseudonym of Papus, published 'Le Tarot des Bohemians' in 1889 using revised Tarot designs by Oswald Wirth. Wirth's cards have Levi's attributions marked upon them.

7. However, the system used by Papus to elucidate the meaning of the Tarot bears no reference to the Tree of life. He uses a septenary system which, in the words of A. E. Waite, who wrote the preface to the English edition, "is arbitrary enough, as it is also contradictory enough". In Waite's opinion "he does what he can, making a brave struggle, but the result is not convincing". Waite further goes on to say that his difficulty arises because, "he does not know what to do with the card which is numbered 0 in the Major Trump series, and his septenary distribution leaves him therefore in the lurch, while his allocation to the Hebrew letters outside those of the Divine Name is also open to question."

8. Here Waite speaks for the main line of the Western Tradition in England, which stems in its modern form from the Order of the Golden Dawn. The system used in this book, (with one or two small modifications), is that which was apparently originated with this Order. The Order was founded in 1886 allegedly as a result of three men, Dr. Wynn Westcott, Dr. Woodford and Dr. Woodman, finding some cipher manuscripts which gave instructions on how to bestow occult initiation by means of ritual. It soon after came under the sole headship of S. L. MacGregor Mathers,

author of 'The Kabbalah Unveiled', a translation of Knorr von Rosenrath's 'Kabbalah Denudata'.

9. According to Aleister Crowley, who became a member of this society in later years, among the cipher manuscripts was an attribution of the Tarot Trumps to the letters of the Hebrew alphabet. The manuscripts, he says, were alleged to date from the early nineteenth century and on one page was a note, apparently in the handwriting of Eliphas Levi, who, Crowley thinks, would probably have seen the manuscript when he visited Bulwer Lytton in England.

10. Dr. Wynn Westcott in the preface to his translation of Levi's 'Sanctum Regnum' (1896) goes even further regarding the date of the manuscript. Speaking of himself in the third person he writes: "he has seen a manuscript page of cypher about 150 years old which has a different attribution, (i. e. from Levi's version G.K.) and one which has been found by several occult students, well known to him, to satisfy all the conditions required by occult science."

11. These occult students were no doubt his fellow leading members of the Golden Dawn. Their attributions run as follows:

O — Fool — *Aleph*	XI — Justice — *Lamed*
I — Magician — *Beth*	XII — Hanged Man — *Mem*
II — High Priestess — *Gimel*	XIII — Death — *Nun*
III — Empress — *Daleth*	XIV — Temperance — *Samekh*
IV — Emperor — *Heh*	XV — Devil — *Ayin*
V — Hierophant — *Vau*	XVI — Blasted Tower — *Peh*
VI — Lovers — *Zain*	XVII — Star — *Tzaddi*
VII — Chariot — *Cheth*	XVIII — Moon — *Qoph*
VIII — Fortitude — *Teth*	XIX — Sun — *Resh*
IX — Hermit — *Yod*	XX — Judgment — *Shin*
X — Wheel of Fortune — *Kaph*	XXI — Universe — *Tau*

12. The Fool is placed at the beginning of the sequence of Trumps thus causing all the attributions except the last to differ from Levi's. Another change is the transfer of Trumps

VIII and XI. When the Trumps are placed in order upon the Paths of the Tree of Life in their traditional numbered sequence, Trump VIII, Justice, falls upon the 19th Path, whose astrological sign is Leo. Trump XI, Strength, (or Fortitude), falls upon the 22nd Path, whose astrological sign is Libra. This is obviously incorrect so the Order of the Golden Dawn, or the unknown author of the cypher manuscript, changed them about.

13. Not only did they change them about but they changed their numbering. Justice was made Trump XI and Strength was made Trump VIII in order to preserve the sequence. This modification has been followed by most subsequent esoteric packs. This seems unfortunate, for it would surely have been better not to have interfered with the actual numbering of the Trumps but simply to have changed the cards about when applying them to the Paths of the Tree. It was not realised that there is an esoteric significance in the numbering of the Tarot when the Tarot is considered as an entity in itself and not as a tributary to the Tree of Life.

14. Crowley is of the opinion that Levi knew the Golden Dawn attributions all along and that he published an incorrect version so as not to break the oath of secrecy he took on Initiation. This may seem far-fetched these days but MacGregor Mathers had done precisely the same thing and A. E. Waite never openly admitted his support of the Golden Dawn attributions until 1923, when, apparently, he had abandoned them for a new and unspecified system. If this state of mind was at all general in nineteenth century occultism—and it probably was—Levi may well have given deliberately false attributions also, but the evidence is only circumstantial.

15. Crowley contends however that it can be proved by analysis of Levi's works. Paul Case agrees on this point, saying that Levi's attribution of The Fool to the letter Shin suggests that he knew the correct version. The letter Shin refers symbolically to Spirit, as does the letter Aleph,

so, according to Case's argument, Levi, not wishing to give the true attribution, gave one which hints at the correct version, namely that The Fool is a card of Spirit and thus ought to be allocated to Aleph. Case also believes that Levi was too intelligent to believe in a system "so patently absurd" as the one he published.

16. All this is open to conjecture, for Levi also mentions quite specifically that Trump I, The Magician or Juggler, is attributed to Aleph because the figure on the card is standing in a position which suggests the letter Aleph. (It could equally be a swastika of course.) What is more, had Levi known of the cypher manuscript it is reasonable to expect that he too would have counterchanged Trumps VIII and XI, which, in fact, he did not do. However, his remarks on the design of Trumps XVII and III seem to indicate an agreement with the Golden Dawn, (See Notes on Trump Design.) though the case is by no means conclusive for his idea of Quintessence of the Triad for Trump III could have been derived from its number and not from its position on the Tree; and the link with Venus of Trump XVII could have been arrived at from the number of smaller stars on the card and not from the Golden Dawn allocation to the 28th Path which leads to Netzach, Sephirah of Venus.

17. The evidence of the cypher manuscript is dubious. Crowley and Westcott give very different estimates of its age, and Waite even goes so far as to suggest that it was post-1860. Crowley again is the only one who mentions a note "which seems to be" in Levi's handwriting. Again, the tradition is that the manuscript emanated from Germany as it contained the address of a certain Fraulein Sprengel, with whom Westcott corresponded and obtained permission to start the Order of the Golden Dawn. If this is the case then Crowley's conjecture that Bulwer Lytton owned it and showed it to Eliphas Levi is a doubtful one.

18. However, whatever the origin of the manuscript, (and the traditional story might well be a cover for an

inner plane communication received perhaps through Mathers) the Golden Dawn attributions have been accepted since their inception by Crowley, (with slight modifications), Regardie and Paul Case. Manly P. Hall has remained neutral though the cards associated with him designed by J. A. Knapp follow Levi's attributions. A. E. Waite has hedged himself about with so many dark hints and apparent contradictions that it is difficult to know precisely what he does favour but close examination of his texts shows that he certainly accepted it at one time though he may have abandoned it since.

19. At any rate, MacGregor Mathers was sufficiently satisfied with the system of attributions to add a footnote to 'Book T' of the Golden Dawn Knowledge Papers, (the one dealing with the Tarot), "In all of this I have not only transcribed the symbolism, but have tested, studied, compared, and examined it both clairvoyantly and in other ways. The result of these has been to show how *absolutely* correct the symbolism of the Book T is, and how exactly it represents the occult Forces of the Universe."

20. Of other former students of the Golden Dawn, Israel Regardie says in 'A Garden of Pomegranates' (1932), "The Tarot trumps furnish a complete set of symbols, but the great difficulty hitherto experienced in their attribution to the 22 letters of the Hebrew Alphabet is that these trump cards are numbered from I to XXI, accompanied by another card marked O, which has always been a stumbling block, being attributed by various people to various letters of the alphabet, depending—apparently—on their whim at any particular moment. It should be quite obvious that the only logical place for this Zero card is antecedent to I, and when so placed the cards assume a definite sequential meaning, profoundly explanatory of the letters."

21. And Crowley, in 'The Book of Thoth' (1944) says: "The secret of the initiated interpretation, which makes the whole meaning of the Trumps luminous, is simply to

put this card marked O in its natural place, where any mathematician would have put it, in front of the number One."

22. Waite's support of the Golden Dawn attributions is evident from examination of his Tarot designs though he never admitted the fact until his Introduction to Stenring's 'Book of Formation' (1923). A passage from his 'Pictorial Key to the Tarot' (1911) however, gives his real ideas on The Fool: "In conclusion as to this part, I will give these further indications regarding the Fool, which is the most speaking of all the symbols. He signifies the journey outward, the state of the first emanation, the graces and passivity of the spirit. His wallet is inscribed with dim signs to shew that many subconscious memories are stored up in the soul." All this, including a double meaning on the word 'speaking', ("In the beginning was the Word"), hints pretty broadly at the 11th Path and the letter Aleph.

23. On the other hand, Manly P. Hall in 'An Encyclopedic Outline of Masonic, Hermetic, Qabbalistic and Rosicrucian Symbolical Philosophy' (1928) cites the argument used previously by Waite in his preface to Stenring's book. "Since Aleph has the numerical value of 1, its assignment to the zero card is equivalent to the statement that zero is equal to the letter Aleph and therefore synonymous with the number 1." This argument does not necessarily follow. To begin with, the numerological attributions assigned to each letter serve a different purpose from the numeration of the Trumps. The numerological attributions (See table in Vol. I.) are for calculating the potencies of Hebrew names. The numbering of the Tarot Trumps, (always in Roman figures except by Wirth and his followers), indicates the sequence of the cards only. So if we try to amalgamate the two separate numbering series, designed for different purposes, we must expect an absurd result.

24. Even so, if we examine the argument a little further, we see that it can only hold good up to Trump X and the 10th letter. The numerological series runs 1, 2, 3, 4, 5, 6,

7, 8, 9, 10, 20, 30, etc. If the letter Yod, whose number is 10, has to have Trump X, the next letter, Kaph, 20, might presumably have Trump XX, but after that we are stuck. There remain Trumps XI to XIX and XXI without letters and the letters numbered 30-90 and 100-400, to say nothing of the final letter forms, 500-900, without Tarot Trumps.

25. The illustrations that appear with Manly P. Hall's essay are based on Wirth's designs and executed by J. A. Knapp. Knapp however, issued a version of his own the following year with an accompanying text by Manly P. Hall. These designs have the Hebrew letters and numbers printed on them and follow Levi's attributions, so Manly P. Hall tends to be associated with this method. This is not necessarily so, for in the text that accompanies the cards he makes quite plain that those who do not agree with the attributions on the cards are welcome to ignore them; and in the 'Encyclopedia' essay he states that Mr. Paul Case's system is, in his opinion, superior to most. Case follows the attributions of the Golden Dawn, which, he says, he worked out independently.

26. This does not mean that Hall approves of this version of the attributions either, for in his view "efforts to assign a Hebrew letter to each Tarot Trump in sequence produce an effect far from satisfying." He thinks it debatable that there is any relation between the two symbol sequences, and even if there were, he thinks it unlikely that the Tarots are in their correct original order.

27. He then goes on to cite Court de Gébelin, who assigned the Zero Trump to Ain Soph, (a very astute attribution), and suggests that a possible arrangement of the Trumps is after the Bembine Tablet of Isis, with 0 as the central Creative Power, surrounded by seven triads of manifesting divinities. He also puts forward the suggestion that The Fool is extraneous to the numbered Trumps and that as this would destroy the numerical analogy between the Hebrew letters and the cards there may be one Trump missing. This, he suggests, could be a card called The

Elements which has become split up into the 56 cards of the Minor Arcana.

28. These are interesting speculations and probably no-one would be wasting his time who experiments with them. But before searching for new cards, missing links, or similar brilliancies, it is best to have a good grounding in the traditional system. Without this there is grave risk of easy superficiality and the inability to judge whether a new consideration is indeed an important contribution to the whole field of study or simply a diverting coincidence of little real import.

29. There is one change in the traditional attributions however since first they became generally known. This change is the transfer of Trumps IV and XVII, The Emperor and The Star, and is a modification put forward by Aleister Crowley. Crowley is, in many respects, the black sheep of the modern esoteric family but he knew his Qabalah. While a change in magical tradition of this nature should be regarded with great circumspection, an examination of all the factors involved seems to indicate that Crowley was right. Hence the change has been followed in this book.

30. The story begins with Crowley's only experience of direct voice mediumship. This took place over three consecutive days, one hour per day, when he was staying in Cairo in 1904. The result of this three hour session was a strange script—Liber Legis, or The Book of the Law—which formed the basis of much of his later teaching.

31. The script is reproduced together with the circumstances of its reception in 'The Equinox' Vol. I. Nos. 7 & 10 (March 1912 and September 1913) and also in 'The Equinox of the Gods' (1936). A full analysis of it is impossible in the present context and it must suffice to say that it is of a most inflammatory and imperious tone, as if dictated by a mystical Nietzsche, and contains much that is enigmatic, a certain amount of rare wisdom, and some material of doubtful worth. On the credit side, it contained those three

main axioms of Crowley's, which are great spiritual truths if understood aright: "Do what thou wilt shall be the whole of the law." "Love is the law, love under will." and "Every man and every woman is a star."

32. Crowley maintained that it was a contact with the Masters of Wisdom and that every word in it was of profound truth. There may well be something in this but the communication does not seem to be that of a Master because of its high handed tone. However this does not discount the possibility that a Master was responsible for its transmission. The Master Morya and the Master Koot Hoomi were definitely in contact with H. P. Blavatsky but their communications were frequently distorted by her mediumship, consciously or unconsciously. Much of the renowned Mahatma letters are filled with evidence of petty spite and a preoccupation with personalities that is completely uncharacteristic of the Masters of Wisdom.

33. When a Master first makes contact with a medium it is rare that he can do it without an intermediary—there is too great a gap between the consciousness of the Master and the consciousness of the medium. A higher type of mediumship is needed than is commonly found. For example, when Dion Fortune first contacted the Masters at Glastonbury in 1922 the contact was first made by a lesser Master, one, in fact, who had very recently been in incarnation, having been killed in the Great War. He was able to forge the initial link which was later utilised by the Greater Masters to put through that abstruse book of teaching 'The Cosmic Doctrine' from a remote inner plane level.

34. It would seem that a similar process occurred with Crowley. In 1904 Crowley was a very bright young man who had passed through several grades of the Order of the Golden Dawn, though this society had already fallen on evil days owing apparently to mismanagement and internal dissensions. It is possible that the Hierarchy felt that it was worth the effort to try to establish direct contact with

Crowley so that the guttering light of the Western Mystery Tradition in England should not go out altogether. It would have been difficult to tell at this time whether he would run off the rails or no, but anyway it seems that the opportunity was considered worth the risk.

35. Crowley was travelling extensively throughout the world at this time, picking up mystical knowledge where he could, and it was quite logical that the highly technical process of a direct contact with him should be attempted while he was in Egypt—the centre from which the Western Mystery Tradition largely stems. The psychic stresses in this region where highly potent ritual magic had been practised for thousands of years would make such an operation easier.

36. It was indeed a tremendous feat that was to be attempted—for a Master operating on high abstract mental levels to concentrate enough force down the planes so as to first attract the attention of, and then pass a message to, a man on the physical plane who had never practised clairaudience before. Nevertheless it was done, and it would seem that in order to do it a technical device known as a 'magical body' was used. That is, what probably happened, *(and it must be realised that all this is conjecture based upon circumstantial evidence only),* was that the Master passed the teaching through an inner plane intermediary who used as a vehicle of etheric manifestation the 'magical body', (a co-ordinated system of psychic stresses like a disembodied Personality which can be used or discarded and 'stored' at will), of an Ancient Egyptian priest.

37. This would account for the hieratic imperious tone of the script, for the original message would be coloured by this magical body in much the same way that a beam of light would be coloured by a stained lens. And as, in order to overcome the technical difficulties, the magical body would have to be one of considerable power, so would the message tend to be biased on the power side. If we add to this bias the possibilities of distortions and interpolations by Crowley's subconscious mind then it will be seen that

in order to interpret the script it will be necessary to try to get at the spirit behind it, rather than to take the letter of it at face value.

38. This, it is evident, Crowley failed to do. He accepted the whole thing literally—including heady references to himself as the prophet for the New Age—references of a type which any medium of even the slightest experience would suspect as being an interpolation of the subconscious mind. To put the matter more occultly, Crowley could not handle the force that was directed onto him by such a contact and consequently lost his magical equilibrium—with the usual result of a gross inflation of the Personality's ideas of its own importance. From accounts of MacGregor Mathers' behaviour in the Order of the Golden Dawn it would seem that he too may have experienced this trouble. It is one of the occupational hazards of occultism and serves to give the subject a bad name with uncommitted observers who naturally have little patience with the disproportionate crowing of occult cocks on their own esoteric dunghills.

39. However, Crowley's biography is another story. What is of relevance here is that in the script there occurred the phrase, "All these old letters of my book are right, but Tzaddi is not the Star." On the Tree of Life Tzaddi is the Hebrew letter assigned to the 28th Path, and using the Golden Dawn system of attributions, the associated Tarot Trump is The Star.

40. Here was a problem. There is no question of Tzaddi not being the Hebrew letter of the 28th Path so the thing to be changed was the Tarot Trump. Yet up till then the current attribution had been accepted, not only by the leading members of the Golden Dawn but also by Crowley himself, who had studied the Tarot extensively in its connection with the Tree of Life and been perfectly satisfied that the Golden Dawn attributions were correct. The distinction to be made was therefore a subtle one.

41. It was many years before Crowley hit upon a solution

to the problem, which was that The Star should be counter-changed with The Emperor just as Justice is counter-changed with Strength. The main authority for this change is a glyph known as the Moebius Ribbon, which, with the Zodiacal signs placed upon it, counterchanges two pairs of them. (See Fig. 6). Leo and Libra revolve about Virgo and Aries and Aquarius revolve about Pisces.

42. In these pairs it is not the astrological signs them-selves which change their positions on the Tree of Life but the Tarot Trumps associated with them. The astrological signs are keyed in with the Hebrew letters. Thus in the first pair Strength and Justice are counterchanged and in the second pair The Emperor and The Star; The Emperor goes to the 28th Path and the Star replaces it on the 15th.

43. Unfortunately, when he made this counterchange in 'The Book of Thoth' Crowley made the faux pas of chang-ing the astrological signs as well so that Aries is on the 28th Path and Aquarius on the 15th. How Crowley should have come to do this is uncertain but an examination of his design of Trump IV suggests a combination of inde-cision, and intractability. (See Notes on the Design of Trump IV)

44. Actually the change of Path and consequently astrolog-ical sign for each Trump is not so revolutionary as might at first appear. The main superficial objection stems from the fact that Trump IV, The Emperor, contains Aries sym-bolism and therefore would go most unhappily on the 28th Path and the sign Aquarius. Reference to the old Mar-seilles Tarot, however, will show no trace of Aries sym-bolism on the card—the fleur-de-lys sceptre, suggestive of Aries perhaps, was Wirth's introduction and all the rams' heads came even later, from Waite. On the Mar-seilles card the sceptre is a Venus one. This is very sig-nificant. The 28th Path leads from Yesod, (whose Magical Image as the Strong Man, suggestive of The Emperor), to Netzach, the Sephirah whose Mundane Chakra is Venus. Furthermore, the Emperor is the consort of the Empress

and she is another Venus figure being on the 14th Path—Daleth—Venus.

45. However, the real justification must be based on how it appeals to the intuition of each individual student. Any who are equipped to disagree with the attributions we use in this book will be capable of reconstituting their own version of the relevant chapters. Indeed, such will have no great need of this book in the first place.

46. It may be asked—if the traditional attribution was wrong—why it should not have been spotted before, by Crowley or MacGregor Mathers and his associates, or subsequently by other commentators following the Golden Dawn tradition. The answer to this is that the change is quite a subtle one. The incorrect placing of Strength and Justice was obvious and so they were counterchanged quite empirically. It was assumed that the numbering of the Tarot cards had become distorted. The counterchanging of The Star and The Emperor is less obvious, particularly as they counterchange onto parallel Paths on the same side of the Tree, so that one is an analogue at a different level of the other. Indeed a fair case could be made for retaining the traditional Golden Dawn attributions though the Yetziratic Texts and Esoteric Titles seem to support the change.

47. When one gets down to basics the only reliable attributions on the Tree of Life are the Hebrew names and letters. All others are later additions to the system and subject to experiment and discussion. Even the astrological signs are open to question though, as it happens, there seems to be little modern controversy on this subject. A casual reference to the Sepher Yetzirah will show that, apart from the general principle of the Elements, Planets and Zodiacal Signs being allocated to the Mother, Double and Single letters respectively, no definite sequence of attributions is given except for Aleph-Air, Mem-Water and Shin-Fire. Medieval commentators gave many varying accounts of the 'true' attributions.

48. A similar situation holds with the Tarot, and by its very nature the pictorial symbols can be interpreted in the light of various contexts. As there are links between various aspects of life so are there links between parts of the Tree of Life. Some symbols can be placed in more than one place. The Planets, for example, have links not only with certain Paths but also with the Sephiroth. Again, The Emperor, to take an example which happens to be under discussion, could, with varying degrees of validity be placed upon Kether, Chokmah, Chesed, Geburah, Tiphareth or Yesod, to say nothing of any of the Paths. There is a considerable degree of tolerance in the meaning of the Tarot images, particularly as most of the finer points of symbolism have been knocked off in its history as a fortune-telling or gaming device. The best versions we have are very corrupt and considerable intuition has to be used to ascertain their possible original form. This, however, is not necessarily a tremendous handicap to us, for, as Oswald Wirth says in his 'Le Symbolisme Hermetique': "By their very nature the symbols must remain elastic, vague and ambiguous, like the sayings of an oracle. Their role is to unveil mysteries, leaving the mind all its freedom."

49. We have reproduced in this book the Marseilles Tarot, for though crude, it is the exoteric Tarot generally considered to be the purest. It represents the cards as they have been passed down to us, untampered with by later occultists. Kurt Seligman in his 'The Mirror of Magic' makes a telling point when he says how curious it is so many occultists believe that a traditional system such as the Tarot should have perpetuated itself through millennia, when these same occultists are ready to distort and add their own cirlicues to it on the slightest pretext, seeming to forget that their own bad habits must have existed before them. The Marseilles Tarot is also devoid of the worst exoteric extravagences that caused some old Tarots to have up to forty Major Trumps, including representations of arts, sciences, virtues, vices, signs of the Zodiac and so

on. Furthermore, Oswald Wirth's designs were based on these, and as he was the first in the modern field to produce a well known esoteric pack most other designers have built on the foundations he laid.

50. Wirth's designs were published in 1889 and received support from the contemporary French occultists Stanislas de Guaita, Gerard Encausse and others. In their symbolism, though based on the Marseilles Tarot, they follow closely the ideas suggested by Eliphas Levi in his books. Most of Levi's ideas are in his 'Dogme et Rituel' together with two plates of his conception of Trumps XV and VII, The Devil and The Chariot. He never got around to drawing up a full set for publication.

51. Contemporary with Wirth's pack would have been the Golden Dawn version but which at this time was withheld from general knowledge and even to this day has never been published. Descriptive details of parts of it are to be found in Crowley's 'Equinox' and Regardie's 'The Golden Dawn.'

52. The next widely known published pack after Wirth's was the 'Rider' pack, so called after their London publishers. These were designed by A. E. Waite and drawn by Miss Pamela Coleman Smith—both members of the now reconstituted Order of the Golden Dawn. This was in 1911. The designs generally follow the traditional pattern but included several innovations that show the influence of the Golden Dawn system of attributions. Apart from the rather crude draughtsmanship it remains one of the best of esoteric packs.

53. Matters rested thus until 1929 when an American version was published by J. A. Knapp in collaboration with Manly P. Hall. In the essay by Manly P. Hall which accompanied it was announced the intention to produce a version of the Tarot based on the original diagrams appearing in Court de Gébelin's 'Le Monde Primitif'. Furthermore they claimed to have added "all that has been

demonstrated as essential from the more modern packs," used colourings "as an effort to emphasise the original symbolic meanings of the cards," and introduced small hieroglyphical figures in order to "link the card with the philosophy of the ancient Qabalah."

54. These two, if anybody, were certainly qualified to attempt such a task, having just finished collaboration on the enormous tome 'An Encyclopedic Outline of Masonic, Hermetic, Qabbalistic and Rosicrucian Symbolical Philosophy' which is perhaps the most comprehensive book on occult subjects ever published. However, the resulting Tarot cards are somehow disappointing. They are in fact what one might have expected from two men who knew probably more than anyone else of their time on occultism in general but not enough about the Tarot in particular. The numeration follows Wirth and the introduction of extraneous hieroglyphic figures is of debatable value, but as Manly P. Hall says, all these additional attributions, if one does not agree with them, can be ignored. The designs are in colour but in spite of this—or more probably, because of it—they do not appeal to the eye. Use of colour is terribly difficult on Tarot cards.

55. About this time another commentator on the Tarot was making his presence felt, Paul Foster Case. He had at first used the Rider version of the Tarot but eventually set to and designed his own with the artistic assistance of Jessie Burnes Parke. In Case's view, his artist followed a little too closely the tricks of style of Pamela Coleman Smith but nevertheless a fine pack resulted—this time openly using the Golden Dawn attributions. With certain exceptions Case followed Waite closely, and the general effect is an all-round improvement upon the Rider pack. Case's book 'The Tarot' has long been the best available elementary text upon the subject too.

56. All the packs hitherto mentioned are continuations of the medieval traditional designs. In 1944 Aleister Crowley

published 'The Book of Thoth' in which were Tarot designs deliberately cast into new forms. It was an attempt to create a modern Tarot as opposed to the usual medieval imitations, which, in Crowley's view, were "gross, senseless, pitifully grotesque" and also "without even the knowledge of the true Attributions."

57. This project took five years, the artist being Lady Frieda Harris. All the designs are reproduced in 'The Book of Thoth', though mostly in black and white. Full colour versions of the whole set have never been published mainly because of the high costs involved in meeting the artist's demands for perfect colour reproduction. Crowley followed the Golden Dawn system of attributions in the main, though with the modification we have already mentioned. He also changed the name of several cards. The general use of the complete pack is marred however for all but Crowley followers in that it incorporates a fair proportion of his private ideas on the New Age, generally correct in principle perhaps, but not in his detailed application and symbolism, which is somewhat warped to his own personal pattern.

58. Such warping is to some extent inevitable in whoever sets down to design a whole pack and so perhaps the only solution to the Tarot problem is for everyone to design his own individual version—modifying it as he develops in realisation.

59. In arriving at colours in which to portray the cards, most attempts are not at all happy. If some system is devised say of tricking out figures in red jackets and blue trousers to represent 'consciousness' and 'subconsciousness,' little is gained, for this type of symbolism tickles only the intellect; it does not speak direct to the soul. In addition to this, earlier designers were severely hampered by the techniques of colour printing available in their day, and even today, with modern photo-lithography, to reproduce colour accurately is an expensive business. Earlier packs often had only bare indications of colour, with areas of

chalky blue, chalky pink, chalky green and chalky yellow.

60. Paradoxically, modern colour printing does not help the designer greatly, it only serves to reproduce his difficulties the more faithfully. A set system of colour symbolism carried through a series of pictorial designs can have an atrocious aesthetic effect—though putting the colours in light pastel shades, as opposed to the old tradition of bright clear colours, (often in fantastic profusion), does reduce the more distressing clashes to a minimum.

61. If, however, one is using a complicated colour system such as the Four Scales of Colour of the Golden Dawn Tradition even more awkward problems assail the designer for the light pastel evasion cannot be pursued. One is faced with cards designed with various shades of red only, or trying to distinguish black figures on indigo backgrounds and so on. The Golden Dawn did get round this difficulty to some extent by use of complementaries of the main colours—so that an all red card could be relieved by pieces of green. The basic complementaries are black-white, red-green, yellow-blue, violet-orange, from which, by reference to the spectrum, all complementaries of intermediate shades can be found by experiment, though it is almost impossible for any artist, however skilled, to get them exact.

62. The Colour Scales are based on clairvoyant investigation but experience shows them to vary somewhat from person to person. Crowley did much original research on these lines when designing his pack and Lady Harris went to immense pains to reproduce the astral colours accurately so her insistence on highly accurate reproduction is understandable. It must be said, however, that it is a virtually impossible task, for many astral colours have no correspondence in physical pigment—the closest approximation being in coloured light, and a stained glass Tarot would be impracticable to produce or use. Again, design in colour has its difficulties even in highly skilled hands as reference to the reproductions in 'The Book of

Thoth' will show. Comparison of the colour reproductions with those in black and white shows that the introduction of colour tends to blur the clear outlines of design.

63. Perhaps the best compromise has been hit upon by Case. His set which is marketed by his group—The Builders of the Adytum—is in black and white line so that students are at liberty to paint in their own colours or leave them blank as they prefer. The colouring of one's own pack, guided by professional line drawing, is perhaps the next best thing to producing one's own pack entirely—a task well worth doing, but beyond the technical accomplishments of many.

64. We should bear in mind another of Oswald Wirth's remarks: "A symbol can always be studied from an infinite number of points of view; and each thinker has the right to discover in the symbol a new meaning corresponding to the logic of his own conceptions." This brings us to a consideration of certain minority views on design and attribution.

65. One large minority prefers to deck out the cards in Egyptian guise. This body of opinion originated in France following the tradition of Court de Gebelin's original hypothesis. This received impetus from writers such as Paul Christian. There is little evidence to prove that the Tarot is of Egyptian origin though information from inner plane sources tends to confirm it. One is on safer, though still uncertain, academic ground to regard it as a medieval Rosicrucian document, though whether originated by them or adapted from an existing tradition is open to question. In any case, the real origin is incapable of definite objective proof.

66. The Frenchman R. Falconnier in 'Les xxii Lames Hermetiques du Tarot Divinatoire' (1896) claimed to have traced the origin of the Tarot from Egyptian monuments, and was taken seriously by a scholar of the calibre of Jessie Weston, ('From Ritual to Romance'), but the evidence is doubtful. However, several 'Egyptian' packs have been produced from various sources. Most of them though,

including the American Zain 'Brotherhood of Light' version, show more evidence of French than Egyptian draughtsmanship. The Ancient Egyptians had a profound knowledge
of the psychological effects of line and angles but these
attributes, (which would have been quite easy to copy
from Egyptian monuments), are conspicuously absent
in the Tarots which follow this tradition.

67. Zain follows the French system of Hebrew letter attributions except that Trump XXI is allocated to Shin and
The Fool— which he calls The Materialist— is numbered 0
or XXII and allocated to the letter Tau. (Knapp, incidentally, is also an odd man out in that he numbers The Universe
XXI and/or XXII.) Zain's astrological attributions differ
from all others mentioned hitherto, namely, using his own
names for the Trumps:

I — The Magus — *Mercury*
II — Veiled Isis — *Virgo*
III — Isis Unveiled — *Libra*
IV — The Sovereign — *Scorpio*
V — The Hierophant — *Jupiter*
VI — The Two Paths — *Vau*
VII — The Conqueror — *Sagittarius*
VIII — The Balance — *Capricorn*
IX — The Sage — *Aquarius*
X — The Wheel — *Uranus*
XI — The Enchantress — *Neptune*
XII — The Martyr — *Pisces*
XIII — The Reaper — *Aries*
XIV — The Alchemist — *Taurus*
XV — The Black Magician — *Saturn*
XVI — The Lightning — *Mars*
XVII — The Star — *Gemini*
XVIII — The Moon — *Cancer*
XIX — The Sun — *Leo*
XX — The Sarcophagus — *Moon*
XXI — The Adept — *Sun*
XXII or O — The Materialist — *Pluto*

68. Another system of attributions we might note is that of the Swedish Qabalist Knut Stenring. He prefers:

ALEPH	— Juggler — Air	LAMED	— Justice — Libra
BETH	— Sun — Sun	MEM	— World — Water
GIMEL	— Moon — Moon	NUN	— Wheel of Fortune — Scorpio
DALETH	— Chariot — Mars	SAMEKH	— Tower — Sagittarius
HE	— Empress — Aries	AYIN	— Fool — Capricorn
VAU	— Emperor — Taurus	PE	— Hierophant — Jupiter
ZAIN	— High Priestess — Gemini	TZADDI	— Hermit — Aquarius
CHETH	— Strength — Cancer	QOPH	— Judgment — Pisces
TETH	— Temperance — Leo	RESH	— Star — Venus
YOD	— Lovers — Virgo	SHIN	— Devil — Fire
KAPH	— Death — Mercury	TAU	— Hanged Man — Saturn

It will be seen that though the Tarot attributions differ, the astrological allocations to the Hebrew letters are the same as the Golden Dawn or British tradition.

69. The Dutchman Thierens has different ideas about the astrological attributions however. He allocates the Zodiacal Signs Aries — Pisces to Trumps I — XII, and Saturn, Mercury, Mars, Uranus, Venus, Moon, Sun, Jupiter, to the remaining Trumps in numerical sequence, with The Fool, (0 or XXII), to Earth or Pars Fortuna.

70. Any who wish for greater details of these systems should refer to Zain's 'Sacred Tarot', Stenring's 'Book of Formation' or Thierens' 'General Book of the Tarot.' In defence of our own system we would say that while Thierens is an eminent astrologer, his knowledge of the Qabalah seems very limited, and that though Zain's propagandising efforts on behalf of esoteric philosophy are highly commendable his Qabalism is somewhat unorthodox to say the least. He considers the Pillars of Manifestation to be representative of Good and Evil for example, and his Sephirothic attributions run, from Kether to Malkuth, Pluto, Neptune, Uranus, Jupiter, Saturn, Venus, Mars, Mercury, Moon and Sun, most of which seem difficult to justify. Stenring, on the other hand, is a Qabalist

of no mean erudition but his knowledge of the Tarot, which is non-Hebraic, seems doubtful.

71. There is a further system of attributions put forward by 'Frater Achad' — a follower of Crowley. This is a little known one for his published works were privately printed in small editions. The relevant ones are 'Q.B.L. or the Bride's Reception' and 'The Egyptian Revival'. He wondered if, as the Serpent of Wisdom *ascends* the Tree, the Tarot cards ought not to be allocated from Path 32 to Path 11 instead of in the usual descending order. He tried this and thought the result an improvement on the lower parts of the Tree but not so on the upper parts.

72. The thing which exited him was that the lower Paths now seemed to show a "wonderful Astrological Harmony, since many of them were now united with their Planetary Rulers, etc., in the Sephiroth." This set him to rearranging all the Trumps is an attempt to extend this "Astrological Harmony" over the whole Tree, which task he found, in his own opinion, to be possible. In order that others may form their own opinions we give the system below with, for easy reference, the Mundane Chakras of the Sephiroth which each Path joins.

11 — KAPH— *Wheel of Fortune*—Jupiter (Zodiac/Primum Mobile)
12 — TAU — *Universe* — Saturn (Saturn/Primum Mobile)
13 — SHIN — *Judgment* — Fire (Sun/Primum Mobile)
14 — TZADDI — *Star* — Aquarius (Saturn/Zodiac)
15 — RESH — *Sun* — Sun (Sun/Zodiac)
16 — SAMECH — *Temperance* — Sagittarius (Jupiter/Zodiac)
17 — AYIN — *Devil* — Capricorn (Sun/Saturn)
18 — PE — *Blasted Tower* — Mars (Mars/Saturn)
19 — NUN — *Death* — Scorpio (Mars/Jupiter)
20 — QOPH — *Moon* — Pisces (Sun/Jupiter)
21 — LAMED — *Justice* — Libra (Venus/Jupiter)
22 — HE — *Emperor* — Aries (Sun/Mars)
23 — YOD — *Hermit* — Virgo (Mercury/Mars)
24 — TETH — *Strength* — Leo (Venus/Sun)
25 — MEM — *Hanged Man* — Water (Moon/Sun)

26 — ZAIN — *Lovers* — Gemini (Mercury/Sun)
27 — VAU — *Hierophant* — Taurus (Mercury/Venus)
28 — CHETH — *Chariot* — Cancer (Moon/Venus)
29 — DALETH — *Empress* — Venus (Elements/Venus)
30 — GIMEL — *High Priestess* — Moon (Moon/Mercury)
31 — BETH — *Magician* — Mercury (Elements/Mercury)
32 — ALEPH — *Fool* — Air (Elements/Moon)

73. The deeper arguments in favour of this system must be sought in 'The Egyptian Revival' but in our own opinion, though this arrangement may make some initial appeal to astrologers, it seems to do so only at the expense of other equally valid esoteric considerations. However, to reject such variations out of hand would serve only to perpetuate the bad old habit of claiming Divine Right for one's own system and pouring contempt on all others. As the Tibetan Master once remarked, it is almost a hallmark of occultists to be "sectarian, exclusive and self-righteous."

74. In any case, apart from the validity of Wirth's remark: "A symbol can always be studied from an infinite number of points of view; and each thinker has the right to discover in the symbol a new meaning corresponding to the logic of his own conceptions." There is also the chance that we might all be wrong—to judge from A. E. Waite's last pronouncements on the subject in 'The Holy Kabbalah' (1929): "The supposed Hebrew symbolism of the Tarot. . . becomes disorganised if there is any doubt as to the attribution of its Trump Cards to the Hebrew Alphabet. Now there is one card which bears no number and is allocated therefore according to the discretion of the interpreter. It has been placed in all cases wrongly, by the uninstructed because they had nothing but their private judgment to guide them, and by some who claimed to know better because they desired to mislead. It happens, however, that they also were at sea. I may go further and say that the true nature of Tarot symbolism is perhaps a secret in the hands of a very few persons, and outside

that circle operators and writers may combine the cards
as they like and attribute them as they like, but they will
never find the right way. The symbolism is, however, so
rich that it will give meanings of a kind in whatever
manner it may be disposed, and some of these may be
suggestive, though illusory none the less. The purpose
of this short paper is therefore to show that published
Tarots and the methods of using them may be serviceable
for divination, fortune telling and other trifles; but they
are not the key of the Kabbalah.''

75. From this, which is enough to strike fear into the
heart of any other poor commentator, it would appear that
Waite had undergone some very high initiation that conferred upon him secrets that few others possess. This
is unlikely in actual fact for initiations are expansions
of consciousness and not dispensations of knowledge.
And we need not take too seriously his claim that we 'will
never find the right way.' His contention is far too defeat-
ist for anyone to take seriously.

76. We do not believe his statement to be true, but there
is much truth in it, namely where he points out that the
symbolism is so rich that it will give meanings of a kind in
whatever manner it may be disposed. It is this difficulty
that makes it unlikely of our ever being *certain* that we
have the once and for all correct attributions. All we can
do is to seek the arrangement which seems to be most
logical and to give the best results in practice. In the present author's view and experience the attributions given in
this book are the best discovered up to now. If we try to
appeal to the past we only find that our medieval predeces-
sors were equally at variance, so we moderns can only do
our best each to perfect his own system and leave others
to do similarly with theirs.

77. There are but two mistakes to avoid: i) the rejection
of the whole subject on account of the divergences of opinion between the 'experts', and ii) the espousement of one
system in a fanatical way with constant denigration of all

other opinions. Each is a mistake of narrow mindedness, or worse, narrowness of soul. And each defeats the principle behind *any* system.

78. It is, on the other hand, important for the beginner to find a system which suits him reasonably and to stick to it for a good length of time. Symbols should not be taken too seriously; they are but representations of reality—though reality can come with continued use of them. After long years of juggling with symbols, meditating upon them, trying out various patterns, experimenting with theories of attribution and so on, one may find that one is arranging the symbols to try to fit a knowledge of reality within oneself. After a realisation such as this, symbolism becomes superfluous at that level. The symbols may however now have a new relevance at the new level of vision and so one may proceed over a series of new horizons until the One Reality which has no symbol, can have no symbol, and needs no symbol — because it just IS — is attained.

79. As a final note, we might list some alternative titles for the Trumps used by F. Ch. Barlet in a section of Papus' 'Tarot of the Bohemians' because they are very suggestive for meditation purposes.

    VI — Liberty
    VII — Osiris
    VIII — Equilibrium
    XI — Force
    XII — The Sacrifice or The Great Work
    XIV — The Two Urns
    XV — Typhon or The Electric Whirlwind
    XVII — The Star of the Magi
    XVIII — Twilight
    XIX — The Resplendent Light
    XX — The Awakening of the Dead
    XXI — The Crown of the Magi

LA · MAISON · DIEV

L'ETOILE

LA · LUNE

LE · SOLEIL

Part II
The Lesser Arcana

THE LESSER ARCANA

1. The Lesser Arcanum of the Tarot is divided into four Suits — Wands, Cups, Swords and Disks. Alternative titles for Wands are Sceptres or Clubs, alternative titles for Cups are Chalices or Goblets and alternative titles for Disks are Pentacles, Circles, Coins, Deniers or Money.

2. It is generally conceded that these suits are the original forms of those of the modern playing cards, though opinion differs widely on the actual correspondence. Papus equates Wands with Clubs, Cups with Hearts, Swords with Spades and Disks with Diamonds; Waite, Wands with Diamonds, Cups with Hearts, Swords with Clubs and Disks with Spades; Mathers, Wands with Diamonds, Cups with Hearts, Swords with Spades and Disks with Clubs; and Thierens, Wands with Clubs, Cups with Diamonds, Swords with Spades and Disks with Hearts. Precedent is thus of little help in making one's choice. Paul Case favours Papus' attributions and we are inclined to agree; however, this line of correspondences is of little importance except perhaps for those who wish to equate the two packs for purposes of fortune telling. It is the links with tradition that are important rather than analogues with modern games, consequently we should look for a set of symbols in myth and legend that correspond to the four Tarot suits.

3. Celtic mythology, and its traces in the Arthurian cycle, is the source from which we can derive the most fruitful correspondences, and Mackenzie, in his 'Celtic Myth and Legend' has listed them in a form which approaches close to poetry: "The living fiery spear of Lugh, the magic ship of Manannan, the sword of Conery Mor which sang, Cuchulain's sword, which spoke, the Lia Fail, Stone of Destiny,

which roared for joy beneath the feet of rightful kings."

4. Lugh was the Celtic god of the Sun, though he was also master of all skills. The latter, however, confirms his standing as a Sun-god, the Sun being representative of the Solar Logos. He was similar in function to The Dagda, and to some extent replaced him. The Dagda was 'Father of All' and 'the Lord of Perfect Knowledge', his main attribute being a huge club. We thus have mythological confirmation of the close link between the club and the fiery spear. This ties in well with the esoteric attribution of Wands being associated with Fire—not only Elemental Fire but the Fire of the Spirit. In the Arthurian cycle we have not only Arthur's spear, called Ron, but also the spear dripping with blood associated with the Holy Grail, the one which was used by Longinus to pierce the body of Our Lord, and which dealt the Dolorous Stroke which maimed the Fisher King and laid a country waste until the advent of a Winner of the Grail. There is symbolism of tremendous depth here which would well repay meditation, particularly the link between the Fisher King and the symbolism of the Christ, one of whose symbols is the Fish and who was also the Great Fisherman. As the legends come from the French there is also the link which is not so obvious in English—Pécheur meaning sinner and Pêcheur meaning a fisherman.

5. Manannan was a Celtic sea god, and the sea over which he ruled was that under which lay Tier nan Og, the Celtic 'other world'—a place which has close links with the astral world of faery and the Garden of Eden—a place of perfection held within the Earth's aura to show the Beginning and the Ending. It is also Avalon—the inner plane place where the dying Arthur was taken in a barque by three mourning queens. And Lancelot, the best knight in the world, father of Galahad, the Grail Winner, was brought up under the waters by the Lady of the Lake, who was in turn closely associated with Merlin, the magician-founder of the Arthurian Table Round. It was she who was the

custodian of Excalibur, Arthur's sword, which arose from the Lake and was eventually returned there by Bedivere. The boat of Manannan needed no sail or oars but went wherever he willed it. Its links with the Cup symbolism derive through the esoteric association of ideas between a boat, an ark, the Ark of the Covenant, the Moon, a chalice, a cauldron, the Cornucopia, the Grail and so on. Such links may seem far fetched to a literary scholar but are obvious to an occultist, artist or depth psychologist—thus meditation rather than ratiocination is recommended in these matters. Manannan also had a flock of pigs which returned to life after being killed and eaten and so provided his people with limitless food. This is an attribute similar to that of the Cauldron of Ceridwen and the Holy Grail. All these associations of the sea, cup, chalice, Grail and so on serve to indicate the Feminine-Side of God. Its close association with the Father Aspect is shown by the Cauldron of The Dagda himself. This was one of the four magical treasures of the Tuatha de Denann, the dwellers in Tier nan Og. The other treasures being Lugh's spear, the sword of Nuada and the Stone of Destiny.

6. The sword of Nuada can be considered the prototype of all other famous swords, whether of Conery Mor, Cuchulain, or any other of the warrior heroes. Nuada was king of the Tuatha de Denann and of a similar category to Lugh and The Dagda. His sword was so powerful that no enemy could escape it when it was unsheathed and so it is again representative of an Aspect of God—God the Destroyer. In Arthurian legend the sword is frequently associated with the stone, as for example in the miracle which caused Arthur to be chosen king and the Grail Winner to be identified. There are other elements of meaning in Excalibur as it appears in the Arthurian cycle but these do not concern us now.

7. The Stone of Destiny, the fourth magical treasure, was the means by which the true king could be identified, and is thus intimately concerned with Divine Rule in Earth—

the tradition of kingship being that the king is God's direct representative, answerable only to God, but responsible for all his people. The feudal tradition, though now outdated, was a fine one in its conception although its high traditions may have been honoured more in the breach than the observance. The same thing could be said, however, regarding the ideals of most forms of government.

8. We can equate these four magical treasures, then, with the four suits of the Tarot and also with the Aspects of God. Wands are indicative of the First or Power Aspect, God the Father. Cups represent the Second Aspect, the characteristic of which is Love or Love/Wisdom, originally worshipped through pagan goddess forms but in the last two thousand years represented by Our Lord and the Virgin Mary. Swords are indicative of the Destroyer Aspect, or Disintegrator, the Fourth Aspect of God, which has received little exoteric acknowledgement and in esoteric circles has often been considered as a part of the First Aspect. Disks, finally, represent that Aspect of God concerned with the actual working out of the Divine Plan and thus the Third Aspect, God the Holy Spirit, the Aspect of Active Intelligence.

9. These, together with the Sephirothic attributions, which are shown by the number of each card, will serve to indicate the reason behind the apparently arbitrary titles of the small cards of the Lesser Arcanum.

10. Previously published commentaries on them have never given very satisfying accounts, mainly because of the blind which announces the Aces to be the Roots of the Elements. This Elemental attribution of the suits is true for the Aces and Court Cards but the Aces have a dual function. Besides representing Kether in the allocation of the Minor Arcana to the Sephiroth they also represent Elemental powers in Malkuth, (strictly speaking, the Kether of Malkuth), when considering the Elemental teaching of the Court Cards. God, in whatever Aspect, in Kether has no attributes, He just IS—so the Ace has no title in the small card attribution.

The Court Cards show modes of manifestation, more particularly of Elemental Force, and it is in relation to these that the Aces have the titles of Roots of the various Elements. The failure to understand this has resulted in attempts to explain the small cards as types of Elemental force at various levels and the explanations have not been convincing.

11. Another system, inaugurated by MacGregor Mathers, though also found in French occultism but with different attributions, is to allocate the small cards to the decans — the 36 ten degree divisions of the Zodiac. This reflects a very commendable synthesising spirit but it sometimes leads to doubtful results, for many symbol systems, correct within themselves, clash with other systems if too close an identification of parts is made. So much attention has been paid by the Golden Dawn and others to the projection of the Tarot and the Tree of Life into a sphere in Space that there is probably much of importance in this line of research, but the pseudo-astrological meanings resulting from the allocation of a small card of the Tarot to each decan do not fit too happily with the traditional titles.

12. The titles of the Lesser Arcana are not in doubt. It is the reason behind the titles that has never been adequately explained. Thus, while the cards have been of some use empirically for divination and such like, a great deal of their deeper implications have been missed. These implications are to be gained by meditation upon the relevant Sephirah and the relevant Aspect of God.

13. Students who have read the Tibetan's books will be familiar with a seven-fold division of God into Rays: I — Will or Power, II — Love-Wisdom, III — Active Intelligence, Adaptability or Higher Mind, IV — Harmony through Conflict, Beauty or Art, V — Concrete Knowledge or Science, VI — Devotion or Idealism, VII — Ceremonial Order or Magic. Of these, three are Rays of Aspect and four are Rays of Attribute, the latter, (Rays IV — VII), being capable of synthesis into Ray III. It is the Rays of Aspect with which

we are here concerned plus a fourth Destroyer or Disintegrator Aspect which, in the Tibetan's system, is considered to be a part of Ray I. In all cases these names of the Aspects tend to cramp rather than expand consciousness so meditation to get at the reality behind the inadequate words will help and also reference to Volume I of Alice Bailey's 'A Treatise on the Seven Rays'.

14. The Aces, as mentioned above, give the four basic divisions of the Godhead in Kether, but it must be understood that all such divisions are in order to make study easier, for God is a Unity, and in the last analysis must be considered as such. So the division of God into Three Persons, Four Aspects, Seven Rays, Ten Sephiroth, Twelve Signs and so on in different systems does not imply contradiction but different ways of studying the same Unity—a Unity so vast that we cannot grasp it in its totality—just as we cannot see all angles and elements of a pot that is standing on a table if our viewpoint is limited to one place. Attempts to paint a picture of such an object from any one angle would necessarily be limited, one could only show one limited part of it unless one were, say, a cubist painter and tried to show various viewpoints at once at the risk of execration by those who cherished their own limited conventional reality. Attempts to give some adequate representation of the Godhead meet similar difficulties.

15. God in Kether is represented at the Formative level by the Four Holy Living Creatures of the Vision of Ezekiel —a Man, a Bull, a Lion and an Eagle. These have their correspondence in astrology and also in the Elements, although the four divisions of the Emanations of God can hardly be called Elemental until Malkuth, the Sphere of the Elements, is reached. All things have their origin in the highest though, so the Four Holy Living Creatures are also Roots of the Elements, but at a very remote level. In view of this, it has never been entirely wrong to try to elucidate the small cards Elementally, but it has been limiting, for the terms of reference have been derived from Malkuth,

not Kether — from the plane of effects instead of the plane of causes.

16. So while we may have in the back of our minds the Elemental attribution of each suit, and these often appear on designs of the Lesser Arcana, we must use the attributions to expand our consciousness, not to limit it. Thus the Fire represented by Wands is the Fire of the Spirit — God Who is a consuming Fire — the Fire of Prometheus stolen from Heaven — Cosmic Fire in all its forms, forces and energies. The Water of Cups includes the Great Sea of Binah with its links in Ain Soph, the whole fluid soul of the world, the Anima Mundi, the Astral Light and so on. The Air of the Swords is the great Dispersing Principle, the nearest Elemental approach to Nothingness, Rarification, which, led to its extreme form, becomes Unmanifestation and thus, from the point of view of manifestation, a Disintegrating or Destroying factor which withdraws life from the form so that the form disintegrates and the life disperses. The Earth of the Disks is, on the other hand, the manifesting principle, the Body of God, and the ways in which Cosmic forces are adapted to manifestation, from the comparative freedom of the Supernals to the dense concrete forms of Malkutn.

17. The Ace of Wands then stands for the first manifestation of the powers of God the Father, the First Aspect of Power, Will or Strength. (The double allocation of the Aces, to Kether and Malkuth, reveals a profound Mystery — the intimate tie between these two Sephiroth.) God the Father in Chokmah is represented by the 2 of Wands, the Lord of Dominion, and as Chokmah is the Prime Masculine Sephirah the attribution is obvious. This Dominion is on a firm footing when the powers of this Aspect manifest through Binah for the first Triangle of Manifestation has been formed, thus the 3 of Wands is the Lord of Established Strength.

18. Chesed, the next Sephirah, is concerned with the establishment of the True Imprint in the lower worlds and hence its association with rulership and the title of the 4

of Wands — Lord of Perfected Work. The function of Geburah being the preservation of balance and eradication of excrescences naturally gives rise to the 5 of Wands being called Lord of Strife; while the establishment of God the Father in Tiphareth, the central Sephirah of the whole Tree and marking the completion of the Second Triad, makes the 6 of Wands the Lord of Victory. In the microcosm the complete Individuality has now been projected by the power of the Spirit — and what follows is of the Personality.

19. The Harmony of Tiphareth is overset to establish manifestation upon the densest levels, and the power of God the Father manifesting in the sphere of Netzach has been likened to 'an army with banners', pressing on towards the Form manifestation of the lower Sephiroth. The 7 of Wands is thus Lord of Valour. In Hod is the mind formed, both macrocosmically and microcosmically, and this flashing method of communication both vertical and horizontal, (there being a close connection between Hermes as magician and messenger), gives rise to the title of the 8 of Wands — Lord of Swiftness. Then the Third Triad is completed in the formation of Yesod, the Foundation, its Magical Image the beautiful naked man, very strong—and so the title of the 9 of Wands is Lord of Great Strength. In Malkuth is the full Crucifixion of the Spirit in dense matter and hence the title which seems strange in a blue-print of Divine Perfection — Lord of Oppression.

20. The Ace of Cups stands for the first manifestation of the powers of God the Son, the Second Aspect of Love-Wisdom, thus the 2 of Cups is Lord of Love. This title derives not only from the inherent qualities of the Second Aspect but also from the duality represented by Chokmah and Kether — reflections one of the other — both called after their fashion Crown of Creation and First and Second Glory. As a result of this union is the third produced, the Sephirah Binah, giving completion and fruition and so the 3 of Cups is the Lord of Abundance.

21. From here the pure Love of God of the Supernals seeks

manifestation and comes into Form in Chesed, a consummation of Spirit and Form represented by the 4 of Cups—Lord of Blended Pleasure. This activity of the Spirit, conforming the Form to its use, gives certain unbalance which has to be corrected, so we have in Geburah the 5 of Cups, Lord of Loss in Pleasure. But inevitably a harmonious manifestation in Form is attained, represented by Tiphareth and the 6 of Cups, the Lord of Pleasure.

22. From here the next objective is the manifestation of the Love of God, or the Christ principle, in Earth or Malkuth. Hence, from the harmony of Love manifesting in Tiphareth the power goes forth to the formation of the next Triangle. Love is an all-inclusive Aspect of Divinity which gives freedom from friction and error owing to its accent on the Unity of all—hence it meets with Success all the way though there are qualifications in Netzach and Hod. The Love in Netzach, the union of disparate objects, is not the final goal, it is a transitory phase, for the function of Netzach is the diversification of the Unity, it acts as a prism which splits one light source into seven, so the title of the 7 of Cups, which represents a complex situation, is Lord of Illusory Success. The Plan is successful in its working out but one has the element of Illusion—the illusion of separateness—which, however is an essential part of the Plan, whose goal is Unity in Diversity.

23. The Sephirah Hod produces a similar situation, for the sphere of the mind is essentially one of differences, it is analytical rather than sythetic, and the differences are implicit—otherwise there would be no need for the Divine Messenger. Hod, in its most synthetic form, is a linker of differences. The magician is one who deals with a universe of differences, bringing such and such a force into such and such a form and so on. There is, however, the old tradition of the man of Love being greater than the magician. One comes upon the theme quite frequently in esoteric fiction. The magician may perform his mighty conjurations to banish an evil entity, but the higher initiate simply draws it into his

aura and annihilates it as evil by the power of unifying Love just by the acceptance of it. There is also the tradition that if, like Christ, one could but look upon a man and see him and accept him as he is, then that man would be healed. None of these Mysteries is within the reach of the mind, so Love manifesting in the sphere of analysis and diversity is represented by the 8 of Cups — Lord of Abandoned Success.

24. The Triangle is completed by the formation of the Sephirah Yesod, and here, in the perfect union of the elements of the Personality, caused by the Love of God manifesting fully in the etheric, subconscious, and passional sphere, we have the 9 of Cups called the Lord of Material Happiness. And when the Christ Imprint is brought down into Earth itself, in the daily living of human beings, then the situation is well described by the title of the 10 of Cups —the Lord of Perfected Success. We have exemplified this on an individual basis but it also applies objectively to the Macrocosm and to humanity as a group. The Love of God operating in dense manifestation, whatever the context, is Perfected Success.

25. The Third Aspect of God, the Holy Spirit, or Active Intelligence, is represented in its First Manifest form by the Ace of Disks. In Chokmah, the 2 of Disks is the Lord of Harmonious Change, indicating the operation of the relationship between the Logos and his projected Universe, or the Cosmic Atom of man and its reflected manifest Spark, according to whether one wishes to assess the matter on a Macrocosmic or microcosmic basis. There is in this duality a mutual process of harmonious change as the Creator regards the created, the contemplation causing changes in the Creator which are reflected in the created reflection, thereby causing further change in the consciousness of the Creator and so on. This is a function of continuous Harmonious Change. The Sephirah Binah is the Form Sephirah of the Supernal Triangle and so is intimately connected with the Third Aspect, which here is the spiritual contemplation of the ends to be achieved in dense manifestation,

and also the means by which this Destiny shall be achieved. Hence the 3 of Disks is the Lord of Material Works.

26. In Chesed the Aspect of Active Intelligence has come into the worlds of Form, manifesting as the more detailed aspects of the ruling principle of Chesed, which governs Form manifestation. Thus the title of the 4 of Disks is Lord of Earthly Power. The close concern with the causes of unbalance and the remedial action needed in Geburah gives the title for the 5 of Disks, Lord of Material Trouble. But achievement of balance is consolidated in Tiphareth, represented by the 6 of Disks, Lord of Material Success. These Sephiroth are not of the material world as we know it in Personality consciousness, but the use of the words Material or Earthly in the titles indicates the close link between organisation of Form and the Third Aspect. Further, strictly speaking, all the Sephiroth up to Chesed are in the worlds of Form.

27. Netzach is however, like Geburah, very much a Sephirah of forces, though within Form manifestation, and so Active Intelligence in this Sephirah is concerned with action which has its results at another level. So the 7 of Disks is known as the Lord of Success Unfulfilled. Active Intelligence in the sphere of mind is well represented by the 8 of Disks as Lord of Prudence, for it is the function of the mind to weigh up possibilities before committing itself to action. The resultant action, once this has been done, gives the completion of the Triangle in Yesod—the perfect form for the force, indicated by the 9 of Disks, Lord of Material Gain. The final concretion of this perfection into Earth gives perfect fruition and reward symbolised by the 10 of Disks, Lord of Wealth, which of course is not confined to monetary wealth, but to health and happiness as well, and enjoyment of the good life in Earth.

28. The suit of Swords refers to the Disintegrator Aspect of God and as its direction of action is thus towards Unmanifestation rather than manifestation it is perhaps better to examine the cards in reverse order.

29. The withdrawal of life forces from the dense form inevitably produces the ruin of the particular form so the 10 of Swords is the Lord of Ruin. This ruin is, however, not evil if under the presidency of a Divine Aspect, but a necessary precursor of new life, for one cannot pour new wine into old bottles. It is thus more in the nature of opportunity when viewed from a higher level, though still ruin when viewed from the plane of effect. Similar considerations apply to the 9 of Swords, the Lord of Despair and Cruelty. This, like the 9 of Spades of the modern fortune tellers, appears to be the great malefic of all the cards, and in the latter, (as for example in the opera 'Carmen'), stands for death —though the Ace of Spades is also commonly credited with this meaning, its Tarot equivalent being the Ace of Swords, the ultimate in Disintegration—return to the Unmanifest. As the Disintegrator acting in Yesod means the complete break-up of a form, and also of the roots of the Personality when applied to man, the applicability of the title of this card will be obvious. It could be regarded as a somewhat shortsighted nomenclature but there is a great Mystery here. It is hinted at by the cry of Our Lord on the Cross: "My God, my God, why hast thou forsaken me?"

30. The 8 and 7 of Swords are the Lords of Shortened Force and Unstable Effort respectively. These indicate the withdrawal of force on the level of mind and the disruption of the Form-giving forces of Netzach so that no lower form is made or maintained.

31. Tiphareth is the Sephirah of the Sacrificed God and the 6 of Swords, the Lord of Earned Success, gives in a phrase the true principle behind sacrifice. In Geburah, a Sephirah which has distinctly destructive aspects, is the 5 of Swords —the Lord of Defeat. Nothing can stand against the destructive might of God when the end of an evolutionary phase is complete. The card of Chesed, the 4 of Swords, is Lord of Rest from Strife. This indicates the final indrawing of the resources of the being which is withdrawing from Form. The processes of involution and evolution in Form even

where there is no Deviation, are essentially ones of struggle, consequently, withdrawal from Form is rest from the strife of the evolutionary journey.

32. The Lord of Sorrow, the 3 of Swords, relates to Binah and of course the Spiritual Experience of this Sephirah is the Vision of Sorrow. This Divine Sorrow is a deep Mystery, and has little to do with the ordinary human sorrow, which is usually the result of limitations on the viewpoint of the Personality brought about by the Deviation. It has much to do with the attitude of the Spirit leaving its Heavenly Home where all is Unity to enter upon differentiated existence in Form. This Sorrow may have caused the human Spirits to try to avoid the full implications of immersion in Form to a greater or lesser extent and thus to enter into Sin or Imperfection. As a consequence of this the Sorrow can also refer to the Sorrow of the Logos at the rejection of the Way, the Truth and the Life of the Divine Plan by the Spirits of the present human evolution. In Chokmah we have a similar situation to Chesed, but at a higher level, where the Spirit contemplates its Creator, microcosmic or macrocosmic, before returning to its Cosmic origins, enriched with the experience of manifest life. Thus the 2 of Swords is the Lord of Peace Restored. The Ace of Swords, as earlier stated, is the final return to the Cosmos, and is the ultimate disintegration, or 'end of the world.'

NOTES ON THE DESIGN OF THE LESSER CARDS

(2 to 10)

As in the whole of the Lesser Arcanum the inner implications of each card are revealed by its title, suit and number rather than by any pictorial element, a close examination of all pictorial variants is not of such importance as with the Trumps. The general designs are limited by the number and type of suit emblems they have to show but the disposition of these suit emblems about the card can indicate the esoteric title quite accurately, especially with the help of a certain amount of ancillary symbolism.

This, on the old cards, took the form of floral decorations. In most of the exoteric packs that have come down to us this flora—and to some extent, fauna—proliferates wildly, but was rectified and put to good use by the Golden Dawn. The use of floral symbolism is, of course, in line with the deep implications of the Garden. The Garden appears in many guises in symbolism, from the Garden of Eden to the Garden of Gethsemane, and the flowers used in the Tarot are the lily and the rose—the lily sometimes under its Eastern form of a lotus or, a compromise between the two, a water-lily.

Most esoteric modern packs take a very simple line; the emblems are ranged in bare geometric figures in much the same way as in modern playing cards. Waite is à notable exception in that he provides pictures for all the cards to suggest the 'divinatory meaning'. The divinatory meaning is, of course, merely a corruption of the esoteric title. Although he states quite plainly that the pictures have no hidden symbolic significance there are in fact deep symbolic elements in many of them — the 3 of Swords, to mention but one, shows a little known Magical Image of the Sephirah Binah. The general disposition of the emblems in the packs we have been considering is shown in Fig. 7, though the ancillary symbolism cannot, for reasons of space, be shown. The more important aspects of it are described below, suit by suit, and for the most part the Aces are dealt with later in conjunction with the Court Cards.

WANDS: This suit, in the old packs, follows a more or less conventional pattern. The huge club of the Ace is replaced by sceptres, divided into three divisions by two encircling rings about the shaft, and with ornate ends. The main addition to basic design is in the form of leaves rather than flowers and in the exoteric packs appears purely decorative. Another feature is the complicated interlacing of the Wands in the centre of the card. This seems to be an Italian innovation.

The Golden Dawn Wands have, in all cases, flames and not leaves, issuing from the points of juncture. They also include radiating angelic hands issuing from clouds and grasping the Wands at the centre where they cross. On the 2 & 3 there is one hand only but on the 4, 5, 6 & 7, two hands issuing from opposite sides of the card, holding each other in the 1st Order grip of the Golden Dawn as well as the diagonal Wands. On the odd numbered cards a similar hand at the bottom of the card holds the upright Wand. With the higher numbered cards two pairs of hands are shown. Additionally, the decanate system peculiar to the Golden Dawn is shown on each card, the planetary sign of the Decan above and the Zodiacal sign below. Starting from the 2 upwards these are Mars, Sun & Venus each with Aries; Saturn, Jupiter, Mars with Leo; and Mercury, Moon & Saturn with Saggittarius.

The Crowley/Harris version also shows these decanate symbols but dispenses with the angelic hands. Tradition has been overthrown to some extent but fertile and intelligent imagination has replaced it. The actual shape of the Wands indicates to some extent the meaning of the card. Thus, those of the 2, Dominion, are great heavy brutal dorjes, those of the 3 are lotuses and those of the 4, ram and dove-headed sceptres. Crowley chose to call the latter two Virtue and Completion. The next three cards have Caduceus, Lotus and Phoenix wands, (the 7 with a club additionally). These are all depicted with flames at the intersections. On card 8 the Wands are forks of lightning, arrow headed, a crystal in the background and a rainbow overhead. The diagonal Wands of the 9 are decorated each with 9 crescent moons, the upright one having a sun at the top and moon below. The diagonals suggest arrows by their shape, presumably of Diana. The last card shows the diagonals like a grating of ordinary Wands with two dorjes lengthened into bars superimposed over them.

The Waite pictures are as follows: The 2 shows a man standing between two Wands looking from his battlements out to sea and holding a globe in his hand while to his left is a lily, rose and cross emblem. The 3 shows a man standing on a clifftop with three Wands, his back turned to us, gazing at ships passing over the sea. The 4 shows a garland suspended on four Wands, with a castle and maidens with more garlands in the background. The 5 shows five youths having a mêlée with staves. The 6 shows a horseman, laurel-wreathed, as is the stave he carries, and accompanied on foot by five others with staves held high. The 7 shows a young man apparently on the edge of a cliff defending himself against the assults of six others whose staves only are visible at the bottom of the card. The 8 shows merely eight Wands flying through the air; open country in the background. The 9 has a man standing on guard before a palisade—the number of staves, his own and those of the palisade are nine in number. Lastly, the 10 shows a man staggering under the weight of a bundle of ten Wands which he is carrying.

There are symbols on Knapp's cards provided by Manly P. Hall. All the Wand cards have radiant triangles but with a different symbol in each. The Ace has a black triangle with a point within a circle in it; the remainder have ordinary line-drawn triangles with, from the 2 upwards, a serpent, a lamp, a Tau, a book, a winged sphere, a leafed branch, a flower, a pillar and a key.

The Zain 'Egyptian' cards have the added interest of having the constellation in the sky which corresponds to the decanate the card is attributed to. The nomenclature of the decans differs from that of the Golden Dawn. Zodiacal and not planetary terms are used so that, for example, the three decans of Aries are called Aries of Aries, Leo of Aries, Saggittarius of Aries instead of Mars of Aries, Sun of Aries and Venus of Aries. This no doubt a better system for the latter can cause confusion. Crowley, for one, made the mistake of thinking the nomenclature could also refer to the influence of a planet in a certain sign, but Mars *in* Aries is a very different thing from Mars *of* Aries. Also, the system of decanate attribution differs from that of the Golden Dawn. Whereas the Golden Dawn system allocated the 2 to 10 to the decanates and considered the Ace to rule over a whole segment of the sky, the Zain system, (which follows the French tradition), allocates the Ace to 9 to the decanates and allocates the 10 to general governorship of the Triplicity. Consequently, every zodiacal attribution is at variance in these two systems, in spite of the general agreement of attributing the Wands suit to the Fire signs—Aries, Leo and Saggittarius.

CUPS: The 2 of the old packs almost invariably shows a pair of dolphins at the top of the card and sometimes a heart at the bottom. This alone should serve to indicate the esoteric origins of the small cards of the Tarot if the attributions are meditated upon.

The Golden-Dawn Cups all show water lilies or lotuses growing in a bunch from the bottom of the card, held by a rayed angelic hand. The flowers overhang the Cups, into which they pour streams of water. Sometimes the Cups are empty, sometimes half filled, sometimes overflowing, or else there may be no waterflow at all from the flowers. The 2 shows a single flower growing out of water at the bottom of the card and held by a hand. Out of this flower grows another, which blooms at the top of the card and from which water gushes as from a fountain, falling in two streams onto two crossed dolphins, one gold and the other silver, and thence into two Cups, side by side, which overflow into the bottom of the card. The 3 shows a hand holding a bunch of lilies from which six flowers rise to overhang each Cup, (two to each), with water flowing from them into the overflowing Cups. One Cup is placed above the other two and overflows into them; these in their turn overflow into the bottom of the card. The 4 has only one flower rising from the bunch held by the hand; this pours water into the two Cups which overflow into two others which do not overflow. From the centre two leaves cross the card transversely to make a kind of cross with the upright stem. On the 5 flowers are falling from the bunch held by the usual angelic hand and so there are only leaves over-hanging the Cups from the fountain-shaped bunch. There is no water flowing and the Cups are empty. The 6 shows the usual figure but with one flower pouring water into each Cup, none of which are full. On the 7 the stems held by the hand rise from the central lower Cup. All the other Cups are overhung by a flower but there is no water flowing. The Cups on the 8 are arranged three, two, three. The top three are empty and have no flowers, nor have the lowest row. The only flowers in the bunch are two in number and overhang the central Cups which are partfilled. The 9 shows a flower flowing water into every Cup, all of which are flowing over. The same applies with the 10 but with an additional flow of water from the topmost sideways tilted Cup which pours water into the top lefthand Cup and is itself filled from a single flower at the top of the card. The decanate symbols are also shown and are, from 2 to 10, Venus, Mercury, Moon of Cancer; Mars, Sun, Venus of Scorpio; and Saturn, Jupiter, Mars of Pisces.

Crowley changed the names of five of the cards in this suit; namely, 4, Blended Pleasure, into Luxury; 5, Loss in Pleasure, into Disappointment; 7,

Illusory Success, into Debauch; 8, Abandoned Success, into Indolence; and 10, Perpetual Success, into Satiety. This reveals himself rather than the inner meaning of the cards, though the Harris pack reflects the meanings very well, erroneous or no. The general design follows the broad pattern of the Golden Dawn versions, though with modifications such as pomegranate Cups and the stems coming round the sides of the card to form a kind of simple wreath on the 3, and the lotus stalks of the 5 forming an inverted pentagram, and the Cups of the 7 and 8 being chipped and broken. Apart from this, the descriptions given of the Golden Dawn cards serve quite well except that on the 10 the Cups are arranged as the Sephiroth on the Tree of Life and the 7 shows a rather peculiar evil looking design. This 7 is a thoroughly vile card, showing poisonous lotuses, green slime instead of water, and the sea below, in Crowley's words, is "a malarious morass." This is Crowley's interpretation of the Love Aspect of God as it manifests in the Sephirah of Beauty and it comes about partly from his faulty quasi-astrological interpretation and partly from his perverted puritanism which regarded anything, particularly Love, as being the greater besmirched the closer it got to Earth.

Waite follows a variant tradition in his 2 of Cups and shows a Caduceus surmounted by a winged lion's head, while below, a youth and maiden, wreathed, pledge each other with two Cups. The 3 shows three maidens pledging each other in a garden. The 4 has a young man seated under a tree discontentedly looking at three Cups on the ground while an angelic hand in mid-air offers him another. The 5 shows a cloaked figure confronting three overthrown Cups while two upright ones stand behind him. The 6 has two children with flower filled Cups in a garden. The 7 has a man confronted by seven chalices with fantastic visions arising out of them, a man's head, a veiled radiant figure, a serpent, a castle on a pinnacle, a pile of treasure, a laurel wreath, and a winged serpent-dragon. The 8 has three Cups on five lined up in the foreground with a man walking disconsolately away between bleak rocks in the moonlight. The 9 shows a fat replete man sitting before a high curtained, arc-shaped shelf supporting 9 Cups; and the 10 shows ten Cups in a rainbow with a man and woman arm in arm hailing it while two children dance by them.

The 'Egyptian' cards, from the Ace to the 9, are allocated to the Cancer, Scorpio, Pisces decanates of Cancer; Scorpio, Pisces and Cancer decanates of Scorpio; and the Pisces, Cancer and Scorpio decanates of Pisces, the 10 presiding over Water generally.

The Knapp cards have a geometrical figure traced behind the actual Cups. On the 2 this is a circle while the other figures correspond to those traced by the Wands suit. Manly P. Hall shows every ancillary symbol in a Vesica Piscis. The Ace shows a radiant crown, the 2 an all-seeing eye, and those following, an H with a flame rising in the centre, a jewel, a fiery serpent, a king, a battle-axe, a four-winged disk, a two-winged disk, and two hands conjoined by a line like three sides of a rectangle.

Case is alone in showing some of the Cups reversed. This occurs in the bottom Cup of the 2, the two lower Cups of the 4, the three lower Cups of the 6 and the four lower Cups of the 8, similarly with the lower three of the 7 and the four of the 9. On the 10 none are reversed and they are placed similarly to the Sephiroth on the Tree of Life.

SWORDS: The traditional Sword cards show long curved Swords interlaced at top and bottom of the card and in the odd numbers, a single straight Sword in the centre, point downward except in the case of the 3. The 10 shows two Swords placed diagonally point downwards between the eight curved interlaced ones. The 2, 4 & 6 have a flower in the centre, face on, upward and reversed respectively. The 3 has flowers about the upward pointing Sword and on all cards there is a flower in each corner.

The Golden Dawn introduce their white radiating angelic hands to hold the Swords, which are all straight. Two hands hold the crossed Swords of the 2 and where they cross is a white radiating Tudor rose. The 3 shows three Swords held point upwards, the central Sword cutting the rose to pieces, which is no longer radiant. The 4 is similar to the 2 except that each hand holds two Swords. The 5 resembles the 3, the central Sword in each case giving the impression that it has knocked the others asunder, the points of the others fall away slightly from the vertical. The 6 again is similar to the 2 and 4. The 7 shows all the Swords almost meeting at a point at the top of the card and the hand that holds the central one also holds the rose. The 8 has four hands with two Swords apiece and the points of the Swords touch at the top of the card; the rose is in the centre of all. The 9 introduces a central Sword disuniting the others and there is no rose at all. On the 10 two Swords held crossed in the centre disunite the other Swords and there is still no rose.

The Crowley/Harris 2 is similar to the above, the 3 shows three Swords, a straight upright one and two curved ones from the top corners piercing a rose. The 4 shows four Swords, one from each corner, meeting in the centre of a rose, while the 5 is of similar design but with curved Swords and the petals of the dismembered rose tracing out an inverted pentagram. The 6 again has all the Sword-points meeting in the centre where there is a rose upon a Calvary Cross. The 7 has a Sword point up, opposed by three smaller Swords each side engraved on their hilts with planetary symbols—the upright one has the Sun. The 8 shows six Indian Swords of assorted shape, the top three pointing in the opposite direction to the lower three and two long downward pointing Swords superimposed on them. On the 9 all the Swords point downward, side by side, and drip blood. The pattern of the 10 suggests the Tree of Life, a Sword-hilt on each Sephirah, with the central Tiphareth Sword broken. There is a complex geometrical background to all these designs, and like the Golden Dawn ones, they are allocated to the decans, the signs of which appear on the cards—from the 2 up: Moon, Saturn, Jupiter of Libra; Venus, Mercury, Moon of Aquarius; Jupiter, Mars, Sun of Gemini. Crowley also renames the 4, 6, 7 & 8, Truce, Science, Futility and Interference.

Waite's 2 shows a seated blindfolded woman, her back to the sea and rocks, a horned moon above, balancing a diagonally held Sword on each shoulder, her arms crossed on her breast to hold them so. His 3 is a profound symbol of Binah, three Swords piercing a heart. He introduces rain and clouds in the background. The 4 shows a knight laid upon a tomb in an attitude of prayer, one Sword beside him and three others, point downward, suspended over his head and breast. The 5 has the sea in the background and two defeated figures walking away, their Swords left lying on the ground. Their victor carries two Swords on his shoulder and holds another point to the ground. Water again appears in the 6, where all the Swords are point downward in a punt in which a man ferries a woman and child across a river. The 7 shows a man stealing off with five Swords, two others left behind, and an armed camp in the background. The 8 has all the Swords stuck into the ground by a bound and blindfolded woman. The 9 shows a woman sitting up in bed, grief stricken, with nine Swords, horizontally placed, dominating the background. The 10 shows a dead man transfixed by ten Swords.

The 'Egyptian' cards, counting up from the Ace, carry the signs of the decanates Capricorn, Taurus and Virgo of Capricorn; Taurus, Virgo and Capricorn of Taurus; and Virgo, Capricorn and Taurus of Virgo. The 10 rules over the Earth quadrant—an unusual attribution for this suit.

The symbol which Manly P. Hall allocates to Swords is a circle surmounting a Tau cross. On the Ace it is winged, the 2 has a straight trumpet behind it, the 3 a radiant eye looking through the circle, the 4 a balance-pan suspended from each arm of the cross, the 5 a flail, the 6 two of the symbols crossed, the 7 a rose twined about it, the 8 two twined serpents to make it a Caduceus, the 9 a crescent moon, and the 10 a serpent impaled upon it and the whole in a circle.

DISKS: All the traditional Disks have floral decoration and additionally there is an S shaped scroll around the Disks of the 2, often bearing the manufacturer's name, and an open book or unicorn in the centre of the 4.

On the Golden Dawn 2 the scroll becomes a green and gold serpent holding its tail in its mouth and an angelic hand holds the centre. There are, however, no roses on the card. The 3 has a hand holding a branch from which two white rosebuds extend to surmount the upper Disk. The 4 has also a branch but with no flowers or buds, though a full blown rose dominates the centre. The 5 similarly has no buds and roses are falling from the branch. On the 6 buds and flowers touch each Disk. On the 7 buds overhang the top five Disks only. On the 8 the Disks themselves have no central cross and roses touch only the lower four. On the 9 and 10 roses touch every Disk but the 9 is the only card on which additional buds are shown.

The Crowley/Harris 2 likewise shows a serpent, though crowned, and the Disks are tai chi tu signs inscribed in the circular countercharges with the Elemental triangles of Fire and Water, Earth and Air. Like the Golden Dawn card, it suggests rotation. The 3 is similarly a card of great movement, the Disks are wheels at the base of a three-dimensional pyramid and are inscribed with the alchemical signs of Mercury, Salt and Sulphur. The 4 shows a plan of a fortress, the Disks being the corner towers and engraved with the Elemental signs as in the 2. The 5 is in the form of an inverted pentagram and there are other strained and bent Disks in the background. The five main Disks carry the Tattva signs. The 6 is in circular/hexagonal form and each Disk is inscribed with a planetary sign, the Sun being represented in the centre with the Rose Cross. The 7 is in traditional formation, which happens to be that of the geomantic sign of Rubeus. The Disks are of lead and engraved with the signs of Earth and Saturn. The 8, also in usual formation, Populus of geomancy, shows the Disks as flowers on a tree, each protected by a huge leaf. The 9 has the central three Disks interlaced in the centre with the others forming upward and downward pointing triangles above and below. The latter are inscribed with the deities of Saturn, Mars, Jupiter, Mercury, Venus, Luna in Sephirothic formation. The 10 represents by its shape the Tree of Life and each Disk is stamped with a different sign but all representative of Mercury. The Disks are shown as coins on the top of a pile of money and the Disk representing Malkuth is larger than the rest. As with the Golden Dawn cards the decanate symbols are included on the cards. These are, from 2 up: Jupiter, Mars, Sun of Capricorn; Mercury, Moon, Saturn of Taurus; Sun, Venus, Mercury of Virgo. Crowley's changes of designation are Worry for the 5 and Failure for the 7. Also he drops the words 'Harmonious', 'Material', and 'Earthly' from the titles of the 2, 3, 4, 6 & 9. This has also occurred in one or two cards of the other suits, namely 'Restored' and 'Despair' from the 2 and 9 of Swords, 'Material' from the 9 of Cups, and 'Great' from the 9 of Wands.

Waite's 2 likewise shows a lemniscate figure round the Disks of the 2 but he shows them being held also by a dancing man in a tall phallic hat. In the background ships bob up and down on a startlingly undulatory sea. The 3 shows a mason working upon a design of three Disks at a double doorway, watched by two monks who hold the plan. The 4 shows a king holding one Disk, another on his head and one under each foot, a city in the background. The 5 has two beggars passing in the snow before a lighted window on which five Disks are inscribed. The 6 shows a merchant, scales in one hand, giving money to one of two kneeling beggars. The Disks are shown overhead. The 7 depicts a man leaning on a staff gazing into a bush in which are seven Disks. The 8 again shows a mason carving the Disks, working on one of them, another at his feet, and the others hung up on display. The 9 has the Disks embedded in prolific grape-vines, a garden and manor in the background. A woman stands in the midst with a bird on her wrist. The 10 shows a man and woman at the gate of a manor house and grounds. They are accompanied by a child who looks at a bearded ancient sitting caressing two dogs. His robe is heavily embroidered with mystic signs and bunches of grapes. The ten Disks are superimposed on the whole picture and suggest by their positioning the Tree of Life.

The Knapp cards have geometric signs inscribed on them. Starting from the 2 these are a pentagram, a hexagram, a pentagram in a diamond and square, a pentagram superimposed on a circle, two triangles of which the lower is reversed, a triangle over a square, two squares, two triangles with a pentagram between, two pentagrams of which the lower is inverted. The actual Disks, as in the Cup suit, follow generally the configuration of these introduced figures. Manly P. Hall has allocated the symbol of a cube to the suit with figures inscribed on it appropriate to each card. The Ace has a pointed lemniscate figure and the 2 a pentagram within a Zodiacal wheel. The cards from 3 to 9 have the planetary symbols of the Mundane Chakras of the relevant Sephiroth—Saturn, Jupiter, Mars, Sun, Venus, Mercury, Moon. The 10 has a symbol of the Four Elements, signifying Earth.

The 'Egyptian' 10 is referred to the Air quadrant. (Earth is more usually aligned with this suit but Zain prefers to give it to Swords.) The other cards, in ascending order from the Ace take the decanates Libra, Aquarius, Gemini of Libra; Aquarius, Gemini, Libra of Aquarius; Gemini, Libra, Aquarius of Gemini.

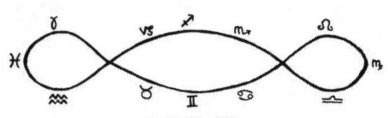

The Moebius Ribbon

Part III

The Court Cards

THE COURT CARDS

1. The Court Cards of the Tarot are sixteen in number—four to each suit and some confusion has arisen over their exact nomenclature. In the modern playing cards there are three Court Cards only to each suit—King, Queen, Knave or Jack. In the Tarot there is additionally a figure on horseback and this has been generally called the Knight.

2. A tradition has thus grown up to call the seated Tarot Court figures the King and Queen; the equestrian figure the Knight; and the standing figure the Page or Princess. This is not altogether a happy arrangement as it obscures the symbolic issues. The suits show the type of force that is manifesting and the figure on the Court Card shows how it manifests.

3. This method of manifestation is summed up in the well known Divine Name of JHVH, and an understanding of the nature of this formula can be most easily obtained, (by anyone who has a smattering of the Qabalah), by placing the first letter, (Yod), on Chokmah; the second, (Heh), on Binah; the third, (Vau), on Tiphareth; and the last, (Heh final), on Malkuth. Alternatively the letters can be allocated to groups of Sephiroth in accordance with the division of the Tree of Life into the Four Worlds. Thus we could put Yod on Kether, which represents Atziluth or the Archetypal World; Heh on Chokmah and Binah, which between them form the Creative World, or Briah; Vau on the Sephiroth of the 'magical circuit' of which Tiphareth is the centre, and which together conform the Formative World, or Yetzirah; and the final Heh on Malkuth, the Material World, Assiah.

4. In these alternative arrangements we have a practical example of the use of correspondences on a flexible basis,

which is essential if one is to get the most out of the Qabalah. We have said that Yod equals Kether and also Yod equals Chokmah. It would be nonsensical to say that because of this Kether equals Chokmah—but it does draw attention to the fact that the one Sephirah is a reflection of the other. Similarly, the first Heh being made representative of Binah in one system and Chokmah and Binah in the other teaches us something about Binah and Briah, the Creative World, although the two are not identical and should not be confused. Again, Vau can represent either Tiphareth or àll the Formative Sephiroth. This indicates the unifying, harmonising function of the central Sephirah, Tiphareth. And the fact that Heh final is attributed to the single Sephirah Malkuth in both systems shows the cardinal importance of that Sephirah and the Material World.

5. Reference to the Sephirothic attribution of the letters will indicate their main characteristics when used in the Divine Name and reference to their attribution to the Four Worlds will serve to expand those key ideas.

6. Chokmah represents the prime movement or energy, the dynamism that gets a thing going. Hence Yod is placed upon it and in the Tarot Court Cards it is represented by the Knight on horseback.

7. Binah represents the reception of this prime energy into Form basis. That is, the initial energy swings in a circle, (to take an analogy from 'The Cosmic Doctrine'), thus forming its own area of limitation so that denser manifestation is possible within that sphere of delimitation—or Ring-Pass-Not. This circumscription of effort is what Qabalists call a Binah condition and to this condition is attributed Heh, and the seated Queen of the Tarot Court. Were the initial force not limited in this way it would disperse into nothingness, no resulting form would be achieved, it would be as a breath of wind in the Cosmos which stirred not the surface of the Waters of Manifestation.

8. Tiphareth represents the establishment of the resultant form in harmonised balance in manifestation, though it has

not reached a dense concrete phase yet, it is still new, creative and fluidic. It is the result of the former processes, and could be said to be the Son of the Knight and Queen, a result of the union of the two former aspects. In fact, the force behind the three is one and the same, it is merely in a different phase of action in each case, as it is actually a Three in One and this may throw some light on the Mystery of the Blessed Trinity. The corresponding Court Card, representing Vau, is what is commonly called the King, but he is the son, not the consort, of the Queen. An alternative name seems necessary for him therefore and the function of force he represents would be better symbolised by having him ride in a chariot rather than sit passively on a throne.

9. Malkuth is the end result, the completion of the original impulse. It is now no longer an impulse or force or energy but an achieved thing, a form in material existence, whether it be a Universe or a simple human gesture motivated by the true self. This is what the Heh final stands for; its corresponding Court Card is the Page or Princess. The latter is the better of the two titles as the figure, representing Form, should obviously be feminine.

10. Applying these concepts to the Four Worlds we have the prime urge to action in the Archetypal World, Kether, which is stabilised in the Creative World of Chokmah and Binah. This is almost an instantaneous process; as soon as the archetypal conception is first manifested in Kether its reflection occurs in Chokmah and the reflection is stabilised in Binah—the Supernal Triad is formed. The further influx of force causes effects in the Formative World because the channel for the force has been formed by the limitation created by the Creative World. Without limitation there can be no manifest creation, and this manifestation takes the form of 'formations'—complications of the original force, which, because of its limitation, acts and reacts upon itself, bringing definition and lower-plane application. The final result is in objective manifestation in the Material World, Malkuth.

11. The true Court Cards of the Tarot are, therefore, in order of manifestation, Knight, Queen, King, Princess, though it would perhaps be better to name them in accordance with the terminology of the Colour Scales: King, Queen, Emperor, Empress. Better still would be to call the Colour Scales and the Cards by the common terminology of King, Queen, Prince and Princess.

12. The Colour Scales are applicable to the manifestation of force in the Four Worlds. Thus the whole Tree in Atziluth may be conceived in the colours of the King Scale, the whole Tree in Briah in the Queen Scale, the whole Tree in Yetzirah in the Emperor Scale and the whole Tree in Assiah in the Empress Scale. In practice, however, it is usual to counterchange the Scales of King and Queen or Emperor and Empress in relating the Sephiroth and Paths. If the Sephiroth are pictured in one Scale then the Paths should be pictured in the other and vice versa.

13. It was the tradition of the Golden Dawn to depict the Court Cards as Elemental forces, that is, to refer them to the Tree in Malkuth. Thus the Aces, the Roots of the Elements, would be referred to the Kether of Malkuth, the Knights to the Chokmah of Malkuth, the Queens to the Binah of Malkuth, the Kings to the Tiphareth of Malkuth and the Knaves to the Malkuth of Malkuth. These attributions would apply to the action of Fire, Water, Air and Earth which are represented respectively by Wands, Cups, Swords and Disks. The esoteric titles for the Court Cards used in this manner are as follows:

WANDS: *Ace* —Root of the Powers of Fire.

          Knight—Lord of Flame & Lightning. King of the Spirits of Fire.

          Queen—Queen of the Thrones of Flames.

          King —Prince of the Chariot of Fire.

          Knave—Princess of the Shining Flame. Rose of the Palace of Fire.

CUPS: *Ace*   —Root of the Powers of Water.

              Knight—Lord of the Waves and the Waters. King of the Hosts of the Sea.

              Queen—Queen of the Thrones of the Waters.

              King —Prince of the Chariot of the Waters.

              Knave—Princess of the Waters and the Lotus.

SWORDS: *Ace*   —Root of the Powers of Air.

              Knight—Lord of the Wind and the Breezes. Lord of the Spirits of the Air.

              Queen—Queen of the Thrones of the Air.

              King —Prince of the Chariot of the Wind.

              Knave—Princess of the Rushing Winds. Lotus of the Palace of Air.

DISKS: *Ace*   —Root of the Powers of Earth.

              Knight—Lord of the Wide & Fertile Land. King of the Spirits of Earth.

              Queen—Queen of the Thrones of Earth.

              King —Prince of the Chariot of Earth.

              Knave—Princess of the Echoing Hills. Rose of the Palace of Earth.

14. However, the Elements have their analogues at every level and so the attributions could be made in every Sephirah besides Malkuth, but particularly the central Sephiroth on the line of the Middle Pillar. The Kerubic forces of Kether descend the central Path from Kether to Malkuth. This is indicated by the Kerubic signs about the corners of The Universe, the Trump of the 32nd Path. Malkuth is, of course, the Sphere of the Elements and Yesod is its Foundation— and being of the Second Plane, the sphere of contact with the Nature Forces. Tiphareth is the Sephirah from which the Elements are controlled; it is the Sephirah of the Elemental Kings, those Elementals which have begun to respond to the spiritual vibrations. An excellent place for the attribution of all the Court Cards would also be the Sephirah Daath. Its associated Archangels are the Archangels of the

Four Cardinal Points, each of which has its Elemental attribution: East and Raphael to Air, South and Michael to Fire, West and Gabriel to Water, North and Uriel to Earth. And in Kether are the Four Holy Living Creatures, Lion/Fire, Eagle/Water, Man/Air, Bull/Earth.

15. A further system of attributions is the placing of the Court Cards down the central Sephiroth. The Aces go on Kether and correspond to the Kerubic Aspects of God, the Knights on Daath corresponding to the Archangels of the Quarters, the Queens on Tiphareth corresponding to the Elemental Kings, and the Kings and Knaves to Yesod and Malkuth corresponding to the higher and lower Elemental beings. This would be a formula of the Heavenly Jerusalem coming down to Earth—the imprint of the perfection of the Planetary Entity upon the primitive Elemental forces of the Planetary Being. (The terminology used is that of 'The Cosmic Doctrine'. The Tibetan would call the Planetary Being the Planetary Entity and he appears to have no term for what is here called the Planetary Entity—the Pattern to which the Planetary Being must attain.) Another system of correspondences on these lines would be to envisage Sanat Kumara, the Lord of the World, in Kether; the Guiding Intelligence of the Earth, the Archangel Sandalphon in Daath; the Planetary Entity in Tiphareth; and the Planetary Being in Yesod and Malkuth.

16. It is possible also, by allocating the Elements themselves to the Tree of Life and following out their correspondences with the suits, to arrive at a system of sub-Elemental categories. The basic Elemental allocation is Fire to Chokmah, Water to Binah, Air to Tiphareth and Earth to Malkuth. It is to these Sephiroth that we have also allocated the four Court figures, so from this line of correspondences we may consider the Knight of Wands to represent Fire of Fire, Queen of Wands to be Water of Fire, King of Wands to be Air of Fire and Knave of Wands to be Earth of Fire. Similar attributions apply to the other suits and so we have a table of sixteen sub-Elements. This is

similar to the Eastern Tattva system and the Tarot Court
Cards could be considered as the Western correspondence
of this system.

17. The Tattva cards are Elemental emblems—a red
triangle, (Agni), for Fire; a silver crescent, (Apas), for
Water; a yellow square, (Prithivi), for Earth; and a blue
circle, (Vayu), for Air. These are formed into representations of the sub-Elements by countercharging each sign
with a small respresentation of every other. Additionally
in the Tattva system there is the black egg, (Akasa), for
Spirit, and this of course corresponds to the Tarot Ace. As
there is no suit representing Akasa the total number of
Tarots in this arrangement is 20 as opposed to 25 Tattvas.
Nonetheless, it is surprising that the Golden Dawn thought
it necessary to introduce an Eastern system into the Western
Tradition when the Court Cards of the Tarot could do just
as good a job—probably better as they are indigenous to
the West.

18. The difficulty may have been over the five 'missing'
cards but it would seem quite easy to make up this number
from the Greater Arcana, calling the new suit Trumps.
There are among the Trumps pictures which amply represent the Court Cards. Thus the Knight of Trumps would be
The Emperor, (who is not on horseback but whose association with Alchemical Sulphur gives him the same potency);
the Queen of Trumps would be The Empress, seated on her
throne as all the other Queens are; the King of Trumps would
be The Chariot, showing a prince in his chariot as all the
Court Cards do, or should do; and the Princess of Trumps
would be The Universe, the single maiden of the other
Court Cards, surrounded by attributions of manifestation
and stability. Finally, the Ace of Trumps would be none
other than The Fool, whose zero cypher is not only representative of Spirit but is similar in shape to Akasa. If it is
worth mentioning, the numbers of the cards mentioned
above are the more important mystical numbers, namely
III, IV, VII, and XXI.

19. There is very much more than mere accident in the numbering of the Tarot Trumps and experimentation along these lines can be very interesting. For example, there could be a case made out for having Temperance as the Princess, in which case the numbering is even more revealing; the first two numbers added together give the third, (III + IV = VII), and the sum of these three reveals the fourth, Temperance. (III + IV + VII = XIV). In such speculations however, let us always remember the reality, that is the Ariadne's thread to prevent us getting lost in a maze of symbolism and cypher. The minotaur, incidentally, who lived in the maze, was the product of an unnatural lust of a human being for a beast whose sacrifice was denied to the gods. It is thus well emblematic of the result of symbol worship. It is also significant that the highly ingenious Daedelus was a party to the perversion and built the intricate wooden cow in which Pasiphae lay to satisfy her lust for the sacred bull. Whatever may be said against symbol worship, (the love for the object and not the reality for which it stands), the methods of the symbol jugglers can never be accused of lacking ingenuity.

20. The Golden Dawn again provides numerous examples of this. The substitution of the letters of the Divine Name, JHVH, for example, renders little but confusion if they are replaced by the corresponding Tarot Trumps or Zodiacal Signs. Yet this was a favourite Golden Dawn device. Whilst it is quite legitimate to experiment along these lines these tentative gropings have been almost exalted to a high and secret place in the Western Mystery Tradition in the minds of many. The reason for this is that many books on the subject are little more than pastiches of the Golden Dawn Knowledge Papers. Genuine results of individual experiment and experience are all too rare and so much that is dead letter is handled blindly on from one generation of occult writers to another.

21. It cannot be emphasised too strongly that the study of symbolism is useless if it is to be a mere intellectual diver-

sion. Though there are some magical techniques with symbols that are not without risk, at least a belief in the powers behind symbols, even if it verges on superstition, is a healthier state than the internal stagnation brought about by the accumulation of intellectual data. This is basically the difference between the esoteric and the exoteric approaches to mysticism.

22. Given the necessary self-discipline and a basic knowledge of the symbols of the Western Tradition the way is open to the heights of spiritual progress and occult knowledge, and no-one else can impose any limitations or bar the way. The only other qualification is that having selected a system one should stick to it, for otherwise confusion and consequent waste of time and energy will almost inevitably follow. To take an example from the substance of this chapter—the Elemental symbols and colours of the Tattva system are different from those of the West. While an experienced occultist can work with either, such eclecticism would be difficult for the beginner. The same applies to other attributions such as whether Fire should be allocated to the sphere of mind and Air to the Spirit or vice versa. All bona fide systems are the product of generations of experimental work and all will bring results, but though broad principles are the same, details differ, and the solitary neophyte has enough to contend with without making matters more difficult for himself.

23. The basic symbolism of the Western Tradition has been propounded in the two volumes of this book in more than adequate profusion. So much can be shown but real progress is up to the application of the individual. Help is never stinted from the inner planes though, for in addition to the well known saying of the Mysteries, "Ask and ye shall receive, seek and ye shall find, knock and it shall be opened unto you", there is the other half of the formula contained in the words of Our Lord: "Behold, I stand at the door and knock: if any man hear my voice, and open the door, I will come in to him, and will sup with him and he with me."

24. No-one is left to struggle unaided, however much appearances may appear to prove the contrary.

NOTES ON THE DESIGN OF
THE ACES AND COURT CARDS

In the medieval packs the Court Cards are the least satisfactory from an esoteric point of view, being highly conventionalised, and this is true for most of the subsequent esoteric designs, for the designers have, on the whole, allowed themselves to be too closely bound by tradition. Thus, for the most part, any esoteric significance is shown purely by ancillary symbolism. It is only in the Golden Dawn and Crowley/Harris packs that any attempt at Elemental 'atmosphere' has been made. Also the varying interpretations of what the Court Cards actually signify make many of the designs of doubtful value. The traditional Ace designs are, on the other hand, very suggestive, and are quite closely followed by the modern versions, this time with happier results.

WANDS: The traditional Ace is a huge club wielded by a radiant angelic hand appearing from a cloud. The club has three lopped off branches and there are either Yods or flowers and fruit falling about it. The Golden Dawn followed this tradition and made the Yods twentytwo in number, divided into groups of three, seven and twelve to indicate the Mother, Double and Single letters of the Hebrew alphabet. As Wands is the suit of Fire they also made the Yods flamelike and gave the whole an appearance of a burning torch. This was followed by the Crowley/Harris card, which is more geometric in shape to give the impression of dynamic force, and with ten Yods, for the Sephiroth, in the form of flames coming from the club-like torch. Waite gives a hand appearing from a cloud holding a stick with budding branches, ten leaves on it and eight falling off. There is usually no intentional significance in Waite's numbers. Case also gives a hand appearing from a cloud but it holds a diamond-headed sceptre with three segments on the shaft, not a club. The diamond at the top of the sceptre is white and surmounted by ten Yods, in pyramid formation, and the diamond at the further end is black. This pattern of sceptre is used throughout the whole suit. Knapp also uses one design for the sceptres of the Ace and of all the other cards of the suit—in his case one with a trefoil top and a pointed base. The Ace has, traditionally, a triangle superimposed on the trefoil and a rising sun in the background, while above the sceptre is a line drawing of a circle over a triangle over a square. The 'Egyptian' Ace is a simple Egyptian phoenix wand without further attributes except for the stars of the appropriate decanate constellation.

The traditional designs of the Court Cards usually show the Knight on horseback with a round club like the Ace, the Queen seated with a huge bulbous sceptre, the King seated with a sceptre more closely resembling the Wands of the small cards, and the Valet or Knave standing with a shorn branch something like the uprights of the gallows on Trump XII, The Hanged Man. The Knight and King have lemniscate hats, the King's being a crown additionally. The Knave has a somewhat nondescript hat and the Queen a crown.

The Golden Dawn Knight is winged and riding on a black horse with fiery mane and tail. He has a winged Norse helmet with crown, mail armour and a scarlet mantle. His crest is a winged black horse's head and he holds a club like the Ace, with flaming ends. The Queen has long red-gold hair and is throned above flames, her robe open to disclose mail armour, but her arms bare. Her crest is a winged leopard's head and a leopard crouches by her side. The Wand has the traditional bulbous conical head. The King has white wings and a golden winged crown. His chariot is drawn by a lion over flames and his crest is a lion's head. Like the Queen, his arms are bare and he has scale armour, while the Wand again resembles the traditional pattern but is flaming. The Knave or Princess is a gold-red haired Amazon with bare arms, shoulders and breasts and a kilt reaching only to the knees. Her armour consists only of a mail belt, broad at front and back, and a Corinthian helmet with crown and plume. Her crest is a tiger's head and she has a tiger skin mantle. At her right hand is a golden or brass altar with fire upon it and decorated with ram's heads. In her left hand is a huge club leaping with flames.

The Crowley/Harris Knight is fully armoured, with winged helmet on a rampant black charger with flaming mane and tail, and his mantle is huge and extends down to the rolling flames at the bottom of the card. The Queen is throned on high over sharp pointed flames, with very long hair and a radiant crown. Her Wand is a shaft headed with a pine cone and she caresses a couchant leopard. The Prince rides a lion drawn chariot amidst flames. On the card he appears to be naked save for a radiant helmet and a phallic sign upon his chest. In his right hand is a phoenix wand and his left arm is extended with the reins loosely draped over the wrist, as if to demonstrate effortless control. His attitude suggests Alchemical Sulphur. As with the Queen, there is a winged globe above his head. Oddly enough, Crowley has described this card as a warrior in chain mail rather than naked as he seems to be on the photographic reproduction of the card in 'The Book of Thoth'. This factor occurs on all the Prince cards of this pack. The Princess is naked and leaping in a Yod-like flame, pulling a tiger skin behind her by the tail and holding a Wand topped with a radiant sun. Her headdress is two flaming plumes and nearby is a ram's head altar with flames upon it.

The Case Knight is armoured, on horseback, though the horse does not appear to be black, and his helmet has a waving plume. In the background is a road leading into the distance past a castle. The sceptre on all the Court Cards is the same design as for the whole suit. The Queen is throned, with mountains in the background, and besides her sceptre, she holds a sunflower. She is crowned and lions and sunflowers decorate the throne. The King is seated likewise but has a robe and throne decorated with salamanders. The Page stands in open country, has a sheathed knife at his belt and a plumed hat. Two trees in the background, like the three on the Knight card, are cypress trees, suggesting, like the plumes, flames.

Most of Case's symbolism follows Waite except that Waite shows pyramids in the background of the Knight card and a salamander design on the Knight's surcoat. Case's and Waite's Queen and King are the same in symbolism if not in draughtsmanship except that Waite shows a salamander by the King and a cat in front of the Queen. The crown of Waite's King also suggests flames. Waite's Page stands in open country with conical hills in the background and has a salamander design on his dress and a flame-like plume to his hat. He bears no dagger as does Case's Page. The Wands of all Waite's Court Cards are his usual rough staff sprouting occasional leaves.

Knapp's Knight is in full armour, his horse's accoutrements, embroidered with crosses. Unlike the previous esoteric cards, the horse is walking, not rearing. His sceptre, as with the other Court Cards is crownheaded and he also bears a red-cross white flag and a shield with a Sun in the centre. He wears a voluminous plume and a castle is in the background. The Queen is throned indoors and there is a chequered pavement about her. Maltese crosses and crowns decorate the altar and a Sun sign hangs about her neck. The King holds a scroll and points with a sceptre to a globe of the world at his feet. His throne is, like the Queen's, at the top of three steps and surrounded by a chequered pavement. The throne has crown symbols, which, like the sceptre heads, suggest by their shape the Hebrew letter Shin. The Throne is also surmounted by a Calvary Cross and Sun disk. The King has a Sun emblem at his breast. The Knave, (signified in this pack by an S — presumably for Serf or Slave — as the Knight is designated W, presumably for Warrior), is kneeling, spade in hand, planting a staff. A sceptre lies beside him but he is obviously a servant or commoner. Manly P. Hall's symbols, all in the triangle he designates to his suit, are, for the Knight, a lingam or ankh; for the Queen, a vesica piscis overlapping the base of the triangle; for the King, a letter Vau, radiant; and for the Knave, a cube. These symbols show he endorses the usual esoteric order of the Court Cards.

The 'Egyptian' Court Cards show a Horseman writing in a scroll with a rainbow in the background, a Queen being offered jewels by a black slave-girl, a King rushing, sword aloft, in his battle chariot, the Horus hawk above him, and the Jack a youth shooting a bow and arrow. This symbolism seems to derive from the attributions peculiar to this pack of allocating the King to Aries, the Queen to Leo, the Jack to Sagittarius and the Horseman to Fire.

CUPS: The traditional Ace in its purest form shows a large Cup shaped something like the traditional idea of the Ark of the Covenant, with four high pillars incorporated in its design and a similar pillar shaped dome at the top. Other versions show a gigantic pumpkin shaped goblet. The Golden Dawn Ace has the Cup supported by the usual angelic hand and with a fountain rising from it with the water falling as spray into a pool beneath in which grow lotuses or water lilies. A Hebrew letter Heh is traced in the spray of the fountain. The Crowley/Harris version shows the Holy Grail mounted in a lotus with a fountain gushing from it, a dove—according to Crowley—descending into it, with a cross-marked Host. There are, according to Waite, four streams gushing from his Ace Cup—though on the card there are five—and falling into the pool at the bottom of the card where water lilies are growing. There are also several Yods in the air and a W or inverted M on the Cup. Case reverts to the Ark like shape—which in fact Waite's design subtly suggests, and also has it supported by an angelic hand but without any other attributions. Knapp's card shows a Cup in the mouth of which is a radiant heart with a rose on a Calvary Cross. The 'Egyptian' card is a simple Cup with usual background stars.

The traditional Knight is bareheaded and, as usual, on horseback. The Queen is crowned and throned under what seems to be a pavilion. The King is throned indoors and has a double lemniscate hat/crown; his Cup is the only one not to bear crosses at the base. The Valet or Knave is bareheaded and carries his hat in one hand; there is, however, a fillet above his brow. A flower blooms nearby.

The Golden Dawn Knight is winged, with flying hair, and rides a white horse over the sea. Through similarly accoutred to the previous Knight, his crest is a peacock with open wings and a crab appears from the Cup in his hand. The Queen is likewise fair and her throne is overflowing water wherein are lotuses or lilies. Her crest is an ibis and one stands beside her upon which she lays her hand. In this hand she holds a lotus or lily and in the other her Cup from whence a crayfish issues. Her general dress resembles the Queen of Wands. The King has a winged crown and, though generally attired like the previous King, his mail resembles feathers. His chariot is drawn by an eagle, which is also his crest. Below is a calm lake and in one hand he holds a lily or lotus and in the other his Cup from which a serpent arises, though with its head drooping down towards the lake. The Princess is another Amazon but standing in the midst of spray on a foaming sea in which swims a dolphin. Her cloak is thin and floating and lined with swan's down, while a swan with opening wings is her crest. In one hand is a lily or lotus and in the other a Cup with an emerging turtle.

The Crowley/Harris cards follow the same basic symbolism except that they have their own unique style. The only differences are minor ones. The Queen is enthroned over, and reflected in, a still lake; the King has tenuous gaseous wings and apart from a minimum of armour, is unclothed, while rain falls into the water below him; the Princess is dancing with a flaming robe embroidered with crystal forms. Crowley has suggested that a scorpion could well be incorporated in the King's card to emphasise its more subtle side.

Waite's Knight has a winged helmet and heels and a river flows into the background of the card. The Queen holds a complicated Ark-like form of the Cup and sits on a sea shore. Her throne is rounded at the top like the inside of a pumpkin and is decorated with representations of mer-children. The King's throne actually floats upon the sea with ship and dolphin in the background. The back of the throne is lotus shaped and he holds in addition to the usual shaped Cup a short lotus sceptre. The Page has a lily-embroidered coat and, standing with the sea in the background, gazes at a fish emerging from his Cup.

Like Waite's Knight, Case's has dolphin-decorated harness but rides by the seashore and has no wings about his person. There is a crayfish design on his breastplate. The Queen sits by the sea shore, cliffs in the background as with Waite, and her throne is decorated with dolphins and crayfish. It loops over at the top in the form of a dolphin-headed canopy. The clasp of her cloak is a shell and in the distance is a ship. The King is also by the sea, perhaps on a sandbank, and his crown and throne are dolphin-decorated. Boats pass in the distance. The Page stands by the seashore armed with a dagger in a dolphin-decorated sheath. A dolphin jumps in the background.

The Knapp Knight is standing with a huge sword and shield before a castle, the sword point down and a Cup emblazoned on the shield. The Queen is enthroned at the top of three steps and holds in one hand a cross-headed sceptre and the Cup in her other hand, issuing flames. The throne has twisted spiral columns and is decorated with Cups. The King is out of doors and holds a flaming Cup in one hand and points to the Earth with the other. The Page is standing barefooted by a broken tree. His wrists are manacled and he hides his Cup under a cloth.

Manley P. Hall has allocated a radiant swastika, a rose, a radiant Vau and a radiant Sun, each within a vesica piscis to these cards in respective order.

The 'Egyptian' cards show a Horseman with Cup, Queen on a moon boat accompanied by two 'Eyes of Horus', King with triangular masonic apron with his foot upon a crab and holding Cup and moon/heart symbol, and the Jack with hands apparently bound, carrying a Cup. The astrological attributions given are Water, Scorpio, Cancer and Pisces respectively.

SWORDS: The traditional Ace shows an angelic hand holding a Sword the point of which enters a crown at the top of the card. A branch of leaves and a branch of berries depend from the right and left hand sides of the crown, and either Yod shaped leaves or else a twig of berries is shown falling. The Golden Dawn made the crown a white radiant celestial one and with an olive branch on the right and a palm branch on the left, with six Vaus falling. The Crowley/Harris crown is a twentytwo-pointed diadem and the word Thelema is engraved on the Sword with two Moons and three Suns and a twined serpent on the handle. There are clouds about the lower part of the card and triangular designs in the background. The Waite card follows tradition but with six Yods falling and a mountainous scene below. Case is similar but without the mountains. The 'Egyptian' version shows a simple curved sword and Knapp a simple straight one, point down, depending from an envisaged Moon.

The traditional Knight follows the usual pattern but has the unusual feature of one crescent Moon epaulette with a face on it. These appear on both shoulders of the King after the manner of Trump XII, The Chariot. The Knight's headgear resembles that of The Emperor, Trump IV, while the Queen has the usual crown, the King a lemniscate hat/crown and the Page also has a hat with lemniscate brim. Additionally the King and Page carry a sceptre in the hand not holding the Sword.

The Golden Dawn Knight, winged, rides a brown horse over dark driving clouds. His crest is a winged six-pointed star and his helmet is crowned and winged. The Queen has grey cumulous clouds beneath her throne and apart from her crest of a winged child's head is attired like the previous Queens. In her free hand she holds a newly severed man's head. The King has wings and a winged crown and drives a chariot over grey nimbus rain clouds. His crest is a winged angel's head with a pentagram on the brow and he carries a sickle in his free hand. Almost naked butterfly-winged youths, (Arch-Elementals), draw the chariot. There are also butterfly wings on their Wands and the fillets they wear; the Wands are each surmounted by a pentagram and the fillets have a pentagram design on them. The Princess is an Amazon giving the impression of great lightness and agility with a Medusa's head crest. By her side is a small silver altar giving off grey incense, and below are grey cirrus clouds.

The Crowley/Harris Knight rushes at breakneck speed through the air on his steed carrying a Sword in one hand and a rapier in the other, held before him. His crest is a revolving fourfold wing. The Queen is naked to the waist and enthroned on a pinnacle of clouds. Her crest is a child's head which gives off rays and she holds a man's severed head. The design of the Prince card is very geometric but the symbolism is principally the same as the Golden Dawn card. The

Princess is helmed and ready to fight. As with the Golden Dawn card, there is a suggestion of Artemis or Minerva. The altar by her has no fire or smoke issuing from it. About her are angry driving clouds.

Waite's Knight also is rushing headlong — but through a windswept scene. The Queen is seated in the open and a winged child's head decorates the throne. The King is also in the open air and appears to be sitting in judgment. The back of his throne has a crescent Moon and butterfly design. The Page is an alert looking youth in a wide plain with many clouds in the sky.

Case follows Waite closely but with a few additions. The Knight has a winged helm and harness embossed with a winged sphere, the Queen has cloud and butterfly emblems about her person, the King is equipped with a book, and the Page has a satchel at his waist similar to that carried by The Fool, Trump 0.

There is little to remark about the Knapp designs as they have little additional symbolism to the bare personages. The Knight is on horseback and the usual thrones of Queen and King are decorated with orbs surmounted by Calvary Crosses. The Knave's wrists are manacled. Hall's symbols are based upon the cross he uses peculiar to this suit—a circle on a line-drawn Tau. The Knight's has another smaller one slanted across it, the Queen's is superimposed by a vesica piscis, the King's has a Vau in the circle and the Knave's transfixes a cube.

The 'Egyptian' cards show the Horseman before a rainbow, the Queen taking an offering to an altar, the King seated before a table on which is a vase and other objects, the Jack kneeling before an empty throne. The Horseman is allocated to Earth and the Queen, King and Jack to Virgo, Taurus and Capricorn.

DISKS: The traditional Ace is a central Disk surrounded by foliage and a flower in each corner of the card. The Disk itself often has a central four petalled flower design and is of four concentric circles with a twelvefold pattern all round. The Golden Dawn complicate matters by having an angelic hand holding a rose branch with the Disk upon it and overhead a small winged circle surmounted by a Maltese cross. There are four roses and two buds on the card. The Disk itself is of five concentric circles with a white centre charged with a red Greek cross and from which twelve white rays radiate. The Crowley/Harris Ace contains some very fine symbolism notwithstanding his personal appropriation of the centre by placing his assumed Magical Name around the Disk and his number, 666, in the middle, with his favourite phallic/philosophic symbol. The Disk is like a rose coloured jewel which, if visualised in three dimensions, would have twentytwo facets. In the centre is a decangle, the ten of Malkuth and the number of the Sephiroth, and also a heptagon, representative of the seven planes. The whole Disk has six wings representing the close relationship between Tiphareth and Malkuth, the Kingdom that is to come to Earth. Waite and Case have an angelic hand holding a Disk on which is inscribed a pentagram and on Waite's card there is also a flower garden with a flowery arch leading to high mountains in the distance. Knapp shows a golden coin superimposed on a pentagram with golden rays and a crown surmounting it. The 'Egyptian' Ace is a simple Disk divided into fourfold symbolism.

The traditional designs of the Court Cards follow the usual pattern for the others. The King and Page have lemniscate hats, the former also with a crown, and the Queen also bears a sceptre.

The Golden Dawn Knight is dark and winged and riding on a light brown horse over fields of ripening corn, bearing a sceptre with a hexagram at the top. His crest is a stag's head. The Queen is also dark and one side of her face dark and the other light. Her crest is a winged goat's head and she has a goat at her side. The Disk appears as a gold orb which she holds, and in the other hand she holds a cube-surmounted sceptre. All about her is dark, sandy, earth. The King's chariot is drawn by a bull and his crest is a winged bull's head. He is winged, and like the Queen, has an orb of gold, but held downwards, and a sceptre surmounted by orb and cross. He drives over a land of flowers. The Princess is an Amazon with red-brown hair standing amid grass and flowers. She suggests Hera, Demeter and Persephone. Her crest is a winged ram's head and she wears a sheepskin cloak; the sceptre she holds is surmounted by a circular disk.

The Crowley/Harris Knight is a short sturdy warrior seated on a heavy shire horse. His stag head crested helmet is thrown back and he bears a large heavy circular shield and a flail. There is luxuriant foliage about him and cultivated fields in the distance. The Queen looks across a desert wherein a stream winds, fertilising it, and oases are springing up. She has huge spiral horns on her helmet and holds besides her Disk of interlaced circles a long sceptre headed with a cube in which is shown a three dimensional hexagram. Her armour consists of small round scales and by her a goat stands upon a globe. The symbolism of the Prince follows that of the Golden Dawn though the style is of course totally different. His orb is a globe marked with mathematical symbols so that it resembles almost a gyroscope. Like the other Princes, he is almost naked; and there are emblems of flowers and fruit all over the chariot and background. The Princess stands in a grove of trees by an altar shaped like a wheatsheaf. Her Disk is like a rose with three rows of twelve petals and a tai chi tu sign in the centre. Her crest is a ram's head and the diamond head of her sceptre is held to the Earth.

Waite's Knight sits on a heavy black standing horse in the midst of rolling ploughed fields. The Queen sits in a flowery bower surrounded by verdant growth. Her throne is decorated with fruits and ram's heads and a rabbit or hare plays nearby. The King likewise is surrounded by fructification and growth and his robe is similarly embroidered. He holds a short globe-headed sceptre and his throne is decorated with bull's heads. Behind him is a low stone wall and a castle instead of the river, trees and distant mountains of the Queen's card. The Page wanders through open green countryside with his Disk hovering just above his hands.

Case's Knight and horse are not so heavy as the foregoing. The Queen and King are similar to Waite's in general symbolism except that the Queen's throne is decorated with a winged child's head and a pomegranate and there is no rabbit or hare. There is no stone wall behind the King but otherwise the symbolism is the same; the globe on his sceptre is more obviously a globe of the Earth. The Page stands on a road with a castle in the background and has flowers in his hat and is armed with a dagger or sword, sheathed.

The Knapp Knight has no horse, but stands with a heavy sword, point down, and has a long shield inscribed with a pentagram in a circle and a red lion rampant. The Queen is throned at the top of three steps, has a cross at her breast, and bears a crowned globe sceptre. The King is standing with a similar sceptre by a chest of gold coins. The Knave is in prison chained by the ankles to a treasure chest. He lifts his hands to the barred windows through which a Sun, emblazoned with a white pentagram, shines. Hall's symbols, all inscribed upon a cube, are the circle surmounted Tau, or ankh; vesica piscis; radiant Vau; cube.

The 'Egyptian' Horseman stands before a rainbow holding a moneybag. The Queen sits holding out in extended arms a sistrum and a balance. The King is Osiris throned and the Jack is reading a scroll. The Horseman bears the sign of Air and the other cards the signs of Libra, Gemini and Aquarius.

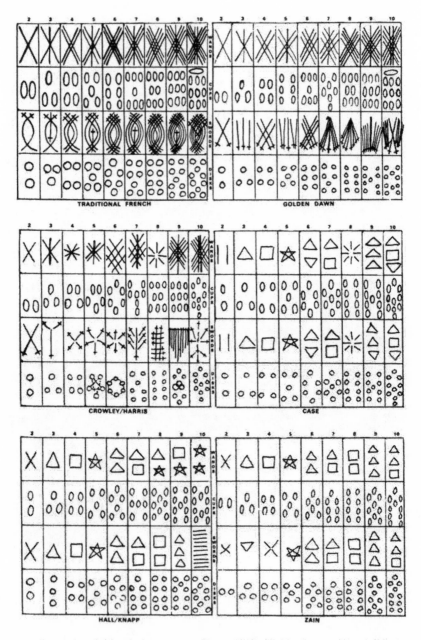

Approximate Symbol Layout in Some of the Better Known Tarot Sets

POSTSCRIPT

Practical Work on the Paths and Tarot

PRACTICAL WORK ON THE PATHS AND TAROT

1. Path-working, without the ability to concentrate, to meditate, or without a good knowledge of the nature, attributions and symbolism of each Sephirah on the Tree of Life is an almost impossible task—an attempt to make bricks without straw. Therefore, before any work of this nature is attempted the student should have studied the first volume of this book and practised, for some months at least, regular concentration exercises and meditation upon the Sephiroth.

2. The work on the Sephiroth will prepare the ground for Path-working, for each Path is influenced to a very large extent by the two Sephiroth it interconnects. Conversely, when the Paths are eventually worked they will throw new light on the nature of the related Sephiroth which in turn will throw new light upon the Paths. The student will thus be well embarked upon a voyage of self-discovery which can last him for a life time and longer, for it should not be thought that once each Sephirah and each Path has been worked over once that the student knows all about the Qabalah—far from it—very far from it!

3. The Paths can be worked in three ways, by astral clairvoyance, by meditation, and in terms of life experience. Each succeeding method can be developed out of the one which precedes it, and in terms of benefits to be achieved they are in increasing order of merit; though when real facility is attained the three methods can be worked one in with the other.

4. Astral clairvoyance is in reality a rather glamorous term for the exercise of the creative imagination. Because of the element of mystery that has overlong surrounded occultism it is commonly throught to be a 'highly esoteric'

272

process. Consequently it is the object of much fascination and curiosity, whereas the almost identical process of psycho-analytic directed reverie evokes far less interest. The fact is that 'astral clairvoyance', 'skrying in the spirit vision', 'directed reverie' and the 'creative imagination' are synonymous terms. The results are also similar and it is of no more interest, save perhaps from an academic point of view, to read another's 'astral experiences' than it is to read the details of case histories in books of analytical psychology. The only direct advantage in the process is to the original participant.

5. There is no necessity for trance in performing the technique in spite of what might commonly be believed by outsiders to esotericism. Trance is a mediumistic faculty which is possessed by a few and is of no advantage in individual esoteric work. It is true that by long and arduous training it is possible to develop concentration to such a pitch that all awareness of the physical environment is temporarily lost, and this condition is probably what is considered by the inexperienced to be full 'astral projection'. However, concentration developed to this pitch is beyond the range of most and it is wasted effort to try to achieve such a state, for equal benefit can be obtained from moderate powers of concentration where full awareness is still retained of the objective physical environment. The object of concentration exercises is not to lose all awareness of the environment but to achieve a state where objective surroundings, or inner instability of mind or emotions, do not disturb the subjective poise and visualisation work in hand. The skilled adept is in fact one who can work subjectively and objectively at the same time, being negative to the inner planes and positive to the outer. It involves no occlusion of consciousness on any level, but rather expanded awareness on all levels—Light in Extension.

6. An Astral Path-working consists first in formulating in the imagination a Temple of the Sephirah in which the Path begins, and it is usual to work from a lower Sephirah

to a higher one, or from left to right on the lateral Paths. The Temple can be visualised how one wishes, though in accordance with the general symbolism of that particular Sephirah. It is as well, though, to include an altar in the centre with a light burning upon it and two pillars on the Eastern side of it—representing the two Pillars of Manifestation,—the left Black or darker colour, the right White, Silver or lighter colour. The gateway of the Path to be worked should be visualised in the appropriate position and across the gateway the appropriate Tarot Trump as if painted on a curtain or veil.

7. After an invocation of the Divine Name and the Archangel of the Sephirah, (made according to one's taste and in one's own words if words are used, for the intention and not the form is important, and creation of one's own form is of more value than using someone else's at second hand), one approaches the picture of the Tarot Trump. As one approaches it should take on a three-dimensional appearance and one walks into the scenery of the card and beyond. One is then upon the Path and any images that arise spontaneously in consciousness should be noted.

8. In order to keep one's bearings, there are two main identification marks or sign-posts along the Path. At the mid-point of the Path is the Hebrew letter, which can be visualised in white light or in the corresponding colour of the Path; while at the far end of the Path is the astrological sign, visualised similarly, and the environs of the further Sephirah. It is not usual to enter this Sephirah unless one is performing a composite journey and traversing, say, the two central Paths from Malkuth to Tiphareth and even beyond. Beginners are advised, however, to stick to one Path at a time. Once one has reached the end of the Path at the environs of the further Sephirah, seeing it possibly as the outside of another Temple, though possibly with open doors so that one can see inside, and with the appropriate Archangel presiding over it, one retraces one's steps and returns to the original Sephirah. Here one closes the

operation with an offering of thanks to the Divine Name and also to the Archangel, who may have accompanied one on the way, and then returns one's consciousness to awareness of physical objective reality. Closing down is most important and some food and drink will help do this. Also, in astral work, the boundaries must be clearly defined and kept to. A figure that is met *may* disappear from sight into a landscape or building but no impression should be fostered of it breaking bounds, thus risking leakage of psychic force or intrusion of alien factors.

9. In the early stages of this kind of work it may be that one will have few spontaneous images arising. This depends upon one's sensitivity, which will develop. A lack of such images in the early stages of practice should not therefore act as discouragement—a completely formal Path-working is not without its advantages.

10. It will be obvious, though, that even where much spontaneous imagery occurs it is of little use if its implications are not realised—one is merely collecting data. Therefore such symbolism should be meditated upon later, if not at the time of its coming up into consciousness. Another method, whilst performing the Path-working, is to identify oneself with the actual symbol—for it is indeed a part of oneself. Such a practice, particularly in regard to the Hebrew letter, astrological sign and Tarot Trump can be very illuminating, and also very disturbing. For this reason it is a method never used in group work. Group work, owing to its greater potency, is, however, a method to be avoided except under skilled supervision.

11. This identification of oneself with a symbol can also be applied to the whole Tree with interesting results. That is, one visualises oneself as if backing into the Tree, with one's Kether above one's head, Daath at the throat level, Tiphareth at the heart, Yesod at the generative organs and Malkuth at the feet. Chokmah, Chesed and Netzach are then

visualised by one's left ear, shoulder and hip respectively and Binah, Geburah and Hod similarly on the right. The Paths can then be included and the whole visualised as radiating with white light. If the colours are used then the King Scale for the Sephiroth and the Queen Scale for the Paths are recommended, to distinguish between their intrinsic objective and subjective states. Such detail is, however, likely to be beyond the visualising powers of most. Whether the Paths and colours are included or not a flow of light should be visualised descending from Kether down one's front, at the periphery of the aura, to Malkuth, beneath one's feet, and ascending up the back to Kether again. This ovoid stream of light represents the involutionary and evolutionary arcs of the manifesting Spirit and clairvoyant investigation has suggested that the downward one represents the past and the upward one the future. This process can be used as a means of clairvoyant investigation by seeing how well the Sephiroth build in the aura; this will reveal the strengths and weaknesses of the individual. Also, past causes can be elicited from the involutionary stream and future potentialities in the evolutionary upward stream, which, in the undeveloped often seems not to complete the circuit back to Kether, but to be used up in building up the Sephiroth, which, as they are visualised as three-dimensional spheres, project into both the past and future areas of the aura, before and behind the central line formed by the point of balance of the body. The Paths are visualised as two dimensional, as of the subjective present, and coincident with the imaginary line.

12. In all this one should not become englamoured with 'astralism.' These are but psychic techniques and by no means infallible. Indeed the use of the intuition can be a surer guide, though it is a more delicate mode of functioning. There is no need to be afraid of astral psychism, on the other hand, as long as one does not fall into the error of regarding it as an end in itself—which, unlike the intuitional technique—is very easy to do. All these methods are but

means to an end and in the midst of glamorous astral colours and forms this is easily forgotten.

13. The Golden Dawn methods of Path-working tended to overemphasise the glamour aspect, whether used in Qabalistic Path-working or investigation of the Tattva symbols and so on. It was their practice, for example, to visualise themselves in full ceremonial robes and accoutrements and to have a complex system of checking whether a symbol or scene arising in consciousness was genuine or not by projecting upon it an appropriate Hebrew letter of a planetary sign to see if it dissolved the picture. These were Tau, (Saturn), for memory; Kaph, (Jupiter), for construction; Peh, (Mars), for anger or impatience; Resh, (Sun), for vanity; Daleth, (Venus), for self-indulgent pleasure; Beth, (Mercury), for over-imagination; Gimel, (Moon), for mind wandering. Such techniques can be useful but are really unnecessary given faith and pure intention. They tend to make matters overcomplicated and spiritual truth is usually to be found in simplicity.

14. Similar factors hold sway with the use of physical regalia and private temples, shrine cupboards and so on. These things have their uses in group working but for individual investigation they can well be so much impedimenta. To one of little experience the physical accoutrements will often serve as distractions and to one who has experience, except for specialised advanced work, they are really unnecessary.

15. The main fault of these accessories is that they tend to divorce occultism from life — and occultism should be very much to do with life. The use of regalia and magical weapons is primarily a ritual matter where various officers represent cosmic forces. But individual work is concerned with broadening oneself as a human being, and this is not to be achieved by narrowing oneself down to the blind potency of a single cosmic force. Such is, in fact, definitely injurious, which is why in Fraternities officers never hold a particular office for any lengthy period, but change round periodically

in order not to become completely identified with a cosmic function—a crippling thing to happen and which has occurred not infrequently in the past. It also happens to a lesser degree in ordinary life of course and Jung's description of the 'persona' and the fate of one in the grip of it is the most commonly held exoteric explanation of the process. Sartre has also described the condition, though from another angle, and its best cure, like so many psychic ills, lies in scientology, though prevention is of course better than cure.

16. It is well, then, not to become too involved in the form side of occultism, a side which has been over-emphasised in the past, and which, together with the mystery and superstition also currently prevalent, it is hoped—and intended—will disappear in the future. Modern esotericism is for sane, healthy, balanced men and women and is a process which should make them saner, healthier and better balanced. Its function should be to teach spirits how to live harmoniously in Earth by intelligent application of higher and lower forces. It is a grave matter that owing to mistakes in the past it should have become the happy hunting ground of the crank and faddist and those who are primarily concerned with trying to escape from Earth conditions.

17. We have said that astral working of the paths should lead on to meditative work. It is quite possible, however, to rely entirely on meditation and to ignore the astral side of things, for whatever results one gets astrally in the form of pictures and symbols to be interpreted, one can get in meditation in the form of direct realisations. Meditation is thus a more efficient, if less spectacular, process.

18. The pictures of the astral are but representations at their own level of higher forces and it is better to work directly with the higher forces if possible than at second hand. There is, for example, the old technique of 'rising on the planes' mentioned quite frequently by Dion Fortune, which, in astral terms, is a Path-working up through the central Sephiroth of the Tree, designed to raise conscious-

ness to a higher level. However, if one sticks to astral imagery one is still on the astral plane, even if one seems to be floating in a brilliant blaze of glory in Kether, with the Kerubim circling all around. This is not to be derided, for very fine results can be obtained in this way, as for example, the Visions of Ezekiel or St. John the Divine wherein real Kether states were attained. However, the Spiritual Experience of Kether is Union with God and from this no-one returns. Thus any real direct experience of this supremely high spiritual awareness we are unlikely to achieve with our brain-limited physical consciousness. We are at liberty though to strive for direct awareness on the level which is within our grasp.

19. This level is the abstract mind or intuition. By abstract mind is not meant the type of mentation that deals with abstract mathematical formulae or first formulations of ideas for future action—this is more the province of the higher levels of the concrete mind. The abstract mind as such has no processes of formal logic—it just knows—it is pure reason, which needs no reasoning to prove itself—it is best referred to, in Western terminology, as Intuition. It is difficult to describe it for in the use of words we are limited to the concrete mind. However, it is important because the forming of the link between the concrete mind and the abstract mind is the forming of the link between Individuality consciousness and Personality consciousness.

20. The same few basic principles apply throughout all life. One of them is that the only way to achieve control of a function is to practise it. This is the reason for meditation. In meditation one confronts an object with the mind. After the concrete mind has had its subjective say one just sits, and after some time sitting regarding the symbolic object with the concrete mind a blank, some fragments of knowledge may filter through from the abstract mind. The process must be assiduously practised for a set time every day until eventually—and it will probably not be for some years, from experience, at least seven—one has the powers of the ab-

stract mind at will and can just switch on, as it were, when one likes, the light of pure reason or intuition.

21. This is, to retain the metaphor, a very illuminating process, but it is very difficult to demonstrate one's illumination to another because in order to communicate, unless both are experts at telepathy, one has to resort to words and these are of the concrete mind. The difficulty is not insuperable though as witness the written wisdom of all races, whether passed down as the sayings of Jesus, Confucius, King Solomon, Hermes or any other. The other form of communication is by visual imagery as in the Revelation of St. John. This is in the form of an astral experience, though it is probable that St. John was quite capable of operating on intuitional and even spiritual levels in direct awareness.

22. Any who read the Revelation however will be aware that it is no easy book to understand, and this demonstrates the two-way aspect of these matters of higher comprehension. In order to understand the deeper astral symbolism one has to meditate upon it, and by meditation one stimulates the channel to the abstract mind and so insight and expansion of awareness is attained. Conversely, in meditation, pictorial symbolism may arise and this may well be the result of intuitional impact which has not registered at the mind level. Once again, meditation is required to elucidate it.

23. The reception of pictorial symbols in meditation is not a bad thing; it is a case of working two planes at once, and if one is receiving such symbols, which are representative not of subconscious elements but of intuitional stimulation of the unconscious then one is working three planes. The ideal would be to have complete functional awareness all the way down—spiritual and intuitional knowledge manifesting in the mind as words of wisdom and astrally as evocative symbolism and being written down physically or drawn in an aesthetically pleasing way. This would represent the perfect human functioning as artist and prophet, Dante,

Leonardo, Shakespeare, St. John or St. Paul are perhaps the closer approaches to such a state.

24. Finally, the Paths can be interpreted as phases of life experience and this is where real insight is needed, aided by symbol and meditation. As the Tree of Life is a glyph of man's whole being and of the Universe, every phase of experience in life has its correlation upon it.

25. In life there are phases within phases, cycles within cycles, and clear definition is often difficult. It is particularly difficult to assess the phase one is going through at the present time for all the factors are not known, and did one have the whole process realised then there would probably be no need to be going through with it. It is perhaps easier to approach this method of occult working—which is the most difficult and also the most worthwhile—by making assessments and reviews of past periods of one's life. It will almost certainly be found that certain difficulties and problems have occurred at different times and in different contexts over and over again. This is the pointer to a karmic cycle operating, to a lesson to be learnt.

26. If such a problem can be detected in this way and defined, and then placed in its appropriate context on the Tree of Life, sustained meditation and astral working upon the relevant symbolism can well bring to light the true nature of the problem and give one the necessary clues to solve it. Once this method has been successfully used in connection with any problems of the past one is the better equipped to apply it to one's problems of the present. The aim of all occult work of any nature is to make happier, more efficient and rounded out individuals. If it does not have these results it is worthless, or rather the way it is being operated is worthless, and possibly injurious.

27. Needless to say, such advanced work is difficult, for it involves the capacity to diagnose one's own failures and shortcomings. It also requires the capacity to regard the potencies of the Tree of Life as living realities, not just as

mere intellectual categories. The attitude towards the Father of Chokmah, the Great Mother of Binah, the Saviour Son of Tiphareth, the 'power behind the throne' or Head Which Is Not of Kether, should be a living relationship, as vibrant and full-blooded as any animal or human family relationship. The inability to feel such a relationship indicates a blockage and it will be found that in most cases the problems of everyday life have their roots in the problems of the soul in its inner life, past and present.

28. Thus one who has always had in the present life a persistently acrimonious relationship with one of the parents would do well to examine his relationship with the Heavenly Father or the Great Mother, Heavenly or Earthly. It will be found that once the real cause of the trouble has been eradicated—the soul's rebellion against God, or an aspect of God, or an aspect of the Divine Plan—then the every day human or social problem clears up. The person can then see his father, or mother, as they really are, simply as closely related human beings. No longer do they carry the projection of his own repressed fears, hates and anxieties about his place in the Universe, no longer does he unconsciously make them scapegoats for the hated or feared Divine Creator.

29. Such hatred of the Divine may be repressed under a cloak of piety of course. The piety though is usually of either a stern 'inhuman' or an obsequious 'unhuman' nature. It is not really the Divinity which is hated or feared however, but a false image of that Divinity which has been mocked up by the separated ego consciousness. The Original Deviation, Sin, or Fall caused a cutting of communication lines, subjectively and objectively, so that the real unity of the Spiritual levels, instead of extending into Form manifestation became broken into separate ego-consciousnesses, not only separate from each other but divided within themselves. The result has been conflict through separation instead of unity in diversity. The breaking of the Tables of the Law when Moses descended from the Daath level of Sinai gives a symbolic indication of this. Basically, all

human problems are problems of communication, either with others, or between the fragmented parts of the self.

30. Apart from this basic rule the complications and over-lays can be legion. Indeed, the phrase "the ways to God are as many as the breaths of men" would be equally true if stated in terms of "the ways *from* God." Further, the father and mother will almost certainly have their own problems, and may, in fact, have their own difficulties in regard to acceptance of God the Son, which prevents them from ever having a satisfactory relationship with their child. In such a case a realisation of his own failings, and correction of them, by the son would have little result on the actual human relationship, for the parents' attitude would still be patho-logical. However, such a possibility should not prevent the son from trying to sort himself out in the first place—and it is probable that if the results of his efforts in this direction were aborted by the unchanging attitude of the other party there would be some deeper factor still at work. These problems are all those of karma, and once a karmic problem is solved, conditions *must* change—that is as inevitable a Cosmic Law as the Law of Gravity. However, there can be a certain time-lag on the physical plane, and if, for exam-ple, a man lost a leg for some karmic reason, no change of realisation after he had lost it would ever bring it back to him. He would have to put up with one leg for the rest of his present physical life.

31. But an overcomplication of the issues at hand must be avoided, for this is but another means of escape from facing up to reality, and the adverse aspects of the soul will do all they can to avoid a reckoning, through the operation of inertia, fear, disbelief, laziness, smugness and in fact every vice in the human repertoire, many of them posing as virtues.

32. In attempting such work then, two simple rules should be observed. 1) A time limit should be set for when the particular work has to be completed, and a timetable made for working upon the particular problem formally every day.

It should be an *easy* timetable—and one *must stick to it.*
2) One should write down, immediately if possible, during
the course of daily life, any reaction in oneself which is
neurotic. A neurotic reaction is one which bears no proportion in its intensity to the thing which engendered it. Thus
to lose one's temper violently, even if one conceals it, because one spills coffee on the breakfast table would be a
neurotic reaction. It is in the so-called trivialities of life
that the true nature of the soul's real difficulties can be
seen. So though the incident may seem trivial in the extreme
it should be noted, (otherwise it will surely be forgotten),
and worked upon at one's next meditation period. One
should try to find the real motives and reasons for one's
neurotic reaction in the light of the principles of the Tree
of Life.

33. As the above paragraph suggests, the Law of Limitation is of tremendous importance in practical occultism,
particularly in work of this nature where the object of investigation is trying to squirm away all the time. By limiting
one's sphere of action, that is, by concentrating upon one
particular problem at a time, and limiting the time in which
one means to achieve a solution, real progress is made. If
the Law of Limitation is not used the whole project will
fizzle out in unfulfilled good intentions—a few more paving-
stones on the road to Hell.

34. Also, a good knowledge of the Tree of Life is a decided
advantage, for it enables the problems to be sorted out the
easier, and correlations to be seen with other aspects of life
where trouble may also have occurred from the same cause.
Thus, the rejection of the Feminine-Side of God, because
perhaps it relates to Form manifestation, would be a Binah
condition primarily, possibly manifesting as complete lack
of Faith or faith—and as Binah is a Sephirah whose Virtue
is Silence it might even result in compulsive communication. Also, the Feminine Principle, although present in all
the Sephiroth, has a strong influence in the Sephiroth
Netzach, Yesod and Malkuth. The Netzach rejection could

cause all kinds of glamour, possibly based on the supposed inferiority of women; the Yesod rejection might cause an intensification of attention on the androgynous perfection of the Machinery of the Universe, thus giving an inhuman tinge to the subject's attitude to other people's feelings—he might have little passional feelings apparently, through repression, or else they might tend to be diverted into a perverted channel. The Malkuth rejection might result in direct ill-health or lack of vitality through a partially expressed refusal to come to terms with the Earth Mother. Indeed, ill health in general might reflect all the above mentioned Sephiroth according to correspondence of function. This, however, is a subject too vast and technical to treat here; the medical profession might do well to pay a little more respect to Paracelsus though.

35. However, where difficulty is experienced in diagnosis and remedial work through the technicalities involved, it is always useful to work upon the Tiphareth Sephirah, for this is the central point of Harmony on the whole Tree. The greatest potency of this Sephirah is expressed through God the Son and this Love Aspect is channeled through the Lord Jesus in the present epoch of the Western world. The Lord Jesus is not the only focus or bearer of this Force but he is the most recent and therefore most comprehensive and therefore the best.

36. It is unfortunate that approximately two thousand years of human misrepresentation have jaded the religious perceptive faculties of many people so that they have little time for the Christian religion. The Christ force nevertheless is the most potent in the whole battery of occultism, to consider things in a purely technical sense, as has been recognised in the popular tradition that the sign of the Cross and the invocation of the name of Christ will banish all demons. This is literally true as it happens, once we divorce it from its melodramatic context. Few are likely to meet hobgoblins or horned devils in haunted houses at midnight but all have 'devils' or 'demons' within themselves—the

errors or sins that cause them so much unhappiness. If it is possible to overcome the automatic revulsion that, tragically, many have from Christianity, due usually to faulty presentation in childhood and after, and to call upon the Christ for help, help will certainly be received. The test of the truth of this statement is quite simple—one only has to try it.

37. The only proviso that obtains to the use of the Christ Force is that the heart must be willing to accept it. It is not a contact that has much to do with the rational mind, but it should cause the heart to 'burn within.' Also it is a contact of Divine Love, so that fear, hatred, suspicion or mental analysis can prevent its work upon the soul. Nor, on the other hand, should any feel too unworthy to try to contact it—as is openly taught in the churches, Christ came to save sinners and there are many parables which also teach this from the prodigal son to the lost sheep.

38. The heart should be willing, though, to face up to its shortcomings and to face the changes necessary. In common Christian parlance this is called Repentance and Redemption, but these words have become so familiar that they no longer convey much meaning to many, and to others they are so tainted by association of ideas with 'churchianity' and 'crosstianity' that their meaning is distorted. As one of the Greater Masters once said: "The greatest barrier to truth is the overfamiliar word."

39. In the overfamiliar terms of the Christian calender is the whole process of any form of human growth and spiritual development, the Birth in the Cave or Stable, the Baptism, the Transfiguration, the Agony in the Garden, the Trial, Crucifixion, Descent into Hell, Resurrection and Ascension. While it is a strange pathology that many nominal Christians seem fixated in one stage of the process — the Crucifixion — it is an equally strange one that with esoteric students great interest can be roused if the same process be tricked out in Alchemistic, Occult or Pagan symbolism, but because Christianity is open and familiar and gener-

ally accepted, immediate rejection is often manifested.

40. The truths are the same and have been the same through all time. It matters little in what form they are accepted but there is a unique and tremendous power in the Christian figures of Our Lord and Our Lady and many of the Saints, and to ignore this power because one has for long been prejudiced against Christianity for one reason or another is to court a very great loss.

41. In matters such as this, expansion of the mind is necessary to get free of the false connotations of overworn and overfamiliar words. To this end meditation is particularly helpful and also the study of other religions to see points of similarity and the reading of the type of esoteric writings which are designed to train the mind rather than to inform it—'The Cosmic Doctrine', 'The Secret Doctrine', 'Treatise on the Seven Rays', 'The Book of Revelations', 'The Stanzas of Dzyan' etc. etc.

42. And now regarding the practical use of the Tarot Cards themselves as a method of divination. This is a thorny subject because there seems to be two opposing camps, which we might call the 'high-minded ignorant' and the 'low-minded superstitious.' As is usual in such situations, there is right — and wrong — on both sides.

43. The 'high-minded' attitude is that divination, even if it should work, is of little worth, and probably harmful, because it can sap the individual of any personal initiative. In other words. it is a process which substitutes the result of chance for the Will of the Sprit. Thus such persons prefer to remain ignorant of the subject and recommend that others follow their example.

44. The 'low-minded' attitude is that here is a means of gauging the psychic factors running at a particular time so that plans can be made accordingly; and the usual metaphor is of a captain of a ship who must know how the tides are running in order to navigate sucessfully. However, the attitude tends, in practice, to revert quickly to superstition, as the opposing faction loses no opportunity to point out.

45. Thus matters have rested for some time. The field has been cursorily investigated in recent times, however, by the psychologist C. G. Jung in his paper 'Synchronicity: An Acausal Connecting Principle' (Vol. 8 Collected Works. 'The Structure and Dynamics of the Psyche.') and in his preface to the Wilhelm translation of the Chinese 'I Ching' —both published by Routledge & Kegan Paul.

46. The principle of divination is based on a philosophy that is no longer currently favourable in the West—though it has always obtained generally in the East and did so in the Occident well into the seventeenth century. This attitude takes little cognisance of the Western scientific structure of the phenomena of causality but views the Universe as a whole, rather than analytically, at any particular moment. Thus it is held that an examination of any part of the Universe at a particular time will reveal by analogy the forces pertaining to the whole, and so to other parts.

47. In order to gauge these forces a small model of the Universe is necessary for examination under 'laboratory' conditions. Such a compendium of the Universe is to be found in the various esoteric systems, the main ones being Astrology, the Tarot, the I Ching, Geomancy and Numerology. The particular practical use of such systems depends mainly upon the number of symbols available. Astrology has the Zodiacal signs, Houses and planets, the Tarot has 78 cards, the I Ching has 64 hexagrams, Geomancy has 16 prick symbols, and Numerology has all numbers plus the letters of the alphabet.

48. Aleister Crowley, who investigated all these systems quite closely, has said that astrology and numerology tend to be too complicated to give consistently accurate results, that Geomancy suffers from having too few symbols, and that the best are the Tarot and I Ching. He personally favoured the I Ching, as the common method takes only a few minutes as opposed to the two hours or so a full Tarot reading by the Golden Dawn method. Nevertheless, he was

much enthused with the Tarot as also were MacGregor Mathers and Paul Case.

49. The difference between fortune. telling and spiritual diagnosis is an important one. In all major systems with the exception of Geomancy, each symbol has a considerable depth of esoteric significance behind it and in its pure form is a philosophical rather that a divinatory structure. So, given the efficacy of the method, which has been fully endorsed by several leading occultists, and sympathetically considered by uncommitted investigators such as Wilhelm and Jung, it could be the vehicle of a profound spiritual and psychological diagnosis. The danger is the all too easy trend towards fatalism and a purely superstitious, arbitrary and superficial meaning being given to the symbols as can be seen by reference to many books on fortune telling and some of the more popular 'occult' magazines.

50. In all matters of divination it is the powers of psychic perception of the diviner that seem to matter more than the actual configuration of the symbols—thus the technique is more of an art than science. Often past events can be explained as being inevitable or at least highly probable from an astrological chart *after* the event has occurred, when the astrologer has the benefit of hindsight. It is not so easy a matter to *foretell* such things and to pick out the relevant data from a very complicated chart.

51. In a full Tarot divination all the cards of the pack are read at least once and so, while the subconscious selection of the right cards in the shuffling *may* play a part in the process, the key to the matter is more likely to be that the focus of attention upon the spread, and the *intention* in the mind at the time, cause the reader to emphasise, consciously or unconsciously, the more important factors of the case.

52. Intention seems an important part of the process as Jung found out in his astrological researches detailed in the paper mentioned above, and as has also been discovered by Dr. J. B. Rhine in his E. S. P. experiments. In the latter, Rhine found that he got better results when the people un-

dergoing the tests were enthusiastic. With subjective tests this is readily understandable, but Jung found to his amazement that enthusiasm tended to affect purely statistical researches. However, this raises questions of too deep and radical a philosophical import to be pursued at length in the present context.

53. The I Ching is a system in which the element of a vast complex of symbolism to be interpreted does not enter, for after the chance tossing of coins or selecting of yarrow stalks, only one hexagram, or at most, two, has to be considered. Here however, the texts that accompany the hexagrams are so obscure that many meanings can be read into any one, and any of them selected at random could afford an answer of sorts. It would seem that is is possible, then, for one to read one's own answer into it and that this might be the mechanics of the oracle, and indeed of all oracles.

54. This seems to be the key to the situation—all speculations of 'synchronicity' apart. If a random selection of deep symbolism is taken it can act as a focus for the projection of the unconscious mind of the reader—and as what is unconscious is often in the process of becoming conscious and affecting objective reality, then divination does work. In astrology there is not the initial random selection but the gifted interpretation of a horoscope probably calls for similar psychic gifts in the reader owing to the great complexity of forces involved.

55. The occultist who disapproves of divination can still say, however, that even if divination does work, such methods are but crutches to be thrown away as soon as possible and a subjective condition striven for whereby the inner trends can be perceived intuitionally without all this artificial paraphernalia. It is quite true of course that divinatory techniques are by no means essential for any course of spiritual development. This has been shown by actual experience over the forty years or so of the existence of

one group known well to the author, which certainly gets results for its members, but which has never used divinatory practices in its methods.

56. However, it would be unreasonable to assert on a priori grounds that such practices are of the Devil. As with most things, so much depends on the uses and abuses to which they are put. It is not proposed to outline any specific methods of Tarot divination because there are so many of them that it is obvious that there is no 'one true way.' Reasoning from first principles it is obvious that just as one's own design of home-made Tarots is of greater personal benefit than any commercially produced one, so is one's own method of divination likely to be more effective than someone else's. This is a principle in fact which is valid throughout the whole range of practical occultism.

57. As a foundation upon which to start however, should any wish to experiment along these lines, the following basic procedure can be highly recommended. One should proceed just as for an ordinary meditation session or Pathworking but the invocation should be made to the 'group soul' of the Tarot, who is known as the angelic being HRU —(probably a corruption of Horus but nevertheless effective and hallowed by tradition). The mental attitude should be as reverent as for any other occult working, it is no game. The method of shuffling is of little importance as long as the mind is kept on the question in hand. It is usual to cut, after shuffling, with the left hand and then to deal off the cards. Six only need be taken and they should be spread to form a Star of David — two interlaced triangles in the order shown in Fig. 8. Anyone who is likely to be any good at Tarot divination will see the significances of this symbol and it is a basic one which can be used to build up bigger spreads if desired when experience is gained. Possible developments from this simple beginning are to complete a structure of the Tree of Life, to deal three or more cards at each point to amplify the meaning, to make several like figures for past, present and future or other aspects of

the problem and so on and so forth. The simple six card spread is quite adequate in itself however.

58. While it is almost always better to try to solve any problem by the light of one's own developing powers of discretion, descrimination, intuition and so on—the development of which, after all, is the main purpose of occult training—there can come a time when no further good can come from worrying away at a problem, it has become overfamiliar, one can no longer get efficiently to grips with it. In such a case it seems that divination would be justified. The prime function of the Tarot is as a philosophical system however, not as an oracle. This is a fact which is often forgotten and leads to many pursuing blind alleys in their esoteric training—particularly if self-taught.

59. But whatever methods of esoteric training are employed it is essential that they be employed systematically otherwise nothing will be achieved. The basic technique for any real and lasting progress is meditation—all other subjective techniques are ancillary to this—and there is enough material given in the two volumes of this book to keep anyone going in meditation subjects almost indefinitely. Also, if one is working on one's own, it is essential, human nature being what it is, to work out a programme or timetable, and stick to it.

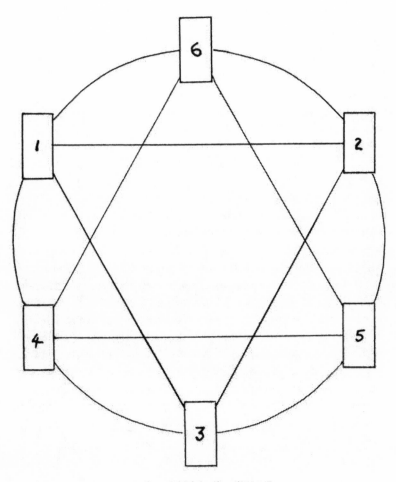

A Tarot Divination Spread

INDEX BY NORMAN D. PETERSON

Roman numerals are used to distinguish between the two volumes. Thus, A in Soph appears on pages 30 and 55 of Volume I, and on pages 100, 143, 190 and 215 of Volume II.

293

294

Astral triangle I-31
Astral world I-215
Astrological attributions, differing
II-228, 229
Astrological harmony and the Tarot
II-230
Astrological signs I-171; see also
Signs, Zodiac
Astrological symbols I-10
Astrology I-134; II-50, 229, 231, 287,
288
Astrology not fully reliable II-50
Atavism I-154
Athanasian creed I-171
Athanor, Trump IV
Atheist existentialism I-121
Athena, see Pallas Athena
Atik Yomin, see Ancient of Days
Atlantis I-199
Atlas I-178
Atom I-27
Atom, cosmic II-66
Atomic bomb I-146; II-35
Atomic consciousness I-201
Atoms, seed II-168, 170, 173
Atomic structure I-230
Attention II-200, 201
Aton, see Solar Disk
Attributes of God II-172
Attributions I-38, 52, 227
Attributions, disagreement as to
I-37, 39; II-211, 221, 222, 227,
232
Attributions, tentative I-205–208
Atum-Ra I-62, 75
Atziluth, see worlds
Aura II-275
Aureole, Trumps V, XIV
Autz Chaiim, see Otz Chiim
Authority I-49, 122
Authority, abuses of II-81
Avalon II-46, 236
Avarice I-99
Avenging Angel I-134, 135
Averse aspects I-9, 167
Awakener I-160
Axiomatics I-166, 170
Axioms I-118
Axioms, Crowley's II-217

Babel I-182; II-61, 82, Trump XVI
Bacchanalian grapes, Trump XV
Bacchus, horns of, see Trump Zero,
and Dionysos
Bailey, Alice A. I-103, 134, 225;
II-27, 42, 85, 128, 134, 169, 182,
240
Balance I-89, 104, 127, 133, 162,
Trump VII

Balder I-109
Balneum Mariae I-231
Banner, Trumps IV, XIII, XIX, XX
Barlet and Papus II-233
Barrie II-182
Barrois Dactylology II-199, Trumps
I, II, V
Basilisk I-228
Bast (Egyptian goddess) II-127
Bat-winged figure, Trump XV
Beat generation II-132
Beauty I-3, 46, 109, 138, 139, 151,
153, 162, 163; see also aesthetics
Beckett, Samuel II-22
Beetle I-63
Behaviourism II-16
Being I-53; see also noumenal being
Beings, non-human II-168
Beltane I-103
Bembine tablet of Isis II-215
Berosus I-182
Besancon Tarot II-15
Bes-headed, black staff, see Trump
Zero
Beth, see Trump II
Bhakti Yoga (devotion) I-17
Bias I-114, 115
Biblical allusions and quotations I-8,
39, 43, 56, 59, 69, 74, 78, 86, 90,
92, 95, 129, 131, 132, 142, 144,
146, 147, 151, 161, 178, 183, 208,
209, 233, 243; II-10, 26, 34, 52,
56, 60, 62, 82, 87, 96, 101, 105,
120, 134, 140, 142, 165, 166, 169,
170, 171, 246, 263
Bibliography II-286, see Asch
Metzareph, Sepher, Zohar, Levi,
Papus, Mathers, Rosenroth,
Waite, Westcott
Big Dipper I-64; see also Great Bear
Binah I-87; II-14, 159, 241
Binah and Ain Soph II-163
Binah, Temple of I-90, 92, 95, 97
Binah, Throne of I-191, 196
Binary symbolism, see Two
Biological roots II-16, 26
Bi-polar duality I-95
Birth I-66
Black Adept I-64
Black and White I-159
Black and white dogs, see Trump
XVIII
Black cross I-146
Black and white pillars, see Trump II
Black Isis II-22
Black Lodges I-85
Black magic I-156, 234; II-108, 132,
195
Blake I-148, 192

298

Indigo, Sephirah 9; Paths 12, 16, 24, 26, 32
Iridescence, Sephirah 2
Lavender, Daath
Leather, Path 17
Maroon, Path 18
Mauve, Paths 17, 28
Olive, Sephiroth 7, 10; Paths 16, 23
Orange, Sephiroth 5, 8; Paths 16, 17, 30, 31
Pearl, Sephirah 2
Pink, Sephiroth 3, 6; Path 29
Plum, Path 20
Primary colours (red, yellow, blue) Sephirah 2
Purple, Sephiroth 4, 8, 9; Paths 12, 19, 21, 23, 28
Red, Sephirah 5; Paths 15, 16, 17, 19, 27, 30
Rose, Sephirah 6; Path 14
Russet, Sephirah 10; Path 18
Salmon, Sephirah 6
Scarlet, Sephirah 5; Paths 15, 27, 31
Sea green, Path 23
Silver, Daath; Paths 13, 29
Slate, Path 20
Spring green, Path 14
Stone, Path 29
Translucent, Path 29
Venetian red, Path 27
Vermilion, Path 31
Violet, Daath, Sephiroth 4, 8, 9; Paths 12, 21, 28
White, Sephiroth 1, 2, 8; Paths 23, 28, 29
Yellow, Daath, Sephiroth 4, 6, 8, 10; Paths 11, 12, 17, 19, 20, 21, 25, 30
Commedia dell'arte II-117
Communality II-182
Communion II-183
Compass points, see cardinal points
Compensation I-127
Compromise I-146; II-96
Compulsive behaviour II-40
Comte de Gabalis I-140
Concealed of the Concealed I-68
Concealment I-91
Concepts vs. realizations I-16
Concretion I-30, 31
Conery Mor II-235
Cone, pine I-107; see also Trump Zero
Conscience I-35; II-109
Consciousness I-27, 57, 67, 108, 194, 196, 198, 212; II-67
Consciousness, dissociation of I-116
Consciousness, mystical II-69
Consciousness, soul II-72
Consciousness, thread of I-83-85

Constant, A. L., see Levi
Consistorial degrees, see Magister Templi and Magus
Constellations I-171
Constellations depicted on the Tarot II-249
Contemplation I-15, 16, 69, 84, 130, 240; II-70, 147, 149
Contemplations of faith I-150
Contemplative order I-22
Contra-sexual image II-132
Contradiction II-84
Controlled conditions I-116
Convention II-97
Copernicus I-63
Cor Leonis II-123, 124
Corinthian Helmet II-265
Corn I-103; II-4, 8, Trump II
Cornucopia II-182, 237
Coronet, iron, Trump VIII
Correspondence courses I-220
Correspondences II-98; see also Attributions
Correspondences as psychological devices I-228
Cosmic atom II-66
Cosmic days I-69; II-28, 41; see also Aeons
Cosmic Doctrine I-44, 53, 54, 66, 134, 193; II-25, 66, 89-93, 111, 135, 165, 167, 217, 256, 260
Cosmic Christ I-91
Cosmic egg I-57
Cosmic law I-104
Cosmic tree II-167
Cosmogony I-197
Cosmology I-53; II-166
Cosmos I-54, 104, 206; see also Universe
Countenance, Lesser (Zoar Anpin, Microprosopos, Adam Kadmon) I-147, 213
Countenance, Vast (Arik Anpin, Macroprosopos) I-73, 213
Countenances, Prince of I-192
Courage I-125, 130; II-69, 70, 99
Courses, correspondence I-220
Court cards of the Tarot II-255
Court cards, esoteric titles of II-258
Court cards of the Trumps II-261; see also Suits
Court de Gebelin, see Gebelin
Covenant II-76
Crayfish in all except Crowley/Harris Tarot, see Trump XVIII
Creative imagination I-84, 160, 161
Creative world I-32, 214
Creativity II-44, 47
Creation I-74

306

308

312

314

316

318

319

320

Made in the USA
Middletown, DE
30 May 2024

55074483R00380